# 2016 CONS LAW UPDATE

MW00977404

Editors

## Neal J. Sweeney
## Chad V. Theriot

Wolters Kluwer

This publication is designed to provide accurate and authoritative information in regard to the subject matter covered. It is sold with the understanding that the publisher and the author(s) are not engaged in rendering legal, accounting, or other professional services. If legal advice or other professional assistance is required, the services of a competent professional should be sought.

—From a *Declaration of Principles* jointly adopted by
a Committee of the American Bar Association and
a Committee of Publishers and Associations

Published by Wolters Kluwer in New York.

Wolters Kluwer Legal & Regulatory US serves customers worldwide with CCH, Aspen Publishers and Kluwer Law International products.

Printed in the United States of America

1 2 3 4 5 6 7 8 9 0

ISBN 978-1-4548-7285-6

ISSN 1054-9331

**FSC**
**MIX**
**FSC® C103993**

# About Wolters Kluwer Legal & Regulatory US

Wolters Kluwer Legal & Regulatory US delivers expert content and solutions in the areas of law, corporate compliance, health compliance, reimbursement, and legal education. Its practical solutions help customers successfully navigate the demands of a changing environment to drive their daily activities, enhance decision quality and inspire confident outcomes.

Serving customers worldwide, its legal and regulatory portfolio includes products under the Aspen Publishers, CCH Incorporated, Kluwer Law International, ftwilliam.com and MediRegs names. They are regarded as exceptional and trusted resources for general legal and practice-specific knowledge, compliance and risk management, dynamic workflow solutions, and expert commentary.

# WOLTERS KLUWER SUPPLEMENT NOTICE

This product is updated on a periodic basis with supplements and/or new editions to reflect important changes in the subject matter.

If you would like information about enrolling this product in the update service, or wish to receive updates billed separately with a 30-day examination review, please contact our Customer Service Department at 1-800-234-1660 or email us at: *customer.service@wolterskluwer.com*. You can also contact us at:

**Wolters Kluwer**
**Distribution Center**
**7201 McKinney Circle**
**Frederick, MD 21704**

---

**Important Contact Information**

- To order any title, go to *www.wklawbusiness.com* or call 1-800-638-8437.

- To reinstate your manual update service, call 1-800-638-8437.

- To contact Customer Service, e-mail *customer.service@wolterskluwer.com*, call 1-800-234-1660, fax 1-800-901-9075, or mail correspondence to: Order Department—Wolters Kluwer, PO Box 990, Frederick, MD 21705.

- To review your account history or pay an invoice online, visit *www.WKLawBusiness.com/payinvoices*.

Wolters Kluwer

# 2016 PREFACE

The feature chapters of the *2016 Construction Law Update*, the 26th book in this *Update* series, reflect the wide range of challenging issues that arise under the broad banner of construction law one and a half decades into the not-so-new millennium.

Construction is a big part of the global economy. Even a construction practitioner who never physically crosses an international border may be called upon to advise on international matters. And, in any event, it is interesting to learn how "construction law" means different things in various parts of the world. Chapter 1 fits the bill by providing a fascinating and informative summary of the differences between U.S. and English common law concepts of construction law, and of Arab law that controls many billions of dollars of construction in the Middle East each year. Co-authored by attorneys trained in English or English common law and/or Arab law, but all with experience in dealing with complex construction disputes in the Middle East, Chapter 1 provides a concise but insightful comparison of those legal paradigms.

Chapter 2 addresses decidedly U.S. domestic issues—Disadvantaged Business Enterprise (DBE) compliance along with other compliance requirements. These are extremely important issues for any contractor or construction lawyer dealing directly or indirectly with government contracts, whether on a federal, state, or local level. As government requirements and scrutiny increase, and prosecutors score big headlines and hefty fines at the expense of contractors, an understanding of how to meet compliance standards and ensuring that they are met is increasingly essential for survival.

The *Spearin* doctrine, considered a cornerstone of U.S. construction law, is a century old. Chapter 3 looks back at the details of the decision and what the U.S. Supreme Court really said and held in that decision. The analysis then returns to the present to survey how the *Spearin* doctrine has actually been interpreted, applied, adapted, or rejected under state law over the last century. The bottom line is that referencing the *Spearin* doctrine may sound definitive and self-explanatory, but the concept and its application is far more complex and nuanced, especially under state law.

The lessons of many successful, as well as troubled, projects and costly disputes over several decades and from around the world are applied in Chapter 4 and used as a crystal ball to identify early warning signs of construction claims and disputes. The authors also suggest steps to take when faced with such early warning signs for the benefit of the project and for the avoidance of disputes.

The importance of surety bonds in construction remains constant, and Chapter 5 looks at recent case law relating to the scope of coverage for both payment and performance bonds in federal, state, and private projects.

As in the past, this year's *Update* addresses in depth the developments in federal contracting, and across the six geographic regions of the nation, in separate chapters. These seven chapters, and the contributing authors who craft them each year, provide the foundation on which the success of the *Update* rests.

The efforts, skill, and dedication of our contributing authors are demonstrated throughout the chapters of this book, and allow the *2016 Update* to maintain and build upon the tradition of excellence established by past contributors.[1] We thank and congratulate them for their efforts. The important assistance of Barbara Detkin at Wolters Kluwer Legal & Regulatory US is also much appreciated. Our sincere thanks also goes to Marion Billingsley for the critical role she plays in the *Update* this year and every year.

Atlanta, Georgia
April 2016

NEAL J. SWEENEY
CHAD V. THERIOT

---

[1] The views and opinions expressed by the contributing authors are not necessarily those of the editors.

# ABOUT THE EDITORS

**Neal J. Sweeney** is an Atlanta partner on the Construction Practice Team of Jones Walker LLP. For over 30 years, he has practiced exclusively in the area of construction law and public contracts, with further concentrations in large infrastructure and industrial projects, federal procurement, and health care construction projects. Mr. Sweeney has been involved with some of the largest public-private partnership projects in the United States. His experience spans the full range of the design and construction process, starting at procurement and bid protests, contract review, and drafting. Much of Mr. Sweeney's time is spent counseling clients during project performance in an effort to mitigate and promptly resolve disputes. He has extensive experience in various forms of construction Alternative Dispute Resolution (ADR) techniques, including dispute review boards, mediation and structured negotiation, as well as extensive work in trial, arbitration and before the federal boards of contract appeal. Mr. Sweeney has written extensively on construction law, government contracts, and related topics. Mr. Sweeney has edited 13 books on construction law, including the annual CONSTRUCTION LAW UPDATE (Aspen) since 1992 and COMMON SENSE CONTRACTING (Wiley 1997). He has also contributed as a co-author to numerous books, including DESIGN-BUILD CONTRACTING HANDBOOK (Aspen, 2d ed. 2001) and PROVING AND PRICING CONSTRUCTION CLAIMS (Wiley, 2d ed. 1996). He also regularly contributes articles to periodicals, including *Development, Constructor, the ASCE Management Journal*, and *Water Environment and Technology* magazines. Mr. Sweeney lectures regularly on construction law for a variety of trade and bar organizations and educational institutions, including American Road and Transportation Builders, Water Environment Federation, the Design-Build Institute of America, American Society of Professional Engineers, Risk and Insurance Management Society, Stanford University, and Georgia Tech. Mr. Sweeney graduated from Rutgers University, *with high honors*, 1979, Rutgers Scholar, and received his J.D. from George Washington University, *with honors*, 1982. Mr. Sweeney has also been recognized in "*Chambers USA—America's Leading Lawyers for Business*" in the area of Construction Law (listed annually since 2009) and *The Best Lawyers in America® 2016* in the area of Construction Law (listed annually since 2007).

**Chad V. Theriot** is an Atlanta partner on the Construction Practice Team of Jones Walker LLP, and focuses his practice on major public and commercial construction projects representing clients across a broad spectrum of construction, contracting, and procurement activities. He represents owners and both commercial and government contractors, major subcontractors, and original equipment manufacturers. Mr. Theriot received a B.S. in finance/economics from Spring Hill College, holds an M.B.A. from South Alabama University, and has a J.D. degree from Tulane. Prior to law school, Mr. Theriot worked as a claims consultant on both commercial and government contracts involving project schedule delivery, schedule risks, inefficiency claims, and delay analyses. As an attorney, Mr. Theriot devotes 100 percent of his practice to construction litigation. He has been involved in several high profile AAA arbitrations and has participated in over 175 arbitration hearing days. He is also a registered AAA arbitrator.

# ABOUT THE CONTRIBUTORS

**Liza Akins** is an associate in the Construction & Infrastructure Projects Group of Kilpatrick Townsend & Stockton LLP in the Atlanta office. Her practice focuses primarily on representing clients in construction litigation and arbitration and government contracting. Ms. Akins received her undergraduate degree in Civil Engineering from Duke University. She received her J.D. from Vanderbilt University. Ms. Akins has represented general contractors, subcontractors, and engineers in disputes regarding contract interpretation, construction defects, and project scheduling and delay. Her representative matters include large power, healthcare, and transportation projects in the United States.

**Michael F. Albers** is a shareholder in the Dallas, Texas office of Hunton & Williams LLP and concentrates his practice in the areas of construction law and commercial real estate development. He has represented owners, developers, contractors, and lenders in construction documentation, dispute resolution, project acquisition, financing, and development activities. Mr. Albers is the practice group leader of the firm's national Construction and Government Contracts Section, is a member of the Texas and the American Bar Associations, and has served on the Texas and Dallas Bar Associations' Construction Law Sections. Mr. Albers serves on the teaching faculty of the Design-Build Institute of America, is on the panel of neutrals for the American Arbitration Association, and is an adjunct professor of law at Southern Methodist University. He has written for and participated in the presentation of various programs concerning construction law, including the Practicing Law Institute's Construction Contracts Seminars, the Texas Bar Advanced Real Estate Program, and the ABA/Joint Program on Bankruptcy in the Construction Industry. He is a contributing author to a number of books published by John Wiley & Sons and Wolters Kluwer, including CONSTRUCTION FAILURES, PROVING AND PRICING CONSTRUCTION CLAIMS, FIFTY STATE CONSTRUCTION LIEN AND BOND LAW, and STATE-BY-STATE GUIDE TO ARCHITECT, ENGINEER, AND CONTRACTOR LICENSING.

**Radwa S. Al Rifai** is an associate in the Dubai office of Squire Patton Boggs LLP where she focuses her practice on mergers and acquisitions and corporate governance, and occasionally supports the construction disputes department. She also regularly works with the Riyadh office where she has advised a number of clients on dispute resolution. Ms. Al Rifai received her LL.M. from the Robert H. McKinney School of Law in 2011. Prior to joining Squire Patton Boggs, she worked with a prominent international firm in Cairo, Egypt for several years.

**Michael Cortez** is Senior Counsel with the law firm of Andrews Myers, PC, located in Houston, Texas. Mr. Cortez is an experienced construction attorney previously with a large, national law firm and in-house counsel in the construction and real estate development industries. His practice is focused on construction-related transactions, energy construction and procurement-related design and construction contracts, project risk management, and lien and bond claims. He has represented owners, architects, contractors, EPCs, and developers on a wide variety of projects, including energy, oil and gas, multi-family, manufacturing, and other commercial and industrial projects. He is a member of the Construction Law, and Oil, Gas & Energy Law Sections of the State Bar of Texas, the Houston Bar Association and the Construction Industry Forum of the American Bar Association, and graduated from Southern Methodist University Dedman School of Law and Texas A&M University. In addition to this publication, he is also a contributing author to Wolters Kluwer's FIFTY STATE CONSTRUCTION LIEN AND BOND LAW and STATE-BY-STATE GUIDE TO ARCHITECT, ENGINEER, AND CONTRACTOR LICENSING. He can be reached at mcortez@andrewsmyers.com.

**Lorraine D'Angelo**, a prominent attorney and nationally recognized expert on legal and regulatory risk management, is the founder and president of LDA Compliance Consulting, Inc. She has more than 25 years' experience in the construction industry, including a recent tenure as senior vice president for ethics and compliance at Dragados USA, a subsidiary of Madrid-based GroupACS. Ms. D'Angelo is an accredited ethics and compliance professional, as well as a frequent speaker to industry audiences. She is a leading expert on small, women-owned, minority and DBE matters, programs and policy implementation, and frequently lectures on the implementation of leading practices for complying with those regulations. Her firm specializes in proactive solutions for legal and regulatory compliance, policy assessments and gap analysis, integrity monitoring, auditing and assurance reviews, education and training, creation of policy and procedures, and investigations.

**Lucy R. Dollens** is a partner in the Indianapolis office of Quarles & Brady LLP. She is licensed to practice in Indiana and West Virginia and serves as the Indianapolis office chair for the Commercial Litigation Group. She has trial experience as well as significant experience in handling appeals before the Indiana Court of Appeals, the Indiana Supreme Court, and the U.S. Court of Appeals for the Seventh Circuit. Ms. Dollens has represented clients in commercial litigation disputes, including breach of contract claims, mechanic's liens defenses, mortgage foreclosures (both commercial and residential), landlord-tenant disputes, U.C.C. matters, lien priority disputes, code violation issues, and defective workmanship matters.

**Meghan A. Douris** is a partner in the Seattle, Washington office of Oles Morrison Rinker & Baker, LLP. Her practice focuses on advising and representing those in the construction and government contracts industries in complex litigation, commercial arbitration, and claims disputes. Prior to joining Oles Morrison in 2010, Ms. Douris was an associate with a firm in New York City, representing design professionals in construction-related disputes, and got her start in construction law as an Associate General Counsel at the New York City Department of Design and Construction. After receiving her undergraduate degree from the College of William and Mary, Ms. Douris earned her J.D. from Brooklyn Law School in 2005, and was a member of the Moot Court Honor Society. Ms. Douris is admitted to practice in New York, Washington, and California.

**Sean P. Dowell** is an associate in the Seattle, Washington office of Oles Morrison Rinker & Baker, LLP. His practice involves all aspects of construction law and litigation. Mr. Dowell received his undergraduate degree in construction management from the University of Washington. Mr. Dowell then worked as a project manager and as an owner's representative on commercial and public construction projects before receiving his J.D., *magna cum laude*, from Seattle University School of Law. During law school, he served as a Lead Article Editor of the *Seattle University Law Review*.

**Eric P. Forner** is an associate in the Seattle, Washington office of Oles Morrison Rinker & Baker, LLP. His practice involves the representation of parties in construction-related disputes. Mr. Forner spent four years in the construction industry before attending University of Washington School of Law where he received his J.D. During law school, he served as a judicial extern for the Honorable Ronald B. Leighton, United States District Court for the Western District of Washington. Mr. Forner also studied international business law at the Université Jean Moulin Lyon 3, in Lyon, France, and holds a B.A. from Seattle University.

**Randall F. Hafer** is head of the Construction and Infrastructure Projects Group at the Atlanta law firm of Kilpatrick Townsend & Stockton LLP. Mr. Hafer's practice is concentrated in the area of construction and public contracts law and dispute avoidance/resolution. Mr. Hafer received a B.S., *cum laude*, from Georgia State University. He received his law degree with high honors from the University of Tennessee College of Law in 1983. He served on the editorial board of the *Tennessee Law Review*, and was elected to the Order of the Coif and the Phi Kappa Phi Honor Society. He has spoken at programs sponsored by the American Bar Association Forum Committee on the Construction Industry, the American Underground Association, the Design-Build Institute of America, and other industry-related groups. Mr. Hafer has also published a number of articles in trade and professional magazines, and has edited or co-authored a number of construction-related books. He is a fellow of the American College of Construction Lawyers where he co-chairs the Alternative Disputes Resolution Committee.

**Charles E. Harper, Jr.** is a partner in the Chicago office of Quarles & Brady LLP. His commercial dispute resolution and litigation practice has an emphasis on real estate and construction litigation. Mr. Harper's trial experience includes bench and jury trials, and his appellate experience includes appeals before the Illinois Court of Appeals and the United States Court of Appeals for the Seventh Circuit. Mr. Harper represents developers, contractors, lenders, and owners in all types of real estate and construction litigation, including construction defect cases, lease and contract disputes, eminent domain, condemnation, zoning, and mechanic's lien enforcement and defense.

**Heather L. Heindel, P.E., Esq.** is a counsel in the Construction & Real Estate Subgroup of the Commercial Litigation Practice Group at Perkins Coie LLP in the Seattle, Washington office. She concentrates her practice in complex construction and infrastructure projects and government contracts. Ms. Heindel received her undergraduate degree in Civil Engineering from Marquette University, a Masters of Science in Environmental Engineering from the Georgia Institute of Technology, and J.D. from Georgia State University. Prior to becoming an attorney, Ms. Heindel was an engineer at a major international engineering firm, designing and overseeing the construction of water and wastewater treatment plants. Ms. Heindel assists clients during the procurement stage of projects, especially on high-profile public-private partnership procurements, analyzing contractual risks and drafting a variety of construction contracts. Ms. Heindel also has extensive experience in advising clients during the construction phase of projects, negotiating changes, preparing claims, and resolving disputes. Ms. Heindel has represented numerous clients in arbitration hearings, mediations, disputes review board hearings, and state and federal trials.

**Guillaume A. Hess** is an associate in the dispute resolution practice in the Dubai office of Squire Patton Boggs LLP. He represents public and private owners and international contractors in resolving disputes arising out of the construction and operation of major projects. Admitted in New York, Mr. Hess has experience in resolving variety of disputes through arbitration, mediation, and other forms of alternative dispute resolution before the International Chamber of Commerce (ICC), the International Centre for Settlement of Investment Disputes (ICSID), the Dubai International Financial Centre—the London Court of International Arbitration (DIFC-LCIA), the Dubai International Arbitration Centre (DIAC), and in the DIFC courts. Mr. Hess graduated from Cornell Law School with an LL.M., focusing on international dispute resolution. He also studied law in France and graduated from the University of Paris 11 with a Masters in international business law as a class valedictorian.

**Scott C. Hutton** is a partner in the Dubai office of Squire Patton Boggs LLP where he focuses his practice on construction and development issues, acting on both contentious and non-contentious matters. He also deals with all property-related matters, including sales, purchases, landlord and tenant, and investment issues. He has a wide-ranging practice with a broad mix of clients both locally and internationally. He has considerable experience in all kinds of dispute resolution in the UAE and has acted in arbitration under the rules of the DIAC, the DIFC-LCIA, the Abu Dhabi Commercial Conciliation and Arbitration Centre (ADCCAC), and Ajman International Arbitration Centre (AIAC). Mr. Hutton was recommended by the Legal 500 for "attention to detail, in-depth knowledge of the applicable laws and interpretation of the law's application in the commercial environment of Dubai." He was also named a "rising star" in the second edition of the GUIDE TO THE WORLD'S LEADING CONSTRUCTION LAWYERS. Mr. Hutton also lectures on property matters at the Dubai Real Estate Institute.

**Peter J. Ippolito** is a partner in the firm of Dentons US LLP in San Diego, California. His practice involves all aspects of construction law, including federal, state, and local government contracts. Mr. Ippolito received a B.A. degree from the Virginia Military Institute, a J.D. degree from the University of Notre Dame, and an LL.M. degree from George Washington University. He is the author of numerous articles and seminar materials regarding construction law and government contracts. Mr. Ippolito represents clients involved in construction disputes and acts as a mediator or arbitrator in national complex construction disputes.

**Kristen M. Jarvis Johnson** is a senior associate at Squire Patton Boggs LLP, based out of the Doha office. Ms. Johnson assists corporations, sovereign governments, and individuals in complex civil litigation and arbitration matters throughout the world. Ms. Johnson's international arbitration practice encompasses both commercial and investor-state proceedings under the rules of UNCITRAL, ICC, ICSID, and QICCA. She has also participated in matters before international tribunals, including the U.N. Human Rights Committee, European Court of Human Rights, and International Criminal Tribunal for the former Yugoslavia. Ms. Johnson was granted a prestigious Fulbright Fellowship to study at Doshisha University in Kyoto, Japan in 2002. She received her undergraduate degree from Michigan State University in 2002, *magna cum laude*, and her Master's degree in international affairs and law degree from American University in 2007, with highest honors.

**Malcolm R. Jezewski** is an associate in the International Dispute Resolution Group at Squire Patton Boggs LLP, with a particular focus on construction and engineering. He has acted for principals and contractors in major infrastructure projects, including airports, hospitals, and oil and gas developments. Originally from the firm's Perth office in Western Australia, Mr. Jezewski has been based in Dubai since early 2015 where he has been gaining valuable experience representing clients in international arbitrations. Mr. Jezewski obtained his Bachelor of Laws from Murdoch University in 2012. He also obtained his Bachelor of Commerce (Finance) at this time. While in law school, Mr. Jezewski worked in-house at UGL Resources where he was involved in claims administration on major liquefied natural gas (LNG) projects. He was also responsible for preparing guidelines for use by on-site project personnel on practical compliance with key contract risk areas. Mr. Jezewski also represented his university in the 2011 Phillip C. Jessup Public International Law Moot competition.

**Shaun C. Kennedy** is an associate with Oles Morrison Rinker & Baker, LLP, in Seattle, Washington. His practice involves representing clients in all aspects of federal contracting law and construction litigation. After receiving his undergraduate degree from the University of Kentucky, Mr. Kennedy obtained his J.D. from American University Washington College of Law.

**Larissa E. Koshatka** is an associate in the Indianapolis office of Quarles & Brady LLP and is a member of the Commercial Litigation Practice Group. Her practice includes representing clients in real estate litigation matters, including eminent domain, mortgage foreclosure, landlord-tenant disputes, and code violations. Her appellate experience includes appeals before the Indiana Court of Appeals and the Indiana Supreme Court. Ms. Koshatka received her J.D., *cum laude*, from Indiana University Maurer School of Law—Bloomington, where she served as a managing editor of the *Indiana Law Journal*.

**Daniel B. Lewin** is an associate in the Chicago office of Quarles & Brady LLP and is a member of the Commercial Litigation Practice Group. Since joining Quarles, he has represented clients in real estate litigation matters, including code violations, mechanics liens, mortgage foreclosure, and landlord-tenant disputes. While in law school, he served as a research assistant for Professor Eve Brensike Primus and worked for the Special Litigation Division of the North Carolina Department of Justice.

**Kevin M. Long** is the national chair of Quarles & Brady LLP's Commercial Litigation Group. His practice focuses on construction and real estate litigation. He is also experienced in U.C.C., condemnation and insurance litigation. Mr. Long's construction litigation experience includes delay damage claims, defective labor/materials/workmanship cases, bid protests, payment disputes, and jobsite injury cases. He has special experience with effect of economic loss doctrine on construction claims, enforceability of liquidated damage provisions in construction contracts and lien priority, perfection, and waiver issues.

**Jennifer S. Lowndes** is a special counsel on Construction Practice Team of Jones Walker LLP in the Atlanta office. Ms. Lowndes routinely assists general contractors, subcontractors, construction managers, and owners in drafting and negotiating construction contracts as well as assisting her clients with obtaining commercial resolutions to issues during construction through the preparation and presentation of claims and dispute resolution board hearings. She has significant experience representing clients in litigation, arbitration, and mediation of disputes related to complex construction projects. Representative claims include breach of contract, extra work, delay, lost productivity and disruption, differing site conditions, acceleration, wrongful termination, and enforcement of performance and payment bonds. Ms. Lowndes also has experience in defending clients against negligence, gross negligence, punitive damages, and RICO claims in both state and federal courts.

**Stanley A. Martin** is the principal of Commonsense Construction Law LLC. His practice focuses on construction and public contract law. Mr. Martin received a degree in architecture from the Massachusetts Institute of Technology and a J.D. degree from Boston College Law School. He is an author of several manuals, articles, and text chapters on construction law issues, and blogs frequently about construction cases and decisions. Mr. Martin has taught construction law courses at M.I.T. and Northeastern University, and has lectured extensively on industry topics. Mr. Martin is a Fellow in the American College of Construction Lawyers. He has served as a board member of the Associated General Contractors of Massachusetts, and on the Corporate Advisory Council of the Boston Society of Architects. Mr. Martin also is a former board member and Secretary of the Boston Architectural College.

**Denise B. McLaughlin** is a Senior Associate in the Doha office of Squire Patton Boggs LLP. She specializes in major construction, engineering, and infrastructure projects, acting in both contentious and non-contentious matters and representing a range of project participants (funders, owners, contractors, and consultants). Ms. McLaughlin received her Graduate Diploma in Legal Practice from the Glasgow Graduate School of Law and is admitted to practice in Scotland. She has acted for clients in contentious and non-contentious matters in Scotland, Australia, and Qatar.

**David P. Muth** is the co-chair of Quarles & Brady LLP's Real Estate & Construction Litigation Group. Mr. Muth has tried numerous bench and jury trials and has significant appellate experience before the Wisconsin Court of Appeals, the Wisconsin Supreme Court, and the United States Court of Appeals for the Seventh Circuit. Mr. Muth has substantial experience in real estate disputes, construction defect claims, lease and contract disputes, scope of work disputes, architect design claims, breach of contract, water intrusion and mold claims, payment disputes, construction liens, and theft by contractor claims.

**Kevin D. Oles** is an associate in the litigation group of Squire Patton Boggs LLP, practicing in the Middle East and Africa (MEA) Region and the United States. Kevin works with clients in a variety of disputes, but focuses on international arbitration, construction litigation, commercial finance disputes, and alternative dispute resolution processes. He received his B.A. from the University of Notre Dame in 2005 and then graduated with honors from the Ohio State University Moritz College of Law in 2010, where he was Editor in Chief of the *Ohio State Journal on Dispute Resolution*. He previously clerked for Chief Judge Charles M. Caldwell, United States Bankruptcy Court for the Southern District of Ohio and worked with an election law think tank in Columbus, Ohio.

**Laurence R. Phillips** is a partner in the San Diego office of Dentons US LLP. Mr. Phillips' significant litigation experience includes the representation of contractors, public entities, real estate developers, manufacturers and other clients and their sureties and insurers in the mediation, arbitration, trial and appeal of complex matters concerning government and private contract disputes, commercial disputes, lease disputes, real estate/land-use disputes and construction disputes: including payment and performance bond claims, changed conditions claims, delay and disruption claims, prompt payment issues, stop notice and mechanic's lien claims, latent and patent defects in construction and design, products liability, and professional liability; bid protests; subcontractor listing issues; termination issues; Miller Act claims; and actions under the California and Federal False Claims Acts. Mr. Phillips also has significant experience in negotiating and drafting public and private works construction contracts, joint venture agreements, commercial leases, work letters, real estate purchase and sale agreements, escrow instructions and related loan documents. Mr. Phillips frequently lectures on issues relating to all stages of public and private works construction. Mr. Phillips received a J.D. degree from Pepperdine University

School of Law. He received a Bachelor of Arts degree from the University of California, San Diego.

**Erich C. Potter** is an attorney in the Seattle, Washington office of Oles Morrison Rinker & Baker, LLP. His practice primarily focuses on discovery and eDiscovery in construction disputes and commercial litigation. After receiving his undergraduate degree from Washington State University, Mr. Potter obtained his J.D. from American University Washington College of Law.

**Melia A. Preedy** is a member of the Seattle law firm Oles Morrison Rinker & Baker, LLP. Her practice focuses primarily on construction law, commercial litigation, and representing creditors and debtors in litigation, debt and insolvency proceedings. Ms. Preedy graduated from Seattle University School of Law in 2014. During law school, Ms. Preedy was a Lead Article Editor for the *Seattle University Law Review*. She externed for the Honorable Thomas S. Zilly at Federal District Court for the Western District of Washington. Prior to law school, Ms. Preedy worked in the construction industry drafting proposals for state and federal contracts. She received her undergraduate degree in English literature from the University of Washington in 2010.

**Gautam Y. Reddy** is an associate in the Construction & Infrastructure Projects Group of Kilpatrick Townsend & Stockton LLP in the Atlanta office. His practice focuses primarily on representing clients in construction litigation and arbitration and government contracting. Mr. Reddy received his undergraduate degree in Industrial Engineering from the University of Michigan. He received his J.D. from Emory University School of Law, where he was a Notes & Comments Editor for the *Emory Law Journal* and graduated Order of the Coif. Mr. Reddy has represented general contractors, subcontractors, and engineers in disputes regarding contract interpretation, construction defects, and project scheduling and delay. His representative matters include large industrial and transportation projects both in the United States and abroad.

**Michael A. Rogers** is an associate in the Indianapolis office of Quarles & Brady LLP, where he focuses his practice on commercial litigation. Mr. Rogers received his undergraduate degree from Purdue University and a J.D. degree from the Indiana University Mauer School of Law. He has bench and jury trial experience, and he represents owners, contractors, and financial institutions in pre-suit negotiations and litigation regarding contract disputes, condemnation and eminent domain, and mechanic's lien enforcement and defense.

**Tyler P. Scarbrough** is a Special Counsel on the Construction Practice Team of Jones Walker LLP in the Atlanta office. He concentrates his practice in construction litigation, contract negotiations, government contracting, and construction and engineering claims avoidance. Mr. Scarbrough received his undergraduate degree from Mississippi State University and J.D. from the University of Alabama. While in law school, Mr. Scarbrough was a lead articles editor for *The Journal of the Legal Profession*. Since joining the firm, Mr. Scarbrough has worked exclusively in construction and general litigation groups. Mr. Scarbrough has represented all types of clients in the construction industry, including private and public owners, general contractors, engineers, EPC contractors, design-build contractors, and subcontractors in various construction trades. Mr. Scarbrough has represented a variety of domestic and international clients throughout many industries, including power, rail, transportation, and high-rise condominium projects.

**Michael J. Schmidt** is an associate with Oles Morrison Rinker & Baker, LLP, in Seattle, Washington. His practice focuses on advising contractors on government and commercial contracts, insurance coverage issues, and representing contractors in litigation. Mr. Schmidt received his B.B.A. degree in Finance and Risk Management from the University of Wisconsin—Madison, and his J.D., *cum laude*, from the University of Wisconsin Law School in Madison, Wisconsin. Mr. Schmidt is admitted to practice in California, Washington, and Wisconsin. Prior to working in law, he worked for several years in corporate finance for a multinational defense contractor.

**Ashley J. Sherwood** is an associate in the Seattle, Washington office of Oles Morrison Rinker & Baker, LLP. Ms. Sherwood's practice focuses primarily on real estate, construction, and commercial litigation. She advises and represents both general contractors and subcontractors on private and public construction projects at the state and federal levels. Her construction experience includes multi-party lien foreclosure actions, differing site condition claims, and construction defect claims for high-rise residential buildings. Ms. Sherwood also advises and represents real estate developers and property management companies with respect to commercial real estate issues, including transactional disputes and litigation. Ms. Sherwood earned both her undergraduate degree and her J.D. from the University of Washington, where she was selected as member of the Order of the Barristers, served as Managing Editor of the *Washington Journal of Environmental Law & Policy* and served as Vice President for the UW Moot Court Honor Board.

**Alix K. Town** is an associate in the Seattle, Washington office of Oles Morrison Rinker & Baker, LLP. Her practice focuses on representing a broad range of clients in the government contracts arena and related litigation, including bid protests, claims, contract disputes, ethical issues, and compliance issues. Prior to joining Oles Morrison, Ms. Town served as an intern with the Air Force General Counsel's Office, where she assisted in suspension and debarment matters, as well as general acquisition law. Ms. Town received her J.D. from the George Washington University Law School and earned her bachelor's degree from Trinity College in Connecticut.

**Richard J. Storrs, Esq.** has practiced construction law and commercial litigation in Atlanta, Georgia since 1984. He received his undergraduate and law degrees from the University of Georgia, where he graduated with honors and served as a Notes Editor of the *Georgia Law Review*. He has served as an arbitrator in numerous construction and commercial matters, and mediates construction, real estate, and business disputes. Mr. Storrs has taught design and construction law since 2006, and is currently an adjunct professor at the University of Georgia School of Law, and Georgia State University College of Law.

**Daniel B. Swaja** is a partner in the Construction & Infrastructure Projects Group of Kilpatrick Townsend & Stockton LLP in the Atlanta office. He concentrates his practice in construction litigation, contract negotiations, government contracting and construction and engineering claims avoidance. Mr. Swaja received his undergraduate degrees from the University of Georgia and J.D. from the University of Georgia School of law. While in law school, Mr. Swaja was a staff member of the *Georgia Law Review*. Since joining the firm, Mr. Swaja has worked exclusively in construction and general litigation groups. Mr. Swaja has assisted public and private owners as well as local, national, and international contractors and engineers regarding contract negotiation, contract management, project execution, claim submittal, bid protests, and dispute resolution. Mr. Swaja has extensive discovery experience including, but not limited to, taking and defending depositions for clients. Mr. Swaja also has represented clients in arbitration hearings, mediations, dispute review boards, and trials.

**Jonathan M. Taunton** is a Senior Associate in the International Dispute Resolution group in the Dubai office of Squire Patton Boggs LLP. Mr. Taunton's practice concentrates on construction disputes and projects in the United States and internationally, with a particular focus on mediation and international arbitration. Mr. Taunton has practiced in U.S. courts, the courts of the Dubai International Financial Centre, and many international arbitral institutions, including ICC, ICE, LCIA, AAA, and DIAC. Mr. Taunton received his undergraduate degree from The Citadel, his Master's degree in Business from Boston University, and his J.D, *magna cum laude*, from Georgia State University College of Law. Prior to attending law school, Mr. Taunton served in the United States Marine Corps and worked in the construction industry as a partner in a small grading and erosion control company. While in law school, Mr. Taunton served as the Executive Editor of the *Georgia State University Law Review*.

**Eric Van Schyndle** is an associate in the Milwaukee office of Quarles & Brady LLP. His commercial dispute resolution and litigation practice has an emphasis on real estate, construction, and government procurement litigation. Mr. Van Schyndle has litigated numerous bid protests and several construction defect and title cases. His appellate experience includes appeals before the Wisconsin Court of Appeals and the Wisconsin Supreme Court. With respect to bid protests, Mr. Van Schyndle represents protestors, intervenors, and procuring municipalities.

**David C. Weaver** is an attorney in the Seattle, Washington office of Oles Morrison Rinker & Baker, LLP. His practice involves representing construction contractors involved in complex disputes. After receiving his undergraduate degree from Harvard University, Mr. Weaver received his J.D. from Santa Clara University School of Law.

**Tom Wilson** heads Squire Patton Boggs LLP's construction and arbitration practices in the Middle East. He advises clients with regard to project delivery systems, contract negotiation, contract compliance, and risk management. Lauded in Legal 500 as "very experienced, capable and practical," and in Chambers as a "top practitioner," Mr. Wilson is among the leading construction disputes lawyers in the Middle East. He represents public and private owners, international contractors, and original equipment manufacturers in resolving disputes over the construction and operation of infrastructure assets. Mr. Wilson has considerable experience resolving disputes through arbitration and alternative dispute resolution and serves as advocate in ICC, LCIA, and DIAC arbitrations, and in DIFC court proceedings. Mr. Wilson also occasionally accepts appointments to sit as arbitrator.

**Joseph Wolenski, Esq.** is an associate attorney at Thompson & Slagle, LLC in Atlanta, Georgia. He is licensed to practice in Georgia, Florida, and Massachusetts. Mr. Wolenski received his undergraduate degree from Boston College and his J.D. from the University of Miami School of Law. He is currently working toward obtaining a Masters in Extension Studies with a Concentration in Sustainability from Harvard University. Mr. Wolenski focuses the majority of his practice on the surety and construction industries.

**James G. Zack, Jr.** is the Executive Director of the Navigant Construction Forum.™ The Forum strives to be the construction industry's resource for thought leadership and best practices on avoidance and resolution of construction project disputes globally. Formerly he was the Executive Director, Corporate Claims Management Group, Fluor Corporation, one of the world's largest EPCM contractors. Mr. Zack was previously Vice President of PinnacleOne and the Executive Director of the PinnacleOne Institute and a Senior Construction Claims Consultant for CH2M HILL, Inc. Mr. Zack has, for more than 40 years, worked on both private and public projects throughout the United States and in 28 countries abroad. Mr. Zack is a Fellow of AACE, the Royal Institution of Chartered Surveyors, and a Fellow for Forensic Analysis with the International Guild of Project Controls. In the construction claims field, he is a recognized and published expert in mitigation, analysis and resolution or defense of construction claims and disputes. Mr. Zack is a Certified Construction Manager (CCM), a Certified Forensic Claims Consultant (CFCC), and a Project Management Professional (PMP).

# CONTENTS

*A complete table of contents for each chapter is included in the beginning of the chapter.*

## Chapter 12
## WEST REGION
## Arizona, California, Hawaii, Nevada, Utah
*Peter J. Ippolito, Laurence R. Phillips*

**Table of Cases**

**Index**

# CHAPTER 1

# CONSTRUCTION LAW IN THE ARAB STATES OF THE GULF COOPERATION COUNCIL[1]

Radwa S. Al Rifai, Guillaume A. Hess,
Scott C. Hutton, Malcolm R. Jezewski,
Kristen M. Johnson, Denise B. McLaughlin,
Kevin D. Oles, Jonathan M. Taunton, Tom Wilson

---

[1] The "Gulf Cooperation Council" or the "Cooperation Council for the Arab States of the Gulf" is a union of Arabian Gulf nations that includes Bahrain, Kuwait, Oman, Qatar, Saudi Arabia, and the United Arab Emirates (UAE) established by treaty on May 25, 1981. *See* "GCC Charter," *available at* http://www.gcc-sg.org/eng/indexfc7a.html?action=Sec-Show&ID=1 (last accessed Nov. 14, 2015).

## § 1.01 INTRODUCTION

Against a backdrop of falling oil prices, the construction sector in the countries of the "Gulf Cooperation Council" or the "Cooperation Council for the Arab States of the Gulf" ("GCC") continues to attract the attention of international contractors and consultants due to the volume of capital projects and major infrastructure development. This is reflected in the figures collated over the last seven years which indicate US$4,500 billion worth of construction work has been awarded since 2007.[2]

The legal environment in the GCC is a particularly diverse one. Large multinational corporations from across the globe enter the market bringing their own legal backgrounds and business practices. Upon arrival, they find an eclectic and sometimes confusing mixture of laws and practices advocated and understood, at varying levels, by attorneys from around the world. The major cities in the GCC are home to a thriving legal industry comprised of both international and local firms. Much of their work is comprised of bridging the gaps between GCC practices and those of foreign clients.

The GCC remains one of the most active areas in the world for construction projects of all sizes, and many construction attorneys will have clients who are, or will be, considering entering this market. This chapter will attempt to introduce western practitioners to some of the issues and practices that could affect their clients' interests when considering projects in the region.

## § 1.02 WHAT LAW APPLIES? CIVIL CODE? CONTRACT? SHARI'AH?

The law in most of the GCC countries is based on civil law through the enactment of a civil code.[3] Civil Codes in the GCC are similar to those found in other regions, but have distinct differences primarily related to the influence of Shari'ah law and the requirement in most GCC countries that any civil law be Shari'ah compliant.

Egypt was the first country in the Middle East to codify its laws and reconcile Shari'ah law within a civil law framework. This trend continued and other GCC countries drafted their own respective civil codes (based on the Egyptian model), which has resulted in many similarities between the GCC codes.

The Kingdom of Saudi Arabia ("Saudi Arabia," "KSA," or the "Kingdom") is a special case in that it has very few statutes apart from the Shari'ah. Shari'ah is not merely the *source* of law in the Kingdom, it is *the law*. As such, it governs many aspects of commercial and contractual relationships as well personal issues. But even here, there are some written statutes and regulations in force. The most

---

[2] GCC Construction Report 2015, MEED.
[3] Excluding Saudi Arabia which has not adopted a civil code.

important to a construction practitioner is likely the Government Tenders and Procurement Law ("GTPL") and its implementing regulations. This law governs all government contracts and, hence, most of the major infrastructure projects in the Kingdom.

Noah Feldman, a law professor at Harvard University, describes Shari'ah as the law which applies the principles of justice on governments and people.[4] Shari'ah law represents the law which is practiced by Islam; it is a word of Arabic origin which means "the right path." Prof. Feldman states, "the word 'Shari'ah' connotes a connection to the divine, a set of unchanging beliefs and principles that order life in accordance with God's will."[5] Shari'ah law is derived primarily from two sources, the Quran and the Sunna.

The Quran is the Islamic holy book and includes the basic standards for human interactions in all perspectives. The Sunna is the teachings which are derived from the Prophet Mohammed and the interpretations of certain Muslim legal scholars.[6] Since the death of the Prophet, Shari'ah law has been re-interpreted by Muslim legal scholars to adapt with the changing times.[7] It is a system of guidelines and duties and is the main source of law in Muslim constitutions. This is especially true in Saudi Arabia where a comprehensive civil code has not been enacted. Shari'ah law is the foundation of the legal system in Saudi Arabia and is the principal source of law.

In comparison, the remaining GCC countries apply civil law as the *primary* source of law, with Shari'ah law being applied if there is a gap in the civil law or a question of interpretation arises. This principle is illustrated in the Federal Law of the UAE which confirms:

> The rules and principles of Islamic jurisprudence shall be relied upon in the understanding, construction and interpretation of [the civil code provisions].[8]

## [A] The Contract Is the Law of the Parties, But . . .

As with other jurisdictions, GCC countries generally take the view that a contract creates the law of the parties,[9] and will be enforced to the extent it does not conflict with the laws of the jurisdiction. Construction practitioners are familiar with the interrelated web of contracts between the parties involved in a project, and this model holds true in the GCC. A practitioner can take some comfort in the

---

[4] Noah Feldman, *Why Shari'ah*, N. Y. Times, Mar. 16, 2008, *available at* http://www.nytimes.com/2008/03/16/magazine/16Shariah-t.html?pagewanted=all&_r=0.

[5] *Id.*

[6] Constitutional Rights Foundation, The Origins of Islamic Law, *available at* http://www.crf-usa.org/america-responds-to-terrorism/the-origins-of-islamic-law.html.

[7] *Id.*

[8] Federal Law No. 5 of 1985 concerning the issuance of the civil transactions law of the UAE.

[9] See § 1.09[C][3], Table 2, Sanctity of Contract under Arab Civil Codes, *infra.*

enforceability of the general terms of the contracts, but, as discussed in the remainder of this chapter, there are nuances in GCC jurisdictions that will affect the rights and obligations of the parties in ways that may not be apparent from the express terms of the contract. These nuances are especially troublesome when standard form contracts from other jurisdictions are adopted without consideration of local law and custom.

Due to the importance placed on Shari'ah law in the GCC, parties entering into commercial contracts should be aware of the issues addressed by Islamic law, including:[10]

- **Interest:** Simple interest is grudgingly allowed in most jurisdictions— Shari'ah does not favor the collection of interest. This is known as "riba" in Islamic economy and is prohibited as it is considered an unjustified, excess form of income which violates the Islamic principles that relate to income distribution.[11] The prohibition is seen explicitly in a number of verses in the Quran, in particular surit 2:275 and 276. But GCC countries have tried to adapt to western commercial norms, and most GCC countries now allow parties to agree to simple interest.

- **Concept of good faith / freedom of contract:** This concept is seen in the first verse of surit al Maida in the Quran, which states "O you who have believed, fulfill [all] contracts." Furthermore, and according to the Quran, all contracts must be entered into and applied in good faith.[12]

- **No uncertainty in contracting:** This is known as "gharar," meaning "risk" in the Arabic language. Whilst risk cannot be completely avoided, gharar means the risk that can be *reasonably* avoided.[13] As such, "gharar will . . . only invalidate a contract if: (i) the risk or uncertainty is significant; (ii) the risk affects the price or the principal objective of the contract; and (iii) the risk cannot be satisfactorily addressed through other available products which are Islamic compliant."[14]

These principles are not always enforced in clear way. Western commercial practices have influenced law in the regions and there are differences and nuances

---

[10] This list is not intended to be exhaustive.

[11] H. VISSER, *The Islamic economy in* ISLAMIC FINANCE: PRINCIPLES AND PRACTICE, 36 (2d ed. Edward Elgar Publishing 2013), *available at* http://0-www.elgaronline.com.mylibrary.qu.edu.qa/view/9781781001738.00010.xml.

[12] "Contract Law," in The Oxford Dictionary of Islam (John L. Esposito ed., Oxford Islamic Studies Online, Oct. 7, 2015), http://www.oxfordislamicstudies.com/article/opr/t125/e454.

[13] H. VISSER, *The Islamic economy, in* ISLAMIC FINANCE: PRINCIPLES AND PRACTICE 52-53 (2d ed. Edward Elgar Publishing 2013), *available at* http://0-www.elgaronline.com.mylibrary.qu.edu.qa/view/9781781001738.00010.xml.

[14] C PROCTER, THE LAW AND PRACTICE OF INTERNATIONAL BANKING 772 (1st ed., OUP 2010).

in how these principles will be applied. For example, many of the GCC jurisdictions do allow interest on amounts due, and while a factor, the concept of gharar will not prevent or invalidate most conventional risk allocation measures seen in contracts.

The law for projects in the GCC will generally be the parties' contract with some notable exceptions described in the following pages. Western clients will usually find the legal environment quite straightforward, and the influence of both Shari'ah and Arab civil law allow great flexibility and will, in most cases, compliment the terms of well drafted contracts. The key, as in any jurisdiction, is that the parties educate themselves and have a common understanding of the risks, rights, and obligations they have agreed to.

## § 1.03  DECENNIAL LIABILITY

Decennial liability is one of the most significant legal clauses that affect construction contracts in civil law jurisdictions. Decennial liability, generally, is strict liability that applies to construction projects, where builders of a work are liable for building defects arising after project completion and delivery to the owner. Decennial liability has roots in the French Civil Code, but has found its way into other civil codes across the globe, including the GCC. In the abstract, decennial liability arises when:

- A valid contract existed;
- The object of that contract is a fixed structure that cannot be transferred without destruction;[15]
- A defect that threatens the safety of the structure and its stability arises after delivery; and
- The defect to the structure was unknown at the time of handover.

When these elements are met, the builder, and sometimes the designer, is strictly liable to the owner for these building defects.

## [A]  Decennial Liability Code

The Qatar formulation of decennial liability, a fair representative of decennial liability provisions in the GCC, states:

> The contractor and the engineer shall be jointly liable for any collapse or defect, either in whole or in part, of the buildings or other fixed structures constructed by them, even if such collapse or defect arises from a defect in the

---

[15] This would exclude ships, cars, and other moveable goods.

land itself or the employer has authorized such defective buildings or structures. Such liability shall include any defects that may appear in the buildings or other structures which may threaten the safety and stability thereof; where the parties intend that the buildings or structures remain on the land for less than ten (10) years, liability shall be valid during any shorter period. In all events, the term shall commence from the date the work was awarded; the provisions of this Article shall not apply to any right of recourse by the contractor against the subcontractors.[16]

## [B] Extent of Decennial Liability

Decennial liability is generally limited to collapses or defects which may cause a collapse. In other words, decennial liability statutes are primarily concerned with structural problems. Mechanical, electrical, plumbing, architectural, fit out, and other types of defects that do not affect the safety and stability of a structure are not covered. Likewise, temporary works used in aid of construction are not covered. There are open questions in several jurisdictions as to how this would affect elements of a process plant.

Under decennial liability, a contractor or designer will be jointly and severally liable even where it has no fault or responsibility for the defect or collapse, but this liability will not extend to subcontractors, suppliers, and subconsultants.[17] Likewise, third parties harmed by a defect or collapse may not have a cause of action under the statute.[18] Some jurisdictions will provide a safe harbor for designers when the structure is not constructed according to the design *and* the designer did not supervise construction.[19]

Decennial liability statutes are generally mandatory, and parties cannot limit or contract out of decennial liability provisions during bargaining.[20] An owner cannot waive its right to seek claims through decennial liability prior to discovery of the defect.[21] Likewise, parties cannot limit the amount of damages available under a decennial liability action. Thus, even where a contract otherwise provides

---

[16] Qatar Law No. 22 of 2004 Regarding Promulgating the Civil Code, Art. 711; *see also* UAE Law No. 5 of 1985, Art. 880.

[17] *See* UAE Law No. 5 of 1985, Art. 880(2) "The said obligation to make compensation shall remain notwithstanding that the defect or collapse arises out of a defect in the land itself or that the employer consented to the construction of the defective buildings or installations."

[18] *Compare* Dubai Court of Cassation Petition No. 150, Year 2007 (holding no third party rights exist under UAE decennial liability statutes) *with* Abu Dhabi Court of Cassation, petition no. 721, Judicial Year 2009 (holding third party rights do exist under UAE decennial liability statutes); *see* discussion *infra*.

[19] *See* UAE Law No. 5 of 1985, Art. 881 ("If the work of the architect is restricted to making the plans and excludes supervision of the carrying out, he shall be liable only for defects in the plans.").

[20] Qatar Civil Law No. 22 of 2004, Art. 715. Note that as decennial liability is a remedy provided to the owner but is not explicitly in the contract, it is considered an extra-contractual remedy.

[21] I. S. ALJIBORI, REGULATION ON THE CONTRACTING CONTRACT 172 (2013).

an agreed limitation on liability, an action under the statute may result in far greater damages than those contemplated or agreed by the parties. This can extend to consequential damages as well. This is a particularly significant issue in a region where the statutes apply to a sizeable portion of the world's oil and gas infrastructure.

Decennial liability has also historically presented difficulty for insurers. France has a decennial liability regime which is covered by an extensive government sponsored insurance regime. This is not the case in the GCC, and standard E&O and CAR policies do not provide specific cover for decennial liability. Such coverage can be purchased, but the market is limited, coverage is costly, and it is advisable to obtain experienced counsel to ensure that there are no gaps.

## [C] Period of Decennial Liability

Despite their name, decennial liability provisions do not always run for 10 years. While many Arab states have decennial liability provisions, they must also be read in conjunction with applicable statutes of limitation and discovery periods. These often combine to operate so that an action under the decennial liability statute may be brought as much as 13 years after handover of a project.[22] The period may also be shorter in some cases. For example, temporary facilities, or buildings that are not intended to last for 10 years, will only be covered for the intended life of the building.[23]

Another critical aspect of decennial liability which must be understood is the point at which it begins. Decennial liability does not commence until after the project is handed over to the employer. Collapses or defects discovered prior to handover are not covered by the statute.

While originally based on the French ideal, decennial liability provisions in the GCC differ from French codes. For instance, under the French code, both the contractor and the engineer are liable only for the defects arising from "large acts." However, most GCC decennial liability provisions do distinguish between "large" and "small" acts, and a contractor and engineer can be liable for any type of structural or construction defects discovered.[24]

---

[22] *See, e.g.,* Qatar Law No. 22 of 2004, Art. 714.

[23] *See* UAE Law No. 5 of 1985, Art. 880 (stating that the liability period applies "unless the contracting parties intend that such installations should remain in place for a period of less than ten years").

[24] *See* Qatar Law No. 22 of 2004, Art. 711 ("the contractor and engineer shall be jointly liable for *any* collapse or defect") (emphasis added); *see also* ALJIBORI at 177.

## [D]  Case Law on Decennial Liability

While civil law systems do not recognize precedent as binding, cases can be persuasive authority and provide insight into how courts are likely to interpret obligations under the civil code.

Qatar courts determined that decennial liability provisions can endure beyond the statutorily provided period in the case of unrectified defects. An owner sued a contractor over a contract worth QAR 515,000 that entailed works for finishing the first floor of a villa and adding a second floor. After handover of the villa, defects arose and the owner brought a claim through decennial liability. The Qatar Court of First Instance found that the contractor was liable for QAR 25,530 for the defects.[25] Then, after the Court entered judgment, additional defects appeared, the building suffered significant cracking, and both walls and ceilings became unstable. The owner brought a second suit against the same contractor for these defects.[26] The Court employed an independent expert who opined that (1) the contractor already compensated the owner for losses and therefore should not be liable for further defects; and (2) the handover occurred beyond the statutory decennial liability period from the date of the claim. However, the Court found the contractor liable for an additional QAR 18,000 in damages because the new defects were related to the defects in the original suit, and therefore any remedy was also related. The contractor appealed this decision to the Qatari Court of Appeals, which affirmed the Court of First Instance's judgment, holding the contractor responsible for the most recent defects, as these defects all stemmed from the original latent defects, and the failure to repair properly was not affected by any statutory time bar.[27]

The Abu Dhabi Court of Cassation addressed the question of when decennial liability begins.[28] The Court held that builders and designers cannot be liable under decennial liability provisions for construction defects that arise during construction and are discovered prior to handover. Additionally, the Court opined in dicta that the latent defect must be one that affects the safety and stability of the building, and does not include minor defects within the ambit of decennial liability.[29]

Turning to determinations of fault, the Dubai Court of Cassation held that decennial liability does not subside with respect to the "but for" cause of the defect.[30] The Court held that it was immaterial whether the defect/collapse arose

---

[25] Qatari Court of First Instance, Petition Number Case #98/900.

[26] Qatari Court of First Instance, Case #1404/202.

[27] Qatari Court of Appeals, Case #408/50 (deciding the case according to Qatar Civil Law No. 22, Arts. 67, 69).

[28] Abu Dhabi Court of Cassation, petition no. 293, Judicial Year 2009.

[29] *Id.* Note that this decision about the scope of defect contrasts with the code that makes no differentiation in the scale of the defect and liability.

[30] Dubai Court of Cassation Petition No. 150, Year 2007.

due to a fault in the ground conditions or whether the employer consented to the construction of a faulty structure, liability applied regardless. This case underlines the strict nature of decennial liability, as the constructing parties are liable to the employer/owner regardless whether they caused the latent defect, failed to discover faulty ground conditions, or attempted any mitigating actions. The Court of Cassation also held that decennial liability rights do not include third parties harmed by a building collapse or defect. Such third parties may pursue their claims, but must pursue them in tort.[31]

In contrast, the Abu Dhabi Court of Cassation opined that damages to third parties can be assessed under decennial liability provisions.[32] The Court held that the Civil Code provides that injuries to third parties are part of the harm that can flow from decennial liability claims. The Court also opined on the calculation of damages, holding that employers and owners can include consequential damages for decennial liability claims, including costs, lost earnings, and lost opportunities in claimed damages.[33]

## [E]   Relevant Statutes

| Jurisdiction | Decennial Liability Provisions |
| --- | --- |
| Qatar | Qatar Law No. 22 of 2004 Regarding Promulgating the Civil Code, Article 711. |
| United Arab Emirates | UAE Civil Code, Law No. 5 of 1985, Articles 880–83 |
| Iraq | Civil Code of Iraq, Law No. 40 of 1951, Article 870–72 |
| Jordan | Jordanian Civil Code No. 43 of 1976, Articles 788–91 |
| Kuwait | Kuwait Law No. 67 of 1980, Article 692 |
| Egypt | Egyptian Civil Code No. 131 of 1948, Article 651 |
| Oman | Civil Code of Oman No. 29 of 2013, Article 634 |

## § 1.04   BONDING AND GUARANTEES IN ARAB CIVIL LAW JURISDICTIONS

U.S. trained lawyers can be vulnerable to a subtle trap when called upon to advise on projects in the Arab Civil Law jurisdictions. Common industry terms sometimes have significantly different meanings when crossing jurisdictions. One example is "bonds." Project bonding in the Middle East is accomplished through guarantees which are more like letters of credit than the insurance-based bonds used in the United States.

---

[31] *Id.*

[32] Abu Dhabi Court of Cassation, Petition No. 721, Judicial Year 2009.

[33] *Id.*

## [A] Bonds in the United States

Bonds in the U.S. construction industry are similar to insurance policies. An obligor enters into a contract under which a guarantor, usually an insurance company, agrees to pay up to a set amount to an obligee/beneficiary if the obligor fails to meet some obligation. In most cases, the guarantor even has the right to step in and perform the work. These bonds commonly guarantee the contractor or subcontractor's performance, and the employer, contractor, or even subcontractor's payments to subcontractors and suppliers.

## [B] Guarantees in ACL Countries

"Bonds" on construction projects in Arab Civil Law countries are very different. Although often referred to as "bonds," they are in fact guarantees. These are more like letters of credit than insurance policies. The guarantor is typically a financial institution such as a bank rather than an insurer, and, unlike the guarantor on a U.S.-style bond, generally has no substantive defenses to payment. A U.S.-style guarantor may step into the shoes of his obligor and assert all of his defenses in addition to any independent defenses the guarantor may have. But the guarantor/bank in an Arab Civil Law jurisdiction is generally obligated to pay on the first written demand. The bank's defenses are usually limited to the expiration of the guarantee and the formalities of presenting the demand letter. As with U.S.-style bonds, the bank often has recourse against the obligor for the amount disbursed.

This lack of meaningful defenses to payment raises the bank's risk level and thus raises the cost of providing the guarantee and the level of collateral or security arrangements that the bank may require from the obligor. This dynamic will affect a contractor's bonding capacity and often tie up cash and securities as collateral for outstanding guarantees. Thus maintaining these bonds for an extended period can be expensive and limit a contractor's ability to take on new work.

A second significant difference is the risk profile for the parties that results from the lower value of the guarantees as compared to U.S.-style bonds. In the United States, a project is often fully bonded and, in many cases, double or triple bonded when one factors in payment bonds and bonds from subcontractors. In Arab Civil Law jurisdictions, only the employer/owner is typically protected, and that protection, though much easier to encash, is customarily only 10% of the contract value.

Where U.S.-style bonds are typically available for both parties, bonds and guarantees in the Middle East generally only protect the employer and sometimes operate more as a means to put pressure on the contractor than as a means of completing the project. A contractor has no strong defenses to prevent an employer from encashing his performance guarantee. Unscrupulous employers often use this as a threat throughout the course of the project. Employers in financial difficulty have even been known to encash contractor's bonds simply to raise money.

## [C]  Types of Guarantees

There are three types of guarantees typically found in Arab Civil Law construction projects: Performance Guarantees, Advance Payment Guarantees, and Retention Guarantees.

Performance Guarantees are intended to guarantee the contractor's performance of the contract. This intentionally broad and vague concept is usually implemented through unconditional bank guarantees for approximately 10% of the contract price. They are found in main contracts,[34] subcontracts, and some professional services contracts. Contracts will commonly require the contractor to increase the performance guarantee to keep pace with variations or change orders which affect the contract price. The Performance Guarantee will remain at full price until the completion certificate is issued, and sometimes remain in force at full or reduced levels after completion until a defects liability period is completed.[35]

Advance Payment Guarantees are intended to secure advances typically made by employers for mobilization. These are usually unconditional guarantees for 100% of the Advance Payment. The Advanced Payment Guarantee is sometimes reduced as the Advanced Payment is recovered through deductions, but more commonly remains at the full amount until the Advance Payment is repaid.[36]

Retention Guarantees are sometimes accepted in lieu of customary 10% retention. These guarantees are less common and often favorable to a contractor because they free up cash flow by allowing the contractor to receive the full value of its interim payments. Some contractors further improve their cash flow by withholding retention from their subcontractors even when the contractor itself is satisfying retention via a guarantee. Retention Guarantees will increase by series of amendments to the guarantee which will increase it in parallel with the contractual retention percentage.[37]

---

[34] *See, e.g.,* FEDERATION INTERNATIONALE DES INGENIUERS-CONSEILS, CONDITIONS OF CONTRACT FOR CONSTRUCTION: FOR BUILDING AND ENGINEERING WORKS DESIGNED BY THE EMPLOYER, [FIDIC Red Book], General Conditions, Cl. 4.2 (1999).

[35] *See, e.g.,* FIDIC Red Book General Conditions, Cl. 11.9.

[36] *See, e.g.,* FIDIC Red Book, General Conditions, Cl. 14.2.

[37] *See, e.g.,* The Joint Contract Tribunal Limited, Retention Bonds 2011, *available at* http://www.jctltd.co.uk/docs/Retention%20Bonds%202011.pdf (last visited Nov. 8, 2015).

## [D]   Resisting Encashment of the Guarantee

Regardless of whether the instruments are referred to as guarantees, securities, or bonds, they are essentially a binding undertaking by the bank, and will generally be interpreted and enforced according to their text.[38] The exception to this is when a party, usually the contractor, tries to prevent encashment through a court action. Courts are reluctant to grant these injunctions permanently,[39] but they sometimes succeed in obstructing and delaying payment of the guarantees for a period of weeks.

While this form of relief is clearly contemplated by most statutes, it is considered exceptional and courts are hesitant to interfere with the clear language of the guarantee. UAE law provides injunctive relief to prevent payment on a guarantee in Article 417 of the Commercial Transactions Law.[40] This is available "in exceptional circumstances" where the obligor has "serious and ascertained reasons to justify the . . . imposition of an attachment."[41]

The Dubai Court of Cassation has further explained the applicable UAE standard in Appeal No. 247/2007. The Court held that a court will not stop a bank from paying under a guarantee unless:

1.   there are exceptional and compelling reasons to do so;

2.   the claim is fully ascertained; and

3.   there are no previous judgments in favor of the principal debtor (obligor) against the beneficiary/obligee based on the same transaction or documentation.

Other commonly used arguments in favor of granting the attachment include:

*   The employer's demand for payment on the bond or advance payment guarantee is made in bad faith;[42]

---

[38] UAE, Abu Dhabi Court of Cassation, 918/Judicial Year 3 (2009) ("It is the wording of the letter of guarantee that determines the obligations of the bank and the conditions under which it must be paid.").

[39] The term "freezing order" is commonly used to refer to an attachment or injunction ordering the guarantor to not to make payment on the guarantee. The court's action is also commonly referred to as a "precautionary attachment" or "seizure." ("In exceptional cases, the court may at the request of the ordering person levy seizure on the guarantee amount with the bank, provided that the ordering person relies for his claim on serious and solid grounds." Federal Law No. 18 of 1993, UAE Commercial Transactions Law, Art. 417(2).) Despite the common term, the action discussed in this chapter is distinct from the "freezing order" commonly understood to refer to an injunction used to secure a defendant's assets for execution of a judgment by "freezing" assets so that a defendant may not deplete or devalue them.

[40] UAE Commercial Transactions Law, Law No. 18 of 1993, Art. 417(2) (2006).

[41] Id.; see also Union Supreme Court, 644/Year 23 (2003).

[42] Art. 172 of the Qatar Civil Code requires that all contracts be performed in good faith.

- the contractor has completed the work and/or has not caused whatever action the employer is asserting forms the basis for encashing the bond; and

- the employer is seeking to encash an amount disproportionate to the justification provided.[43]

If an injunction is obtained, it is usually temporary. The procedure for obtaining an injunction is similar to procedures in common law jurisdictions. It is usually an ex-parte hearing in which the party seeking relief will plead some equitable reason for the court to maintain the status quo by blocking payment. This is often granted on a preliminary basis, following which the party making a demand on the guarantee may file an objection. This process can delay payment by several weeks or even months.

It should be remembered that the bank's customer is the party purchasing the guarantee, usually the contractor. When a demand is made upon a guarantee, even one payable immediately upon demand, banks will often delay payment in order to give their customer an opportunity to negotiate or seek an injunction to stop payment. The bank would always rather retain the funds than seek recourse from the contractor, and has little to lose by delaying payment even where it constitutes a clear breach of the guarantee.

## [E]   Qatar

The situation in Qatar is legally different, but the same in practice. Qatar law allows banks to raise substantive defenses to an employer's demand to encash a bond, but banks are reluctant to do so without a court order.

Qatar law incorporates by reference the United Nations Convention on Independent Guarantees and Stand-by Letters of Credit ("CIGSLC").[44] Article 413 of Law No. 27 (2006), Commercial Code, provides that "The rules of international transactions concerning the letter of guarantee shall apply in respect of any matter not specifically provided for in this section." Banks may refuse demands for payment on guarantees under this law, if circumstances allow; however, banks are typically hesitant to refuse such demands for fear of breaching the terms of the guarantee. This could have both contractual and regulatory consequences.

---

[43] While no justification is required by the bank, a prima facie case by the contractor will shift the burden to the employer sufficiently that the court may enquire as to the employer's reasons for both the fact and amount of the encashment.

[44] Qatar has incorporated the CIGSLC by reference, but is not listed as a signatory. Kuwait joined the convention by accession in 1998.

## [F] Statutory References

| Jurisdiction | Relevant Statutes |
|---|---|
| Bahrain | Articles 331-336 of the Law of Commerce (Decree Law No. 7 of 1987, as amended) (the "Commercial Law") |
| Oman | Oman Commercial Law, Royal Decree 55 of 1990, Art. 238 *et seq.* |
| Qatar | Commercial Code, Law No. 27 (2006), Art. 406-413 (incorporating by reference the United Nations Convention on Independent Guarantees and Stand-by Letters of Credit ("CIGSLC") |
| United Arab Emirates | Commercial Transactions Law (Law No. 18 of 1993), Arts. 411-419 |

## [G] Sample Guarantee and Demand Letter[45]

---

SAMPLE PERFORMANCE GUARANTEE

Date: _____

[Beneficiary Name]
[Beneficiary Address]

**Subj:** Our Performance Security No. ABC123 for USD $_____
**Contract:** [Identify underlying construction contract]
**Project:** [Identify Project]

Dear Sirs,

[Name of Contractor], the Contractor, have described that their tender for the above named Works has been accepted. We hereby undertake to hold at your disposal the sum of **USD** _____ ([amount in words] United States Dollars), 10% of the Contract Price, as Performance Security. This Security shall be free of interest and payable in cash on your first demand in the manner ordered, without the Contractor or any person on his behalf or ourselves having the right to suspend or delay payment or to object thereto for any reason whatsoever.

This Security is valid until the Contractor has executed and completed the Works and remedied any defects therein in accordance with the Contract and shall, before expiry, be automatically renewed until a Defects Liability Certificate has been issued or until advised by you that the Contract has been fulfilled. No claim shall be made against the Security after the issue of the Defects Liability Certificate.

---

[45] As discussed above, banks sometimes ignore their obligations to pay immediately. A GCC bank recently notified the contractor/obligor that it would delay payment for a week on a guarantee with exactly the same payment terms as those in this example. The delay allowed the contractor to obtain a preliminary attachment and allowed the bank to temporarily avoid payment.

Yours Faithfully,

_____

[Bank's Authorized Signatory]

*\*\*\*This sample is adapted from an actual performance guarantee which was encashed. The names, account numbers and currencies have been changed to preserve confidentiality, but the terms are accurately reproduced.*

---

SAMPLE LETTER OF DEMAND ON PERFORMANCE GUARANTEE

**Ref: [Employer Reference]**
**Date: _____**

**[NAME OF BANK]**
[Address of Bank]
**By Hand**

Dear Sirs,

WRITTEN NOTICE OF DEMAND FOR PAYMENT
PERFORMANCE SECURITY NO :      ABC123 FOR USD $_____
CONTRACT NO                    :      [IDENTIFY UNDERLYING CONSTRUCTION
                                      CONTRACT]
PROJECT:                       :      [IDENTIFY PROJECT]

---

Pursuant to your Performance Security No. ABC123, dated the ___ day of April _____, you, [BANK], as the Guarantor, have undertaken to pay us, the [Name of Beneficiary] (the **Beneficiary**), the sum of USD _____ (the **Guarantee Sum**) in cash upon our first demand. The original instrument of the Performance Security is attached to this written demand for your attention and acknowledgement hereof.

Further, take notice that the Contractor has not completed the Works, and no Defects Liability Certificate has been issued. Your Performance Security remains valid according to its terms.

In the exercise of our legal and contractual rights as the Beneficiary under the Performance Security, we, [Name of Beneficiary], **HEREBY DEMAND FROM YOU**, [Bank], as the Guarantor, the full and immediate payment of the Guarantee Sum to us in cash or into our bank account as per the following details:

Bank Name/Branch:        _____
Account Beneficiary:     [Name of Beneficiary]
IBAN/Account No:         _____

Pursuant to the terms of the Performance Guarantee, you, as the Guarantor, are obliged to pay the Guarantee Sum to us immediately, without any delay whatsoever, and without reference or recourse to or any objection of the Contractor or any other person thereof.

Kindly acknowledge your acceptance of this written demand on the duplicate copy of this letter and return the same to our office.

Yours faithfully,
**FOR AND ON BEHALF OF [BENEFICIARY]**

**[name & designation of the authorized signatory]**

## § 1.05   FIDIC IN ARAB CIVIL CODE JURISDICTIONS

The most commonly used standard form contracts for construction projects in the Middle East are those of the FIDIC suite of contracts. They are rarely used as published, and are more often encountered with a variety of amendments which often alter the balance of risk in the original FIDIC document.

The term "FIDIC" is an acronym of *Federation Internationale Des Ingenieurs-Conseils* (i.e., International Federation of Consulting Engineers) which drafted and published the FIDIC suite of contracts. The contracts forming the FIDIC suite have each been printed with a different color on the cover page,[46] and the contracts are referred to by their allotted color.

FIDIC has been utilized in the Middle East for several decades;[47] however, the following contracts from the suite are used the most frequently:

   i.   **The Red Book**—This is "traditional" or construct-only form of contract for building and engineering works where the employer undertakes design;

   ii.  **The Yellow Book**—This is a design and build contract for electrical and mechanical engineering works;

   iii. **The Silver Book**—This is an EPC[48]/turnkey contract;

   iv.  **The Gold Book**—This is a design, build and operate form of contract; and

   v.   **The White Book**—This is a Model Services Agreement for the appointment of consultants.

In the private sector, FIDIC is the most widely used standard form of contract across the GCC. Even where it is not used, its influence can be seen in the structure and provisions of bespoke contracts. FIDIC's influence is also apparent

---

[46] Often referred to as the "rainbow suite."
[47] Since the 1970s.
[48] Engineer, procure, and construct.

in the public sector where many employers favor bespoke forms of contract *based* on FIDIC but modified to comply with local law. For example, in Saudi Arabia,[49] the government uses a Public Works Contract[50] ("**PWC**") when contracting with the private sector. The PWC is based on a very early version of the Red Book.[51]

## [A]  Using FIDIC in GCC Countries

Whilst FIDIC's objective is no doubt to have a workable contract that does not require material amendment, the reality in the Middle East is that FIDIC forms are heavily adapted. FIDIC's terms are based on common law principles[52] and often require significant modifications before they can be used to resolve various conflicts between the common law and local laws in the Middle East (including Shari'ah law). Additionally, disparate bargaining power often results in amendments which skew the balance of risk away from that envisioned by the authors.

## [B]  Labor and Employment Targets

Many GCC countries have codified government initiatives intended to increase the number of their citizens[53] employed in the public and private sectors (usually in managerial or professional roles). In Saudi Arabia, employers are required to attract and employ Saudis to ensure the number of Saudi nationals does not drop below 75% of the workforce (unless otherwise agreed by the Labor Minister).[54]

To further boost the number of Saudi nationals employed in the Saudi Arabian private sector, the Ministry of Labor introduced the "nitaqat" program which classifies each company depending on the number of Saudis employed. If the number of Saudis employed falls below a certain threshold,[55] the company risks being classified "red" and its permissions to operate in Saudi Arabia may be withdrawn.

---

[49] In accordance with Government Tenders and Procurement Law (Royal Decree No. M/58 4 *Ramadan* 1427H/27 September 2006).

[50] 1988 version. It is worth noting that the PWC is expected to be replaced with a new contract called the General Construction Contract Form ("**GCCF**"). The GCCF (which has not yet been enacted) will also take its influence from the Red Book (most likely the 1999 version) and is expected to amend the standard form to comply with local law.

[51] Third edition (1977).

[52] Adam Webster, FIDIC IN THE MIDDLE EAST (2009), Society of Construction Law (Gulf).

[53] Particularly the young citizens of GCC countries.

[54] Article 26, Saudi Labour (Royal Decree No. M/46 of 05/06/1436).

[55] This will depend on the size of the organization and the sector.

Qatar has a similar plan ("Qatarization") which is part of its vision for 2030. The initiative was undertaken by the industrial and oil and gas sectors in an effort to increase the number of Qatari nationals in the public workforce. The Qatari Labor Law[56] incorporates the principle of Qatarization in the private sector; its aim is to increase the number of Qataris in the industrial sector by 50% by 2020.

The UAE established (some time ago) an "Emiratization" plan. Various federal ministerial decisions in the banking, insurance, and other business sectors stipulate required thresholds for local hiring, generally in the range of 3-5% of the total workforce. Similar policies exist in Bahrain, Kuwait, and Oman.

Employers, especially government or quasi-government employers, will often include these statutory requirements in the contract.

## [C] Decennial Liability

Decennial liability is a statutory regime that applies strict liability to defects in the building which threaten (or are likely to threaten) the building's safety and stability, and total or partial collapse of the building.[57] The concept of decennial liability is one of the key nuances in the Middle East and is often overlooked by many foreign contractors and consultants.[58] The key points for contractors and consultants to be aware of in relation to decennial liability when pricing works and considering the risk allocation are as follows:

- decennial liability protects against (i) defects in a building which threatens (or are likely to threaten) the building's safety and stability; and (ii) total or partial collapse of the building;

- liability is not limited to the main contractor, it is also imposed on architects, engineers, and project managers;

- decennial liability continues for a period of 10 years, which is far greater than a standard defects liability period;

- the usual defects liability regime under standard form contracts, including FIDIC, is distinct from (and in addition to) decennial liability;

- there is a growing practice of inserting contract terms that appear to mimic decennial liability, but in fact increase the scope of a contractor or designer's liability to provide full defects coverage, irrespective of whether the defects threaten (or are likely to threaten) the structural integrity of the building. Often, contractors and designers accept this

---

[56] Law No. 14 of 2004.

[57] Discussed in more detail in section 1.02 of this chapter.

[58] Particularly those from common law backgrounds where the concept of decennial liability does not exist.

more onerous provision due to a lack of understanding in relation to the limited scope of their obligations under the decennial liability regime;

- professional indemnity insurance and "contractors' all risks" insurance are unlikely to cover decennial liability;[59] and

- it is not possible to limit or discharge decennial liability obligations.

## [D]  Limiting Liability

It is not possible to limit all liability under civil law in the GCC, such as decennial liability (see paragraph [C] above).

General Condition 17.6 of the Red Book[60] limits the liability of the parties under the contract by excluding liability for indirect and consequential loss suffered in connection with the contract; however, the exclusion is subject to several carve outs which essentially reintroduce liability for indirect and consequential loss (if one or more of the carve outs are satisfied). These carve outs conflict with Shari'ah law in Saudi Arabia which only permits *actual* (direct) losses to be recovered; as opposed to indirect and consequential losses. Furthermore, the civil law in Bahrain, Oman, and the UAE does not address indirect and consequential loss or define what is meant by these terms. This can be contrasted with the Qatar civil code which follows the common law by defining "consequential damages" as those which were "reasonably foreseeable or within the contemplation of the parties at the time of the conclusion of the contract."[61]

Notably, the civil codes in Bahrain[62] and Qatar[63] allow parties to claim indirect and consequential losses in the event of liability arising from fraud or gross negligence.

Thus parties should be aware that the clear language of the FIDIC suite regarding consequential damages and limitations on liability may not be enforceable in all situations. Some of these issues are unavoidable, but others can be addressed by careful drafting. To avoid a dispute over what constitutes indirect and consequential loss, parties should consider adding a definition of "indirect and consequential loss" to the FIDIC standard form. In all cases, some level of client education is advised.

---

[59] It is possible to procure insurance to cover decennial liability however this will be expensive to maintain.

[60] 1999 edition.

[61] Art. 263(2), Qatar Civil Code (Law No. 22 of 2004).

[62] Art. 223, Bahrain Civil Code Law No.19 of 2001.

[63] Art. 263, Qatar Civil Code (Law No. 22 of 2004).

## [E]  Boycott Clause

Several GCC countries have sanctions in place in relation to contracting with Israel. For example, in Qatar:

> A person, whether natural or juristic, shall not enter into agreement, directly or by proxy, with bodies or persons residing in Israel or holding Israeli nationality or working on behalf or in favor of Israel, wherever they lived, whether the subject of the agreement is commercial or financial transactions or any other transaction of whatever nature.[64]

Importantly, Oman, Jordan, and Bahrain are all parties to the United States "Free Trade Agreement" (**FTA**). As such, any provision that purports to restrict or limit trade when contracting in Oman, Jordan, or Bahrain will be unenforceable. Conversely, when contracting in Qatar, Kuwait, the UAE, and Saudi Arabia, one will often encounter amendments to the FIDIC standard form to include provisions that address the boycott rules. Care must also be taken by U.S. companies to ensure they do not run afoul of U.S. law by entering into these agreements.

## [F]  Language and Choice of Law

From a practical perspective, it is useful to know that laws, regulations, decisions, and decrees across the GCC (excluding the UAE) are published in Arabic with no official English translation. As a result, legal professionals and other interested parties must engage the services of a recognized interpreter to review and translate the relevant law, regulation, decision, or decree. Whilst this is currently the only available option, it is important to remember that the Arabic version will control if there is a question of interpretation or an inconsistency between the official Arabic version and a translation.

It is also important to note that General Condition 1.4 of the Red Book[65] allows the contracting parties to select the law and language applicable to the contract. This right reflects the concept that parties should be free to negotiate and draft contract terms as they see fit (i.e., "freedom of contract"), which is enshrined in civil law.

Notwithstanding freedom of contract, parties should be aware that selecting the law of another jurisdiction (in relation to domestic works procured using a public sector contract) in Saudi Arabia is prohibited.[66] Furthermore, an English

---

[64] Art. 5 of Law No. 13 of 1963, Qatar. The UAE includes a similar sanction in Law No. 15 of 1972.

[65] 1999 edition.

[66] Unless consent is received from the governing authority. Art. 1, Governmental Competition and Purchase Statute, Law No. 58 of 2006.

translation of a government contract cannot be relied upon in court in Saudi Arabia as the agreement between the parties is governed by the Arabic version (and the contract must be interpreted and written in Arabic before signing takes place).[67]

### [G] Liquidated Damages

General Condition 8.7 of the Red Book[68] entitles the employer to levy liquidated damages against the contractor for each day of delay between the Time for Completion and the date stated in the Taking-Over Certificate.[69]

Despite inserting a daily rate of liquidated damages in the Appendix to the FIDIC standard form (and any corresponding aggregate cap), the courts in GCC countries are entitled to review the level of liquidated damages. Arguably, this power undermines "freedom of contract" and circumvents the primary benefit of including liquidated damages in the first instance (i.e., financial certainty in respect of the level and limit of damages that will be imposed in the event of a delay to completion).

Article 266 of the Qatar civil code provides a defense against a claim for liquidated damages[70] as it allows the court to reduce the level of liquidated damages to reflect the *actual* loss suffered (and can reduce the level of liquidated damages to zero if there has been no loss). A similar provision applies in the Bahrain Civil Code.[71] Contractors should also be aware that the courts in the UAE also have the capacity to increase the level of liquidated damages applied. The official commentary on Article 390 of the UAE Civil Code[72] provides:

> If the compensation is due and the same is equal to the loss sustained, then the liquated damages agreement in question shall be upheld. However, if the due compensation is not equal to the loss sustained, the judge shall have the right, upon the request of one of the parties, to *increase or decrease* the amount of such compensation in order to reflect the loss. This in the line with the Sharia'h principles under which compensation shall be equal to actual loss suffered.

(Emphasis added.)

---

[67] Art. 27, Governmental Competition and Purchase Statute, Law No.58 of 2006.

[68] 1999 edition.

[69] The cap on liquidated damages should be included in the Appendix to the Red Book.

[70] James Bremen, English Law Concepts in the Gulf Cooperation Council Countries (Society of Const. Law April 2009).

[71] Arts. 225-227, Bahrain Civil Code, promulgated by Decree No. 19 of 2001.

[72] Issued by the UAE Ministry of Justice.

## § 1.06   DISPUTE RESOLUTION FORUMS IN THE GCC

### [A]   Litigation

The court systems of the GCC countries are generally organized into a three tier structure consisting of: (1) a Court of First Instance; (2) Court of Appeal; and (3) a Court of Cassation or Supreme Court. The notable exceptions are the Kingdom of Saudi Arabia, the Dubai International Financial Centre ("DIFC"), the Abu Dhabi Global Market ("ADGM"), and the Qatar Financial Centre ("QFC"), each of which will be discussed individually below. Some peculiarities of each system are discussed below while general discussion is relevant to all courts other than the common law courts found in the DIFC, ADGM, and QFC.

Shari'ah courts exist in all GCC countries and they deal with all matters relating to the personal status of Muslims (with an extended jurisdiction in Saudi Arabia). Separate criminal courts and, in some jurisdictions, military courts also exist. Civil courts do not have specialist courts such as construction courts and there are no specialist judges. For this reason, the importance of court-appointed experts cannot be understated and is discussed below.

### [1]   Jurisdiction and Cross-Border Enforcement

Local courts generally have jurisdiction through domicile or place of performance/contract. They often also have exclusive jurisdiction in certain types of commercial matter, including commercial agencies or distributorship agreements, real estate, employment, and government contracts. Local courts do, in theory, recognize the principle of freedom of contract but often choose to reject a choice of foreign law where they deem that they have jurisdiction to hear the matter or on public policy grounds, which have been widely construed.

The GCC countries are all signatories to two important conventions relating to recognition and enforcement of judgments and awards, namely, the Riyadh Convention of 1983[73] and the GCC Convention of 1996.[74] Article 1 of the GCC Convention states that "Each of the GCC countries shall execute the final judgments issued by the courts of any member state in civil, commercial and administrative case."

In order for a judgment to be enforceable, the originating court must have had jurisdiction, within the definition provided in the Convention.[75] Importantly, the conventions cover the recognition and enforcement of judgments and arbitral awards without re-examination of the merits, so long as leave to enforce has been granted by a competent court in the home jurisdiction.

---

[73] The Inter-Arab Convention on Judicial Co-operation, 1983.

[74] Agreement on the Execution of Judgments, Delegations and Judicial Notifications, 1996.

[75] The various jurisdictional gateways are set out in Art. 4 of the Convention.

Most GCC courts will not enforce a foreign judgment from a non-GCC country where they would have had original jurisdiction to hear the underlying dispute. For these purposes, original jurisdiction is often broadly defined by local courts.

Further, the enforcement of certain judgments granting remedies of a non-pecuniary nature, for example an injunction, may not be possible because such remedies are not ordinarily available in the local court. To enforce such a judgment would require the filing of a new claim in the local court. The foreign judgment would be used as evidence in such a claim.

All of the countries of the GCC are signatories to the 1958 New York Convention on the Recognition and Enforcement of Foreign Arbitral Awards with the UAE being the last to sign in 2006.

### [2]  Court Practice (Excluding DIFC, ADGM, and QFC)

All court proceedings are conducted in Arabic and only licensed practitioners may appear in court.[76] In each jurisdiction, licensed practitioners are, in large part, Arab lawyers. Legal representatives must be formally appointed through a written Power of Attorney, which will be presented to the court in its original form. If executed locally, the Power of Attorney must be notarized but if executed abroad, the Power of Attorney must be notarized, legalized, and authenticated.

Court proceedings are conducted in an inquisitorial manner through a number of hearings where the parties present written pleadings to the court and there is little in the way of oral argument. Witnesses may be called to give oral testimony where it is deemed to be in the interests of justice and the court considers it necessary or where requested by either party. But the rules of evidence governing both written and witness testimony are significantly different from those in arbitration or common law jurisdictions.[77]

### [3]  Rights of Appeal

Courts of Appeal will hear appeals against a judgement of the Court of First Instance on matters of fact or law, but appeals to the Court of Cassation/Supreme Court[78] are only permissible on points of law.

---

[76] Saudi law allows non-licensed practitioners to appear, exceptionally, in limited circumstances including: (1) in their personal capacity, (2) as the legal representatives of juristic persons, (3) representing family members, or (4) in any other cases provided that such non-licensed practitioners are subject to a limit of three cases.

[77] A discussion of the rules of evidence is beyond the scope of this article, but for example in UAE courts, a party or an employee of a party cannot testify as a witness.

[78] Or Supreme Judicial Council/Board of Appeal in the Kingdom of Saudi Arabia.

## [4]  Precedent

There is no concept of binding case precedent in most legal systems of the GCC. Court judgments are often referred to and are persuasive but they are not binding. Local courts are public courts and are open to the public although, in practice, proceedings are, to a large extent, confidential. Court files that contain the record of proceedings, pleadings, orders, etc. may only be available to the parties to the litigation and are not available to the public.

## [5]  Statute of Limitations

Under Shari'ah principles, "a just claim never expires"; however, each jurisdiction has a number of time bars which exist in relation to different forms of claims. All of the GCC countries, with the exception of Saudi Arabia, recognize a 10-year time limit on commercial claims but these can be reduced to as little as 60 days depending on the precise nature of the claim.

## [6]  Interest

Shari'ah principles prohibit the charging or payment of usury interest but the GCC countries, excluding Saudi Arabia, include legislation specifically allowing the payment of interest and many courts have upheld agreements which include the payment of interest. Court practice varies but courts generally apply the rate agreed in the contract up to a reasonable maximum which is determined in accordance with law or at the discretion of the court. Interest rates tend to vary between 7% and 15% simple interest. Compound interest is generally not accepted.[79]

DIFC and QFC law provide for interest at the contractual rate or the average bank short-term lending rate to prime borrowers prevailing for the currency of payment at the place of payment.[80]

Qatar law allows for the provision of interest in the amount of the lost opportunity in case of failure by the debtor to pay the due amount.[81] There are exceptions to this rule, however, which are dealt with by statute. For example, financial institutions licensed by the Central Bank may apply interest to loans and may benefit from default interest.[82]

---

[79] Dubai Court of Cassation has, however, accepted the principle of compound interest where it was agreed in the contract.

[80] S.118(2) DIFC Contract Law (DIFC Law No.6 of 2004) and Art. 104 of QFC Contract Regulations, 2005.

[81] Art. 268 of the Civil Code provides that "If the obligation concerns an amount of money which the debtor fails to pay after being notified and the creditor proves that he has suffered damage as a result, the court may order the debtor to pay damages observing the principles of justice."

[82] Cf. Decree-Law No. 33 of 2006 on the Central Bank of Qatar and subsequent regulations of the Central Bank.

Similarly, in Saudi Arabia, interest in the strict usury sense is not awarded in the courts, Committees, or the Board of Grievances. Some judges have, however, been known to award compensation or damages in the amount of the loss suffered as a result of non-payment.[83] Interest provisions in agreements are severable and therefore agreements containing interest provisions are not automatically void for reason of the interest provision.

### [7]  Court-Appointed Experts

As there are no specialist courts, court-appointed experts play a crucial role in many court cases in the GCC. This is especially true in construction matters. Provision is made for the parties to agree on the identity of an expert but, in practice, the appointment is generally made by the court from a list of independent consultants maintained at the Ministry of Justice. In some jurisdictions, such as Kuwait, the experts are directly employed by the Ministry of Justice and are not, therefore, independent.

### [8]  Costs

Courts are at liberty to award the recovery of court costs to the winning party and often do so. They also have the power to make an award of legal costs but, typically, such awards are only in a nominal amount of up to $500. In Saudi Arabia, there are no costs for filing a claim and, therefore, such costs are not appropriate.

### [9]  Liquidated Damages

The courts of the GCC generally recognize the concept of liquidated damages but it should be noted that the Civil Codes of each jurisdiction,[84] or the Shari'ah in Saudi Arabia, specifically empower the courts to increase or decrease the amount of liquidated damages to reflect the actual damage suffered.[85]

### [10]  United Arab Emirates (Excluding DIFC)

In the UAE, all emirates are part of a federal court system with the exception of Dubai and Ras Al Khaimah, which have their own independent judicial

---

[83] For example, provision for a late payment fee or compensation of 10% of the amount due may be recognized but interest on a loan would not be.

[84] Excluding DIFC and QFC.

[85] Art. 390(2) of the UAE Civil Code (Federal Law No. 5 of 1985); Art. 266 of the Qatari Civil Code (Law No. 22 of 2004); Art. 223 Bahrain Civil Code (Law No. 19 of 2001); Art. 267 of the Oman Civil Code (Royal Decree No. 29 of 2013).

systems. The Federal and Dubai systems each have a Court of First Instance, Court of Appeal, and Court of Cassation or Supreme Court. Ras Al Khaimah has only a Court of First Instance and a Court of Appeal. The rules of the Civil Procedure Code[86] apply equally to the federal courts and to the courts of Dubai and Ras Al Khaimah.

It should be noted that in Dubai, before a party can take action against the Government of Dubai or a government entity, it must first seek leave to do so from the Dubai Department of Legal Affairs ("DLAD"). The DLAD will attempt to mediate the dispute and resolve matters without recourse to the courts. If there is no resolution within two months, the claimant is entitled to resort to the competent court.

### [11]  Dubai International Financial Centre ("DIFC")

The DIFC is a financial free zone in Dubai offering a unique, independent legal and regulatory framework aimed at creating an environment for growth, progress, and economic development in the UAE and the wider region.[87] It is one of many free zones in the UAE established to allow 100% foreign ownership and offering guarantees of tax exemption for up to 50 years.

In 2006, the DIFC opened its own judicial forum with the opening of the DIFC Courts,[88] which are presided over by experienced judges from around the world.[89] Unlike other courts in the region, DIFC Court proceedings are conducted in English and are based on court rules that closely follow the Civil Procedure Rules used by the Courts of England and Wales.[90] Legal precedent applies in the DIFC Courts and judgments are published online.

The DIFC Courts operate a Court of First Instance and a Court of Appeal as well as a Small Claims Tribunal for claims of under $136,000.[91]

Jurisdiction of the courts was initially limited to matters or parties which had a sufficient connection to the DIFC. This jurisdiction was extended to an "opt-in" jurisdiction in 2011 enabling all contracting parties to include DIFC Courts jurisdiction clauses in their agreement without the requirement of any nexus to the DIFC.[92]

---

[86] Federal Law No. 11 of 1992.

[87] As described on www.difccourts.ae. Financial free zones were made possible by amendment of the UAE Constitution and Federal Law No. 8 of 2004 regarding the Financial Free Zones in the UAE.

[88] Dubai Law No. 12 of 2004 established the Judicial Authority of the DIFC.

[89] Including former Court of Appeal, Commercial Court, and High Court judges of the Courts of England and Wales.

[90] Rules of the DIFC Courts, 2011.

[91] 500,000 UAE Dirhams.

[92] Dubai Law No. 16 of 2011.

Judgments of the DIFC Courts can be enforced in Dubai via Dubai Courts provided certain procedural steps are followed.[93] As the DIFC Court is constitutionally a part of the Dubai judicial system, the same applies to arbitral awards or judgments that have been ratified by the DIFC Courts.

Licensed practitioners in the DIFC Courts include lawyers from both common and civil law backgrounds including many from international law firms.

DIFC Courts have no prohibition on the awarding of interest as the courts are not influenced by the Shari'ah.

DIFC Courts have discretion to award both court and legal costs to a party and regularly make such awards on either a standard or indemnity basis.[94]

DIFC Courts have signed a number of Memoranda of Guidance with fellow common law jurisdictions in relation to the reciprocal enforcement of judgments.[95] Recently, the DIFC Courts signed such a document with the United States District Court for the Southern District of New York on March 29, 2015.[96] These Memoranda have no binding legal effect but do provide some helpful guidance.

### [12]   Abu Dhabi Global Market

A further independent judicial system will be opened in Abu Dhabi in the near future. The Abu Dhabi Global Market[97] ("ADGM") is described as "a broad-based international financial centre for local, regional and international institutions" and bears many similarities to the DIFC. Like the DIFC, ADGM will operate an independent judicial system based on English Common Law and will accept English court precedents on a limited basis. At the time of writing, the ADGM had declared itself open for business although the Courts are not yet open.

### [13]   Kingdom of Saudi Arabia

Generally speaking, the Saudi court system is divided into the Shari'ah Courts (including the General Courts and the Criminal Courts) and the Board of Grievances (the "BoG").

---

[93] As detailed in Dubai Law No. 16 of 2011.

[94] Part 38 of Rules of the DIFC Courts, 2011.

[95] The Commercial Court of England and Wales on January 23, 2013 (27), the Supreme Court of New South Wales on September 9, 2013 (28), and the Federal Courts of Australia on March 28, 2014 (29); the MOG with the High Court of Kenya (Commercial & Admiralty Division) on November 27, 2014, the Supreme Court of Singapore on January 19, 2015, and with the Supreme Court of the Republic of Kazakhstan on August 28, 2015 (the first memorandum with a civil law jurisdiction).

[96] A copy of this memorandum is *available at* http://difccourts.ae/memorandum-of-guidance-between-the-difc-courts-united-states-district-court-for-the-southern-district-of-new-york-sdny/.

[97] ADGM is established in accordance with the Federal Law No. 8 of 2004, Federal Decree No. 15 of 2013, Cabinet Resolution No. 4 of 2013, and Abu Dhabi Law No. 4 of 2013.

The General Courts have jurisdiction over all civil matters except where specifically excluded. The BoG generally has exclusive jurisdiction over administrative law issues and currently also has exclusive jurisdiction over commercial disputes.

A number of specialized quasi-judicial committees and administrative tribunals ("Committees") also exist in Saudi Arabia, which have jurisdiction over specific disputes and some of which issue final and binding decisions. Such Committees usually operate under administrative bodies of the Saudi Government. Examples of such Committees include the Committee for the Resolution of Banking Disputes (administered by the Saudi Arabian Monetary Agency (SAMA)), the Committee for the Resolution of Securities Disputes (under the Capital Market Authority), The Labor Dispute Settlement Committees (under the Ministry of Labor), and the Commercial Papers Office (under the Ministry of Commerce and Industry).

In 2007, the Saudi Government enacted a restated Judiciary Law ("Judiciary Law") and Grievance Board Law ("Grievance Board Law"). Under the Judiciary Law, the Shari'ah Courts are segregated into specific subject matters. Furthermore, the appellate courts are reorganized and a final and supreme appellate court for the Shari'ah court circuit is established (known as the Supreme Court). It also established a Supreme Judicial Council to administer the Judiciary and the courts in this circuit. To date, this has been only partially implemented.

The Judiciary Law contemplates a segregation of the Shari'ah Courts of first instance whereby they are divided into: (i) General Courts (i.e., civil matters); (ii) Personal Status Courts; (iii) Commercial Courts; and (iv) Labor Courts. A decision of the courts of first instance shall be subject to appeal to the Appellate Courts for the respective jurisdiction, with final appeal to the Supreme Court.

The BoG is reorganized under the Grievance Board Law. It, like the Supreme Court, has an Administrative Judicial Council, which is responsible for the management and administration of this circuit. It is divided into administrative tribunals of first instance, appellate tribunals, and a penultimate and final Administrative Supreme Court. Notably, commercial matters remain within the jurisdiction of the BoG until such time as the Commercial Courts are established under the Judiciary Law.

## [14]  QFC

Similar to the DIFC, the QFC was set up in 2005 as an onshore centre that provides a platform for domestic, regional, and international growth and in which foreign entities can exercise 100% ownership rights.[98] The QFC established its

---

[98] http://www.qfc.qa/about-qfc/Pages/about-qfc.aspx. The QFC is established by the Qatar Financial Centre Law (Law No. 7 of 2005), as amended by Law No. 2 of 2009.

own civil and commercial court in 2006[99] which is a creature of Qatar statute and is a Qatari institution[100] which seeks to operate on the basis of international best practice.

The court operates as a court of first instance and an appeal court. Proceedings are usually conducted in English but the court shall pay due respect to the fact that Arabic is the official language of Qatar and parties are entitled to conduct proceedings in Arabic if they wish to do so.[101] Hearings are conducted on an adversarial basis.

Jurisdiction of the court is restricted to matters involving entities of the QFC or where a contract is performed within the QFC.[102] Claims must be raised within six years of the date on which the cause of action accrued.[103]

The QFC Court has discretion to award costs as it deems fit and proper but the general rule is that the unsuccessful party shall bear the costs of the successful party.[104]

### [15]   Table of Court Systems

The table below provides summary information on each court system.

| Jurisdiction | Court Structure | Legal System | Procedural Rules |
|---|---|---|---|
| UAE | Court of First Instance<br>Court of Appeal<br>Supreme Federal Court | Civil &<br>Shari'ah | Civil Procedures Law - Federal Law No. 11 of 1992 |
| DIFC Courts (UAE) | Court of First Instance<br>Court of Appeal | Common Law | Rules of the DIFC Courts 2011 |
| Kingdom of Saudi Arabia (Shari'ah Courts) | Court of First Instance<br>Court of Appeal<br>Supreme Court | Shari'ah | Judiciary Law, 2007[105] |

*continues*

---

[99] Qatar Financial Centre Law (Law No. 7 of 2005), as amended by Law No. 2 of 2009.

[100] This is specifically stated in the QFC Civil and Commercial Court Regulations and Procedural Rules (issued by Resolution No. 1 of 2011) and was confirmed in the *Silver Leaf* case of 2009 (Case No. 0001/2009).

[101] Art. 3.2 of the Civil and Commercial Court Regulations and Procedural Rules (issued by Resolution No.1 of 2011).

[102] Art. 8.3 of the QFC Law (Law No.7 of 2005).

[103] Art. 11.2 of the QFC Civil and Commercial Court Regulations and Procedural Rules (issued by Resolution No.1 of 2011).

[104] Art. 33 of the QFC Civil and Commercial Court Regulations and Procedural Rules (issued by Resolution No.1 of 2011).

[105] Royal Decree No. (M/78). 19 Ramadan 1428H (1 October, 2007).

| Jurisdiction | Court Structure | Legal System | Procedural Rules |
|---|---|---|---|
| Kingdom of Saudi Arabia (Board of Grievances) | Court of First Instance<br>Court of Appeal<br>Board of Appeal | Shari'ah | Law of the Board of Grievances, 2007 |
| Qatar | Court of First Instance<br>Court of Appeal<br>Court of Cassation | Civil & Shari'ah | Qatar Civil and Commercial Code of Procedure – Law No.13 of 1990 |
| Qatar Financial Courts (Qatar) | Court of First Instance<br>Court of Appeal | Civil Law | QFC Civil and Commercial Court Regulations and Procedural Rules (issued by Resolution No. 1 of 2011) |
| Bahrain | Court of First Instance<br>Court of Appeal<br>Court of Cassation | Civil & Shari'ah | Civil and Commercial Procedures Act – Amiri Decree No. 12 of 1971 |
| Kuwait | Court of First Instance<br>Court of Appeal<br>Court of Cassation | Civil & Shari'ah | Code of Civil and Commercial Procedure – Law No. 38 of 1980 |
| Oman | Court of First Instance<br>Court of Appeal<br>Court of Cassation | Civil & Shari'ah | Civil and Commercial Procedure Law – Royal Decree No. 29 of 2992 |

## [B] Arbitration in the GCC

Commentators often note that arbitration in the GCC has a long and complicated history. Although a favored method of dispute resolution in traditional Arabic societies, the perception of arbitration was affected in more recent times by a series of arbitral decisions rendered in favor of international companies against GCC states or state owned entities in the 1950s and 1960s. GCC countries have however moved on. Recent years have seen significant developments which have decidedly put GCC countries on the map of modern international arbitration.

### [1]   Accession to International Instruments

As noted above, all of the GCC countries have acceded to the New York Convention on the Recognition and Enforcement of Foreign Arbitral Awards (1958) together with the Riyadh Convention[106] and the GCC Protocol.[107]

Finally, all of the GCC countries are signatories to the 1965 Convention on the Settlement of Investment Disputes between States and Nationals of Other States (also called ICSID Convention), with Qatar acceding in 2011.

### [2]   Adoption of Modern Arbitration Legislation

While some of the GCC countries, such as Bahrain[108] and Saudi Arabia,[109] have recently adopted a modern legislative framework inspired by the UNCI-TRAL[110] Model Law, others have yet to reform older statutes. At the time of writing, both the UAE and Qatar are understood to be in advanced stages of preparing modern arbitration statutes based on the UNCITRAL Model Law.

In the UAE, it is further worth noting that the DIFC has adopted a separate arbitration law which is based on the UNCITRAL Model Law. The DIFC thus offers a credible modern alternative to an arbitration seat located in "onshore" UAE.

### [3]   Courts' Approach to Arbitration

In general terms, the courts of the GCC countries have in recent years adopted a more favorable and less interventionist approach to arbitration. For instance, the Dubai Court of Cassation has affirmed since 2012 that the enforcement of foreign arbitral awards in the UAE is governed by the New York Convention and not by the provisions of the UAE Civil Procedure Code.[111] Positive developments have however been too few, inconsistent or recent, to draw any general conclusions. Some widely publicised recent decisions have had a negative impact on the perception of the GCC courts' approach to arbitration. For instance, in 2012, the Qatari Court of Cassation held that arbitral awards are null unless issued in the name of His Highness the Emir of Qatar, thus treating arbitral awards as national court judgments.[112]

---

[106] The Inter-Arab Convention on Judicial Co-operation, 1983.

[107] The Agreement on the Execution of Judgments, Delegations and Judicial Notifications, 1996.

[108] Bahrain Legislative Decree No. 9/2015.

[109] Saudi Royal Decree No. M/34.

[110] United Nations Commission on International Trade Law.

[111] Dubai Court of Cassation Decision No. 132/2012 in Airmech Dubai LLC v. Macsteel International LLC.

[112] Qatar Court of Cassation, Petition No. 64/2012.

## [4]  Arbitration Institutions

Recent years have witnessed a significant development of arbitration institutions in the GCC, with each of the GCC countries having developed one or more arbitration centers. The most active institutions currently are the Dubai International Arbitration Centre, the DIFC-LCIA, and the Bahrain Chamber for Dispute Resolution (BCDR-AAA).

## § 1.07  INTELLECTUAL PROPERTY IN ARCHITECTURE AND DESIGN ENGINEERING

Intellectual property (IP) means the rights resulting from intellectual activity in the industrial, scientific, literary, or artistic fields, such as copyright rights, trademark rights, patent rights, and others.

Although there are some differences between Common Law and Civil Law in the approaches and processes for the protection of IP, the goals remain the same. This section focuses on general practical aspects to consider when seeking to protect IP rights that arise in the context of construction projects in the GCC.[113]

## [A]  General Intellectual Property Concerns in the Context of Construction Projects

Architects, designers, engineers, and clients may have a number of intellectual property rights in their work product. In the context of construction projects, IP-related disputes most frequently arise in respect of copyright claims, which is the primary focus of this section.

## [1]  Copyright Protection

Copyright exists to prevent the unauthorized copying of works and subject matter other than works protected by copyright laws. Copyright only protects certain expressions of ideas, not the ideas themselves.

As early as the engagement of consultants for the development of conceptual designs and design briefs, copyright attached to any of these works will generally rest with the consultant. The terms and conditions of the consultant's engagement may, however assign the copyright to the client. To limit copyright liability, it is recommended that architects and designers become aware of what

---

[113] The jurisdictions are Bahrain, Kuwait, Oman, Qatar, Kingdom of Saudi Arabia, and the United Arab Emirates.

copyrighted materials might influence their design decisions and how these copyrighted materials can be used.

### [2]  Patent Protection

Patent protection is available to anyone who "invents or discovers any new and useful process, machine, manufacture, or composition of matter or any improvement thereof."[114] As plans develop, designers and architects may innovate to achieve the constructability of a design. Patents are available for building systems, building technologies, details, and products. Obtaining patents in architecture is also possible,[115] but the patentability of architectural works remains difficult.

### [3]  Trademark Protection

Trademark laws protect consumers from risks of confusing brands of companies they trust for the purchase of goods and services with other brands. In the context of construction, trademarks will generally become important when selecting a business, trade name, or logo.

Trademarks can also protect the physical interior or exterior of a business, which is commonly known as "trade dress" protection. Also, "The three dimensional configuration of a building is able to be registered only if it is used in such a way that it is or could be perceived as a mark."[116] This is particularly applicable in a region racing to construct landmark or iconic structures and developments.

### [B]  The Early Influence of Islamic Shari'ah in IP[117]

The Islamic Shari'ah contained principles to protect intellectual property[118] long before the United States empowered Congress to "promote the progress of science and useful arts by securing for limited times to authors and inventors the exclusive rights to their respective writings and discoveries."[119] Shari'ah principles provide that ideas must be properly attributable to its source. This concept arises from the necessity to accurately transmit the Prophet's teachings.

---

[114] 35 U.S.C. § 101 (1952).

[115] Apple successfully getting an architectural patent for the design for its store in the Upper West Side in New York City on November 15, 2011, *available at* http://www.archdaily.com/197061/architectural-patents-on-what-grounds (last visited Nov. 9, 2015).

[116] *See* United States Patent and Trademark Office, Trademark Manual of Examining Procedure § 1301.02 (c).

[117] Please note that there are a number of different schools of thought for the interpretation of Islamic Shari'ah. This section relies on the most liberal interpretation.

[118] Shari'ah protections preceded the United States by approximately 1300 years.

[119] U.S. Const. § 8, cl. 1.

Islamic Shari'ah doctrines established the right for individuals to exploit creations for their own benefit and for the benefit of the wider society. The only limitation Islam placed with respect to enjoyment of intellectual property rights are that creations be within the permitted articles in Islam.

The main principles established under the Islamic Shari'ah include continuous benefit of the intellectual property rights that outlive the right holder[120] and financial benefits. Similar to most civil jurisdictions, Shari'ah recognizes the moral and financial rights dichotomy. These principles of personal property together form the overarching doctrine for protecting IP rights.[121]

Even though all GCC countries that have adopted civil law systems espouse that their statutes are in keeping with Shari'ah, the statutes do not treat IP issues as seriously as Shari'ah. Infringing IP rights is akin to theft under the Islamic Shari'ah and it is sanctioned by severe punishment, which serves as a deterrent to commit any infringement. But, the statutory provisions that govern IP infringements in the GCC hardly provide for any meaningful deterrent.[122]

With the exception of the Kingdom of Saudi Arabia, GCC countries only apply Shari'ah Law in discrete matters because it has been gradually replaced by secular-type legislation. However, as explained above, it is important to note that the infringement of IP rights in most of the GCC is considered to be not only a potential breach of the applicable statutes but also a breach of religious principles.[123]

---

[120] The Hadith of Prophet Mohammed "works of a person that do not cease even after death are three: continuing charity, a beneficial know-how or a worthwhile son." The Hadith is one of the main sources of legislation in Islam.

[121] See, e.g., Nehad Mohamed Eweda, *Intellectual Property in Architecture Between Legislations and Ethical Manifestations with Special Reference to the Egyptian Case*, 5 Int'l. J. of Arch. Res. (2011).

[122] Most of the ACLs sanction IP Infringement with short imprisonment sentences and fines. However, the courts very rarely sentence an infringer to a prison sentence. It is also worth noting that some jurisdictions (the UAE for example) will grant interim relief in the context of IP infringements whereas this emergency measure is generally unavailable in the GCC. For the applicable penalties, please refer to the following examples: Art. 37 of the Copyright and Neighboring Rights Law, Law No. 7 of 2002 (UAE) and Art. 46 of the Copyright and Neighboring Rights Law, Law No. 7 of 2002 (Qatar).

[123] The references to "public order" and "morality" in all of the statutes of the GCC are generally interpreted in light of Shari'ah principles (see for example Articles 2 and 3 of the UAE Civil Code). More importantly, the exercise of one's rights shall not be contrary to the rules of the Islamic Shari'ah (see Article 106 of the UAE Civil Code). For more detailed information on this topic, the author recommends reading SILVIA BELTRAMETTI, *The Legality of Intellectual Property Rights under Islamic Law, in* THE PRAGUE YEARBOOK OF COMPARATIVE LAW 2009 at 55-94 (Mach, T. et al. eds., 2010).

## [C]  Protecting IP Rights in the GCC Countries

In a number of GCC countries, the protection of patents, trademarks, and copyrights is perceived as inadequate by Western standards. While most of the jurisdictions have ratified the main IP-related treaties, protectable works may require cumbersome and expensive registration processes.

When seeking the protection of IP rights in the GCC, it is important to understand that these protections may not be granted if an administrative body considers that the IP rights violate public order or morals. The concept and content of public order and morals arise primarily from Shari'ah principles. It is important to note that these notions are very broadly interpreted in GCC countries and are regularly relied upon to support judicial and administrative decisions. For example, in the context of trademark registration, it is obvious that some classes are not accepted in their entirety, such as class 33 (alcoholic drinks). However, in light of the broad interpretation of public order, other potential violations of public order may not be obvious.[124]

### [1]  Copyright

The two main differences between Common Law and Civil Law on the protection afforded by copyright in the context of construction projects are (i) ownership of the rights attached to copyright in work-for-hire situations[125] and (ii) the assignability of moral rights attached to copyrights.

The doctrine of "work for hire" does not exist in the GCC. An agreement to transfer economic rights attached to copyright in any work must be explicit and specifically grant the right to continue to copy, transfer, or exhibit the work. The author remains the owner of all the rights that have not been specifically granted. In other words, where the architect was hired to prepare designs and drawings, he, individually, continues to own the copyright unless he transfers or assigns it.

Unlike other rights inherent to a copyright, the owner may not assign its moral rights. While, in the United States, the author of a work protected by copyright laws can assign all of its rights, moral rights in Civil Law countries are inalienable. The moral rights arising out of copyright are born in the author at the moment the whole work takes shape.[126] Due to its extra-patrimonial nature, the

---

[124] Trade Marks Law, Art. 8, (2) (Qatar): "indecent expression, picture, or sing or anything that is in conflict with public order." One example of a controversy in the UAE is the shape of the sea-facing side of the Burj Al Arab. The shape is claimed by some to be the world's largest Christian cross. Whether this was intentional is still open to debate.

[125] "Work for hire" is a legal concept applicable in many jurisdictions that governs situations in which an employer automatically owns the copyright to works prepared by its employees in the scope of their employment. *See, e.g.*, 17 U.S.C. § 101 (2012).

[126] The moral rights attached to the author are interpreted as extension of the author itself.

moral rights are not assignable and are only transferrable to the author's heirs.[127] An author can agree to waive its right to attribution and integrity of the works (having its name on the works for example). It is important to note that it is generally accepted that such waiver can be revoked at any time by the author.

As a practical illustration, it is extremely rare to see the name of architect or designer affixed to a building. One of the common problems specific to the architectural profession is that most projects are attributed to a firm, but the name of the architect is not officially mentioned. In the GCC, this is potentially a violation of the architect's moral rights of attribution.[128] In practice, employers should consider seeking a written waiver from the architect specifically stating that it waives the right of attribution of a building.[129]

The copyright laws of the GCC generally provide for specific protection of design and architectural works. The UAE Ministry of Economy, for example, specifies that architectural works can be protected by copyright.[130] This specific definition of the protection afforded to architects and designers is not found throughout the GCC. For example, Qatar only provides for copyright protections for architectural works, which inevitably triggers the debate of what types of works can be protected by copyright.[131]

The existence of a copyright is not conditioned upon any requirement to register the copyright, but many GCC countries do provide for registration services, such as the UAE. While registration process can be costly and lengthy, it will generally grant greater rights to the owner.[132]

It is also important to understand the local registration requirements. In Qatar, for example, every published, displayed, or circulated work is required to be accompanied by a certificate of origin, and a declaration (by the importer or

---

[127] Art. 5 of the Federal Law Concerning Copyrights and Neighboring Rights, Law No. 7 of 2002 (UAE).

[128] For example, Jumeirah Group owns the copyrights to the Burj Al Arab in Dubai and the name of the architect (Tom Wright) is, to the author's knowledge, never mentioned. The author understands Jumeirah Group may seek to sue an Indian hotel that reproduced the shape of the Burj in India. Tom Wright should also have a course of action to sue on the basis that the integrity of his design has been altered. *Available at* http://www.arabianbusiness.com/owner-of-india-s-fake-burj-al-arab-replica-reports-thriving-trade-591398.html#.VlGDh08cS9J (last visited Nov. 22, 2015).

[129] As noted above, however, the waiver can be revoked by the author at any time.

[130] Art. 2(7) of the Federal Law Concerning Copyrights and Neighboring Rights, Law No. 7 of 2002 (UAE).

[131] Arts. 2-4 of the Copyright and Neighboring Rights Law of Qatar, Law No. 7 of 2002 do not specifically set out the protection for architects and designers. Article 5 provides for the protection of "architectural works constructed in Qatar" but again the types of works that benefit from the protection is not clear.

[132] In the UAE, the registration of a copyright will, in practice, provide greater guarantees for the enforcement of the rights attached to a copyright because the certificate delivered to the author is instant proof of ownership.

owner) specifying the geographic area/place within which the display or circulation is authorized.[133] In Saudi Arabia, however, there are no procedures for the
registration of copyrights, which means the authors hold the entirety of their
rights from the first moment of creation, and no additional rights are conferred
through a registration process.

### [2]  Trademark

A trademark is broadly defined in GCC trademark laws as anything that
takes a distinctive form.[134] This includes, *inter alia*, names, words, signatures, figures, symbols, and combinations thereof used to distinguish goods, products, or
services, to show ownership by the trademark's owner, or to indicate service performance.

Some GCC countries, such as the UAE, have no specific laws for unregis-
tered trademarks, and it is generally difficult to successfully claim the ownership
of a trademark by demonstrating the use of the mark in commerce.[135] This is particularly the case for "trade dress." However, owners of well-known trademarks
may be able to protect them under international conventions, particularly the Paris
Convention.[136] The Paris Convention was the first international agreement to help
innovators ensure that the product of their intellectual works was protected in
other signatory States.

The State of Qatar provides specific protection for "design rights." Inventive designs or industrial models can be registered under the Trademarks Law.[137]
Some aspects specific to designs are not set out in the Trademarks Law, which
results in little or no clarity on what can be protected by a registered design and
what mandatory criteria the design must comply with.

### [3]  Patents

GCC countries have specific patent laws and most are signatories to the
major international patent-related treaties.[138] In Saudi Arabia, however, the statute

---

[133] Art. 6, Copyright and Neighboring Rights Law, Law No. 7 of 2002 (Qatar).

[134] Please note that the Gulf Cooperation Council Unified Trademark Law of 2006 harmo-
nizes the trademark laws of Saudi Arabia, Bahrain, Kuwait, Oman, Qatar, and the UAE. The GCC
Trademark Law was approved in May 2014 and the implementing regulations were issued in
21 December 2015.

[135] Under Common Law principles, however, the use of a mark in the commerce for prolonged
period of time can result in the ownership of a trademark.

[136] Paris Convention (International Union), 1883–1967. Note: Qatar is the only ACL that is not
a signatory to the Paris Convention.

[137] Art. 6, Trademarks Law, Law No. 9 of 2002 (Qatar). Qatar has a specific protection labelled
"Design Rights" but the definition of what is included under these design rights is unclear.

[138] Please refer to the table in § 1.07[D], below.

that governs patents applies not only to patents but also layout designs of integrated circuits, plant varieties, and industrial models.[139]

As set out below with the example of the UAE, seeking and obtaining patents in the GCC can be technical and cumbersome.

Patents in the UAE are issued through a deed of protection, which is a document confirming the patentability of the invention, industrial drawing, or industrial design. Such deeds take the form of either a letter patent or a utility certificate. A letter patent will generally be awarded by the IP Administration in the name of the UAE for a new invention that results from an innovative idea or inventive step in all fields of technology that have a scientific basis and a potential useful industrial application.[140] A utility certificate is issued by the IP Administration in the name of the UAE "for an invention that does not result from intellectual effort sufficient for granting a letter patent."[141] A utility certificate is often issued for new inventions capable of industrial application but having no innovative character warranting patentability.[142] Finally, it is important to note that, in the UAE, industrial drawings and designs follow a registration that slightly differs from the letter patent and the utility certificate. To benefit from patent-type protection, the industrial drawing or design must be new, innovative, must have an industrial or vocational application, and must not violate the public order or morals of the UAE.

### [4]  Works by Employees

Unlike the laws governing copyrights, if an employee invents a product or a process in the context of an employment contract and the invention relates to the employee's scope of employment, or other contractual "work-for-hire" situation, the employer will be the owner of any patents covering such inventions unless otherwise provided for in the agreement between the parties.[143] However, if the economic value of the invention surpasses the expectations of the parties at the time of the contract's execution, a civil court may determine that the employee who created the invention is entitled to additional compensation.[144]

---

[139] Royal Decree No. M/27 (July 17, 2004).

[140] Federal Law No. 17 of 2002, Art. 4 (UAE). The term of protection under a letter patent is 20 years.

[141] Federal Law No. 17 of 2002, Art. 1 (UAE).

[142] Federal Law No. 17 of 2002, Art. 1 (UAE). The term of protection under a utility certificate is 10 years.

[143] Please note that this is a fundamental difference with most of the Copyright Laws in the GCC.

[144] Art. 9, Industrial Regulation and Protection of Patents, Industrial Drawings, and Designs, Federal Law No. 17 of 2002, as amended by Federal Law No. 31 of 2006 (UAE).

As of this writing, the State of Qatar does not have a direct patent registration system. Patent protection in Qatar is extended through the Gulf Cooperation Council Patent Office in Riyadh, Saudi Arabia.

## [D]  Statutory References

| Jurisdiction | Relevant Statutes and Treaties |
| --- | --- |
| Bahrain | **National Laws**<br>— Patent and Utility Models Law No. 1 of 2004<br>— Patent and Utility Models Law No. 14 of 2006 (amending the Patent and Utility Models Law No. 1 of 2004)<br>— Trade Marks Law No. 11 of the year 2006<br>— Law No. 22 of 2006 on the Protection of Copyright and Neighboring Rights<br>**Treaties:**<br>— Paris Convention (International Union), 1883–1967<br>— Patent Cooperation Treaty (PCT) of 1970<br>— Patent Law Treaty of 200, since December 15, 2005<br>— Madrid Protocol relating to the Madrid Agreement Concerning the International Registration of Marks of 1891, since December 15, 2005<br>— Nice Agreement Concerning the International Classification of Goods and Services for the Purposes of Registration of Trade Marks of 1957, since December 15, 2005 |
| Egypt | **National Laws:**<br>— Law No. 82/2002 dated June 2, 2002 concerning Protection of Intellectual Property Rights<br>— Ministerial Decree No. 1366 of 2003 concerning Executive Regulations of Law No. 82/2002<br>**Treaties :**<br>— Convention Establishing the World Intellectual Property Organization (WIPO Convention) of 1967, since April 21, 1975<br>— Agreement concerning the Trade Related aspects of Intellectual Property (TRIPS Agreement) of 1994, June 30, 1995<br>— Paris Convention (International Union), 1883–1967, since July 1, 1951<br>— Madrid Agreement concerning International Registration of Trademarks of 1891, since July 1, 1952<br>— Madrid Agreement (Indication of Origin), since July 1, 1952<br>— Madrid Protocol of 1989, since September 3, 2009<br>— Nice Agreement Concerning the International Classification of Goods and Services for the Purposes of Registration of Trade Marks of 1957, since June 18, 2005<br>— Trademark Law Treaty of 1994, since October 7, 1999 |

*continues*

| Jurisdiction | Relevant Statutes and Treaties |
|---|---|
| Kuwait | **National laws:**<br>— Law No. 4 of 1962 relating to Patents, Designs and Industrial Models, as amended in 1999<br>— Patents, Designs and Industrial Models Regulations of 5 December 1965, as amended<br>— Commercial Code (Book I, Part III), issued by Law Decree No. 68 for 1980 (replacing Law No. 2 of 1961 relating to Trade Marks, as amended by Law No. 7 of 1962), as last amended by Law No. 1 of 2001<br>— Trade Mark Regulations of March 5, 1961, as amended by Ministerial Decree No. 8 of 1995<br>— Law No. 64 of 1999 concerning Intellectual Property Rights<br>**Treaties:**<br>— Convention Establishing the World Intellectual Property Organization (WIPO Convention)of 1967, July 14, 1998<br>— Agreement concerning the Trade Related aspects of Intellectual Property (TRIPS Agreement) of 1994, January 1, 1995<br>— Paris Convention (International Union), 1883–1967, since December 2, 2014 |
| Oman | **National Laws:**<br>— Industrial Property Rights and their Enforcement for the Sultanate of Oman (Royal Decree No. 67/2008) (2008)<br>— Royal Decree No. 65/2008 promulgating the Law on Copyright and Related Rights (2008)<br>— Ministry of Trade and Industry Ministerial Decree No. 103/2008 issuing the executive regulations of the Law on Copyright and Neighboring Rights (2008)<br>— Regulations No. 105/2008 under the Law on Industrial Property Rights & Their Enforcement for the Sultanate of Oman (2008)<br>**Treaties:**<br>— Paris Convention (International Union), 1883–1967 (with the declaration provided for in Article 28(2) of the Stockholm Act concerning the International Court of Justice), since July 14, 1999<br>— Convention Establishing the World Intellectual Property Organization (WIPO Convention) in 1967, since February 19, 1997<br>— Patent Cooperation Treaty (PCT), 1970 (with the declaration provided for in Article 64(5)), since October 26, 2001<br>— Agreement concerning the Trade Related aspects of Intellectual Property (TRIPS Agreement) of 1994, since November 9, 2000 |

*continues*

| Jurisdiction | Relevant Statutes and Treaties |
|---|---|
| Qatar | **Nationals Laws:**<br>— Qatar by Law No. (9) of 2002 (Trade Marks Law)<br>— Copyright and Neighboring Rights Law No. 7 of 2002 (the "Copyright Law")[145]<br>**Treaties:**<br>— World Trade Organization<br>— Convention Establishing the World Intellectual Property Organization (WIPO Convention) of 1967<br>— Nice Agreement Concerning the International Classification of Goods and Services for the Purposes of Registration of Trade Marks of 1957 |
| Kingdom of Saudi Arabia | **National Laws:**<br>— Royal Decree No. M/41 (Aug. 30, 2003) and published in the Official Gazette No. 3959, dated September 19, 2003 (the Copyright Law)<br>— Royal Decree No. M/21, 28 Jumada I 1423H (Aug. 7, 2002) (the Trademark Law)<br>**Treaties:**<br>— Universal Copyright Convention of 1952<br>— Berne Convention for the Protection of Literary and Artistic Works of 1896<br>— Paris Convention (International Union), 1883–1967 |
| United Arab Emirates | **National Laws:**<br>— Federal Law No. 7 of 2002 Concerning Copyrights and Neighboring Rights (Copyright Law)<br>— Federal Law No. 37 for the year 1992 (Trademark Law)<br>— Federal Law No. 17 of 2002 pertaining to the Industrial Regulation and Protection of Patents, Industrial Drawings, and Designs, as amended by Federal Law No. 31 of 2006 (Patent Law)<br>**Treaties:**<br>— Berne Convention for the Protection Literary and Artistic Work of 1896<br>— Paris Convention (International Union), 1883–1967, since September 19, 1996<br>— Gulf Cooperation Council Unified Trademark Law of 2006<br>— Convention Establishing the World Intellectual Property Organization (WIPO Convention) in 1967, since September 24, 1974<br>— Patent Cooperation Treaty of 1970, since March 10, 1999<br>— Agreement concerning the Trade Related aspects of Intellectual Property (TRIPS Agreement) of 1994, since April 1996 |

---

[145] At the time of this paper, the implementing regulations of the Copyright Law No. 7 of 2002 have not yet been issued; thus delaying the implementation of the law.

## § 1.08   MANAGER LIABILITY IN ARAB CIVIL LAW JURISDICTIONS

Company managers and board members in GCC countries may be personally and even criminally liable for the actions of their company. If a company violates a law or is negligent, the managers may find themselves personally liable or even imprisoned for mistakes or wrongdoing by their employees.

### [A]   What Is a "Manager"?

The term "manager" is typically interpreted differently in the GCC than in western jurisdictions, and for the purposes of this discussion, applies to individuals named in memorandums of association or listed on business licenses as mangers of the entity. The manager of a limited liability company (LLC) or the chairman of a joint stock company is the legal representative of the company and can be held personally responsible for some of its actions. This is especially relevant where the company causes, or seems to cause, injuries or damage in violation of labor or environmental laws.

### [B]   Financial Liability

Some of the manager's obligations will seem familiar to western practitioners. Managers and directors are subject to civil liability for fiduciary issues such as fraud, improper distributions, and breaches of confidentiality. They are also generally liable to both shareholders and third parties for the ambiguous offense of "mismanagement." In some situations, managers may also be responsible for bounced checks and directors can become personally liable in an insolvency.[146]

### [C]   Criminal Liability

Also of clear concern to companies seeking to do business in the region is the possibility that a manager or director may be responsible under criminal laws. A company's violations of labor laws or environmental regulations usually carry the possibility of personal fines and imprisonment for both the supervisors immediately responsible and for those further up the chain of command.

### [D]   Examples of Manager Liability in the UAE

- Under the UAE Federal Commercial Companies' Law No. 2 of 2015 (UAE Companies' Law), managers of LLC can be liable for bounced checks. The Dubai Court of Cassation has established that a crime which

---

[146] UAE Penal Code and Commercial Transaction Law.

has been committed by a representative of the juristic person or its directors or agents for its account or in its name does not exempt the perpetrator of the crime from punishment.[147]

- The Labor Law states that criminal proceedings may be filed against the general manager who is responsible for the management of an establishment and against the employer if circumstances give the belief that he was not unaware of the facts constituting violations.[148]

### [E] Examples of Manager Liability in the Kingdom of Saudi Arabia

- Board members are jointly liable for damages sustained by any of the company or its shareholders or third parties as a result of their mismanagement or violating the Companies Law or the bylaws of the company.[149] The same is applicable for managers of an LLC.[150]

- An employer is required to maintain a healthy and hygienic workplace. The employer is also required to undertake necessary measures to protect its workers from hazards and diseases that arise from the type of work and equipment used. Employers violating this obligation shall be subject to a fine of not less than SAR 3,000 and up to SAR 10,000 for each violation or temporary closure of the entity for a period not exceeding 30 days or permanent closure; the fine and closure(s) may be combined in addition to resolving the source of hazard.[151]

### [F] Examples of Manager Liability in the Egypt

- A manager shall be liable for imprisonment of not less than two years and a penalty of up to EGP 10,000 (that he must bear personally) if he distributes profits in a manner that does not comply with the Companies' Law or the company's by-laws.[152]

- Managers violating occupational health and safety regulation may be sentenced to three months of jail and payment of a penalty of not less than EGP 1,000 (approximately USD 127) and not exceeding EGP 10,000 (approximately USD 1,270) or either one of these penalties.[153]

---

[147] Dubai Court of Cassation 87/1997 (46).

[148] Art. 184 of Federal Law No. 8 of 1980 on Regulation of Labour Relations.

[149] Art. 78 of the Saudi Companies' Law, Royal Decree No. M/6.

[150] Art. 165 of the Companies' Law.

[151] Art. 121, Saudi Labor Royal Decree No. M/51.

[152] Art. 162, Egyptian Labor Law, Law No. 12 of 2003.

[153] *Id.* at Art. 256.

## [G]  Examples of Manager Liability in the Qatar

- Managers who do not ensure proper ventilation and hygiene measures at the workplace including potable water and proper lighting may be sentenced to one month in prison and payment of a penalty ranging between 2000 and 6000 Qatari Riyals or either of these penalties.[154]

- Where a violation is committed in the name of a juristic person or for its benefit, its legal representative shall be considered a partner in such violation and penalized in accordance unless he can evidence that he was unaware of such violation or that he has exerted sufficient effort to avoid such violation. Penalties include fiscal penalties and imprisonment.[155]

## § 1.09  MANDATORY AND RESTRICTED CONTRACT PROVISIONS IN ARAB CIVIL LAW

Projects in the Middle East are procured on a variety of bases, including lump sum turnkey, construction management and management contracting variants, EPCM, and traditional direct contracting. The presence of multinationals and the large number of common law trained lawyers practising in the Middle East means that the understanding of the various contract types is often significantly influenced by common law expectations.

This can create issues. The region is predominantly governed by Civil Codes,[156] and not all contract provisions that are otherwise customary to common law jurisdictions fit within Arab Civil Law. The result, many may be unworkable or ultimately unenforceable to the detriment of the common law lawyer expecting to rely on them.

In particular, mandatory and restricted contract provisions in the Middle East can have a significant impact on the operation of otherwise customary principles. This chapter summarizes some of the mandatory and restricted contract provisions in Arab Civil Codes.

## [A]  Public Policy Exceptions to the Sanctity of Contract

Sanctity of contract is recognized throughout the Middle East,[157] and construction contracts are recognized and enforceable in the usual way—the contract, if clearly drafted, will apply to define the rights of the parties. However, such rights are subject to mandatory provisions of law and will be unenforceable

---

[154] Art. 145, Qatari Labor Law No. 14 of 2004.

[155] Art. 74, Qatari Environment Protection Law, Law No. 30 of 2002.

[156] *See* § 1.09[C][3], Table 1: Arab Civil Codes governing contract.

[157] *See* § 1.09[C][3], Table 2: Sanctity of Contract under Arab Civil Codes.

to the extent that they conflict with public order or decency.[158] These mandatory and restricted contract provisions in the Middle East can have a significant impact on the operation of otherwise customary principles. This chapter looks at such examples of mandatory and restricted contract provisions in Arab Civil Codes.

## [B]  Mandatory Provisions of the Law

### [1]  Choice of Law—Arbitrability

Arab Civil Law provides parties the freedom to choose and agree on the governing law of the contract that they intend to enter into. However, in certain circumstances, the law of the contract may be influenced or determined by the identity of one or more of the parties.

For example, in the UAE, while parties are allowed the freedom to select the laws which govern their agreements, if certain provisions of the chosen law are contrary to Shari'ah law or UAE public order,[159] the chosen governing law will not be applied and UAE law will be applied instead.[160]

This is similar across the Arab Civil Law jurisdictions—choice of law provisions will be rendered inoperable if the provisions of the foreign law are deemed contrary to public policy or morality.

In KSA, the situation under the applicable *Government Tenders and Procurement Law* is similar—contracts must be interpreted and executed in Arabic, even if drafted in another language.

### [2]  Limiting Liability Under Contract—Liquidated Damages and Decennial Liability

Financial and temporal limitations of liability clauses are subject to a number of statutory exceptions under Arab Civil Law. This includes the courts' inherent power to adjust levels of agreed compensation (liquidated damages) and decennial liability.

---

[158] *See* § 1.09[C][3], Table 3: Exceptions to sanctity of contract under Arab Civil Codes.

[159] Article 3 of the Federal Law of Civil Transactions (No. 5 of 1985) defines public policy as: "Public policy shall be deemed to include matters relating to personal status such as marriage, inheritance, and lineage, and matters relating to systems of government, freedom of trade, circulation of wealth, rules of individual ownership and the other rules and foundations upon which society is based, in such a manner as to not conflict with the definitive provisions and fundamental principles of Islamic Shari'a."

[160] *See* § 1.09[C][3], Table 4: Exceptions to choice of law under Arab Civil Codes.

### [a] Liquidated Damages

In common law jurisdictions, parties are free to commercially agree rates of liquidated damages. The courts will enforce whatever is agreed provided that it is determined to be a genuine pre-estimate of the loss suffered.

In Arab Civil Law jurisdictions, a court (or arbitral tribunal) can, regardless of any agreement to the contrary, override a contractually agreed compensation arrangement and adjust the specified compensation to make it equal to the actual loss suffered.[161]

A court's power to adjust the agreed compensation includes both downward and *upward* adjustments—in practice, application of the former is more commonly sought (by the contractor seeking to reduce damages), while the latter is rarely exercised unless one party has suffered fraud or gross error at the hands of the other.

### [b] Decennial Liability

Decennial liability is a strict form of liability imposed on contractors and design professionals (architects and engineers) in all Arab Civil Law jurisdictions for the cost of rectifying a structural defect appearing in a building or installation within 10 years of hand over (five years in Bahrain). It cannot be excluded or capped by contract, save for in Bahrain and Saudi Arabia.[162]

### [c] Doctrine of Changed Circumstances

In common law jurisdictions, the general principle is that unilateral modification of contractual terms is not permitted.

The doctrine of changed circumstances is a mandatory provision of many civil law countries, and the GCC countries are no exception.[163] While there is considerable uncertainty surrounding the circumstances in which the doctrine can be successfully invoked in practice, in theory, there are four conditions necessary for the doctrine to apply:

1. *Exceptional events*: such as a general strike, substantial increase or decrease in the price of raw materials.

2. *General in nature*: not specific to a particular project or contract but affecting the whole industry.

---

[161] *See* § 1.09[C][3], Table 5: Courts' power to adjust agreed compensation under Arab Civil Codes.

[162] *See* § 1.09[C][3], Table 6: Decennial liability under Arab Civil Codes.

[163] *See* § 1.09[C][3], Table 7: Doctrine of changed circumstances under Arab Civil Codes.

3. *Unforeseeable*: the event is unexpected and could not have been fore-seen; and

4. *Excessively onerous*: as a direct result of exceptional event, the party's obligation is unduly onerous, threatening excessive loss but not making it impossible to perform.

If all the above conditions apply, Arab Civil Law permits a court to reduce party's obligations until they become more bearable to perform or to add counter-obligations to the "creditor" party in return for maintaining the more difficult obligation of the "debtor."

The Egyptian Civil Code has a provision which addresses the doctrine of changed circumstances specifically in the context of construction contracts.[164] This provision is significant because it provides for the possibility of termination, which is not permissible under the doctrine of changed circumstances in the other Arab Civil Codes.

## [C]  Public Policy or Morals

### [1]  Good Faith and Fairness

In common law jurisdictions, good faith in construction contracts is most commonly reflected in the implied term that an employer must not prevent or hinder a contractor from completing its work. In practice, the application of good faith and fair dealing is difficult and it often falls short of the lofty ideals with which it is associated.

The doctrine of good faith is taken seriously under Arab Civil Law. It applies to all contracts and imposes on each party a legal obligation to exercise good faith in the performance of its contractual obligations and its dealings with the other party.[165] As outlined below, the principles of good faith and fairness may apply to modify the contractual rights and obligations in certain circumstances. This can have significant practical implications.

### [2]  Exclusive Remedies Clauses

In Arab Civil Code jurisdictions, a party's reliance on an exclusive remedies clause can be restricted, or completely precluded, if it is deemed to be contrary to

---

[164] Egyptian Civil Code, Art. 658(4): "if the economic equilibrium between the obligations of the employer and the contractor has collapsed due to exceptional circumstances of a public nature which could not have been foreseen at the time of contracting, removing the financial basis for the contract of works, then it is open to the judge to decide to increase the fees or terminate the contract."

[165] *See* § 1.09[C][3], Table 8: Enshrinement of good faith and fairness under Arab Civil Codes.

public policy principles. Each of the Arab Civil Codes contains express prohibitions[166] against a party exercising its right in circumstances where:

1. it is intended to infringe the rights of another party;

2. the outcome is contrary to the rules of Islamic Shari'ah, the law, public order, or morals;

3. the desired gain is disproportionate to the harm suffered by the other party; or

4. it exceeds the bounds of custom or practice.

In practice, this restriction is particularly relevant in circumstances where a contractor relies on an exclusive remedies clause where it would be clearly prejudicial to the employer's interest. For example, to preclude an employer from obtaining redress in respect of a defective design or to preclude recovery of additional costs required to remedy the harm caused.

Consequently, the protection afforded by an exclusive remedies clause (which by its nature is negotiated to benefit one party's interest over another's) is rendered questionable at best and can result in contractors being left precariously exposed if an exclusive remedies clause that they seek to rely upon is struck out.

### [3]  Appendix 1—Tabled Extracts from Arab Civil Codes

The following tables provide a nonexclusive list of some of the statutes governing the issues discussed above.

### TABLE 1

| Arab Civil Codes governing contract |
|---|
| (full citation and abbreviated citation used in subsequent references) |

| | |
|---|---|
| **Bahrain** | The Civil Code promulgated by Legislative Decree No. 19 of 2001 (**Bahrain Civil Code**). |
| **Egypt** | The Egyptian Civil Code promulgated by Law No. 131 of 1948 (**Egyptian Civil Code**). |
| **KSA** | The Kingdom of Saudi Arabia (**KSA**) has no civil code. Saudi Government contracting is regulated by the *Government Tenders and Procurement Law* (2006) and the *Implementing Regulations* (2007). As the majority of construction spending in Saudi Arabia is government sector, the *Government Tenders and Procurement Law 2006* is referred to (**Government Tenders and Procurement Law**). |

*continues*

---

[166] *See* § 1.09[C][3], Table 9: Restriction on the exercise of rights under Arab Civil Codes.

| | |
|---|---|
| **Kuwait** | Decree/Law No. 67/1980 Promulgating the Civil Law (**Kuwait Civil Code**). |
| **Oman** | Omani Civil Transactions Law (promulgated by Sultani Decree 29/2013) (**Oman Civil Code**). |
| **Qatar** | Law No. 22 of 2004 (**Qatar Civil Code**). |
| **UAE** | Law of Civil Transactions of the UAE (Federal Law No. 2 of 1987) (**UAE Civil Code**). |

## TABLE 2

| Sanctity of Contract under Arab Civil Codes | |
|---|---|
| **Bahrain** | **Article 128, Bahrain Civil Code:**<br><br>The contract makes the law of the parties. It can be revoked or altered only by mutual consent of the parties or for reasons provided for by the law. |
| **Egypt** | **Article 147(1), Egyptian Civil Code:**<br><br>The contract makes the law of the parties. It can be revoked or altered only by mutual consent of the parties or for reasons provided for by law. |
| **KSA** | n/a |
| **Kuwait** | **Article 196, Kuwait Civil Code:**<br><br>The contract is the doctrine of both contracting parties, and neither of both may separately revoke or modify the provisions thereof, except within the limits permitted by the agreement or unless otherwise decided by law. |
| **Oman** | **Article 167, Oman Civil Code:**<br><br>The contracting parties may not rescind or modify a contract that is valid and binding unless by mutual agreement or legal action. |
| **Qatar** | **Article171(1), Qatar Civil Code:**<br><br>A contract is the law of the contracting parties and cannot be revoked or modified except that the agreement of the parties or for such reasons that are prescribed by the law. |
| **UAE** | **Article 267(1), UAE Civil Code:**<br><br>If the contract is valid and binding, it shall not be permissible for either of the contracting parties to resile from it, nor to vary or rescind it, save by mutual consent or an order of the court, or under a provision of the law. |

TABLE 3

| Exceptions to Sanctity of Contract under Arab Civil Codes | |
|---|---|
| **Bahrain** | **Article 109, Bahrain Civil Code:**<br><br>A contract is void if its object is contrary to public order or morality.<br><br>**Article 110, Bahrain Civil Code:**<br><br>(a) A contract may include any condition agreed upon by both contracting parties, provided that such condition shall not be forbidden by law or contrary to public order or morality.<br><br>(b) If the condition included in the contract is unlawful, it is void and the contract is valid. The contract shall be void if a contracting party proves that the contract would not have been entered into without such condition. |
| **Egypt** | **Article 136, Egyptian Civil Code:**<br><br>A contract is void when an obligation is assumed to be without cause or for a cause contrary to public policy or morality. |
| **KSA** | n/a |
| **Kuwait** | **Article 172, Kuwait Civil Code:**<br><br>If the subject of the obligation is in violation of law or public order or good ethics, the contract shall be void.<br><br>**Article 175, Kuwait Civil Code:**<br><br>(1) The contract may include any stipulation approved by the two contracting parties, unless it is legally prohibited or in violation of public order or good ethics.<br><br>(2) If the stipulation included in the contract is illegitimate, the stipulation shall be invalid yet the contract shall be valid, unless either of the contracting parties proves that he cannot accept the contract without his stipulation whereupon the contract shall be annulled. |
| **Oman** | **Article 116, Oman Civil Code:**<br><br>The subject-matter must be a matter to which the provisions of the contract can be applied, possible, deliverable, and not prohibited by the Shari'ah or law, otherwise the contract shall be deemed null and void.<br><br>**Article 121, Oman Civil Code:**<br><br>If a contract is without cause, or the cause of which is contrary to the Islamic Shari'ah or public order or public morals, it shall be void. |

*continues*

| Qatar | **Article 151, Qatar Civil Code:**<br><br>A contract shall be void if the subject matter of the obligation breaches public order or morality.<br><br>**Article 154, Qatar Civil Code:**<br><br>(1) The contract may include any provision agreed to by the contracting parties, unless such provision is prohibited by law or in breach of the public order or morality.<br><br>(2) Where a provision in the contract is illegal, however, such provision shall be invalid, even if the contract is valid, unless either party proves that it would not have agreed to enter into the contract without such provision, in which event the contract shall be revoked. |
|---|---|
| UAE | **Article 31, UAE Civil Code:**<br><br>A mandatory provision of law shall take precedence over a contractual stipulation. |

## TABLE 4

| Exceptions to choice of law under Arab Civil Codes | |
|---|---|
| Bahrain | **Article 110, Bahrain Civil Code:**<br><br>(a) A contract may include any condition agreed upon by both contracting parties, provided that such condition shall not be forbidden by law or contrary to public order or morality. |
| Egypt | **Article 28, Egyptian Civil Code:**<br><br>The provisions of a foreign law applicable by virtue of the preceding articles shall not be applied if these provisions are contrary to public policy or to morality in Egypt |
| KSA | **Article 27, Government Tenders and Procurement Law:**<br><br>Contracts, their documents and annexes shall be drafted in Arabic. Another language besides Arabic may be used, provided that Arabic is the prevailing language for interpretation and execution of the contract as well as for determination of its specifications, plans and communications relating thereto. |
| Kuwait | **Article 175(1), Kuwait Civil Code:**<br><br>The contract may include any stipulation approved by the two contracting parties, unless it is legally prohibited or in violation of public order or good ethics. |
| Oman | **Article 28, Oman Civil Code:**<br><br>The provisions of a foreign law specified by the previous Articles may not be apply if said provisions be inconsistent with the Islamic Sharia or the public order or morals in the Sultanate of Oman. |

*continues*

| Qatar | **Article 38, Qatar Civil Code:** |
|---|---|
| | The provisions of a foreign law applicable by virtue of the preceding Articles shall not be applied if they conflict with the public order or morals in Qatar. In such event, the Qatari law shall apply |
| UAE | **Article 27, UAE Civil Code:** |
| | It shall not be permissible to apply the provisions of a law specified by the preceding Articles if such provisions are contrary to Islamic Shari'a, public order, or morals in the State of the United Arab Emirates. |

## TABLE 5

| **Courts' power to adjust agreed compensation under Arab Civil Codes** | |
|---|---|
| **Bahrain** | **Article 226, Bahrain Civil Code:** |
| | Damages fixed by agreement are not due, if the debtor establishes that the creditor has not suffered any loss. |
| | The court may reduce the amount of these damages, if the debtor establishes that the amount fixed was grossly exaggerated or that the principal obligation has been partially performed. |
| | An agreement contrary to the provisions of the two preceding paragraphs is void. |
| | **Article 227, Bahrain Civil Code:** |
| | When the loss exceeds the amount fixed by the contract, the creditor cannot claim an increased sum, unless he is able to prove that the debtor has been guilty of fraud or gross negligence. |
| **Egypt** | **Article 224, Egyptian Civil Code:** |
| | Damages fixed by agreement are not due, if the debtor establishes that the creditor has not suffered any loss. The judge may reduce the amount of these damages, if the debtor establishes that the amount fixed was grossly exaggerated |
| **KSA** | n/a |
| **Kuwait** | **Article 303, Kuwait Civil Code:** |
| | The agreed upon indemnity shall not be due if the debtor proves that no detriment is incurred to the creditor. The Court may decrease the indemnity than the agreed upon if the debtor provides that the estimation is extremely exaggerated, or that the obligation is partially executed, and any agreement to the contrary shall be invalid |
| | **Article 304, Kuwait Civil Code:** |
| | If the detriment exceeds the value of the agreed upon indemnity, the creditor may not claim more than this value, unless it is provide that the debtor has committed fraud or a major fault. |

*continues*

| Oman | **Article 267, Oman Civil Code:** |
|------|-----------------------------------|
|      | (1) If the subject matter of obligation is not a sum of money, the contracting parties may determine the amount of compensation in advance by making a provision of same in the contract or in a subsequent agreement. |
|      | (2) In all cases, the court may, upon the application of either of the parties, amend such agreement to make the compensation equal to the damage, and any agreement to the contrary shall be null and void. |
| Qatar | **Article 266, Qatar Civil Code:** |
|      | The agreed compensation will not be payable if the debtor shows that the creditor has not incurred loss. The court may reduce the compensation from what is agreed if the debtor shows that this is grossly excessive or that the obligation has been partially fulfilled. Any agreement to the contrary shall be null and void. |
| UAE | **Article 390, UAE Civil Code:** |
|      | (1) The contracting parties may fix the amount of compensation in advance by making a provision therefor in the contract or in a subsequent agreement . . . |
|      | (2) The judge may in all cases, upon the application of either of the parties, vary such agreement so as to make the compensation equal to the loss, and any agreement to the contrary shall be void. |

## TABLE 6

| **Decennial Liability under Arab Civil Codes** | |
|------|-----------------------------------|
| Bahrain | **Article 615, Bahrain Civil Code:** |
|      | (a) The architect and contractor are jointly and severally responsible for the total or partial demolition of constructions or other permanent works erected by them for a period of five years from the date of completing the building or construction subject always to the following articles. |
|      | (b) However, if it is proved that the intent of the contracting parties that the buildings or constructions shall last for less than five years, the warranty shall be for the period during which they are intended to last. |
| Egypt | **Article 651(1), Egyptian Civil Code:** |
|      | The architect and contractor are jointly and severally responsible during a period of ten years for the total or partial collapse of contraction of other fixed works erected by them even if such destruction is due to a defect in the ground itself . . . |
| KSA | **Article 76, Government Tenders and Procurement Law:** |
|      | A contractor shall provide a ten-year warranty against partial or full collapse of what he constructs starting from the date of final handover to the Government Authority, if such collapse is due to a construction defect, unless the two contracting parties agree on a shorter period. |

*continues*

| Kuwait | **Article 692(1), Kuwait Civil Code:** |
|---|---|
| | The contractor and engineer shall guarantee any whole or partial destruction or damage that may incur to the buildings or the fixed constructions built by them during ten years from the time of completion of the building or construction, provided that the provisions of the following Articles shall be observed. |
| | . . . |
| | **Article 697, Kuwait Civil Code:** |
| | Any condition exempting the engineer or the contractor from the guarantee or restricting thereof shall be invalid. |
| Oman | **Article 634(1), Oman Civil Code:** |
| | The engineer and the contractor shall both be jointly liable for a period of ten years for the total or partial collapse of the buildings that they have constructed or the other fixed structures established thereof even if the collapse is the result of a defect in the land itself or the landowner has permitted the establishment of the defective structures unless the two contracting parties in said case were willing that such structures shall stay for a period of less than ten years. |
| | . . . |
| | **Article 636, Oman Civil Code:** |
| | Any agreement tending to exclude or limit the decennial liability of the engineer and the contractor shall be void. |
| Qatar | **Article 711(1), Qatar Civil Code:** |
| | The Contractor and the designer will be jointly liable for any total or partial collapse or any defect in buildings or fixed installations even if such collapse or defect is the result of a fault in the land or if the building owner has approved such buildings or installations. Such liability will cover any defects appearing in the building or installations that threaten their stability and safety. |
| UAE | **Article 880(1), UAE Civil Code:** |
| | If the subject matter of the contract is the construction of buildings or other fixed installations, the plans for which are made by an architect, to be carried out by the contractor under his supervision, they shall both be jointly liable for a period of ten years to make compensation to the employer for any total or partial collapse of the building they have constructed or installation they have erected, and for any defect which threatens the stability or safety of the building, unless the contract specifies a longer period. The above shall apply unless the contracting parties intend that such installations should remain in place for a period of less than ten years. |
| | . . . |
| | **Article 882, UAE Civil Code:** |
| | Any agreement tending to exclude or limit the decennial liability of the engineer and the contractor shall be void. |

TABLE 7

| Doctrine of changed circumstances under Arab Civil Codes | |
|---|---|
| **Bahrain** | **Article 130, Bahrain Civil Code:** |
| | When, however, as a result of exceptional and unpredictable events of a general character, the performance of the contractual obligation, without becoming impossible, becomes excessively onerous in such way as to threaten the debtor with exorbitant loss, the judge may, according to the circumstances, and after taking into consideration the interests of both parties, reduce to reasonable limits by lessening its extent or increasing its consideration, the obligation that has become excessive. Any agreement to the contrary is void. |
| **Egypt** | **Article 147(2), Egyptian Civil Code:** |
| | When, however, as a result of exceptional and unpredictable events of a general character, the performance of the contractual obligation, without becoming impossible, becomes excessively onerous in such way as to threaten the debtor with exorbitant loss, the judge may according to the circumstances, and after taking into consideration the interests of both parties, reduce to reasonable limits, the obligation that has become excessive. Any agreement to the contrary is void. |
| **KSA** | n/a |
| **Kuwait** | **Article 198, Kuwait Civil Code:** |
| | Should public exceptional circumstances occur, after concluding the contract and before completion of implementation thereof, which were impossibly expected upon concluding it, and the occurrence thereof ensues that the implementation of the obligation resulting therefore from, becomes though not impossible, yet becomes more burdensome to the debtor, such that it threatens him by a great loss, the judge after comparison between the interest of the two parties may return the burdensome obligation to the reasonable limit by decreasing its range or increasing the consideration thereof, and any agreement to the contrary shall be invalid. |
| **Oman** | **Article 159, Oman Civil Code:** |
| | If general exceptional accidents that were unforeseen at the time of contracting occur and result in that the execution of the contractual obligation, even if not impossible, become burdensome to the debtor and threaten the latter with serious loss, the court may, according to the circumstances and after balancing the interests of both parties, reduce the burdensome obligation to a reasonable limit. Any other agreement to the contrary shall be void. |

*continues*

| Qatar | **Article 171(2), Qatar Civil Code:** |
|---|---|
| | However, if public exceptional incidents occur which could not have been expected, the occurrence of which makes the fulfilment of the contractual obligation though, though not impossible, but exhausting to the debtor and threatens him of grave loss, the judge may, taking into consideration the circumstances and after weighing the interests of the parties, reducing the exhausting obligation to a reasonable margin. Any agreement to the contrary shall be void. |
| UAE | **Article 249, UAE Civil Code:** |
| | If exceptional circumstances of a general nature which could not have been foreseen occur as a result of which the performance of the contractual obligation, even if not impossible, becomes oppressive for the obligor so as to threaten him with grave loss, it shall be permissible for the judge, in accordance with the circumstances and after weighing up the interests of each party, to reduce the oppressive obligation to a reasonable level if justice so requires, and any agreement to the contrary shall be void. |

**TABLE 8**

| Enshrinement of good faith and fairness under Arab Civil Codes | |
|---|---|
| Bahrain | **Article 127, Bahrain Civil Code:** |
| | A contract is not only limited to its expressed conditions, but also as regards everything which according to law, usage and equity is deemed in view of the nature of the obligation, to be a necessary sequel to the contract, taking into consideration custom and usage, requirements of equity, nature of business, good faith and honesty. |
| | **Article 129, Bahrain Civil Code:** |
| | A contract must be performed in accordance with its contents and in compliance with the requirements of good faith and honesty. |
| Egypt | **Article 148, Egyptian Civil Code:** |
| | A contract must be performed in accordance with its contents and in compliance with the requirements of good faith. |
| | A contract binds the contracting party not only as regards its expressed conditions, but also as regards everything which, according to law, usage and equity, is deemed, in view of the nature of the obligation, to be a necessary sequel to the contract. |

*continues*

| KSA | **Article 77, Government Tenders and Procurement Law:** |
|---|---|
|  | Contractors and government authorities shall execute their contracts in accordance with contract terms, in good faith and as the proper functioning and interest of the public utility. |
|  | Ministries, government departments and agencies with independent corporate personality shall inform the Ministry of Finance of cases of deceit, fraud and manipulation immediately upon discovery and provide it with decisions made in this respect, including decisions of withdrawal of work. |
| Kuwait | **Article 197, Kuwait Civil Code:** |
|  | The contract must be implemented in accordance with the provisions included therein and in such a manner in compliance with the requirements of food faith and honour of dealing. |
| Oman | **Article 156, Oman Civil Code:** |
|  | The contract must be executed in accordance with its content and not restricted to the obligation of the contracting party as specified therein, but it may also involve whatever is deemed of its requisites according to the law, the custom and justice, and pursuant to the nature of the disposition. |
| Qatar | **Article 172, Qatar Civil Code:** |
|  | (1) The contract must be performed in accordance with its contents and in a manner which consistent with the requirements of good faith. |
|  | (2) The contract is not confined to obliging a contracting party to its contents, but also includes its requirements in accordance with the law, custom and equity as per the nature of the obligation. |
| UAE | **Article 246, UAE Civil Code:** |
|  | (1) The contract must be performed in accordance with its contents, and in a manner consistent with the requirements of good faith. |
|  | (2) The contract shall not be restricted to an obligation upon the contracting party to do that which is (expressly) contained in it, but shall also embrace that which is appurtenant to it by virtue of the law, custom, and the nature of the transaction. |

TABLE 9

| Restriction on the exercise of rights under Arab Civil Codes | |
|---|---|
| **Bahrain** | **Article 28, Bahrain Civil Code:**<br>The exercise of a right shall be unlawful in the following cases:<br>(a) If the sole aim thereof is to harm another person.<br>(b) If it is aimed to achieve unlawful interest or interests.<br>(c) If the benefit or benefits it is desired to realise is out of proportion to the harm caused thereby to another person.<br>(d) If it is designed to cause a serious and unfamiliar damage to third parties. |
| **Egypt** | **Article 5, Egyptian Civil Code:**<br>The exercise of a right is considered unlawful in the following cases:<br>(a) if the sole aim thereof is to harm another person;<br>(b) if the benefit it is desired to realize is out of proportion to the harm caused thereby to another person; or<br>(c) if the benefit it is desired to realize is unlawful. |
| **KSA** | n/a |
| **Kuwait** | **Article 30, Kuwait Civil Code:**<br>The use of a right is illegal if its owner deviates thereby from the purpose of the social function therefor, particularly:<br>(a) If the interest ensuing therefrom is illegal.<br>(b) If it only intends to incur detriment to third parties.<br>(c) If the interest ensuing therefrom is absolutely incompetent with the detriment incurred to third parties.<br>(d) If it is expected to incur great unfamiliar detriment to third parties. |
| **Oman** | **Article 58, Oman Civil Code:**<br>The public damage shall be averted by the private damage and the greater damage by the lesser one.<br>**Article 59, Oman Civil Code:**<br>Whoever abuses his right shall be held liable for compensation; the abuse of right shall be in the following instances:<br>(1) Should the intent of infringement be available.<br>(2) Should the intended benefit of the act be unlawful.<br>(3) Should the benefit be not proportionate to the damage sustained by third parties.<br>(4) Should it exceed the bounds of custom and habit. |

*continues*

| Qatar | **Article 63, Qatar Civil Code:** |
|---|---|
| | The exercise of right shall be unlawful in the following cases: |
| | (1) If the interest to be achieved is unlawful. |
| | (2) If it was only intended to cause damage to others. |
| | (3) If the interest to be achieved is at all disproportionate with the damage inflicted on others. |
| | (4) If it inflicts on others severe unfamiliar damage. |
| UAE | **Article 106, UAE Civil Code:** |
| | (1) A person shall be held liable for an unlawful exercise of his rights. |
| | (2) The exercise of a right shall be unlawful: |
| |     (a) if there is an intentional infringement (of another's rights); |
| |     (b) if the interests which such exercise of right is designed to bring about are contrary to the rules of the Islamic Shari'a, the law, public order, or morals; |
| |     (c) if the interests desired are disproportionate to the harm that will be suffered by others; or |
| |     (d) if it exceeds the bounds of usage and custom. |

CHAPTER 2

# ARE YOU COMPLYING WITH THE DBE REGULATIONS? HOW AND WHY AN ETHICS AND COMPLIANCE PROGRAM CAN BE A PREVENTATIVE TOOL IN LIGHT OF CURRENT ETHICS AND COMPLIANCE TRENDS

Lorraine D'Angelo

## § 2.01 INTRODUCTION

One of the biggest issues facing the construction industry today is complying with the requirements of the United States Department of Transportation's ("USDOT") Disadvantaged Business Enterprise ("DBE") program and/or state or locally mandated minority or woman-owned ("M/WBE") programs. In contracting with the government on certain public works projects (on USDOT projects: the Federal Transit Administration, Federal Aviation Administration, and Federal Highway Administration), the government mandates that a specific portion of the contract work be awarded to a business that has been certified as socially or economically disadvantaged as a DBE. The goals are required to be set based upon proof of continued discrimination and the availability and capacity of DBE or M/WBE firms. Where a contract sets a goal, the government expects that contractors working on a contract financed in whole or in part with taxpayer dollars shall take all necessary and reasonable steps to ensure that designated firms have an opportunity to compete for, and participate in, a project. The government expects that contractors will pay more money and take specific actions to provide opportunities and to use certified firms to promote the social policy goal of eliminating past discrimination and denial of opportunity in government contracting.

DBE and M/WBE programs are collectively referred to as XBE programs in this chapter. "XBE" is a term coined by the author to indicate any program that requires the use of small, disadvantaged, minority, locally-based, woman-owned firms, or other business designated by the government as eligible to participate in such a program. It must be noted that the regulations that apply to a specific contract or program must be consulted and applied. XBE program concepts are similar from program to program but there are differences and those differences can be critical to properly claiming participation or attainment dollars in connection with the specific regulation.

How to achieve goals with legitimate XBE firms and monitor, assess, and document XBE compliance has become a critical issue for contractors and governmental agencies.

Generally, a contractor will aspire to use contractors that have been certified to reach the percentage of participation established by the agency for the contract, but that certification does not assure ability to perform a commercially useful function ("CUF"). A socially or economically disadvantaged business enterprise must be responsible for the execution of a distinct element of work and carries out its responsibilities by actually performing, managing, and supervising the work using its own resources. A XBE does not perform a CUF if its role is limited to that of an extra participant in a transaction, contract, or project through which funds are passed in order to obtain the appearance of participation.

In recent years, the government has stepped up its efforts to detect and punish those contractors who commit fraud in this area and often form joint and coordinated task forces between different departments of the government. A tool often employed is to commence a civil or criminal action under the False Claims Act.

The USDOT Inspector General Calvin Scovell has stated publicly that 29% of his staff attorney's time is now spent investigating XBE fraud cases. Major contractors have paid millions of dollars to resolve XBE fraud issues. In addition to the fines and penalties, a corporation accused of XBE fraud or who has paid a fine, with or without admitting liability, must continually prove its "responsibility" to avoid suspension or debarment from government contracting work. Suspension and debarment proceeding have consistently increased since 2009 under the continued legislative pressure to do business only with those firms that exhibit integrity in their business practices. The U.S. Attorney stated that the Department of Justice ("DOJ") is using civil and criminal prosecutions of individual corporate officers to "deliver the message" to private industry that they will be held accountable for illegal corporate activity. In addition, as part of a settlement many corporations are required to implement compliance programs subject to third-party scrutiny, hire additional compliance staff, hire an IPSIG or independent monitor to review future corporate activities, all adding to the company's overhead.

Hardly ever is there a report that a contractor used a firm that was not on the government's certified list. The reality remains that it is up to the contractor engaging the XBE firm to monitor that firm's performance and make sure that amounts claimed for participation/attainment are in conformance with the appropriate regulation. With the level of scrutiny given by law enforcement agencies on these socio-economic programs, the old adage that an ounce of prevention is worth a pound of cure could not ring truer. An ethics and compliance program that contains a specific procedure to address XBE compliance has become a necessity for those operating in the government contracting arena.

Federal and state governments have established programs that promote the utilization and growth of small, socially and economically disadvantaged business enterprises. The social policy goals of such programs is to increase participation in government contracting by groups that are identified as socially or economically disadvantaged, to create a level playing field to compete for contracts that are funded with public dollars, to assist in the development of firms that can compete successfully outside the program, and to help remove barriers to participation by engaging in nondiscrimination in the solicitation and award of contracts. Federal and state small business programs are varied and impose limitations on large businesses when contracting. The government expects that each contractor, subcontractor, manufacturer, trucker, and supplier working on a contract financed in whole or in part with federal funds shall take all necessary and reasonable steps to ensure that designated firms have an opportunity to compete for, and participate in, performance on project contracts and subcontracts. The government may establish goals for award to small businesses which meet the specific qualifications of the state or federal program. For the purposes of this chapter, when discussing general program concepts, these socially or economically disadvantaged firms are called "XBEs," and when discussing a specific program, like the DBE program or a local M/WBE program, the specific reference is used.

The government expects that contractors will pay more money to use certified firms to promote the social policy goal of eliminating discrimination. Generally, a contractor will aspire to use contractors that have been certified to reach the percentage of participation established by the agency for the contract. Although the requirements for counting participation vary certain concepts are implicit in each program. Generally, independence from non-XBE businesses and control of all aspects of the day-to-day business operations must be in the hands of the small or disadvantaged business owner. A small, socially or economically disadvantaged business enterprise must be responsible for the execution of a distinct element of work and carry out its responsibilities by actually performing, managing, and supervising the work generally using labor and equipment it has procured or owns. A XBE does not perform a CUF if its role is limited to that of an extra participant in a transaction, contract, or project through which funds are passed in order to obtain the appearance of participation.

Although state and federal regulations differ in interpreting how a contractor can reach the established goal and count the participation of a socially or economically disadvantaged business enterprise, the general concept is that a contractor can count the amount paid to such concern provided the business provides a CUF on the project. Typically, a socially or economically disadvantaged firm must itself perform a specified percentage of the work required by the subcontract or purchase order agreement. The scope of work to be performed should be meaningful and add value to the overall performance of the project. A contractor is required to make every good faith effort to achieve the contract goal, either by meeting the goal or by documenting adequate good faith efforts to meet the goal. All efforts made are to be sincere, aggressive, and documented.

The DBE Regulations, 49 CFR Parts 26 and 23, apply to USDOT federal-aid or federal financial participation projects. Federal-aid or federal financial participation includes, but is not limited to, any funds directly or indirectly received by State Departments of Transportation (Recipients), or authorized for distribution to or through the State DOT, by the USDOT, or any operating administration within the USDOT. As a condition of receiving the contract, the contractor promises to advance certain social and economic programs. The XBE program objective is to provide contracting opportunities, either through race neutral or race conscious measures, to firms that have been certified as socially or economically disadvantaged because of past discrimination as evidenced and supported by a study that demonstrates the firms are not getting their fair share of opportunities. Many state and local governments have implemented their own programs that require contractors on public works to use, or attempt to use, businesses that are defined as eligible to participate in a program. These programs operate similarly to the federal DBE program. By providing the firms with preferential status to compete for opportunities, these programs seek to create a level playing field for opportunities for these firms to participate in publically funded projects.

The federal DBE program concepts regarding performance and participation of DBEs are generally applicable to the other government programs. Under a XBE program, both the contractor and the governmental agency receives credit toward the established goal (contract and overall) only when a XBE working on a contract performs a CUF. XBEs generally can perform work as a subcontractor, a subconsultant (i.e., professional services), a trucker, a material supplier (a regular dealer), a manufacturer, or other than manufacturer or regular dealer. While each of these categories is evaluated differently when determining whether the XBE has performed a CUF, there is one guiding principle that must be met. Under the terms established in 49 CFR 26.55, a DBE firm performs a CUF when it is:

> Responsible for execution of the work of the contract or a distinct element of the work . . . by actually performing, managing, and supervising the work involved.

What are the management, supervision, and performance actions of a XBE firm that satisfactorily meets this requirement? As discussed herein, evaluating these areas will form the basis to render a determination that a XBE subcontractor or subconsultant has in fact performed a CUF and, therefore, its participation dollars can be claimed under the appropriate regulation.

In general, the Contractor's obligation is to meet the contractual and regulatory requirements by meeting or exceeding the XBE goal expressed in the contract and applicable XBE program or to demonstrate its good faith efforts proving it was unable to achieve the goal despite its sincere, aggressive efforts. It has also become the responsibility of the contractor to assure that those firms it claims for participation are eligible to participate in the program and are performing a CUF. Certification and counting XBE participation are two separate and distinct concepts. The contracting agency has an oversight responsibility to ensure that the prime contractor has effectively met this responsibility under his or her contract and is supposed to set clear directives and standards for monitoring. Often the monitoring function is limited to seeing that required paperwork regarding XBE participation is submitted and payments are made. However, due to the heightened enforcement environment, more agencies are devoting attention to CUF reviews. Certification lists are often inaccurate and cannot be relied upon by a contractor as its sole source for determining CUF. Despite the increased CUF scrutiny by the agencies, it appears difficult to remove non-bona fide XBE firms from participation in the XBE programs. All of these factors make it more important than ever for the contractor to establish a process and procedure for compliance with the regulations.

Also, failure to carry out the requirements of the XBE regulations is often made a material breach of the contract with the public agency and can result in remedies imposed by the contracting agency which include, but are not limited to, termination of the contract, withholding of progress payments, assessing sanctions, liquidated damages, imposition of integrity monitors, strengthening of a contractor's compliance program, or disqualification from future biddings (suspension and debarment).

Certifications and submissions made by the contractor regarding amounts paid to XBE contractors often form the basis for proceeding against a contractor or its employees. All employees must understand certifications and representations that the company obligates itself, such as: XBE requirements, EEO/AA requirements, wages, immigration, safety, environmental, gift giving restrictions, etc. Contractual obligations must be understood and timelines identified, such as dates when reports need to be submitted to agency and assignment of responsibility for submission. All project personnel must also understand what actions are required in order to meet agreed obligations and that others within a company may be relying upon each employee taken the requisite level of due diligence to assure compliance.

> The certification that the signer of a . . . statement adopts creates a duty to investigate. . . . One who signs a certification cannot choose to remain unaware of the veracity of that certification like the proverbial ostrich who buried its head in the sand so as to see no evil, hear no evil and speak no evil. Thus, a failure to conduct a proper investigation before making a false statement may be sufficiently reckless to yield False Claims Act liability.[1]

This chapter will highlight the basics of the regulations, the overarching program concepts, and suggestions on the elements that should be contained in a "best practices" XBE compliance policy.

## § 2.02 THE BASICS YOU NEED TO KNOW IN ORDER TO MEET THE REGULATORY REQUIREMENTS

The contractor needs to familiarize itself with the specific XBE program and applicable regulations. For instance, although the DBE program oversight is through an operating administration (FAA, FTA, or FHWA), each state agency is required to obtain approval of its own "DBE program." As a result, and although the DBE programs are governed by the federal regulation, 49 CFR Parts 26 and 23, state agencies may insert requirements that are additional to those included in the federal regulations. It is important to carefully review the approved state DBE program. Usually, the proposal or contract documents will inform the contractor about these additional requirements. The same is true for local, city or municipal governmental authorities.

---

[1] United States v. Raymond & Whitcomb Co., 53 F. Supp. 2d 436, 446-47 (S.D.N.Y. 1999).

Only firms certified by the appropriate certifying agency can be claimed by the contractor for participation. For the DBE program, this is done under the State's Uniform Certification Program ("UCP"). State and local governments will separately certify firms for participation in their programs and maintain their own, separate lists of certified firms. Separate certifications are required for participation in the DBE, M/WBE, or local programs. Recently, the DBE program permitted recipient state agencies to offer reciprocity for out-of-state DBE certified firms but this creates its own issues with respect to verifying the credentials of the out-of-state DBE firm.

Usually, a XBE firm is a for-profit small business concern, owned at least 51% by individuals defined as socially or economically disadvantaged, and those individuals are actually responsible for and control the management and daily business operations of the DBE firm. The business is also required to be independent of other businesses in all respects: financially, operationally, etc. Under the current DBE regulations, African Americans, Hispanics, Native Americans, Asian-Pacific and Subcontinent Asian Americans, and women are presumed to be socially and economically disadvantaged. Other individuals can also qualify as socially and economically disadvantaged on a case-by-case basis. State and local programs have similar eligibility requirements and identify eligible groups usually based upon disparity studies.

Disparity studies are widely used to prove the need for government imposed racial preferences in government contracting policies in order to remediate past discrimination against historically disadvantaged racial and ethnic groups. Simplistically, the studies gather both statistical and anecdotal evidence regarding the availability of certain firms to participate in opportunities and compare the actual participation. Target goals are then set by governmental agencies based upon the findings of the studies.

The rules for claiming participation are different depending on whether the firm is used as a subcontractor or subconsultant, material or equipment supplier (regular dealer, manufacturer, or broker), or trucker. It is important to recognize which category the XBE falls under because the amount of participation that can be claimed is different. In all categories, the participating DBE firm must perform a CUF.

"Commercially Useful Function" is defined as "[r]esponsible for execution of the work of the contract or a distinct element of the work . . . by actually performing, managing, and supervising the work involved."[2] If the firm is an extra participant in the transaction and adds no value or commercial purpose, then it not performing a CUF and participation for those services cannot be claimed. To help determine if a firm is performing a CUF, ask: whether the DBE firm would be performing in the manner it is if there was no DBE program. Stated another

---

[2] 49 C.F.R. § 26.55.

way, does the DBE firm perform this work, this way when working outside of the DBE program?

XBE participation may be claimed only for firms that provide value to the contracting process. This concept is commonly referred to as a commercially useful function ("CUF"), a concept that came out of the DBE program but is now finding its way into any state and local M/WBE programs. A contractor is responsible for every dollar of participation it claims for attainment, whether the participation is claimed through direct contracts with the DBEs or lower tier agreements. Care must be taken in creating a XBE policy and procedure that attention is given to these lower tier agreements and the contractor is not turning a blind eye to its lower tier contractors' actions.

In determining whether a XBE is an extra participant in a transaction, you must examine similar transactions, particularly those in which XBEs do not participate. A XBE must have a necessary and useful role in the transaction, of a kind for which there is a market outside the context of the program. The firm's role must not be a superfluous step added in an attempt to obtain credit towards the goal.

To help determine whether a CUF is being performed, assess five areas and review for red flags:[3] management, performance, workforce, materials and equipment, and trucking. Generally, the contractor should evaluate the amount of work proposed to be given to see if it is consistent with normal industry practices and if the amount to be paid under the contract is commensurate with the work that is actually being performed by the XBE and to be credited towards the goal. Take care when relying on normal industry practices. If the practice is generally acceptable in the industry but compromises other attributes of CUF (i.e., independence), then it still might not be acceptable to claim attainment for that particular firm.

In a competitive bid process and in determining whether to award a contract to a low bidder, the agency must consider whether the contractor met the XBE goal. In assessing the contractor's good faith efforts, an agency is permitted to look to the XBE utilization plans submitted by the other bidders. An agency is permitted to reject a low bid and award to the second bidder where a low bidder was submitted a XBE utilization plan that did not meet the goal upon the grounds that the low bidder did not meet its good faith effort requirement.

Several recent cases illustrate the importance of being able to demonstrate the efforts taken to try to achieve the goal.[4]

---

[3] Red flags are questionable practices, which may warrant further review. The presence of a "red flag" does not mean that the XBE is not *bona fide* but it does blur some aspect of the XBE regulations and should not be ignored.

[4] *See* Midwest Fence Corp. v. U.S. Dep't of Transp., 2010 CV 05627 (N.D. Ill. 2015); C.S. McCrossan v. Minnesota Dep't of Transp., 946 F. Supp. 2d 851 (D. Minn. 2013); Dunnet Bay v. Hannig, 10 CV 3051 (C.D. Ill. 2011).

Certification and CUF are separate and distinct issues. Certification decisions address the nature of a firm's ownership and structure while CUF primarily
concerns the role a firm has played in a particular transaction. Failure to perform
a CUF can be considered by the agency during the certification process; however,
it must not necessarily be the sole factor considered by the certification agency in
making the determination to certify a firm.

Contractors and individuals have been prosecuted for not using the XBE
firm in accordance with the regulations and intent of the XBE program. The prosecutions usually rest upon the contractor's certification made in connection with
its monthly request for payment. Contracts typically contain multiple certifications that a contractor is in compliance. The certification should never be treated
as a mere formality. Process needs to be put in place to address verifying that the
XBE is eligible to participate and that it performs a CUF during performance.

The most common XBE schemes involve the use of "pass through" or
"front" companies. In the "pass through" scheme, the DBE firm typically receives
a fee (3-5%) and the services are performed by a non-DBE firm. The work
"passes through" the DBE to give the appearance of participation. In the "front"
company scheme, the DBE owner is a figurehead and the firm performs little or
no work. Again, the actual work is performed by a non-XBE or the prime contractor. Thus, it is critical to understand the regulations as well as to exercise diligence during the performance of the work.

## § 2.03  ESSENTIAL INFORMATION FOR THE BIDDING, ESTIMATING, AND PURCHASING FUNCTIONS

### [A]  Identification, Solicitation, and Selection of the DBE

A contractor should formulate its participation plan by relying upon the
appropriate agency certified list since those are the only firms that a contractor
will be able to count for attainment toward the established goal. XBEs are firms
that have been certified by an agency charged with the responsibility for evaluating the firm's application and for determining whether the firm meets the basic
criteria and requirements established for certification. Generally, the certifying
agency does not make a determination regarding the firm's capacity or capability
to perform the work it states it can perform. Such work is typically assigned a
code that is associated with a system for identifying work. For example, the DBE
program uses the North American Industrial Classification System ("NAICS").
Certification is the firm's "foot in the door" and only entitles it to participation in
the XBE program. It remains the contractor's obligation to check if the firm can
perform the scope of work it wants to award to the firm as well as a CUF. A contractor should not rely on the firm's certification as the only criteria for claiming
participation.

Considering that the designation of a XBE firm on a participation plan is viewed as a firm commitment to enter into a scope of work with the XBE at the price listed, a contractor should investigate the capacity and capability of the XBE firm in advance of the submission. At a minimum consider the following steps:

- Obtain a copy of the DBE's certification:

    1. Check the appropriate certification list (e.g., UCP list) to make sure firm currently appears on the list;

    2. Print and retain a copy of the certification listing as often the certification listed are not historical and searched performed on specific past date cannot be replicated;

    3. Check the NAICS Codes assigned to the firm and determine if the proposed scope of work is consistent with the NAICS Code. Work done by a XBE outside its code cannot be claimed for attainment credit;

    4. Review and determine that the work proposed to be given to the XBE is *not* outside its known capability;

    5. Ascertain if the XBE firm is financially capable of supporting the work based upon the payment cycle of the contract;

    6. Ascertain if the XBE firm possesses the manpower, equipment, and ability/knowledge to perform the work; and

    7. Ascertain that the XBE firm can operate independently of a non-XBE business and is not dependent upon another business in its operation (e.g., possesses the necessary licenses).

## [B]  Bidding and Preconstruction

Under most current regulations, once a XBE is submitted to the agency as part of the contractor's participation plan, the contractor must use that firm and often written agency approval is required to remove or substitute the XBE firm. Thus, it is imperative that the vetting of the proposed XBE firm's capacity and capability be done in advance of submitting the XBE as part of any participation plan. DBEs may only be claimed for attainment if they are certified, appear on the state UCP list, and intend to perform a scope of services for which it has a NAICS Code.

In addition, a contractor should carefully review the contract requirements for any additional requirements (e.g., agency approval of subcontractors, approval of truck leases, pre-qualification of regular dealers).

A contractor cannot reject a XBE's quote on the basis of price alone or value associated with self-performance of the work. If a XBE's quote is rejected, the contractor must document the reason why the quote was rejected. There is no established criterion for determining when a XBE firm's price becomes commercially "unreasonable."

XBEs should always have a written agreement that sets forth the scope of its services and agreed price. This information often has to be submitted by the contractor to the agency or made available to the agency upon request. All written agreements should clearly define the scope of services to be provided by the XBE. Items of work that are to be excluded should also be identified and process implemented with the contractor's accounting department to make certain that if deductions are to be made attainment credit should not be mistakenly taken (e.g., use of a crane, loading and unloading materials, storage of equipment and materials, supervision and inspection of work).

Written confirmation should also be obtained from the XBE that indicates the scope of services to be provided and the agreed price. More often than not, this information must also be submitted to the agency within the rules guidelines.

Second tier and lower tier agreements, if permitted, call for increased vigilance by the contractor. The same rules that apply to direct contracts apply to lower tier agreements.

Under the DBE regulations, a contractor may not count participation for work a DBE subcontracts to a non-DBE. Closely associated with this concept is the requirement that a DBE perform a certain amount work. A DBE does not perform a CUF if it performs less than 30% of the total cost of its work or subcontracts more work than would be expected based upon normal industry practice. State or local requirements may require a DBE to perform greater than 30%.

As soon as you are able, get to know the agency personnel responsible for the oversight of the agency XBE program. (Note: many contracts restrict contact with agency officials in advance of contract award. Take care not to violate the "point of contact" procurement rules.) Use their knowledge and expertise as a resource. Be transparent. The XBE program rules are not always black and white; seek agency guidance. They can be a tremendous resource.

The contractor's XBE policy should strive to create a participation plan that meets or exceeds the XBE goal, making sure to address the following:

1.  Identify work that may be subcontracted and the estimated value of the work;

2.  Breakdown work into packages that make it possible for a XBE to participate (commonly referred to as "unbundling");

3.  Determine if vetted, certified, and capable XBEs are available;

4.  Solicit those firms through variety of methods including printed advertisements, targeted advertisement in publications that reach the intended minority community, direct solicitation via email, certified mail, or telephone calls, etc.;

5. Provide assistance without compromising the XBE's independence in performing, managing, or supervising the work;

6. Determine if second tier participation is permitted and, if so, discuss with non-XBE subcontractors flowing down the same requirements to lower tiers that the agency is requiring the contractor to abide by;

7. Determine if material or equipment supply is permitted and, if so, the percentage of participation that may be claimed (e.g., 100% vs. 60%); and

8. Create a XBE utilization plan that meets or exceeds the goal, or consider requesting a waiver or modification of the goal if it cannot be met.

## [C]  Good Faith Efforts

Good faith efforts ("GFE") are all sincere, aggressive efforts made that one would anticipate would result in achieving the XBE goal. A contractor must be able to prove that it was actively and aggressively looking for XBEs. The agency will evaluate the quality, quantity, and intensity of the contractor's efforts. A contractor must be able to show that it could not achieve the contract goal despite its aggressive and sincere efforts. Good faith efforts are not mere pro forma efforts ("going through the motions" or "checking a box"). Good faith efforts are determined by the agency on a case-by-case basis and are often made in hindsight.

Under the DBE regulations that became effective November 3, 2014, bidders are required to submit:

1. The names and addresses of DBE firms that will participate in the contract;

2. A description of the work to be performed and NAICS Code;

3. Contractor's commitment to use the listed DBEs;

4. Written confirmation from the DBE;

5. Good faith efforts, if the goal was not met;[5] and

6. If the DBE goal was not met, all DBE and non-DBE quotes where a non-DBE was chosen over a DBE and documented reasons why the DBE was not chosen.

A contractor may not have a strict low bid policy and price alone is not a reason for rejecting a DBEs bid, as long as it is not unreasonable. Desire to self-perform is also not a reason for rejecting a DBE bid.

Under the DBE regulations, the agency has the choice to make the submission of GFEs a matter of responsiveness or responsibility. If a matter of responsibility,

---

[5] 49 CFR Pt. 26, Appendix A contains a non-exclusive list of items that are considered to be actions that evidence good faith efforts.

the GFE documentation supporting the contractor's efforts are due seven days after bid opening. (Effective January 1, 2017, the seven-day period is reduced to five days.) If a matter of responsiveness, the GFEs are due at the time of bid submission.

Under the DBE regulations, negotiated procurement (i.e., Design-Build, P3) is excluded from the above requirement. The agency is permitted to accept a contractually binding commitment that the DBE goal will be met or GFEs documented. However, before final selection of the bidder, it must provide items 1-6, above.

The contractor must use the DBEs it submits and lists unless it obtains written consent from the agency to remove or substitute the DBE firm. If a contractor terminates or replaces a DBE without obtaining written consent, the contractor is not entitled to payment for the work performed.

If a DBE is removed for any reason, the contractor must demonstrate GFEs to replace the same amount of work with another DBE, document its efforts, and submit such GFEs to the agency. The agency is required to issue a written determination evaluating the contractor's GFEs.

A contractor is expected to engage in real, aggressive actions that, if taken, would expect to achieve the established goal. These are typically referred to as "good faith efforts." 49 CFR Part 26, Appendix A includes a non-exhaustive list of actions a contractor can take to demonstrate that it engaged in efforts designed to meet the participation goal. Suggestions for soliciting DBE firms are included in 49 CFR Part 26, Appendix A. These efforts include: outreach (general and targeted), advertisement in publications designed to reach a broad DBE community, solicitation of firms from the list to ascertain their interest in bidding the work, breaking down the work into pieces that DBEs may be able to perform and support, requiring non-DBE subcontractors and suppliers to commit to use DBE firms, providing assistance in meeting the bonding or insurance requirements (a note of caution: although assistance is listed as a GFE, any assistance given by a contractor must be carefully balanced so that the line of independence between the DBE and the contractor is not crossed), etc.[6] All of the factors listed in any regulation describing what the agency considers to be GFEs should be considered during the solicitation process and documented.

Many state and local governments have their own definitions of GFEs. For instance, New York State Regulations, 5 NYCRR 142.8, defines GFEs as follows:

(a) The contractor must document its good faith efforts toward meeting certified minority- and women-owned business enterprise utilization plans by providing, at a minimum:

(1) Copies of its solicitations of certified minority- and women-owned business enterprises and any responses thereto;

---

[6] *See* 49 C.F.R. pt. 26, Appendix A.

(2) If responses to the contractor's solicitations were received, but a certified minority- or woman-owned business enterprise was not selected, the specific reasons that such enterprise was not selected;

(3) Copies of any advertisements for participation by certified minority- and women-owned business enterprises timely published in appropriate general circulation, trade and minority- or women-oriented publications, together with the listing(s) and date(s) of the publication of such advertisements;

(4) Copies of any solicitations of certified minority- and/or women-owned business enterprises listed in the directory of certified businesses;

(5) The dates of attendance at any pre-bid, pre-award, or other meetings, if any, scheduled by the State agency awarding the State contract, with certified minority- and women-owned business enterprises which the State agency determined were capable of performing the State contract scope of work for the purpose of fulfilling the contract participation goals;

(6) Information describing the specific steps undertaken to reasonably structure the contract scope of work for the purpose of subcontracting with, or obtaining supplies from, certified minority and women-owned business enterprises.

(b) In addition to the information provided by the contractor in paragraph (a) above, the State agency may also consider the following to determine whether the contractor has demonstrated good faith efforts:

(1) whether the contractor submitted an alternative utilization plan consistent with the subcontract or supplier opportunities in the contract;

(2) the number of certified minority- and women-owned business enterprises in the region listed in the directory of certified businesses that could, in the judgment of the State agency, perform work required by the State contract scope of work;

(3) The actions taken by the contractor to contact and assess the ability of certified minority- and women-owned business enterprises located outside of the region in which the State contract scope of work is to be performed to participate on the State contract;

(4) whether the contractor provided relevant plans, specifications or terms and conditions to certified minority- and women-owned business enterprises sufficiently in advance to enable them to prepare an informed response to a contractor request for participation as a subcontractor or supplier;

(5) the terms and conditions of any subcontract or provision of suppliers offered to certified minority- or women-owned business enterprises and a comparison of such terms and conditions 38 with those offered in the ordinary course of the contractor's business and to other subcontractors or suppliers of the contractor;

(6) whether the contractor offered to make up any inability to comply with the certified minority and women-owned business

enterprises goals in the subject State contract in other State contracts being performed or awarded to the contractor; and (7) any other information that is relevant or appropriate to determining whether the contractor has demonstrated a good faith effort.

A contractor should carefully review the XBE regulations it typically operates under and incorporate, at a minimum, those actions the agency regulations identify as a GFE. Remember that changes to contract value (additions or deletions) or scope may impact the contractor's ability to meet the goal and, if the goal falls below the contract requirements, GFEs are going to be needed.

## § 2.04  ESSENTIAL INFORMATION FOR THE FIELD OPERATIONS

Both the prime contractor and the governmental agency receive credit toward the XBE goal (contract and overall) only when a XBE working on a contract performs a CUF.

CUF means that the DBE is "responsible for execution of the work of the contract or a distinct element of the work by actually performing, managing, and supervising the work involved."[7] The responsibility to make sure that only those DBEs that perform a CUF are claimed for participation has been place upon the contractor. Thus, monitoring performance to determine if DBE firms listed on the participation/utilization plan are performing a CUF is critical to a XBE policy.

### [A]  Subcontracting

What are the management, supervision, and performance actions of a DBE firm that satisfactorily meet the requirement to perform a CUF? Evaluating these areas will form the basis to render a determination that a DBE has in fact performed a CUF. The subcontract is the starting point for any evaluation. The subcontract should clearly define the scope of work and effectively describe the work to be performed by a DBE. It is also a legally recognized and binding document that gives the relationship added credibility in the agency's eyes.

The federal government has described the following key factors in its DBE regulations to help determine whether a CUF is being performed and they provide useful guidance for other XBE programs:

1. Evaluation of the amount of work subcontracted, whether it is consistent with normal industry practices;[8]

---

[7] 49 C.F.R. pt. 26.

[8] A note about "normal industry practice": Normal industry practice is determined largely by non-DBE firms and is often simply a practice repeated enough to set the normal industry practice. For purposes of CUF, a DBE's role is evaluated with reference to normal industry practice. **However, if normal practices in fact erode the ability of the DBE to control its work and remain**

2.  Whether the amount the firm is paid under the contract is commensurate with the work that is actually being performed to be credited towards the goal;

3.  When the DBE furnishes materials, the DBE must be responsible for negotiating the price, for determining the quality and quantity of the material, ordering the material, and paying for it. As a contractor, a DBE firm may be contracted to furnish and install or just to install an item in the contract.

4.  Whether the DBE's role is limited to that of an extra participant in a transaction, contract, or project through which funds are passed through in order to obtain the appearance of DBE participation. In essence, was the role merely a contrived arrangement for the purpose of meeting the DBE contract goal?

Typically, a subcontract will require the subcontractor to both "furnish and install." In order to claim 100% of the subcontract value, with respect to the purchase of the materials or equipment, the DBE must be responsible for all of the following: (1) negotiate price; (2) determine quality and quantity; (3) order the materials; and (4) pay for the materials itself. Any involvement by the contractor in the procurement of the materials or equipment can erode or eliminate the CUF of the DBE subcontractor. The DBE must negotiate directly with the supplier. The supplies should relate directly to the scope of work to be provided by the DBE and should be installed by the DBE's workforce. The ability to pay for the materials is also a consideration. Often a supplier may be hesitant to rely upon the credit of the XBE and will request the contractor to issue a joint check to the XBE and the supplier. Caution must be exercised with these requests. Joint check arrangements are not per se prohibited but they do raise a red flag regarding the ability of the XBE to financially support the subcontract work. Transparency with the agency regarding the arrangement and a written joint check agreement between the XBE and the contractor can be actions a contractor may employ should the XBE request that payment for supplies be made with a joint check.

The contractor cannot participate in any of the above listed activities. This means that if the contractor had negotiations with the supplier, it cannot share the results of the conversation with the XBE. Some examples of activities to be avoided include providing to the XBE draft purchase orders specifying the items to be purchased or quantity, requiring contractor approval of purchase orders between the XBE and supplier, and negotiating directly with the supplier on

---

independent, the practice is inconsistent with the DBE program. In such cases, the DBE program requirements prevail. Such application of the regulations in this manner often make it difficult for a contractor to treat a DBE firm in the same manner as a non-DBE firm when it comes to labor and equipment use or other practices.

behalf of the XBE. Engaging in any of the listed activities compromises the ability of the contractor to receive full credit for the XBE participation as a subcontractor.

Knowing the regulations is imperative. For example, a contractor may not count participation for work a DBE subcontracts to a non-DBE. Under state or local programs, this may not be the rule. Another example, a DBE does not perform a CUF if it performs less than 30% of the total cost of its work or subcontracts more work than would be expected based upon normal industry practice. State or local requirements may require a DBE to perform greater than 30%. A good practice for the contractor is to ask the agency for its rules or regulations during the bidding or proposal period.

## [B] Monitoring Commercially Useful Function ("CUF")

Although an agency is charged with monitoring XBE participation, a contractor should establish its own procedures to periodically monitor XBE performance in the field for CUF. It should create a CUF observation checklist and provide it to its project supervisors and managers to complete based upon their real time observations. Once completed, the CUF form should be reviewed and retained. If at any time a XBE is observed not performing a CUF or if there are any items that are suspicious, red flags, or warrant further attention, this should be reported to a designated individual within the contractor's organization. This will permit early detection, investigation, and, if necessary, corrective action by the contractor. The following areas should be reviewed in assessing CUF: (1) management and performance, (2) workforce, (3) materials and equipment, and (4) trucking.

### [1] Management and Performance

The XBE must manage the work that has been contracted to his or her firm. Management includes, but is not limited to, scheduling work operations, ordering equipment and materials, preparing and submitting certified payrolls, hiring and firing employees. The XBE owner must supervise daily operations, either personally or with a full time, skilled, and knowledgeable superintendent employed by and paid wages by the XBE. The superintendent must be under the XBE owner's direct supervision. The XBE must be responsible for the performance, management, and supervision of a distinct element of the work, in accordance with normal industry practice (except where such practices are inconsistent with the XBE regulations).

The XBE owner cannot be a figurehead but its participation in the management of the firm must be real, substantial, and continuing. The XBE owner should make all day-to-day operational and managerial decisions for the firm. Mere performance of administrative duties is not supervision of daily operations.

## [2]  Workforce

In order to be considered an independent business, a XBE firm must keep a regular workforce. XBE firms cannot "share" employees with non-XBE contractors, particularly the contractor. The XBE shall perform its work with employees normally employed by and under the XBE's control.

All work must be performed with a workforce the XBE firm controls, with a minimum percentage of the work to be performed by the XBE firm's regular employees, or those hired by the firm for the project from a source other than the contractor. The XBE, in all instances, must have direct supervision of all employees. The XBE firm must be responsible for all payroll and labor compliance requirements for all employees performing on the contract and is expected to prepare and finance the payrolls. Direct or indirect payments by any other contractor are not allowed.

Union contractors may face a particular challenge in this area since the workers for XBE and non-XBE firms are drawn from the same union pool of labor. Workers may appear on the prime, non-XBE firm, and XBE firm's payroll which may create the appearance of "sharing employees." A recommendation is that the contractor should communicate with and engage the agency XBE representative making sure that the union assignment and hiring process is well known to the representative.

## [3]  Material and Equipment

The XBE must assume the actual and contractual responsibility for the provision of the material to be incorporated into the item of work being performed by the XBE. The XBE must negotiate the cost, arrange delivery, and pay for the materials and supplies for the project. The XBE must prepare the estimate, quantity of material, and be responsible for the quality of materials. Invoices for material should show the payee as the XBE.

A contractor should guard against performing any of the material supply procurement activities by the DBE. The contractor should not negotiate the price of the materials, pay for the materials, or call for delivery of the materials. Doing so may erode the CUF and participation should be carefully reviewed as to what amount may be claimed for attainment.

## [4]  Manufacturer

As described in 49 CFR § 26.55(e)(1)(ii), a manufacturer is a firm that operates or maintains a factory or establishment that produces, on the premises, the materials, supplies, articles, or equipment required under the contract and of the general character described by the specifications. Webster's dictionary defines a manufacturer as a process or operation carried out systematically with division of labor and the use of machinery for making any material product from raw material by forming, shaping, and altering it into a form suitable for use. Examples of such items could be a concrete ready mix plant, a crushing operation, fabricating plant either steel or concrete, etc.

A contractor may count 100% of the manufactured materials toward its DBE participation.

### [5]  Regular Dealers

In order for a firm to be deemed a regular dealer under the DBE regulations, it must be an established, regular business that engages, as its principal business and under its own name, in the purchase and sale or lease of the products in question. In addition, a regular dealer is a firm that owns, operates, or maintains a store, warehouse, or other establishment in which the materials, supplies, articles, or equipment of the general character described by the specifications and required under the contract are bought, kept in stock, and regularly sold or leased to the public in the usual course of business. DBEs can be regular dealers for one item and not for others. There is no NAICS Code for regular dealers and the DBE will usually possess a wholesaler NAICS Code. Regular dealer status must be determined on a contract-by-contract basis and, even, an item-by-item basis.

It is important to make a distinction between a regular dealer and a firm that supplies a product on an ad hoc basis in relation to a particular contract or contractor. The latter does not meet the requirements of a regular dealer because supplier-like functions are performed on an ad hoc basis or for only one or two contractors with supplier relationships. A regular dealer has a regular trade with a variety of customers. One of the key considerations of being a regular, established dealer is the presence of an inventory of materials and/or supplies. A regular dealer assumes the actual and contractual responsibility for the provision of the material and/or supply.

A firm may be a regular dealer in such bulk items as petroleum products, steel, cement, gravel, stone, or asphalt without owning, operating, or maintaining a place of business if the firm both owns and operates distribution equipment for the products. Any supplementing of regular dealers' own distribution equipment shall be by a long-term lease agreement and not on an ad hoc or contract-by-contract basis.

Drop shipping raises a particular concern primarily because the DBE firm does not take possession of the materials as part of its inventory. Therefore, whenever the DBE firm wants to drop ship items from the manufacturer directly to the project, care must be taken to analyze whether the DBE firm is still performing a CUF. One of the factors that should be used in this analysis is industry practice. You must assess whether there is an industry practice and whether that practice exists for all contractors irrespective of DBE/non-DBE status. In such instances, the general rule is that the industry practice, as one element of consideration, will not save a practice that conflicts with the DBE Program requirements. For example, if an industry practice erodes the control or independence of the DBE, the DBE Program requirements take preference over the industry standard.

### [a] Dealers in Bulk Items

A firm may be a regular dealer in such bulk items as petroleum products, steel, cement, gravel, stone, or asphalt without owning, operating, or maintaining a place of business if the firm both owns and operates distribution equipment for the products. Any supplementing of regular dealers' own distribution equipment shall be by a long-term lease agreement and not on an ad hoc or contract-by-contract basis.

In accordance with 49 CFR Part 26.55(e)(2)(B), a regular dealer of bulk items must be an established, regular business that engages in (as its principal business and in its own name) the purchase/sale/lease of products in question. Unlike a regular dealer of non-bulk items, a dealer in bulk items (petroleum products, steel, cement, gravel, stone asphalt) does not have to necessarily own, operate, or maintain a place of business if the dealer BOTH *owns* and *operates* the distribution equipment for the products. Supplementation of the dealer's own distribution equipment must be by long-term lease and NOT on a contract-by-contract basis.

Packagers, brokers, manufacturers' representatives who arrange or expedite transaction ARE NOT regular dealers.

Therefore, in order to count DBE participation for bulk items such as fuel oil, the DBE must prove: (1) It engages in the sale and distribution of fuel oil (for example); and (2) it owns, operates, or maintains the place of business from where the product ships. Alternatively, if the bulk item regular dealer does not own, operate, or maintain the place of business, it can still qualify if it both *owns* and *operates* the distribution equipment for the products. The bulk item regular dealer can lease the distribution equipment but only as a supplement to its own distribution equipment and not on a project-by-project basis.

To determine if a firm is a bulk item regular dealer, ask the following questions:

1. Does it engage in the sale and delivery of BULK ITEM as part of your regular business? (This question is most likely going to be self-evident from business cards or other literature.)

2. Does it own, operate, or maintain a place of business from where the BULK ITEM is made or shipped? If not,

3. Does it own the distribution equipment? i.e., trucks. (Ownership should be proven by vehicle registration, insurance, title.)

4. If so, how many vehicles?

5. Does it supplement the distribution equipment by any long term leases? (Please provide a copy.) (Leases cannot be for a specific project or a specific contract.)

6. Does it employ the drivers/operators of the vehicles?

If the answer to question 2 is No, you must see if the firm can answer YES to both questions 3 and 6. If answer to either question 3 or 6 is No, then the firm *does not* qualify as a regular dealer of the bulk item and the contractor cannot count amounts paid to it for DBE participation.

### [b] Packagers, Brokers, Manufacturers' Representatives, Transaction Expeditors

Packagers, brokers, manufacturers' representatives, or other persons who arrange or expedite transactions are **not** regular dealers. Typically, the fees and commission and cost of transportation are the only amounts that may be claimed for DBE attainment.

### [c] Equipment

A XBE firm may lease specialized equipment, but not from the prime contractor or its affiliate, if it is consistent with normal industry practices and at rates competitive for the area. A rental agreement should specify the terms of the agreement. The lease must be for a short period of time and involve a specialized piece of equipment readily available at the job site. The lease may allow the operator to remain on the lessor's payroll, if this is a generally acceptable practice within the industry. The operation of the equipment must be subject to the full control of the XBE.

The XBE is expected to provide the operator for non-specialized equipment and is responsible for all payroll and labor compliance requirements. A separate lease agreement is required.

Equipment leased and used by the XBE firm with payment deducted from the prime contractor's payment(s) to the XBE is not allowed.

### [d] A Special Focus on Material Supply

The latest enforcement trend focuses on XBE suppliers. Typically, investigators and prosecutors have found instances of straight pass-through arrangements where the XBE supplier adds no value and performs no CUF, but instead merely lends its name in exchange for a small percentage of the contract value.

As discussed above and below, the rules for claiming participation are different depending on whether the firm is used as a subcontractor or subconsultant, material or equipment supplier (regular dealer, manufacturer, or broker), or trucker. It is important to recognize which category the firm falls under because the amount of participation that can be claimed for each is different and those differences can be significant when attempting to satisfy the project goals. In addition, agency rules complicate claiming credit for suppliers because agencies treat suppliers differently.

The Federal DBE regulations define a regular dealer as "an established, regular business that engages, as its principal business and under its own name, in the purchase and sale or lease of the supplies or products in question. Additionally, a regular dealer owns, operates, or maintains a store, warehouse, or other establishment in which the materials, supplies, articles or equipment of the general character described by the specifications and required under the contract are bought, kept in stock, and regularly sold or leased to the public in the usual course of business." The commentary to the regulation goes on to state: "a firm that supplies a product on an ad hoc basis to a few contractors with whom it has a special relationship, rather than to the general public as a whole, is not a regular dealer." Packagers, brokers, manufacturers' representatives, or other persons who arrange or expedite transactions are not regular dealers.

The Federal DBE regulations essentially leave it up to the contractor to determine whether a supply firm is a regular dealer or a broker on a contract-by-contract basis (really an item-by-item basis, a daunting task). The distinction is significant because the amount that can be claimed for participation as a regular dealer is 60% of the cost of the materials vs. a broker where the fee/commission, typically 3-5%, is all that can be claimed. Regular dealers of bulk item supply (e.g., petroleum products, steel, cement, gravel, stone, or asphalt) have different qualifying rules, but limit the participation to 60% of the cost of the materials. The state regulation (N.Y. Executive Law Article 15-A) provides little guidance about how to count suppliers. The rules for claiming material suppliers on a project funded through the NY State Revolving Loan Fund on an EPA project can be 100% of the cost of the material supply up to 25% of the total contract value. The N.Y. City Regulations (Local Law 1) do not permit counting material suppliers in the construction setting.

Under any of the applicable regulations, the participating firm must still perform a "commercially useful function." If you are using material supply to satisfy a contract goal, it is imperative that you understand the particular rule that applies to your contract. Assuming a supplier is performing a CUF, the chart[9] attempts to summarize how attainment participation may be claimed for suppliers in New York State (not manufacturers or fabricators):

---

[9] Note that the chart is intended as an example. Specific contract provisions or regulations may impact how attainment may be claimed. If you are in doubt, you should seek assistance.

| Regulation | Supplier Credit |
|---|---|
| DBE, USDOT, 49 CFR Part 26.55 | 60% |
| NYS, M/WBE Article 15A | 100% |
| NYC M/WBE (Local Law 1) | 0% |
| State University Construction Fund (Based upon contract language) | 25%, if firm has the designation "certified broker" |
| Dormitory Authority of the State of New York (Based upon contract language) | 25%, if firm has the designation "certified broker" |
| Department of Environmental Protection Projects (funded through the NYS Revolving Loan Fund), 33 CFR Part 103 | 100% of the cost of the materials, up to 25% of the total cost of the construction |

A recent case highlights the importance of getting it right. On August 14, 2015, the USDOT Office of the Inspector General reported that HD Waterworks, an Atlanta-based company described as the "nation's largest supplier of water, sewer, fire protection and storm drain products" paid $4.9 million to settle civil allegations made under the False Claims Act that it used a DBE as a "pass through." According to the USDOT-IG, contractors reported that they were using American Indian Builders & Suppliers, a now defunct DBE, for supply. However, it appears, based on invoices, that HD Waterworks was supplying the materials to the contractors, who would then pass its invoices—with a mark-up—through American Indian Builders & Suppliers. This settlement was reported to be the largest of its kind involving a third-party supplier in a DBE fraud case.

### [6] Trucking

To be certified in the DBE program as a trucking firm, the DBE firm is only required to own and operate at least one fully licensed, insured, and operational truck used on the contract.

To perform a CUF, a DBE firm must also be responsible for the management and supervision of the entire trucking operation on a contract-by-contract basis. There cannot be a contrived arrangement for the purpose of meeting DBE goals.

A DBE can lease a truck(s) from an established equipment leasing business open to the general public. The lease must indicate that the DBE has exclusive use of and control over the truck. This requirement does not preclude the leased truck from working for others during the term of the lease with the consent of the DBE, so long as the lease gives the DBE absolute priority for use of the leased truck. Otherwise, the DBE does not receive full credit for DBE participation.

Count DBE trucks toward a contract goal, as follows:

1. The DBE may lease trucks from another DBE firm, including an owner-operator who is certified as a DBE. The DBE can count all the leased trucks.

2. The DBE may also lease trucks from a non-DBE firm. The DBE can count the number of trucks it leases from the non-DBE firm if it employs the drivers.

3. Additional DBE participation can be achieved from non-DBE trucks up to the number of truck that qualify under items 1 and 2 plus the fee or commission it receives as a result of trucks that exceed the 1:1 ratio. NOTE: this counting is ONLY permitted if allowed by the agency under the DBE program and if approved by the operating administration.

When the DBE firm leases trucks, a contractor should request the valid lease agreement. To be considered valid, the lease agreement must include such items as the lessor's name, list of trucks to be leased by Vehicle Identification Number (VIN), and the agreed upon amount of the cost and method of payment. It should be the responsibility of the DBE to provide the operator's fuel, maintenance, and insurance for all leased trucks.

## [7] Terminating or Substituting a XBE

Typically, the contractor must use the XBEs it submits in its participation/utilization plan unless it obtains written consent from the agency to terminate or substitute the XBE contractor. If a contractor terminates or replaces a DBE without obtaining written consent of the agency, the contractor may not be entitled to payment for the work performed.

If a XBE is terminated or replaced, the contractor must make GFEs to find another XBE to perform the work or at least the same amount of work needed to meet the contract goals.

Under the current DBE regulations, if requested by the agency, the contractor must submit evidence of its GFEs to find a replacement DBE within seven days, subject to an extension of seven days, and the agency must provide to the contractor, within seven days, written determination of the sufficiency of the GFEs.

### [a] Consequences of Failing to Achieve the Goal

Socio-economic programs have consistently struggled with providing opportunities for legitimate XBE firms and keeping those that want to game the system out of the programs. Programs have come under tremendous criticism for not achieving their objectives and graduating more firms. "Front" and "pass through" schemes are regularly reported. It seems the government has stepped up its efforts to detect and punish those contractors who commit fraud in this area. From October 1, 2003 through September 30, 2008, the Department of Transportation, Office of the Inspector General ("OIG") reported that investigations of DBE fraud allegations resulted in 49 indictments, 43 convictions, nearly $42 million in recoveries and fines, and 419 months of jail sentences. From 2009 to 2010, the number of open OIG investigations related to DBEs increased by almost 70%. DBE investigations accounted for approximately 25% of OIG's open procurement/grant fraud caseload in 2010. Also, DBE fraud represented over one-third of OIG's open ARRA cases in 2010.[10] Reports and letters such as the following examples are likely to result in increased scrutiny and result in more enforcement proceedings against corporations and individuals.

In April 2013, the Office of the Inspector General published a scathing report on the XBE program.[11] The audit was conducted from April 2011 to October 2012. It sought to establish whether the USDOT (1) provides adequate XBE program management, (2) whether the operating administrations sufficiently oversee and implement the XBE program, and (3) achieves its program objectives to help develop XBEs to operate in the commercial marketplace. The report identified major weaknesses in the XBE program and implementation. On May 15, 2013, Congress sent a letter signed by 30 members to Secretary LaHood stating Congress is "deeply concerned" with the OIG's report conclusions that the Department is not effectively managing its multi-billion dollar DBE program.

On June 12, 2014, the Office of the Inspector General published a report titled "New Disadvantaged Business Enterprise Firms Face Barriers to Obtaining Work at The Nation's Largest Airports." The report seemed to indicate that barriers still exist for new DBE/ACDBE firms to participate in FAA contracts finding that relatively few new firms had been awarded contracts despite efforts by the FAA to encourage new firms to participate, including (1) unbundling major contracts and leases into smaller components, (2) entering into direct contracts or leases with DBE/ACDBE firms, (3) conducting outreach, and (4) providing financial assistance. All too familiar obstacles were noted as barriers to participation, including (1) limited opportunities for and infrequent turnover of disadvantaged firms, (2) access to capital and high entry costs, and (3) firms' lack of experience with the airport bidding process. In addition, the report noted that inaccuracies were detected in reporting making it difficult to assess whether the FAA DBE program meets its objectives.

---

[10] DOT Office of Inspector General, Audit of DOT's Disadvantaged Business Enterprise (DBE) Program, Federal Audit Executive Council Procurement Training Conference, Washington, DC (June 12, 2013).

[11] Weaknesses in the Department's Disadvantaged Business Enterprise Program Limit Achievement of Its Objectives, Office of the Inspector General (Apr. 23, 2013).

On November 24, 2014, Manhattan District Attorney Cyrus R. Vance, Jr., issued a press release announcing the issuance of New York State Grand Jury Report on contractor fraud and misuse in the MWBE program in New York State.[12] According to DA Vance:

> The evidence gathered revealed criminal conduct in the construction industry spanning at least a decade and, within the relatively small sample of cases reviewed, found that the amount of money intended for MWBEs that instead went to non-MWBEs exceeded $10 million. As a result of these findings, the Grand Jury recommended significant reforms to the MWBE procurement process, including stronger accountability for contractors and MWBEs, increased resources for certifying and contracting agencies, changes to the Scheme to Defraud statute, and increased fines.[13]

In addition, and despite these programmatic shortcomings, various enforcement agencies are leveraging their resources and forming joint and coordinated task forces between different departments of the government like the Offices of the Inspector General, Department of Justice, Internal Revenue Service, prosecutors, and agency representatives. Recently, on August 5, 2015, "the Manhattan District Attorney's Office, the New York City Department of Investigation ("DOI"), the Port Authority of New York and New Jersey ("PANYNJ") Office of the Inspector General, the Metropolitan Transportation Authority ("MTA") Office of the Inspector General, and the Business Integrity Commission for the City of New York ("BIC") . . . announced the Construction Fraud Task Force ("Task Force") to identify and prosecute citywide corruption and fraud in the construction industry."[14] The Eastern District of New York has operated such a task force for a number of years.

On September 9, 2015, the U.S. Attorney announced that it has implemented new guidelines for the DOJ in assessing a corporation's cooperation with a government investigation with a focus on individual accountability—now, commonly called the "Yates Memorandum." The gist of the memorandum is that a corporation will not be given full credit for cooperation unless it actively seeks out and identifies those within the corporation who were responsible for the corporate misbehavior and turn over evidence against them, "regardless of their position, status or seniority." The guidance directs the DOJ to focus on individuals from the beginning of an investigation, not to release the individuals from liability in the absence of departmental policy or extraordinary circumstances and directs that the civil and criminal divisions should be "in routine communication

---

[12] http://manhattanda.org/press-release/da-vance-grand-jury-report-recommends-significant-reforms-assist-minority-and-women-ow.

[13] http://manhattanda.org/press-release/da-vance-grand-jury-report-recommends-significant-reforms-assist-minority-and-women-ow.

[14] http://www.nyc.gov/html/doi/downloads/pdf/2015/Aug15/pr_citywide_construction_taskforce_80515.pdf.

with each other." The memorandum guidance applies to all pending and future cases. It remains to be seen how (or if) DOJ will enforce these guidelines but it certainly signals an increased focus on individual accountability.[15]

Where a government contract includes minimum "XBE" participation requirements or goals, the consequence of failing to achieve those goals (or be able to establish GFEs) could have a material adverse impact to the company's ability to complete the project or be fully compensated for the work, to perform on future government contracts (suspension or debarment), or have material adverse impacts to its financial position, its ability to control its commercial process, cash flow or profitability, as well as reputational risk. A policy specifically devoted to a compliant approach to XBE participation that seeks to prevent, detect, and correct non-compliant activity is an effective preventative tool.

### [8] Establishing Policy and Procedures to Address and Detect XBE Fraud and the Warning Signs

Although the contracting agency has the responsibility to ensure that a XBE meets the certification criteria and performs in accordance with the appropriate regulations, the primary responsibility to ensure that the XBE firm is performing a CUF, a useful business function, or otherwise adding commercial value in the performance of its contract seems to fall upon the contractor. Certification of a XBE (a/k/a eligibility to participate in the program) and CUF are separate and distinct issues. Certification decisions address the nature of a firm's ownership and structure while CUF primarily concerns the role a firm has played in a particular transaction. Most of the recent prosecutions and settlements have involved the incorrect use and reporting of the XBEs participation in the program. Therefore, any contractor with a government contract that requires XBE participation would be wise to establish a policy and procedure to manage and address the risk. At a minimum, the policy and procedure should be written, assign accountability and responsibility across the organization, include regular training and education of the employees on the specific regulatory and contractual requirements as well as appropriate regulations, be fully supported from the top, be consistently enforced, and well documented. Consideration should be given to educating and training third parties (both joint venture partners and subcontractors, suppliers, and vendors) as well as governmental agency representatives. A contractor should also have an established mechanism for anonymous reporting. In other words, it is incumbent upon the contractor to recognize and establish procedures to monitor to prevent and detect fraud.

---

[15] Yates Memorandum, U.S. Department of Justice, *Individual Accountability for Corporate Wrongdoing* (Sept. 9, 2015), http://www.justice.gov/dag/file/769036/download.

The following are some indicators or "red flags" of XBE fraud:

1. A business owner lacking background, expertise, or equipment to perform sub-contract work;

2. A situation where employees are shuttling back and forth between prime contractor and a XBE business' payrolls;

3. Business names on equipment and vehicles have temporary signage covering the legal owner which is not a certified XBE;

4. Orders and payment for necessary supplies made by individuals who are not employed by XBE business;

5. A contractor facilitated purchase of XBE business;

6. A XBE business owner is never present at the job site;

7. A contractor always uses the same XBE;

8. Financial ownership agreements between contractor and XBE contractors exist beyond the contractual relationship;

9. Joint bank accounts exist between contractor and XBE subcontractors;

10. Joint check arrangements;

11. Absence of a warehouse or inventory of a particular item;

12. Drop shipping materials;

13. Workers move back and forth between XBE and non-XBE;

14. Order and/or payment for suppliers handled by non-XBE;

15. XBE owner is former employee of non-XBE company;

16. XBE firm does work exclusively for one company;

17. Third party obtains price from supplier before bid and gives the XBE benefit;

18. An absence of written contracts between contractors and XBE business;

19. The DBE provides little or no supervision of the work;

20. The DBE's superintendent is not a regular employee of the firm or supervision is performed by personnel associated with the contractor, or another business;

21. Key staff and personnel are not under the control of the DBE firm;

22. The DBE firm's owner is not aware of the status of the work or the performance of the business;

23. Inquiries by department or agency representatives are answered by the contractor;

24. Work that is being done jointly by the DBE and another contractor;

25. The work to be performed by the DBE is outside of the DBE's known experience or capability;

26. Any portion of the work designated to be performed by a DBE subcontractor is performed by the contractor or any other firm;

27. The DBE is working without a subcontract agreement;

28. A DBE subcontracts more than 30% of the contract value;

29. Any agreement that erodes the ownership, control or independence of the DBE subcontractor;

30. The volume of work is beyond the capacity of the DBE firm;

31. Work is not performed by employees of the DBE but by employees of the contractor or non-DBE;

32. Employees are paid by the DBE and the contractor;

33. Certified payroll is prepared by someone other than the DBE;

34. Employees appear on the payrolls of the DBE and non-DBE contractors;

35. Materials or supplies necessary for the DBE firm's performance are delivered to, billed to, or paid by another business;

36. Invoices addressed to the contractor or non-DBE firm or otherwise indicating that the DBE is not the customer;

37. Contact person on the invoice is not an employee of the DBE;

38. Materials provided to DBE from the contractor;

39. DBE performs little or no work related to the materials;

40. Materials for the DBE are ordered or paid for by the contractor;

41. Two party checks or joint checks are sent by the contractor to the supplier or manufacturer;

42. Payment for materials is deducted by the contractor from payments to DBE for work performed;

43. Equipment used by the DBE firm belongs to the contractor or another firm with no formal lease agreement;

44. The equipment signs and markings cover another owner's identity, usually through the use of magnetic signs; and

45. A DBE trucking business utilizes trucks owned by the prime contractor.

Contractors will be well-served to establish and implement policies and procedures for the utilization and use of such small businesses. Two key areas to address are contract administration/procurement and monitoring field performance. Contract administration/procurement focuses on elements related to the certification and capacity of the XBE firm. A contractor would be well-served to exercise a certain level of due diligence in verifying that a XBE can perform the anticipated scope of work. Remember, certification and CUF are two separate concepts.

The concepts from the Federal Sentencing Guidelines for Organizations ("FSGO") as to what constitutes an effective ethics and compliance program are helpful in creating a "best practices" program for XBE participation and claiming attainment. Particular attention should be given to training and education of employees regarding the applicable rules as well as to the monitoring and proper documentation and use of such subcontractors, manufacturers, truckers, or suppliers.

Here are some proactive measures you can take followed by some practical advice for implementing the elements:

- Review your internal procedures and controls. Have a written XBE compliance program that specifies the company process in areas such as outreach, GFEs, verification, assurance reviews, CUF, and modifications to utilization plans.

- Make sure you understand the rules for what can or cannot be claimed for participation. Engage in training and education (early and often and when changes to the policy or regulations occur hitting all employees involved in the process and third parties).

- Assign accountability and responsibility within your organization (If everyone is responsible, no one is.).

- Determine the capacity/capability of XBE firms in advance.

- Be able to demonstrate your real actions you took to meet, or to try to achieve, contract goals.

- Engage agency representatives and third-party stakeholders in the process. Be transparent.

- Be vigilant during project performance and address any concerns or issues as they are noticed (Are we following the policy? Is it working?). Monitor behavior and timely correct it, if necessary.

### [9]  Written Standards

The written program should include assignment of responsibility, definition of procedures to be implemented at all stages of the procurement process: bid/proposal phase, pre-award and performance as well as establishing an overall outreach effort where the contractor engages in activities geared to meet XBE firm to establish a relationship and determine capabilities which will create opportunities for firms in existing and future projects. The written program should address issues such as outreach efforts, vetting, documentation of efforts and retention, reporting, and what to do if a red flag is noticed.

### [10]  Responsibility and Accountability

If everyone is responsible, no one will be responsible. Prepare a written program that defines not only policies and procedures but makes specific individuals or positions responsible for the proper management of the XBE program. A recommendation is that a high level officer of the company sign the certifications required by many of the agency programs. Remember that most government contracts will include an extremely broad certification that the claims for payment being made by the contractor are done in full accordance with the contract documents, plans and specifications.

Not only should the contractor be held accountable but the contractor should make the XBE accountable for its own performance. Some ways of doing this is to flow down the contract requirements to all lower tier subcontractors, suppliers, and truckers require a monthly certification from the XBE that the work it performed was in full accordance with the rules, regulations, and contract documents, require participation in education and training and making compliance with the regulations a material requirement of the agreement with the XBE.

### [11]  Communication, Training, and Education

Key is employee awareness of the rules as well as company procedure. The rules and regulations related to such programs are not necessarily intuitive or exactly the same. It is imperative that all employees understand what is permitted and what activity will run afoul of the regulations. Regular training should be held on the contractor's policy and procedure as well as the regulations. Consideration should be given to holding training company-wide as well as project specific. The contractor may want to invite the subcontractors, major suppliers, and government officials to project specific trainings. Records should be maintained.

Plain language communications that regularly bring attention to XBE programs should be employed. Wallet cards or red flag posters could be used as a method of keeping the "red flags" in the minds of the employees responsible for project performance.

Also useful to bring home the point that serious consequences may flow from a breach of the regulations is using some examples of violations of the rules. Use of government presentations (which can be found on the Internet) or press releases issued by enforcement agencies (OIG, DOJ, local District attorneys) is particularly effective.

### [12] Transparency and Collaboration with the Government and Stakeholders

Keeping the government officials informed and up to date about the progress of XBE attainment and any issues encountered will well serve the contractor. It is also recommended that the civil rights office be included in any discussions. Regular updates will also assist the contractor when changes need to be made to an existing utilization plan.

A contractor should also look to engage the minority community and other important stakeholders keeping them informed about progress and asking for assistance if goals are not being met.

### [13] Monitoring and Auditing

Vetting of the XBE firms is critical to ascertain that the firm is properly certified, capable of performing the contemplated scope of work, and has the ability to support the work. Documentation should be kept which may include written materials provided by the subcontractor demonstrating the scope and size of the last projects performed, information related to bonding capacity, workforce, equipment, and management. An XBE must have a necessary and useful role in the transaction, of a kind for which there is a market outside the context of the program.

The firm's role must not be a superfluous step added in an attempt to obtain credit towards the goal. Key to this check are home office site visits of the XBE and interviews with the principal owners to assess that they possess the requisite knowledge to manage the work and run the day-to-day operations of the business. In addition, a contractor may want to run a background check on the firm or its principals. Such check can be a formal or an informal check of information that is available in the public domain (Google searches, OIG, DOJ press releases, newspaper articles, etc.).

Next, the agreement with the XBE should be in writing and outline the particular scope of work to be performed by the XBE and define any special provisions or concessions that the contractor makes in order to encourage participation. This practice makes it easier to evaluate whether the XBE is performing a CUF as well as to encourage transparency in the commercial process. Contract language can also be included alerting the XBE to the contractor's intent to use the firm for participation and emphasizing the applicable regulations and rules.

Detailed project-level or field monitoring is important to help ensure that (1) only work done by certified businesses is credited towards a contract's project participation goal and (2) suspicious arrangements are detected, investigated, and if required, dealt with expeditiously to preclude contractors from unfairly benefitting from the program. Monitoring reviews should be conducted periodically and, at times, unannounced, as a further check to assure compliance. Monitoring includes review of the XBE's qualifications, project documentation, site visits, and interviews with contractors and their employees before and during performance. Of course, any such review should be documented.

CUF field checks are also a mandatory best practice. Prepare a checklist that can be used by field personnel that covers each of the red flag areas. Such checks can alert the contractor to possible "red flag" areas and allow the contractor the opportunity to correct the issue, educate the XBE, and inform the agency of the issue and the resolution. Perform the checks randomly and periodically.

### [14]   Corrective Action

Almost as important as detecting actions that do not comply with the regulations is what the organization does once it detects such activity. Errors in reporting should be corrected and discussed with the agency. Additional training may be warranted to correct misconceptions about the XBE regulations. Taking corrective action could mean the difference between a criminal and civil proceeding.

### [15]   Documentation

Above all, document your efforts. Remember, if you cannot show what you did, it did not happen. It is critical that you (and others) are able to prove and verify your actions. Bringing in a neutral third party to provide an objective analysis of your current process and procedures can be an effective technique for proving effectiveness of your program and to ensure that your business is keeping up with best practices.

To sum up the importance of documentation: "If it is not in writing it did not happen." If it becomes necessary to perform an evaluation of the contractor's efforts, such review will be performed after the fact and at a time where the contractor will have no ability to correct the situation. Thus, it is imperative that all steps a contractor takes be appropriately documented.

## [C]   Conclusion

Know the XBE program. Know the Rules. Recognize the "red flags." Know the XBE. Provide the appropriate tone at the top to support the program and provide an avenue for employees to raise concerns. Impress upon them the consequences for the company and individuals for a breach of the rules. Document actions taken. Correct deficiencies. Report violators and violations. Be proactive and not reactive.

## § 2.05   HOW AND WHY AN ETHICS AND COMPLIANCE PROGRAM CAN BE A PREVENTATIVE TOOL IN LIGHT OF CURRENT ETHICS AND COMPLIANCE TRENDS[16]

Enron, WorldCom, the collapse of the financial markets in 2008 reinvigorated the debate on how to improve compliance programs and drive positive change within the public and private sector, particularly in the area of preventing and mitigating excesses and scandals. One only has to pick up a newspaper today to know that government scrutiny of corporations and a hyper regulatory environment abound. It is becoming easier for regulators and prosecutors to charge and convict both corporations and their "responsible corporate" officers. In 2015, "culture" was the word of the year and there was an increased focus on accountability for both the corporation and the individuals. The DOJ has reported that, since 1987, it recovered $30.3 billion under a single federal statute, the False Claims Act. False Claims Act settlements and judgments in the FY ending September 30, 2015 were in excess of $3.5 billion. Although down from the $5.7 billion collected the year before, it was the fourth highest since 1988.[17] It must be noted that these monies reflect federal losses only under a single statute. Additional amounts were collected under state and local FCA statutes. Although the largest contributing market sector was the healthcare industry, government contracting rose to claim the number two spot, totaling $1.1 billion. For those in government contracting, an ethics and compliance program can be a vital tool in helping companies detect and prevent unlawful conduct by their employees.

### [A]   Understanding the Basics of an Ethics and Compliance Program

In a nutshell, compliance is the minimum that is required to follow all laws, rules, and regulations in a particular market sector. Ethics is "doing the right thing, even when no one is looking" and is values based. Leading practice compliance programs are moving away from rules-based programs to values-based programs. The goal of the compliance program should be (1) to establish an ethical culture that fuses business practices with the organization's core values and

---

[16] This chapter is not intended to be a dissertation on ethics and compliance programs in general but to briefly identify the requirements of an ethics and compliance program and then to frame the 2015 issues and 2016 emerging trends.

[17] http://www.justice.gov/opa/pr/justice-department-recovers-over-35-billion-false-claims-act-cases-fiscal-year-2015.

ethical principles, (2) to prevent and manage misconduct, (3) to uphold the organizational commitment to integrity, and (4) to minimize legal and/or regulatory difficulty, operational, financial, or reputational risk. The purpose of a compliance program is to assist and ensure that the business and all of its employees understand and adhere to all contractual requirements, laws, rules, and regulations in the conduct of its business and to assist and ensure that all employees understand and adhere to the Code of Business Ethics and Code of Conduct. Ignorance of the law is no excuse. A compliance program is not static but is a living, breathing, adaptive program continuously developing in response to emerging issues as well as specific industry risks. If used effectively, it can be a significant risk mitigation strategy.

Compliance programs should be designed by the organization to be appropriate for the market sector that the business operates in and should be appropriate for the scope and size of the business organization. There is an abundance of literature on the elements of a compliance program but the FSGO[18] is accepted as the baseline for establishing an ethics and compliance program. If you are creating one, you may want to also consult with the following: the Federal Sentencing Guidelines for Organizations, Organisation for Economic Cooperation and Development ("OECD") Guidelines for Multinational Enterprises,[19] Committee on Sponsoring Organizations ("COSO") of the Treadway Commission Standards[20] on Internal Controls-Integrated Framework, and the Federal Acquisition Regulations ("FAR") 52.203-13, Contractor Business Code of Ethics, or other government regulations or governmental requirements. In 2014, the International Standards for Organizations ("ISO") published its guidelines for ethics and compliance management systems, ISO 19600:2014. The guidance is framed as being applicable to all types of organizations and is based on the principles of good governance, transparency, and sustainability. Although not yet an ISO "standard," the issuance of this compliance management guidance signals a global focus on moderating corporate behavior and the prevention and detection of organizational misconduct.

The FSGO, published in 1991 by the U.S. Sentencing Commission, contain the prosecutorial guidelines that seek to encourage businesses to establish ethics and compliance programs that prevent and detect organizational wrongdoing. If a business establishes a program that contains the "seven elements," then, in the event of wrongdoing, it could be eligible for a lesser penalty. Since 1991, there have been a number of modifications to the guidelines (the Thompson Memorandum, the Holder Memorandum, and most recently, the Yates Memorandum). These modifications sometimes happen in response to significant compliance crisis. These guidelines combined with the regulations that follow such crisis (SOX,

---

[18] http://www.ussc.gov/training/organizational-guidelines/2013-ussc-guidelines-manual.
[19] http://www.oecd.org/daf/inv/mne/48004323.pdf.
[20] http://www.coso.org/ic.htm.

Dodd-Frank, etc.) inform businesses as to what regulators and government agencies consider as the elements required for an effective risk mitigation strategy. In addition to a risk assessment, the so-called eighth element,[21] the seven elements are:

1. Organization must *establish standards and procedures* to prevent and detect violations of law (Sec.8B2.1(b)(1));

2. Program Oversight:

   - *Board must be knowledgeable* of content and program operation and *exercise reasonable oversight* of program and program effectiveness (8B2.1(b)(2)(A));

   - *High-level Individuals* must have *overall program responsibility* to ensure implementation and effectiveness (8B2.1(b)(2)(B));

   - Specific *Individuals* must have day-to-day *operational responsibility* for program and have *adequate resources*, appropriate authority and direct access to the Board or Audit Committee (8B2.1(b)(2)(C));

3. *Exclude from authority* those who have engaged in illegal activities or *who act inconsistent with program* (8B2.1(b)(3));

4. *Communicate standards and procedures* to board, senior leaders, and other employees, and, as appropriate, to its agents, by *conducting training* and *disseminating information* (8B2.1(b)(4)(A));

5. Ensure compliance and ethics *program is followed*, including monitoring and auditing, *evaluate its effectiveness*, and *publicize a system of reporting* or seeking guidance regarding criminal conduct without fear of retaliation (8B2.1(b)(5));

6. *Program must be promoted* and enforced through *incentives* supporting compliance and *discipline* for engaging in criminal conduct (8B2.1(b)(6)); and

7. After the criminal conduct is detected, organization must respond appropriately and take steps to prevent similar conduct (8B2.1(b)(7)).

A compliance program has many parts and should be designed to educate employees, ensure compliance with the Code, foster an ethical corporate environment, establish a mechanism to detect and identify violations of the Code or other unethical behavior, and monitor (audit) the company's and its employees' compliance and adherence to the Code and applicable laws, rules, and regulations.

---

[21] Organization must periodically assess risk of criminal conduct and design, implement, or modify program to reduce risk of illegal conduct. USSG, 8B2.1(c).

Corporations must focus not only on having a Code of Conduct, reporting mechanisms, and employee training, but also on *the prevention and detection of criminal conduct*, effectiveness of internal controls, independence of auditors and directors/managers, and financial reporting disclosures. The "kumbaya" moment does not happen in organizations; it takes dedication, the fortitude to act, and ongoing commitment from senior leaders to "lead by example" and support the Compliance Officer in his or her obligations to the company. (Compliance will not magically happen after implementation of the Code of Conduct, reporting mechanism, and training.)

A compliance program should be formalized into a written procedural document that addresses such procedural issues as the role of the Compliance Officer, reporting, frequency of audits or assurance reviews, meetings, investigations, etc. A compliance program should address five major areas:

1. Risk Assessment and Evaluation;

2. Standards, Policies, and Procedures;

3. Communication, Education, and Training;

4. Assurance Reviews, Internal Controls, and Monitoring; and

5. Investigations.

## [B] The Risk Assessment

A risk assessment is a fundamental component of any ethics and compliance program not only because it is required by the U.S. Sentencing Federal Guidelines but because it lays the foundation for the compliance program by identifying those risks (reputational risks, financial risks, or risks that may impact the company's ability to do business). A compliance risk assessment looks to identify the risks that have the greatest potential for causing harm to the company by assessing the likelihood of occurrence with the severity of the impact. Any violation of laws, regulations, or contract that would result in suspension or debarment from contracting with the government must be constantly monitored and addressed by the Compliance Officer. Anything that impacts the reputation of the organization should fall in the ethics and compliance world. The Code of Conduct is the gateway to beginning to educate employees about organizational values and expected behavior. Policy, procedures, laws, and regulations further define how the employee's behavior should be shaped.

One of the greatest risks a company operating in the construction industry faces relate to the submission of a false statements or false claims. The certifications and representations made by construction companies in obtaining contracts (i.e., pre-qualification applications and proposal submissions), payment requisitions (i.e., " . . . by submitting this request for payment to the government the Company is in complete and full compliance with all contract requirements, the contract plans and specifications"), compliance with socio-economic goals (like disadvantaged business enterprise requirements), lobbying and political contributions, and prevailing wage law are all areas of high risk for the company with the possibility of suspension or debarment, or huge financial, reputational, and operational risks. By conducting periodic risk assessments, the company can determine where its greatest risks lie and, if necessary, develop a risk mitigation plan that may include implementing a policy or procedure that addresses the risk. Finally, a company can raise employee awareness through training and education.

At the conclusion of the risk assessment, the Board of Directors and the senior management should address the results and determine whether any corrective action or mitigation plans should be implemented, whether additional policies and procedures are required, whether changes need to be made to communication, education or training, or any other aspect of the compliance program.

Three key concepts for an ethics and compliance program are detection, prevention, and response. The following sections discuss critical elements of a compliance program.

## [C]  Standards, Policies, and Procedures

The Code of Business Ethics and Code of Conduct ("Code") is the foundation of your ethics policy. The Code should provide employees with clear guidance regarding behavior that is expected of them as representatives of the company and that which will not be tolerated. The Code should provide a statement of the organizations' ethical principles and core values. It should relate those core values to the laws, regulations, and workplace policies and procedures that the organization must follow. These many laws, rules, and regulations which, if violated, could cause substantial operational, financial, and/or reputational risk to the company and adversely impact its ability to do business with federal, state, and local governmental owners. The Code also provides guidance on employee interaction with other employees, business partners, government officials, and other external parties. The compliance program should seek to integrate integrity with proper business conduct (core values/standards by which the organization behaves and interacts with others).

The second component of the compliance program is the other policies, procedures, and systems that have been established to support the Code and the organization's core values/ethical principles. These core values/ethical principles, policies, systems, and internal controls should be periodically evaluated and updated to ensure the compliance program is in line with leading practices, legal and regulatory requirements, and the organization's ethical standards. The compliance program is not static and changes or implementation of additional policies, systems, and internal controls is an ongoing process made in response to challenges, changes in laws, rules, or regulations, and/or ethical or compliance lapses.

The compliance program should also provide a means of reporting without fear of retaliation—the anonymous reporting mechanism. In addition to the Code, an anonymous reporting system (i.e., Hotline) needs to be established for reporting suspected fraud, violations of law or of the Code. The reporting mechanism(s) as well as the Code should be communicated to all employees and advertised at the company and at project sites. Alternate reporting avenues like email and written memorandum may also be established.

*Qui Tam* ("Whistleblower") litigation is on the rise and the threats and harm to business organizations are no different in the construction industry than in any other industry. A *Qui Tam* case can be brought by private individuals on behalf of the government under the federal, state, or local Civil False Claims Act, which could include claims for up to treble damages. Further, if a company fails to comply with any of the regulations, requirements, or statutes or if it has a substantial number of accumulated Occupational Safety and Health Administration, Mine Safety and Health Administration, or other workplace safety violations, its existing government contracts could be terminated and it could be suspended from government contracting or subcontracting, including federally funded projects at the state level. Should one or more of these events occur, it could have a material adverse effect on its financial position, operations, cash flow, and liquidity.

Retaliation and corporate inaction increase the likelihood that an employee will report wrongdoing outside the company, discourages reporting of misconduct, and allows misconduct to persist and grow. Relationships and personal employee comfort with senior leadership appears to impact reporting, pressure to compromise standards, and observation of misconduct. When companies go through mergers and acquisitions and changes in leadership, employees feel greater pressure to compromise standards. These findings and observations should be taken into consideration when fashioning non-retaliation policy.

In November 2015, OSHA issued draft guidance on anti-retaliation training. OSHA enforces the whistleblower protection provisions of the Occupational Safety and Health Act. The agency's draft guidance lists five steps to creating an effective anti-retaliation compliance program, which are applicable to non-retaliation policies in general:

1. Ensure leadership commitment.

2. Foster an anti-retaliation culture. OSHA recommended eliminating all workplace incentives that discourage reporting.

3. Implement a system for responding to reports of retaliation.

4. Conduct anti-retaliation training.

5. Monitor progress and program improvement.

It is important to address employee's concerns regarding confidentiality should he or she report suspected misconduct. It takes courage to step forward and report, especially if the supervisor or other manager is one of the individuals engaging in possible misconduct. Research shows that communicating to employees exactly what steps will be taken when a complaint is made and implementing procedures to guard against retaliation are two steps a company can take that will encourage reporting.

## [D]  Communication, Education, and Training—Because All Compliance Is Not Intuitive

Once the Code and reporting mechanisms are established, they should be published to the employees and other third parties. In-person training is most effective and, if done by the Compliance Officer, gives visibility to the ethics and compliance function within the organization. The purpose of the training sessions should be to introduce the ethics and compliance function, the Compliance Officer, the Code, and the reporting mechanisms and to educate and train employees on laws, rules, regulations, company policies, and expected behavior. Communication and awareness are vital components of a robust compliance program.

An integral part of any compliance program is the development and execution of suitable regular and periodic training programs designed to educate employees on the Code and other laws, rules, and regulations that impact or effect the company's business, such as socially and economically disadvantaged business enterprise requirements, prevailing wage, wage and hour compliance, anti-corruption compliance, antitrust compliance, immigration compliance, environmental requirements, health and safety requirements, and EEO/AA compliance.

To communicate, educate, and train, the ethics and compliance department should train on the Code at least annually, train on specific risk areas on a regular or as-needed basis, consider weekly/monthly/periodic compliance communications, and provide notification to appropriate employee groups on changes in laws, articles of interest, and other information.

## [E]  Assurance Reviews, Internal Controls, and Monitoring

Key to success of the compliance program is making compliance with the Code and all laws, rules, and regulations everyone's responsibility. This involves active communication among all the groups responsible for implementing the Code and all applicable laws. The Compliance Officer and staff interact and provide oversight of all functional areas within the company. The Compliance Officer is the agent of the Board of Directors in ensuring that its officers and management are upholding the Code and all laws, rules, and regulations. Consider embedding compliance responsibilities in the functional group that has responsibility for the particular regulatory area thereby engaging them in the monitoring process.

Effective compliance programs include proactive monitoring and auditing functions that are designed to test and confirm compliance with the legal requirements within each department and with the organization's written compliance standards, internal policies and procedures and with federal, state, and local laws, regulations, and rules. Proactive monitoring and auditing assist an organization's compliance activities by identifying possible misconduct or criminal activity and providing the company with the opportunity to take corrective and, if necessary, disciplinary action.

Internal controls are those tailored to prevent the kind of conduct that puts a company at risk and avoid trouble. An *assurance review (audit)* is typically a more formal review of compliance with a particular set of internal (e.g., compliance policies) or external (e.g., laws and regulations) standards. Assurance reviews are typically conducted by individuals who are independent from the area being audited—usually compliance department staff or outside auditors. *Monitoring* refers to reviews that are repeated on a regular basis during the normal course of operations, either with or without advance notice. An organization may monitor its activities as part of a corrective action plan, to assure that corrections implemented continue to be effective. Monitoring may also be initiated when no specific problems have been identified to confirm and document ongoing compliance. Conducting both assurance reviews and monitoring are hallmarks of an effective compliance program.

A company must monitor, test, assess, and audit to determine if its management is complying with laws, rules, regulations, and contractual requirements and its compliance policies and procedures are a "living and breathing program" and not just a paper tiger. Internal controls are necessary to prevent, detect, and help remedy any situation. A company that has a set of written standards that was not followed is typically dealt with more harshly because the regulators and enforcement attitude is that the company knew better and should have acted.

Proactive monitoring may also provide the corporation and its officers, Board of Directors with shelter from legal/regulatory authorities in the event that there is a legal or ethical lapse. The assurance review and monitoring function of the compliance program can also be used to test the completion and effectiveness of functions at the heart of the compliance program, such as compliance training programs, employee and vendor screening, or whether disciplinary action is occurring and is appropriate. This function also provides a unique opportunity for a compliance program to measure and benchmark its own effectiveness.

Compliance assurance reviews are typically structured to test compliance in a finite cross section or functional area of the organization. It is, therefore, generally possible to repeat the same audit periodically, and thereby to measure not only the organization's current level of compliance, but also its progress in attaining higher levels of compliance as the compliance program matures.

Self-evaluation that occurs as a result of a compliance assurance review and monitoring is often critical in identifying areas where compliance standards have not been fully understood or fully implemented or have been incorrectly applied. An effective monitoring and auditing program may allow an organization to correct any oversight or resulting non-compliance before it creates significant risk to the organization.

Decisions to indict or not prosecute the corporation, the responsible corporate officers, or Board of Directors will determine whether an organization has a system of internal controls and procedures monitored by the compliance function and designed to ensure wrongdoing is discovered.

## [F] Investigations

An integral part of any ethics and compliance program is the duty to investigate reports of suspected fraud, illegal or unethical conduct, Code violations, or other suspected violations of laws and regulations and make independent determinations as to whether a violation occurred and report the finding to the CEO/President and/or Board of Directors. Furthermore, it is the Compliance Officer's duty, to the extent possible, to safeguard the confidentiality of all reports of suspected violations and investigations.

Investigations of suspected fraud, illegal or unethical conduct, Code violations, or suspected violations of laws and regulations may be the result of Helpline complaints, complaints made directly to the ethics and compliance department, or learned from other sources or detected as a result of an assurance review or monitoring activities.

In line with the increased focus on accountability, an organization must be able to prove that it undertook a real investigation that looked to identify the source of the wrongdoing and that it took the appropriate corrective action in response to the results of the investigation.

## § 2.06 TRENDS FROM 2015 AND WHAT CAN BE EXPECTED IN 2016

### [A] Culture: What's Culture Got to with It?

Everything since culture can trump any policy or procedure an organization tries to establish. Misconduct can be expensive. Under U.S. law, companies are responsible for the actions of their employees. Risks associated with misconduct can include (1) reputational damage; (2) exposure to legal liability (criminal, civil, fines, penalties); (3) reduced efficiency and profitability; and (4) impact access to capital, stock prices, and cause increased costs on loans.[22] A well-implemented ethics and compliance program and strong ethical culture have been found to be the two drivers of reducing risks in organizations.[23] The risk of misconduct is reduced because those within the organization felt less pressure to compromise standards. When employees noticed or observed misconduct, they reported it confident that the organizational culture would support the decision to report and not ostracize the reporter. Finally, with a strong organizational culture, the employees observed less retaliation.

Culture can be defined as the typical attitudes, habits, and behavior of a group or subgroup. Often it is described as the way things are really done around an organization. Merriam Webster announced in December 2014 that the word of the year was "culture." What did that mean? It was the word that most people searched its site for the definition. Interestingly, Merriam-Webster noted that culture was not associated with any single event but dominated the headlines in many different ways: entertainment industry, sports, pharmaceutical industry, financial, automotive, and company culture overall. Culture drives the viability of an ethics and compliance program and is critical to the success of an ethics and compliance program. Culture can trump your ethics and compliance efforts. So, not only do you have to have all the elements necessary to create an effective program but you also have to promote an organizational culture that uphold compliance with the law.

Current research supports the conclusion that culture is also a profit driver. Research by James L. Heskett indicates that "culturally unremarkable competitors suffer a 20-30% drop in performance."[24] Other research from organizations that have studied ethics and compliance, the Ethics Compliance Initiative and the Ethics Resource Center, point to savings achieved by longer employee retention periods and less misconduct. Strong ethical cultures reinforce employee commitment to the organization which results in a measurable benefit to the company: they remain and "go the extra mile" to make the company successful and profitable. Employee engagement and commitment to the organization are directly related to the strength of the ethical culture.

Visible and continuing commitment by senior leadership is also important to the strength of the ethical culture. Employee perceptions about management are critical to the organization's ability to detect misconduct, investigate, and correct it. Employees are not guided by the organizational chart and often include more

---

[22] See Ethics Resource Center, 2012 National Business Ethics Survey of Fortune 500 Employees: An Investigation into the State of Ethics at America's Most Powerful Companies.

[23] Ethics Resource Center, National Business Ethics Surveys, 2011 and 2012.

[24] James L. Heskett, The Culture Cycle (2011).

managers in their definition of senior leadership.[25] So an organization should not forget about its middle level managers and supervisors. When senior leaders are respected and known for his or her ethical decisions, observed misconduct is significantly reduced, reporting is increased, which increases the probability that an organization can correct misconduct before it reaches a critical juncture.

Trending in 2016 will be an increased focus on how the organization takes steps to promote an ethical culture and whether its leadership takes visible action to uphold its ethical principles. Boards of Directors and leadership will be charged with having a substantive role in the "doing" of compliance. It is not enough to say "we have the correct tone at the top." An organization will have to be able to demonstrate that it does. "Do as I do" will become the norm. Board of Directors and senior management will be expected to lead the ethics and compliance function.

Some recommendations for promoting an ethical culture are:

1. Focus senior leaders and supervisors on the development of the ethics and compliance message.

2. Make ethics and compliance awareness a part of ordinary business meetings.

3. Shift the focus away from more controls (the "stick") to better training of leaders that teaches and imparts the importance of ethical decision-making.

4. Raise risk awareness of unintentional but unethical behaviors through frequent targeted ethics and compliance communication and educational training.

5. Recognize that behavior will be influenced by what is measured and rewarded. If necessary, re-design the employee performance evaluation to make ethics and compliance a prominent feature of the evaluation. Also, impose disciplinary measures on leaders and supervisors who do not support the program or continually send the wrong message (i.e., fail to show up for code of conduct training):

   a. Connect career advancement to ethics signals; and

   b. Give the Compliance Officer the opportunity to weigh in on employee evaluation (raise, bonus, promotion) decisions.

6. Address fear of speaking up:

   a. Create and communicate strong support from the top;

---

[25] According to the 2012 NEBS Survey of Fortune 500 Employees, senior Leaders are: The head of your location (38%), the head of your region (13%), the head of your business unit (22%), the President of CEO of the company (24%), the Board of Directors (2%).

        b.   Actively engage senior management (participate in Ethics and Compliance campaign, video messages from senior leaders, guest writers);

        c.   Implement rewards/incentives, recognition; and

        d.   Educate mangers to be responsive.

    7.   Address Retaliation perception:

        a.   Actively protect employees from retaliation;

        b.   Be transparent about problems and how they were addressed;

        c.   Think out loud. Explain the reasoning behind key business decisions and how ethics and integrity factored into the decision (build trust);

        d.   Periodically check in with employees who report misconduct to make sure they have not been negatively impacted by their decision to blow the whistle; and

        e.   Include retaliation warning signs as part of ethics and compliance training.

## [B]   Proper Support for the Ethics and Compliance Program at All Management Levels (Otherwise Known as "Tone at the Top")

Two criteria are key to an effective ethics and compliance program—tone at the top and embedding the program within the business organization. Central to the success of the compliance program is the "tone at the top." The tone at the top is the ethical atmosphere that an organization's leadership creates in the workplace. A company's senior leaders are responsible for the culture they create, and must be faithful to the same set of rules they set out for other employees. They must lead by example. Whatever tone senior management sets has a direct impact on the employees of the company. If the tone set by senior management is one of integrity, employees are more inclined to uphold the same values; however, if senior management appears unconcerned with ethics and focuses solely on the bottom line, employees are less likely to believe ethical conduct is important to the organization and therefore are more likely to commit fraud. If making the numbers is all that seems to matter, managers and employees may turn back to their old tricks and turn their back on values. Research has shown that employees pay close attention to the behavior and actions of their superiors, and they follow their lead. In short, *employees will do what they witness their superiors doing.* The point to be made here is that the "top" can also include your middle level managers, do not forget about them.

Some strategies for promoting the right tone are:

1. Celebrate employee acts of ethical leadership, in team meetings and in other company communications;

2. Adapt program to changing business needs;

3. Focus on validity and improvement of metrics to really prove program effectiveness;

4. Focus on people as a key element of risk assessment;

5. Include social responsibility in code of conduct; and

6. Involve the Compliance Officer in senior management performance and promotions.

## [C] And Now Even the DOJ Has a Conscience (i.e., Compliance Expert)

In November 2015, The Fraud Section of the Department of Justice announced that it was hiring a "full time compliance expert." This individual is expected to bring private practice compliance practice insights to the DOJ public sector particularly related to expectations as to what a compliance program can realistically be expected to achieve in a corporation.

Two trends that might result from this focus on the compliance function are (1) the elevation of the importance of the compliance function and (2) the DOJ's compliance expert's focus in evaluating effectiveness of a corporate compliance program. These trends were discussed partially by Andrew Weissman, Chief of the Fraud Unit of the DOJ, at the Ethics Compliance Initiative Best Practice Conference in New Orleans this past fall. He discussed an expectation that a corporation be represented by "compliance counsel" in addition to its general counsel at DOJ presentations. He also discussed what will be reviewed in terms of program effectiveness and going beyond the numbers in evaluating the program. DOJ's compliance officer will look to see that your compliance program goes beyond aspiring to the minimum.

## [D] Effectiveness and Metrics: Beyond the Hotline Numbers—Everyone Has a Code of Conduct but How Do We Know It's Working?

Proving you have a Code of Conduct is no longer enough; now you must be able to prove it is effective. In 2010, the FSGO criteria for determining whether a compliance program is "effective" were revised. Now, an effective program is one where the Compliance Officer has direct reporting obligations to the governing authority (i.e., Board of Directors or a subset thereof), ferrets out wrongdoing; self-reports misconduct or illegal conduct and where no individual with operational responsibility for the program participated in or turned a blind eye to the illegal conduct.[26]

The Yates Memorandum makes it more incumbent on the Board of Directors and senior leadership to be able to demonstrate knowledge of the program beyond the fact that you have a program and the number of hotline calls. The new aggressive environment where the regulators are seeking to modify corporate behavior through enforcement calls for demonstrable actions/activities on the part of leadership.

Review you program to ascertain whether the organization's directors and senior management provide strong, explicit, and visible support for its ethics and compliance program and whether they have a role in determining the structure and framework of the program. Care should also be taken to evaluate what demonstrable evidence could be provided to support their efforts.

### [E]  Is There More to Cooperation Than Just Being Cooperative? According to the Latest Guidance from DOJ, Yes! The Yates Memorandum . . .

The DOJ has a long-standing policy that a company's cooperation in an investigation could impact the resolution of the case and have a mitigating impact upon a business that is facing criminal or civil penalties. Beginning in 2014 and perhaps in response to the public outcry seeking individual corporate officer accountability for the financial crisis, the DOJ has made public statements explaining that there is more to "cooperation" than just being cooperative. Recently, the DOJ has said in order to be seen as cooperating with the government the corporation needs to do more than just turn over its documents.

Cooperation is now defined by taking an active role in investigating and uncovering evidence of the actual individual corporate "wrongdoers." In September 2014, Leslie Caldwell, chief of the DOJ criminal division, stated that companies seeking cooperation credit "must root out the misconduct and identify the individuals responsible, even if they are senior executives." In another speech, Caldwell reiterated these sentiments that in order "to receive cooperation credit, we expect companies to conduct appropriately tailored investigations designed to root out misconduct, identify wrongdoers and provide all available facts." About one year later, on September 10, 2015, the U.S. Attorney announced that it has implemented new guidelines for DOJ in assessing a corporation's cooperation with a government investigation. The gist of the memorandum is that a corporation will not be given full credit for cooperation unless it actively seeks out and identifies those within the corporation who were responsible for the misbehavior and turn over evidence against them, "regardless of their position, status or seniority." The guidance directs the DOJ to focus on individuals from the beginning of

---

[26] USSG Section 8C2.5(f)(3)(A)-(C).

an investigation, not to release the individuals from liability in the absence of departmental policy or extraordinary circumstances and directs that the civil and criminal divisions should be "in routine communication with each other."

The Yates Memorandum identifies six key steps to strengthen the government's pursuit of individual accountability for corporate wrongdoing:

(1) in order to qualify for any cooperation credit, corporations must provide to [DOJ] all relevant facts relating to the individuals responsible for the misconduct;

(2) criminal and civil corporate investigations should focus on individuals from the inception of the investigation;

(3) criminal and civil attorneys handling corporate investigations should be in routine communication with one another;

(4) absent extraordinary circumstances or approved departmental policy, [DOJ] will not release culpable individuals from civil or criminal liability when resolving a matter with a corporation;

(5) Department attorneys should not resolve matters with a corporation without a clear plan to resolve related individual cases, and should memorialize any declinations as to individuals in such cases; and

(6) civil attorneys should consistently focus on individuals as well as the company and evaluate whether to bring suit against an individual based on considerations beyond that individual's ability to pay.

The Yates Memorandum Guidance applies to all pending and future cases. It remains to be seen how DOJ will enforce these guidelines but it certainly signals an increased focus on individual accountability for an organization's misconduct. The following is a link to the memorandum, http://www.justice.gov/dag/file/769036/download.

## [F] Empowering the Compliance Officer-Positioning, Budget, and Staff

Where ethics and compliance was once a silo of an organization or relegated to a division in the general counsel's, chief finance officer's department or other department, today's leading practices dictate that this model no longer be followed. The responsibility for the ethics and compliance function should extend from the board of directors down and across to all business units and departments: operations, legal, finance, internal audit, human resources, safety and risk management. Current leadership thought in the compliance community has rejected the earlier models regarding placement of the Compliance Officer and more organizations are seeing the value in positioning the Compliance Officer outside the general counsel's office. The FSGO prescribe the designation of a high level individual with the ability to effect change who reports directly to the governing body of the organization outside of any other departments that exist in the corporation (legal, human resources, audit or financial departments). Current leading practices call for establishing the Compliance Officer role as a member of executive management team. The role should be a proactive, as opposed to reactive role. A Compliance Officer adds value to the extent that he or she helps an organization stay out of trouble and is expected to engage in active monitoring of a company's compliance with laws, policies, and standards and has a "seat at the table." A recent Deloitte/Compliance Week survey (11/2015 Volkov) reported that now 60% of the Compliance Officers report directly to the CEO and are part of the Executive Management Team.

The Compliance Officer position must be adequately structured (high level, senior management position) with sufficient authority, *autonomy*, and responsibility to carry out its functions. The minimum requirements are:

- *Independent* to raise matters of concern without fear of reprisal or a conflict of interest. A Compliance Officer must objectively monitor the decisions and conduct of management, based on the standards of the organization and the law. "When so much as the possibility of wrongdoing surfaces, it is the duty of the CO to respond."[27]

- *Connected to the company operations* to build an ethical culture that advances the overall objectives of the business. The Compliance Officer should not be isolated from the daily activity of the company.

- Given the *authority to have decisions and recommendations taken seriously* at all levels of the organization. Compliance cuts across functions and transcends levels. "If corporate leaders are serious about ethics, they will have to empower their ethics officials to develop tough programs that *challenge and monitor* senior executives at a level of intensity commensurate with the power that they wield."[28]

- *Financial and human resources* to monitor, promote standards, and educate the workforce. Financial and human resources and authority of the Compliance Officer should be reviewed and determined by the Board of Directors.

A key consideration in determining a program's effectiveness is the program's ability to prevent and detect criminal conduct.[29] According to the FSGO, the Board of Directors must assign responsibility for *internal controls* to someone "at a sufficiently high level" possessing "adequate resources" to implement the program which includes periodic reviews to detect wrongdoing. Part and parcel of prevention and detection is the adequacy of the Compliance Officer's staff and budget. Does the ethics and compliance office have enough resources to

---

[27] *Leading Corporate Integrity: Defining the Role of the Chief Ethics & Compliance Officer (CECO)*, Ethics Resource Center, August 2007, p. 15.

[28] *Leading Corporate Integrity: Defining the Role of the Chief Ethics & Compliance Officer (CECO)*, Ethics Resource Center, August 2007, p. 9.

[29] USSC Section 8B2.1(a).

adequately and effectively perform this function? Is the compliance staff sufficient to audit, document, and analyze the corporation's compliance efforts?[30]

Some key considerations:

1. Is compliance the first cut made by an organization in a down economy or period of low profitability?

2. Does the Compliance Officer have access to technology and staffing sufficient to achieve the corporate purpose?

3. Is the Compliance Officer visible? Will the executives listen? One often hears that a compliance matter is an "operational issue" or a "business decision." While sometimes it can be, take care because more often than not it is a code word for not following recommendation of the Compliance Officer.

4. Where is the Compliance Officer positioned? Delegation of authority? Who can fire? Senior level? How is the Compliance Officer empowered? Is the Compliance Officer invited to meetings or excluded? Does senior management include the Compliance Officer in interviews for high level executive positions? Is the Compliance Officer allowed to conduct exit interviews?

One suggestion for garnering senior level support is to create a committee where its members are not directly subordinate to the functional head of the department. All departments can be represented on the committee. The committee should meet regularly and its charter should define "significant compliance issues." These issues could be referred to the committee for review and recommendation.

## [G] The Expanding Role of the Compliance Officer—Agent of the Board of Directors

In light of the Yates Memorandum (measuring cooperation credit and personal liability), it is more important than ever to assess whether your Board of Directors is exercising independent judgment. Make certain that it is provided with information that will enable it to exercise this independent judgment. Is the Board of Directors asking the tough questions? Does it know the risks in light of the company's overall compliance strategy/framework?

According to the FSGO, the Board of Directors must assign responsibility for *internal controls* to someone "at a sufficiently high level" possessing "adequate resources" to implement the program which includes periodic reviews to detect wrongdoing. Internal reporting mechanism, *e.g.*, a hotline; disciplinary

---

[30] 1999 Holder Memorandum.

action for offenders and those who fail to take "reasonable steps to prevent or detect improper conduct." The FSGO require that the Board of Directors have knowledge about the program—both the content and its implementation. It is the CEO/President's responsibility to run the organization; the Board of Directors are charged with ensuring that the management team serves the company's and the shareholder's long term interests. The Compliance Officer is seen as acting as an agent for the Board of Directors in assuring that the company meets its regulatory responsibilities. Board of Directors backed independence for the Compliance Officer is equated with appropriate authority for the position to carry out its fiduciary obligations and vice versa.

Case law has discussed personal liability for members of the Board of Directors if they fail to ensure appropriate information and reporting systems are instituted by management.[31] This can extend to cases involving the improper submission of representations or certifications, false claims, false statements, as well as other violations of laws or regulations.

At least annually (and perhaps more often), the Board of Directors should address the company's ethics initiatives with the Compliance Officer and other key executives; asking questions beyond the metrics about how many employees were trained and focusing on the issue of compliance program effectiveness. Examples of such questions are:

1. What is done to ensure that every employee understands the Code? Does each employee, manager, executive, and member of the Board of Directors make an annual commitment to abide by the Code?

2. Is the Code alive and real, or are the people merely going through the motions?

3. What are the established practices for handling Code violations? Does Board of Directors know what it would do if a senior executive were allegedly involved in serious wrongdoing?

4. What are the established practices for incentivizing compliance with the Code?

5. Do the employees perceive the Helpline as a safe way to speak up?

6. Are the reports and findings of ethical lapses from internal assurance reviews, the Helpline and throughout the company collected into one place and regularly analyzed for trends?

7. Is Code training provided to employees? What is taught to whom and with what frequency? Is effectiveness measured?

---

[31] Caremark Int'l Inc. Derivative Litig., 698 A.2d 959 (Del. Ch. 1996); Stone v. Ritter, 911 A.2d 362 (Del. 2006).

8. Are confidential surveys administered periodically to measure employee attitudes and perceptions about management style and ethical climate?

9. Do hiring practices employ integrity screens or background checks?

10. Are departing employees provided an anonymous exit interview?

11. Does the executive leadership team establish the proper Tone at the Top?

12. Does the executive leadership team make sure that the proper Tone at the Top is communicated throughout the organization? How?

13. Are all departments cooperating and collaborating with the Compliance Officer to monitor all operations to ensure that the company is following the Code and all applicable laws, rules, and regulations?

One current trend is the creation of a Board of Directors level "Compliance Committee" that is separate from and in addition to the Audit Committee. The focus here is looking beyond the establishment of a direct reporting line to the determination of whether the reporting is "unfiltered." In other words, is the Board of Directors only hearing the message that the executive management wants the Board to receive? This Board Level Compliance Committee can advise and guide the Board of Directors on risks like XBE, FCPA, AML, Kickbacks. Such a committee can facilitate Board of Directors oversight and serve as a check and balance on the company leadership. The Compliance Committee can also assist the Compliance Officer with reporting obligations to the Board of Directors.

## § 2.07 KEY 2016 TRENDS IN THE ETHICS AND COMPLIANCE FIELD

- Move away from a rules-based ethics and compliance program (compliance with rules and regulations) toward a values-based ethics and compliance program that focuses on ensuring ethical behavior by aligning culture, decision making, and conduct with core values;

- Assessing ethics and compliance program effectiveness;

- Empowerment of the Compliance Officer through positioning, budget, and resources;

- Individual accountability;

- Focus on Board of Director knowledge and involvement with the ethics and compliance program;

- More sustained impact on the ethical culture. Key to this is the visible support of the top management that goes beyond mere attendance annual training. They should be able to articulate and demonstrate by their words and actions their support for the program; and

- Consistent, visible corrective and disciplinary action for ethics and compliance failures (and incentives for good behavior):

  — Improve the visibility of the program;

  — Implement rewards for ethical conduct;

  — Provide more information and reassurance about the reporting process; and

  — Watch for retaliation.

CHAPTER 3

# SPEARIN—THE IMPLIED WARRANTY OF DEFECT-FREE PLANS AND SPECIFICATIONS—ONE HUNDRED YEARS AND COUNTING

Heather L. Heindel, P.E.,* Esq.†

§ 3.01 Introduction
    [A]   George B. Spearin and the 1916 Court of Claims Case
    [B]   The 1918 Supreme Court Decision in *United States v. Spearin*
    [C]   While Originally a Federal Project Concept, the *Spearin* Doctrine Has Been Applied to Both Public and Private Contracts at the State Level
    [D]   States Accepting the *Spearin* Doctrine and Confirming the Existence of an Implied Warranty of Plans and Specifications of Owner Provided Designs
        [1]  Arizona
        [2]  Arkansas
        [3]  California
        [4]  Colorado
        [5]  Florida
        [6]  Illinois
        [7]  Kentucky
        [8]  Louisiana
        [9]  Maine
        [10] Maryland
        [11] Massachusetts
        [12] Minnesota
        [13] Mississippi
        [14] Missouri
        [15] Montana
        [16] Nevada
        [17] New Mexico

---

* Professional Engineer licensed in Georgia.
† Attorney licensed in Georgia and Washington.

## § 3.01  INTRODUCTION

One hundred years ago, the Court of Claims published its opinion in *Spearin v. United States*, ruling in favor of George B. Spearin, paving the way for the proclamation of an owner's implied warranty of defect-free plans and specifications. Two years later, the U.S. Supreme Court affirmed the Court of Claims decision and the *Spearin* doctrine would become a fundamental part of the construction lawyer's vocabulary. George B. Spearin could hardly have known 100 years later, in the day of computer aided design, cloud computing, fast-track construction, high-speed rail, space travel, and wireless communications, his name would have become a doctrine, known by contractors, owners, and designers near and far. Few cases have the staying power of one hundred years, and in honor of the one hundredth year anniversary of *Spearin* we examine some of the more unique state applications of the *Spearin* doctrine—a creature of federal government contract law.

Commentators often generally describe the *Spearin* doctrine as universally accepted; however, when reading the cases that cite to *Spearin* the acceptance of the *Spearin* doctrine varies widely and in some states, has been explicitly rejected. Here we examine opinions interpreting the laws of the states throughout the United States to clarify the boundaries of the purported universal acceptance of the *Spearin* doctrine. We focus on the cases rather than the commentators. This approach is not without limitations, with thousands of citations to *Spearin* it's impossible to even cover the majority of those citations in one chapter. The focus here is to discuss the application of the *Spearin* doctrine on a state-by-state basis and discuss some of the more unique state interpretations.

### [A]  George B. Spearin and the 1916 Court of Claims Case

In 1905, George B. Spearin entered into a contract with the U.S. government for the construction of a Navy dry dock, including the relocation of a 6-foot sewer running through the site.[1] Spearin followed the owner-provided plans and specifications for the 6-foot sewer and made a reasonable inquiry with the Navy to review information about the site before bidding. Unknown to Spearin, but known to the Navy and the civil engineer in charge of the Brooklyn sewer system (portions of the sewer system were joint Navy-Brooklyn undertakings), there was a large dam in an interconnected 7-foot sewer and both the 6- and 7-foot sewers had overflowed as the result of the dam during sudden and heavy downpours of rain. "For a number of years preceding this occasion, under exactly similar circumstances, these very sewers in the navy yard had overflowed, blowing the iron tops off catch basis and manholes and flooding the yard itself with water to a

---

[1] Spearin v. United States, 51 Ct. Cl. 155 (1916) (herein referred to as *Spearin 1916*).

considerable depth."[2] Spearin constructed the intercepting 6-foot sewer as required by the plans and specifications, and began excavation of the dry dock. Almost a year into the project, a heavy rain occurred at the same time as high tide. The new 6-foot sewer failed, flooding the excavation. The Navy attempted to force Spearin to fix the sewer, which had failed due to a design error. Spearin refused, demanding that the Navy fix its design. Ultimately, Spearin was terminated and filed claims for recovery of unreimbursed costs and his anticipated profit. The Navy relet the contract twice and changed the defective design substantially, finally "designed to overcome and forestall the recurrence of a disaster similar to the one of which [Spearin] complained."[3]

The Court of Claims found that the government knew of the condition of the sewers and had actually disclosed the condition to some bidders, but withheld the same information from Spearin.[4] The Court of Claims found the government, "by [its] plans and specifications warranted their efficiency and the contractor had a right to rely upon them as correct representations of good and sufficient engineering skill and ability without an independent investigation of previous local conditions which might have warned him otherwise."[5] *Spearin 1916* methodically examined the issue of defective plans and specifications and decisions throughout the country.

### [B]   The 1918 Supreme Court Decision in *United States v. Spearin*

Both Spearin and the government appealed the amount of damages awarded in the Court of Claims ruling. The Supreme Court thus confirmed the implied warranty of defect-free plans and specifications and coined the *Spearin* doctrine as we know it today, stating:

> The general rules of law applicable to these facts are well settled. Where one agrees to do, for a fixed sum, a thing possible to be performed, he will not be excused or become entitled to additional compensation, because unforeseen difficulties are encountered. Thus one who undertakes to erect a structure upon a particular site, assumes ordinary risk of subsidence of the soil. But if the contractor is bound to build according to plans and specifications prepared by the owner, the contractor will not be responsible for the consequences of defects in the plans and specifications. This responsibility of the owner is not overcome by the usual clauses requiring builders to visit the site, to check the plans, and to inform themselves of the requirements of the work.

***

---

[2] *Spearin 1916*, 51 Ct. Cl. at 166.
[3] *Spearin 1916*, 51 Ct. Cl. at 167.
[4] *Spearin 1916*, 51 Ct. Cl. at 177.
[5] *Spearin 1916*, 51 Ct. Cl. at 180.

> [T]he insertion of the articles prescribing the character, dimensions and location of the sewer imported a warranty that if the specifications were complied with, the sewer would be adequate. This implied warranty is not overcome by the general clauses requiring the contractor to examine the site, to check up the plans, and to assume responsibility for the work until completion and acceptance.[6]

And thus for the past 98 years, the concept that the implied warranty of defect-free plans and specifications *cannot* be overcome by requiring a contractor to examine the site and assume the responsibility for the work has been known as the *Spearin* doctrine.[7]

## [C]  While Originally a Federal Project Concept, the *Spearin* Doctrine Has Been Applied to Both Public and Private Contracts at the State Level

Much of the body of construction law throughout the states has its roots in federal government contract cases. While federal cases are not necessarily binding on private construction projects or state or local government projects within a given state, the federal cases are often instructive on key issues raised in construction project disputes. Commentators often opine that the *Spearin* doctrine has virtually universal acceptance in the United States. Upon closer examination, the nuances of state courts' application, rejection, and modification of the *Spearin* doctrine and its progeny are anything from "universal acceptance." In particular, many courts cite to only the first part of the *Spearin* doctrine, "Where one agrees to do, for a fixed sum, a thing possible to be performed, he will not be excused or become entitled to additional compensation, because unforeseen difficulties are encountered" and never reach the most important element of the *Spearin* doctrine, the implied warranty of defect-free plans and specifications.[8]

Construction lawyers are confronted with issues of defective plans and specifications on both public and private construction projects. In order to assess the applicability of the *Spearin* doctrine to a particular dispute, three questions come to mind:

(1)   Is the defective plan or specification a performance specification or a design specification (the *Spearin* doctrine implied warranty of defect-free plans and specifications is not applicable to performance specifications)?

---

[6] United States v. Spearin, 248 U.S. 132, 136-37 (1918) (herein referred to as *Spearin*) (internal citations omitted).

[7] *Spearin*, 248 U.S. at 137.

[8] *Spearin*, 248 U.S. at 136.

(2)  Has the *Spearin* doctrine's implied warranty of defect-free plans and specifications been applied to the type of project at issue in the jurisdiction having authority (check applicability to public and private construction projects)?[9]

(3)  Have the courts of the jurisdiction recognized any language sufficient to operate as a waiver to the implied warranty of plans and specifications?

This chapter attempts to address these questions by examining reported cases in each of the fifty states. The state-to-state application of the *Spearin* doctrine's implied warranty of defect-free plans and specifications varies, as some have embraced it unconditionally, while others have developed their own rules, and a number of states have never addressed the issues. Keen readers may observe some overlap between cases discussing the implied warranty of defect-free plans and specifications and those discussing differing site conditions. The author has recognized this as well, but remained focused on the court's handling of the implied warranty of defect-free plans and specifications. Overall, there are thousands of cases, administrative decisions, trial court materials, and secondary sources citing to *Spearin*: not bad for a 1916 case with humble beginnings.

## [D]  States Accepting the *Spearin* Doctrine and Confirming the Existence of an Implied Warranty of Plans and Specifications of Owner Provided Designs

### [1]  Arizona

The *Spearin* doctrine's implied warranty of defect-free plans and specifications is recognized in Arizona for both private and public construction projects.[10] The Arizona Supreme Court adopted this "principle in construction law" with relatively little written analysis.[11] Later, the Arizona Supreme Court further analyzed the *Spearin* doctrine's implied warranty of defect-free plans and specifications and confirmed that it is inapplicable to performance specifications.[12] In an unreported case, the Court of Appeals of Arizona refused to extend the implied warranty of defect-free plans and specifications to a contractor who installed work

---

[9] This distinction may or may not be significant in a particular jurisdiction depending upon the courts of that jurisdiction and the robustness of the jurisdiction's public contract laws.

[10] *See* Chaney Bldg. Co. v. City of Tucson, 716 P.2d 28, 31 (Ariz. 1986); Kubby v. Crescent Steel, 466 P.2d 753, 754 (Ariz. 1970).

[11] *See Chaney Bldg.*, 716 P.2d at 31.

[12] Willamette Crushing Co. v. State By & Through Dept. of Transp., 932 P.2d 1350, 1352 (Ariz. 1997).

in deviation of the specifications.[13] In *Jonovich*, the contractor argued that it had not deviated from the specification because the owner's consultants verbally approved the deviation—the court relying on the contract language requiring written change orders disagreed with the contractor's interpretation of its deviation.[14]

## [2]  Arkansas

Arkansas recognizes an exception to the general *Spearin* doctrine: "[A] competent and experienced contractor cannot rely upon submitted specifications and plans where he is fully aware, or should have been aware, that the plans and specifications cannot produce the proposed results."[15] The "should-have-been-aware" exception is unique, and it essentially shifts the burden of the implied warranty onto the experienced contractor, who should have known the plans and specifications were defective, to prove it could not have known the plans and specifications were defective.[16] It is important for contractors performing work in Arkansas to understand the should-have-known standard.

In addition, a contractor's express warranty and implied warranty of sound workmanship and proper construction take precedence over the owner's implied warranty of defect-free material, plans, and specifications in Arkansas.[17] In *Graham*, the contractor verbally warranted that the roof would not leak, which the trial court found negated all the implied warranties:

> The [trial] court found that there was in fact an express warranty that the roof would not leak, and that said expressed [sic] warranty negates and makes inoperative any implied warranties, including the implied warranty that the job would be done in a workmanlike manner as alleged in the plaintiff's complaint. There was a general warranty that the roof would not leak, and the court finds no evidence that the skylights were excluded from the warranty that the roof would not leak. The proof was clear that the roof leaked.[18]

The appellate court confirmed the trial court's holding, an additional cautionary tale to contractors offering verbal express warranties. *Graham* exposes the dangers of simple warranties shifting the risk of defective design from the owner to

---

[13] Jonovich Cos., Inc. v. City of Coolidge, No. 2 CA-CV 2011-0029, 2011 WL 5137180, at *3 (Ariz. Ct. App. Oct. 31, 2011).

[14] *Jonovich*, 2011 WL 5137180, at *4.

[15] Housing Auth. of the City of Texarkana v. E.W. Johnson Constr. Co., 573 S.W.2d 316, 322 (Ark. 1978) (holding that the generally dilapidated condition of the roof was readily apparent, but not addressing the implication of the implied warranty of defect-free plans and specifications because the owner assumed responsibility to repair the roof).

[16] *See* Graham Constr. Co., Inc. v. Earl, 208 S.W.3d 106 (Ark. 2005).

[17] *Graham Constr.*, 208 S.W.3d at 111.

[18] *Graham Constr.*, 208 S.W.3d at 111.

the contractor. The Arkansas courts have not addressed if the should-have-been-aware standard requires a contractor to identify something less than a patent defect.

### [3]  California

There is a long history of conflicting appellate decisions related to the application of the *Spearin* doctrine on public projects in California. The Supreme Court of California examined the historical cases and held the following:

> [T]hat a contractor on a public works contract may be entitled to relief for a public entity's nondisclosure in the following limited circumstances: (1) the contractor submitted its bid or undertook to perform without material information that affected performance costs; (2) the public entity was in possession of the information and was aware the contractor had no knowledge of, nor any reason to obtain, such information; (3) any contract specifications or other information furnished by the public entity to the contractor misled the contractor or did not put it on notice to inquire; and (4) the public entity failed to provide the relevant information. The circumstances affecting recovery may include, but are not limited to, positive warranties or disclaimers made by either party, the information provided by the plans and specifications and related documents, the difficulty of detection the condition in question, any time constraints the public entity imposed on proposed bidders, and any unwarranted assumptions made by the contractor. The public entity may not be held liable for failing to disclose information a reasonable contractor in like circumstances would or should have discovered on its own, but may be found liable when the totality of the circumstances is such that the public entity knows, or has reason to know, a responsible contractor acting diligently would be unlikely to discover the condition that materially increased the cost of performance.[19]

*Los Angeles Unified School District* details at length the limitations of the application of the *Spearin* doctrine to public projects in California and clarifies how the implied warranty of defect-free plans and specifications can be waived. A number of states look to California for guidance on construction law issues, so it will be interesting to see if other states adopt California's four-part test going forward. California appellate courts have not analyzed if the *Spearin* doctrine applies to private construction projects, but have opined that "authorities appear to support" the application.[20]

---

[19] Los Angeles Unified Sch. Dist. v. Great Am. Ins. Co., 234 P.3d 490, 499 (Cal. 2010).
[20] Atowich v. Zimmer, 25 P.2d 6, 9 (Cal. 1933).

### [4]  Colorado

Without significant analysis, Colorado acknowledges the application of the *Spearin* doctrine's implied warranty of defect-free plans and specifications to public projects.[21] Colorado appellate courts have not examined whether the *Spearin* doctrine is applicable to private construction projects.

### [5]  Florida

The *Spearin* doctrine's implied warranty of defect-free plans and specifications is generally applied to public projects in Florida.[22] "Florida law recognizes a public owner's implied duty to provide bidders with information that will not mislead them, comparing it to the implied duty of good faith."[23] The United States District Court for the Northern District of Florida, when given the opportunity to address if the *Spearin* doctrine's implied warranty of defect-free plans and specifications applied on a private construction project did not address the issue. In an instance where there was no contractual privity, the court did not address the issue, thus leaving the application of the *Spearin* doctrine to private construction and parties not in privity still unsettled in Florida.[24]

### [6]  Illinois

Illinois law on the implied warranty of defect-free plans and specifications predates the *Spearin* doctrine and applies to private construction projects as well as public construction projects.[25] More recently, the Illinois Court of Appeals found that contractual attempts to shift responsibility for the sufficiency and

---

[21] *See* BRW, Inc. v. Dufficy & Sons, Inc., 99 P.3d 66 (Colo. 2004).

[22] *See* Jacksonville Port Auth. v. Parkhill-Goodloe Co., Inc., 362 So. 2d 1009, 1012 (Fla. Dist. Ct. App. 1978) (holding that "[i]n furnishing bidders with information as to the nature of the materials likely to be encountered in dredging to the required depth, [the owner] had a duty to furnish information which would not mislead prospective bidders and to not withhold from prospective bidders information that another dredging contractor, in an adjacent area, had encountered extensive rock." *Jacksonville Port Auth.*, 362 So. 2d at 1013).

[23] Martin K. Eby Constr. Co., Inc. v. Jacksonville Transp. Auth., 436 F. Supp. 2d 1276, 1309 (M.D. Fla. 2005).

[24] Lincoln v. Florida Gas Transmission Co., No. 4:13-cv-74-MW/CAS, 2014 WL 3057113, at *5, n.11 (N.D. Fla. July 7, 2014) (refusing to extend *Spearin* "to a contractor that installs a pipeline in a location that has been selected by others and approved and mandated by a regulatory agency" clearly stating that "because Plaintiff is a third-party, not in a contractual relationship with USPI, and the contract is not before this Court, there is no need to enter the quagmire of the *Spearin* doctrine in a unique case when Plaintiff's claim of negligence is insufficient for another reason").

[25] *See* Clark v. Pope, 70 Ill. 128 (1873) (holding that a private project (church) contractor who builds according to plans and specifications furnished to him and performs in a good and workmanlike manner will not be responsible for defects in such plans and specifications).

adequacy of the plans and specifications to the contractor are impermissible "without providing the contractor the corresponding benefit of having something to say about the plans which he is strictly bound to follow."[26] Illinois, thus recognizes the ability to waive the implied warranty of defect-free plans and specification, but that waiver must provide benefit to the contractor in the form of the ability to contribute to the development of the plans and specifications. Illinois' approach to the waiver of implied warranty of defect-free plans and specifications is unique and has not been found in other jurisdictions.

### [7] Kentucky

A slightly modified *Spearin* doctrine is recognized on public projects in Kentucky, where the owner has a "duty . . . to furnish to the [contractor] all material information it has in its possession, obtained either by borings or from past experience . . . and if it failed to do so, and as a result thereof the [contractor was] put to large additional expense in completing the contract, [the contractor is] entitled to recover the reasonable damages sustained by them."[27]

### [8] Louisiana

The Louisiana supreme court specifically adopted the *Spearin* doctrine for private construction projects in *Louisiana Shipbuilding Co. v. Bing Dampskibsaktieselskab.*[28] Likewise, the *Spearin* doctrine applies to public construction projects in Louisiana.[29] In 1958, the Louisiana legislature first codified the implied warranty of defect-free plans and specifications:

> No contractor, including but not limited to a residential building contractor as defined in R.A. 37:2150.1(9), shall be liable for destruction or deterioration of or defects in any work constructed, or under construction, by him if he constructed, or is constructing, the work according to plans and specifications furnished to him which he did not make or cause to be made and if the destruction, deterioration, or defect was due to any fault or insufficiency of the plans or specifications. This provision shall apply regardless of whether the destruction, deterioration, or defect occurs or becomes evident prior to or after delivery of the work to the owner or prior to or after acceptance of the

---

[26] W.H. Lyman Constr. Co. v. Village of Gurnee, 403 N.E.2d 1325, 1332 (Ill. App. Ct. 1980).

[27] Davis v. Commissioners of Sewerage of City of Louisville, 13 F. Supp. 672, 681 (W.D. Ky. 1936).

[28] 104 So. 364 (La. 1925).

[29] Brasher v. City of Alexandria, 41 So. 2d 819 (La. 1949) (holding that the contractor was entitled to a change order, in accordance with the *Spearin* doctrine, when the plans and specifications, prepared by the City Engineer, were insufficient and defective).

work by the owner. The provisions of this Section shall not be subject to waiver by the contractor.[30]

While this statute provides more protection to contractors in Louisiana than in many other states, it will not protect a contractor who enter into express written guarantees or warranties. A contractor, who seeks relief due to a defective roof design, but "voluntarily undertook to execute a written ten year guarantee against roof leakage" is not protected by the *Spearin* doctrine or statute in Louisiana.[31] Louisiana highlights the unintended consequences of warranties for leak-free roofs.

### [9]  Maine

The Supreme Court of Maine adopted *Spearin* and the implied warranty of defect-free plans and specifications in 1981. In *Marine Colloids, Inc. v. M.D. Hardy, Inc.*, the court found that an owner designed a fire wall by specifying the height, width and materials and that the subsequent failure of the fire wall was due to the owner using it for a purpose other than its intended purpose (owners used it as an exterior wall, which was not part of the design).[32] An engineer's testimony supported that the contractor's work was performed in a workmanlike manner and in compliance with the Owner's specifications, and the court summarily acknowledged that the contractor fulfilled any duty he may have had to warn the owner in specification defects.[33] The Supreme Court of Maine identified an exception to *Spearin* doctrine that had been adopted by some courts, but expressly refused to address the issue:

> Some jurisdictions have established an exception to the general rule for situations in which the owner's specifications contain defects that should reasonably have been apparent to the contractor. When such a defect appears, the contractor is held to have a duty to warn the owner of the defect before proceeding with construction. *e.g., Lewis v. Anchorage Asphalt Paving Co.*, 535 P. 2d 1188 (Alaska 1975); *Cooperative Cold Storage Builders, Inc. v. Arcadia Foods, Inc.*, 291 So. 2d 403 (La. App. 1974); *Dobler v. Malloy*, 214 N.W. 2d 510 (N.D. 1973). We need not now decide whether that exception to the general rule should be introduced into Maine law. . . .[34]

---

[30] La. R.S. § 9:2771 (2001).

[31] New Orleans Unity Soc'y of Practical Christianity v. Standard Roofing Co., 224 So. 2d 60, 63 (La. Ct. App. 1969) (holding that the roofing contractor that installed roof according to architect's plan was liable under written guarantee against roof leakage, notwithstanding La. R.S. § 9:2771).

[32] Marine Colloids, Inc. v. M.D. Hardy, Inc., 433 A.2d 402 (Me. 1981).

[33] *Marine Colloids*, 433 A.2d at 406.

[34] *Marine Colloids*, 433 A.2d at 406.

By the early 1990s, Maine had gotten further away from establishing a contractor's duty to warn, focusing on the workmanlike manner of a contractor's construction rather than duty to warn, even when a referee from a lower court teed up the issue.[35] In *Paine*, an owner hired an unlicensed designer who in turn hired an unlicensed engineer to design a "dream home."[36] During construction, and after framing, a steel beam protruded out of the roof and the contractor cut it off and added additional supports. The court found that this was not workmanlike and again confirmed that in Maine, a contractor does not have a duty to recognize design defects.[37] In Maine, the *Spearin* doctrine's implied warranty of defect-free plans and specifications applies equally to public and private projects.

### [10]  Maryland

The Maryland Court of Special Appeals adopted the *Spearin* doctrine's implied warranty of defect-free plans and specifications generally for public construction projects, but included an element of justifiable reliance to be proven by the contractor, showing that it indeed relied upon the owners' plans and specifications.[38] The court found that on a underwater repair project for bascule piers of a bridge, the contractor justifiably relied on the plans and specifications and the owner's representations regarding the project conditions:

> The record extract established that the specifications as prepared by [engineer] on behalf of [owner] were materially wrong and substantially inaccurate. * * * [The engineer] and the [owner] knew or shown have known the representations regarding the deterioration of the piers and the quantities of concrete necessary for the repairs were inaccurate as [engineer] had been engaged by the [owner] over a period of years to inspect the underwater portions of the bascule piers. [Engineer] actually had thirteen contracts with the [owner] between 1968 and 1972 which required the [engineer] to make underwater inspection of the bascule piers, tremies and piles, and field supervision of the piers.[39]

The court held that the contractor's reliance on the plans and specifications was justifiable because the contractor should not have had to conduct diving tests in order to verify the information given in the plans and specifications that it took an engineer four years to compile.[40]

---

[35] *See* Paine v. Spottiswoode, 612 A.2d 235 (Me. 1992).

[36] *Paine*, 612 A.2d at 237.

[37] *Paine*, 612 A.2d at 239.

[38] Raymond Int'l, Inc. v. Baltimore Cnty., 412 A.2d 1296 (Md. App. 1980).

[39] *Raymond*, 412 A.2d at 1302.

[40] *Raymond*, 412 A.2d at 1302.

## [11]  Massachusetts

The year 2015 was an important year for the *Spearin* doctrine in Massachusetts, prior to a historic decision by the Massachusetts Supreme Court, the future of the *Spearin* doctrine's implied warranty of defect-free plans and specifications on alternative delivery method projects seemed bleak. Historically, for public design-bid-build projects, "[i]t is well established that where one party furnishes plans and specifications for a contractor to follow in a construction job, and the contractor in good faith relies thereon, the party furnishing such plans impliedly warrants their sufficiency for the purpose intended."[41] The implied warranty imposes requirements on contractors as well, when a contractor encounters an "obvious omission, inconsistency, or discrepancy, he should take steps, by way of his own investigation, or by putting questions to the owner (or owner's representative), to bridge gaps in the documents."[42]

In 2005, the Massachusetts legislature authorized design-build and construction management at risk ("CM-at-risk") as alternative delivery methods for public construction projects.[43] In 2015, the Massachusetts Supreme Judicial Court held that the implied warranty of plans and specifications applies to public CM-at-risk projects, overturning a controversial lower court decision.[44] The Massachusetts Supreme Judicial Court found that differences between the responsibilities of a general contractor in a traditional design-bid-build project and CM at risk project impact the scope of the implied warranty, but not the actual existence of the implied warranty.[45] "The greater the CMAR's [construction manager at risk] design responsibilities in the contract, the greater the CMAR's burden will be to show, when it seeks to establish the owner's liability under the implied warranty, that its reliance on the defective design was both reasonable and in good faith."[46]

The court next examined whether waiver of the implied warranty had occurred, and found that the contract (between the owner and the CM-at-risk contractor) did not include an express disclaimer of the implied warranty of defect-free plans and specifications.[47] Gilbane (the CMAR) undertook a number of responsibilities including:

> [T]o "carefully study" and "carefully compare" all design-related documents; "'take field measurements and verify field conditions," compare them to the designs, and "report to the Designer any questions, errors, inconsistencies, or omissions." . . . "review" the designs "on a continuous basis" with a group of

---

[41] Alpert v. Commonwealth, 258 N.E.2d 755, 763 (Mass. 1970).

[42] Richardson Elec. Co. v. Peter Frances & Son, 484 N.E.2d 108, 111 (Mass. App. Ct. 1985).

[43] *See* Mass. G.L. c. 149A § 15.

[44] Coghlin Elec. Contractors, Inc. v. Gilbane Bldg. Co., 36 N.E.3d 505 (Mass. 2015).

[45] *Coghlin Elec.*, 36 N.E.3d at 514.

[46] *Coghlin Elec.*, 36 N.E.3d at 514.

[47] *Coghlin Elec.*, 36 N.E.3d at 514.

architects or engineers in order to "discover inconsistencies, errors and omissions," and "review the design documents for clarity, consistency, constructability, maintainability / operability and coordination among the trades" . . . attend Project meetings with [owner] and the Designer concerning planning for construction of the Project.[48]

None of those responsibilities resulted in a waiver of the implied warranty of defect-free plans and specifications. In the absence of an express disclaimer, the owner's implied warranty of defect-free plans and specifications still applies to CM-at-risk projects.[49]

### [12]  Minnesota

In Minnesota, "where a contractor performs according to the plans and specifications supplied to him, he is not responsible for defects in those plans and specifications."[50]

The Minnesota Supreme Court adopted *Spearin* with limited exceptions, in *Friederick v. County of Redwood*:[51]

> Where a contractor makes an absolute and unqualified contract to construct a building or perform a given undertaking it is the general, and perhaps universal, rule that he assumes the risks attending the performance of the contract, and must repaid and make good any injury or defect which occurs or develops before the completed work has been delivered to the other party. But where he makes a contract to perform a given undertaking in accordance with prescribed plans and specifications, this rule does not apply. Under such a contract he is not permitted to vary from the prescribed plans and specifications even if he deems them improper and insufficient; and therefore cannot be held to guarantee that work performed as required by them will be free from defects, or withstand the action of the elements, or accomplish the purpose intended. Where the contract specifies what he is to do and the manner and method of doing it, and he does the work specified in the manner specified, his engagement is fulfilled and he remains liable only for defects resulting from improper workmanship or other fault on his part, unless there be a provision in the contract imposing some other or further obligation.[52]

---

[48] *Coghlin Elec.*, 36 N.E.3d at 514-15.

[49] *Coghlin Elec.*, 36 N.E.3d at 515; Daniel O'Connell's Sons v. Commonwealth, 212 N.E.2d 219, 221 (Mass. 1965) ("express disclaimer" of responsibility for accuracy of geological data invalidates implied warranty); D. Federico Co. v. Commonwealth, 415 N.E.2d 855, 857 (Mass. App. Ct. 1981) (no implied warranty "where the contract terms specifically precluded warranty of, or reliance on" quantity estimates).

[50] Hayle Floor Covering, Inc. v. First Minnesota Constr. Co., 253 N.W.2d 809, 811 (Minn. 1977) (citing *Spearin*).

[51] 190 N.W. 801 (Minn. 1922).

[52] *Friederick*, 190 N.W. at 802.

Historically, a contractor had no obligation to inquire if the information in the plans and specifications were improper or incomplete. A more modern, but unreported case, tends to indicate that additional inquiry by the contractor is warranted. In an unreported case, boring logs which were mentioned, but not included, in specifications, and contract documents which had clear indications of the potential of unsuitable soils invalidated the contractor's claim of breach of implied warranty of defect-free plans and specifications when unsuitable soils were found during construction.[53] In this instance the contractor had an obligation to ask for the boring logs that weren't included in the contract documents. This obligation differs in Minnesota than other states where an owner would be obligated to provide the known information. Because this case is unreported, its precedential value is limited, but it should be considered when confronting these types of issues in Minnesota.

### [13]  Mississippi

Without citing to the *Spearin* doctrine by name, Mississippi courts recognize an owner's implied warranty of defect-free plans and specifications for both public and private construction projects.[54] An express guarantee that includes "repair" to "a defect due to design" is the type of express warranty that trumps the owner's implied warranty of defect-free plans and specifications.[55]

The presence of weathered rock in quantities larger than represented in subsurface reports was not a defective specification, where the information regarding the subsurface conditions was "not guaranteed by [owner] to represent all conditions to be encountered in constructing the drilled pier foundations at the site."[56] The court found that the owner had "fully disclosed all the information it had in regard to the site conditions in the subsurface investigation reports and had no further obligations with respect to such conditions."[57] *Richard Goettle* is an interesting case because the contract included unit prices per linear foot of pier that were tied to the soil conditions, and the owner had been paying the contractor

---

[53] *See* Starry Constr. Co., Inc. v. Hubbard Cnty., No. C898341, 2001 WL 1647344, at *5 (Minn. Ct. App. Dec. 26, 2001).

[54] *See generally* Trs. of First Baptist Church of Corinth v. McElroy, 8 So. 2d 138, 141 (Miss. 1955) (confirming that an implied warranty of defect-free plans and specifications exists, but does not survive any express warranty as to defects in plans and specifications); Southerland Enters., Inc. v. Newton Cnty., 838 So. 2d 286, 298-90 (Miss. 2003); Mayor & City Council of the City of Columbus, Miss. v. Clark Dietz & Assocs.-Eng'rs, Inc., 550 F. Supp. 610, 625 (N.D. Miss. 1961) (finding that warranty as to "materials and workmanship" did not "guarantee the adequacy of the design" and therefore implied warranty prevailed); Harvard v. Board of Supervisors, 70 So. 2d 875 (Miss. 1954).

[55] Greenbriar Digging Servs., Ltd. P'ship v. South Central Water Ass'n, Inc., No. 3:07CV601, 2009 WL 812241, at *4 (S.D. Miss. Mar. 26, 2009).

[56] Richard Goettle, Inc. v. Tennessee Valley Auth., 600 F. Supp. 7, 10 (E.D. Miss. 1984).

[57] *Richard Goettle*, 600 F. Supp. at 11.

the weathered rock unit prices in the increased quantities, yet the contractor still pursued a breach of implied warranty claim.

### [14] Missouri

Missouri has adopted and expanded the *Spearin* doctrine's implied warranty of defect-free plans and specifications.[58]

In an unreported case, the U.S. District Court for the Eastern District of Missouri examined whether under Missouri law, the *Spearin* doctrine's implied warranty of defect-free plans and specifications extends to products specified by the owner.[59] In *Travelers*, the owner of a new electronics store hired a contractor for the interior build out of a new store.[60] The owners specified four possible electrical cabinets to be installed, shortly after the work was completed a meltdown in the cabinet occurred destroying the cabinet and other property.[61] The contractor argued that he could not be held liable for a latent defect in a product that was specified by the project owner, citing to *Spearin*.[62] The court found that only the Third Circuit had addressed this issue, and analyzed that decision.[63] The Eastern District opined that the Missouri Supreme Court would likely follow the dissent in the Third Circuit case because "Missouri courts generally take the view that contractors should not be held liable for circumstances which are beyond their control."[64] Because the owner impliedly warranted to the contractor that the product and materials specified in the plans and specifications were adequate, the contractor cannot be held liable for a defect that was beyond its control.[65]

While we focus on construction disputes, many of the practitioners reading this book likely do government contract work as well. Importantly, the Missouri Court of Appeals further extended the applicability of the *Spearin* doctrine to government contracts outside of construction.[66] This is an important, and

---

[58] *See, e.g.,* Sanders Co. Plumbing & Heating, Inc. v. City of Independence, Missouri, 694 S.W.2d 841, 848 (Mo. Ct. App. 1985) ("Generally, when a contractor is to construct a project according to another's plans it does not insure that the plans are sufficient to obtain the result sought"); Eveready Heating & Sheet Metal, Inc. v. D.H. Overmyer, Inc., 476 S.W.2d 153 (Mo. Ct. App. 1972) (where contractor is to build a specified structure according to another's plans and specifications, contractor does not insure that plans and specifications are sufficient to obtain the result sought).

[59] Travelers Indem. Co. v. S.M. Wilson & Co., 4:04 CV 01365 ERW, 2005 WL 2234582 (E.D. Mo. 2005).

[60] *Travelers Indem.,* 2005 WL 2234582, at *1.

[61] *Travelers Indem.,* 2005 WL 2234582, at *1.

[62] *Travelers Indem.,* 2005 WL 2234582, at *9.

[63] *Travelers Indem.,* 2005 WL 2234582, at *9 (analyzing Rhone Poulenc Rorer Pharm., Inc. v. Newman Glass Works, 112 F.3d 695 (3d Cir. 1997)).

[64] *Travelers Indem.,* 2005 WL 2234582, at *10.

[65] *Travelers Indem.,* 2005 WL 2234582, at *10.

[66] *See* Missouri Consol. Health Care Plan v. Community Health Plan, 81 S.W.3d 34, 52-53 (Mo. Ct. App. 2002) ("The rationale behind all of the construction cases equally applies to incorrect

relatively unusual finding—providing additional security to entities dealing with the state government in Missouri.

### [15]  Montana

The established Montana law provides that a contractor on a public construction project can rely on the plans and specifications provided by an owner.[67] The owner providing the plans and specifications "warrants and is responsible for the accuracy of the descriptions in the plans and specifications of the contract that are issued."[68] In *Sornsin*, the owner pointed to the following contract clause putting the contractor on notice to inquire further, and thus as the owner argued, eliminating the owner's responsibility for any inaccuracies in the plans and specifications:

> The Contractor shall be responsible for having taken steps reasonably necessary to ascertain the nature and location of the work, and the general and local conditions which can affect the work or the cost thereof. Any failure by the Contractor to do so will not relieve him from responsibility for successfully performing the work without additional expense to the Contracting Local Organization. The Contracting Local Organization assumes no responsibility for any understanding or representations concerning conditions made by any of its officers or agents prior the execution of this contract, unless such understanding or representation are expressly stated in the contract.[69]

The court found that as a matter of law, the language in the contract did not "waive, eliminate, or modify the contractor's right to rely on the representations made in the plans or specifications. . . ."[70] In *Sornsin*, Montana affirms the adoption of the *Spearin* doctrine's implied warranty of defect-free plans and specifications for public construction projects.

### [16]  Nevada

The U.S. Court of Appeals for the Ninth Circuit has applied the *Spearin* doctrine to public projects in Nevada.[71] There is no published Nevada appellate court decision confirming the application of the *Spearin* doctrine under Nevada law.

---

representations made by a governmental entity to induce a contractor to enter into any type of government contract or lease * * * Governmental entities may not make false representations and avoid suits in contract merely because the theory behind such suits smack of tort. . . .").

[67] *See* Haggart Constr. Co. v. State Highway Comm'n, 427 P.2d 686 (Mont. 1967); Sornsin Constr. Co. v. State, 590 P.2d 125 (Mont. 1978).

[68] *Sornsin Constr.*, 590 P.2d at 129.

[69] *Sornsin Constr.*, 590 P.2d at 128.

[70] *Sornsin Constr.*, 590 P.2d at 129.

[71] Frank Briscoe Co. Inc. v. Clark Cnty., 857 F.2d 606 (9th Cir. 1988).

### [17]  New Mexico

As it did with its lien law, New Mexico adopted California's interpretation and application of the *Spearin* doctrine.[72] Exculpatory clauses waiving the implied warranty of defect-free plans and specifications will not preclude liability for data included in plans and specifications in New Mexico.[73]

### [18]  New York

Courts of New York have recognized the applicability of the *Spearin* doctrine's implied warranty of defect-free plans and specifications to both public and private projects.[74] The application to private projects has been without analysis on relatively small residential projects. The issue of performance versus design specifications was discussed at length in *Fruin-Colnon*. The court determined that based on the language and structure of the contract as a whole and the parties' usage and course of performance under the contract, that the contractual water tightness requirement, while read in isolation may have appeared to be a performance specification, was in fact a design specification.[75] The court found that "complex and exacting standards for design and construction of the tunnel * * * the contract contemplat[ing] that waterproofing would be accomplished by means of fissure grouting, which also was to be carried out pursuant to detailed specifications * * * Bidders had no input into the design of the tunnel, nor did [contractor] exercise any independent design judgment . . . " were all factors that weighed in favor of a design specification and the application of the *Spearin* doctrine to the water tightness issue.[76]

### [19]  North Carolina

North Carolina expressly adopted the general rule that a contractor who follows the plans and specifications furnished by the owner will not be responsible for the consequences of defects in those plans or specifications.[77] The burden is on the contractor to prove that it complied with the plans and specifications, that

---

[72] *See* Vinnell Corp. v. State of New Mexico, 512 P.2d 71, 72-73 (N.M. 1973) (citing Souza & McCue Constr. Co. v. Superior Ct. of San Benito Cnty., 370 P.2d 338 (Cal. 1962)).

[73] Western States Mech. Contractors, Inc. v. Sandia Corp., 798 P.2d 1062, 1065 (N.M. Ct. App. 1990).

[74] *See* Ferrari v. Barleo Homes, Inc., 112 A.D.2d 137 (N.Y. App. Div. 1985); Fruin-Colnon Corp. v. Niagara Frontier Transp. Auth., 180 A.D.2d 222 (N.Y. App. Div. 1992).

[75] *Fruin-Colnon*, 180 A.D.2d at 230.

[76] *Fruin-Colnon*, 180 A.D.2d at 230-31.

[77] Board of Educ. v. Constr. Corp., 273 S.E.2d 504 (N.C. App. 1981).

the plans and specifications were defective, and that the defects were the proximate cause of the deficiency in the completed work.[78]

### [20]  Ohio

In Ohio, the "*Spearin* doctrine holds that, in cases involving government contracts, the government impliedly warrants the accuracy of its affirmative indications regarding job site conditions."[79] While Ohio has acknowledged and adopted the *Spearin* doctrine on public projects, the Ohio Supreme Court has specifically refused to extend the *Spearin* doctrine to delays that arise out of inaccurate, incomplete, and changed plans and specifications.[80]

The U.S. District Court for the Southern District of Ohio specifically declined to extend the *Spearin* doctrine to projects involving private owners.[81] The court detailed the reason for its decision:

> In deciding whether the *Spearin* doctrine applies to this case between private entities and governed by the laws of Ohio, this Court must apply the substantive law of Ohio as set forth by the Ohio Supreme Court. If the Ohio Supreme Court has not directly addressed the issue, this Court must determine what the Ohio Supreme Court would decide if faced with the issue and should not disregard a decision of an Ohio appellate court on point.
>
> In this case, the Ohio Supreme Court has not directly determined that the *Spearin* doctrine applies to contracts between private parties. However, the *Spearin* doctrine grew out of a case involving contract specifications prepared by a government entity and the reasoning used to set forth the *Spearin* doctrine is based upon cases involving contract specifications prepared by a government entity. Further, Ohio courts, including the Ohio Supreme Court, have applied the *Spearin* doctrine only to cases involving contract specifications prepared by government entities. Finally, an Ohio appellate court has determined that there is no implied warranty of the correctness of plans.
>
> Therefore, this Court finds no basis for extending the *Spearin* doctrine to include cases involving private entities and elects to not do so. The *Spearin* doctrine does not provide an implied warranty for defects in plans and specifications in this contract action between Wal-Mart and Thomas & Marker, both private entities.[82]

It is worth noting that the Ohio appellate court case referred to above is not a construction case, but a complex wrongful death action involving multiple

---

[78] Gilbert Eng'g Co. v. City of Asheville, 328 S.E.2d 849, 857 (N.C. App. 1985).

[79] Sherman R. Smoot Co. v. Ohio Dep't of Admin. Servs., 736 N.E.2d (Ohio App. 2000).

[80] Dugan & Meyers Constr. Co. Inc. v. Ohio Dep't of Admin. Servs., 864 N.E.2d 68 (Ohio 2007).

[81] Thomas & Marker Constr. Co. v. Wal-Mart Stores, Inc., No. 3:06-cv-406, 2008 WL 4279866 (S.D. Ohio Sept. 15, 2008).

[82] *Thomas & Marker*, 2008 WL 4279866, at *19.

tortfeasors and extensive analysis of indemnity and contribution under Ohio law.[83] In addition, a number of Ohio courts have subsequently acknowledged that the implied warranty of defect-free plans and specifications does in fact exist.[84]

Ohio also provides a framework for public owners to disclaim the implied warranty of defect-free plans and specification.[85] Further clarifying that a contractor "cannot rely upon the Spearin doctrine where the contractor had unique knowledge that the plans were obviously flawed and did not inform the owner."[86]

### [21]  Oklahoma

Oklahoma recognizes the application of the *Spearin* doctrine's implied warranty of defect-free plans and specifications to public projects, but limited the implied warranty by excusing an owner from disclosing information that is discoverable through the type of investigation contemplated by the contract.[87]

### [22]  Oregon

Oregon courts appear to recognize the *Spearin* doctrine's implied warranty of defect-free plans and specifications, but have not offered relief on *Spearin* doctrine grounds to contractors in any reported cases. A contractor working on a private home "receives no protection under the *Spearin* Doctrine" when he did not follow the owner's plans and specifications.[88] This case leaves the question open in Oregon as to whether or not the *Spearin* doctrine applies to private owners at all.

When the owner deferred to the judgment of a contractor as to which of the authorized methods he would use for cleaning and painting of a structural steel bridge, a claim for additional costs because the chosen method of sandblasting

---

[83] Lattea v. City of Akron, 458 N.E.2d 868 (Ohio App. 1982).

[84] *See Dugan & Meyers*, 864 N.E.2d at 73; Trucco Constr. Co., Inc. v. City of Columbus, No. 05AP-1134, 2006 WL 3825262 (Ohio App. Dec. 29, 2006); Central Ohio Joint Vocational Sch. Dist. Bd. of Educ. v. Peterson Constr. Co., 716 N.E.2d 1210 (Ohio App. 1998).

[85] S&M Constructors, Inc. v. City of Columbus, 434 N.E.2d 1349, 1352 (Ohio 1982) (requiring clear and unambiguous language for disclaiming implied warranty such as "are not warranted" and "agrees that he will make no claim").

[86] *Central Ohio Joint Vocational Sch. Dist. Bd. of Educ.*, 716 N.E.2d at 1216 (holding that the "obviously flawed" exception to the *Spearin* doctrine did not apply when an organic soil problem was not obvious—"an expert in soil excavation, did not immediately recognize the organic soil problem").

[87] Cook v. Oklahoma Bd. of Pub. Affairs, 736 P.2d 140, 147 (Okla. 1987) (finding that *Spearin* doctrine did not apply to a project where the owner failed to disclose that there were wet conditions, when the project entailed the renovation of fish ponds—which are obviously wet—and bidders were advised to investigate and determine the site soil conditions).

[88] Country Mut. Ins. v. Gyllenberg Constr. Inc., No. CV-03-856-ST, 2004 WL 1490326, at *9 (D. Or. July 2, 2004).

was enjoined because of damage to neighboring properties is not supported by the *Spearin* doctrine.[89]

### [23]  Pennsylvania

The genesis of the application of the *Spearin* doctrine in Pennsylvania is interesting and identifies an area that is likely ripe for appellate review on a future case. In the late 1990s it was clear that the Pennsylvania state courts had not expressly adopted the *Spearin* doctrine's implied warranty of defect-free plans and specifications.[90] Despite that clear assertion, both the U.S. District Court and the U.S. Court of Appeals authored decisions "affirming" that Pennsylvania law required the *Spearin* doctrine to apply to private projects in Pennsylvania, even though no such supporting decisions existed. The Third Circuit discussed the *Spearin* doctrine at length in a dispute between a contractor and a glass subcontractor, and ultimately decided that the expressed warranty governed the relationship.[91] The subcontract at issue specified the type of glass to be installed and listed three approved manufacturers.[92] Defendant purchased and installed the glass in conformance with the specifications.[93] The subcontract contained an express warranty that required the subcontractor to "take down all portions of the work . . . which the Architect or [Plaintiff] shall condemn as unsound, defective or improper or as in any way failing to conform to this Agreement or the Plans, Specifications or other Contract Documents, and the Subcontractor, at its own cost and expense shall replace the same with proper and satisfactory work and materials. . . ."[94] The Plaintiff demanded that the subcontractor remove and replace glass that was defective, even though it complied with the specifications.[95] The court decided that it did not need to predict how the Pennsylvania Supreme Court might apply the *Spearin* doctrine here, because the true conflict was between the express and implied warranties:

> We need not predict how the Pennsylvania Supreme Court might define the contours of the implied warranty of specification, however. Assuming arguendo, that the implied warranty of specification normally would absolve Defendant of liability for the defective glass, we are presented here with a conflict between the implied and the express warranties. We conclude that the

---

[89] C.H Savage v. Peter Kiewit Sons' Co., 437 P.2d 487 (Or. 1967).

[90] Stabler Constr. Inc. v. Commonwealth, 692 A.2d 1150, 1153 (Pa. Commw. Ct. 1997) ("The instant case does not involve or require the application of federal law. Therefore, *Spearin* is not binding on this court.").

[91] Rhone Poulench Rorer Pharm., Inc. v. Newman Glass Works, 112 F.3d 695 (3d Cir. 1997).

[92] *Rhone*, 112 F.3d at 696.

[93] *Rhone*, 112 F.3d at 696.

[94] *Rhone*, 112 F.3d at 697.

[95] *Rhone*, 112 F.3d at 696.

Pennsylvania Supreme Court would find that the express warranties must prevail.[96]

The Third Circuit found that any implied warranty of defect-free specifications of the type and manufacturer of the glass were superseded by the subcontractors express warranties against defective materials.[97] This case is a cautionary tale regarding the depth and breadth of express warranties in subcontracts. Here, the court found that the subcontract express warranty required the subcontractor to replace, at its own cost, glass that was specifically required by the subcontract, but improperly specified. The subcontractor had "virtually no discretion in carrying out its contractual obligations in light of the exacting specifications in the subcontracts."[98]

By 2009, the U.S. District Court for the Eastern District of Pennsylvania unilaterally and emphatically applied with *Spearin* doctrine's implied warranty of defect-free plans and specifications to a private owner, "under Pennsylvania law, the project owner warrants to the contractor . . . that the plans and specifications are accurate and complete, and suitable for use in construction work."[99] Despite what the *Eastern Electric* court stated, Pennsylvania courts had never, prior to this case, applied the *Spearin* doctrine across the board to all "project owners"— previously, only public owners had been held to the standard of the implied warranty.[100] In the future, the applicability of the implied warranty of defect-free plans and specifications to private construction disputes in state courts may be decided. For now, some conflicts between federal and state courts exist.

Interestingly, the Commonwealth Court held that "the mere identification of a product or manufacturer does not create a design specification. Where a government agency identifies a particular product or manufacturer by name, but permits substitution of 'an approved equal,' such a specification is 'performance' in nature and, as a result carries no implied warranty."[101]

### [24]   Rhode Island

Acknowledges the *Spearin* doctrine's implied warranty of defect-free plans and specifications on public construction projects, but allows for special disclaimers of implied warranty.[102]

---

[96] *Rhone*, 112 F.3d at 697.

[97] *Rhone*, 112 F.3d at 698.

[98] *Rhone*, 112 F.3d at 702.

[99] Eastern Elec. Corp. of New Jersey v. Shoemaker Constr. Co., 657 F. Supp. 2d 545, 549 n.3 (E.D. Pa. 2009).

[100] *See Stabler*, 692 A.2d 1150.

[101] A.G. Cullen Constr., Inc. v. State System of Higher Educ., 898 A.2d 1145, 1158 (Pa. Comm. Ct. 2006).

[102] Fondedile, S.A. v. C.E. Maguire, No. C.A. PC 83-3809, 1989 WL 1110563 (R.I. Sept. 7, 1989).

### [25] South Carolina

When a public owner includes locations and logs of test auger borings on the plans, that is considered a representation that the subsurface information revealed is accurate and fully disclosed on the plans.[103]

### [26] Utah

Like New Mexico, Utah followed California's lead, quoting with approval the California Supreme Court in *Souza & McCue Constr. Co. v. Superior Court*:

> It is a reasonable principal of law that:

> A contractor of public works who, acting reasonably, is misled by incorrect plans and specifications issued by public authorities as the basis for bids and who, as a result, submits a bid which is lower than he would have otherwise made may recover [damages] in an contract action for extra work or expenses necessitated by the conditions being other than represented.[104]

Like the *Spearin* doctrine, in Utah, general disclaimers are ineffective to qualify specific misleading information contained within plans and specifications.[105]

The Court of Appeals of Utah considered similar issues on a private construction project and determined that the specific facts prevented the implied warranty of defect-free plans and specifications from being applied to private projects.[106] In *Frontier Foundations*, boring logs were provided from "a representative area near the site" with a specific disclaimer that the logs were not part of the contract documents and "not a warrant of subsurface conditions."[107] The court found that "the construction contract, read as a whole, unambiguously provides that Layton count not rely on the boring logs as representing the soil to be encountered at the construction site and, therefore Layton is not entitled to damages incurred because of differing soil conditions."[108]

---

[103] Robert E. Lee & Co. v. Commission of Pub. Works of City of Greenville, 149 S.E.2d 55, 58 (S.C. 1966).

[104] Thorn Constr. Co., Inc. v. Utah Dept. of Transp., 598 P.2d 365, 368 (Utah 1979) (quoting Souza & Mc Cue Constr. Co. v. Superior Court, 370 P.2d 338, 339-40 (Cal. 1962)).

[105] *See* Jack B. Parson Constr. Co. v. State, 725 P.2d 614 (Utah 1986) (remanding case for determination of reasonableness of bidder's reliance on misleading information in the plans and specifications).

[106] Frontier Founds., Inc. v. Layton Constr. Co., Inc., 818 P.2d 1040 (Utah Ct. App. 1991).

[107] *Frontier Founds.*, 818 P.2d at 1042.

[108] *Frontier Founds.*, 818 P.2d at 1043.

### [27]  Virginia

In Virginia, the implied warranty of defect-free plans and specifications is limited. It was first approved in 1927 by the Virginia Supreme Court for application to private construction projects.[109] It does not protect contractors who are negligent or who make express guarantees or warranties that the specifications are sufficient or free from defects.[110] Standard contract provisions like: agreeing that the construction documents are "complete and sufficient for bidding, negotiating, costing, pricing, and construction of the Project" or the contractors "continuing duty to review and evaluate the Construction Documents" do not constitute express warranties and by agreeing to these terms the contractor is not seen as affirmatively accepting the burden of defects in the construction documents.[111]

### [E]  States Developing Their Own Implied Warranty of Defect-Free Plans and Specifications or Rejecting the *Spearin* Doctrine, at Least in Part

#### [1]  Alabama

Alabama acknowledged that an implied warranty of defect-free plans and specifications exists under certain circumstances on private projects.[112] Interestingly, *Broyles* excused architects from the same accountability that it imposed on engineers:

> Architects must have as a part of their competency a keen aesthetic sense to enable them to design structures of beauty and dignity; they must have a technical knowledge of many structural factors which lend strength and stability to their designs. The materials they recommend for use are produced by agencies beyond the control and influence of the architect. His work . . . depends . . . on production of materials by others. . . . The texture of the soil for a foundation, a factor beyond his control, must be considered. For those reasons

---

[109] *See* Southgate v. Sanford & Brooks Co., 137 S.E. 485 (Va. 1927).

[110] Greater Richmond Civic Recreation, Inc. v. A.H. Ewing's Sons, Inc., 106 S.E.2d 595 (Va. 1959) (acknowledging the application of the *Spearin* doctrine to public projects and detailing appropriate waivers of the implied warranty); Modern Cont'l South v. Fairfax Cnty. Water Auth., 72 Va. Cir. 268 (2006) (holding *Spearin* inapplicable where express contract language required the contractor to "verify all . . . details shown on the drawings" and to "notify [the engineer] of all errors, omissions, conflicts and discrepancies").

[111] Costello Constr. Co. of Md., Inc. v. City of Charlottesville, 97 F. Supp. 3d 819, 826 (W.D. Va. 2015).

[112] Broyles v. Brown Eng'g Co., 151 So. 2d 767 (Ala. 1963) (finding that a civil engineering firm provided an implied warranty because the nature of its work and its engagement justified the assumption that an implied warranty existed, and both parties agreed that the civil engineering firm warranted its design results).

and others which we will not undertake to enumerate, our courts have not held architects to a strict accountability of guaranty.[113]

The Alabama Supreme Court later expressed the limits of *Broyles*, stating that "*Broyles* was limited to the facts of that case and did not state any broad general rule."[114]

Likewise, related to a dispute on a public project, the U.S. District Court for the Southern District of Alabama refused to apply the *Spearin* doctrine, because the court believed that parties understanding that the plans would likely be modified once additional information was gathered raised a question of fact as to whether an implied warranty of defect-free plans and specifications could actually exist.[115]

### [2]  Alaska

While the issue of implied warranty of defect-free plans and specifications has been brought to the Alaskan Supreme Court, the court found that factually it was unable to apply the *Spearin* doctrine, leaving open the possibility that it "might be persuaded to apply the rule enunciated in the *Spearin* cases" under the right factual circumstances.[116]

Over time, Alaska adopted its own implied warranty of defect-free plans and specifications without explicitly relying on *Spearin*.[117]

The temporal proximity of *A.R.C. Industries* and *Northern Corp.*, warranted a closer look at *Northern Corp.*— which later was cited to support the application of the *Spearin* doctrine in Alaska. While *Northern Corp.*, cites to *Spearin* in a footnote, the disputed issue was actually not the implied warranty of defect-free plans and specifications, but the impossibility of performance and the owner's insistence of performance even after trucks and workers fell through the ice and died trying to haul the rock over the frozen lake:

> This case presented a novel question with reference to alleged damages arising out of attempts to perform a public contract by a specified method (hauling rock across a frozen lake). Most cases presenting analogous problems involve situations where the government has set forth in the contract certain specifications which proved to be impossible. Based on the government's

---

[113] *Broyles*, 151 So. 2d at 771-72.

[114] K.B. Weygand & Assocs., P.C. v. Deerwood Lake Land Co., 812 So. 2d 1165, 1168-69 (Ala. 2001).

[115] Southern Elec. Corp. v. Utilities Bd. of City of Foley, Ala., 643 F. Supp. 2d 1302 (S.D. Ala. 2009).

[116] A.R.C., Indus., Inc. v. State, 551 P.2d 951, 960 (Alaska 1976).

[117] *See* Fairbanks North Star Borough v. Kandik Constr., Inc. & Assoc., 795 P.2d 793, 797 (Alaska 1990) (relying on Northern Corp. v. Chugach Elec. Ass'n, 532 P.2d 1243, 1246 (Alaska 1974), *appeal after remand*, 562 P.2d 1053 (Alaska 1977)).

implied warranty of its specification, recovery has been allowed. Here, however, the ice haul method was determined by agreement of the parties, so that initially neither warranted the method any more than the other.[118]

The court held that once the contractor informed the owner of the impossibility of performance, and the owner insisted the contractor perform any way that the owner impliedly warranted the ice haul method as if it had unilaterally established the specification at the time the contract was executed.[119] It is a challenge to reconcile the 1976 *A.R.C. Industries* holding where the Alaska Supreme Court believed it still had not applied the *Spearin* doctrine, with the later *Fairbanks North* holding that relies on the 1974 *Northern Corp.*, case (pre-dating *A.R.C. Industries*) to argue that the implied warranty of defect-free plans and specifications is recognized in Alaska.

### [3]  Georgia

In 1928, the Georgia Supreme Court held that a contractual clause providing for an allowance if there was a change in elevation of piers was sufficient to indicate that the county did not intend to warrant that the designed piers could be built at the elevations show on the plans.[120]

The Northern District of Georgia denied summary judgment because of material factual disputes as to whether the owner had made a material misrepresentation as to the amount of rock excavation required by a project and as to whether the contractor could not have discovered the true facts through a reasonable investigation.[121] While courts in Georgia have cited to the *Spearin* doctrine in opinions, the decisions offer little guidance as to predict whether or not the *Spearin* doctrine's implied warranty of defect-free plans and specifications is recognized in Georgia.

### [4]  Indiana

Indiana has not embraced the *Spearin* doctrine's implied warranty of defect-free plans and specifications. "[T]he Spearin Doctrine, [ ] differs from the Indiana case law recognized by the trial court in *St. Paul Fire & Marine* imposing a duty on contractees to discover and disclose defects in plans or specifications."[122]

---

[118] *Northern Corp.*, 532 P.2d at 1244.

[119] *Northern Corp.*, 532 P.2d at 1246.

[120] Decatur Cnty. v. Praytor, Howton & Wood Contracting Co., 142 S.E. 73, 81-82 (Ga. 1928) (citing the *Spearin*, but not establishing an implied warranty of defect-free plans and specifications in Georgia).

[121] Robert E. McKee, Inc. v. City of Atlanta, 414 F. Supp. 957, 961 (N.D. Ga. 1976) (requiring the contractor on remand to show that the underlying factual data was inaccurate).

[122] The Blakley Corp. v. EFCO Corp., 853 N.E.2d 998, 1005, n.6 (Ind. Ct. App. 2006).

The court in *St. Paul Fire & Marine* held, "[a] contractor has a duty to discover defects in plans or specifications, that are reasonably discoverable or patent, and to warn the contractee or architect of the defects, even if the plans and specifications are supplied by the contractee."[123]

### [5]  Michigan

Michigan law is rather nuanced when it comes to the adoption of the *Spearin* doctrine. Michigan law essentially applies an implied warranty of material information pertinent to the bid. The decisions historically decided in Michigan courts in joint tortfeasor cases have held that a contractor cannot be held liable for others errors. *Spearin* has not been adopted, absent concurring opinion dicta. A footnote in unreported 2014 decision, sums up the Michigan court's position on the issue:

> Each party makes extensive reference to *US v. Spearin*, which is the seminal case recognizing a cause of action for breach of contractual warranty of specifications
>
> * * *
>
> Here, this analysis has the effect of reinforcing what is already the rule from Michigan cases . . . [contractor] cannot be held liable for the alleged design errors or omissions committed by [designers] beyond those allocated to [contractor] for its *own* active fault in building and overseeing the construction as general contractor.[124]

"Michigan law implies in every construction contract a duty to inform bidders of all material information pertinent to the bid."[125] The implied warranty cannot be avoided or waived by disclaiming the warranty or directing contractors to go visit the site.[126]

Notably, the only private owner case in Michigan incorporating the implied warranty is unreported. Therefore, it is unsettled whether Michigan's implied warranty of material information is applicable beyond public projects.

---

[123] St. Paul Fire & Marine Ins. Co. v. Pearson Constr. Co., 547 N.E.2d 853, 858 (Ind. Ct. App. 1989).

[124] Sachse Constr. & Dev. Co, LLC v. AZD Assocs., Inc., No. 11-121946-CH, 2014 WL 1351397 at *3, n.7 (Mich. Ct. App. Apr. 3, 2014) (internal quotations omitted).

[125] Performance Abatement Servs., Inc. v. Lansing Bd. of Water & Light, 168 F. Supp. 2d 720, 738 (W.D. Mich. 2001).

[126] *Id.*, *see also* Valentini v. City of Adrian, 79 N.W.2d 885 (Mich. 1956).

### [6]  New Jersey

Like Michigan, New Jersey has been resistant to adopt the *Spearin* doctrine wholesale, but New Jersey public contracting law has generally evolved to provide for some level of implied warranty:

> [W]hen the State actually makes false representations in its contract documents that are more than gratuitous and amount to positive averments of site conditions, it will remain liable to the public contractor despite a general exculpatory clause in the contract. In some cases, actual concealment of information may be considered a false factual representation. Inferential conclusions from contract documents, however, shall not be considered a false factual representation in the face of sufficiently clear and unambiguous disclaimers of liability by the State.[127]

Thus, in New Jersey it is possible to have a valid waiver of the implied warranty of defect-free plans and specifications. The court identified two questions to determine if there is in fact no warranty of defect-free plans and specification:

> (1) Is the disclaimer sufficiently specific, i.e., is it straightforward and unambiguous as applied to the contract interpretations at issue, or conversely, (2) Are the statements in the contract themselves ambiguous and not descriptive of the actual working conditions, i.e., are they not positive averments purporting actually to describe the land?[128]

Therefore, a unambiguous disclaimer may be sufficient to waive the implied warranty of defect-free plans and specifications in New Jersey.

### [7]  Tennessee

Tennessee has not yet adopted the *Spearin* doctrine's implied warranty of defect-free plans and specifications. Its courts have stated that the *Spearin* doctrine does not extend to estimated excavation quantities contained in contract, where the contract warned the bidders that they "shall rely exclusively upon their own estimates, investigation and other data which are necessary for full and complete information upon which the proposal may be based."[129] The language of the Tennessee Court of Appeals decisions indicate that it's likely that there are very few circumstances in which it would find the *Spearin* doctrine to be appropriate:

> In the case of *United States v. Spearin*, 248 U.S. 132 (1918), the Supreme Court stated the general contract rule for allocation of risk: "Where one agrees

---

[127] P.T. & L. Constr. Co., Inc. v. State of N.J., Dept. of Transp., 531 A.2d 1330, 1342 (N.J. 1987).

[128] *P.T. & L.*, 531 A.2d at 1337.

[129] Brown Bros., Inc. v. Metro. Gov't of Nashville, 877 S.W.2d 745, 745 (Tenn. Ct. App. 1993).

to do, for a fixed sum, a thing possible to be performed, he will not be excused or become entitled to additional compensation because unforeseen difficulties are encountered." *Spearin* at 136. While this general rule may appear to be one sided, the courts of many states, including Tennessee, have recognized that it is not:

> . . . contracting is a risk business. On some jobs contractors are able to make large profits. On others their losses are of the same magnitude. In those latter instances they are bound by contracts which inure to the benefit of the owners just as we believe the state as owner was bound to the express terms of a contract which in this case insured to the benefit of the contractor. *Purcell Enterprises v. State*, 631 S.W. 2d 401 (Tenn. App. 1981).[130]

### [8]  Texas

Everything is bigger in Texas, including the number of conflicting decisions related to the application of the *Spearin* doctrine's implied warranty of defect-free plans and specifications. In Texas, the *Lonergan* rule is followed for public and private construction. In *Lonergan,* a contractor was sued by an owner because a house it constructed collapsed and the contractor refused to replace it because the damage was due to defects in the plans and specifications provided by the owner.[131] The Texas Supreme Court sided with the owner, finding that when contractors bid on the contract they assumed liability:

> The trust company was willing to risk the skill of the architect and submitted the specifications to bidders for inspection and for their own determination as to whether or not they were willing to bind themselves to build the house in pursuance of an in accordance with the specifications prepared. The owner being satisfied with the specifications, the contractors were called upon to exercise their own judgment, and if they were not competent to judge for themselves, it became their duty to protect their interests by procuring such aid as was necessary to put them in possession of the facts. There is no more reason why the loan and trust company should be held responsible for the alleged defects in the specifications that it did not discover for want of skill and knowledge of the business of an architect, than there is for holding [the contractor] to be bound by their acceptance of the defective plans which they understood as well as the [owner] did, and in all probability much better. The fact that [the contractor] contracted to construct the building according to the specifications furnished implied that they understood the plans.[132]

---

[130] *Brown Bros.*, 877 S.W.2d at 747.
[131] Lonergan v. San Antonio Loan & Trust Co., 104 S.W. 1061 (Tex. 1907).
[132] *Lonergan*, 104 S.W. at 1065.

The Texas Supreme Court held that "specifications are, as a matter of law, not guaranteed by either party to the other. . . ."[133] In 2005, the Fifth Circuit for the United States Court of Appeals, decided that the *Lonergan* rule not only was still valid, some 99 years later, but it also applied to public projects.[134] The Fifth Circuit, based on a review of the Texas court decisions and other federal court cases applying Texas law, held that the *Lonergan* rule was still very much in force, essentially rejecting the *Spearin* doctrine:

> We conclude the Texas Supreme Court would require contractual language indicating an intent to shift the burden of risk to the owner in order to find an owner breached a contract by providing defective plans. The contrary rule [that failing to provide adequate or correct plans and specifications is a breach of contract in and of itself] is simply not well reasoned.[135]

"In order for an owner to breach a contract by supplying inadequate plans to a contractor, *Lonergan* and its progeny require that the contract evidence an intent to shift the burden of risk of inadequate plans to the owner."[136] Thus, a *Spearin*-style implied warranty of defect-free plans and specifications is not recognized in Texas, unless it is an expressed warranty—i.e., there is express contractual language indicating an intent to shift the burden of defects in the plans and specifications.

### [9]  Washington

Because the original implied warranty of defect-free plans and specification case in Washington predates the *Spearin* doctrine, Washington courts have not cited to *Spearin* in upholding the implied warranty of defect-free plans and specifications. Washington courts have adopted the implied warranty of defect-free plans and specifications on both private and public construction projects:

> It is a well established rule in Washington that when [ ] a contractor is required to building accordance with plans and specifications furnished by the owner, it is the owner, not the contractor, who impliedly guarantees that the plans are workable and sufficient. *Armstrong Construction Co. v. Thomson*, 390 P.2d 976 (Wash. 1964) (affirming the rule of *Ericksen v. Edmonds School Dist. No. 15*, 125 P.2d 275 (Wash. 1942), (*see E. g. Ward v. Pantages*, 131 P. 642 (Wash. 1913) (held failure of a plumbing and heating system installed by subcontractor in conformity with plans and specifications as required by the architect would not defeat right of subcontractor to mechanics lien); *Huetter v. Warehouse & Realty Co.*, 142 P. 675 (Wash. 1914) (contractor excused from

---

[133] *Lonergan*, 104 S.W. at 1066.

[134] Interstate Contracting Corp. v. City of Dallas, Texas, 407 F.3d 708 (5th Cir. 2005).

[135] *Interstate Contracting*, 407 F.3d at 720.

[136] *Interstate Contracting*, 407 F.3d at 720-21.

completing contract for large fill and viaduct, whose walls collapsed during construction state, where plans and specifications prepared by contractee city's engineer were defective); *Novelty Mill Co. v. Heinzerling*, 81 P. 742 (Wash. 1905) (contractor not liable for collapse or weakening of piers, where concrete was well tapped underwater as contract required, and where damage was caused by fault of contract in requiring that to be done); *Clark v. Fowler*, 363 P.2d 812 (Wash. 1961) (contractor not a guarantor of proper functioning of furnace installed in accordance with contractee's plans and contract); *Teufel v. Wienir*, 68 Wash.2d 31, 411 P.2d 151 (Wash. 1966) (contractor not liable for leak of curtain wall where wall was constructed in accordance with specifications which called for design improper for intended use); *Tyee Construction Co. v. Pacific Northwest Bell Telephone Co.*, 472 P.2d 411 (Wash. Ct. App. 1970) (contractor not responsible for damage to conduits for power lines resulting from operation necessary to fulfill requirements of contractee's plans).[137]

More recently the United States District Court for the Western District of Washington rejected a contractor's *Spearin* doctrine claim, when the contractor sued an engineer for professional negligence.[138] *Pacific Boring* is an important reminder that the *Spearin* doctrine invokes the ability to assert either a breach of implied warranty or breach of contract claim against the entity with whom you have privity, not a negligence claim against the designer.

### [10]   Wisconsin

The Wisconsin Supreme Court case, *Bentley v. State*,[139] was described as "strikingly similar" to *Spearin*.[140] In *Bentley*, a contractor was engaged to construct an addition to the state capitol building.[141] The contractor followed the plans and specifications yet, one of the partially completed wings failed due to defects in the plans and specifications.[142] Subsequently, the architects plans and specifications were extensively modified, adding more strength to the design and additional cost and expenses to construction.[143] The state refused to pay the contractor for the wall and the contractor sued, the court awarded the contract judgment for the full amount claimed stating:

---

[137] Weston v. New Bethel Missionary Baptist Church, 598 P.2d 411, 415 (Wash. Ct. App. 1978).

[138] Pacific Boring, Inc. v. Staheli Trenchless Consultants, Inc., C14-187RSM, 2015 WL 5794260 (W.D. Wash. Oct. 5, 2015).

[139] 41 N.W. 338 (Wis. 1889).

[140] *Spearin 1916*, 51 Ct. Cl. at 172.

[141] *Bentley*, 41 N.W. at 339.

[142] *Bentley*, 41 N.W. at 341.

[143] *Bentley*, 41 N.W. at 343.

Under the contract it is very manifest that, had the plaintiffs departed from such plans and specifications and refused to follow the directions of the architect, there could have been no recovery or the building of the south wing, even had they in the first instance built it as they were finally directed by the architect to do. On the contrary, they could only recover by furnishing materials and doing the work according to such plans, specifications, and directions as they allege they did.[144]

In the years that passed since *Bentley* and *Spearin*, the Wisconsin Supreme Court has evolved and adopted an interesting position on the implied warranty of defect-free plans and specifications. Now, even if the plans and specifications are admittedly defective, if the work anticipated under the defective specifications was proposed as unit cost work, the contractor is held to that unit cost regardless of the additional work caused by the defective specification.[145] The City of Wausau developed plans and specifications for the construction of a garage and storage building near a river.[146] The construction site had previously been a slough of the river and filled in by the City, the contractor did not know this, but the city's director of public works did.[147] The city and its architect dug test holes for the footing design, and ultimately the bottom of the footings was designed to be at 1157 feet above sea level.[148] The contractor was required to include a unit price per cubic yard of concrete for the footings in his bid, the contractor investigated the water table and determined that based on the elevation of the bottom of the footings, he would have to dewater only one foot, to 1156 feet elevation, to construct the footings.[149] The architect's specifications ultimately were wrong and 87% of the 70 footings had to be lowered, resulting in an additional six feet of dewatering across the entire construction site.[150] The dewatering operation was substantially more involved, complex, and costly than anticipated under the original specifications, upon which the unit price was based (10 days, with 27 well points, and one small pump, versus 3 months (24 hours a day, 7 days a week), with 71 well points, and a much larger pump).[151] The court held that the unit price provision of the concrete was enforceable regardless of the fact that the specification, upon which the unit price provision was based, was defective, thus leaving the contractor responsible for the additional dewatering scope.

---

[144] *Bentley*, 41 N.W. at 343.

[145] Thomsen-Abbot Constr. Co. v. City of Wausau, 100 N.W.2d 921 (Wis. 1960).

[146] *Thomsen-Abbot*, 100 N.W.2d at 922.

[147] *Thomsen-Abbot*, 100 N.W.2d at 922.

[148] *Thomsen-Abbot*, 100 N.W.2d at 922.

[149] *Thomsen-Abbot*, 100 N.W.2d at 924.

[150] *Thomsen-Abbot*, 100 N.W.2d at 924.

[151] *Thomsen-Abbot*, 100 N.W.2d at 924.

## [F]  States That Have Not Explicitly Adopted the *Spearin* Doctrine or an Implied Warranty of Plans and Specifications More Generally

### [1]  Connecticut

Without fully acknowledging whether or not the *Spearin* doctrine has been adopted in Connecticut for public projects, the Connecticut Court of Appeals found that a waiver stating that the subcontractor agrees "not to assess any delay damages or claims against the [contractor] unless the Owner accepts responsibility, and payment" was sufficient to supersede any implied warranty of defect-free plans and specifications (if it exists in Connecticut).[152]

### [2]  Delaware

Delaware courts have not addressed the application of the *Spearin* doctrine.

### [3]  Hawaii

The Hawaii Supreme Court cites to the *Spearin* doctrine, and over simplifies the *Spearin* holding to be a simple case of "withholding of a material fact, a misrepresentation which misled."[153] In *Lord*, a contractor was hired to build a wharf, which required 330 piles be driven into the ocean floor. The plans and specifications contained boring log data and submarine contours, and the following note, "although [the drawings] indicate approximately the conditions that are likely to be found, intending bidders must examine the site of the work, and should satisfy themselves as to the depths to which the piles will have to be driven."[154] 155 *Lord* never reaches the fundamental *Spearin* doctrine issue of the implied warranty of defect-free plans and specifications, because the contractor in *Lord* was required to design the depth of the piles, the depth of the piles was not mandated by the owner's plans and specifications. There are no modern cases analyzing the applicability of the *Spearin* doctrine's implied warranty of plans and specifications in Hawaii.

### [4]  Idaho

Idaho courts have not cited to the *Spearin* doctrine, nor decided whether an implied warranty of defect-free plans and specification exists when between an owner and a contractor. Idaho courts have concluded, however, that "a general

---

[152] Suntech of Connecticut, Inc. v. Lawrence Brunoli, Inc., 72 A.2d 1113, 1119 (Conn. App. Ct. 2013).

[153] Lord v. Territory, 27 Haw. 792, 809 (1924).

[154] *Lord*, 27 Haw. at 798.

contractor does not impliedly warrant to a subcontractor the sufficiency of the plans and specifications provided by the owner."[155]

### [5]  Iowa

While the Iowa Supreme Court has cited to *Spearin*, it has not actually applied the *Spearin* doctrine to a case.[156]

### [6]  Kansas

Kansas state courts have not explicitly decided whether or not the *Spearin* doctrine is recognized under Kansas law.[157]

### [7]  New Hampshire

Neither the *Spearin* doctrine, nor the implied warranty of plans and specifications have been analyzed by New Hampshire courts.

### [8]  South Dakota

In a split decision, South Dakota's Supreme Court found that "unambiguous language of a contract defeats an implied warranty claim."[158] The unambiguous language of the contract required the Contractor to investigate the gravel pipe provided by the Department of Transportation for sufficiency for use on the project before bidding.[159] Two judges concurred in the result, but specifically challenged the majority's opinion that South Dakota had already embraced the implied warranty of the accuracy of plans and specifications.[160] Justice Henderson, concurring in the result stated, "When this Court has decided cases in the past pertaining to this type of action, we never alluded to—nor cited—nor adopted *United States v. Spearin*, 248 U.S. 132, 39 S.Ct. 59, 63 L.Ed. 166 (1918). We did not sanction *Spearin* as authority."[161]

---

[155] Gillingham Constr., Inc. v. Newby-Wiggins Constr., Inc., 42 P.3d 680 (Idaho 2002).

[156] *See generally* Midwest Dredging Co. v. McAninch Corp., 424 N.W.2d 216 (Iowa 1988); Employers Mut. Cas. Co. v. Collins & Aikman Floor Coverings, Inc., No. 4:02-CV-30467, 2004 WL 840561 (S.D. Iowa Feb. 13, 2004).

[157] *See generally* Roof-Tech Int'l, Inc. v. State, 57 P.3d 538 (Kan. Ct. App. 2002).

[158] Mooney's Inc. v. South Dakota Dept. of Transp., 482 N.W.2d 43, 46 (S.D. 1992).

[159] *Mooney's*, 482 N.W.2d at 46.

[160] *Mooney's*, 482 N.W.2d at 47.

[161] *Mooney's*, 482 N.W.2d at 47.

## [9]  Vermont

No Vermont courts have cited to *Spearin* as authority.

## [10]  West Virginia

While technically, West Virginia courts have not addressed whether or not the *Spearin* doctrine applies to construction contracts, they have generally opined on the implied warranty of defect-free plans and specifications. For public construction projects in West Virginia, "a contractor may pursue a claim for the breach of an implied warranty of plans and specifications in the absence of privity" directly against a designer.[162] The court held:

> Due to the special relationship that exists between a design professional and a contractor . . . we believe a similar conclusion is warranted in the case of an implied warranty of plans and specifications. While, in a technical sense, the plans and specifications are prepared for the owner of a project, a design professional nonetheless knows that they will be relied upon by contractors vying for the project, and ultimately will be further relied upon by the contractor who is hired to perform the actual work. Furthermore, errors and inadequacies in the specifications will foreseeably work to the financial detriment of the contractor. Consequently, an innocent contractor should be protected by a warranty, and design professionals thereby held accountable for their work.[163]

Because *Eastern Steel* rejected the concept that claims for breach of implied warranty of plans and specifications sound in contract, it also shortened the statute of limitations for those implied warranty claims.[164] Thus, claims for breach of the implied warranty of plans and specifications are subject to a shorter, two-year statute of limitations in West Virginia.[165] West Virginia treats implied warranty of defect-free plans and specifications very differently than any other state.

## [11]  Wyoming

Wyoming courts have not addressed the *Spearin* doctrine.

---

[162] Eastern Steel Constructors, Inc. v. City of Salem, 549 S.E.2d 266, 277 (W. Va. 2001) (noting special duties owed to contactor hired by the same owner that hired the engineer and holding that the breach of implied warranty of plans and specifications is a tort claim in West Virginia).

[163] *Eastern Steel*, 549 S.E.2d at 276.

[164] Hensel Phelps Constr. Co. v. Davis & Burton Contractors, Inc., No. 3:11-1020, 2013 WL 623071, at *3 (S.D. W. Va. Feb. 19, 2013).

[165] *Hensel Phelps*, 2013 WL 623071, at *3.

## § 3.02  CONCLUSION

The *Spearin* doctrine has stood the test of time. A review of its application on a state-by-state basis reveals that some states have embraced the implied warranty of defect-free plans and specifications with open arms, while other have flat-out rejected it. Others have crafted unique waiver provisions and carved out exceptions. Some states have even codified the implied warranty and expanded it to non-construction projects. The common thread throughout the states, is that the *Spearin* doctrine and its implied warranty of defect-free plans and specifications will continue to be relevant for the next 100 years.

# CHAPTER 4

# A CRYSTAL BALL—EARLY WARNING SIGNS OF CONSTRUCTION CLAIMS & DISPUTES[1]

James G. Zack, Jr., CCM, CFCC, FAACE, FRICS, FFA, PMP

---

[1] This Chapter is adapted from a Research Perspective issued by the Navigant Construction Forum™ in June 2015 under the same title. Navigant Consulting, Inc. established the Navigant Construction Forum™ in September 2010. The mission of the Navigant Construction Forum™ is to be the industry's resource for thought leadership and best practices on avoidance and resolution of construction project disputes globally.

[4] Changes in Major Subcontractors

[5] Inability to Ramp Up Planned/Needed Craft Levels

[6] D/B or EPC Contractor "Going to Field Too Early"

[B] Early Warning Signs for Contractors

[1] At Pre-Construction Meeting, the Owner Announces "There Will Be No Change Orders on this Project"

[2] Multiple Prime Contractors on Site

[3] Lack of Site Access, Property, Easements, or Rights of Way

[4] Lack of Necessary Permits

[5] Unanticipated Work Hour Restrictions or Limits on Work Areas

§ 4.04 Early Warning Signs—Construction Phase

[A] Early Warning Signs for Owners—Scheduling Issues

[1] Contractors Not Submitting Monthly Schedule Updates

[2] Key Milestone Dates Missed but Project Completion Still on Time

[3] Schedule Updates That Focus Primarily on Owner Caused Delays and Impacts

[4] Need to Rebaseline the Schedule

[5] Constant Resequencing of Work

[6] Continual Schedule Slippage and Float Consumption

[B] Early Warning Signs for Owners—Change Issues

[1] Excessive Number of Notices of Change and/or Delay

[2] Change Orders Do Not Address Time and Impact Costs or the Contractor Refuses to Sign Change Orders and Will Perform Changed Work Only on a Time and Material Basis

[3] Contractor Working on T&M Changes Does Not Submit Daily T&M Records

[4] Excessively High Change Order Cost Proposals and/or Lump Sum Cost Proposals with No Supporting Documentation

[C] Early Warning Signs for Owners—Project Management Issues

[1] Excessive and Frivolous Requests for Information

[2] Massive Letter Writing Campaign or Change in Style of Contractor's Project Correspondence

[3] Change in Character and Content of Progress Meetings and Meeting Minutes

[4] Inflated Payment Applications

[5] Complaints from Subcontractors and Suppliers Concerning Slow or Late Payments

[6] Attorney or Claim Consultant Attending Project Meetings

[D] Early Warning Signs for Owners—Field Issues
[1] Late Delivery of Materials & Equipment
[2] Lower Than Expected Manpower Levels or Contractor Ramps Down Manpower Prior to the End of the Project
[3] Turnover in Contractor Project Management Staff
[4] Decline in Labor Productivity
[5] Excessive Quality Disputes

[E] Early Warning Signs for Contractors—Scheduling Issues
[1] Requests for Recovery Schedules
[2] No Responses to Notices of Delay
[3] Multiple Suspension of Work Directives

[F] Late or Incomplete Delivery of Owner Furnished, Contractor Installed Items

[G] Early Warning Signs for Contractors—Change Issues
[1] Excessive Number of Changes
[2] Owner Refusal Negotiate Time or Impact Costs with Change Orders
[3] Disagreements over "Scope of Work" Items and/or Contract Interpretation Disputes

[H] Early Warning Signs for Contractors—Project Management Issues
[1] Turn Over in Owner Project Management Staff
[2] Payment Problems
[3] Change in Style of Owner's Project Correspondence
[4] Delayed Submittal Reviews and Responses
[5] Owners Correcting Design Deficiencies Through the RFI Process
[6] Design Professional Advises "Coordination of Details Will Be Done Through the Shop Drawing Process"
[7] Exclusion of Design Professional from Project Meetings
[8] Attorney or Claim Consultant Attending Project Meetings
[9] Contractor Told Not to "Put Things in Writing"
[10] Owner Advises "We'll Take Care of This at the End of the Job"
[11] Negative Cost Trends
[12] Lack of Reasonable Evidence Concerning Financial Arrangements
[13] Owner Unreasonably Withholding Issuance of the Certificate of Substantial Completion
[14] Receipt of Cure Notice or Default Notice from Owner

## § 4.01 INTRODUCTION

Construction projects over the past few decades have become increasingly complex. As a result, disputes[2] have grown in direct relation to the size and complexity of projects. One recent study reported that the value of the average dispute in the United States is approximately $34.3 million.[3] A slightly older survey of claims and disputes determined that, in the 2009–2011 timeframe, there were 65 international contract arbitrations in which at least US$1 billion was in controversy.[4] The amounts in controversy ranged from US$1 billion to US$20 billion. The total value of these 65 disputes was US$174.8 billion with the median value being US$2.73 billion.[5] These claims and disputes did not appear out of nowhere. Experience indicates that when a dispute occurs, there is a history of events, decisions, lack of decisions, etc. that can be traced back from a few weeks to several years. These are "early warning signs" of claims and disputes and are all too frequently only recognized in hindsight after the project has devolved into disputes and costly arbitration or litigation. One key to delivering a dispute-free project is the early identification of potential claims and disputes by being alert to these early warning signs and taking action in response to them.

Experience shows that the parties to a contract are often in a dispute long before they realize it. Before owners and contractors can deal with a dispute, both must see into the future and recognize that one is in the offing. This chapter identifies and dsicusses numerous "early warning signs" of potential disputes based on the collective observations of numerous construction claims consultants. These early warning signs are organized into typical project phases, and recommended claims and dispute avoidance actions are recommended for each. The keys to successful dispute avoidance and resolution are (1) to recognize a potential dispute as it starts and (2) to take appropriate action to resolve whatever the issue is. Waiting, in the hope that the problem or dispute will resolve itself rarely, if ever, succeeds.

---

[2] For the purposes of this chapter, the term "claim" is defined as a request for additional time or money or some other modification to the contract which is in the hands of the owner and contractor representatives and is still in some form of negotiations. The term "disputes," for the purposes of this chapter, refers to a claim which has *not* been resolved via negotiations and has been removed to some form of legal proceedings such as mediation, arbitration, or litigation.

[3] PwC, *Resolving Capital Project Disputes: Adopting a Business Case Approach*, September 2014.

[4] Michael D. Goldhaber, *2011 Arbitration Scorecard*, americanlawyer.com/focuseurope, Summer 2011.

[5] The "amount in controversy" represented the sum of both the claims and the counterclaims.

## § 4.02  EARLY WARNING SIGNS—BID & PROPOSAL PHASE

It has been the author's experience that some early warning signs of claims and disputes are apparent as early as the bidding or proposal (for a design/build ["D/B"] or engineer-procure-construction ["EPC"] contract) phase of a project. All too often, owners and bidders overlook or ignore these warning signs as they are focused exclusively on awarding the contract or on winning the next project. Such early warning signs during this very early phase of the project are outlined in more detail in the following section.

### [A]  Early Warning Signs for Owners

#### [1]  First Time Experience with the Project Delivery Method

If the owner has decided to employ a new project delivery method, the chances of claims and disputes increase. Experience shows, and research by the Construction Industry Institute confirms, that claims and disputes are likely to increase significantly when an owner decides to use a new or different project delivery method for the first time.[6] New project delivery methods require owner representatives to change their thinking, their work processes and procedures, etc. For example, if the owner typically contracts for projects using the design-bid-build ("DBB") process and for this new project decides to deliver the project using the D/B or EPC process, the owner's staff has a huge learning curve to overcome. Such shifts in project delivery methods often lead to claims and disputes.

- **Recommended Claims and Dispute Avoidance Actions:** In such situations, the owner should invest heavily in educating and training the owner's staff on the new project delivery method. The owner may also want to hire a few key personnel who are experienced in the chosen project delivery method. In the alternative, the owner may want to retain the services of a consulting construction management firm that has experience with D/B or EPC. Employing either, or both, of these recommendations may very well reduce impact damage and delay claims resulting from owner actions or inactions.

#### [2]  Lack of Biddability and Constructability Review

Design professionals are typically experienced with preparing plans, specifications, and other related technical documents. However, design professionals are not constructors and may have limited experience being in the field while a

---

[6] *Special Publication 23-3—Disputes Potential Index*, Disputes Prevention and Resolution Team, Construction Industry Institute, The University of Texas at Austin, February 1995.

project is built. Furthermore, design professionals often have no experience bidding hard dollar work or preparing a proposal in response to an invitation to bid for an EPC project. Additionally, design professionals frequently find themselves in an unenviable position. They are required to perform a quality control check on documents they themselves prepared. Experience shows that it is very difficult to objectively review work we performed ourselves; not because we do not know our business but because, in our minds, as a reviewer we are reviewing what we think we wrote or drew which may not be what was actually written or drawn. Finally, plans and specifications are prepared for the end user (i.e., the contractor) and *not* the design professional. A contractor may review and interpret drawings and specifications differently than design professionals, thus increasing the likelihood of changes, claims, and disputes.

- **Recommended Claims and Dispute Avoidance Actions:** To reduce the level of change orders during the construction phase and to decrease the chances of claims and disputes, owners ought to have a biddability and constructability review performed on the contract documents prior to bidding or issuing an invitation to propose for an EPC project. A "biddability review" is a review of the bidding documents by a team of construction experienced and oriented individuals who had nothing to do with the design, in order to determine if there is sufficient information included in the bid package to allow a bidder to prepare and submit an intelligent bid. A "constructability review" is performed by a similar team of construction-oriented individuals to determine if there is enough clear, concise information in the bid documents that will allow the contractor to build the project the owner wants. In this regard, the constructability review team is looking for errors, omissions, ambiguous requirements, conflicts, and impossible or impracticable requirements. These two reviews should, if implemented with the proper team(s), go a long way toward decreasing the need for changes during construction and mitigate the potential for constructive change claims and disputes.

## [3]  Known Internal or External Constraints Not Identified in Contract Documents

Design professionals generally know a great deal about architecture or engineering but often know little about the details concerning operating facilities. It is not uncommon that when construction is being performed in an operating facility there are operational needs that must be met but which a contractor is unaware because the constraints are **not** included in the bidding documents. The author was once involved in a hospital expansion project that involved constructing a mirror image mid-rise building immediately adjacent to the existing facility. The drawings called for sky bridges from the second through fifth floors. Once the contractor erected the steel and decks were installed on the new building, the contractor prepared to install the sky bridges. At that point, the owner's representative advised, for the very first time, that work on the sky bridges could only be performed between midnight and 6:00 AM so as not to endanger surgical procedures through potential vibrations to the existing building. While the explanation and reasoning made perfect sense to everyone, there was no mention of this requirement in the contract documents. As a result, the contractor had no budget for the additional night work labor cost, the added work lighting, etc.

- **Recommended Claims and Dispute Avoidance Actions:** Owners need to think through and identify all potential project constraints such as work hour restrictions or requirements; operational constraints such as the contractor may take only one clarifier off line at a time and must return each clarifier to full service before taking the next unit off line; site access restrictions; construction sequences such as Building 1 must be completed within 270 days after issuance of Notice to Proceed ("NTP"), Building 2 must be completed within 360 days; etc. In the event the design professional is contracted to design a project expanding or modifying an existing operating facility and the owner does **not** provide a list of constraints, the design professional needs to meet with the owner's staff to learn about constraints that may impact construction and include these constraints clearly in the contract documents. Such action helps avoid delay and impact claims from arising during the performance of the work when the constraints are finally identified to the contractor.

## [4]  Lack of Operability Review

If the project involves an operating facility (either new, an expansion, or a modification), project owners should have an operability review performed on the bidding documents prior to bidding. Similar to the previous reviews discussed, an "operability review" is a review of the bidding documents by a group of senior, experienced operators to ascertain that the facility design incorporates everything needed to successfully operate the constructed facility. As mentioned earlier, design professionals are **not** operators and thus are at a distinct disadvantage when trying to incorporate operational needs into the project during the design process. The failure to perform such a review is likely to lead to numerous end-of-the-job change orders once the operating staff starts to take possession of the project.

- **Recommended Claims and Dispute Avoidance Actions:** Owners of operating facilities should assign one or two senior operators to the design review team in order to make certain that the project design team incorporates all operating and maintenance needs of the project. This action should help avoid late change orders which are all too common toward the end of construction when the operators start commissioning the project and transfer of care, custody and control of the work process is underway. End of the job change orders are inordinately expensive as they almost always involve delay which is exacerbated by the fact that craft labor has been demobilized by the site and must be remobilized to perform such changes. This review is intended to avoid these changes.

### [5]  Rushed Design

Public works owners often operate under schedules driven by fiscal year constraints, an annual goal of bidding and awarding "x" number of projects per year, and other artificial requirements to "put the project out for bid no later than June 30th." Such scheduled bid dates often result in a rushed design. Private owners often push their design professionals to complete design faster in order to convert construction financing to permanent financing; to complete the project design and begin manufacturing sooner in order to meet a time-to-market deadline; to avoid inflationary costs; etc. Experience teaches that rushed design frequently leads to more change orders as overlooked details during design come to light during construction. Further, rushed design often sacrifices appropriate time allotted for quality control and quality assurance reviews, leaving the design incomplete or full of flaws. This in turn may lead to delay and attendant impacts.

- **Recommended Claims and Dispute Avoidance Actions:** If the project owner is faced with internal or external time constraints (i.e., court ordered deadlines; contractual timeframes; time to market considerations; etc.), the owner may want to consider alternative project delivery methodologies in order to speed up the design and construction process. If the owner is **unable** to extend the program schedule, then the owner should at least alert bidders to the shortened timeframe to help them prepare and submit realistic bids. If internal and external constraints are not project drivers, when an owner reaches a decision to construct a new project, the owner's should consult with designers and experienced construction-oriented professionals to determine the reasonable amount of time needed to properly design and construct the project. Planning for the project should include the information obtained from this consultation **plus** a contingency. If necessary, the owner should extend the overall project or program plan for design completion, bidding, contract award, and project completion. Owners need to remember the old adage that, "No one ever remembers whether the project was bid on time, but everyone always remembers whether it was completed on time!"

### [6]   Poor Estimate During Bid Process

Owners should review the cost estimate prepared by the design professionals to determine that it is complete, thorough, realistic, and takes into account all
known factors concerning the project and its surrounding circumstances. Design
professionals undoubtedly do their best to prepare good estimates for bidding purposes. However, as noted previously, they may not have construction experience
and tend to look at drawings and specifications differently than potential bidders.
Initially, this type of situation is likely to lead to bids coming in higher than the
approved budget. Should this happen, the owner may have to revise the approved
budget by reallocating project contingency funds and/or management reserve
funds. If this action is taken, the funds initially planned for handling changes during the work may well be exhausted before construction even commences. The
alternative to this would be for the owner to reject all bids, have the project rede-
signed, and then rebid the work. This, of course, results in additional design and
bidding costs as well as delay to the entire project.

- **Recommended Claims and Dispute Avoidance Actions:** If the owner
  does **not** have experienced internal resources to review the design professional's project cost estimate, the owner would be well advised to
  retain such service either from a construction management firm or an
  estimating consultant. While this action will add to the project costs
  somewhat, it may more than repay the owner by helping set a realistic
  estimate of the work prior to bidding.

### [7]   Bidders Requesting for Project Duration Extension

If, during the bidding period, potential bidders complain that the time for
performing the work is too short and ask that it be extended, owners need to pay
close attention. Such situations arise generally when the owner has **not** performed any pre-bid scheduling, or when the project's schedule is driven by some
outside force (i.e., a court order, time to market concerns, commercial agreements, etc.). In the latter event, there may be nothing the owner can do to revise
the time of performance duration. However, in the former event, the owner may
want to take appropriate action to prevent potential delay claims from arising during the performance of the work. Owners should realize that if contractors believe
the time of performance is unreasonable, they will (1) prepare higher bids based
on overtime work, added labor, and/or added construction equipment and/or (2)
be on constant look out for potential owner-caused delays, or delays caused by
situations for which is owner is contractually liable (i.e., differing site conditions). Some years back, the author was involved in a project to upgrade a large
wastewater treatment facility. Bidders requested that the project duration time be
extended during the bidding period. The owner did **not** do so. The contractor who
ultimately won the project mobilized to the site and prepared and submitted a

baseline schedule. The schedule showed the contractor initiating underground work at a specific location of the plant site. When excavation commenced, the contractor encountered uncharted utilities and had to stop work and demobilize from that area of the site to another area. Much to the owner's surprise, the contractor again encountered uncharted utilities and had to remobilize to yet another area where the contractor, again, encountered uncharted utilities. By the time the time extensions for these three differing site condition claims were resolved, the time of performance was substantially extended—even beyond what bidders had initially requested. In hindsight, it would have been less expensive to extend the project duration by bid addendum than it was to negotiate the three claim settlements.

- **Recommended Claims and Dispute Avoidance Actions:** Owners should prepare, or have prepared, a pre-bid schedule that allows the owner and design professional to establish a reasonable time of performance for the work about to be bid. Experience shows that design professionals typically establish the project duration without such pre-bid scheduling because this work is **not** typically included in their scope of work or their planned cost. If the owner is **not** experienced with construction of such projects and does **not** have experienced in-house staff to prepare such a schedule, the owner may want to engage the services of a construction management or a scheduling firm to do this work.

### [8]  Ineffective Project Controls

Owners about to begin construction of a capital improvement project need to assess the capabilities of their work processes and in-house staff to determine whether they have a robust internal project control system as well as the staff necessary to run the system. In the context of this chapter, a "project control system" includes scheduling, schedule monitoring, and the ability to perform and/or analyze schedule delay analyses; cost estimating including the capability to negotiate change order costs and evaluate the proposed cost savings of value engineering proposals; cost management including the tools and ability to assess the contractor's proposed schedule of values as well as monitor ongoing construction in order to properly assess the contractor's payment requests or draw requests; cost trending including earned value management if the contract requires costs be monitored in that manner; and the ability to perform manhour analysis in order to perform impact analysis and assess loss of productivity and efficiency claims. The failure to have an effective project controls system and sufficient experienced personnel to run the system is likely to lead to claims or disputes concerning delay, constructive acceleration, and impact damages.

- **Recommended Claims and Dispute Avoidance Actions:** If the owner's self-assessment indicates that the owner does **not** have an adequate project controls system in place and/or does **not** have experienced staff to manage such a system, then the owner needs to either hire staff to put a system in place and manage it or retain the services of a construction management firm to prepare, implement, and operate such a system.

### [9]  Inadequate Change Management Procedure

As the ancient Greek philosopher, Heraclitus said, "There is nothing permanent except change."[7] This statement still holds true today, especially during the construction of a capital project. Owners often decry change orders on a project as something bad and some owners even start new projects by informing their contractor that "There will be no change orders on this job!" Owners with this attitude miss the point. The Changes clause of a contract is for the benefit of the owner, **not** the contractor. The Changes clause allows the owner to change his or her mind, to make changes to the work in progress, to modify the project to fit the owner's changing needs, etc. Change is inevitable. As a result, the owner prior to beginning a new project needs to review his or her change management system internally as well as in the contract documents. The change management procedure must provide for timely notices of change; timely submittal of change order submittals; in-depth review of such proposals including both time and cost; etc. Further, the owner needs to examine the experience and capabilities of his or her project team to see that the team can properly operate the change management system. The failure to implement such a system will likely result in the owner overpaying for needed changes or facing claims and disputes over the time and cost of changes on the project.

- **Recommended Claims and Dispute Avoidance Actions:** Should the owner's self-evaluation lead to the conclusion that the owner's change management procedure is inadequate and/or the owner's staff lacks the experience and capability to implement a good change management system, the owner should consider hiring additional experienced staff or retain the services of a construction management firm to create, implement, and staff a good change management system. Again, as with some of the previous recommendations, the cost of this recommendation may pale in comparison to the cost of a poorly managed change management procedure.

---

[7] Heraclitus, On Nature, 6th Century BCE.

### [10] Bid Amount Substantially Below All Other Bids

Provided that the project is well designed, the time of performance is reasonable, and biddability and constructability reviews have been performed, most projects should have a fairly tight grouping of bids. When bids are opened and the apparent low bidder is substantially below the other bidders, chances are there is something wrong with the bid. All too many owners believe they should snatch up the bid as soon as possible and enjoy the money saved due to the low bid. This approach ignores the fact that if they award the contract on the basis of the very low bid, they are buying into a set of unknown problems starting the day the contract is awarded and NTP issued. The contractor in this situation will move onto the project looking for changes, claims, and potential disputes.

- **Recommended Claims and Dispute Avoidance Actions:** If such a situation arises, it is recommended that the owner follow a procedure similar to that employed by the federal government, described below:

  > After the opening of bids, contracting officers shall examine all bids for mistakes. In cases of apparent mistakes and in cases where the contracting officer has reason to believe that a mistake may have been made, the contracting officer shall request from the bidder a verification of the bid, calling attention to the suspected mistake... To assure that the bidder will be put on notice of a mistake suspected by the contracting officer, the bidder should be advised as appropriate -That its bid is so much lower than the other bids or the Government's estimate as to indicate a possibility of error.[8]

If the owner follows this course of action and the low bidder verifies there are no errors in its bid, the owner will likely be protected from claims based on a "mistaken bid." If the low bidder finds a mistake, the bidder should identify it to the owner and the owner should follow State statutes, local ordinances, or internal policies concerning the handling of mistaken bids. The sum and substance of this recommendation is that owners are best served by avoiding contract awards to contractors based on mistaken bids.

## [B] Early Warning Signs for Contractors

### [1] Onerous Contract Language

When reviewing a set of bid documents, contractors should review the General and Supplemental Conditions of the contract as carefully as they examine the drawings and specifications. This review should look for inappropriate risk

---

[8] Federal Acquisition Regulations (FAR) 14.407, Mistakes in Bids.

assignment or exculpatory clauses. For example, contracts declaring that concurrent delay is inexcusable delay; force majeure clauses that exclude a large number of typical force majeure causes; No Damages for Delay clauses; Differing Site Condition clauses that provide contractors may only recover the cost of overcoming the situation, but **not** the delay related to the situation; clauses declaring that the owner owns the float in the schedule; etc.[9] Such clauses may or may not be enforceable in the jurisdiction where the project is located and thus are likely to be the cause of claims and disputes. Owners must also be mindful that disputes cannot be avoided by simply drafting and issuing a contract that attempts to shift all risk of delays and costs to the contractor. Contractors and their legal counsel will likely find some way around such contract terms. As the old saying goes, "what one man can invent another man can circumvent."[10]

- **Recommended Claims and Dispute Avoidance Actions:** If the contractor does **not** have the in-house capability to perform this sort of review, the contractor should have an experienced construction litigation attorney to perform the review. If the contract is very onerous, the contractor has two options. First, the contractor may decide **not** to bid the project on the basis that the risk of bidding may wipe out any potential profit that can be earned on the project. Or, second, if it is risky, but the contractor believes the risk is manageable, the contractor may want to add to his or her bid contingency.

## [2] Apparent Lack of Pre-Bid Scheduling

As part of the contract review during the bidding phase, the contractor's staff should review the time of performance clause. If the schedule is too short or too long, this indicates that the owner did **not** perform any pre-bid scheduling. Projects based on a schedule that is too long are likely to have increased bid costs as most contractors preparing a bid assume owners have performed pre-bid scheduling and that the time of performance is reasonable. On the other side of the coin, if the project duration is too short but the contractor assumes this time has been reasonably estimated, then the contractor will likely **not** bid the required acceleration costs necessary to complete the work on time. If the contractor does realize that the time is too short, the bids will be significantly higher than necessary.

- **Recommended Claims and Dispute Avoidance Actions:** Despite the fact that bidding construction projects is quite expensive, contractors are well advised to have a team consisting of one of their experienced project

---

[9] James G. Zack, Jr., *Trends in Construction Claims and Disputes*, Navigant Construction Forum™, Boulder, CO, December 2012.

[10] *The Illustrated London News*, April 12, 1856.

managers or superintendents and an experienced construction scheduler review the drawings and specifications and then prepare a summary plan and construction schedule. In a DBB project, the bidder has a complete set of drawings and specifications available for review. In a D/B or EPC project, the bidder is more likely to be reviewing the front end engineering documents ("FEED") or Bridging Documents. Notwithstanding, the bidder should be in a position to prepare a Class 4 or Class 5 schedule to assess whether the contract's time of performance is reasonable and achievable without extraordinary cost and efforts by the contractor.[11]

### [3]   Insufficient Disputes Clause

Another indicator of a good potential for disputes is a contract that does **not** have a well thought out Disputes clause. This type of Disputes clause typically calls for project level negotiations which, should they fail to reach resolution, takes the project participants directly to binding arbitration or litigation in a court of competent jurisdiction. A well-crafted Dispute clause should include a two-step negotiation process (with the first step being project level negotiations and the second being executive level negotiations). The clause ought to stipulate one or more alternative dispute resolution ("ADR") methods such as mediation or a Dispute Resolution Board ("DRB") **prior to** arbitration or litigation.[12] The lack of a thorough Disputes clause is an obvious early warning sign of potential disputes, as the contract does **not** provide for more than one opportunity to resolve an issue if it cannot be negotiated on the project site.

- **Recommended Claims and Dispute Avoidance Actions:** If the contractor's review shows this to be the case, there is little the contractor can do to change the situation. The contractor's project risk analysis review needs to take this into consideration when deciding whether to bid the project or not.

### [4]   Poor Definition of Scope of Work

If the contractor's review of the bidding documents shows that the project's scope of work is poorly defined, this too is an early warning sign of claims and disputes. Indicators of an inadequate scope of work may include an excessively

---

[11] See *AACE International Recommended Practice No. 27R-03, Schedule Classification System*, Revised November 12, 2010, which describes the methods for preparing a Class 4 or 5 schedule as "Top down planning using high level milestones and key project events. Semi-detailed."

[12] Adam K. Bult, David W. Halligan, Jonathan Pray and James G. Zack, Jr. *Delivering Dispute Free Projects: Part III—Alternative Dispute Resolution*, Navigant Construction Forum™, Boulder, CO, June 2014.

high number of submittals required; language in the quality control portions of specifications indicating that, " . . . work must be accomplished to the satisfaction of the engineer or the architect"; the bidding documents do **not** contain any subsurface conditions report where one typically would be required for a project of this type; the invitation to bid contains wording similar to, " . . . neither the Owner nor the Architect assumes responsibility for errors or misunderstandings resulting from the use of incomplete information"; or includes language such as, "The work includes any other items necessary to provide a complete, useable building even if not shown or specified in the bid documents." A poor definition of the project scope of work is likely to result in an abnormally high number of change orders and constructive changes claims as well as the resulting delay and disruption.

- **Recommended Claims and Dispute Avoidance Actions:** If indications such as the above are found, the bidder may consider not bidding the project. In the alternative, the bidder may prepare and submit a written list of detailed questions concerning the proposed scope of work to the owner during the bidding process and in accordance with the instructions contained in the invitation to bid. The owner is generally compelled to respond to these questions to all potential bidders and may be required to issue a bid addendum. In either event, the contractor is allowed to rely upon the owner's response, thus eliminating some potential change orders, claims, and disputes during the performance of the work.

### [5]  Defective Design

Just as owners should perform their own constructability review, so should bidders. In the process of analyzing the bidding documents for estimating and pricing purposes, the bidder's staff must stay alert for indications of defective design including errors, omissions, ambiguities, and impossible or impractical requirements. While there may be some of these items even in the most carefully prepared set of bid documents, if the bidder's review indicates numerous design deficiencies, this may be an early warning sign of major claims and disputes. Claims and disputes arising from defective design include constructive changes as well as suspension of work, delay, and impact damages.

- **Recommended Claims and Dispute Avoidance Actions:** If review of the bidding document reveals a large number of design defects, the bidder has but two choices. Either the bidder decides **not** to bid the project or the bidder prepares a written list of design deficiencies found, in the form of questions, and submits this list to the owner seeking responses prior to bidding. If the owner responds, then bidders are entitled to rely on the owner's responses. Should the owner take the position "Bid these items as you see them," then the contractor may want to reconsider his or her earlier decision and not submit a bid.

## § 4.03  EARLY WARNING SIGNS—EARLY CONSTRUCTION PHASE

At times, there are no early warning signs during the bidding period. However, once the contract is awarded and the NTP issued, early warning signs start popping up. Among them are the following.

### [A]  Early Warning Signs for Owners

#### [1]  Problems Concerning the Baseline Schedule

Typically contracts call for submittal of a project schedule within a short time after issuance of the project's NTP (i.e., 30 or 45 days). Most owners believe this is adequate time to prepare a schedule and most contractors attempt to submit their as-planned or baseline schedule within the mandated timeframe. However, some contractors play games with the baseline schedules for a variety of reasons.[13] Inadequately planned schedules, late schedule submittals, poor level of details, lack of procurement information, etc. are often found within the initial baseline schedule submittals. It is not uncommon to find that the baseline schedule is not accepted or approved by the owner for several months after issuance of the project's NTP. Should this happen, it may lead to disputes over project delays, especially for those events that occurred prior to acceptance of the baseline schedule.

- **Recommended Claims and Dispute Avoidance Actions:** In order to obtain timely submittal of a good baseline schedule, owners may modify their contract documents in the following ways: crafting and including a detailed Scheduling specification in the contract documents; tying mobilization payments to submittal and approval of the baseline schedule; requiring that the contractor's scheduling effort start at Notice of Award, **not** NTP; employing a Two-Step NTP process; etc.[14]

#### [2]  Early Need to Tap into Contingency Fund or Allowances

Typically, project owners establish contingency funds or allowances for use by the project team to cover the cost of potential changes. Some owners may also

---

[13] Amanda Amadon, Emily Federico, Steve Pitaniello and James G. Zack, Jr., *Construction Scheduling Games—Revisited & Updated*, Navigant Construction Forum™, Boulder, Colorado, 2014.

[14] *Ibid.*

set up a management reserve for each project to have funds available in the event there is a major change to the work. Experience indicates that owners typically rely on past project experience when establishing such funds (e.g., anticipated cost of change orders or delays). These funds are almost always intended to last for the duration of the project. However, on occasion, owners find themselves in a situation where the project is only partially complete but the contingency funds and allowances are nearly exhausted. This is an early warning sign of potential claims and disputes centering on future changes and their impacts.

- **Recommended Claims and Dispute Avoidance Actions:** It is recommended that the owner carefully review the remaining work to determine whether more changes will be needed. If so, then the owner needs to estimate the projected cost to complete the work, including identified changes. At this point, the owner needs to determine whether to terminate the project, complete the necessary redesign and rebid the remaining work, or continue to complete the work by change order, after adjusting the project budget and re-establishing the contingency and reserve funds. If this is done proactively, the owner may be able to restate the project budget, including the needed changes and complete the work within the revised budget and schedule.

### [3]  Bid Breakdown Excessively Front End Loaded

On hard dollar bid projects, the normal procedure is to require the contractor to submit a bid breakdown shortly after NTP. This breakdown allocates the contract value across all pay items on the project. One of the owner's challenges in dealing with a proposed bid breakdown is to determine that the proposed pay items are not unbalanced. Accepting an unbalanced bid breakdown or a cost loaded schedule and making project payments based on either, may lead to a dispute with the contractor's surety in the event the contractor is defaulted and the owner calls on the surety pursuant to the Performance Bond. It also places the owner at risk should there be changes on work that is carrying excessively high costs. An unbalanced bid breakdown is an early warning sign of claims and disputes especially over the cost of potential future change orders.

- **Recommended Claims and Dispute Avoidance Actions:** Owners and their representatives need to review proposed bid breakdowns very carefully to eliminate unbalanced pay items to the maximum extent possible. Each proposed pay item needs to be reviewed individually in order to avoid such a situation. If some items are determined to be unbalanced, the owner needs to negotiate more balanced items.

## [4]   Changes in Major Subcontractors

It is not uncommon, especially on public works projects, that bidders are required to list all or almost all subcontractors in the bid. Almost all contracts that require subcontractor listing also set forth a formal procedure for subcontractor substitutions. Such requirements are intended to prevent potential bid shopping and/or bid peddling. If, after contract award and NTP issuance, an owner finds that the contractor is requesting substitution of one or more major subcontractors, then this may be an early warning sign of claims and disputes. Experience indicates that substitutions after award frequently stem from contractor/subcontractor disputes over the subcontractor's scope of work or the terms and conditions of the subcontract. In either event, such disputes will disrupt the project and lead to disputes concerning work scope issues and change orders.

- **Recommended Claims and Dispute Avoidance Actions:** There probably are times when subcontractor substitutions are clearly warranted and entirely justified. However, owners are well advised to make certain that the subcontractor substitution procedure contained in the contract documents is well defined and thorough. In the event that such a substitution is requested, owners need to make certain that both the contractor and the owner themselves follow the contract procedure exactly.

## [5]   Inability to Ramp Up Planned/Needed Craft Levels

One key to a successful project is labor productivity. Labor productivity depends entirely upon the contractor's ability to provide the right number of qualified craft labor to the project. Many scheduling specifications require that the contractors "resource load" their baseline or as-planned schedule. Resource loading often is defined to include cost and labor by trade and craft. If the contractor's baseline schedule is labor loaded, the owner has the ability to analyze the labor needed to complete the project on time and track the labor actually on the project site. If the owner reviews a labor loaded baseline schedule and calculates what labor is needed on site over time, the owner can review certified payrolls or obtain site labor data from the contractor or the contractor's construction management staff to determine if the contractor has the planned labor on-site. If the owner determines that the contractor has **not** ramped up to the needed level of labor, this is an early warning sign of claims and disputes. Claims and disputes concerning delay and lost labor productivity are likely to result.

- **Recommended Claims and Dispute Avoidance Actions:** As soon as an owner determines that the actual labor on site has fallen below the planned level, the owner should meet with the contractor and discuss the issue and inquire how the contractor intends to rectify the situation. The owner may also want to calculate the actual labor productivity achieved and extrapolate actual labor productivity into the schedule for the remaining work to determine what project delay is likely. If this is done, then this should be brought to the contractor's attention to demonstrate the contractor's potential exposure to liquidated damages.

### [6] D/B or EPC Contractor "Going to Field Too Early"

A common issue with D/B or EPC contracts is the need to complete sufficient design work to allow the contractor to move to the field and progress the contractor's construction efforts efficiently and effectively. All too often owners fail to understand the value of the contractor waiting until there is enough approved design to allow them work effectively. When owners get impatient with waiting for the contractor to move to the field, they start complaining to the contractor about the "lack of real progress." If the contractor moves to the field at the owner's request and the owner finds that the contractor is working haphazardly and ineffectively, then this may be an early warning sign of claims and disputes. Claims of project delay, lost productivity, and attendant impact damages are likely to arise from this type of situation.

- **Recommended Claims and Dispute Avoidance Actions:** The situation is avoidable if the owner and contractor work together in accordance with the project plan and schedule. If, however, the owner convinces the contractor to move to the field earlier than planned and then observes inefficient work in the field, the owner and the contractor need to meet and discuss the situation and work out a plan to allow the contractor to proceed efficiently or, potentially, suspend the work in the field until the design effort catches up.

## [B] Early Warning Signs for Contractors

### [1] At Pre-Construction Meeting, the Owner Announces "There Will Be No Change Orders on this Project"

For the contractor, this is clearly an early warning sign of potential claims and disputes as it is an indicator that the owner has unrealistic expectations concerning design and construction and/or has **not** read their own contract. The type of claims and disputes likely to grow from this attitude include constructive changes, delays and constructive suspensions of work, disputed differing site condition claims, and constructive acceleration.

- **Recommended Claims and Dispute Avoidance Actions:** Contractors dealing with an owner with this attitude must review the contract very carefully to determine what clauses provide the right of recovery and what the required procedure is. Paying very careful attention to notice requirements is critical as is documentation of all events leading to a request for change order or filing a claim. The communications procedure on the project must also be well documented as the attitude on the part of the owner is unlikely to be swayed by verbal commitments and handshake deals in the field.

### [2] Multiple Prime Contractors on Site

Several states (approximately ten) require that all or some contracts be bid as multiple prime contracts. Under this project delivery method, the project is bid in several different packages such as civil and architectural, electrical, plumbing and heating, and ventilating and cooling. Other states allow public works owners to bid multiple prime contracts (California, for example).[15] It is also the author's experience that some state agencies and municipalities opt to bid work using multiple primes in order to "keep the work local" and some major oil, gas, and chemical project owners utilize this project delivery method to complete projects faster and, perhaps, decrease their own risk exposure. Contractors bidding on a multiple prime contract should view this delivery method as an early warning sign of potential claims and disputes. Since there is no privity of contract (contractual relationship) between the independent prime contractors when one prime contractor delays or impacts another, the only option the impacted contractor has is to file a request for change order or a claim against the project owner. Experience indicates that owners in situations such as this frequently resist issuing such change orders on the basis that "We didn't impact you, the electrical prime did!" Such refusal to deal with claims of this nature often leads to larger claims concerning lost productivity and/or constructive acceleration.

- **Recommended Claims and Dispute Avoidance Actions:** There is **not** a lot a contractor can do to insulate themselves from potential claims or disputes on multiple prime contract projects. Since the situation arises from a well-known prebid condition, the contractor's opportunity to claim unrevealed superior knowledge on the part of the owner (a classic starting point for many claims) is **not** available. The contractor's best defense is to insist that all baseline schedules and schedule updates be circulated to all multiple prime contractors and that the owner hold frequent coordination meetings with all prime contractors in an effort to identify potential problems early and come to a coordinated agreement on how to avoid such problems or mitigate them.

---

[15] Neal J. Sweeney and Peter C. Brown, *Coordination Responsibilities on Multi-Prime Projects*, Federal Publications, Inc., Washington, D.C., September 1998.

### [3]   Lack of Site Access, Property, Easements, or Rights of Way

Owners should **not** bid projects until all property, easements, and rights of way ("ROW") are acquired and all site access issues clearly resolved. Having said this, the author's experience is that owners frequently bid a project prior to resolution of site access and other property issues. This is **not** uncommon in Public Private Partnership ("P3") highway projects which are typically bid on a D/B basis prior to the final vertical and horizontal alignment being fully established. Contractors bidding on projects where property acquisition issues are **not** fully resolved are typically advised of this in the bidding documents. An early warning sign of potential claims and disputes would be if the needed property acquisitions, easements, or ROW do **not** become available in accordance with the property acquisition schedule contained in the bid document or if there is no property acquisition schedule included in bidding documents. The types of claims and disputes are likely to be delay, suspension of work, and/or constructive suspension of work and their attendant impacts.

- **Recommended Claims and Dispute Avoidance Actions:** Assuming the owner acknowledges in the bid documents that **not** all property acquisition will be completed as of the bid date, the owner should include a property acquisition schedule in the bidding documents. If one is **not** included, bidders should request such a schedule be added by addendum. If the owner does **not** provide a schedule, bidders may want to rethink their decision to bid this project. If the project is bid, awarded, and NTP issued without such a schedule at the preconstruction meeting, the contractor should demand this information and advise the owner that a baseline schedule cannot be prepared on a rational basis without this knowledge. Should the owner still refuse, the contractor should prepare the contractor's baseline schedule using the contractor's internal plan and placing the completion of each property acquisition or easement activities at logical dates in the schedule but do so as milestone dates or complete no later than dates and annotate each such schedule activity as an owner responsibility. Should the owner **not** make the property or easements available on those dates, written notice of potential delay should be filed on that date to preserve the contractor's right to file a claim at a later point in time.

### [4]   Lack of Necessary Permits

As with the property issue above, owners should **not** put projects out for bids until they have received all necessary permits the owner is obligated to obtain. Some owners, however, acting on the belief that the permits will be issued quickly and wanting work on their project to start sooner, may bid the project without the required permits. It is the author's experience that when this occurs, owners often do **not** tell the bidders on the presumption that all permits will be available prior to NTP. It is also the author's experience that frequently this is not the case. Thus, there is a potential for project delays, suspensions of work, and/or constructive acceleration. But, how can contractors learn about this during the bid phase?

- **Recommended Claims and Dispute Avoidance Actions:** As a matter of routine, bidders ought to submit a written question to the project owner prior to the prebid conference asking if all owner-furnished permits were already in hand. A follow on written question should be, "If the answer is no, when does the owner believe the permits will be issued?" If the response is "no" the permits are **not** yet issued, and the owner refuses to provide a response, or cannot tell bidder when the permits are likely to be issued, then any of these are early warning signs of potential claims and disputes. Such claims as delay, constructive suspension, constructive acceleration, and the impacts of these claims are likely. Similar to the lack of site access and property availability discussed above, the contractor would be well advised to obtain information concerning the permits from the owner and include it in the baseline schedule. In the absence of any owner-furnished information concerning permit issuance, the contractor should create a baseline schedule and include receiving the permits by dates certain. If the permits are not available by those dates, a written notice of potential delay should be provided to the owner on that day.

### [5] Unanticipated Work Hour Restrictions or Limits on Work Areas

If, after contract award and/or NTP, the owner advises the contractor of work hour restrictions or limitations on work areas that were **not** identified in the bidding documents, this is an early warning sign of potential claims and disputes. The most likely claims arising from this situation are constructive changes, delays, suspensions of work, constructive suspensions, and constructive acceleration.

- **Recommended Claims and Dispute Avoidance Actions:** As soon as these new work restrictions are identified, the contractor needs to provide written notice of potential delay. The contractor should then analyze the contractor's baseline schedule and plan and modify it accordingly to account for these new restrictions. Once this is done, the contractor should be in a position to estimate the project delay, if any, and the impact costs caused by the previously unidentified work restrictions. This analysis must be performed promptly and an appropriate change order request for additional time and/or damages be filed with the owner.

## § 4.04   EARLY WARNING SIGNS—CONSTRUCTION PHASE

Early warning signs continue as the project progresses. They are **not** limited to the early phase of construction. In fact, there are more warning signs as the project progresses but due to the pressure of other business on the project, owners and contractors frequently do **not** recognize the warnings when they first occur. For the purposes of this chapter, the author has classified and presented these early warning signs in the following four categories:

- Scheduling Issues
- Change Issues
- Project Management Issues
- Field Issues

## [A]   Early Warning Signs for Owners—Scheduling Issues

## [1]   Contractors Not Submitting Monthly Schedule Updates

Once the project baseline schedule has been approved or accepted, it is typical for the contract to require a routine schedule update on a regular basis (i.e., monthly, quarterly, or by milestone). One schedule-related early warning sign is when the contractor does **not** submit routine schedule updates despite clear requirements in the scheduling specification. This is an early warning sign of potential claims and disputes and it is likely that delay and impact damage claims will arise as a result.

- **Recommended Claims and Dispute Avoidance Actions:** This situation is avoidable if the owner adopts appropriate defenses in the scheduling specification including making schedule update submittals a pay item on the schedule of values, implementing a Pay Off the Schedule specification, stipulating liquidated damages for late schedule submittals, or crafting a clause allowing the owner to withhold payment for the failure to submit schedule updates. If any of these defenses are included in the scheduling specification, the owner needs to enforce them. If none of these defenses were included in the contract documents, then the owner needs to meet with the contractor to discuss the situation and convince the contractor to submit these updates. The theme of this meeting should be that the project will run more smoothly if the contractor submits the required updates and the owner performs a detailed analysis. The owner may also point out that it is impossible to agree with any time extension requests unless they are based on a current, updated schedule.

### [2]  Key Milestone Dates Missed but Project Completion Still on Time

When the project records show that the contractor has missed one or more milestones, or when analysis indicates that a large number of planned activity start dates have **not** been achieved on time **but** the project completion date has **not** moved, this is an early warning sign of claims and disputes. "Scheduling away delay" typically is accomplished by changing durations of remaining activities, deleting activities from the schedule, using leads and lags, using constraints, changing logic or schedule calendars, etc. The type of claims arising out of this situation will be delays, impacts, and lost productivity.

- **Recommended Claims and Dispute Avoidance Actions:** Similar to the early warning sign above, this sort of situation can be mitigated by including some or all of the following in the scheduling specification: require and review carefully a Schedule Change Report with every update; require joint update meetings with the contractor, owner, and all major subcontractors; require electronic schedule update submittals; and/ or obtain the contractor's weekly scheduling documents typically provided to trade superintendents. If none of these defenses are in the scheduling specification, the owner needs to meet with the contractor to discuss the situation and convince the contractor to submit properly updated schedules. The meeting should focus on the need for properly updated schedule submittals. The owner needs to point out that time extension requests cannot be assessed unless they are based on accurately updated schedules.

### [3]  Schedule Updates That Focus Primarily on Owner Caused Delays and Impacts

If all schedule updates focus primarily on alleged owner delays and impacts, this is obviously an early warning sign of claims and disputes, especially if this sort of update starts very early in the project. The typical way to accomplish this sort of schedule update is for the contractor to insert new "owner caused delays" in the schedule updates. The types of claims likely to be asserted sometime during the project include delays, constructive suspensions of work, impacts, and lost productivity.

- **Recommended Claims and Dispute Avoidance Actions:** One way to mitigate this type of schedule update is to include a strict written notice requirement in the Delay clause and a well thought out Time Impact Analysis ("TIA") requirement in the scheduling specification. If these are in the contract documents, then owners should enforce them. If not, the owners may want to use their construction management team to create and maintain a Ghost Schedule that more accurately reflects the real status of the project.[16]

### [4]   Need to Rebaseline the Schedule

There are occasions on a project when a schedule may need to be rebaselined. Typically, this becomes necessary when changes or delays have rendered the original project plan meaningless. This type of situation and its causation is generally obvious to both the owner and the contractor. However, if the contractor unilaterally rebaselines the contractor's schedule on several occasions, this is an early warning sign of potential claims and disputes. Claims of delay, constructive suspensions of work, and other impacts are likely to be raised as justification for rebaselining the schedule.

- **Recommended Claims and Dispute Avoidance Actions:** A classic way to mitigate this situation is to include a requirement in the schedule specification that any schedule rebaseline effort must be supported by a Schedule Rebaseline Report which justifies the need for a rebaseline and must be done in a joint review meeting with the owner, the contractor, and all major subcontractors and that unilateral rebaselined schedules will **not** be accepted by the owner. In the absence of such a contract requirement, any time a schedule rebaseline is submitted, the owner should convene a joint review meeting involving the contractor, the owner's representatives, and all major subcontractors. The owner and contractor should discuss the need for a schedule rebaseline and, if **not** justified, the owner should refuse to accept a rebaselined schedule. As noted above, the owner may also want to have the owner's representatives create and maintain a Ghost Schedule for the owner's use in the event delay claims are later filed.

### [5]   Constant Resequencing of Work

Critical Path Method ("CPM") schedules are dynamic in nature. That is, as the project proceeds, it is likely that not everything will go as planned. Some activities will start earlier or later than planned; labor productivity may not come up to the planned level; labor shortages may occur; equipment and material deliveries may be later than planned; weather or differing site condition delays may be encountered; etc. When events such as these arise, the schedule must be adjusted to accommodate such occurrences. Under circumstances such as these, resequencing of work activities may well be justified. However, if every schedule update

---

[16] Scott A. Beisler and James G. Zack, Jr., *Ghost Schedules—What, Why & What's the Risk?*, Navigant Construction Forum™, Boulder, CO, March 2015.

contains resequencing of work activities without apparent justification, then this is an early warning sign of claims and disputes. Claims arising from this sort of scheduling generally include delay, constructive suspensions of work, constructive changes, and loss of productivity.

- **Recommended Claims and Dispute Avoidance Actions:** Owners should review every schedule update carefully. Whenever resequencing of a number of activities is encountered, the owner needs to meet with the contractor and any affected subcontractors to question the need for resequencing of each activity resequenced. If the answers are logical and justified, then there would appear to be no problem accepting such resequencing. On the other hand, if there is no justification, the owner should reject the schedule update. If the contractor refuses to abandon the resequencing efforts, the owner should document this and consider the possibility of creating and maintaining a Ghost Schedule.

## [6] Continual Schedule Slippage and Float Consumption

As noted above, CPM schedules are dynamic and should always be responsive to changes in the project plans in the current schedule update. However, if the owner's update review encounters constant schedule slippage and a continual erosion of float in the schedule, this is an early warning sign of potential delay claims.

- **Recommended Claims and Dispute Avoidance Actions:** When an owner observes this happening in a schedule, rather than ignoring this trend or refusing to approve or accept the schedule update submittal (which effectively leaves the project with **no** schedule), the owner could include in the schedule specification a requirement for a TIA for every identified delay, and the owner may be justified in requesting a TIA for each schedule slippage in the update. Additionally, the schedule specification should contain a Schedule Update Narrative submittal with every update. The specification should outline the contents of this narrative report, one item of which should be an explanation of all schedule slippage including the event(s) causing the slippage (i.e., who or what caused the activity to slip, how that impacted the activity, etc.). If the specification has such a requirement, carefully review the narrative report to see if the slippage is justified. If the schedule specification has neither requirement, the owner ought to perform a joint schedule update review with the contractor and all major subcontractors to review the update, ask about schedule slippage and justification for the same, and deal with the situation at this joint meeting.

### [B]   Early Warning Signs for Owners—Change Issues

#### [1]   Excessive Number of Notices of Change and/or Delay

Virtually all construction contracts contain written notice requirements in both the Changes and the Delay clauses. The purpose of such notice requirements is to keep the owner apprised of potential problems and allow the owner to get involved in resolving such issues. Contractors submitting such written notices are complying with the terms and conditions of the contract and should **not** be faulted for doing so. On the other hand, if the contractor is constantly filing spurious or questionable notices of change and delay, this is likely an early warning sign of potential claims and disputes.

- **Recommended Claims and Dispute Avoidance Actions:** One contractual defense that may be employed is a requirement in both the Changes and the Delay clauses that requires the contractor to submit a complete change order proposal or claim submittal within a specified number of days after the notice is filed (i.e., 30 calendar days). If such a requirement is included in the contract, the clause should identify what must be included in a "complete change order proposal or claim submittal." In order to make this clause realistic, the clause should include language to the effect that if the delay event or changed work is **not** completed within this timeframe, the contractor must still file the request for change or claim within the specified time, but may note the submittal is not complete and may file an amended request within 30 calendar days after the event or work is completed. Absent such a requirement, the owner should review each notice promptly and carefully to determine whether the notice if justified or not. If it is justified, the owner should work with the contractor to craft the most cost effective solution to the issue. If it is **not** justified, the owner should respond to the notice, advising the contractor that the notice is not warranted and include detailed reasons or justifications as to why not. The owner should continue to track each identified situation carefully to determine potential liability and the eventual outcome.

#### [2]   Change Orders Do Not Address Time and Impact Costs or the Contractor Refuses to Sign Change Orders and Will Perform Changed Work Only on a Time and Material Basis

Both situations discussed here are common in construction and either one is an early warning sign of future claims and disputes. Many contractors are loathe to provide a complete change order proposal which includes all hard dollar costs, the projected time extension and delay costs, and any related impact damages. While they are willing to propose, negotiate, and settle the hard dollars costs, they either do not know how to estimate time and impact or are unwilling to take on the risk of doing so and signing a change order with no reservation of rights. This type of contractor is likely to only be willing to perform changed work under a change order with a reservation of rights or, if the owner is not willing to allow this, perform changed work on a time and material ("T&M") or cost reimbursable basis. This latter scenario is tantamount to a complete reservation of rights to hard dollar costs, delay and impact costs. Situations such as this are likely to lead to claims concerning the cost of directed changes, delay, and delay impact. Of course, this situation is exacerbated in many instances by an owner who refuses to deal with requested time extensions and/or impact damages. Owners who want to deal with hard dollar costs only open themselves up to such claims every time they take this course of action.

- **Recommended Claims and Dispute Avoidance Actions:** One preventive measure that can be included in the Changes clause is a requirement defining what must be included in all change order proposals—scope of work, hard dollar costs, time extension request, and impact costs—all of which must be justified by a complete breakdown of the requested costs and a TIA demonstrating the need for a time extension. Absent such a contractual requirement, the owner and the contractor should first negotiate the scope of the change order work in detail, to make certain both parties are preparing estimates on the same work. The owner may then prepare the owner's own cost estimate including impact damages and own TIA. Once this is completed, the owner and contractor should meet to compare estimates and TIAs. If agreement cannot be reached through reconciliation of the two estimates and TIAs, the owner should challenge the contractor to "correct" the owner's estimate on a line-by-line basis and do the same concerning the owner's TIA. If this is done, rather than the traditional method of "attacking" the contractor's estimate, the more likely it is that the owner and contractor can reach a mutual satisfactory resolution of the scope, time, and cost of a change before work proceeds in the field.

### [3]  Contractor Working on T&M Changes Does Not Submit Daily T&M Records

Should the owner decide to issue T&M change orders, the owner is at risk for all time, all costs, and all impacts as this is an open ended work order.[17] The only way the owner can exercise some degree of control over the time and cost

---

[17] While some owners attempt to limit their risk by issuing T&M changes with a Not to Exceed ("NTE") cost, this does not totally resolve the issue as contractors are *not* required to perform all the changed work for the NTE cost but, rather, they are only required to perform the changed work

of such changes is to obtain contemporaneous information on the time and cost of the change. When contractors do **not** submit daily T&M records, the owner is at increased risk. This lack of information should serve as an early warning sign of a forthcoming claim or dispute. The nature of this claim would be a claim for disputed change order costs.

- • **Recommended Claims and Dispute Avoidance Actions:** The best defensive measure against this sort of situation is to include clear language in the Changes clause of the contract requiring a contractor to submit daily T&M records for each T&M change separately, at the end of each shift of work, to the owner's representative. Such a requirement should also mandate the information that must be submitted daily (i.e., labor forces by trade for both the contractor and any subcontractor working on the T&M change, equipment, materials, etc.). Owner representatives must be trained to observe T&M work closely and compare their daily observations to the daily T&M submittals from the contractor. Should the owner representatives disagree with some portions of the daily T&M submittals, they should mark up the contractor's submittal in a different color ink and attach a record of their own observations. Such submittals, reviewed and marked up documents, and owner's records should be filed daily and used to reconcile the final cost when the T&M work is completed. If the contract does **not** contain such a requirement, then the owner should assign one or more inspectors to the T&M work with the direction to record everything concerning the T&M work from start to finish. While this may require the employment of more inspectors on-site, it will likely cost far less than not having any contemporaneous documentation of the actual cost of the T&M work.

### [4]  Excessively High Change Order Cost Proposals and/or Lump Sum Cost Proposals with No Supporting Documentation

Often times, contractors, when the opportunity presents itself, will submit one-line lump sum proposals in response to an owner's request for a change order cost proposal. When the owner receives such a proposed lump sum cost, it may significantly exceed the cost the owner anticipated and/or have no supporting documentation which would afford the owner the opportunity to analyze the proposed cost. Contractors may do this because they perceive themselves to be in the driver's seat. That is, they may believe the owner needs this change made and feel that they are the only one on site who can perform the changed work. Thus, they

---

up to the NTE cost and then "drop tools." Should the owner want to complete the changed work, the owner will be required to change the NTE cost. Thus, the owner is not really protected in this situation.

may try to coerce the owner into either accepting the proposed cost or issuing a T&M change order. If this happens, it is an early warning sign of a pending claim or dispute concerning the cost and impact of a specific change or group of changes.

- **Recommended Claims and Dispute Avoidance Actions:** The most effective tool to prevent this situation from occurring is a clear requirement in the Changes clause that the contractor must submit a breakdown of all elements of the proposed cost separately (i.e., labor, materials, equipment, subcontractor costs [broken down in the same manner], small tools and consumables, etc.). The clause ought to make clear that even though the owner intends to issue lump sum change orders, the lump sum value of the changed work will be derived from negotiations based on the individual elements of cost. If such a requirement is **not** contained in the contract, then the owner should prepare the owner's own detailed estimate as a counter proposal and challenge the contractor to show the owner's estimate is erroneous, on a line-by-line basis.

## [C] Early Warning Signs for Owners—Project Management Issues

### [1] Excessive and Frivolous Requests for Information

Requests for Information ("RFI") are a typical communication mechanism on most construction projects. An RFI is typically a question raised by a contractor and submitted to the owner and/or design professional concerning some requirement or provision of the drawings or specifications that the contractor is not clear on. However, numerous claims games have been created revolving around the use and abuse of RFIs.[18] Should the owner start to see numerous RFIs that are actually submittals; routine project correspondence; requests for substitutions; responses to notice of nonconformance; RFIs that are easily answered by reviewing the specifications and/or drawings; or RFIs asked more than once, these are early warning signs of pending claims and disputes. Claims arising from RFIs are typically constructive change claims including the attendant delay and impact costs. Having noted this, the author has observed situations where the design was not complete at the time of bidding and the owner and design professional opted to complete the design through the submittal and RFI process rather than delay awarding the contract. In the event this happens, the number of RFIs is certain to increase radically.

---

[18] Nigel Hughes, Christopher L. Nutter, Megan Wells and James G. Zack, Jr., *Impact & Control of RFIs on Construction Projects*, Navigant Construction Forum™, Boulder, CO, April 2013.

- **Recommended Claims and Dispute Avoidance Actions:** One of the more effective ways to avoid situations such as this is to incorporate a well thought out RFI clause and system in the contract documents, intentionally designed to control the RFI process.[19] If the contract does **not** have such a clause, the owner's team needs to set up a process similar to that outlined in the referenced report (i.e., strict review of all documents labeled as an RFI immediately upon receipt; rejection of those documents that are not truly RFIs; and classification and tracking of all documents submitted as an RFI by category; and tracking all justified RFIs to insure prompt response).

### [2]   Massive Letter Writing Campaign or Change in Style of Contractor's Project Correspondence

The technique is frequently referred to as "papering the job." It involves flooding the owner with a large number of letters providing notices; complaining of poor design, slow responses to notices, requests for change orders, RFIs, submittals, or time extensions; multiple complaints concerning designer or CM performance; etc. The object of this tactic is to put the owner on the defensive from the outset of the project and fill the project files with "documentation of unresolved issues." A variant of this tactic may be observed when the contractor's attorneys or claim consultants start writing such letters to the owner. When any of these situations arise, they should be taken as early warning signs of pending claims and disputes. Such claims will typically revolve around constructive changes, constructive suspensions of work, delay, and the attendant impact of such claims.

- **Recommended Claims and Dispute Avoidance Actions:** If some of the contractor's letters demonstrate entitlement to a change order as a result of an event, the owner should issue such change orders as promptly as possible to demonstrate that the owner complied with the provisions of the contract. As expensive as it sounds, the most effective way to deal with the remaining spurious or questionable correspondence is to make certain each letter is responded to promptly, objectively, and professionally. All project correspondence must be logged and tracked to document prompt responses. This course of action will create a more accurate record of what happened on the project, when, who caused each issue, etc. If necessary, the owner may need to increase the size of the project staff to achieve this result. However, this additional cost will likely be substantially less than a drawn out dispute.

---

[19] *Ibid.*, see pages 21–28 for an example.

## [3]   Change in Character and Content of Progress Meetings and Meeting Minutes

Another early warning sign of potential claims and disputes is if there is a radical change in the character or content of routine progress meetings or meeting minutes (if the contractor kept them) or in objections to draft meeting minutes (if the owner kept them). This may be an early warning sign of simmering claims and disputes—even though the contractor may **not** have provided written notice. When this occurs, it is nearly impossible to predict what sort of claims may be lurking in the background but there is a near certainty some problem(s) is causing the change of attitude.

- **Recommended Claims and Dispute Avoidance Actions:** The challenge for the owner in a situation like this is to get the contractor to open up so the owner can ascertain what the problem(s) are. If this is a Partnered Project then the owner may be able to use the partnering facilitator to learn about the unresolved issues.[20] If partnering is **not** part of the project management process, the owner may want to recommend bringing in a turnaround partnering facilitator to initiate a partnering process on the project and improve project communications.[21] If this is done, the owner should be able to determine the underlying unresolved issues. Once the issues are identified, perhaps the owner can work with the contractor to resolve the issues.

## [4]   Inflated Payment Applications

It is not uncommon on lump sum projects with a negotiated list of pay items to encounter disagreements on monthly payment applications between the owner and the contractor. Typical disagreements tend to center on the contractor's estimate of the percentage of work completed on various pay items. For example, where the contractor may estimate that Pay Item No. 13 is 55% complete, the owner's representatives may assert that it is only 52% complete. This type of dispute is more or less common and can be worked out on the site. However, when the owner starts seeing monthly payment applications or loan draws that are substantially inflated, or that include disputed pay items, this may be an early warning sign of a pending claim or dispute. This may indicate a serious cash flow problem for the contractor. If there are a number of ongoing disputes over ambiguities in the contract where the owner directed the contractor to proceed with the

---

[20] Sue Dyer, *Partner Your Project*, Pendulum Publishing, Livermore, CA, 1997. Ralph J. Stephenson, *Project Partnering for the Design and Construction Industry*, John Wiley & Sons, Inc., New York, 1996.

[21] International Partnering Institute, *Collaborative Construction—Lessons Learned for Creating a Culture of Partnership*, Livermore, CA, June 2008.

work in accordance with the owner's interpretation, this may, in part, explain the contractor's cash flow problems. The type of claim growing out of this situation is likely to be a series of constructive change claims.

- **Recommended Claims and Dispute Avoidance Actions:** If there are a number of ambiguous specification claims on the project, the owner should reexamine the previous determinations to make certain his or her earlier decisions were correct. If the owner determines some decisions were incorrect, issuance of a change order may help alleviate the cash flow problem. If this is **not** the case, owners ought to confer with their legal counsel to determine if the owner should notify the contractor's surety to get them involved in trying to resolve or mitigate the situation.

### [5] Complaints from Subcontractors and Suppliers Concerning Slow or Late Payments

Similar to the above situation, if the owner starts to receive complaints from subcontractors and/or suppliers about slow or late payments from the contractor, this too is an early warning sign of claims and disputes. Like the above, the typical claim arising from this scenario is one of constructive changes to the work.

- **Recommended Claims and Dispute Avoidance Actions:** The owner should examine the owner's payment process to see that it is not extremely slow thus exacerbating the situation. If it is, the owner needs to quickly modify the payment system appropriately. And, like the above situation, the owner should confer with the owner's legal counsel and consider notifying the contractor's surety.

### [6] Attorney or Claim Consultant Attending Project Meetings

Obviously, this is an early warning sign of pending claims and disputes. Owners probably cannot prohibit the contractors from bringing their legal counsel and/or claims consultant to progress meetings. So, the challenge for the owner is to ascertain what are the simmering claims and disputes. The type of claims arising from this situation need to be discovered and addressed as quickly as possible so as to avoid a dispute at the end of the project.

- **Recommended Claims and Dispute Avoidance Actions:** While the owner cannot prevent this action, the owner should not be intimidated. The owner should still run the progress meeting in the normal fashion, using the owner's standard meeting format. The owner should still focus the discussion on the contractor and the subcontractors are typically included in the meeting and maintain thorough meeting minutes. In the meeting, the owner should ascertain what issues are unresolved and work on a plan to resolve these issues.

## [D]   Early Warning Signs for Owners—Field Issues

### [1]   Late Delivery of Materials & Equipment

It is axiomatic that construction cannot proceed effectively or efficiently unless materials and equipment are on site as planned. This may even involve delivery to the correct working space on the site. For example, in a high rise office structure having thousands of sheets of drywall on site does not help progress the work if they are stored inside on the first floor when the crews need several hundred sheets each on the seventeenth and eighteenth floors. If material and equipment delivery is proceeding in this manner and the owner notes idle crews waiting for delivery to their work area, this is an early warning sign of potential claims and disputes. The likely type of claims growing out of this will be delay, constructive suspension of work, and/or lost productivity.

- **Recommended Claims and Dispute Avoidance Actions:** One way an owner can track this issue from the outset of the project is to require in the scheduling specification that all equipment and material procurements activities be included in the baseline schedule and coded in the Work Breakdown Structure ("WBS") accordingly. If this is done, the owner can isolate the delivery activities using the correct WBS codes and print out a delivery schedule. This delivery schedule can be used by the owner's representatives in the field to track such deliveries and deliveries should be discussed in the weekly project meetings.[22] In the absence of such a contract requirement, at each weekly update meeting, the owner should ask the contractor to list what activities will be starting over the next two- to three-week period and then inquire about the necessary material and equipment deliveries required to support this planned effort.

### [2]   Lower Than Expected Manpower Levels or Contractor Ramps Down Manpower Prior to the End of the Project

Similar to the above, the project cannot be completed on time nor the work proceed efficiently unless the contractor has the appropriate numbers and type of qualified craft labor on site when, and, as needed. If the owner observes that the anticipated manpower levels have **not** been met, or notes that the manpower on site is dropping off even though there is a large amount of work remaining to be

---

[22] *Ibid.*, Amadon, Federico, Pitaniello and Zack, *Construction Scheduling Games—Revised & Updated.*

accomplished, this is an early warning sign of potential claims and disputes. The most likely type of claim arising from this situation is one of productivity loss.

- **Recommended Claims and Dispute Avoidance Actions:** One way to track the labor required to meet the schedule is for the scheduling specification to require that the baseline schedule be manpower loaded. If this is done, the owner can extract a set of histograms by craft for the duration of the project and then observe on a weekly basis whether the contractor and each subcontractor have the required amount of labor on site to support the schedule. If not, the owner can surface this issue at the weekly project meetings to find out what is happening, why and what can be done about it. Without such a contract requirement, the owner is somewhat at a loss to create predictive histograms, but can still track ongoing productivity of key activities (i.e., activities on the schedule's critical path and any subcritical paths of 30 calendar days or less) and measure progress of these activities. Using these two metrics, the owner can adjust the durations of the remaining key activities' work to determine whether they will complete on time and achieve the contract completion date. If they will **not** meet the required date, the owner can address this issue at routine project meetings, showing the owner's calculations and address with the contractor how to remedy this situation.

### [3]   Turnover in Contractor Project Management Staff

Yet another early warning sign of potential claims and disputes is a turnover in the contractor's key project management staff during the course of construction and with **no** apparent logical reason. The owner should directly contact the contractor's executives to determine what is happening and why. There may, however, be a logical reason. For example, the contractor may have been awarded a large new contract and needs to staff it immediately while this project is past its most critical points and can be completed with another project management team.

- **Recommended Claims and Dispute Avoidance Actions:** One effective way to prevent a situation like this is to include in the contract a listing of "contractor key project management personnel" (e.g., project manager, project scheduler, project quality control manager, and others as appropriate) with the requirement that **no** "key personnel" can be removed from the project until substantial completion is achieved without advance written approval of the owner. Lacking such a contractual requirement, the owner should meet with the contractor's executives to learn why the shift in project management personnel is taking place. If the reason revolves around the current staff's lack of resolving issues, obtaining adequate labor, managing subcontractors, etc., the owner may want to engage in a discussion of how they can assist in resolving such issues.

## [4]   Decline in Labor Productivity

Again, like the two indicators above, if labor productivity has dropped off or is declining slightly month after month, this is an early warning sign of potential claims and disputes. Obviously, the type of claim likely to be generated is one of productivity loss.

- **Recommended Claims and Dispute Avoidance Actions:** If the scheduling specification included manpower loading, then baseline productivity can be calculated from this data. If the contract required the use of Earned Value, the planned and actual productivity can be calculated easily. If neither of these techniques was specified, the owner's field representatives ought to observe and make some recording of labor productivity. Such observations should be made after the "learning curve effect" has diminished. Further observations of labor productivity should take place routinely throughout the project and compared to the baseline metrics. If a drop off in labor productivity is observed, the owner should bring this to the attention of the contractor and initiate discussions on why this may be occurring and what can be done to resolve the problem.

## [5]   Excessive Quality Disputes

It is fairly typical that there will be a limited number of quality disputes on any project. All nonconformance reports should be received and reviewed by the owner in order to minimize the amount of rework on the project.[23] Contractor responses typically propose means and methods of resolving the nonconformance issue. If, however, the contractor refuses to provide a proposed fix to the nonconformance report and correct deficiencies, this is an early warning sign of pending claims and disputes. The type of claim most likely to result from this situation is one of constructive changes.

- **Recommended Claims and Dispute Avoidance Actions:** If a situation like this arises, the owner needs, in the first instance, to review the nonconformance report in contention to see if it is correct. Assuming it is correct in all respects, the owner needs to meet with the contractor's project manager (and perhaps contractor's executives) to determine the

---

[23] Jason M. Dougherty, Nigel Hughes, James G. Zack, Jr., *The Impact of Rework on Construction & Some Practical Remedies*, Navigant Construction Forum™, Boulder, CO, August 2012.

nature of the problem and find a way to get the quality dispute resolved without a claim being filed.

## [E]  Early Warning Signs for Contractors—Scheduling Issues

### [1]  Requests for Recovery Schedules

Almost all scheduling specifications provide that the owner may require submittal of a recovery schedule when a schedule update shows a projected late project completion. If, however, the contractor has filed multiple requests for time extensions that the owner has **not** yet responded to but still demands a recovery schedule, this is an early warning sign of pending claims and disputes. The type of claim arising from this situation is most likely to be one of constructive acceleration.

- **Recommended Claims and Dispute Avoidance Actions:** Should this situation arise and assuming the contractor has properly filed notices of delay and time extension requests in accordance with the terms of the contract for each delay event, then the contractor should file a notice of constructive acceleration upon receipt of the owner's request for a recovery schedule. If the owner ignores this notice or responds with a continued demand for a recovery schedule, the contractor should proceed to plan the contractor's acceleration efforts, provide the recovery plan to the owner, initiate the recovery efforts (only after the owner approves the recovery plan), and then initiate tracking of all time, costs, and impact arising from this effort.

### [2]  No Responses to Notices of Delay

Typical construction contracts require written notices of delay to be filed with the owner for every event the contractor believes **may** cause a delay and for which the contractor **may** be entitled to a time extension. The purpose of these notices is to keep the owner apprised of what is happening on the project and to give the owner the opportunity to get involved with solutions to such problems. However, some owners are loathe to deal with delay claims until the end of the project when the owner can actually see "how much time does the contractor really needs." When notices of delay are filed and **no** response is received, this is an early warning sign of potential claims. As with the above warning, the type of potential claim is likely to be a constructive acceleration.

- **Recommended Claims and Dispute Avoidance Actions:** When a situation such as this arises, the contractor needs to meet with the owner and explain the potential of a constructive acceleration claim. The contractor needs to convince the owner to deal with the notices of delay in a timely manner in order to avoid a later dispute. If this approach is ineffective, the contractor should confer with the contractor's legal counsel.

### [3]  Multiple Suspension of Work Directives

Virtually all construction contracts contain a Suspension of Work clause. This clause gives owners the right to direct a work stoppage, of all, or a portion of the work, at any time. Owners are **not** required to justify the issuance of such stop work orders but contractors are required to comply with such orders. It is the author's experience that stop work orders are **not** common on the typical project. Therefore, if the contractor encounters multiple suspension of work orders on a project, this is an early warning sign of potential claims and disputes. The type of claim would likely center on the stop work orders and the resulting project delay.

- **Recommended Claims and Dispute Avoidance Actions:** Whenever a stop work order is issued (especially if the order is to "stop all work" on the project) the contractor needs to meet with the owner to discuss how long the suspension is likely to last and whether the owner wants the contractor to remain on "hot standby" or demobilize **all** resources (labor, equipment, and project management staff). Agreement on this aspect of the stop work order is critical in order to establish what damages are owed at the end of the work stoppage.

### [F]  Late or Incomplete Delivery of Owner Furnished, Contractor Installed Items

Many owners prepurchase major pieces of equipment for a project to save time and/or cost. Some owners of large programs may even prepurchase some of the bulk commodities common to several projects on a program (e.g., rail and concrete ties for a large light rail system program). If this is done, the bid documents will reflect the fact that the owner is purchasing certain items of equipment and/or material and will furnish them to the contractor when needed. This is commonly referred to as Owner Furnished, Contractor Installed ("OFCI") items. When owners employ OFCI, they either stipulate delivery dates in the contract documents or provide them to the contractor after contract award. Contractors must include such dates in their project plan and the schedule. Should the OFCI equipment or material **not** be delivered on time, or if the deliveries are incomplete or not as represented by the owner, this is an early warning sign of potential claims and disputes. The type of claims likely to arise include delay and constructive changes.

- **Recommended Claims and Dispute Avoidance Actions:** If a situation such as this arises, the contractor must file written notice of delay and/or change in strict accordance with the terms of the contract. At this point, the contractor should commence tracking all time and cost impacts cause by this situation, separately from base scope time and cost. Ultimately, the contractor must perfect and submit an appropriate claim. Should the owner refuse to deal with the claim or is unwilling to resolve the claim, contractors should seek advice from their legal counsel.

## [G] Early Warning Signs for Contractors—Change Issues

### [1] Excessive Number of Changes

Virtually all contracts have a Changes clause providing the owner with the right to make needed changes within the general scope of the work. This clause allows the owner to make changes to the work, as needed. Virtually all projects have at least a few change orders. However, the contractor may encounter a project with an excessive number of changes. The author was involved in a project that ultimately had 900+ change orders, some of which involved multiple changes. This is an early warning sign of potential claims and disputes. The type of claims likely to arise would be claims for disputed cost of changed work, delay, lost productivity and attendant impact costs.

- **Recommended Claims and Dispute Avoidance Actions:** The contractor must always be alert to changes and the need to file written notice of change in a timely manner. Once the contractor becomes aware of the potential for an excessive number of changes, the contractor needs to tighten up the contractor's change management procedure and system including written notifications, negotiation of the scope of changed work, the ability to prepare and submit timely adequate cost and time estimates, and the ability to negotiate agreements on scope, time, and cost. The contractor may need to retain additional project management staff (i.e., estimators, schedulers, document control personnel, etc.) to deal with a large number of changes. If this becomes necessary, the contractor would be well advised to provide notice to the owner that additional site staff are being assigned to the project due to the large number of changes and the contractor anticipates that the owner will compensate them for the added staff.

### [2] Owner Refusal Negotiate Time or Impact Costs with Change Orders

Despite the fact that almost all owners say they want to settle all change orders full and final and with no reservation of rights on change orders, all too often owners refuse to deal with delay arising from changes or impact costs such as changes to unchanged work. If an owner takes this approach to change orders, this is a clear warning sign of forthcoming changes and claims. Obviously, the resulting type of claim will involve the cost of changes, time and other cost impacts, and perhaps constructive acceleration.

- **Recommended Claims and Dispute Avoidance Actions:** When an owner starts to take this position, the contractor needs to open a discussion of what the downside risk of this approach is. The contractor needs to advise the owner that this position will result in all change orders having a reservation of rights and if this is the case then there will be a major claim at the end of the project for all delay and all impact costs. Should the owner persist in this approach, the contractor needs to be vigilant in recording all costs and all time impacts arising from each change order. If the owner refuses to allow reservation of rights language on the face of each change order, the contractor should confer with the contractor's legal counsel concerning the viability of including reservation language in the cover letter when returning the change order to the owner. If this technique is not acceptable, the contractor may want to adopt the position that the contractor will not sign any change order and if the owner wants work changed, the owner will have to issue a unilateral change on a T&M basis. Finally, if the owner refuses to deal with the potential delay of each change, the contractor should make certain that the time extension section on the face of the change order does **not** state "0 days." It should be annotated "To Be Determined" or "TBD."

### [3] Disagreements over "Scope of Work" Items and/or Contract Interpretation Disputes

This type of disagreement is typically unpredictable at the outset of the project and generally does not manifest itself until a submittal of some sort is provided for review by the contractor. At this point, if the owner's design professional rejects the submittal or directs a substantial revision, the contractor only then realizes that there is a disconnect between themselves and the owner as to what the contract actually requires. The author's experience is that more times than not, the specification governing the submittal has an ambiguity which was **not** identified until the submittal was provided. Up to that point, both the owner and contractor thought they understood the requirement clearly. Now, they know there is a disagreement concerning what exactly is in the scope of work for this specification section. This is an early warning sign of potential claims and disputes. The type of claim ordinarily arising from this situation is a constructive change claim.

- **Recommended Claims and Dispute Avoidance Actions:** As soon as a submittal is rejected or the contractor is told to substantially revise the submittal to include "x, y, and z," the contractor needs to review the contractor's submittal to see if the contractor made an error. If this review indicates that the submittal reflected exactly what the contractor thought was required, the contractor needs to send a written notice of change to the owner. This is important to preserve the contractor's rights and to emphasize to the owner and the owner's design professional that the contractor's objection must be taken seriously. Subsequently, the contractor needs to meet with the owner and the owner's design professional to discuss the different interpretations of the specification in contention. If the owner and design professional insist upon their interpretation of the specification and direct the contractor to proceed accordingly, the contractor must do so or face a potential default interpretation. The contractor must obtain this direction in writing and carefully track all time and cost impacts separately from base scope work so that when the disputed work is complete, a properly documented claim can be filed and supported.

## [H]   Early Warning Signs for Contractors—Project Management Issues

### [1]   Turn Over in Owner Project Management Staff

If the owner suddenly and without apparent reason replaces the owner's project management staff, this is an early warning sign of potential claims and disputes as it is illogical for an owner to take this action if the owner is satisfied with what is happening on the project. Unfortunately, the type of claim and dispute likely to arise cannot be predicted and it is up to the contractor to suss out the issue(s) behind this decision.

- **Recommended Claims and Dispute Avoidance Actions:** The most obvious way to find out what caused the change out of project personnel is to meet with the outgoing project team and ask the question "Why is this happening?" This should be done before they depart the project if at all possible. Depending on the information received, the contractor ought to meet with the owner's executives to ask the same question. Once the real issues are tabled, the contractor can, hopefully, work with the owner to resolve the issues without need to resort to claims or disputes.

### [2]   Payment Problems

If the contractor encounters slow or late payments, this is an early warning sign of pending claims and disputes. This may indicate that the owner's staff is not doing a good job of tracking the progress in the field which, in turn, causes them to dispute the percentages complete claims by the contractor. On the other hand, this may also mean that the owner is running out of funds to complete the work of the project. In either event, this is an early warning sign of claims and disputes. If allowed to go on too long, the type of claims likely to result will include delay or constructive suspension of work.

- **Recommended Claims and Dispute Avoidance Actions:** If the slow or late payments stem from disagreements over progress, the contractor needs to meet with the owner's staff that reviews payment applications to discuss the issue. The owner and the contractor may need to renegotiate and revise the Schedule of Values. If there is no apparent reason for such payment delays, the contractor needs to seek advice from the contractor's legal counsel to see what options are available (i.e., terminate involvement in the contract if the contract provides for contractor termination; take action under the relevant Prompt Payment Act, if there is one in the State that covers this project; etc.).

### [3]   Change in Style of Owner's Project Correspondence

If, during the performance of the work, the owner's correspondence changes radically, this may indicate that the owner has an attorney or claim consultant writing the owner's letters. If, unlike earlier correspondence, there are constant references to poor contract performance on the part of the contractor, or there are multiple complaints concerning contractor noncompliance with contract requirements, this is obviously is an early warning sign of claims and disputes. The type of claim or dispute likely to result will be a default termination.

- **Recommended Claims and Dispute Avoidance Actions:** The contractors need to notify their legal counsel and, perhaps, their surety of the situation and seek their advice. Additionally, the contractors should convene a meeting with the owner and the owner's staff or construction managers to discuss the situation and determine the underlying issue(s). If issues are clearly revealed, then the contractor can work with the owner to resolve the issues and avoid disputes.

### [4]   Delayed Submittal Reviews and Responses

One of the major changes in the construction industry over the past few decades is the radical increase in the number of shop drawings and submittals that must be provided by the contractor. This change, when combined with the contract requirement that " . . . materials and/or equipment may not be imported to the site nor work proceed . . . " until the submittal is approved, means that each submittal has the potential to create a delay to the work and, perhaps, the critical path of the schedule. The author has noted that, to protect the owner, many contracts have a stipulated time for review and response to each submittal (typically 30 calendar days). In some instances, the contract may contain a "submittal metering clause" prohibiting the contractor from submitting more than "x" submittals per week or per month. Given the potential for delay, the contractor must monitor the submittal review and response process very carefully. When submittal responses are not as prompt as called out in the contract or as they should be, this is an early warning sign of claims and disputes. The typical claims are likely to be delay or constructive suspension of work.

- **Recommended Claims and Dispute Avoidance Actions:** At the outset of the project, when preparing the baseline schedule, the contractor should consider putting all required submittals in the schedule including either the contract stipulated review time or a "reasonable period of time" for review. If this is done and assuming the contractor utilizes a robust WBS system such that all submittals and submittal review times are coded separately from other activities, the contractor can print out the contractor's own "submittal schedule" documenting when each submittal is due to the owner and when the response is scheduled. This provides the contractor with the beginnings of a good tracking system concerning submittals. Some owners may ask the contractor to remove the submittal review times from the schedule but since each review and response may be the source of a delay, contractors may rightfully decline such a request. Contractors must stay alert to submittal responses and each time the scheduled period has lapsed without a response, should submit a written notice of potential delay to the owner and track, in the schedule, the actual response time in order to track the consumption of schedule float.

### [5]   Owners Correcting Design Deficiencies Through the RFI Process

The RFI process is used widely in construction as a communications tool. The intended use of an RFI is for the contractor to ask a question of the owner, construction manager, and/or design professional concerning some requirement of the contract. The response should **not** be a change to the requirements of the contract, but rather, a clarification. The exception to this statement is when the RFI has identified an issue that requires a change to the work and then the response should indicate that a change order is forthcoming. It is the authors' experience that all too often owners and their representatives attempt to use RFI responses to correct errors or deficiencies in the contract documents without issuing a change order.[24] Should the contractor encounter situations such as this, this is a clear early warning sign of potential claims and disputes. The type of claim resulting from this sort of action is a constructive change claim.

- **Recommended Claims and Dispute Avoidance Actions:** Contractors must review each RFI response to determine whether it is simply a clarification or a change to the work. Any time a response appears to cause changed work, written notice to the owner must be filed in strict accordance with requirements of the contract. If the owner persists with the owner's interpretation and directs the contractor to proceed, the contractor should do so under protest, tracking all time and cost impacts separately from base scope work so as to be able to file and document a claim for damages when the changed work is completed.

### [6] Design Professional Advises "Coordination of Details Will Be Done Through the Shop Drawing Process"

Coordination of trade subcontractors in the field is typically the role of the general contractor. However, coordination of design details between trades (especially mechanical, electrical, plumbing, and control systems) should be performed by the design professional and/or construction manager prior to the project being bid. This type of coordination should be included in the drawings such as one line electrical conduit runs, plumbing and HVAC runs, wall penetrations, etc. When a designer advises the contractor that coordination of these details will be accomplished through the submittal process, this is an early warning sign of claims and disputes as it indicates that the project design is **not** complete. The typical claim growing out of this situation is a constructive change claim.

- **Recommended Claims and Dispute Avoidance Actions:** Given this attitude by the design professional, the contractor must review each submittal and/or RFI response thoroughly and cautiously. The review should be oriented at whether the response will cause a change to the work. If it appears to do so, the contractor should provide timely written notice of change to the owner. If the owner directs contractor compliance with the response from the design professional without a change order, the contractor should comply, under protest, carefully documenting all time and cost impacts in order to be able to compile a well-documented claim at some later point in time.

---

[24] Nigel Hughes, Christopher L. Nutter, Megan Wells and James G. Zack, Jr., *Impact and Control of RFIs on Construction Projects*, Navigant Construction Forum™, Boulder, CO, April 2013.

### [7]   Exclusion of Design Professional from Project Meetings

Design professionals should be included in all project update meetings as contractors frequently have questions concerning the project design which can be addressed in the meeting by the design team. When the design team is excluded from the project site meetings by the owner, even when design input is needed, this should be taken as an early warning sign of claims and disputes. The types of claims likely to result include constructive changes, delays, and/or constructive suspensions of work.

- **Recommended Claims and Dispute Avoidance Actions:** The contractor probably will not be advised why the owner has excluded the design professional from project meetings. And, the reason may not matter. In a situation such as this, a contractor in need of an opportunity to meet with and discuss issues with the design professional should specifically notify the owner in writing that the contractor needs to have the design professional present at the next project meeting to discuss certain issues that require resolution. The written request should briefly identify each issue and the contractor should request that each issue be specifically included in the meeting agenda. If the owner continues to exclude the designer, the contractor should pose the contractor's inquiries as best the contractor can through the RFI process but each should be accompanied by a written notice of potential delay on the basis that " . . . the issue could have been resolved at this week's project meeting rather than awaiting a response to RFI #35."

### [8]   Attorney or Claim Consultant Attending Project Meetings

It is quite apparent that having the owner's legal counsel and/or claims consultant attend routine project meeting is an early warning sign of claims and disputes. What sort of claim is likely to be raised is, however, unknown to the contractor. It is up to the contractor to ascertain this information.

- **Recommended Claims and Dispute Avoidance Actions:** If the contractor has filed several claims, none of which are yet resolved, the owner may have these additional individuals at project meeting to discuss the claims. This is logical and understandable. However, if there are no pending claims from the contractor, then the contractor should ask the owner why the owner's attorney and/or claims consultant was invited. If the owner fails to provide a reasonable response, perhaps the contractor ought to advise the owner that if the owner is going to have the owner's attorney attend all meetings, then the contractor will do likewise. Hopefully, at this point, each party will consider the cost of such actions and adopt a more reasonable manner to proceed.

### [9]  Contractor Told Not to "Put Things in Writing"

The author was involved in a project where the owner specifically told the contractor **not** to put things in writing. The owner's direction included meeting minutes, RFIs, and notices of change and/or delay. This project was a gigaproject[25] with a huge potential "award fee" based upon completion of the work **under** budget and **earlier** than required. The author, upon arriving at the site, learned that the project was under budget and ahead of schedule. The author also learned that this directive was a mechanism used by the owner to direct extra work (which absorbed the cost and time savings the contractor had achieved to date and inflated the project cost and extended the project time) thus lessening the chances of the contractor achieving the award fee. If a directive like this is provided by the owner, the contractor should recognize this as an early warning sign of potential claims and disputes. Virtually any type of claim may result from this sort of action.

- **Recommended Claims and Dispute Avoidance Actions:** If given such a directive, the contractor should request that the directive be put in writing by the owner's project manager or executive. If the owner fails to do so, the contractor ought to document the directive by writing a letter to the owner repeating the directive, stating the date upon which the directive was given, and asking the owner to confirm the directive in writing. Whether the owner confirms the directive or not, the contractor should keep and distribute meeting minutes, submit written RFIs and document the responses in written form, and provide all contractually required notices in writing and as specified in the contract. If the owner continues to object, the contractor should remind the owner of the unchanged contract requirements.

### [10]  Owner Advises "We'll Take Care of This at the End of the Job"

Many owners are loathe to grant time extensions and/or pay impact costs while the project is in progress. Owners who take this approach generally claim that they want to deal with real, documented damages, not speculative projected damages. What they fail to realize or acknowledge is that impact damages are real and are paid by the contractor on a daily basis so the refusal to deal with impact damages on an ongoing basis harms the contractor's cash flow. Such owners also fail to understand that contractors need to protect themselves against the potential imposition of liquidated or late completion damages and, thus, may accelerate the

---

[25] A "gigaproject" is generally defined as any project costing more than US$1 billion. See Patricia D. Galloway, Kris R. Nielsen and Jack L. Dignum, *Managing Gigaproject: Advise from Those Who've Been There, Done That*, ASCE Press, Reston, VA, 2013.

work to avoid the imposition of late completion damages. When an owner asserts this position, this is an early warning of potential claims and disputes. The most likely claims growing from this scenario are lost productivity damages and constructive acceleration claims.[26]

- **Recommended Claims and Dispute Avoidance Actions:** To protect themselves, contractors must adhere to the written notice requirements of the contract at all times and in all situations. As soon as notice is provided to the owner of any event, contractors need to open new job cost accounts in order to accrue all related costs to the event. Likewise, contractors should include a new activity related to the event in the current project schedule. The new schedule activity should be connected to a logical predecessor activity or activities and its end date should be allowed to float free until the event has past. At that point, the schedule activity should be connected to appropriate follow-on activities (successors) on the schedule. This process allows the contractor to prepare a schedule delay analysis to determine whether the event impacted the critical path or not. Even if the event did not impact the critical path, this process will track the consumption of float within the schedule such that later delays can be proven.

### [11]  Negative Cost Trends

Contractors must employ a robust cost control system on each project to protect themselves.[27] At least monthly, all job cost accounts on the project should be updated. Each account should be trended to see if the costs associated with that account are tracking the estimate, or are overrunning the planned cost. If the trend for one or more cost accounts is overrunning, the individuals responsible for that account should be queried as to what is causing the potential overrun. Additionally, project controls personnel should prepare an "estimate at complete" for the entire project to ascertain the net effect of all trends. If there are multiple potential negative trends and/or the project's estimate at complete indicates a potential cost overrun, the contractor needs to take this as an early warning sign of potential claims and disputes. The types of claims growing from this type of situation will be defined by the causes of the negative trends.

---

[26] James G. Zack, Jr., *Constructive Acceleration—A Global Tour*, Navigant Construction Forum™, Boulder, CO, 2011.

[27] Construction Management Association of America, *Cost Management Procedures*, 2001 Edition, McLean, VA.

- **Recommended Claims and Dispute Avoidance Actions:** The contractor needs to examine each cost account showing a negative trend and determine causation. If the negative trend is being caused by something the contractor, or one of the contractor's subcontractors, is responsible for (i.e., bad bid, material cost increases, lower than planned labor productivity, etc.), then the contractor needs to create a plan to reverse the negative trend and execute this plan. On the other hand, if the negative trend is being caused by something for which the owner is liable, the contractor must prepare and submit timely written notice(s) to the owner and begin preparing a change order proposal or claim submittal.

## [12]  Lack of Reasonable Evidence Concerning Financial Arrangements

If the contractor is performing work under a FIDIC contract[28] and has any concerns about the owner's ability to finance and pay for the entire project, the contractor has the right to request " . . . reasonable evidence that financial arrangements have been made and are being maintained which will enable the Employer to pay the Contract Price in accordance with Clause 14 *[Contract Price and Payment].*"[29]

- **Recommended Claims and Dispute Avoidance Actions:** Pursuant to this clause, the owner (employer) has 42 calendar days to provide the requested "reasonable evidence." The failure of the owner to do so may result in a number of follow on actions. If " . . . the Employer fails to comply with Sub-Clause 2.4 *[Employer's Financial Arrangements]* . . . the Contractor may, after giving not less than 21 days' notice to the Employer, suspend work (or reduce the rate of work) unless and until the Contractor has received . . . reasonable evidence . . . "[30] Continuing, "The Contractor shall be entitled to terminate the Contract if: (a) the Contractor does not receive the reasonable evidence within 42 days after giving notice under Sub-Clause 16.1 *[Contractor's Entitlement to Suspend Work]* in respect of a failure to comply with Sub-Clause 2.4 *[Employer's Financial Arrangement].*"[31] Thus, there is a clear 105-calendar-day process in place to obtain satisfactory evidence, the owner has the wherewithal to pay for the project, or the contractor may withdraw from the project. During this period, a contractor is well advised to

---

[28] Federation Internationale de Ingenieurs-Conseils ("FIDIC") contract.

[29] Sub-Clause 2.4, *Employers Financial Arrangements,* FIDIC Conditions of Contract for Construction for Building and Engineering Works Designed by The Employer, 1998 Edition.

[30] Sub-Clause 16.1, *Contractor's Entitlement to Suspend Work,* FIDIC Conditions of Contract.

[31] Sub-Clause 16.2, *Termination by Contractor,* FIDIC Conditions of Contract.

notify and seek guidance from the contractor's own legal counsel and, perhaps, the contractor's surety.

### [13]  Owner Unreasonably Withholding Issuance of the Certificate of Substantial Completion

Substantial completion (sometimes referred to as mechanical completion) is that point in the project where work is sufficiently complete such that the owner can begin using the project for its intended purpose.[32] Substantial completion is also when liquidated or late completion damages cease, unless the contract specifically states otherwise. Typically, construction contracts require the contractor to file a notice of substantial completion. Upon receipt of such notice, the owner is generally required to inspect the work. If the owner agrees the work is substantially complete, the owner is generally required to notify the contractor in writing to this effect. This written notice is often referred to as a certificate of substantial completion. If the owner is unreasonably withholding issuance of the certificate of substantial completion (i.e., for no stated reasons at all or for very flimsy reasons), then this is an early warning sign of potential claims and disputes. The type of claims growing out of this situation will generally revolve around constructive changes and project delay. The type of disputes likely to arise will resolve around a substantial punchlist including items the contractor does **not** believe are in the scope of work.

- **Recommended Claims and Dispute Avoidance Actions:** In order to avoid such last minute project disruption, a contractor should start working with the owner staff sometime prior to substantial completion to have them perform preliminary substantial completion inspections on a floor-by-floor or system-by-system basis. If this can be arranged and punchlists provided after each preliminary inspection, legitimately incomplete work can be completed before the final inspection. This will help avoid major project delay and disruption. In any event, whenever the owner provides the contractor with a punchlist, it must be carefully examined to determine that all allegedly "incomplete work" items are truly within the scope of work. If some are **not**, the contractor should provide prompt written notice of change. Should the owner demand the contractor complete the disputed work items, the contractor should perform with work under written protest, keep track of all time and cost impacts, and file a claim when the disputed work is complete.

---

[32] That is, unless the contract documents provide a more specific or detailed definition.

### [14] Receipt of Cure Notice or Default Notice from Owner

Should the owner send a cure notice or show cause notice to the contractor (either of which is a precursor to a default termination), this is a clear warning sign of a large dispute in the making. The claim and dispute is likely to be one of wrongful termination.

- **Recommended Claims and Dispute Avoidance Actions:** Upon receipt of a cure notice, the contractor should immediately confer with the contractor's legal counsel and seek their advice. Depending upon their advice, the contractor may also need to provide notice to the contractor's surety. The contractor needs to examine the claimed contract breaches to determine whether the contractor actually breached the contract. Additionally, each alleged breach should be examined to determine whether the owner caused, in whole or in part, the alleged breach. If it is determined that the owner is at least partially responsible, the owner may not have clean hands and thus may not be able to terminate the contractor for default. The results of all such internal examinations must be provided to and discussed with legal counsel. The contractor, at this point, should place himself or herself in the hands of his or her legal counsel, following their advice carefully so as to minimize the damage from this type of claim.

### [I] Early Warning Signs for Contractors—Field Issues

### [1] Multiple "Holds" on Drawings or Work

Contractors tend to assume that once they are in the field performing work, the design effort is complete. It is the author's experience that this is **not** always true. For example, the author was involved with the construction of a courthouse in the Midwest. The work was speeding toward an on-time, in-budget completion with a minimum of change orders. A few weeks before project completion—when interior finishes were nearing completion—the chief judge toured the building and ended up putting a hold on some 15% of the rooms in the project. These were all rooms for use by defendants and their attorneys during trials. The complaint relayed to the contractor by the contracting officer was that the judge was "extremely upset" that the interior finishes in these spaces were equivalent to the finishes in spaces used by prosecutors and judges. He found this unacceptable even though the interior finish schedules had been approved more than two years previously and were unchanged. Should something like this happen on a project, this is an early warning sign of pending claims and potential disputes. The typical claims are likely to be change and delay claims.

- **Recommended Claims and Dispute Avoidance Actions:** As soon as a hold notice[33] is provided, the contractor must provide a written notice of potential delay. Again, and as noted previously, the contractor needs to open new job cost accounts to accrue the cost damages growing from this action and add a new schedule activity (or more than one if necessary) to track the potential delay and/or the consumption of float within the schedule. Once the holds are released, the contractor should complete the documentation, prepare and submit a claims for cost and/or time, as appropriate.

### [2]  Lack of Responses to RFIs

As noted earlier, an RFI is a communications vehicle whereby the contractor asks a question and receives a response. Assuming this is a legitimate RFI[34] on the contractor's work, at least on the portion of the project where the question arose, the work is probably stopped or at least slowed down. The longer it takes for the owner or the owner's representatives to respond, the greater the likelihood of a delay or constructive suspension of work claim. Thus, the failure to respond to RFIs should be considered an early warning sign of claims and dispute.

- **Recommended Claims and Dispute Avoidance Actions:** If the contract stipulates a turnaround time for RFI responses, then on the day this time has expired, the contractor should provide written notice of potential delay. If no such time is contained in the contract and the owner and contractor did not negotiate a turnaround time for RFIs at the outset of the project or during an early partnering meeting, the contractor should provide written notice of potential delay after a reasonable period of time for a response has expired.[35] A new project cost account code should be opened to capture the impact costs (such as demobilizing crew(s) from this area of work to another and remobilizing them back to this area once the response is received). And, a new schedule activity should be included in the current schedule starting the date the RFI was submitted and continuing to the date when the response is received. When all is said and done, these actions will serve as the basis of the damages in the claim to the owner.

---

[33] A "hold notice" under some contracts is similar to a directed Suspension of Work on many projects but is typically *not* accompanied by all the paperwork that accompanies suspension orders.

[34] *Ibid.*, Hughes, Nutter, Wells and Zack, *Impact & Control of RFIs on Construction Projects.*

[35] Research into the management of the RFI process indicates that 10 working days should be a reasonable amount of time to respond to most RFIs. *Id.*, *Impact & Control of RFIs on Construction Projects.*

### [3]  Owner Refusal to Acknowledge Differing Site Conditions

Most construction contracts contain a Differing Site Condition ("DSC") clause[36] under which the owner assumes liability for latent site conditions in order to reduce contractor contingencies at the time of bidding. All such clauses require a written notice of DSC as soon as a materially different condition is encountered and direct the contractor to cease work in the area of the alleged DSC until the owner has the opportunity to investigate. Most such clauses require the owner investigate "promptly." Once the owner makes the owner's investigation, it is not at all uncommon for the owner to simply advise the contractor to go back to work. That is, a standard DSC clause does **not** require the owner to tell the contractor whether the owner believes the condition is, or is not, a DSC before directing the contractor to return to work. In most such cases, the contractor will work the contractor's way through the condition at the contractor's own expense. Obviously, to perfect a DSC claim, the contractor will, among other things, have to document the time and cost damages resulting from the DSC. Thus, careful tracking of time and cost is mandatory. However, most owners will likely advise the contractor within a reasonable period of time whether they believe the condition is, or is not, a DSC. If the owner remains silent for some period of time on the owner's decision concerning the alleged DSC, this is an early warning sign of claims and a potential dispute.

- **Recommended Claims and Dispute Avoidance Actions:** If this situation occurs, the contractor should formally write to the owner seeking the owner's final decision on the DSC either under the Disputes clause or the DSC clause. If no decision is still forthcoming and the contractor is working on a contract that has established either a Dispute Resolution Board ("DRB") or a Dispute Adjudication Board ("DAB"), the contractor can take the issue to the Board and obtain a decision. Alternatively, if the contract embodies a Project Neutral, Individual Decision Maker, or an Early Neutral Evaluation process, the contractor can seek their input on the issue.[37]

### [4]  Unreasonable Disapproval of Contractor's Ordinary and Customary Means and Methods

Many owners employ "standard specifications" for their projects changing them only occasionally. And many contractors bid to the same owners time after

---

[36] Sometimes referred to a Changed Conditions or Unforeseeable Physical Conditions. *See* Steven A. Collins and James G. Zack, Jr., *Changing Trend in Risk Allocation—Differing Site Conditions*, Navigant Construction Forum™, Boulder, CO, September 2014.

[37] *Ibid.*, Bult, Halligan, Pray and Zack, *Delivering Dispute Free Projects: Part III—Alternative Dispute Resolution.*

time. As such, contractors who have executed several projects for the same owner using the same specifications, gain a right of reliance concerning the specifications. If a contractor is working on a project for an owner the contractor has worked for previously and, again, using the same specifications, has a submittal rejected even though it is based on the contractor's ordinary and customary means and methods used on previous projects, this should be considered as an early warning sign of claims and a potential dispute. The type of claim likely to result would be a constructive change claim.

- **Recommended Claims and Dispute Avoidance Actions:** If the submittal is rejected, or the contractor is directed to make substantial changes to the submittal in accordance with review comments, the contractor should review the response carefully. If it looks like the contractor is being directed to make a change, then a written notice of change should be filed with the owner. This notice should be followed up with a meeting where the contractor provides documentation that what the contractor proposed on this project is exactly what the contractor did on several previous projects, using the same specification. Unless there is some special need for modified means and methods, the owner should approve the contractor's submittal. If there is a special need requiring changed means and methods, the contractor and owner can negotiate a change order using the contractor's base bid for this piece of work as the basis or floor for the damages.

### [5] Over Inspection or Changes to Inspection Criteria after Contract Award

Most technical specifications are based on building codes or on recognized and published industry practices. And, many technical specifications contain detailed inspection criteria so the contractor understands the standard the work will have to meet in order to get paid. However, at times the owner's inspection team may decide to use a different inspection technique or procedure **after** the project is awarded. For example, the welding specification may state that certain type of weld will be inspected using the Magnetic Particle technique and, after award of the contract, decide to use Ultrasonic testing in its place. Ultrasonic testing is more sophisticated and likely to find much smaller welding flaws, thus negatively impacting welding productivity.[38]

---

[38] Charles Hayes, *The ABC's of Nondestructive Weld Examination*, NDTnet, Vol. 3, No. 6, June 1998.

- **Recommended Claims and Dispute Avoidance Actions:** Should the owner make a change to inspection standards after contract award, the contractor, upon becoming aware of this, should file a written notice of change with the owner. Subsequently, the contractor should closely monitor the productivity of the activities impacted by the change in inspection techniques. If a drop in productivity is observed, the contractor needs to document the loss of productivity probably using the classic Measured Mile technique.[39] Once the issue is past, this data can be used to prepare and submit a claim for lost productivity and, perhaps, delay.

### [6] Excessive Quantity Variations

If the contractor is working on a unit price contract and the units vary excessively, this is an early warning sign of claims and a potential dispute.

- **Recommended Claims and Dispute Avoidance Actions:** Once the quantities start to vary, although generally not specifically required to do so, the contractor ought to give notice of change to the owner citing both the Changes clause and the Quantity Variation clause. The contractor should document the contractor's as-bid quantities and track and document actual quantities. The contractor should also carefully review the Quantity Variation clause to determine at what point (typically expressed as a percentage of the as-bid quantities) the contractor may claim a quantity variation and how such a variation can be calculated. If the quantities vary because the contractor encounters an "entirely different job"[40] or there is an unforeseen need for an unusual construction methodology,[41] then the DSC clause **may** be employed in lieu of the Quantity Variation clause. If it can be demonstrated that the owner's estimate was negligently performed[42] or if owner-issued change orders substantially increase the estimated quantities[43] again, the DSC clause may override the Quantity Variation clause when it comes to pricing such variations. And, material variations on owner-provided quantity estimates may become a Type 1 DSC if they resulted from a differing site condition.[44]

---

[39] Recommended Practice No. 25R-03, *Estimating Lost Labor Productivity in Construction Claims*, AACE International, Morgantown, WV, April 2004.

[40] *Brezina Construction, Inc.*, ENG BCA No. 3215, 75-1 B.C.A. ¶ 10,989.

[41] *Dunbar & Sullivan Dredging Co.*, ENG BCA No. 8265, 73-2 B.C.A. ¶ 12,285.

[42] *John Murphy Construction Co.*, AGBCA No. 418, 79-1 B.C.A. ¶ 13,836.

[43] *Leavell & Co.*, ENG BCA 3492, 75-2 B.C.A. ¶ 11,596.

[44] *United Contractors v. United States*, 177 Ct. Cl. 151, 368 F.2d 585 (1966).

## § 4.05   CONCLUSION

This chapter highlights a large number of early warning signs concerning potential claims and disputes. This is not an exhaustive list, certainly, but the chapter lists many of the most common early warning signs. Having said this, the author wants to reiterate a point made earlier in the chapter. That is, the real key to dispute avoidance is (1) early recognition of potential claims and (2) prompt action on the part of both the owner and the contractor to identify the issue and work together to craft an acceptable resolution based upon the terms and conditions of the contract. If both parties focus on achieving project success rather that positioning, then the likelihood of delivering a project on time and in budget substantially increases.

# CHAPTER 5

# SURETY LAW UPDATE

Richard J. Storrs, Esq., Joseph Wolenski, Esq.

## § 5.01   INTRODUCTION

This chapter explores recent developments in surety law. We have included cases decided, for the most part, in 2015. The authors first provide an update on the law of payment bonds, including coverage and defense issues. The authors then turn to performance bonds, and examine recent developments involved with performance bond claims and defenses. Finally, the authors discuss indemnity claims and defenses, as well as cases involving the rights between sureties and third parties.

## § 5.02   PAYMENT BONDS

### [A]   Coverage—Who Is Entitled to Protection?

In *U.S. for the Use of Pilecor, Inc. v. Slurry Systems, Inc.,*[1] the claimant was a broker who leased a large 40-ton piece of construction machinery to the prime contractor. After a dispute arose over the machine's rental cost, the claimant sued the prime contractor and its surety under the Miller Act for non-payment of the machine's rental cost. The prime contractor filed a counter-claim and, after an eight-day trial, the jury returned a confused verdict that awarded the prime contractor $0 in compensatory damages but $20 million in punitive damages. The verdict was contrary to Illinois law.[2] After a second trial, the jury returned a verdict in the claimant's favor against both the prime contractor and its surety.

The surety appealed, arguing that only the claimant's parent company, which manufactured the equipment, could sue under the Miller Act (as opposed to the claimant, which was the broker), as it was the one that technically "furnished" the equipment to the prime contractor, a phrase the surety argued meant "supplied directly."[3] The court disagreed with the surety's definition of "furnish" under the Miller Act and held that the claimant, a broker, could recover in its contract against the prime contractor.[4]

In *APAC-Kansas, Inc. v. BSC Steel Inc., et al.,*[5] the plaintiff supplied equipment and labor to a third tier subcontractor who, in turn, was partially responsible for steel erection at a new Army hospital. The first tier subcontractor furnished a payment bond to the prime contractor. The claimant sued the first tier subcontractor and its surety (the defendants) for payment under the payment bond and moved for summary judgment.

---

[1] 804 F.3d 889 (7th Cir. 2015).
[2] 804 F.3d 889, 891.
[3] 804 F.3d 889, 893.
[4] 804 F.3d 889, 894.
[5] 2015 WL 866898 (D. Kan. Mar. 2, 2015).

The defendants contended the claimant was not within the scope of the bond's coverage and thus was not a proper claimant.[6] The defendants based this argument on the bond's language that it was conditioned on payment for labor and material "reasonably required for use in the performance of this Subcontract, for all or any part of which the Contractor and Owner is liable."[7] Initially, the defendants contended this phrase meant the bond covered obligations for which the owner and the prime contractor were both liable. After the plaintiff pointed out that based upon that interpretation of the clause, no one would qualify as a claimant because there is no one to whom both the prime contractor and owner could be directly liable, the defendants changed their argument so as to interpret "Contractor *and* Owner" to "Contractor *or* Owner,"[8] thus affording coverage if one or both were potentially liable to the claimant.

The court disagreed with the defendants, explaining that the "appropriate construction of the phrase 'for all or any part of which the Contractor and Owner is liable' is a general reference to the costs of constructing the project. Claimants can seek recovery under the Payment Bond only if they are seeking costs and expenses for labor and materials used in the performance of a subcontract for which [the prime contractor and owner] would be liable."[9]

The defendants further argued that even if the plaintiff was covered under the bond, it could only recover after it showed that an upper-tier contractor was paid for the work or supplies sought by them (i.e., pay-if-paid).[10] The court again disagreed and held that the contract language was intended as a pay-when-paid timing clause, not a condition precedent. Therefore, the court ruled the claimants did not have to show payment to an upper-tier subcontractor.

In *JSI Communications v. Travelers Casualty & Surety Co. of America*,[11] several second-tier subcontractors filed claims against the prime contractor's payment bond for unpaid materials on a public works project in Mississippi. The prime contractor filed an interpleader action and deposited the balance of the contract funds owed to the first-tier subcontractor with the court's registry. Subsequently, the prime contractor obtained a judgment releasing it from any further liability on its subcontract with the first-tier subcontractor.[12]

Shortly after the prime contractor obtained this judgment, a new claimant (and ultimately the plaintiff in this case) notified the prime contractor and its surety that it was seeking payment under the payment bond for non-payment of

---

[6] 2015 WL 866898 at *4.
[7] 2015 WL 866898 at *4.
[8] 2015 WL 866898 at *5 (emphasis added).
[9] 2015 WL 866898 at *5.
[10] 2015 WL 866898 at *5.
[11] 807 F.3d 725 (5th Cir. 2015).
[12] 807 F.3d at 726.

supplies (the notice was timely under Mississippi's Little Miller Act). In response, the prime contractor amended its complaint for interpleader to include this new claimant, and, that same day, obtained an amended judgment extending the previous release of liability. The plaintiff-claimant then sued the surety to recover its unpaid balance.

The surety argued that it was no longer liable to the claimant on the bond because the prime contractor's liability to the claimant was extinguished by the entry of judgment on the interpleader action. The court disagreed, holding that the interpleader action did not subvert the purpose or enforceability of Mississippi's Little Miller Act:

> Under Mississippi's Little Miller Act, second-tier subcontractors . . . can sue on a payment bond absent a direct contractual relationship with the contractor. . . . Accordingly, that [the prime contractor] has been released of liability to [the first-tier subcontractor] has no effect on [the claimant's] ability to recover under the bond.[13]

Likewise, the court rejected the surety's argument that its bond obligation was discharged by the interpleader judgment. The court reasoned that the funds held in the interpleader action (i.e., the "stake") represented only the remaining balance due on the subcontract, not the extent of the surety's liability.[14] Therefore, the "stake" was separate and distinct from any obligations the prime contractor and it surety had on the first-tier subcontract, and did not "shield the surety from liability that arises under its bond obligation." Finally, the court concluded that the prime contractor's indemnity obligation to the surety was "irrelevant" and had "no bearing" on the surety's bond obligation to the claimant under Mississippi's Little Miller Act.[15]

Given the foregoing, the court reversed the district court and remanded with instruction to enter summary judgment in favor of the claimant.

In *Selective Insurance Co. of America v. Glen Wilde, LLC*,[16] the surety executed a payment bond, delivered it to the principal, and collected a premium. The principal did not sign the bond or deliver it to the owner. The principal sent the owner a change order to increase the contract price by the amount of the premium plus a 10% markup; however, the owner rejected the proposed change order.[17]

---

[13] 807 F.3d at 727.
[14] 807 F.3d at 728.
[15] 807 F.3d at 729.
[16] 2015 WL 1471186 (W.D.N.C. Mar. 15, 2015).
[17] 2015 WL 1471186 at *2.

The claimant was an unpaid subcontractor. The surety argued that there was no payment bond because there was no contract—the parties failed to reach a meeting of the minds and there was no acceptance. The surety argued that the bond was not signed by the principal or delivered to the obligee.[18]

The court found factual issues as to delivery of the payment bond but granted the surety summary judgment on the argument that the obligee did not accept the bond. The court reasoned that the obligee expressly rejected bonding by failing to approve the aforementioned change order, which the court believed represented the offer.[19] In rejecting the change order, the obligee rejected bonding altogether and thus terminated the offer. Therefore, there was no payment bond, which meant there could be no claim against the payment bond by the subcontractor.[20]

The dispute in *U.S. for the Use of Pacific Western Inc. v. Liberty Mutual Insurance Co.*[21] concerned whether the claimant provided transportation services to a subcontract (thus falling under the purview of the Miller Act) or to a materialman (in which case the Miller Act would not afford coverage). The prime contractor ordered an asphalt pavement material from a supplier. The claimant-plaintiff transported the asphalt material, but was not paid by the supplier. The claimant made a claim against the payment bond. The defendants moved to dismiss on grounds that the plaintiff was not within the coverage of the Miller Act because the supplier met the definition of a materialman, not a subcontractor. The court analyzed factors that distinguish between whether a party is a subcontractor or materialman and found that the facts alleged in the complaint did not support a finding that the supplier was a subcontractor.[22] Therefore, the Miller Act did not afford coverage and the court granted the defendants' motion to dismiss.

## [B]   Damages Covered Under Payment Bonds

*Ergon Asphalt & Emulsions, Inc. v. Capriati Construction Corp., Inc. et al.*,[23] arose out of a dispute over the payment of escalation costs for an asphalt product sold by the plaintiff-supplier to the defendant-prime contractor. The prime contractor's contract with the Nevada Dept. of Transportation (NDOT) contained an "escalation provision" that required NDOT to increase its payments to the prime contractor if the price of asphalt increased during the project.[24] Meanwhile,

---

[18] 2015 WL 1471186 at *7.
[19] 2015 WL 1471186 at *9.
[20] 2015 WL 1471186 at *9.
[21] 2015 WL 3407873 (E.D.N.Y. May 26, 2015).
[22] 2015 WL 3407873 at *3.
[23] 2015 WL 1959851 (D. Nev. Apr. 29, 2015).
[24] 2015 WL 1959851 at *1.

the supplier and prime contractor exchanged various proposals to provide the asphalt but did not execute a formal contract.[25] The supplier ultimately provided the asphalt but the prime contractor refused to pay the increased price as the project went on.

The court held that under a theory of unjust enrichment the supplier was entitled to receive escalation payments made by the NDOT, and granted summary judgment accordingly. The court further held that prime contractor's sureties should be held liable based on the prime contractor's failure to pay for labor and materials related to the project.[26]

In *Bond Restoration, Inc. v. Ready Cable, Inc.*,[27] a supplier sold material to a subcontractor on a street improvement project for the City of Houston. The subcontractor failed to pay the supplier, so the supplier contacted the prime contractor and asked for information on the payment bond. The prime contractor, however, did not respond to the supplier's request. Thereafter, the supplier sought similar information from the City. The City was unable to provide the requesting information without a project name or a project number. The supplier had no such information.[28]

Eventually, the deadline to submit a claim against the payment bond expired. The supplier sued the prime contractor and alleged under Texas law, the prime contractor was obligated to provide the requested bond information and that its failure to do so caused the supplier damages. Included in the supplier's damage claim was a claim for "consequential damages" that included an amount equal to the unpaid invoices that would have been paid had the prime contractor timely provided the requisite bond information.[29]

The court held that the statutory remedy for failing to provide the bond information was liability "to the requesting person for that person's reasonable costs incurred in getting the requested information."[30] Thus, there was no private cause of action available to the supplier to recover consequential damages. The court reversed judgment for the supplier because the judgment was based on the supplier's claim for consequential damages only.

The issue of consequential damages came up again via lost profits in *The Erection Co. v. Archer Western Contractors, LLC.*[31] In that case, a dispute arose between a prime contractor and a subcontractor on a Miller Act project. The subcontractor sought lost profits from the prime contractor's surety. The court

---

[25] 2015 WL 1959851 at *2-3.

[26] 2015 WL 1959851 at *8.

[27] 462 S.W.3d 597 (Tex. App. 2015).

[28] 462 S.W.3d at 599.

[29] 462 S.W.3d at 602.

[30] 462 S.W.3d at 603.

[31] 2015 WL 926782 (D. Nev. Mar. 4, 2015).

granted the surety's summary judgment motion holding "the Miller Act . . . bars a subcontractor . . . from recovery of unrealized profits."[32]

## [C]  Notice Requirements

In *St. Louis Housing Authority ex rel. Jamison Electric, LLC v. Hankins Construction Co.*,[33] a subcontractor sued the prime contractor and its surety for various back-charges, delays, acceleration costs, and other costs. The court addressed whether there was any breach of the payment bond because the plaintiff filed its lawsuit before waiting 90 days after it last worked on the project. The court ruled that because the subcontractor did not fulfill its obligation under the payment bond "by waiting 90 days to file suit, neither [the prime contractor nor the surety] can be said to have breached the bond, at least not yet."[34] Likewise, the court held that the subcontractor's premature suit barred any claim for vexatious refusal to pay by the surety.

## [D]  Timeliness of Actions and Limitations

In *U.S. for the Use of Asphalt Contractors & Site Work, Inc. v. KAR Contracting, LLC*,[35] a first-tier subcontractor sued the prime contractor and its Miller Act surety under the payment bond. The defendants moved to dismiss the complaint for failure to state a claim upon which relief can be granted because the suit was not filed within the Miller Act's one year limitations period.

After a succinct explanation of the standard of review under a Rule 12(b)(6) motion, the court stated that to survive such a motion, a complaint "must contact sufficient factual matter, accepted as true, to state a claim to relief that is plausible on its face."[36] Applying that standard, the court noted that it was not clear from the face of the complaint that the final invoice represented the last date the plaintiff provided labor or materials on the project (alluding that labor or materials could have been provided after the date of the invoice).[37] Thus, the court reasoned, it was not clear from the face of the complaint that the statute of limitations ran before the plaintiff filed its complaint.[38] The court further held that the complaint alleged additional work had been performed at the request of the prime contractor and the owner, which may have extended the deadline to file suit.[39] Given

---

[32] 2015 WL 926782 at *5.
[33] 2014 WL 7408944 (E.D. Mo. Dec. 31, 2014).
[34] 2014 WL 7408944 at *15.
[35] 2015 WL 3651279 (S.D.W. Va. June 11, 2015).
[36] 2015 WL 3651279 at *1.
[37] 2015 WL 3651279 at *2.
[38] 2015 WL 3651279 at *2.
[39] 2015 WL 3651279 at *3.

the foregoing, the complaint stated claims for breach of both the payment bond and subcontract, and the defendants' motion to dismiss was denied.

In *U.S. for the Use of Stuart C. Irby Co. v. Pro Construction, Inc.*,[40] an electrical material supplier on a federal project sued the prime contractor and its Miller Act surety. On the supplier's summary judgment, it argued that it had properly met all requirements of a valid claim under the Miller Act. The defendants cross-moved for summary judgment and argued (i) the plaintiff-supplier did not have a good-faith belief that all of the materials for which the plaintiff sought payment were provided to the job site because the last delivery of material was to the subcontractor's office, not the job site, and (ii) because the plaintiff-supplier was on an open account, it was required to provide notice of its claim within 90 days of each invoice, which the supplier had not done (it had filed one notice of claim at the end of the project).[41]

In evaluating the cross-motions for summary judgment, the court held that the supplier's good-faith belief that the supplies were for a bonded job was all that was needed and that "delivery to the job site or actual use in the prosecution of the work is immaterial to a right of recovery."[42] The court rejected the defendants' argument that the 90-day notice requirement had to be met separately for each invoice. The court stated "when there is an open account, a ninety-day notice is timely even when it includes material furnished more than ninety days before the notice."[43] Thus, a single notice within 90 days of the final delivery was sufficient.[44] The court granted the plaintiff-supplier's motion for summary judgment.

## [E]  Payment Bond Defenses

### [1]  Estoppel by Conduct

In *Travelers Casualty & Surety Co. of America, et al. v. Cummins Mid-South, LLC*,[45] a subcontractor's supplier sued the general contractor and its surety on a public construction contract. The plaintiff-supplier sought payment for a generator supplied to the subcontractor. The prime contractor had earlier paid the supplier for service work done to the generator and subsequently furnished an "Unconditional Waiver and Release" to the supplier, which stated it "covers the full and final payment of the contract amount for labor, services and equipment,

---

[40] 2015 WL 3671731 (M.D. Ga. June 15, 2015).
[41] 2015 WL 3671731 at *3-4.
[42] 2015 WL 3671731 at *3 (internal citations omitted).
[43] 2015 WL 3671731 at *5 (internal citations omitted).
[44] 2015 WL 3671731 at *4-5.
[45] 2015 Ark. App. 299, 460 S.W.3d 308 (2015).

or material furnished [on the project."[46] The supplier's chief financial officer signed the release but later testified that he failed to check whether the supplier had been paid in full before doing so (the supplier was owed almost $60,000). The court held that the release was unambiguous and barred the claim against the payment bond. In addition, the court rejected the supplier's claim for unjust enrichment because there was a written contract and "unjust enrichment has no application when an express contract exists."[47]

In *J&B Boat Rental, LLC v. JAG Construction Services, Inc.*,[48] the claimant rented a tugboat to a subcontractor for use on a Miller Act project. The subcontractor and claimant entered into an oral contract concerning the hourly rate for the tugboat rental. Naturally, a dispute over the rental rate arose and the claimant provided notice of its claim to the prime contractor and its surety pursuant to the Miller Act. The claimant then filed a lawsuit seeking the unpaid balance of the rental agreement. After the lawsuit was filed, the subcontractor filed for bankruptcy. The claimant filed a notice of claim in the bankruptcy court, and ultimately the bankruptcy judge ruled that the claimant was owed only 7.6% of its claimed amount, leaving a substantial balance.[49]

After the bankruptcy ruling, the claimant moved to lift the stay on the civil litigation, and moved for summary judgment arguing that the bankruptcy court's judgment established both the existence of the oral contract and the value of the services provided under that contract.[50]

The defendants cross-moved for summary judgment on grounds the Miller Act suit was barred under the doctrine of claim preclusion. The defendants pointed out that they were not parties to the bankruptcy proceeding, and that the proper procedure would have been for the claimant to bring its claim as an adversary proceeding in the bankruptcy court against both the subcontractor and prime contractor (and the surety) as necessary parties.[51]

The court held that claim preclusion did not bar the Miller Act suit because the parties to the action were not the same as the parties in the bankruptcy, and the Miller Act claim was separate from the breach of contract action that was adjudicated in bankruptcy court. The court further ruled that because a subcontractor can pursue a Miller Act claim for payment on the bond against a surety without joining the contractor as a defendant, the claimant in this case was not required to bring its Miller Act claim in the context of the adversarial proceeding.[52]

---

[46] 460 S.W.3d at 311.
[47] 460 S.W.3d at 315.
[48] 2015 WL 2376004 (E.D. La. May 15, 2015).
[49] 2015 WL 2376004 at *2.
[50] 2015 WL 2376004 at *2.
[51] 2015 WL 2376004 at *5.
[52] 2015 WL 2376004 at *5.

### [2]  Set-off Defenses

In *Mason v. International Fidelity Insurance Co.*,[53] the claimant rented equipment to a subcontractor on a public works project. After work commenced, the prime contractor became dissatisfied with the subcontractor's performance and obtained permission from the project's owner to remove the subcontractor from the project.[54] The claimant-supplier then rented equipment to the prime contractor directly. Eventually, however, the claimant issued a stop-notice on the project and alleged that it had not been paid in full by the subcontractor who had been terminated previously (the prime contractor was not responsible for the subcontractor's failure to pay the claimant, but the stop notice affected the prime contractor's ability to receive its own payment).

Thereafter, the prime contractor settled the stop-notice claim. The settlement included a complete release for all rentals to the subcontractor but did *not* include a release for rentals made to the prime contractor directly. When the claimant received only a partial payment for its rentals from the prime contractor, it sued the prime contractor's surety under the payment bond. The surety argued the claimant had to show it was underpaid for "*all* of the equipment it rented during the course of the project, *including* the equipment it had rented subcontractor."[55] The surety sought a set off on this basis against the claim amount.

The court disagreed, and held the settlement between the prime contractor and the claimant as to the *subcontractor's* debt (which was paid by the prime contractor not the surety) resolved what was owed for rentals to that subcontractor with no liability to the surety. Therefore, the court reasoned, the settlement was a standalone arm's-length negotiated agreement to resolve a claim and could not be re-opened for purposes of the surety's calculations.[56]

### [3]  Other Defenses

*United States v. KAR Contracting, LLC*,[57] addressed the defense of "unilateral mistake" in the context of surety law. Here, the subcontractor incorrectly estimated the amount of asphalt it needed (it reviewed the incorrect drawing with an incorrect scale).[58] The subcontractor completed the job and sued the prime contractor and its surety (the defendants) for the value of the additional asphalt. The defendants moved for summary judgment arguing, among other things, that there

---

[53] 2015 WL 5453929 (Cal. App. Sept. 16, 2015).

[54] 2015 WL 5453929 at *1.

[55] 2015 WL 5453929 at *3 (emphasis added).

[56] 2015 WL 5453929 at *4.

[57] 2015 WL 8074073 (S.D.W. Va. Dec. 4, 2015).

[58] 2015 WL 8074073 at *2.

was no breach of contract because it paid the subcontractor the full amount of the subcontract. The court agreed and granted summary judgment because the claimant-subcontractor could show neither a breach of the subcontract nor payment bond.[59]

In *Conviron Controlled Environments, Inc. v. Arch Insurance Co.,*[60] a subcontractor on a state public works project sued the prime contractor's surety on the payment bond. The subcontract contained a provision stating that retainage would be released upon several conditions being met, which included acceptance of the subcontractor's work by the owner.[61] The prime contractor alleged backcharges were applicable against any sum owed the subcontractor. Regardless, the subcontractor moved for summary judgment for the unpaid subcontract balance less any dispute back-charges.

The surety argued it had no responsibility to pay the subcontractor until such conditions in the subcontract had been met. To that end, the surety claimed that the subcontract was incorporated into the payment bond.[62] The court disagreed with this position, stating that the payment bond specifically acknowledged and incorporated only the *prime* contract, and that there was no similar language expressly incorporating the subcontract.[63] Having held that the bond did not incorporate any of the conditions to payment set forth in the subcontract, the court turned to whether the prime contract contained grounds sufficient to raise a genuine issue of fact concerning the subcontractor's entitlement to the unpaid balance on the subcontract.

The defendants argued summary judgment was not appropriate because the release of the remaining subcontract balance was conditioned on written acceptance by the owner.[64] The court found this was a mere timing provision (to fix payment) and not a condition precedent to payment. Moreover, New York state law only provided delay for "a reasonable period of time after completion of the subcontract work."[65] And because the prime contract dictated that the owner would "promptly" make the final inspection, the owner's delay to do precisely this for more than two years prohibited the surety's use of this contract language as a justification to withhold the subcontractor's payment.

In *Allen Engineering Contractor, Inc. v. United States,*[66] a contractor filed suit against the government, claiming improper default termination of three construction contracts awarded by the Navy. The Navy alleged the contractor failed

---

[59] 2015 WL 8074073 at *5.
[60] No. 2014-cv-2030 at DE10 (E.D.N.Y. Nov. 13, 2015).
[61] 2014-cv-2030 at *2.
[62] 2014-cv-2030 at *11.
[63] 2014-cv-2030 at *11.
[64] 2014-cv-2030 at *13.
[65] 2014-cv-2030 at *14.
[66] 611 Fed. Appx. 701 (5th Cir. 2015).

to maintain valid performance and payment bonds after replacement bonds were found to be fraudulent and the contractor did not obtain new bonds.[67] The Federal Court of Claims dismissed the lawsuit and the contractor appealed. On appeal, the contractor argued the Government failed to follow its own regulations in approving the bonds that turned out to be fraudulent. The court disagreed, however, holding that the Navy's "review and approval of the bonds is for the government's benefit—not for the benefit of [the contractor]."[68] The court concluded the government's termination for default was justified.

*Advance Industrial Coating, LLC v. Westfield Insurance Co.*[69] reminds parties of the requirements on pleading diversity jurisdiction. Here, the plaintiff alleged a claim on a public construction bond but relied on diversity of citizenship for federal jurisdiction. The plaintiff alleged it was a Florida Limited Liability Company but did not allege the citizenship of its members.[70] Moreover, the plaintiff alleged the surety was an Ohio corporation but did not allege the location of the surety's principal place of business. Thus, the court dismissed the complaint without prejudice.

## [F] Arbitration

In *Irving Materials, Inc. v. Angelo Iafrate Construction Co.*,[71] a concrete supplier to a second-tier subcontractor sued the subcontractor and its surety. The basis of the lawsuit was a contract between the parties that consisted of a credit application and a purchase order. Both forms contained arbitration provisions but, when read together, were wholly contradictory. One provision placed the choice of whether or not to arbitrate in exclusive control of one party to the agreement and the other provision determined whether or not a dispute is resolved by arbitration based upon the subject matter in question.[72]

The court ruled that the purchase order controlled due to its higher level of specificity and higher overall amount of information as to the intentions of the parties to formulate a contract.[73] This holding, however, did not end the dispute as the subcontractor had written to the supplier earlier, and stated that in deciding whether to arbitrate or litigate, the subcontractor chose litigation in Michigan. The supplier thus argued that nothing in the agreement allowed the subcontractor to choose the forum for the litigation, and in choosing "litigation," the subcontractor waived its right to compel arbitration. The court agreed with this argument and

---

[67] 611 Fed. Appx. at 703-04.
[68] 611 Fed. Appx. at 707.
[69] 2015 WL 1822510 (M.D. Fla. Apr. 16, 2015).
[70] 2015 WL 1822510 at *2.
[71] 2015 WL 5680488 (W.D. Ky. Sept. 25, 2015).
[72] 2015 WL 5680488 at *4.
[73] 2015 WL 5680488 at *6.

denied the subcontractor's motion to compel arbitration.[74] The court further agreed that the surety could no longer chose arbitration as the surety's derivative rights could not rise higher than the rights of its principal.[75]

*Lasco, Inc. v. Inman Construction Corp., et al.,*[76] dealt with the issue of awarding attorneys' fees in the context of arbitration. Here, the claimant's subcontract provided for arbitration "in accordance with the Construction Industry Arbitration Rules of the American Arbitration Association. . . ."[77] The issue of attorneys' fees was not addressed anywhere else in the subcontract. The arbitrator awarded attorneys' fees to the prime contractor and its surety. The subcontractor appealed to the trial court, which vacated the fee award as having exceeded the power of the arbitrator. The prime contractor and surety then appealed that decision to the court of appeals.[78]

The court held that the incorporation of the Construction Industry Rules by reference made the rules part of the subcontract. Accordingly, Rule 45 of the Construction Rules provided for attorneys' fees if "all the parties have requested such an award or it is authorized by law or their arbitration agreement."[79] Applying Rule 45 to the case at hand, the court stated that the subcontractor requested attorneys' fees in its initial demand for arbitration, and later asked for fees again in its post-hearing brief. The court noted that it was "only after [the prime contractor and its surety] were awarded their attorneys' fees did [subcontractor] take the position that Rule 45 did not authorize such an award."[80] Thus, the court of appeals reversed the trial court and remanded for an entry confirming the arbitrator's award of attorneys' fees.

In *Five Star Electric Corp. v. Federal Insurance Co.,*[81] a subcontractor on a public construction project sued the prime contractor's sureties to recover on the payment bond. The principals on the bond were a two company "consortium" of Siemens Industry, Inc. (Siemens) and Transit Technologies LLC (Transit).[82] The subcontractor's contract with Transit called for arbitration. Siemens, which was not contractually bound to arbitrate, agreed to be bound by arbitration anyway. The subcontractor-claimant, however, would only permit Siemens' participation on what "could only be described as extortionate terms which Siemens could not rationally accept."[83] The trial court granted summary judgment and held that two

---

[74] 2015 WL 5680488 at *7.
[75] 2015 WL 5680488 FN2 at *7.
[76] 467 S.W.3d 467 (Tenn. App. 2015).
[77] 467 S.W.3d at 469.
[78] 467 S.W.3d at 469.
[79] 467 S.W.3d at 473.
[80] 467 S.W.3d at 474.
[81] 2015 WL 1781968 (N.Y. App. Div. Apr. 21, 2015).
[82] 2015 WL 1781968 at *1.
[83] 2015 WL 1781968 at *1.

sureties were bound by the results of the arbitration between the subcontractor-claimant and Transit. The appellate court reversed, holding "with one of the surety bond's principals unable to participate in the arbitration [i.e., Siemens], the sureties cannot be collaterally estopped from contesting the result."[84]

## [G]  Other Stays of the Payment Bond Action

*U.S. for the Use of DVBE Trucking & Construction Co., Inc. v. McCarthy Building Cos., Inc.*[85] addressed the issue of waiver of the Miller Act. In this case, work on the project was delayed due to the issuance of a notice of suspension by the project's owner, the VA. The claimant's subcontract stated that in the event of a claim based on actions of the owner, the subcontractor would follow procedures set forth in "FAR 52.233—1 DISPUTES (JUL 2002). [The subcontractor] shall be bound by the result of any such dispute resolution procedure with [the owner, VA] or others to the same degree as [the prime contractor]."[86] As such, the prime contractor submitted the subcontractor's claims and, upon inaction (and "deemed denied") by the contracting officer, appealed to the board of contract appeals.[87] Subsequently, the subcontractor sued the prime contractor and its sureties under the Miller Act for recovery under the payment bond. The defendants moved to stay proceedings under the Miller Act pending the outcome of the claim against the owner.

The court analyzed waiver of the Miller Act. To be effective, a waiver of the Miller Act must be "(1) in writing; (2) signed by the person whose right is waived; and (3) executed after the person whose right is waived has furnished labor or material for use in the performance of the contract."[88] Because the subcontract was not signed after work began, the waiver was not only void, but insufficiently clear and explicit. Thus, the court denied motion to stay the Miller Act litigation on grounds the waiver was unenforceable.

In a similar case on the other side of the country, in *Marenalley Construction, LLC, et al. v. Zurich American Insurance Co., et al.*,[89] the subcontractor filed suit under the Miller Act against the prime contractor and its surety seeking to recover for additional materials provided on project for the VA. The prime contractor and its surety (the defendants) argued the subcontractor's payment bond suit should be dismissed or stayed pending resolution of the prime contractor's Contract Dispute Act claim against the VA for additional compensation.[90]

---

[84] 2015 WL 1781968 at *1.

[85] 2015 WL 4198794 (N.D. Cal. July 10, 2015).

[86] 2015 WL 4198794 at *2.

[87] 2015 WL 4198794 at *2.

[88] *Id.* (internal citations omitted).

[89] 99 F. Supp. 3d 543 (E.D. Pa. Mar. 13, 2015).

[90] 99 F. Supp. 3d at 546.

The court disagreed with the defendants on the argument that the subcontractor waived its Miller Act rights, stating "the Subcontract was entered into before [subcontractor] began work on the Project and, therefore, even if the terms on which [the defendants] rely do state a waiver of [subcontractor's] right to proceed against the Payment Bond at this time . . . that waiver would be void."[91]

In regards to the defendants' motion to stay or dismiss, the court stated:

> a stay would subject [subcontractor] to a substantial, indefinite delay as [prime contractor's] claim passes through the administrative process and court review, only to be left at the end of that process to begin again here to litigate its rights against [prime contractor]. Congress made clear in the Miller Act its concern for providing government subcontractors the right to prompt payment by allowing them to sue against the payment bond ninety days after completion of their work rather than the previously required six months after completion of the entire project.[92]

Thus, the court denied the motion to stay or dismiss as contrary to the purpose of the Miller Act.

## [H]   Actions of the Public Owner

In *City of College Park v. Sekisui Americas, LLC*,[93] the city did not obtain a payment bond for a sewer project, and a subcontractor that worked on the project brought action against the city when the prime contractor failed to pay the subcontractor for work performed. The subcontractor alleged the city was liable because it failed to ensure the prime contractor obtained a payment bond; the subcontractor also asserted claims for unjust enrichment and implied obligation to pay.

The city argued that the subcontractor failed to give proper pre-suit notice under Georgia law. The court rejected this argument because the "plain text of the statute makes clear that it applies only to tort claims regarding personal injury or property damage."[94]

Like most states, Georgia law requires a payment bond for public projects with an estimated cost greater than $100,000; however, that requirement does not apply to projects that are "necessitated by an emergency; provided, however, that the nature of the emergency shall be described in the minutes of the governing authority."[95] An "emergency" was defined as "any situation resulting in imminent

---

[91] 99 F. Supp. 3d at 549.
[92] 99 F. Supp. 3d at 551.
[93] 331 Ga. App. 404 (2015).
[94] 331 Ga. App. at 407.
[95] 331 Ga. App. at 408.

danger to the public health. . . ."[96] Here, the court held that there is no requirement that the "emergency" be justified by the city, only that the nature of the emergency be described in the minutes of the governing authority, which was the case with the failure of a 10-inch sanitary sewer line. The court thus ruled in the city had no obligation to obtain a payment bond and thus was not responsible for the subcontractor's claim.

In *Selective Insurance Co. of America v. Ohio Department of Rehabilitation & Correction (ODRC)*,[97] a subcontractor on a public project sent the owner an affidavit of claim for the unpaid balance of a subcontract to provide and then repair a generator. Pursuant to Ohio law, upon receiving the affidavit, the owner should have detained from the balance of the funds remaining in the contract with the prime contractor an amount that did not exceed the claim.[98] When the owner received the affidavit of claim, there were sufficient funds on the contract balance to pay the subcontractor. Despite this mandate, the owner did not detain the funds but instead dispersed the majority of the remaining balance to the prime contractor.

The subcontractor and the surety settled their dispute and, as part of that settlement, the subcontractor's claim was assigned to the surety.[99]

On appeal, the court rejected the owner's argument that the surety was asserting a subrogation claim, stating "under [Ohio Statute] R.C. 2743.02(D), the statute cited by the owner, [the surety] is the claimant and had no collateral recovery. Therefore, there is no reduction of any recovery against the state."[100] The court also rejected the owner's argument concerning the validity of the subcontractor's lien, stating that the "affidavit of claim constitutes a stop notice due to the public authority, preventing the payment of moneys due to the principal contractor . . . [the owner] cannot ignore the mandate of the statute because it doubts the validity of the lien."[101] Finally, the court rejected the owner's argument that the surety is statutorily required to indemnify the owner against the prime contractor's failure to perform the contract according to its provisions. The court stated "[the owner] is not entitled to recover damages from [the surety] for its own negligence in failing to detain funds."[102] Thus, the court affirmed the trial court's decision to grant the surety summary judgment.

---

[96] 331 Ga. App. at 408.

[97] 2015 WL 872972 (Ohio App. 2015).

[98] 2015 WL 872972 at *1.

[99] 2015 WL 872972 at *2.

[100] 2015 WL 872972 at *3.

[101] 2015 WL 872972 at *4.

[102] 2015 WL 872972 at *5.

## § 5.03  PERFORMANCE BONDS

### [A]  Damages

In *Hartford Casualty Insurance Co. v. City of Marathon*,[103] the City of Marathon sued the contractor's performance bond surety. The court awarded the city the amount by which the completion contract exceeded the original defaulted contract—$43,042.88. The court also awarded the city $335,199.00 for outstanding payables that the principal owed to its subcontractors, finding that the amount was reasonable and "no more than Hartford was obligated to pay under its payment bond."[104] The court also approved expenses paid to an engineering firm for additional work associated with completion of the contract and $2,808.00 needed to maintain the job site while the job was idle.

Bond obligees often seek an award of liquidated damages against the surety as a result of the principal's delay. In *Hartford Casualty Insurance Co. v. City of Marathon*[105] discussed above, the city also sought liquidated damages after the surety declined to take over work without a completion agreement. The city contracted with a new contractor and after completion of the project, the city made a claim for liquidated damages against the performance bond surety for 471 calendar days in a liquidated damages amount of $1,500.00 per day. The court found that, under Florida law, a party claiming liquidated damages has the burden to introduce evidence to apportion the fault for delay if the parties share responsibility for the delay. The city made no effort to present such evidence, and the surety showed that at least some portions of the delay were the city's responsibility. Specifically, the surety argued that 64 days of the delay were during settlement negotiations and 44 days of delay were due to change order work that was beyond the scope of the original contract. Finding that the city failed in its burden, the court declined to award liquidated damages.[106]

In *Davis Group, Inc. v. Ace Electric, Inc.*,[107] the prime contractor sued the subcontractor and its surety for liquidated damages withheld by the owner, and for other delay damages. After the work was completed, the prime contractor apportioned the damages and demanded that the subcontractor and surety pay an amount for 82 days of delay. When the money was not paid, the prime contractor declared a default and demanded payment from the surety. The surety moved for summary judgment on the ground that the prime contractor failed to provide notice of default under the terms of the performance bond.[108] The prime contractor disagreed with the surety's argument, denying that the bond required any such

---

[103] 2015 WL 4633683 (S.D. Fla. July 31, 2015).
[104] 2015 WL 4633683 at *4.
[105] 2015 WL 4633683.
[106] 2015 WL 4633683 at *6.
[107] 2015 WL 3935422 (M.D. Fla. June 26, 2015).
[108] 2015 WL 3935422 at *3.

notice and contending that the surety's "default" was its failure to pay the liqui-dated damages and delay damages. The court found that whether and how the subcontractor defaulted and the date upon which the default occurred were genu-ine issues of material fact precluding the entry of summary judgment.[109] The court found that the general contractor provided reasonable notice when it sent notice to the surety on February 12, 2014, because the subcontractor's default arguably occurred 72 hours after February 6, 2014, when the general contractor demanded that the subcontractor pay its share of the liquidated damages assessed by the owner, and the subcontractor failed to pay.[110]

### [1] Jurisdictional Amount

In *Frederick Quinn Corp. v. West Bend Mutual Insurance Co.*,[111] the obligee prime contractor sued the surety, and alleged that the cost to complete the sub-contract work, less the admitted subcontract balance, was less than the $75,000.00 jurisdictional amount. The court granted the surety's motion to dismiss, finding that interest should not be included in the calculation for the jurisdictional amount, but that any attorney's fees incurred prior to the filing of the complaint could be used as part of the jurisdictional amount. The court granted the plaintiff leave to file an amended complaint, including whatever details it deemed neces-sary to establish the amount in controversy.

### [2] Attorney's Fees and Consequential Damages

In *King County v. Vinci Construction Grands Projets/Parsons RCI/Frontier-Kemper, JV*,[112] a public owner and contractor pursued claims including differing site conditions, defaults, and damages. Ultimately, the owner recovered a sub-stantial net judgment against the contractor (over $100 million), and almost $15 million in attorney's fees. The sureties appealed the award of attorney's fees and the trial court's holding that they were jointly and severally liable for damages under the contract against the contractor. The court analogized insurance policy cases to the performance bond issues, noting that the county was forced to pursue litigation in order to obtain the benefit of the performance bond. The sureties also argued that they should not be liable for the entirety of the attorney's fees award, but only the attorney's fees incurred for the claims against the sureties. The court found that the fees to litigate the issues with the sureties could not be segregated from the owner's fees in general. The court found that the owner had to prove its claim against the contractor in order to recover against the surety, and the county

---

[109] 2015 WL 3935422 at *3.
[110] *Id.*
[111] 2015 WL 2210336 (N.D. Ill. May 8, 2015).
[112] 2015 WL 6865706 (Wash. App. Nov. 9, 2015).

"could only obtain the benefit of the bond by defeating [the contractor's] defenses."[113]

## [B] Performance Bond Defenses

### [1] Identity of Principal

In *Choate Construction Co. v. Auto-Owners Insurance Co.*,[114] the Georgia Court of Appeals addressed payment and performance bond claims against Auto-Owners Insurance Co. ("AOIC"). Choate was the general contractor for construction of fraternity and sorority houses at the University of Georgia in Athens, Georgia. Choate subcontracted the electrical work to Dedmond Electrical Services, and provided its bond forms to Thad Dedmond, the sole proprietor of Dedmond. About a month after Dedmond started working on the project, Choate received payment and performance bonds that designated AOIC as the surety and D.E.S. Electrical Contractors ("DES") as the principal. After Dedmond's default, performance and payment bond claims were made against AOIC. Choate and AOIC both moved for summary judgment in the case.

In a previous decision, the court of appeals reversed the trial court's grant of summary judgment to AOIC. Specifically, the court of appeals agreed with Choate that the evidence, when viewed in Choate's favor, presented a jury question as to "whether Dedmond and DES were the same company and/or whether Payne acted as an agent or "on behalf of" Dedmond when she procured the bonds." The court also found that jury questions existed as to whether AOIC had actual or constructive knowledge of, or participated, in a possible fraud by Thad Dedmond and Ms. Payne, and whether AOIC intentionally or recklessly misrepresented to Choate one or more material facts when it issued the bonds.

In this decision, the court was confronted with Choate's motions for summary judgment against AOIC. The court of appeals noted that in its previous decision, it had reversed the trial court's grant of summary judgment to AOIC. In addressing Choate's motion for summary judgment, the court explained that it had already considered Choate's arguments, reviewed the bonds and the subcontract, and determined that there were numerous material factual disputes regarding AOIC's liability to Choate under the bonds. The court based its ruling on the law of the case rule, which Georgia has formally abolished except as it applies to rulings by one of the appellate courts. Under the Georgia law of the case rule, an appellate court ruling is binding and in all subsequent proceedings in that case.[115]

Choate also appealed the trial court's grand of summary judgment to AOIC on Choate's claim for surety bad faith. Choate made a bad faith claim based upon

---

[113] 2015 WL 6865706 at *18.
[114] 779 S.E.2d 465 (Ga. App. Nov. 18, 2015).
[115] 779 S.E.2d at 469-70.

an insurance statute, which provides that where an insurer fails to pay a claim within 60 days after demand has been made, and upon a finding that such refusal is in bad faith, the insurer is liable to pay the claimant, in addition to the loss, not more than 50 percent of the liability of the insurer for the loss or $5,000.00, whichever is greater, and all reasonable attorney's fees for prosecution of the claim.[116] Since the court found that there were genuine issues of material fact as to whether Choate was entitled to coverage under the payment and performance bonds, the court found that AOIC had reasonable grounds to contest Choate's claims, and thus could not be in bad faith.[117] Similarly, the court affirmed the grant of summary judgment to AOIC on Choate's attorney's fees claim.[118]

### [2]  Limitations

Sureties may invoke their principal's limitations defense. For example, in *Nacimiento Water Co., Inc. v. International Fidelity Insurance Co.*,[119] the court granted the surety summary judgment based on the surety's statute of limitations defense. Cal. Code of Civil Procedure § 359.5 provides: "The expiration of a statute of limitations with respect to the obligations of the principal, other than the obligations of the principal under the bond, shall also bar an action against the principal or surety under the bond. . . ." The obligee argued that the claim against the surety was not barred by the statute of limitations because the obligee and surety entered into a tolling agreement. The court granted the surety's motion for summary judgment, finding that the statute of limitations to sue the principal had expired, and this relieved the surety of liability.[120]

In *Peekskill City School District v. Colonial Surety Co.*,[121] the surety filed a declaratory judgment action against the obligee and the obligee did not file a counterclaim against the surety. Later, the surety dismissed the declaratory judgment action and the obligee filed suit against the surety after the two-year contractual limitations period had run. The court found that the declaratory judgment action did not toll the limitations period and pointed out that the obligee could have protected his rights by answering and asserting a counterclaim in the declaratory judgment action or by filing its own lawsuit within the limitations period.

---

[116] 779 S.E.2d at 471-72.

[117] 779 S.E.2d at 472. It is unclear why, this case involving bond claims, the Court cited to Georgia's bad faith insurance statute, O.C.G.A. § 33-4-6(a), rather than O.C.G.A. § 10-7-30, which specifically applies to bad faith by sureties.

[118] 779 S.E.2d at 472.

[119] 2015 WL 4554288 (C.D. Cal. July 28, 2015).

[120] 2015 WL 4554288 at *2-3.

[121] 595 Fed. Appx. 91 (2d Cir. Mar. 2, 2015) (affirming summary judgment for surety at 6 F. Supp. 3d 372 (S.D.N.Y. 2014)).

Another surety defended a performance bond claim based on the bond's two-year contractual limitations period in *Travelers Casualty & Surety C. of America v. City of Pittsburg, Tennessee.*[122] In that case, the surety argued that the action was barred by the two-year limitations provision in the bond. Under the bond language, the two-year limitations period commenced on the earlier date that the principal ceased work, the date of contractor default, or the date that the surety refused or failed to perform its obligations. The court found that there was an issue of fact as to the date that the principal ceased work. The surety argued that it was still entitled to summary judgment because the principal's alleged failure to comply with the contract was more than two years prior to the suit against the surety, and the bond defined "contractor default" as "failure of contractor, which has been neither remedied nor waived, to perform or otherwise comply with the terms of the contract."[123] The court held that the contractor default for the purposes of the two-year limitation period was the date that the obligee formally declared the contractor default pursuant to Paragraph 3 of the bond, and that the action was filed within two years of the contractor's default. Accordingly, the court denied the surety's motion for summary judgment.[124]

In a New York decision, the surety argued that the obligee's claim was barred because the obligee failed to file the claim within the two-year contractual limitation period. The court found that, while the obligee's claim was filed more than two years after the surety's principal completed work on the project, the principal claimed it had installed windows after final completion to comply with industry standards. Accordingly, the court found a disputed issue of material fact as to whether the principal had remained working on the project and extended the limitations period.[125]

### [a]   Limitations-Timeliness of Claim After Final Completion

In *JJK Group, Inc. v. VW International, Inc.,*[126] the prime contractor on a federal project sued a subcontractor and the subcontractor's performance bond surety. After completion of the project, the government had revoked acceptance of the subcontractor's work because of alleged latent defects and demanded a replacement of the work. The surety argued that once the work was completed, it had no further obligations. The court rejected that argument, finding that under Maryland law, the liability of the surety was coextensive with that of its principal and did not cease upon the initial completion of the work.[127] The court found that the subcontractor was obligated to perform the replacement work in installing and

---

[122] 2015 WL 414053 (Tenn. App. Jan. 30, 2015).

[123] 2015 WL 414053 at *6-7.

[124] 2015 WL 414053 at *7.

[125] Niagra Univ. v. Hanover Ins. Co., 2015 Slip Op. 1028 (N.Y. App. Div. Feb. 6, 2015).

[126] 2015 WL 1459841(D. Md. Mar. 27, 2015).

[127] 2015 WL 1459841 at *13.

replacing the nurse call system. Since the subcontractor was liable, the surety, First National, would be obligated to cure the default.[128] Similarly, the court found that the surety's obligations under the performance bond were not null and void upon the government's final acceptance of the original nurse call system. The court found ample authority in Maryland law for the proposition that surety obligations extend beyond acceptance and final payment. [129]

### [3]   Conditions Precedent and Declaration of Default

In *Howard Robson, Inc. v. Town of Rising Sun*,[130] the prime contractor and its surety sued the obligee and the obligee counterclaimed, alleging that it "fully complied with the terms and conditions of the performance bond." The surety moved to dismiss the counterclaim based on the obligee's failure to comply with conditions precedent in the bond. The court ruled that for the purposes of a motion to dismiss under Rule 12(b)(6), the obligee had alleged performance of all conditions precedent sufficient to survive the motion and that the surety could assert the obligee's failure to comply with the conditions precedent as part of its affirmative defenses. The court cautioned that the surety could renew its contentions regarding the conditions precedent defenses at a later time.

In *Heckler Electric Co. v. Liberty Mutual Insurance Co.*,[131] a contractor pursued a subcontractor and its surety for both a performance bond claim for the cost of completing its work and a payment bond claim for the amount claimed to the sub-subcontractor. The court found that there were issues of fact as to whether the contractor complied with conditions precedent in the performance bond and what amounts, if any were owed to the subcontractor for work it performed under the subcontract, and accordingly denied both parties' motion for summary judgment.

In *Cardi Corp. v. State*,[132] the court denied the surety's motion for summary judgment. The surety argued that the claim was barred by a two-year statute of limitation contained in the bond, that the plaintiff was not a proper claimant under the performance bond, and that the plaintiff failed to satisfy conditions precedent to recovery outlined in the performance bond. The court found that while the payment bond failed to define the term "claimant," this action arose out of their performance bond and that the claimant was entitled to bring a claim under the performance bond. As to the conditions precedent argument, the court found that the alleged lack of notice by the obligee did not present a defense, because the claim involved latent defects, and the surety suffered no prejudice from the lack of notice. Last, with respect to the limitations, argument, the court noted that

---

[128] 2015 WL 1459841 at *19.
[129] 2015 WL 1459841 at *13.
[130] 2015 WL 424773 (D. Md. Jan. 30, 2015).
[131] 2015 WL 7313860 (D.N.J. Nov. 20, 2015).
[132] 2014 R.I. Super. LEXIS 103 (R.I. Super. Ct. 2014).

under Rhode Island law, the limitations period is measured from the date the contract work is completed and is not extended by any repair or corrective work. The court found that there were fact issues concerning when the work was completed, and accordingly denied the motion for summary judgment on the limitations issue.

In *Archstone v. Tocci Building Corp. of New Jersey, Inc.*,[133] the owner sued the general contractor and its performance bond surety, Liberty Mutual, on an AIA A312 performance bond. Liberty moved for summary judgment, claiming that the owner failed to comply with certain express conditions precedent. The appellate decision does not identify the conditions precedent at issue. However, the court held that Paragraph 3 of the A312 performance bond does contain certain express conditions precedent to the liability of the surety under the bond and further found that the plaintiff failed to strictly comply with the conditions of the bond. Accordingly, the court upheld the trial judge's grant of summary judgment to Liberty.[134]

A court granted the performance bond surety's summary judgment where it found that (1) the owner was in default and (2) the owner failed to adhere to notice and meeting requirements of Article 3 of the performance bond. The court found that the bond in this case was highly similar to the A312 performance bond form. The court rejected the obligee's position that since the surety had not suffered harm arising from the deficient notice, the bond should not be discharged.[135]

Sureties sometimes defend performance bond claims based upon the obligee's failure to timely declare a default of the bonded contract and to terminate that contract. Such a failure by the obligee resulted in the court granting a surety summary judgment in *Curtiss-Manes-Schulte, Inc. v. Safeco Insurance Co. of America*.[136] In that case, the obligee prime contractor completed the bonded subcontract work without terminating the subcontract or giving notice to the surety. In ruling on a motion for reconsideration by the surety, the court noted that the bond language "[w]henever the Principal [Balkenbush] shall be, and is declared by the Obligee [CMS] to be in default under the Subcontract" is a provision that stipulates for notice, acts as a condition precedent to any duty owed by Safeco, and is inserted into performance bonds "to avoid the common-law rule that a secondary obligor such as [the surety] is not entitled to notice when the time for its performance is due."[137] In essence, the court found that language required an

---

[133] 119 A.D.3d 497, 990 N.Y.S.2d 44 (2d Dep't 2014).

[134] *Id.* at 497.

[135] Eddystone Borough v. Peter V. Pirozzi General Contracting, LLC, 2015 WL 1542284 (E.D. Pa. Apr. 7, 2015).

[136] 2015 WL 2062566 (W.D. Mo. May 4, 2015).

[137] *Id.* at *3.

unequivocal termination for default and demand on the surety.[138] Since there was no dispute that the obligee failed to declare the subcontractor to be in default, the court granted summary judgment to the surety.

An opposite result was reached by a California appeals court in *JMR Construction Corp. v. Environmental Assessment & Remediation Management, Inc.*,[139] when the court rejected the surety's argument that the prime contractor was required to provide notice of default. In *JMR*, the court construed a performance bond provided by the subcontractor, EAR, and its surety, Suretec. The bond contained predictable language providing: "'Whenever the Principal shall be, and is declared by the Obligee to be in default under the Subcontract, with the Obligee having performed its obligations in the Subcontract, the Surety may promptly remedy the default, or shall promptly' (1) '[c]omplete the Subcontract in accordance with its terms and conditions'; (2) retain a new subcontractor to complete the Principal's work under the subcontract; (3) pay the Obligee the amount for which the Surety is liable; or (4) deny liability in whole or in part, providing an explanation for doing so."[140] Suretec argued that this language created a condition precedent requiring notice by the general contractor, even though the language does not stipulate that it is a "condition."

The court found that the bond lacked the requisite "clear, unambiguous language" that would support a finding that the contractor must provide notice as a condition precedent to the surety's liability under the bond. The court noted the absence of any specific, express notice requirement in the bond, and premised its decision in part on a California statute that courts, in construing an instrument, must take care "not to insert what has been omitted, or to omit what has been inserted."[141] The court rejected other case authority, including the Florida cases discussed in this chapter, and found them inconsistent with California law.

### [4]  Standing to Bring Performance Bond Claim

In *Liberty Mutual Insurance Co. v. Travelers Casualty & Surety Co. of America*,[142] the prime contractor's surety sued a subcontractor's surety, after the prime's surety took over the work. The prime's surety claimed that the subcontractor's work was defective, demanded that the subcontractor's surety remedy it,

---

[138] *Id.* at *4-6. The Court quoted from an earlier case, in which the court explained: "Interpreting the notice of default provision, the Fifth Circuit stated that the performance bond imposed liability on the surety for the subcontractor's breach "only if two conditions exist[ed]. First, [the subcontractor] must have been in default of its performance obligations under the subcontract. Second, [the general contractor] must have declared [the subcontractor] to be in default." L & A Contracting Co. v. Southern Concrete Servs., 17 F.3d 106, 111 (5th Cir. 1994).

[139] 2015 Cal. App. LEXIS 1172 (Dec. 30, 2015).

[140] *Id.* at *42-43.

[141] *Id* at *47, *quoting* Cal. Code Civ. Proc. § 1858.

[142] 2015 WL 1737811 (S.D. Miss. Apr. 16, 2015).

and sued the subcontractor and its surety when the surety declined to do so. Travelers moved to dismiss, arguing that Liberty lacked standing to bring the claims. The court denied the motion to dismiss, finding that under the allegations of the complaint, the prime contractor's surety had standing to assert the claims. The court relied not only on specific subcontract language, but also on Liberty's subrogation argument, explaining that Liberty properly stepped into the shoes of its principal to seek the benefits of the bond.[143]

Several interesting issues were presented in a case involving a claim by a general contractor against a subcontractor's performance bond surety. In *Allied Products Corp. v. J. Strober & Sons, LLC*,[144] the surety sought to defend a third-party complaint by the general contractor, arguing that a general contractor was not a proper claimant under the bond, that the general contractor failed to accept the performance bond, and that there was no obligation for the surety to comply with the bond form acquired under its principal subcontractor's contract because it never received or read the contract.

As to the first issue, whether the general contractor was the true obligee or a proper claimant under the performance bond, the court noted that the contract was incorporated by reference into the bond, and the bond identified all other aspects of the project directly. Accordingly, the court reviewed the bond and contract as one document and held that the general contractor was the true obligee.[145] The court also rejected the surety's arguments that it was relieved from liability because the general contractor did not accept the bond form, and that it was not bound by the bond form submitted by the general contractor. The court ruled that the surety was bound to the bond form required under the contract by contracting with its principal and accepting the premium.[146] Finally, the court found that acceptance of a performance bond by an obligee is not a condition precedent to the surety's liability under the law of New Jersey.[147]

### [C]    Extracontractual Claims and Bad Faith

In *Clark County School District v. Travelers Casualty & Surety Co. of America*,[148] the obligee moved to reconsider the court's ruling that the surety lacked a special relationship with the obligee that would support a claim for tortious breach of the covenant of good faith and fair dealing. The court noted various Nevada Supreme Court decisions which involved bad faith claims by principals, but found that the reasoning in those decisions, including the lack of equal bargaining power, would not apply to a claim by the obligee.

---

[143] 2015 WL 1737811 at *2-3.
[144] 437 N.J. Super. 249, 97 A.3d 1169 (App. Div. 2014).
[145] 97 A.3d at 1176.
[146] 97 A.3d at 1176-77.
[147] 97 A.3d at 1179.
[148] 2015 WL 1578163 (D. Nev. Apr. 8, 2015).

The court found that the Nevada Supreme Court had held in two prior decisions that bad faith claims against sureties are not maintainable. The court noted that the cases disallowing bad faith claims involved cases brought by principals and not obligees. However, the court found the precedent instructive and ruled that the bad faith claim by an obligee against a surety is barred as a matter of law. The court found that the prior case law refusing to apply a tortious bad faith claim to a surety was equally applicable in a case against the obligee, because the court focused on the absence of a special relationship in the surety context noting that a "special element of reliance" and "vastly superior bargaining power" were not present.[149]

The obligee sued the performance bond surety for bad faith in *C&I Entertainment, LLC v. Fidelity & Deposit Co. of Maryland.*[150] The claim against the surety in federal court was stayed pending state court litigation against the principal. Once judgment was entered against the principal in the state court action, the surety moved for summary judgment on the bad faith claim, and argued that it had no liability to the obligee because of the obligee's failure to satisfy conditions precedent contained in the A312 performance bond.

Ultimately, the principal satisfied the state court judgment in favor of the obligee. In any event, the court denied the surety's motion to dismiss, finding that the surety was bound by the reason it gave for denying the obligee's claim—a two-year limitations argument. Accordingly, the court denied the surety's motion to dismiss the bad faith claim.[151]

## § 5.04   INDEMNITY ISSUES AND OTHER SURETY RIGHTS

After incurring a loss, the surety seeks to be made whole by filing an indemnity claim against the principal and other indemnitors who signed the general agreement of indemnity. The surety may also take other action, including asserting its claim to contract proceeds or filing actions against other potential third parties. This section first explores various defenses raised in indemnity cases, and then proceeds to examine other recent developments involving the surety's assertion of equitable or legal claims against the indemnitors or other third parties.

---

[149] 2015 WL 1578163 at *5.

[150] 2014 WL 3640790 (N.D. Miss. July 22, 2014).

[151] 2014 WL 3640790 at *14-15. The *C&I* court also discussed at length the surety's defenses that the obligee failed to comply with conditions precedent triggering its liability. The decision contains an interesting discussion about whether the conditions precedent applied and whether the conditions were waived by the surety. The court found disputed fact issues concerning such waiver.

## [A]  Indemnitor Defenses

### [1]  Forgery

A surety battled with its indemnitors over several different issues, including alleged fraud committed by a husband in forging his wife's signature on an indemnity agreement in *Travelers Casualty & Surety Co. v. HUB Mechanical Contractors, Inc.*[152] In *HUB*, the court granted the wife's motion for summary judgment on the basis of the fraudulent signature. The court granted partial summary judgment to the surety, Travelers, on Traveler's claim against the husband, rejecting the husband's argument that because the surety agent knew about the fraud, that knowledge should be imputed to Travelers.[153]

### [2]  Termination of Indemnity

In the *Hub* case discussed above, the court denied all motions for summary judgment on the husband's remaining liability for claims under performance and payment bonds, in part because the husband claimed to have sent a letter stating that he would be "no longer responsible for any performance bonds issued on Hub Mechanical Contractor's behalf after March 27, 2008."[154] Initially, the court granted Travelers' summary judgment as to the payment bond claim, asserting that the letter written by the husband would not have affected his liability to repay Travelers for the payment bond claims it paid. However, one day later, the court issued a revised opinion in which it found support under Mississippi law for the proposition that there were disputed issues of fact as to whether the payment bond claims could be maintained as well.[155]

*Developers Surety & Indemnity Co. v. Barlow*[156] dealt with the liability of indemnitors who were no longer affiliated with the principal. The indemnitors signed the indemnity agreement in 2004 and asserted that they had sold their interest in the principal in 2006. The indemnitors failed to comply with the indemnity agreement's requirements for terminating the indemnity—they failed to provide the surety with written notice of the termination of the indemnity agreement. The court found that whether phrased as lack of consideration, failure of consideration or failure to mitigate damages, the indemnitors' arguments failed because while the indemnitors may not have had a beneficial interest in the specific bond sued on, there was nevertheless consideration for the indemnity agreement.[157] The court focused on the language of the indemnity agreement, and rejected the

---

[152] 2015 WL 6158826 (S.D. Miss. Oct. 19, 2015).
[153] 2015 WL 6158826 at *7.
[154] 2015 WL 6158826 at *8.
[155] 2015 WL 6158826 at *8.
[156] 2015 WL 6075709 (10th Cir. Utah Oct. 15, 2015).
[157] *Id.* at *2-3.

indemnitors' claim that they must have a specific interest in the bond in order to have the obligation to indemnify. The court explained:

> The Agreement is not ambiguous. No provision releases an Indemnitor if the Indemnitor lacks a sufficient interest in the bonds. If an Indemnitor is no longer interested in whether [the principal] obtains a bond, the Indemnitor need only provide notice to Developers to end his or her liability on future bonds. The Indemnitors' warranty that they have a specific and beneficial interest in the bonds is an obligation of the Indemnitors; it does not bind Developers.[158]

In *Liberty Mutual Insurance Co. v. Integrated Pro Services*,[159] the indemnitors argued that they were not bound by the indemnity agreement because they had sold their interest in the principal shortly after the indemnity agreement was signed. The surety countered that the indemnitors failed to provide written notice in accordance with the provision in the indemnity agreement that was required to be relieved of responsibility for future bonds. The court denied the motion for summary judgment by the surety, finding that there were disputed issues of fact as to whether the surety terminated the indemnitors' obligations even though they did not follow the procedure in the agreement.[160] In so ruling, the court criticized Liberty's argument that the indemnitors failed to follow the requirements in the agreement for terminating their indemnity:

> Liberty Mutual's argument proceeds from the faulty premise that paragraph 19 is the sole means of terminating an indemnitor's obligation. To be sure, an indemnitor who unilaterally seeks to terminate his obligations must do so pursuant to paragraph 19. However, paragraph 16 of the Indemnity Agreement states, "The Indemnitors and Principals shall continue to remain bound under the terms of the [Indemnity] Agreement, Other [surety] Agreements, and any other agreements containing indemnity obligations, *even though the Surety [that is, Liberty Mutual] may from time to time heretofore or hereafter, with or without notice to or knowledge of the Indemnitors and Principals, accept, release, or reduce any indemnity obligations or collateral of current or future Indemnitors and Principals for any reason*." Clearly, Liberty Mutual has the right to terminate any indemnitor's obligation at any time "for any reason," and there are genuine issues of material fact with respect to whether Liberty Mutual did so.[161]

In *Arch Insurance Co. v. Nizar & Nuha Katbi Family Trust, et al.*,[162] the indemnitors signed an agreement of indemnity in 2006. The next year, in 2007,

---

[158] *Id.* at *2.

[159] 2015 WL 3620147 (E.D. La. June 9, 2015).

[160] 2015 WL 3620147 at *5.

[161] 2015 WL 3620147 at *5 (emphasis in original).

[162] 610 Fed. Appx. 622 (9th Cir. 2015).

the indemnitors wrote a letter to the surety informing it that he was switching sureties. Two years later, the indemnitors returned to the original surety but the parties did not execute a new indemnity agreement, but the surety issued new bonds.[163] Presumably, claims arose on the bonds and the surety called upon the provisions of the indemnity agreement to indemnify the surety and post collateral. The defendants took the position that the 2007 letter terminated the indemnity agreement. The court rejected that argument stating "the parties never abandoned the contract, and [the indemnitor] is estopped from claiming that they did."[164]

### [3]   Bad Faith, Good Faith

In *Great American Insurance Co. v. RDA Construction Corp.*,[165] the court rejected the indemnitors' bad faith claims and granted the surety summary judgment on its claims for indemnity, specific performance of the collateral deposit provision of the indemnity agreement, *quia timet*, and exoneration. The indemnitors challenged the obligee's termination of the bonded contract, and also challenged the surety's reprocurement of the work. The court rejected these challenges, finding that the indemnity agreement required only that the surety not act with a dishonest purpose, conscious wrongdoing, or ill will. The court found that bad faith requires more than bad judgment, negligence, or insufficient zeal.

A federal district court took a somewhat anti-surety view of "good faith" in *Liberty Mutual Insurance Co. v. Integrated Pro Services, LLC.*[166] The obligee terminated the bonded contract for default and the surety took over completion of the work. The principal disputed the termination in state court litigation. The surety sued the principal and individual indemnitors for its losses to date and for an order requiring the defendants to deposit collateral for additional expected losses. Under the indemnity agreement, Liberty was "entitled to charge for any and all disbursements made by it in good faith . . . under the belief that it is, or was, or might be liable for the sums and amounts so disbursed or that it was necessary or expedient to make such disbursements, whether or not such liability, necessity or expediency existed."[167] The indemnitors challenged their liability on the basis that the termination was not proper. The court conceded that the surety did not have to prove that it was liable to the obligee and that the indemnity agreement required indemnity for payments made in good faith. The court noted that the indemnity agreement failed to define good faith, and looked to the Louisiana Procurement Code which defines good faith as "honesty in fact in the conduct or

---

[163] 610 Fed. Appx. at 622.
[164] 610 Fed. Appx. at 623.
[165] 2015 WL 5163043 (D. Miss. Sept. 3, 2015).
[166] 2015 WL 3620147 (E.D. La. June 9, 2015).
[167] 2015 WL 3620147 at *3, quoting from Indemnity Agreement, ¶ 2.

transaction concerned and the observance of reasonable commercial standards of fair dealing."[168]

Examining the good faith issue, the court examined a Liberty email produced in discovery. IPS submitted an internal email between Liberty Mutual employees, dated October 14, 2013, that discusses the levee construction project. The email states that the obligee advised Liberty that it "is going to terminate the contract today"; "that the job is virtually subcontracted out"; that the subcontractor "is doing a good job and . . . will remain on the job and complete it for the same price"; and that "this is good for [Liberty Mutual]." The court noted: "[t]his email, dated over five months before IPS was actually terminated from its contract by Plaquemines Parish, may raise an inference that Liberty Mutual did not act in good faith because it was not conducting itself with 'honesty in fact in the conduct or transaction concerned' and/or because it did not 'observ[e] . . . reasonable commercial standards of fair dealing.'"[169] The court denied Liberty's motion for summary judgment because issues of fact existed regarding Liberty's exercise of good faith.

### [4] Other Defenses

In *Developers Surety & Indemnity Co. v. Krause*,[170] the surety filed two different actions—one against the surety's agent claiming that the bonds issued by the surety were unauthorized and a second action against the principal and indemnitors. The court rejected the indemnitors' argument that collateral estoppel or judicial estoppel barred the surety's claims, and found that, as a practical matter, the surety's pleadings were consistent between the two cases.

In *Ohio Casualty Insurance Co. v. Copps*,[171] the court granted summary judgment against the indemnitor, disallowing the indemnitor's argument that the indemnity agreement was unenforceable because it failed to comply with Kentucky law by stating a maximum amount and a termination date. The court differentiated the indemnity agreement from a guarantee obligation that is limited by K.R.S. 371.065.

In *Bond Safeguard Insurance Co. v. National Union Fire Insurance Co. of Pittsburgh*,[172] the court granted summary judgment to an insurance company in an action filed by the surety on a series of subdivision bonds. The surety sued the indemnitor for negligence and misrepresentation in administering the projects and securing the bonds, rather than for breach of the general agreement of indemnity.

---

[168] 2015 WL 3620147 at *4.

[169] 2015 WL 3620147at *11-12.

[170] 2015 WL 3962287 (N.D. Ill. June 29, 2015).

[171] 2015 WL 5612175 (E.D. Ky. Sept. 22, 2015).

[172] 2015 WL 5781002 (11th Cir. Oct. 5, 2015).

The indemnitor reached a settlement with the surety, allowing the surety a judgment and then assigning to the surety the indemnitor's rights under a director's and officer's liability insurance policy.

The insurer defended the action based on an exclusion in the policy providing that the insurer "shall not be liable to make any payment for Loss in connection with a Claim made against an Insured . . . alleging, arising out of, based upon or attributable to any actual or alleged contractual liability of the Company or any other Insured under any express contract or agreement." Exclusion 4(h).[173] The insurer argued that this exclusion barred the surety's claims because they arose out of the indemnity agreement. The court agreed, holding that the surety's "pleading of its claim in tort does not alter the fact that all of its asserted losses arose from [the indemnitors'] contractual breaches of the development contracts and the GAI. . . . Given the Florida Supreme Court's broad interpretation of the unambiguous phrase 'arising out of,' we find sufficient causal connection between Bond—Lexon's purported negligence claim and the contractual liability of [the indemnitors] to enforce the exclusion according to its terms."[174]

In *Lexon Insurance Co. v. Naser*,[175] the Court of Appeals affirmed the district court's decision that an indemnitor was personally liable to the surety. Here, the defendant claimed he never became personally liable under the indemnity agreement though he signed the agreement twice: once as an officer on behalf of the corporation and again as a co-owner of that same corporation. In signing a second time, the defendant did not include his corporation title, but did include his social security number next to his signature. The court held the defendant's second signature made him personally liable to the surety stating "[the defendant] offers no reason why he would sign the indemnification agreement twice if he did *not* intend to hold himself personally liable."[176]

The court in *Liberty Mutual Insurance Co. v. Sumo-Nan, LLC, et al.*,[177] rejected the argument that a surety has an obligation to pursue recovery again some indemnitors before others. Here, the court labeled two distinct group of indemnitor-defendants: The "Sumo Defendants" and the "Nan Defendants." The Nan Defendants argued the surety had an obligation to first pursue the Sumo Defendants. The court disagreed, stating "nothing in any of the agreements offered by the parties' obligation [the surety] to pursue each of its indemnitors, or each of its indemnitors in any particular order. . . ."[178] The court ultimately granted summary judgment in favor of the surety.

---

[173] 2015 WL 5781002 at *1.
[174] 2015 WL 5781002 at *6.
[175] 781 F.3d 335 (6th Cir. 2015).
[176] 781 F.3d at 341 (emphasis in original).
[177] 2015 WL 7303523 (D. Haw. Nov. 18, 2015).
[178] 2015 WL 7303523 at *4.

## [B]   The Surety's Extraordinary Remedies and Equitable Relief

A federal district court ruled on the surety's request for extraordinary remedies in *Platte River Insurance Co. v. Premier Power Renewable Energy, Inc.*[179] The court ruled that the surety was entitled to a writ of attachment against the indemnitors' property, but the court found that, to a large extent, the surety had failed to successfully prove what specific non-exempt property it could actually attach. The surety also sought a motion for a temporary protective order, in order to freeze the indemnitors' assets while the surety conducted discovery. The court found that the TPO would not be appropriate because the purpose would be to freeze the defendants' assets until the court ruled on a motion to attach, and the court had already ruled on that motion.[180]

In *Atherton v. Gopin*,[181] the court addressed the surety's request for extraordinary relief in the form of the common law writ of ne exeat and a bond to assure that the defendant would remain within the jurisdiction of the court. The trial court ordered the defendant to post a ne exeat bond in the amount of $100,000.00, and subsequently increased the amount of the bond to $500,000.00. When the defendant failed to post a bond, the court had the defendant arrested and released him only after he posted a ne exeat bond in the reduced amount of $250,000.00. The appellate court held that the bond was an inherent part of the writ of ne exeat, and that the court could detain the defendant's property, as well as his person, and that there was substantial evidence supporting the trial court's actions

In addressing the surety's injunctive remedies, a federal district court granted the surety's motion for a preliminary injunction requiring the indemnitors to provide access to their books and records as required by the indemnity agreement. In *Travelers Casualty & Surety Co. of America v. Padron*,[182] the court denied the surety's motion for the indemnitors to deposit collateral in the amount of $2,000,000.00. The court distinguished between inadequate remedy at law and irreparable harm. The court agreed that since the surety had not made payments it did not have any remedy at law and could seek specific performance of the collateral provision of the agreement. However, the court thought that the surety could enforce the provision by means of a specific performance and so it would not be irreparably harmed if the preliminary injunction did not include a deposit of collateral.[183]

Other district courts have likewise focused on the "irreparable harm" requirement of a preliminary injunction in the context of a surety collateral demand. In *Ohio Casualty Insurance Co. v. Campbell's Siding & Windows,*

---

[179] 2015 WL 5474344 (E.D. Cal. Sept. 17, 2005).

[180] 2015 WL 5474344 at *11.

[181] 355 P.3d. 804 (N.M. App. 2015).

[182] 2015 WL 1981563 (W.D. Tex. May 1, 2015).

[183] 2015 WL 1981563 at *10-11.

*et al.*,[184] the surety moved for a preliminary injunction requiring the deposit of collateral as provided in the indemnity agreement. The defendants did not oppose the motion. The court, however, denied the motion on grounds that the surety did not establish "irreparable harm." The court noted:

> The injury complained of in the Motion for Preliminary Injunction is economic. . . . Such relief is economic and does not establish irreparable injury that cannot be remedied later. . . . At this stage, the injury alleged in the Motion is that [the surety] will have to pay the bond claims before receiving collateral. That is an economic injury and does not establish irreparable harm for purposes of granting an injunction.[185]

The court denied the surety's motion for issuance of a preliminary injunction.

### [C] Other Indemnity Issues

In XL *Specialty Insurance Co. v. Truland*,[186] the court granted the surety summary judgment in its claim against individual indemnitors and held that an indemnitor's retirement accounts were pledged in the indemnity agreements and that such pledge was valid and enforceable. The court also found that, while the indemnity agreement excluded the indemnitor's residence, the exclusion did not extend to a larger contiguous parcel of property that had a different address.

*Fidelity & Deposit Co. of Maryland v. M. Hanna Construction Co., Inc.*[187] was unique because the defendants filed a motion for partial summary judgment and asked the court to void the "homestead waiver provision" of the indemnity agreement as illegal under Texas law.[188] The court agreed and declared the homestead waiver provision void and unenforceable.

---

[184] 2015 WL 6758137 (D. Idaho. Nov. 4, 2015); *see also* Insurance Co. of the State of Pennsylvania v. Lakeshore Toltest JV, LLC, 2015 WL 8488579 (S.D.N.Y. Nov. 30, 2015) ("Because [the surety's] motion for preliminary injunction seeks an easily quantifiable monetary award, it fails to establish extreme or very serious and irreparable harm."); *but see* Great Am. Ins. Co. v. JMR Constr. Corp., 2015 WL 8328267 (D. Nev. Dec. 8, 2015) (a "security arrangement is a critical aspect of an indemnity agreement; monetary damages for breach of those security obligations cannot make plaintiff whole. Without injunctive relief in the form of specific performance of the collateral security obligation in the indemnity agreement and freezing assets, plaintiffs may suffer from irreparable harm."); Safeco Ins. Co. of Am. v. Lawrence Brunoli, Inc., 599 Fed. Appx. 9 (2d Cir. 2015) ("Under the terms of the parties' agreement, collateral security is not limited to actual losses.").

[185] 2015 WL 6758137 at *3.
[186] 2015 WL 2195181 (E.D. Va. May 11, 2015).
[187] 2015 WL 632047 (E.D. Tex Feb. 13, 2015).
[188] 2015 WL 632047 at *3.

## [D]  Other Surety Rights

### [1]  The Surety's Right to Contract Proceeds

In *Hartford Fire Insurance Co. v. Columbia State Bank*,[189] the surety sued the principal's bank, alleging that a progress payment received by the bank and applied to a loan was a trust fund pursuant to the indemnity agreement. The court found that the contract language did not establish a trust and that the indemnity agreement's trust provision was not triggered until the surety starting making payments under the bond. The surety also argued that it possessed an equitable lien on the progress payment funds under the theory of equitable subrogation. The court rejected that argument, because the surety had not incurred a loss at that time.[190]

In *Carter Douglas Co., LLC v. Logan Industrial Development Authority, Inc.*,[191] a Kentucky District Court granted the surety's motion for leave to intervene in its principal's suit against the obligee. The surety had entered into a takeover agreement and claimed the right to payment of the contract balance including a fund held by the owner's counsel. The court found that the surety met the requirements for intervention under the Federal Rules of Civil Procedure.

In *Safeco Insurance Co. of America v. JAAAT Technical Services, LLC*,[192] the surety sued its principal, a general contractor, seeking to freeze the contractor's assets. The contractor had subcontracted "essentially all of the work" on many different projects in several states to Tetrus Tech Tesoro, Inc. (TTT). The court entered a consent order for a preliminary injunction directing that any payment be made as directed by the surety. In the meantime, however, the court found that both JAAAT and Safeco failed to tell the court about other lawsuits arising from other projects, including a North Carolina project in which the court entered an order requiring that JAAT not spend any of its money on anything or any entity *except for TTT*. Based on notions of comity and the court's equitable concerns, the court vacated its preliminary injunction and denied the general contractor's request for an injunction against TTT.[193]

In *Dwyer v. Insurance Co. of the State of Pennsylvania*,[194] the surety made claims against the bankruptcy trustee for contract funds held by the principal's bank. The bank held one category of funds as a "preexisting balance," which was in the principal's bank account when a second category of funds, the "September payment," was received on September 17, 2013. As of September 17, 2013, the

---

[189] 183 Wash. App. 599, 334 P.3d 87 (2014).

[190] 334 P.3d at 93.

[191] 2015 WL 4554741 (W.D. Ky. July 27, 2015).

[192] 2015 WL 3886149(E.D. Va. June 23, 2015).

[193] 2015 WL 3886149 at *4-5. The Court also noted that under the Rooker-Feldman Doctrine, a federal court should not interfere with an injunction issued by a state court.

[194] 529 B.R. 414 (Bankr. D. Mass. Apr. 14, 2015).

surety had received claims, and the principal had abandoned work on bonded public projects. The principal filed its bankruptcy proceeding on September 20, 2013. While recognizing the surety's subrogation rights, as well as the rights of the principal's assignment made under the indemnity agreement, the court found that genuine issues of material facts existed as to when the principal first defaulted so as to trigger the surety's rights. Further, the court held that the facts were not sufficient to support an argument by the surety that the principal held the contract funds in a constructive trust under Massachusetts law.

In *Selective Insurance Co. of America v. Environmental Safety & Health, Inc., et al.,*[195] the surety sought a preliminary injunction for deposit of collateral, deposit of proceeds of bonded contracts into trust account, and access to books and records. The indemnitors did not oppose the motion for injunctive relief, but the defendant bank objected on grounds that the requested relief interfered with the bank's collateral rights. The bank also moved to dismiss the surety's complaint for Conversion for failure to state a cause of action against the bank.

The court denied the bank's motion to dismiss, stating "the court finds that the GAI creates an express trust upon bonded contract proceeds, and because of this finding, the court finds that [the surety] has properly alleged itself as the true owner of the property at issue."[196] Thus, having properly alleged itself as the "true owner" of the funds in question, the court held the surety properly alleged a claim for Conversion under Tennessee law. The court denied the bank's motion to dismiss and entered the order agreed to by the other defendants in regards to the deposit of funds to a designated account and access to the indemnitors' books and records.

### [2]  Subdivision Bonds

In *Camden County v. Lexon Insurance Co.,*[197] the County obligee on a subdivision bond accepted alternative security from the successor developer in order to release the surety. The property owners in the development intervened in the action and sought to assert claims against the surety and argued that the County's release of the bond was an *ultra vires* act and void. The court granted the surety's motion for summary judgment to dismiss the intervenor's complaint, finding that the County acted within its authority.[198]

The surety on a subdivision bond battled a successor developer who purchased the property from the bankrupt principal in *Camino Properties, LLC v. Insurance Co. of the West.*[199] The City, which was the original bond oblige,

---

[195] 2015 WL 914824 (E.D. Tenn. Mar. 3, 2015).
[196] 2015 WL 914824 at *8.
[197] 2015 WL 515734 (S.D. Ga. Sept. 1, 2015).
[198] 2015 WL 515734 at *4-6.
[199] 2015 WL 2225945 (D. Nev. May 12, 2015).

assigned its rights to the successor developer. The court first ruled against the surety on a statute of limitations argument, finding that the case was governed by the six-year statute of limitations applicable to contract matters, not the three-year limitations period which applies to statutory liabilities.[200]

The surety also defended on the basis that the City could not assign its rights under the bond. The court found that the City could assign its rights, at least in order to facilitate completion of the improvements.[201] The court noted that the surety appeared to agree the City could assign its right under the Bond if the assignment was for the purpose of completing the improvements. The court noted that the surety argued that the City did not assign its rights for the purpose of completing the improvements, but rather that the City assigned its rights for Plaintiff's sole financial benefit. The court found that the developer provided evidence raising a genuine dispute about whether the City assigned its rights under the Bond, at least in part, to facilitate completion of the off-site improvements. As the Court noted, the assignment's language indicates the assignment was made to facilitate the off-site improvements. It stated the assignee "intends to complete" the improvements and that it is in the "best interests of the Parties to complete" the improvements.[202]

Finally, the court rejected the surety's argument that the bond required the City to notify the surety that the work that it performed did not complete the improvements. The court found that the bond did not clearly require notification.[203]

### [3] Surety vs. Insurer

A Pennsylvania court examined the interplay between a commercial general liability (CGL) policy and the performance bond surety's obligations in *Pennsylvanian National Mutual Casualty Insurance Co. v. Retirement Systems of Alabama.*[204] The obligee sued the prime contractor and its surety, alleging defective construction of a firewall and consequential mold infestation. The court found that the improperly constructed firewall was not an occurrence as defined in the CGL policy. The court also found that the mold infestation would be excluded by the CGL policy's fungi or bacteria exclusion.

---

[200] 2015 WL 2225945 at *2-4.
[201] 2015 WL 2225945 at *4.
[202] 2015 WL 2225945 at *4.
[203] 2015 WL 2225945 at *5.
[204] 2015 WL 1814316 (N.D. Ala. Apr. 21, 2015).

## [E] Arbitration and the Surety's Rights

In *Hanover Insurance Co. v. Atlantis Drywall & Framing, LLC*,[205] the Eleventh Circuit, after rehearing, ruled that the surety was not required to arbitrate its indemnity claims. The court found that it did not need to reach the question of whether the indemnity agreement was part of a single transaction with the bond and the bonded subcontract, or whether the agreements were so intertwined that the indemnitor could demand arbitration. The court also felt it unnecessary to examine whether the indemnitor was a third-party beneficiary of the arbitration provision. Rather, since the arbitration provision required arbitration only at the option of the prime contractor and here the prime contractor was not involved, there was no basis to compel the surety to arbitrate. The court noted: "Under the plain language of the arbitration provision, only Brice [the prime contractor] can compel arbitration and Brice has not done so here."[206]

The Texas Court of Appeals granted a surety's motion to compel arbitration in *Granite Re v. Jay Mills Contracting Co.*[207] The subcontractor's surety moved to compel arbitration of the prime contractor's claims on the basis that the blanket agreement between the parties contained an arbitration provision and the specific work order on this project incorporated the blanket agreement. Thus, the court supported invoking arbitration based on the string of incorporations by reference.

The court reversed an arbitration award in favor of the surety in *Asia Pacific Hotel Guam, Inc. v. Dongbu Insurance Co., Ltd.*[208] The surety had completed work after the principal's default and recovered an arbitration award against the obligee. The trial court had affirmed the Award, including pre-judgment interest. On appeal, the court concluded that the trial court properly affirmed the Award but set aside the trial court's summary judgment for the surety enforcing the Award because it found issues of fact as to the meaning of some of the amounts in the Award and the amount to which the surety was entitled by subrogation. In effect, a dispute existed as to whether the surety had been awarded more as subrogee of the contractor than the surety had actually paid out the bond obligations.[209]

---

[205] 611 Fed. Appx. 585 (11th Cir. May 26, 2015).
[206] 611 Fed. Appx. at 591.
[207] 2015 WL 1869216 (Tex. App. Apr. 23, 2015).
[208] 2015 WL 582955 (Guam Terr. Feb. 3, 2015).
[209] 2015 WL 582955 at *11.

CHAPTER 6

# GOVERNMENT CONTRACTS

Tyler P. Scarbrough, Gautam Y. Reddy

§ 6.09　Recent Federal Regulations
　　　　[A]　Requirement of Federal Contractors to Provide Paid Sick Leave
　　　　[B]　Cyber Security Rules Issued by Department of Defense
　　　　[C]　Amendment to FAR Anti-Trafficking Regulations
　　　　[D]　FCA and OSHA Civil Penalties Set to Increase in 2016

## § 6.01  INTRODUCTION

In this year's update, we address recent decisions in standard areas of construction and procurement law such as claim and certification requirements under the Contract Disputes Act ("CDA"), recovery of attorneys' fees and costs under the Equal Access to Justice Act ("EAJA"), the timeliness of bid protests, and the conduct required for the government to terminate a contractor for cause. With respect to the CDA, a line of case law is examined where it is now the case that the CDA's six-year statute of limitations period is not jurisdictional in nature and the government must plead the appellant's failure to satisfy the limitations period as an affirmative defense. We also address significant developments in False Claims Act ("FCA") jurisprudence, tracking the development of the "implied certification" theory in two circuit court rulings and speculating on how the Supreme Court will ultimately settle the issue. Finally, we discuss recent developments that potentially impact all federal contractors related to the requirements to now provide employees with paid sick leave, new Cyber security reporting requirements imposed by the Department of Defense ("DoD"), more stringent anti-trafficking regulations, and a potentially significant increase in FCA and Occupational Safety and Health Administration ("OSHA") penalties.

## § 6.02  ISSUES ARISING UNDER THE CONTRACT DISPUTES ACT

### [A]  Jurisdictional Requirements and the Six-Year Statute of Limitations: An Analysis of *Sikorsky*

In December 2014, the Court of Appeals for the Federal Circuit issued a significant ruling in *Sikorsky Aircraft Corp. v. United States*,[1] holding that the six-year time limit under the CDA was not jurisdictional in nature. Because lower courts had previously held that the six-year limitations period was jurisdictional, if the deadline was missed, courts could not consider the appellant's claim for lack of jurisdiction. The claim at issue was void, but the *Sikorsky* decision is considered a sea change in this regard.

The facts in *Sikorsky* are as follows. Sikorsky Aircraft Corporation ("Sikorsky") held a number of government contracts in which it would furnish helicopters and other goods and services to the government and those contracts were subject to the government Cost Accounting Standards ("CAS"). The CAS standards govern the allocation of costs among various contracts being performed by government contractors with an allocation between government and non-government (commercial) contracts.[2] Between 1999 and 2005, Sikorsky allocated

---

[1] 773 F.3d 1315 (Fed. Cir. 2014).
[2] *Id.* at 1318.

costs in a certain manner but subsequently changed that allocation method effective January 1, 2006.[3] The government's contracting officer approved Sikorsky's new allocation method as compliant with the CAS.[4] However, in March 2007, the contracting officer issued a notice of potential noncompliance for the period from 1999 to 2005 covering Sikorsky's prior allocation method.[5] The government ultimately determined that Sikorsky owed nearly $65 million in principal and $15 million in interest to the government.[6]

On December 8, 2009, Sikorsky appealed the government's claim to the Court of Federal Claims.[7] Sikorsky filed a separate lawsuit asking the court to determine the validity of certain affirmative defenses it had asserted against the government.[8] The suits were consolidated and the government counterclaimed for $65 million plus interest.[9] The court characterized the statute of limitations issue as an affirmative defense, assigning the burden of proof to Sikorsky. Sikorsky's statute of limitations defense was then rejected because Sikorsky failed to show that the government had actual or constructive knowledge of a potential claim more than six years before the government submitted the claim to Sikorsky. On the CAS claim, the Court determined that there was no violation by Sikorsky. The Court of Federal Claims granted judgment for the contractor and the government appealed.

On appeal to the Federal Circuit, the issues presented were (1) whether the government's claim was time barred by the CDA's statute of limitations and (2) whether Sikorsky violated the CAS. The Federal Circuit addressed the six-year statute of limitations claim as set forth in the CDA, 41 U.S.C. § 7103(a). Under the CDA, the court noted that:

> *[e]ach claim by a contractor against the Federal Government* relating to a contract and each claim by the Federal Government against a contractor relating to a contract *shall be submitted within 6 years after the accrual of the claim. A claim accrues as of the date when all events, that fix the alleged liability of either the Government or the contractor and permit assertion of the claim, were known or should have been known.* For liability to be fixed, some injury must have occurred. However, monetary damages need not have been incurred. *A claim is submitted by the government when the contracting officer renders a final decision to the contractor.*[10]

---

[3] *Id.*
[4] *Id.* at 1319.
[5] *Sikorsky*, 773 F.3d at 1319.
[6] *Id.*
[7] *Id.* at 1319.
[8] *Id.*
[9] *Id.*
[10] *Sikorsky*, 773 F.3d at 1319-20 (emphasis added) (internal citations omitted).

There was no dispute that the date of the government's submission of the claim was December 11, 2008, the date the contracting officer issued its final decision to Sikorsky. Thus, the "statute of limitations was satisfied if the claim accrued within the six years before December 11, 2008."[11] Sikorsky argued that the court must address the statute of limitations issue before the merits of the claim because the limitations period identified in the CDA was jurisdictional. The court disagreed with Sikorsky, relying on the United States Supreme Court's decision in *Sebelius v. Auburn Regional Medical Center.*[12]

In *Auburn Regional*, the court held that a 180-day limit for filing appeals to the Provider Reimbursement Review Board was not jurisdictional.[13] The Supreme Court noted that it has "repeatedly held that filing deadlines ordinarily are not jurisdictional" and instead they are "quintessential claim processing rules."[14] The Court in *Auburn Regional* articulated a "readily administrable bright line" rule with respect to whether a filing deadline was jurisdictional, in which the inquiry is:

> ***whether Congress has clearly stated that the rule is jurisdictional***; absent such a clear statement, [the Court has] cautioned [that] courts should treat the restriction as nonjurisdictional in character. Congress need not incant magic words ["jurisdictional"] in order to speak clearly, and render the provision jurisdictional. ***The statutory language, the placement of the provision within the statutory scheme, and context, including [Supreme Court] interpretations of similar provisions in many years past, are indicative of whether the provision is jurisdictional.***[15]

In light of this precedent, the *Sikorsky* court determined that the CDA did not "speak in jurisdictional terms."[16] Furthermore, the language of the CDA did not suggest that the provision was meant to carry jurisdictional consequences and the placement within the CDA did not indicate that the provision was jurisdictional.[17] The court noted that to the extent that the statute applies to claims by the government, the statute pertains to the submission of claims by a contracting officer to a contractor, rather than to a government body.[18] Ultimately the court held that CDA "§ 7103 is not jurisdictional and need not be addressed before deciding the merits."[19]

---

[11] *Sikorsky*, 773 F.3d at 1320.

[12] 133 S. Ct. 817, 184 L. Ed. 2d 627 (2013).

[13] *Sikorsky*, 773 F.3d at 1321.

[14] *Id.* at 1321 (*quoting* Sebelius v. Auburn Reg'l Med. Ctr., 133 S. Ct. 817, 184 L.Ed.2d 627 (2013)).

[15] *Sikorsky*, 773 F.3d at 1321 (internal quotations and citations omitted) (emphasis added).

[16] *Sikorsky*, 773 F.3d at 1321.

[17] *Id.*

[18] *Id.*

[19] *Sikorsky*, 773 F.3d at 1322.

In *Systems Management & Research Technologies Corp.*,[20] the Civilian Board of Contract Appeals analyzed a claim under the framework articulated in *Sikorsky*. In *Systems Management*, the Department of Energy ("DOE") filed a motion to dismiss, as time barred, for a portion of the appellant's claim submitted to the contracting officer in March 2014. The DOE claimed that because the services under the contract were performed on an annual or bi-annual basis between 2004 and 2008, Systems Management and Research Technologies Corp.'s ("SMARTECH") 2014 claim for fixed fees earned from 2004 through 2007 was untimely because it had not been submitted within six years of the date in which the claim accrued as required by the CDA.[21]

The facts in *Systems Management* were as follows. On September 30, 2003, the DOE awarded SMARTECH an undefinitized time-and-materials letter contract. The contract was finalized by the parties on March 17, 2005. On March 6, 2008, DOE advised SMARTECH that it had awarded a new contract for document review services to another entity, that DOE did not expect to issue further work to SMARTECH, and that SMARTECH should take all necessary steps to complete phase-out of the contract by March 31, 2008. The DOE never terminated the contract and it expired by its own terms on September 29, 2008. On September 29, 2010, SMARTECH submitted a request for an equitable adjustment ("REA"). In the REA, SMARTECH, for the first time, sought payment for unpaid portions of invoices of its fixed fees under the contract. The contracting officer indicated that DOE would not pay the remaining unpaid fixed fees on May 18, 2011.[22] On March 28, 2014, SMARTECH submitted a certified claim and the contracting officer denied that claim on May 22, 2014.[23] SMARTECH filed an appeal. In its answer to the complaint, the DOE asserted the CDA six-year statute of limitations as an affirmative defense.[24]

Under the post-*Sikorsky* standard of review, the Board recognized that the Federal Circuit originally interpreted the CDA's six-year statute of limitations period to be jurisdictional.[25] However, the Board noted that the Federal Circuit recently changed this framework in *Sikorsky Aircraft Corp.*[26] when the Court determined that "§ 7103 'does not speak in jurisdictional terms' or refer in any way to . . . jurisdiction," and does "not suggest, much less provide clear evidence, that the provision was meant to carry jurisdictional consequences." It therefore "conclude[d] that § 7103 is not jurisdictional."[27]

---

[20] CBCA 4068, 15-1 BCA ¶ 35976.
[21] *Id.*
[22] *Id.*
[23] *Id.*
[24] *Systems Management*, 15-1 BCA ¶ 35976.
[25] *Id.*
[26] 773 F.3d 1315 (Fed. Cir. 2014).
[27] *Systems Management*, 15-1 BCA ¶ 35976 (citations omitted) (*citing* Sikorsky Aircraft Corp. v. United States, 773 F.3d 1315 (Fed. Cir. 2014)).

In *Systems Management,* the Board fully recognized that the:

transformation of the ***CDA's six-year statute of limitations from jurisdictional to non-jurisdictional changes how we must approach a motion to dismiss a case for failure to meet that deadline***. No longer can the Government, through a motion to dismiss, challenge the factual allegations that the contractor has made in its complaint and require the contractor to prove jurisdictional facts by a preponderance of the evidence. Instead, ***the CDA's six-year statute of limitations is now an affirmative defense that the Government must plead in its answer to the appellant's complaint. [F]ailure to plead an affirmative defense . . . in a timely fashion generally results in the waiver of that defense***. In addition, the burden is on the Government, not the appellant, to prove its affirmative defense that the contractor's claim is time-barred. Further, because the statute of limitations issue is no longer jurisdictional, ***the party seeking to enforce the limitations period must do so using the same procedural rules that the Board applies to other non-jurisdictional issues: motions for failure to state a claim, summary relief procedures, and, if there are genuine issues of material fact relating to the statute of limitations issue, a hearing or record submission to resolve competing versions of the facts***.[28]

Notably, with the *Sikorsky* framework in place, the government must now plead the CDA's six-year statute of limitations as an affirmative defense. Failure to do so may result in waiver of the argument all together. Additionally, now that the statute of limitations under the CDA is no longer considered jurisdictional, parties have the ability to toll the limitations period which could have added benefits including avoiding protracted litigation to mutually resolve pending claims.

## [B] Timely Appeals Under the Contract Disputes Act

Whether an appeal is filed timely under the CDA is always a concern for any contractor. Under the CDA, the Board or Court will have jurisdiction over a claim only if it is taken within 90 days of the contractor's receipt of a contracting officer's final decision. However, what happens if the contractor fails to appeal the final decision to the Board of Contract Appeals or the Court of Federal Claims and instead sends the appeal to some other government entity or employee? In *Axxon International, LLC,*[29] the Board dealt with this exact issue. In *Axxon* the contracting officer issued a written decision terminating Axxon's contract for cause on January 27, 2014.[30]

---

[28] *Systems Management*, 15-1 BCA ¶ 35976 (emphasis added) (citations omitted).
[29] ASBCA Nos. 59497, 59498, 15-1 BCA ¶ 35864 (Jan. 21, 2015).
[30] *Id.*

In that decision, the contracting officer stated that it was the "final decision [of] the Contracting Officer" and notified Axxon of its rights to appeal to "the agency board of contract appeals' or to the U.S. Court of Federal Claims."[31] On March 3, 2014, Axxon submitted a document characterized as an "appeal of the wrongful termination of the Contract," but did not submit it to the Board or the Court of Federal Claims, instead it was submitted to the "U.S. Army Materiel Command, Office of the Command Counsel."[32]

On appeal, Axxon stated "that it thought the Command Counsel was an appropriate recipient because the solicitation advised that if it had 'complaints about this procurement,' it could 'protest to Headquarters (HQ), Army Materiel Command (AMC).'"[33] The Command Counsel forwarded the submission to the contracting officer. On May 16, 2014, the contracting officer issued a written decision denying the monetary claim, declining to reconsider the termination, and again notified Axxon of its appeal rights. Evidence showed that Axxon received the contracting officer's final decision on May 19, 2014. Axxon then submitted notices of appeal to the Board, which were received by the Board on August 18, 2014.[34]

The Board noted that Axxon presented a familiar issue of the "misdirected appeal" when it submitted the appeal to the Command Counsel instead of the Board on January 27, 2014. Specifically, on similar facts,[35] the Board held that a "misdirected appeal" sent to agency counsel in timely fashion was not fatal to jurisdiction, thus, the Board upheld its jurisdiction over the appeal.[36] The Board stated that Axxon's March 3, 2014 letter was transmitted to Command Counsel on March 3, 2014, within 90 days after the January 27, 2014 contracting officer's termination decision. The fact that Axxon's submission "expresses dissatisfaction with the termination and an intention to appeal, stating that it is *'an appeal of the wrongful termination' of the contract*," supported the affirmation of jurisdiction by the Board.[37]

The "misdirected appeal" argument does not always pan out for a contractor and can have its pitfalls just as the contractor found in *Bahram Malikzada Construction Co.*[38] In *Bahram*, on June 8, 2010, the government awarded two contracts to Bahram Malikzada Construction Co. ("BMCC") for the construction of headquarters buildings on Bagram Airfield, in Afghanistan.[39] On November 29,

---

[31] *Id.*
[32] *Id.*
[33] *Id.*
[34] *Id.*
[35] *See Brunner Bau GmbH*, ASBCA No. 35678, 89-1 BCA ¶ 12315.
[36] *Id.*
[37] *Id.* (emphasis added).
[38] ASBCA No. 59613, 15-1 BCA ¶ 36134.
[39] *Id.*

2010, the contracting officer, Daniel R. Tatro, issued two final decisions terminating both contracts for default. The record contained two other final decisions from another contracting officer, Michael Washington, dated July 14, 2012, denying BMCC's "claim[s] for additional payment" under the terminated contracts.[40] Notably, neither final decision provided any information regarding BMCC's right to appeal.[41]

After Washington issued his final decisions, BMCC continued to seek payment under both contracts. The government subsequently emailed BMCC notifying BMCC that it should submit its claim to a "Major Locklear" who was then designated as the contracting officer for the action. BMCC issued two documents to Colonel Glen E. Christensen titled "Actual Bill of Quantities Completed as Per Site."[42] The documents were then forwarded by the government to Major Locklear. On June 8, 2013, Major Locklear directed BMCC to provide a certification and supporting documentation for its claims.[43] The record also contained a CDA certification, signed by BMCC's president, certifying claims for $286,139 under one contract and for $243,534 under the other contract for a total of $529,673.[44] Contracting officer Locklear issued a final decision on September 25, 2013, denying BMCC's claim. In the final decision, contracting officer Locklear stated:

> This is the final decision of the Contracting Officer. You may appeal this decision to the agency board of contract appeals. If you decide to appeal, you must, within 90 days from the date you receive this decision, mail or otherwise furnish written notice to the agency board of contract appeals and provide a copy to the Contracting Officer from whose decision this appeal is taken.[45]

In a September 27, 2013 email, BMCC's president responded to the contracting officer stating that it "will start my [a]ppeal."[46] Additional email correspondence was exchanged between the parties, and on December 16, 2013, the government notified BMCC that if it did not agree with the final decision, it could contact the Armed Services Board of Contract Appeals and provide BMCC with the mailing address and email address of the Board. BMCC did not contact the Board and continued to resolve the issue without filing an appeal. On October 6, 2014, the Board received BMCC's letter, dated September 22, 2014, and postmarked September 25, 2014, titled "Bahram Malikzada Construction Company (BMCC) Appeal."[47] The Board subsequently docketed the appeal.

---

[40] *Id.*
[41] *Id.*
[42] *Id.*
[43] *Id.*
[44] *Id.*
[45] *Id.*
[46] *Id.*
[47] *Id.*

The government then moved to dismiss the appeal for lack of jurisdiction, arguing that the September 22, 2014 letter was not filed within the 90-day statutory deadline. BMCC argued that the Board could exercise jurisdiction relying upon the misdirected appeal case precedence. The Board noted that "[w]e have long held that filing an appeal with the contracting officer is tantamount to filing an appeal with the Board."[48] To be effective, "a writing filed within the requisite time period *must express dissatisfaction* with the contracting officer's decision *and indicate an intention to appeal the decision to a higher authority*."[49] Specifically, the contractor communication must "express an election to appeal to this Board" and this intent has been inferred if the communication to the contracting officer uses the term "appeal."[50]

In reviewing the correspondence between the parties, the Board determined that BMCC's emails did not indicate an intention to appeal the contracting officer's final decision. Specifically, "[a]lthough BMCC stated that it 'will start [its] Appeal,' the record does not reflect an intent by BMCC to appeal to this Board through that email."[51] Notably, the record reflected that BMCC would continue to seek compensation through local channels in Afghanistan and the Board declined to attribute intent to appeal to the Board in BMCC's September 27, 2013 email. The bottom line is that "the record reasonably must demonstrate an intent to appeal to the Board" for jurisdiction to attach.[52]

The decisions in *Axxon* and *Bahram* are instructive. It is always recommended that a contractor submit its appeal directly to the appropriate Boards of Contract Appeals or Court of Federal Claims when initiating an appeal. Appeals can be filed electronically via the Board or Court websites. While it is highly discouraged, an appeal can be submitted to the government instead of the Board or Court and nonetheless satisfy the jurisdictional requirements under the CDA if the contractor expresses a clear and unambiguous intent to initiate an appeal. Otherwise, there is a significant risk that the contractor's claims will be denied just as the contractor in *Bahram* unfortunately discovered.

Another issue related to the timing of appeals deals with a situation where more than one copy of the contracting officer's final decision is issued to a contractor. In *TTF, LLC*,[53] the Board held that the 90-day period in which to file an appeal began on the contractor's receipt of the first copy of the contracting officer's final decision.

In *TTF, LLC*, the government terminated three separate contracts for default all on April 30, 2014. The contracting officer issued three separate letters each stating:

---

[48] *Id.*

[49] *Id.* (emphasis added).

[50] *Id.*

[51] *Bahram*, 15-1 BCA ¶ 36134 (internal citations omitted).

[52] *Id.*

[53] ASBCA No. 59511, 15-1 BCA ¶ 35883 (Feb. 5, 2015).

> This notice constitutes a final decision of the contracting officer from which you have the right of appeal. You may appeal this decision to the Armed Services Board of Contract Appeals. If you decide to make such an appeal, you must mail or otherwise furnish written notice thereof to the Board within 90 days from the date you receive this decision. . . .[54]

The contracting officer transmitted the termination decision for all three contracts on May 1, 2014. A copy of each certification was also sent to the appellant via certified mail. The certified mailings took various routes to reach the appellant such that the appellant signed for one on May 8, 2014, and the other two on May 19, 2014. The appellant via letter submitted its notice of appeal for all three final decisions dated August 14, 2014, and post marked August 18, 2014. In the submission, the appellant stated that the appeals are taken from the April 30, 2014 final decisions in which the appellant claimed that the decisions were received in "late 19 May 2014," "19 May 2014," and "late May 2014."[55]

The government moved to dismiss the claims arguing that the Board lacked jurisdiction over the appeals because the appellant received the termination decisions by email on May 1, 2014, but did not appeal until August 18, 2014—more than 90 days later. The government further argued that if the Board chose to consider the date in which the appellant signed for certified mail copies of the termination decisions, more than 90 days had passed before the one signed for on May 8, 2014 was filed. The appellant argued that the appeals were not untimely because the contracting officer could not have rendered a decision absent an affirmative claim by the contractor.[56] In the alternative, the appellant argued that because it did not sign for the copies of the termination decisions until May 19, 2014, the appeals were timely.

With respect to its affirmative claim argument, the Board stated that "[i]t is well settled that the decision to terminate a contract for default is considered to be a government claim against the contractor for which the contractor may appeal to the Board without the necessity of filing an affirmative claim."[57] "Thus, a contractor may appeal from the decision to terminate its contract for default, and, provided the contractor seeks to challenge only the propriety of the termination decision, no affirmative claim by the contractor is required."[58]

The Board next addressed the issue: "when, for the purposes of determining the Board's jurisdiction under the CDA, did appellant receive the termination decisions in these appeals?" The Board noted that "[t]he day the contractor receives the final decision is not counted in determining the 90-day period, while

---

[54] *Id.*
[55] *Id.*
[56] *Id.*
[57] *TTF, LLC*, 15-1 BCA ¶35883(*quoting Amina Enterprise Group, LTD*, ASBCA Nos. 58547, 58548, 13 BCA ¶35376 at 173,580; *Lisbon Contractors, Inc. v. United States*, 828 F.2d 759, 764 (Fed. Cir. 1987)).
[58] *Id.*

the day the contractor mails or delivers its appeal is included."[59] It is the government's burden to establish the date the final decision was received, but the burden of proof is on appellant to establish that its appeal was timely filed.[60]

The record contained copies of the email sent from the contracting officer to the appellant, all dated May 1, 2014, which attached copies of the termination decisions as well as copies of the delivery receipts signed by the appellant showing that the appellant signed for them on May 8, 2014 and May 19, 2014. In performing its analysis, the Board noted that:

> We have previously held that sending multiple copies of a contracting officer's final decision without indicating which of them is intended to begin the running of the appeal period confuses a contractor as to the date for appeal of the decision, entitling the contractor to compute the date from receipt of the last copy. However, where appellant had previously requested to receive correspondence by means of a particular medium, an earlier copy of the decision received through that medium may start the 90-day appeal clock.[61]

There was nothing in the record indicating that the contracting officer instructed the appellant which termination decision was intended to begin the running of the 90-day appeal period. Also, there was nothing indicating that the appellant specifically requested to receive correspondence by a particular medium, such as email. Consequently, the Board held that the 90-day period began with the appellant's actual receipt of the mailed copies of the termination decisions sent by certified mail. Based on this reasoning, the Board determined that the two appeals received on May 19, 2014 were timely, but the one received on May 9, 2014 was not and refused to exercise jurisdiction over that appeal.

*TTF, LLC* provides several noteworthy lessons. First, a contractor must be mindful of the precise medium in which it has elected to receive official correspondence from the government. If email has been requested, a contractor will likely be unable to take advantage of a later mailed final decision of the contracting officer, as the 90-day clock for purposes of jurisdiction, would begin to run when the email is received. Second, it is simply not good practice to procrastinate when appealing a contracting officer's final decision. While there may be specific business reasons that would prevent a contractor from firing off an appeal under certain circumstances, it is always recommended to submit the notice of appeal well in advance of the 90-day deadline. Unlike the CDA's six-year statute of limitations discussed earlier in this chapter, the 90-day deadline is jurisdictional and can never be waived.

---

[59] *Id.* (*citing* Board Rule 5(b); *Eastern Computers,* ASBCA No. 49185, 96-2 BCA ¶ 28343 at 141,549).

[60] *TTF, LLC,* 15-1 BCA ¶ 35883.

[61] *Id.* (internal citations omitted).

## [C]  Defining Claims Under the Contract Disputes Act

Defining the scope of a claim can be problematic for contractors. For example, if the complaint contains broader language than the certification in which the contracting officer has rendered a final decision, the result can be a dismissal for lack of jurisdiction. This precise issue was addressed in *K-Con Building Systems v. United States*,[62] where a contractor discovered the jurisdictional pitfalls that can occur from expanding on previously certified claims. In *K-Con*, the contractor entered into a contract with the government to construct a "cutter support team building" for the Coast Guard in Port Huron, Michigan for $5,982,641.[63] Upon completion of the project, the Coast Guard withheld $109,554 in liquidated damages amounting to 186 days of delay at a rate of $589 per day.[64] There was no dispute with the liquidated damages calculations.[65] K-Con sent a letter to the contracting officer requesting remission of the liquidated damages "wrongfully withheld from the contract" asserting that the "liquidated damages [constituted] an impermissible penalty" and that the Coast Guard "failed to issue extensions of the completion date as a result of the changes to the contract."[66] The contracting officer denied the claim and K-Con sued in the Court of Federal Claims under the CDA.[67]

While the litigation was underway, K-Con submitted a second letter to the contracting officer and extensively detailed the contract changes made by the Coast Guard during the contract term and asked for a new remedy—$196,126.38 for additional work—and an extension of time to the contract.[68] These requests were denied by the Contracting Officer.[69] K-Con then amended its complaint filed in the Court of Federal Claims to "add allegations about the matter covered in its second letter and to seek, beyond the liquidated-damages relief, a judgment of $196,126.38 and a 186-day extension."[70] The Court first ruled that the liquidated damages clause was enforceable. It then held that K-Con did not provide valid written notice regarding the contract changes and therefore had not satisfied a precondition to claiming additional compensation under the contract's changes clause.[71] Thus, it dismissed K-Con's time-extension claim for the remission of liquidated damages for lack of jurisdiction. K-Con appealed all three rulings to the Court of Appeals for the Federal Circuit.

---

[62] 778 F.3d 1000 (Fed. Cir. 2015).

[63] *Id.* at 1003.

[64] *Id.*

[65] *Id.*

[66] *Id.*

[67] *Id.* at 1004.

[68] *Id.*

[69] *Id.*

[70] *Id.*

[71] *Id.*

Before turning to the merits, the Federal Circuit was required to determine whether the Court of Federal Claims had jurisdiction under the CDA. Under the CDA, jurisdiction is granted to the Federal Circuit over "actions brought on claims within twelve months of a contracting officer's final decision."[72] For jurisdiction to extend to the Court of Federal Claims, a claim meeting certain requirements must be submitted to the contracting officer and the contracting officer is required to issue a final decision on that claim. The contracting officer's final decision on a claim may either be written or implied from the contracting officer's failure to issue a decision on a contract claim within the period required.[73] With respect to identifying individual claims, the Court stated:

> *We have long held that the jurisdictional standard must be applied to each claim, not an entire case*; jurisdiction exists over those claims which satisfy the requirements of an adequate statement of the amount sought and an adequate statement of the basis for the request. *Claim identification is important also for application of the rule that, once a claim is in litigation, the contracting officer may not rule on it—even if the claim is not properly in litigation because it was not properly submitted to and denied by the contracting officer before it was placed in litigation.*
>
> ***
>
> Our longstanding demand that a claim adequately specify both the amount sought and the basis for the request implies that, at least for present purposes, *we should treat requests as involving separate claims if they either request different remedies (whether monetary or non-monetary) or assert grounds that are materially different from each other factually or legally.* This approach, which has been applied in a practical way, serves the objective of giving the contracting officer an ample pre-suit opportunity to rule on a request, knowing at least the relief sought and what substantive issues are raised by the request.[74]

The Court expressly stated that its prior holding was not meant to impose such a rigid standard as to preclude all litigation adjustments in amounts based upon matters developed in litigation.[75] It recognized that there are situations where the Court has differentiated claims seeking different types of remedy, such as expectation damages versus consequential damages.[76] Furthermore, adding factual details or legal arguments does not create a different claim, "but presenting a materially different factual or legal theory (e.g., breach of contract for not

---

[72] *K-Con Building Systems*, 778 F.3d at 1005 (*citing James M. Ellett Constr. Co. v. United States*, 93 F.3d 1537, 1541 (Fed. Cir. 1996)).

[73] *K-Con Building Systems*, 778 F.3d at 1005.

[74] *K-Con Building Systems*, 778 F.3d at 1005 (emphasis added) (internal citations omitted).

[75] *Id.*

[76] *Id.*

constructing a building on time versus breach of contract for constructing with the wrong materials) does create a different claim."[77]

In *K-Con*, the amended complaint presented three discrete claims: (1) the allegation that the liquidated damages clause was unenforceable, (2) a requested time extension that the Coast Guard never provided, and (3) changes made by the Coast Guard entitled K-Con to $196,126.38 over and above the liquidated damages.[78] While the Court agreed with the Court of Federal Claims that it had jurisdiction over the unenforceability of the liquidated damages and alleged changes claims, it held that it did not have jurisdiction over K-Con's requested time extension.[79] With respect to the liquidated damage enforceability claim, jurisdiction was never disputed by the government. The government disputed that jurisdiction existed over the alleged changes claim, arguing that there was no authorized final decision before litigation commenced in the action because of K-Con's second letter after the filing of its original complaint. The Court disagreed, noting that while the original complaint mentioned contract changes and included some factual assertions shared by the contract changes claim presented in the second letter, the remedies requested in the two documents were categorically different making the requests different claims.

As for the time extension claim, there was no jurisdiction because K-Con squarely placed that claim in litigation when it requested the remission of liquidated damages through its original complaint thus divesting the contracting officer of the authority to issue a final decision. Ultimately, things got worse for K-Con on the merits as the Federal Circuit held that the liquidated damages clause was enforceable and that it failed to comply with the contract's written notice requirement with respect to its alleged changes claim.

*K-Con* provides valuable information for a contractor who is considering amending its complaint or adding claims. If claims are added to present materially different factual or legal theories, then the contractor should take caution in deciding the proper course of action. If there is any doubt as to whether the newly developed claims are broader than those previously submitted to the contracting officer for a final decision, the prudent course of action, while taking longer to resolve, is to separately submit those claims for a final decision and then subsequently move to consolidate the appeals after they have been filed. Though not ideal, it is much better to be safe than sorry if the claims are later barred for lack of jurisdiction several years later.

---

[77] *Id.* at 1006.
[78] *Id.*
[79] *Id.*

## [D]  Attorneys' Fees Under the Equal Access to Justice Act

The cost of litigation is a significant concern for litigants and attorneys' fees can easily exceed hundreds of thousands of dollars in what may seem to be very straightforward claims. Very few small businesses or individuals have funds to set aside for a "legal budget," but in the context of government contracting, a litigant has the ability to offset a portion of its costs and attorneys' fees under the Equal Access to Justice Act ("EAJA") provided that certain elements are satisfied.[80] In *Systems Integrations & Management*,[81] the Civilian Board of Contract Appeals recently addressed a litigant's request for attorneys' fees under the EAJA.

In *Systems Management*, there was a dispute between Systems Integration Management, Inc. ("SIM") and the government over the payment of invoices. SIM certified a claim and then filed an appeal after the contracting officer's denied SIM's claim. In May 2009, the parties engaged in settlement discussions and the Board conducted a mediation in July 2009 where the parties agreed that they could resolve the dispute.[82] By March 2010, the parties agreed that the General Services Administration ("GSA") would pay SIM $960,000, inclusive of interest and attorneys' fees. Of that amount, $525,000 would be offset to satisfy a judgment against SIM that had been obtained by the government in a civil false claims action.[83] The terms of the settlement were memorialized on March 23, 2010.[84] After the parties reached this agreement, SIM attempted to change various terms.[85] GSA did not agree to the changes and SIM refused to finalize the settlement agreement and the parties returned to the Board for assistance.

Another mediation session was conducted on March 9, 2011, and the parties again agreed to a new tentative settlement.[86] GSA's draft settlement agreement was essentially identical to the March 2010 agreement.[87] SIM subsequently amended the agreement to add a demand for additional interest and when GSA refused, SIM withdrew the proposed change. In August 2011, SIM's counsel presented the agreement to SIM's CEO, but the CEO refused to sign the agreement. SIM subsequently hired new counsel and rejected the settlement agreement.[88]

---

[80] Under the EAJA, attorneys' fees shall not be awarded in excess of $125 per hour unless the court determines that an increase in the cost of living or a special factor, such as the limited availability of qualified attorneys for the proceedings involved, justifies a higher fee. 28 U.S.C. § 2412(d)(2)(A).

[81] CBCA Nos. 3815-C, 3816-C,15-1 BCA ¶ 35886.

[82] *Systems Integrations and Management*, 15-1 BCA ¶ 35886.

[83] *Id.*

[84] *Id.*

[85] *Id.*

[86] *Id.*

[87] *Id.*

[88] *Id.*

A trial was conducted and the Board granted SIM's appeal finding that GSA owed SIM $1,058,722.23, plus interest. SIM then submitted an application for reimbursement under the EAJA seeking $1,410,261.94 in attorneys' fees and $43,313.23 in costs. GSA opposed the application noting, among other things, that the application sought over $600,000 in fees incurred before December 18, 2008, the date of the contracting officer's final decision.[89] SIM subsequently revised the application down to $235,401 in attorneys' fees and expenses of $26,830.68. GSA's argument for the rejection of fees was based on the position that it was substantially justified in the dispute.[90]

In performing its analysis, the Board stated that under the EAJA, "[a]n agency that conducts an adversary adjudication *shall award*, to a prevailing party other than the United States, fees and other expenses incurred by that party in connection with that proceeding, unless the adjudicative officer of the agency finds that the position of the agency was substantially justified or that special circumstances make an award unjust."[91] The "purpose of the law is 'to eliminate barriers that prohibit small businesses and individuals from securing vindication of their rights in civil actions and administrative proceedings brought by or against the Federal Government.'"[92] The Board then noted that several requirements must be met before a litigant can recover under the EAJA:

(1) have been a prevailing party[93] in a proceeding against the United States;

(2) if a corporation, have not more than $7,000,000 in net worth and five hundred employees at the time the adversary adjudication was initiated;

(3) submit its application within thirty days of a final disposition in the adjudication;

(4) in that application (a) show that it has met the requirements as to having prevailed and size (numbers (1) and (2) above) and (b) state the amount sought and include an itemized statement of costs and attorney fees; and

(5) allege that the position of the agency was not substantially justified.[94]

---

[89] *Id.*

[90] *Id.*

[91] *Id.* (emphasis added).

[92] *Systems Integrations & Management*, 15-1 BCA ¶ 35886.

[93] To qualify as a "prevailing party" under the EAJA, it is not enough that a party has achieved its desired result. The appellant must show that there was a Board decision sustaining the appeal, or a Board decision in the nature of a consent judgment, effecting a material alteration in the legal relationship of the parties. *Military Aircraft Parts*, ASBCA No. 59632, 15-1 BCA ¶ 35897 (*citing Lasmer Industries, Inc.*, ASBCA No. 56411, 10-2 BCA ¶ 34491).

[94] *Systems Integrations & Management*, 15-1 BCA ¶ 35886 (*citing* 5 U.S.C. § 504(a)(1), (2), (b)(1)(B)).

The only issue for the Board consideration in *Systems Management* was whether the government's position was not "substantially justified." In making a determination, the Board should ask whether the agency's position was "'justified in substance or in the main'—that is, justified to a degree that could satisfy a reasonable person" and "[u]nder this standard, the trier of the case must determine whether the Government's position had a reasonable basis in both law and fact."[95]

GSA argued that the passage of time between the performance of SIM's work covered by the invoices at issue and when it submitted the claims limited GSA's ability to pay the amounts sought by SIM.[96] The Board held that GSA's failure to adequately explain its refusal to pay the invoices required a finding that the government's position was not substantially justified.[97] The next issue was whether the government's position became substantially justified when SIM rejected GSA's settlement offer.

Under the EAJA, "[i]f, after a certain point in time, the Government's position on the issues involved in a case becomes substantially justified, reimbursement of costs incurred by the contractor in prosecuting the case further is not appropriate under the EAJA."[98] GSA contended that its position became substantially justified after SIM unreasonably rejected the settlement offer of $960,000 in March 2010. The Board agreed, holding that SIM's actions "unduly and unreasonably protracted the final resolution of the matter in controversy."[99] Specifically, the Board noted that SIM's insistence on a hearing and a decision, which resulted in no better of a result than what GSA had offered after deducting litigation costs incurred after the offer on April 9, 2010 was a key factor. The Board thus determined that SIM was only entitled to those litigation expenses incurred from December 18, 2008 until April 9, 2010.[100] Consequently, SIM was only entitled to $32,150, a mere fraction of the total fees and costs incurred.

In *JM Carranza Trucking Co*,[101] the Postal Service Board considered an application for attorneys' fees under the EAJA. The underlying litigation in *JM Carranza Trucking* involved five consolidated appeals: (1) an appeal of the termination for default of Contract No. HCR 33547, (2) an appeal of the termination for default of Contract No. HCR 33749, (3) Carranza Trucking's claim for $678,285.73 for the balance of the contract proceeds for Contract No. HCR 33547, (4) Carranza Trucking's claim for $45,402.84 for work on Contract No. HCR 33749 performed before termination, and (5) the Postal Service's claim

---

[95] *Id.*
[96] *Id.*
[97] *Id.*
[98] *Systems Integrations & Management*, 15-1 BCA ¶ 35886.
[99] *Id.*
[100] *Id.*
[101] PSBCA No. 6354, 15-1 BCA ¶ 35994.

against Carranza Trucking for $285,549.24 for excess fuel.[102] The Board rejected JM Carranza Trucking's challenge of the two terminations for default, denied its claim for $678,285.73, granted $43,147 of Carranza Trucking's $45,402.84 claim, and ultimately allowed the Postal Service to collect $81,389.90.

JM Carranza subsequently filed an application for fees seeking $23,645.[103] The application under the EAJA did not break down the amount of attorneys' fees associated with each appeal or each litigation issue. The Postal Service challenged the application arguing that JM Carranza Trucking was not a prevailing party with respect to three of the five cases before the Board and that, in the appeals where JM Carranza Trucking was the prevailing party, the Postal Service's positions before and during the litigation were substantially justified. Despite the total number of appeals, the underlying litigation centered on three basic issues: (1) Did the Postal Service act in bad faith or otherwise breach the contracts when it withheld contract proceeds because Carranza Trucking exceeded its fuel allowance?, (2) Was the Postal Service justified in terminating the two contracts for default?, and (3) Did the Postal Service breach its duty of good faith and fair dealing by allowing damages to continue to accrue once it had actual knowledge of the monthly fuel overages? On these issues, the record showed that the parties spent approximately 1/3 of their time on each issue.

On the first two issues, the Board held that the Postal Service did not act in bad faith. However, on the third issue, the Board ruled that the Postal Service breached its duty of good faith and fair dealing and was thus not substantially justified.[104] In awarding fees to JM Carranza Trucking, the Board stated that "[a] reduced fee award is appropriate if the granted relief is a portion of the litigation as a whole."[105] Success rate is one indicator of the proportion of fees that should be awarded and because JM Carranza Trucking prevailed on one of the three issues, it was awarded a third of the amount sought.[106]

While the EAJA can provide benefits to contractors and individuals, *Systems Management* and *JM Carranza Trucking* demonstrate that an award is not absolute even if the appellant is the prevailing party and the government's position is not substantially justified. Specifically, an appellant must be sensitive to the value of its claim when receiving a settlement offer from the government. Failing to accept a reasonable offer can potentially curtail the appellant's ability to recover a portion of its fees under the EAJA even if it is successful in

---

[102] *Id.*; *see* JM Carranza Trucking Co. v. United States Postal Serv., PSBCA Nos. 6354, et al., 14-1 BCA ¶ 35776.1.

[103] *JM Carranza Trucking Co.*, 15-1 BCA ¶ 35994.

[104] *Id.*

[105] *JM Carranza Trucking Co.*, 15-1 BCA ¶ 35994 (*citing* Hensley v. Eckerhart, 461 U.S. 424, 433 (1983)).

[106] *JM Carranza Trucking Co.*, 15-1 BCA ¶ 35994 (*citing Haselrig Constr. Co., Inc.*, PSBCA No. 4609, 03-2 BCA ¶ 32325) (holding that the Postal Service was not justified in opposing half of the appellant's claim, but was justified in opposing the other half).

prosecuting its claims in the underlying lawsuit. Additionally, *JM Carranza Trucking* is instructive, suggesting that attorneys should separately track fees incurred on each appeal or particular issue so that the fees can be allocated accordingly if an application is submitted under the EAJA. Doing so will make it easier to ensure that the litigation expenses that are potentially recoverable can actually be recovered for the client.

## [E] Certifications Under Contract Disputes Act

A relatively minor issue that seems to consistently plague contractors under the CDA is the sum certain requirement when certifying a claim. The Board of Contract Appeals precedent makes clear that extraneous factors impacting the value of an appellant's claim does not divest the Board of jurisdiction. Under the CDA, the sum certain requirement is measured at the time the contractor submits its claim to the contracting officer. Whether an appellant is ultimately entitled to the amount sought in its certification is the subject of the appeal process, not the threshold issue of jurisdiction. The CDA's sum certain requirement was specifically addressed in the 2014 update of this chapter where it was recognized that:

> The Contract Disputes Act (CDA) requires that a contractor submit a written claim to the contracting officer for decision. Since the Act does not define the term "claim," the definition that is set forth in Federal Acquisition Regulation (FAR) 2.201, 48 CFR 2.201 (2007), is relied on by tribunals. FAR 2.201, in pertinent part, defines a claim as "a written demand or written assertion by one of the contracting parties seeking, as a matter of right, the payment of money in a sum certain." No particular wording is required for a claim, but the demand must contain "a clear and unequivocal statement that gives the contracting officer adequate notice of the basis and amount of the claim." To comply with the sum certain requirement for a valid claim, a fixed amount must be stated.[107]

In *Ari University Heights, LP*,[108] the contractor failed to state a fixed amount when submitting its certification to the contracting officer. In *Ari University*, there was a dispute over the payment of utility expenses by the government where ARI submitted a claim to the contracting officer on November 10, 2014, stating:

> [P]er the information provided, the cost to the landlord, based on the average of the last 3 years of use, which includes annualizing 2014 year to date, the estimates are that *the cost is likely to be around $20,140 per year*, without taking into account the uncontrollable aspect of utility cost increases. Based on a [capitalization (cap)] rate of 7.5%, this reduces the value of the property by approximately $268,533.

---

[107] *ASP Denver, LLC*, CBCA 2618, 12-1 BCA ¶ 35007.
[108] CBCA 4660, 15-1 BCA ¶ 36085.

Based on the above, [ARI] makes this claim and respectfully requests that the lease be interpreted so that it requires that the GSA or USGS pay the service provider directly for electrical usage in the Premises and that the rental consideration specifically excludes electrical consumption at the Premises; and that a lease amendment be executed specifically that memorializing [sic] same. Alternatively, *[ARI] makes this claim for payment of a minimum of $268,533* for the diminution of the property's value as a result of the inclusion of the cost of electrical service in the rental consideration.[109]

The contracting officer denied the claim in its entirety and Ari University appealed the final decision.

GSA moved to dismiss the claim on the basis that Ari University failed to state a sum certain. Ari University opposed, arguing that its monetary claim is a sum certain derived from calculations presented in its claim. With respect to the sum certain issue, the Board noted that a "contractor must 'submit in writing to the contracting officer a clear and unequivocal statement that gives the contracting officer adequate notice of the basis and amount of the claim' to submit a monetary claim in a sum certain. A claim for monetary relief is not clear and unequivocal when a contractor's 'qualifying language leaves the door open for the request of more money on the same basis.' In short, the sum certain requirement demands a fixed amount be stated in the claim."[110]

The Board held that "ARI's monetary claim is not stated as a sum certain because the dollar amount is preceded by the phrase 'of a minimum.'"[111] Ari University argued that the minimum reference was sensitive to the fact that additional reduction in value of the property may occur at a future date and that the sum certain could be extrapolated from the formula provided in its claim.[112]

However, the Board stated that "[t]he purpose behind the sum certain requirement 'is to facilitate negotiations and the final and fair resolution of [a] claim by the [[[contracting officer].' If a contractor were permitted to demand a minimum or otherwise indefinite amount, the contracting officer would be precluded from resolving the dispute with any finality because, upon payment of the claim, the contractor could simply claim some greater amount."[113] The Board held that a sum certain was not stated here and rejected Ari University's formula argument because it was dependent upon *prospective* utility expenses and not amounts that had been assessed and paid.

In *Ari University*, it was clear that the contractor failed to meet the sum certain requirement. While it may seem that Ari University made a prudent decision to prospectively calculate the costs, the better route would have been to

---

[109] *Ari University Heights, LP,* 15-1 BCA ¶ 36085 (emphasis added).
[110] *Ari University Heights, LP,* 15-1 BCA ¶ 36085 (internal citations omitted).
[111] *Id.*
[112] *Id.*
[113] *Ari University Heights, LP,* 15-1 BCA ¶ 36085 (internal citations omitted).

specifically identify an amount due without the qualifying language or simply wait until the costs were **actually incurred** before certifying the claim. While Ari University may have ultimately lost the appeal on the merits, failure to properly assert a sum certain cost Ari University its day in court.

In *Equine Architectural Products, Inc.*,[114] the jurisdictional sum certain requirement was decided when the contractor simply failed to include any sum whatsoever. In February 2012, the government awarded a contract to Equine Architectural Products, Inc. ("EAP") for the demolition and removal of railroad and related facilities in Maryland.[115] The government subsequently issued a stop work order and later notified the appellant that it was being terminated for convenience. EAP issued a letter on January 7, 2014 to the government, certifying its claim as follows:

> Please accept this letter as an official claim under the above contract pursuant to the [CDA].
>
>                          ***
>
> This claim is for return to Equine of all property which existed within that 15 foot area, including the 14 miles of rail, at the time of that mobilization. Much of this equipment is noted per drawings titled APG: North Rail Lines dated March 27, 2012. By the direct language of the contract, title to this property passed to Equine at the time of contracting. This claim is for possession and return of all such property which now belongs to Equine and which it has been prevented from removing by the government.
>
>                          ***
>
> I certify that I have reviewed this claim and that it is made in good faith, the supporting data is accurate and complete to the best of my knowledge and belief, that the property requested is accurately reflected in the contract under which Equine believes the Government is liable; and that I am duly authorized to certify this claim on behalf of Equine.[116]

There were no other documents referenced in EAP's letter. Several weeks later, the parties discussed the quantum of EAP's claim in which the appellant's counsel advised the government that it believed the materials at issue were worth "approximately $6,986,832.00."[117] EAP's counsel then issued a letter to the government captioned "FOR SETTLEMENT PURPOSES ONLY" setting forth that the "estimate of the total value of these costs and impacts is $9,250,000.00"[118] EAP did not certify this amount. After no final decision was issued, EAP filed a notice of appeal to the Board on a deemed denied basis on or about December 12,

---

[114] ASBCA No. 59743, 15-1 BCA ¶ 36004.
[115] *Id.*
[116] *Id.*
[117] *Id.*
[118] *Id.*

2014 "stating that its total losses exceeded $10,000,000.00."[119] On December 15, 2014, the contracting officer denied EAP's claim dated January 7, 2014 with the estimated value being $6,986,832.00.[120]

Under the CDA, the Board noted that the term "claim" is not defined, but the FAR does state:

> *Claim* means a **written demand or written assertion by one of the contracting parties seeking**, as a matter of right, **the payment of money in a sum certain**, the adjustment or interpretation of contract terms, or other relief arising under or relating to the contract. However, **a written demand or written assertion by the contractor seeking the payment of money exceeding $100,000 is not a claim** under the Contract Disputes Act of 1978 **until certified as required by the Act**.[121]

The Board noted that it believed EAP's claim is essentially a monetary claim and was therefore required to submit its claim to the contracting officer in a sum certain. There was no amount identified in EAP's January 7, 2014 certification letter and the Board held that it did not have jurisdiction over the claim based upon that single submission.[122]

EAP argued that the Board should go beyond its January 7th letter and view other communications to determine whether a proper claim had been submitted under the CDA. Specifically, EAP directed the Board to its counsel's email in which a value of $6,986,832.00 was asserted and the letter in which the appellant stated that the claim was in the amount of $9,250,000.00.[123] The Board did not entertain the argument because EAP failed to provide any certification for the monetary claims it did request over $100,000. Thus, the Board was without jurisdiction for this reason as well. In *EAP*, it was abundantly clear that the contractor failed to present the value of its claims to the contracting officer. This error cost the contractor its claim. Even if the amount stated is later proven wrong, a dollar figure *must* be submitted. Otherwise, the CDA requirements are not satisfied and the claim will be dismissed for lack of jurisdiction.

## [F] Time for Government to Respond to Contractor's Certified Claim

In federal procurement disputes, contractors must submit a certified claim to the government, then wait until the government has issued a final decision before pursuing a lawsuit. The CDA specifies the amount of time the government has to respond to a contractor's certified claim. In a recent Court of Federal

---

[119] *Id.*
[120] *Id.*
[121] *Id.*
[122] *Id.*
[123] *Id.*

Claims decision, the court clarified the standard for when the government's failure to issue a final decision is deemed a constructive denial of that claim.

In *Rudolph & Sletten, Inc. v. United States*,[124] Rudolph & Sletten, Inc. ("Rudolph") contracted with the government to construct a laboratory in La Jolla, California. After starting construction, Rudolph submitted a certified claim on August 20, 2013, seeking a compensable time extension and costs for government-caused delays. Two months later, on October 30, the contracting officer wrote to Rudolph stating: "Due to the complexity and extensive nature of your claim, we anticipate a final Contracting Officer's decision to be issued 9 months from the date of this letter."[125]

On November 4, 2013, Rudolph responded to the contracting officer, stating that the nine-month time period to issue a final decision was excessive and unreasonable. The contracting officer replied on November 8, attempting to justify the delay and providing a timeline to issue a final decision by July 15, 2014. On July 8, 2014, the contracting officer informed Rudolph that a final decision would not be reached by July 15, 2014, and that the government would need until March 15, 2015.

Rudolph then filed suit in the Court of Federal Claims on July 23, 2014. The government moved to dismiss the case, arguing that the court lacked jurisdiction because Rudolph had not obtained a final decision from the contracting officer. The court first delineated the requirements for subject matter jurisdiction for the Court of Federal Claims under the CDA:

> For the Court to have subject-matter jurisdiction to hear a dispute under the CDA, the plaintiff must meet two prerequisites: (1) submit a proper claim to the relevant contracting officer, which must be properly certified if the amount requested is above $100,000, and (2) obtain a final decision on that claim.
>
> Under the CDA, a contractor may obtain either an actual or a deemed final decision on the claim. *For claims over $100,000, the CDA provides that the contracting officer shall, within 60 days of receipt of the submitted certified claim, "(A) issue a decision; or (B) notify the contractor of the time within which a decision will be issued." The decision must be "issued within a reasonable time,"* which is calculated by "taking into account such factors as the size and complexity of the claim and the adequacy of information in support of the claim provided by the contractor." If the contracting officer denies the claim within the required time period, that claim is actually denied. *However, a failure to issue a decision within the required time "is deemed to be a decision by the contracting officer denying the claim."* A denial, actual or deemed, authorizes an "appeal or action on the claim as otherwise provided in [the CDA]."[126]

---

[124] 120 Fed. Cl. 137 (2015).

[125] *Id.* at 139.

[126] *Id.* at 141 (emphasis added) (internal citations omitted).

In support of its motion to dismiss, the government argued that the contracting officer properly and timely extended the deadline to March 15, 2015 once he determined that the government could not meet the original deadline, and that this new deadline was reasonable. The court first looked to the plain language of the relevant statute, 41 U.S.C. § 7103(f)(2), noting that it requires either a decision within 60 days or the establishment of a firm deadline for issuing a final decision within 60 days.[127]

Next, the court looked to prior case law for further guidance. In particular, the court considered a 2014 case in the United States District Court for the District of Columbia holding that a contracting officer is entitled to only a single deadline extension under the CDA.[128] Here, the contracting officer set an initial deadline of July 15, 2014 and then later sought to extend this deadline into March 2015. The court held that "no language in the CDA provides the government with the right to a second extension."[129] Thus, the government's failure to issue a final decision by July 15, 2014 constituted a denial of Rudolph's claim.

The court then addressed the government's argument that the contracting officer had the right to a second extension due to the complexity of the claim. Under 41 U.S.C. § 7103(f)(2) though, the government's deadline must take into account "such factors as the size and complexity of the claim and the adequacy of information in support of the claim provided by the contractor."[130] Thus, the court disregarded the government's complexity argument and held that it had subject matter jurisdiction over the claim.

Finally, the court decided to stay the case and retrocede authority to the contracting officer to issue a final decision before proceeding with the case.[131] The court reasoned that the contracting officer had devoted substantial resources to the review and that these results would clarify the issues and promote judicial economy. Because the review was near completion, the court found that there was no undue hardship imposed on the parties because of this short delay.

Ultimately, *Rudolph* is a favorable decision for government contractors. The clear rule now is that the government must issue a final decision within 60 days or provide a hard deadline within 60 days. The government cannot seek additional time extensions as that now constitutes a deemed denial of the claim. Contractors should note though that courts may allow jurisdiction but then cede authority to the contracting officer to finish his review, as the court did here. In effect, this serves as an additional time extension for the contracting officer.

---

[127] *Id.*

[128] Tuba City Reg'l Health Care Corp. v. United States, et al., 39 F. Supp. 3d 66 (D.D.C. 2014).

[129] *Rudolph*, 120 Fed. Cl. at 142.

[130] *Id.*

[131] "[W]hen the Court does possess jurisdiction over a claim based upon a deemed denial, it is specifically granted discretion to retrocede authority to the contracting officer [by the CDA]." *Id.* at 143 (*citing* United Partition Sys., Inc. v. United States, 59 Fed. Cl. 627, 643 (2004)).

## [G]   Directing the Government to File the Initial Pleading in a Contract Appeal

In the past two years, the ASBCA has explored the issue of when it should direct the government to file a complaint instead of the contractor. Typically, the contractor is required to file a claim before the ASBCA or similar contract boards of appeals, regardless of whether the dispute arises from the contractor's affirmative claim or a government claim. Indeed, under the CDA, both contractor and government claims must be subjected to a contracting officer's final decision,[132] but only the contractor can initiate contract board proceedings.[133] This approach can be unwieldy and confusing when the dispute involves a government claim as it forces the contractor to file a complaint based on what it assumes the government is claiming. In some cases, it is difficult for the contractor to discern what exactly the government is claiming based solely on the dealings between the parties and the contracting officer's final decision.

After issuing two decisions on this topic in 2014,[134] the ASBCA continued to develop this area of contract board practice in 2015 in *Kellogg Brown & Root Services, Inc.*[135] Under its contract with the government, Kellogg Brown & Root ("KBR") was required to provide workers' compensation insurance for its own employees and to flow down this requirement to its subcontractors. Because it was responsible for ensuring that subcontractor employees were covered, KBR elected to provide insurance for its subcontractors to ensure compliance. After paying KBR, the government alleged that the $33.9 million KBR spent on this insurance was an unallowable cost and demanded repayment.

The contracting officer issued a final decision on this claim in favor of the government. Notably, the contracting officer's written decision was brief and cursory, stating only:

> This is my final decision asserting a Government claim for $33,851,868, pursuant to FAR 52.233-1, Disputes, due to the inclusion of unallowable Fiscal Year (FY) 2007 direct costs claimed and billed to the Government. My decision was based on FAR 31.201-2, Determining Allowability, due to KBRSI's computation of subcontract DBA insurance costs claimed and billed under contract no. DAAA-09-02-D-0007. The cost billed was not based on actual subcontractor labor incurred during FY 2007. The following documents are referenced and relied upon in making this decision:

---

[132] 41 U.S.C. § 7103.

[133] 41 U.S.C. § 7104.

[134] Beechcraft Defense Co., ASBCA No. 59173, 14-1 BCA ¶ 35592; BAE Systems Land & Armaments Inc., ASBCA No. 59374, 15-1 BCA ¶ 35817.

[135] ASBCA No. 59557, 15-1 BCA ¶ 35865.

      (a) DCAA Audit Report No. 3321-2007K10100001 dated May 30, 2014

      (b) KBRSI' s response dated, May 19, 2014[136]

KBR argued in its ASBCA appeal that the ASBCA should direct the government to file the complaint, stating:

> unless the government is required to file the complaint, it will have been excused from "having to proffer a basic legal and factual rationale for its demand of the significant sum at issue in this Appeal, resulting in a [KBR] complaint simply disagreeing with the bare-bones conclusions of the Final Decision and a Government answer simply denying these . . . positions. Such pleadings would do little, if anything, to advance this Appeal."[137]

In response, the government argued: (1) that its position was apparent from communications between it and KBR; (2) that KBR is the party that bears the burden of proof to show that its costs are allowable; and (3) KBR has knowledge of the facts regarding the reasonableness of its costs.

In reaching its decision, the board first noted that a government claim is alone not enough to justify requiring the government to file the appeal. Instead, "the Board may exercise its discretion to require the government to file the complaint, if doing so will facilitate efficient resolution of the appeal."[138] The board reviewed the contracting officer's decision, the two documents referenced within it, and other communications between the parties, ultimately finding that there was not enough information for KBR to fully understand the basis of the government's claim. The board held that KBR "should not have to speculate about the basis for the government's claim in its complaint" and directed the government to file the initial pleading in the appeal.[139]

This decision, along with similar preceding ones, is significant for contractors dealing with the ASBCA. When dealing with a government claim, contractors should now analyze whether the government provided enough information in the contracting officer's final decision and other communications. If not, contractors have the strategic option of motioning the ASBCA to direct the government to file the initial appeal pleading. In doing so, the contractor gains the advantage of being able to respond to the government's allegations instead of having to defend itself based on what it believes the government is alleging. Further, this decision may prompt the government to express more detail in the contracting officer's final decision, potentially fostering a more efficient contract appeal process.

---

[136] *Id.*
[137] *Id.*
[138] *Id.*
[139] *Id.*

Less than two months after the *KBR* decision, the ASBCA issued another decision on a contractor's motion for the government to file the complaint. In *Carro & Carro Enterprises, Inc.*[140] ("CCE"), the contractor performed construction work for the Army Corps of Engineers on a flood control project in Puerto Rico. The Corps withheld some amounts from its progress payments to CCE because of supposed issues with CCE's work. CCE submitted a certified claim to the contracting officer and, after its denial, appealed the decision to the ASBCA.

CCE then motioned the ASBCA to direct the government to file the complaint because the Corps' withholding was a government claim for a reduction to the contract price. CCE argued that the government thus has the burden of proving that its withholding was proper. The Corps conceded that it did assert a claim against CCE but argued instead that CCE had sufficient information to file the complaint and determine the extent of damages due to its alleged defective work.

First, the board ignored the Corps' concession and held that this was not in fact a government claim, stating: "Since the Corps' CO has not made a specific monetary demand on CCE, but simply retained a portion of the monies sought by CCE pursuant to a contract clause based on unsatisfactory progress, and the CO final decision does not fall within the Disputes clause's other provisions (i.e., the adjustment or interpretation of contract terms or other relief), there is no factual or legal basis to conclude that this appeal presents a 'government' claim."[141] Thus, the board noted that CCE, and not the government, has the burden of proof on this appeal. The board then found that CCE had enough information to file the complaint itself and that thus there was "no reason why filing of the initial pleading (complaint) by the Corps would facilitate further proceedings in this appeal."[142]

With the *CCE* decision, the ASBCA has made clear that the two main considerations in determining whether the government should file the complaint is: (1) whether there is sufficient information for the contractor to file the complaint; and (2) whether having the government file the complaint will facilitate efficient resolution of the appeal. Indeed, the board in *CCE* considered the burden of proof issue but ultimately conditioned its holding on these two considerations.

---

[140] ASBCA No. 59485, 15-1 BCA ¶ 35915.

[141] *Id.*

[142] *Id.*

## § 6.03  CIRCUIT SPLIT IN VALIDITY OF "IMPLIED CERTIFICATION" THEORY IN FALSE CLAIMS ACT LITIGATION

### [A]  Fourth Circuit Imposes Liability on Contractor Under "Implied Certification" Theory

The False Claims Act ("FCA") is a powerful government tool to combat fraud and other deceitful business practices in federal procurement. Contractors must tread carefully when submitting claims to the government to avoid potential FCA liability. Since its inception in 1863, the FCA has undergone numerous revisions and been the subject of extensive litigation. In recent years, the "implied certification" theory of liability has been at the forefront of FCA litigation. Under the FCA, there are two broad categories of false claims: (1) factually false claims (e.g., a contractor billing for services not provided); and (2) legally false claims (e.g., a contractor certifying a claim that violates an applicable statute, regulation or contract provision). Under the implied certification theory, a contractor impliedly certifies its compliance with all legal provisions (whether statutory or contractual) when submitting a claim for payment. Thus, an explicit certification of compliance with a law is not required for liability to attach.

This issue was at the forefront of FCA litigation this year with both the Fourth and Seventh Circuit Courts of Appeals joining other circuits in addressing this issue. The Fourth and Seventh Circuits deepened the circuit-wide split on this issue by reaching opposite results. Based on the flurry of activity in this area and the split among circuits, the Supreme Court granted certiorari late in the year to hopefully clarify this area of law.[143]

In *United States v. Triple Canopy, Inc.*,[144] the Fourth Circuit recognized the implied certification theory and used it to impose FCA liability on a contractor. The contractor, Triple Canopy, was hired by the government in 2009 to provide security services at an airbase in Iraq. Triple Canopy's contract with the government contained individual task orders containing responsibilities for Triple Canopy. One of these requirements was to "ensure that all employees have received initial training on the weapon that they carry, [and] that they have qualified on a U.S. Army qualification course."[145] Triple Canopy hired around 300 Ugandan guards whose personnel files indicated that they met the required marksmanship qualifications. However, upon arrival at the airbase, Triple Canopy supervisors realized that these guards were incapable of performing to the level of their purported qualifications. Despite this, Triple Canopy submitted monthly

---

[143] On December 4, 2015, the U.S. Supreme Court granted certiorari in the appeal of United States v. Universal Health Servs., Inc., 780 F.3d 504 (1st Cir. 2015), *cert. granted in part*, 136 S. Ct. 582 (2015).

[144] 775 F.3d 628 (4th Cir. 2015).

[145] *Id.* at 632.

invoices for the guards. None of these invoices required Triple Canopy to make any certification or endorsement regarding the task order responsibilities.

After a failed training attempt, Triple Canopy began falsifying qualification scorecards and placing them in the Ugandan guards' personnel files. Triple Canopy continued falsifying scorecards while submitting monthly invoices for these guards. A Triple Canopy employee then filed a *qui tam* action under the FCA in the Eastern District of Virginia, prompting the government to intervene and prosecute Triple Canopy for violating the FCA. The government alleged that Triple Canopy knew that its guards did not meet the task order's marksmanship qualification requirement but still submitted invoices for those guards, and falsified scorecards for its guards. Thus, by simply submitting the invoices, the government claimed that Triple Canopy was liable under the implied certification theory. The district court dismissed the government's claims, finding that: (1) Triple Canopy never submitted a demand for payment that contained an objectively false statement; and (2) the government never reviewed and thus never relied on the falsified scorecards.

On appeal, the Fourth Circuit held that "the Government pleads a false claim when it alleges that the contractor, with the requisite scienter, made a request for payment under a contract and 'withheld information about its noncompliance with material contractual requirements.'"[146] The court also recognized that the implied certification theory could be abused to impose FCA liability for mere, unintentional breaches of contract. Cognizant of this possibility, the court instructed that "[t]he best manner for continuing to ensure that plaintiffs cannot shoehorn a breach of contract claim into an FCA claim is 'strict enforcement of the Act's materiality and scienter requirements.'"[147]

The court then applied these principles to the facts at issue and held that the government sufficiently alleged a false claim under the FCA. The court reasoned that Triple Canopy was required to meet the marksmanship requirement, had actual knowledge that it failed to do so, and then fraudulently attempted to obscure its failure. Next, the court analyzed whether the marksmanship requirement was a material contractual requirement. To establish materiality, the government must allege that the falsity had "'a natural tendency to influence, or be capable of influencing' the Government's decision to pay."[148] Here, the court reasoned that the government established materiality for two reasons: (1) common sense dictates that the government's decision to pay for security would be influenced by the fact that the contractor's guards could not shoot accurately; and (2) Triple Canopy's cover up of the guards marksmanship scores suggests its materiality.

---

[146] *Id.* at 636.
[147] *Id.* at 637.
[148] *Id.* (*citing* 31 U.S.C. § 3729(b)(4)).

Finally, the court reversed the trial court's holding that Triple Canopy's falsification of the score cards was irrelevant. The court held: "The district court thus erred in focusing on the actual effect of the false statement rather than its potential effect. A false record may, in the appropriate circumstances, have the potential to influence the Government's payment decision even if the Government ultimately does not review the record."[149] The court then remanded the case to the trial court, concluding that "[t]he FCA is 'strong medicine in situations where strong remedies are needed' . . . when, as here, a contractor allegedly engages in a year-long fraudulent scheme that includes falsifying records in personnel files for guards serving as a primary security force on a United States airbase in Iraq."[150]

Thus, the Fourth Circuit recognized and used the implied certification theory to impose FCA liability on a contractor despite that contractor never expressly certifying its requests for payment. Contractors operating in the Fourth Circuit should be aware of this development and its potential consequences, at least until the Supreme Court rules on this issue. If the Supreme Court embraces this expanded scope of FCA liability, the government may become increasingly aggressive in pursuing claims against contractors. However, contractors should take solace in the *Triple Canopy* court's imposition of stringent scienter and materiality requirements to curb overzealous use of the theory by the government, and the court's conclusion, emphasizing the egregiousness of the contractor's behavior. Contractors should hope that the Supreme Court will follow this rationale and limit the theory to such extreme circumstances.

## [B] Seventh Circuit Rejects Government's Usage of "Implied Certification" Theory

A few months after the Fourth Circuit's *Triple Canopy* decision, the Seventh Circuit went the opposite direction and rejected the government's false certification theory. In *United States v. Sanford-Brown, Ltd.*,[151] the defendant, Sanford-Brown College, was a for-profit educational institution receiving federal subsidies from the Department of Education ("DOE"). To receive these subsidies, Sanford-Brown had to enter into a Program Participation Agreement ("PPA") that was conditioned on participants meeting and continuing to meet a plethora of statutory, regulatory, and contractual requirements.

As Sanford-Brown continued to receive federal funding, a former employee filed a *qui tam* action, alleging that Sanford-Brown's practices violated numerous regulations imposed by the PPA and that its applications for subsidies were false claims. The former employee argued that by entering the PPA, Sanford-Brown

---

[149] *Id.* at 639.
[150] *Id.* at 640.
[151] 788 F.3d 696 (7th Cir. 2015).

represented that it would comply with the required laws and regulations. By submitting claims while in violation of these laws, Sanford-Brown was submitting false claims, even though it never certified its compliance in any submission to the government.

After the district court rejected this implied certification argument, the former employee, joined by the government, appealed to the Seventh Circuit. The Seventh Circuit affirmed the trial court's ruling, stating: "we conclude that it would be . . . unreasonable for us to hold that an institution's continued compliance with the thousands of pages of federal statutes and regulations incorporated by reference into the PPA are conditions of payment for purposes of liability under the FCA. Although a number of other circuits have adopted this so-called doctrine of implied false certification . . . we decline to join them."[152] The court elaborated that "[t]he FCA is simply not the proper mechanism for government to enforce violations of conditions of participation contained in—or incorporated by reference into—a PPA."[153]

The *Sanford-Brown* decision offers an alternate path for the Supreme Court to take. A Supreme Court decision supporting the Seventh Circuit's line of reasoning would be a clear victory as *Sanford-Brown* limits contractor liability under the FCA, limiting the possibility of an FCA action in the absence of an explicit certification.

## § 6.04   THIRD CIRCUIT CLARIFIES LOSS CALCULATION FOR DISADVANTAGED BUSINESS ENTERPRISE FRAUD

Programs that offer incentives to certain categories of businesses (e.g., minority or veteran-owned businesses) are ubiquitous in federal contracting. Along these lines, the Department of Transportation ("DOT") has long operated a Disadvantaged Business Enterprise ("DBE") program, intended to ensure a level playing field for social and economically disadvantaged contractors. To that end, the DBE program offers benefits and subsidies to qualifying contractors. Like other similar initiatives, the DBE program is subject to abuse from unqualified contractors seeking to take advantage of these benefits.

In *United States v. Nagle*,[154] the Third Circuit considered the amount of loss attributable to a contractor found guilty of DBE fraud. The two *Nagle* defendants owned a construction business in Pennsylvania and entered into an arrangement with a certified DBE to fraudulently obtain DBE benefits. Under the arrangement, the DBE would bid on jobs that had DBE participation requirements but the defendants' company would perform all the work. The defendants paid the DBE a fixed fee and kept the remaining profits for themselves. The defendants

---

[152] *Id.* at 711-12.
[153] *Id.* at 712.
[154] 803 F.3d 167 (3d Cir. 2015).

perpetuated this fraud from 1993 to 2008, obtaining over $100 million in government contracts intended for DBEs.

After the government discovered the fraud and brought criminal charges, the defendants pled guilty to a variety of charges. Under the government's sentencing guidelines, the length of the sentence depends on the amount of loss the defendants are responsible for.[155] As part of this process, the district court issued an opinion holding that the amount of loss was the total face value of the contracts the DBE received ($135.8 million for one defendant and $53.9 million for the other).

On appeal, the defendants challenged the district court's loss calculation, claiming that it erred in not considering the value of the services they performed. The Third Circuit looked to district precedent in other fraud cases for guidance, noting that: "Our case law makes clear that, in a normal fraud case, 'where value passes in both directions [between defrauded and defrauder] . . . the victim's loss will normally be the difference between the value he or she gave up and the value he or she received.'"[156] Applying this principle here, the Third Circuit held that the defendants were entitled to a credit for the fair market value of the work they performed, and remanded this issue to the district court. The court then advised that in calculating the fair market value, district courts should consider the value of the materials supplied, the labor required for construction, and the cost to transport and store the materials. Finally, the court advised that "[i]f possible and when relevant, the District Court should keep in mind the goals of the DBE program that have been frustrated by the fraud."[157] However, the court did not elaborate on this vague statement.

*Nagle* establishes an important principle in DBE fraud cases. In sentencing contractors guilty of DBE fraud, courts must credit the value of the services performed for the sentencing calculation and not simply rely upon the face value of the contracts at issue.

## § 6.05   DCAA PROTECTED FROM NEGLIGENT AUDIT CLAIM BY SOVEREIGN IMMUNITY

The Defense Contract Audit Agency ("DCAA") is a common foe for contractors prosecuting claims against the government. The DCAA is used by the government to audit contractor claims and determine the reasonableness and accuracy of the claimed costs. Contractors and the DCAA often disagree on the audit and evaluation of these costs. In a recent decision, a contractor filed suit against the government, alleging that the DCAA's negligent audit violated the Federal Tort Claims Act ("FTCA").

---

[155] *See* U.S.S.G. § 2B1.1.
[156] *Nagle*, 803 F.3d at 180 (*citing* United States v. Dickler, 64 F.3d 818, 835 (3d Cir. 1995)).
[157] *Id.* at 183.

In *Kellogg Brown & Root Services, Inc. v. United States*,[158] Kellogg Brown & Root ("KBR") filed suit in federal district court, seeking to recover $12.5 million in attorneys' fees incurred due to the DCAA's negligent audit. KBR alleged two counts, one for each dispute with the government related to the DCAA audit. The two disputes were a contract appeal before the ASBCA and a subsequent Department of Justice ("DOJ") action under the False Claims Act. The government countered that the district court lacked subject matter jurisdiction because of sovereign immunity.[159] The court noted that the FTCA waives this sovereign immunity for tort claims seeking monetary damages. However, this waiver is subject to the discretionary function exception under which "the government retains sovereign immunity for '[a]ny claim . . . based upon the exercise or performance or the failure to exercise or perform a discretionary function or duty on the part of a federal agency or an employee of the Government, whether or not the discretion involved be abused.'"[160]

Per the United States Supreme Court's seminal decision in *Berkovitz v. United States*, courts apply a two-part test to determine if the discretionary function exception applies: (1) whether the action at issue "involves an element of judgment or choice"; and (2) whether the judgment exercised "is of the kind that the discretionary function exception was designed to shield."[161] The exception is designed to shield "governmental actions and decisions based on considerations of public policy."[162]

First, the court applied the test to KBR's count regarding the ASBCA appeal, holding that both the contracting officer and the DCAA performed discretionary functions. KBR argued that the contracting officer and the DCAA acted in lockstep and that the DCAA's audit did not involve discretionary judgment because the auditors failed to comply with mandatory auditing standards and practices. The court rejected this argument, countering that those standards allow auditors to exercise professional judgment, thus making the audit a discretionary action. Next, the court turned to the second prong of the *Berkovitz* test to determine whether the discretionary action involved considerations of public policy. The court reasoned that the audit was in "direct response to a congressional investigation addressing PSC [Personal Security Contractor] costs" and that this decision "involved Congress's budgetary concern, which is a fundamental matter of public policy."[163] Thus, the court held that the discretionary function exception applied to the ASBCA-related count.

---

[158] 102 F. Supp. 3d 648 (D. Del. 2015).

[159] "Sovereign immunity not only protects the United States from liability, it deprives a court of subject matter jurisdiction over claims against the United States." *Id.* at 652 (*citing* Richards v. United States, 176 F.3d 652, 654 (3d Cir. 1999)).

[160] *Id.* (*citing* 28 U.S.C. § 2680(a)).

[161] Berkovitz v. United States, 486 U.S. 531, 536 (1988).

[162] *Id.* at 537.

[163] *Kellogg, Brown & Root Servs.*, 102 F. Supp. 3d at 655.

Second, the court applied the test to KBR's count regarding the DOJ's lawsuit. The court reasoned that the DOJ's decision to initiate the lawsuit was clearly a discretionary act. However, KBR argued that its injury was caused instead by the DCAA's negligent audit. In response to this argument, the court looked to *General Dynamics Corp. v. United States*,[164] a Ninth Circuit case where the plaintiff similarly argued that its injuries were caused by the DCAA instead of the prosecuting authority. The *General Dynamics* court rejected this argument, stating that the prosecutors "had a report from the DCAA, but the decision to prosecute was all their own" and that they "were not required to prosecute, and were not forced to do so."[165] Attempting to distinguish *General Dynamics*, KBR alleged that the DOJ and DCAA acted in lockstep (as it alleged that the contracting officer and the DCAA did in its ASBCA count) and that their actions were intertwined. The court rejected this argument, stating that the DOJ had "the ultimate decision" regarding prosecution of KBR and that the decision to file was "all their own."[166] Moving to the second prong, the court again referenced congressional interest in PSC spending as evidence of public policy considerations. Thus, the court dismissed both of KBR's counts for lack of subject matter jurisdiction.

*Kellogg, Brown & Root Services* is a blow to contractors as it seemingly broadens the scope of the discretionary function exception under the FTCA. The court's holding suggests that a DCAA audit is always a discretionary function as it involves professional judgment, even if, as here, the DCAA did not follow certain standard practices. Thus, it appears that contractors have no judicial recourse against the DCAA for damages resulting from errors made in a DCAA audit.

## § 6.06  BID PROTEST ISSUES

### [A]  Court of Federal Claims Dismisses Contractor's Protest of Patent Error as Untimely

Timing of filings is a critically important aspect of federal procurement law and bid protests in particular. Indeed, there are numerous statutory and common law deadlines that practitioners need to be aware of. In a recent Court of Federal Claims decision, an otherwise valid bid protest was dismissed as untimely.

In *Visual Connections, LLC v. United States*,[167] the contractor bid on a task order to perform IT services for the Department of Health and Human Services ("HHS"). The solicitation listed several evaluation factors and also stated that bids would be evaluated for price reasonableness. However, the solicitation did not address the relative importance of the non-cost and cost factors. After HHS

---

[164] 139 F.3d 1280 (9th Cir. 1998).

[165] *Id.* at 1286.

[166] *Kellogg, Brown & Root Servs.*, 102 F. Supp. 3d at 656.

[167] 120 Fed. Cl. 684 (2015).

awarded the task order to another contractor, Visual Connections filed a protest with the Government Accountability Office ("GAO"). The GAO denied the protest on its merits prompting Visual Connections to file a protest with the Court of Federal Claims. Visual Connections claimed that HHS's decision lacked a rational basis and was "neither reasonable nor lawful because [the solicitation] does not disclose, as required by 41 U.S.C. § 3306(c)(1)(C), the relative importance of the Price and non-Price evaluation factors."[168]

In response, the government filed a motion to dismiss the complaint because Visual Connections did not challenge the terms of the solicitation prior to the quote submission deadline. The government relied on *Blue & Gold Fleet, L.P. v. United States*,[169] a Federal Circuit decision holding that:

> [A] party who has the opportunity to object to the terms of a government solicitation containing a patent error and fails to do so ***prior to the close of the bidding process*** waives its ability to raise the same objection subsequently in a bid protest action in the Court of Federal Claims.[170]

Visual Connections countered that *Blue & Gold* does not apply when the solicitation violates a statutory requirement, as it allegedly did here. The court rejected this argument, stating that "the Federal Circuit did not limit its decision in *Blue & Gold* to non-statutory violations."[171] Thus, the court held that because Visual Connections had the opportunity to challenge this patent error but failed to do so, it waived its ability to raise the same issue in a bid protest. Finally, the court addressed Visual Connections' alternative argument that the error was latent and thus not subject to the *Blue & Gold* holding. The court disposed of this argument by citing Visual Connections' own response to the government's motion to dismiss, which alleged that the government committed "an '*obvious* statutory violation'" in its solicitation.[172]

Thus, the court did not even consider the merits of Visual Connections' protest since it was untimely and had to be dismissed. In light of this decision, contractors that suspect a patent defect in a solicitation must raise that issue before the bid deadline. Otherwise, regardless of the nature of the patent defect, the Court of Federal Claims must dismiss a subsequent bid protest as untimely.

---

[168] *Id.* at 688.
[169] 492 F.3d 1308 (Fed. Cir. 2007).
[170] *Id.* at 1313 (emphasis added).
[171] *Visual Connections*, 120 Fed. Cl. at 695.
[172] *Id.* at 698.

## [B]  The Government Must Conduct Discussions with All Competitive Bidders

Government agencies must tread carefully when communicating with bidders to avoid accusations of bias or impropriety. A recent GAO decision held that the government improperly communicated with a bidder because it communicated only with that bidder and not other competitive bidders.

International Waste Industries ("IWI") filed a protest with the GAO regarding the Air Force awarding a bid to Mahto Construction for a solid waste incinerator.[173] Initially, the Air Force received 11 proposals in response to its Request for Quotation ("RFQ"). Mahto's proposal contained several terms that conflicted with the RFQ. For example, Mahto proposed a per diem payment scheme for installation instead of a fixed price as required by the RFQ. To resolve these discrepancies, the Air Force sent Mahto an e-mail asking various questions about its proposal. After the parties exchanged e-mails, the Air Force concluded that Mahto's proposal was technically acceptable. Although Mahto submitted the most expensive proposal, the Air Force awarded it the bid because it determined that the other 10 proposals were technically unacceptable. Notably, the Air Force did not communicate with any of the other 10 bidders.

After receiving a debriefing, IWI filed an agency-level protest which was denied. IWI subsequently filed a protest with the GAO, contending that the Air Force improperly communicated with Mahto. IWI argued that "had the agency conducted discussions with all of the vendors, IWI could have clarified the issues in its proposal that led to the agency's conclusion that its quotation was technically unacceptable."[174]

The GAO first referenced FAR § 15.306, which governs agency communications with bidders during procurements.[175] Under this statute, there are two main classifications for such communications: clarifications and discussions. The GAO stated that "clarifications are 'limited exchanges' between an agency and an offeror for the purpose of eliminating minor uncertainties or irregularities in a proposal, and do not give an offeror the opportunity to revise or modify its proposal."[176] Conversely, discussions are used for "obtaining information essential to determine the acceptability of a proposal" or providing the offeror "an opportunity to revise or modify its proposal in some material respect."[177] Generally, when an agency conducts a discussion with a bidder, it must give all other competitive bidders an opportunity to engage in a discussion as well.

---

[173] *Int'l Waste Indus.*, 2015 CPD ¶ 196, 2015 WL 4265303 (Comp. Gen.).

[174] *Id.* at *3.

[175] 48 C.F.R. § 15.306

[176] *Int'l Waste Indus.*, 2015 WL 4265303 at *3.

[177] *Id.*

The GAO then rejected the Air Force's contention that its communications with Mahto were simply clarifications. The record showed that Mahto was permitted to revise and alter parts of its quotation based on its communications with the Air Force. The GAO held that these actions were "quintessentially the nature of discussions, and not clarifications."[178] Thus, the Air Force was required to also conduct discussions with the 10 other bidders. Based on the Air Force's failure to do so, the GAO sustained IWI's protest. As for a remedy, the GAO concluded that termination of Mahto's contract was unfeasible because Mahto had already started performance. Instead, the GAO recommended that the Air Force reimburse IWI its bid preparation costs and its costs to file and prosecute its protest.

In light of this decision, contractors should keep in mind that agency communications with a bidder may constitute grounds for a valid bid protest. Conversely, contractors communicating with the government regarding a bid should pay close attention to the nature of these communications. If these communications rise to the level of "discussions" under the GAO definition, there is a risk that other contractors may file a bid protest if the government does not afford them an opportunity to conduct discussions as well.

## § 6.07 FEDERAL CIRCUIT RULES AGAINST GOVERNMENT'S TERMINATION FOR CAUSE

Government contracts often include a provision allowing for the government to terminate the contract for a variety of reasons—for example, poor performance or violation of a material contract term. In *EM Logging v. Department of Agriculture*,[179] the Federal Circuit held that the government improperly terminated a contractor because it did not establish that the contractor showed "flagrant disregard" for the terms of its contract.

EM Logging and the U.S. Forest Service entered a timber sale contract that contained terms regarding maximum load limits for EM Logging's trucks, the routes its trucks could use, and what notice EM Logging was required to provide if a load was delayed. Before performance, EM Logging notified the Forest Service that working time regulations would make it difficult to meet the notice requirement. The Forest Service denied EM Logging's request to modify this clause.

During EM Logging's performance of the contract, the Forest Service became aware of several instances where it appeared that EM Logging had violated either the load limit requirement or the route requirement. After each instance, the Forest Service issued notifications of breach to EM Logging. The

---

[178] *Id.* at *4.
[179] EM Logging v. Dep't of Agric., 778 F.3d 1026 (Fed. Cir. 2015).

Forest Service eventually terminated EM Logging for "repeated and ongoing disregard for the terms of [the] contract almost from the start of logging and hauling operations. . . ."[180]

EM Logging appealed the termination to the CBCA, who held that EM Logging's breaches amounted to "blatant and flagrant violations of material contract provisions."[181] On appeal, the Federal Circuit overturned the CBCA's ruling in a unanimous panel verdict. The Federal Circuit first looked to the termination clause, which allowed for termination when the contractor had "engaged in a pattern of activity that demonstrates a flagrant disregard for the terms of this contract."[182] In interpreting the term "flagrant disregard," the court reasoned that examples of such conduct would include repeated suspensions for breach or causing significant environmental damage. Notably, the court held that both the plain meaning of the word "flagrant" and its usage in the contract make clear that "termination for 'flagrant disregard' must be predicated on more than technical breaches of minor contract provisions or isolated breaches of material contract provisions which caused no damage."[183]

The court then walked through the alleged violations of the load limit requirement, the route requirement, and the notice requirement. Based on its review of the record, the court summarized that "there was one instance of route deviation necessitated by illness, one load limit violation, and two instances of delayed notifications."[184] The court held that none of these violations, considered either alone or together, showed "substantial evidence of a pattern of activity demonstrating that EM Logging's actions were in flagrant disregard of the contract."[185] The court thus reversed the CBCA's upholding of the Forest Service's termination.

This case is a victory for contractors as it makes it more difficult for the government to terminate a contractor for cause. The Federal Circuit found that the government was overzealous and unjustified in holding a contractor in "flagrant disregard" of the contract for several minor breaches. Contractors with identical or similar language in their termination clauses should be aware of this decision and the type of contractor conduct now required for the government to justify termination for cause. In addition, this case is a valuable reminder for contractors to be scrupulous in documenting the relevant facts when the government issues a notification of breach. This case turned on EM Logging's ability to factually show that its alleged breaches were minor violations and in some cases justified by the circumstances at the time.

---

[180] *Id.* at 1029.

[181] *EM Logging*, CBCA 2397, 2427, 13 BCA ¶ 35350.

[182] *EM Logging*, 778 F.3d at 1030.

[183] *Id.* at 1031.

[184] *Id.* at 1033.

[185] *Id.*

## § 6.08  THE GOVERNMENT'S DUTY OF GOOD FAITH AND FAIR DEALING

In last year's update, we discussed the Federal Circuit's landmark decision in *Metcalf Construction Co. v. United States*,[186] which expanded the scope of the government's implied duty of good faith and fair dealing and revived the use of this doctrine as a weapon against the government. Indeed, since the decision, contractors have seized on *Metcalf* to bring claims against the government. So far, lower courts have faithfully applied *Metcalf*, confirming the vitality of the duty of good faith and fair dealing. This was exemplified in a recent Court of Federal Claims ruling.

In *Mansoor International Development Services v. United States*,[187] the contractor alleged that the government breached the implied duty of good faith and fair dealing by refusing to pay valid invoices. Mansoor contracted with the government to provide trucking services in Afghanistan. The government later terminated Mansoor for default, after which Mansoor submitted a certified claim seeking payment for 519 task orders that the government had refused to fully pay for. The government replied that it was willing to discuss a settlement for these task orders and the parties subsequently began negotiations. After several offers and counteroffers, the parties reached a stalemate.

The contracting officer then issued a final decision stating that based on an audit, Mansoor was entitled to only a portion of its claim amount. The referenced audit was based on an "Aggregate Claims Adjudication" ("ACA") method which used historical data and statistical analysis to evaluate Mansoor's claim.[188] Mansoor then appealed to the Court of Federal Claims, alleging two counts: (1) breach of contract by refusing to fully pay for Mansoor's task orders; and (2) breach of the implied duty of good faith and fair dealing because the contracting officer "failed to 'fairly and independently consider the merits of the contractor's claim'" and improperly applied an undisclosed statistical analysis to the claims.[189]

In response, the government motioned to dismiss the count regarding the duty of good faith and fair dealing for lack of subject matter jurisdiction. Broadly, the government's logic was that: (1) under the CDA, the court must review a denied claim *de novo*, without regard for the contracting officer's final decision; (2) Mansoor's count centered on the manner in which the contracting officer reached its final decision; and (3) Mansoor's count is thus irrelevant to this appeal

---

[186] 742 F.3d 984 (Fed. Cir. 2014).
[187] 121 Fed. Cl. 1 (2015).
[188] *Mansoor Int'l Dev. Servs.*, 121 Fed. Cl. at 4.
[189] *Id.*

because it focuses on the contracting officer's analysis instead of the "fundamental facts of liability and damages."[190] Indeed, it concluded that "'Mansoor's allegations reflect a disagreement with the contracting officer's approach to Mansoor's claim' and are insufficient to invoke this court's jurisdiction."[191]

The court rejected this argument as "sophistic and untenable."[192] The court noted that while parties do start with a clean slate when appealing a contracting officer's decision, "*de novo* consideration of a claim does not entirely ignore what the contracting officer actually did."[193] Thus, it held that it had jurisdiction to determine whether the government breached its duty of good faith and fair dealing in evaluating Mansoor's claim.

Next, the court addressed the government's argument that Mansoor had failed to state a claim upon which relief could be granted. The government claimed that "the implied duty of good faith and fair dealing 'is limited to ensuring compliance with the express terms of the contract and, thus, does not create obligations not contemplated in the contract itself.'"[194] The court rejected the notion that the duty applies only to express terms, stating that it also addresses "reasonable expectations that may not have been embodied in explicit contractual language."[195]

The court cited to *Metcalf* for the principle that the implied duty exists "because it is rarely possible to anticipate in contract language every possible action or omission by a party that undermines the bargain."[196] The court noted that although the duty is most often raised in response to parties' performance obligations, it applies equally to enforcement as well. In addition, it cited to the *Restatement (Second) of Contracts* § 205, which states that bad faith is not a necessary element and that the duty extends to "dealing which is candid but unfair."[197] Based on these principles, the court held that Mansoor's allegation that the contracting officer breached the duty of good faith and fair dealing by using the ACA method to analyze its claims was a viable claim for relief.

Importantly for contractors, this case both embraces *Metcalf* and expands on it. The duty of good faith and fair dealing applies not only to the government's dealings during the performance of the contract, but also afterwards when addressing and evaluating contractor claims. Indeed, the court took a broad view of this duty, holding that its application is not limited to express contract terms and that it extends to "candid but unfair" dealings. The imposition of this duty on

---

[190] *Id.* at 5.

[191] *Id.* at 6.

[192] *Id.*

[193] *Id.* (emphasis in original).

[194] *Id.*

[195] *Id.*

[196] *Id.* at 7 (*citing Metcalf*, 742 F.3d at 991).

[197] *Id.* at 7 (*citing* Restatement (Second) of Contracts § 205 (1981)).

a contracting officer is perhaps the most important takeaway, as contractors can now use the duty to attack how the contracting officer evaluates their claims.

## § 6.09   RECENT FEDERAL REGULATIONS

### [A]   Requirement of Federal Contractors to Provide Paid Sick Leave

On September 7, 2015, President Obama signed Executive Order 13706 ("Order") requiring all federal contractors and subcontractors to provide paid sick leave to their employees.[198] The President's order seeks to "increase efficiency and cost savings in the work performed by parties that contract with the Federal Government by ensuring that employees on those contracts can earn up to 7 days or more of paid sick leave annually, including paid leave allowing for family care."[199] The Order applies to government contracts entered after January 1, 2017 that are:

- A procurement contract for services or construction;

- A contract for services covered by the Service Contract Act;

- A contract for concessions, including any concessions contract excluded by Department of Labor regulations at 29 CFR 4.133(b); or

- A contract in connection with Federal property or lands and related to offering services for Federal employees, their dependents, or the general public.[200]

Under the Order, all executive departments and agencies are required to include a clause in a covered contract requiring the contractor and any subcontractors to incorporate into lower-tier subcontracts, specifying, as a condition of payment, that all employees shall earn at least 1 hour of paid sick leave for every 30 hours worked for a minimum of 56 hours per year.[201] The paid sick leave will carry over from year to year. Contractors are not required to make payment to an employee upon separation from employment for accrued sick leave that has not been used, if the employee is rehired by another contractor within 12 months of job separation.[202]

Paid sick leave is required upon an oral or written request of an employee which provides the expected duration of the leave, is made at least seven calendar days in advance where the need for the leave is foreseeable, and in other cases, as

---

[198] Exec. Order No. 13706, 80 Fed. Reg. 54697, 2015 WL 5251503 (Sept. 7, 2015).
[199] *Id.* at 54697.
[200] *Id.* at 54699.
[201] *Id.* at 54697.
[202] *Id.*

soon as practicable. Sick leave may be used for an absence resulting from any of the following:

- physical or mental illness, injury, or medical condition;

- obtaining diagnosis, care, or preventive care from a health care provider;

- caring for a child, a parent, a spouse, a domestic partner, or any other individual related by blood or affinity whose close association with the employee is the equivalent of a family relationship who has any of the conditions or needs for diagnosis, care, or preventive care; or

- domestic violence, sexual assault, or stalking, if the time absent from work is for the purposes otherwise described in the Order to obtain additional counseling, to seek relocation, to seek assistance from a victim services organization, to take related legal action, including preparation for or participation in any related civil or criminal legal proceeding.[203]

Importantly, a contractor need not to revise an existing paid leave policy if the amount of paid leave is sufficient to meet the requirements of the Order and it may be used for the same purposes and under the same conditions described in the Order.[204]

While paid sick leave appears to have clear benefits for the employees of federal contractors, the new Order does not come without consequence. For example, not all contractors will be able to afford the excess costs which may result in lower salaries, lower profits, and the elimination of jobs. Additionally, the Order could have the unintended effect of increasing contract prices because contractors may now attempt to defray the added costs by passing them back to the government at bid time.

## [B] Cyber Security Rules Issued by Department of Defense

The DoD recently issued an interim rule ("Rule") to amend the Defense Federal Acquisitions Regulations Supplement ("DFARS"). The interim rule, effective August 26, 2015, relate to the reporting of cyber network penetrations and the implementation of cloud computing services.[205] The Rule requires contractors and subcontractors to "report cyber incidents that result in an actual or potentially adverse effect on a covered contractor information system or covered defense information residing therein, or on a contractor's ability to provide operationally critical support."[206]

---

[203] *Id.*

[204] *Id.* at 54698.

[205] 80 Fed. Reg. 51739 (Aug. 26, 2015).

[206] *Id.*

Under the Rule, when a contractor discovers a Cyber incident,[207] the contractor is required to:

> (i) Conduct a review for evidence of compromise of covered defense information, including, but not limited to, identifying compromised computers, servers, specific data, and user accounts . . . ; and
>
> (ii) Rapidly report cyber incidents at http://dibnet.dod.mil.[208]

To comply with the rapid reporting requirement, the contractor must do so within 72 hours of the discovery of any Cyber incident. Additionally, contractors are required to include a clause in all subcontracts that require subcontractors to rapidly report cyber incidents directly to DoD at http://dibnet.dod.mil and the prime Contractor by providing the incident report number to the prime contractor or next higher-tier subcontractor as soon as possible.[209]

The new Rule also adds a provision related to cloud computing services to allow the offeror to represent its intention to utilize cloud computing services in performance of the contract or not.[210] If the contractor chooses to use cloud computing services, the contractor must "implement and maintain administrative, technical, and physical safeguards and controls with the security level and services required in accordance with the Cloud Computing Security Requirements Guide (SRG)" and "maintain within the United States or outlying areas all Government data that is not physically located on DoD premises, unless the Contractor receives written notification from the Contracting Officer to use another location."[211] Contractors are required to report all Cyber incidents that are related to the cloud computing service provided under this contract directly to the DoD at http://dibnet.dod.mil/. While the 72-hour rapid reporting requirement is not referenced in this portion of the Rule, contractors should adhere to a similar deadline in the event of a Cyber incident.

The DoD's implementation of the Cyber reporting requirements is significant to government contractors. Contractors not only have the burden of implementing safeguards to ensure that sensitive information is protected from attacks, but also will now have the administrative burden of reporting security breaches that result in an actual or potentially adverse effect to the sensitive information. Because the Cyber security definitions are broadly defined in the Rule to include "potentially adverse effects," contractors must perform a detailed analysis in determining whether they will ultimately be required to submit a report to the DoD. The implications of reporting a security breach to the DoD are not entirely

---

[207] Cyber incident is defined under the Rule as "actions taken through the use of computer networks that result in a compromise or an actual or potentially adverse effect on an information system and/or the information residing therein." DFARS 252.204-7009(a).

[208] DFARS 252.204-7012(c)(i) & (ii).

[209] DFARS 252.204-7012 (m)(1) & (2).

[210] DFARS 252.239-7009.

[211] DFARS 252.239-7010(b)(2) & (3).

clear. However, it is safe to assume that the DoD will not take the reports lightly which could have lasting impacts on future work of contractors who are required to submit a report under the new Rule.

## [C] Amendment to FAR Anti-Trafficking Regulations

On January 29, 2015, the FAR council amended the FAR to incorporate two recent rulings: (1) Executive Order 13627, titled "Strengthening Protections Against Trafficking in Persons in Federal Contracts";[212] and (2) Title XVII of the 2013 National Defense Authorization Act.[213] These amendments apply to all federal contracts awarded after March 2, 2015 and future orders under existing indefinite-delivery/indefinite-quantity contracts.

These amendments greatly expand on two existing FAR sections that address human trafficking—FAR Subpart 22.17 and FAR 52.222-50. The largest change was the addition of six prohibited activities to FAR 52.222-50(b), in which contractors now shall not:

- "Destroy, conceal, confiscate, or otherwise deny access by an employee to the employee's identity or immigration documents, such as passports or drivers' licenses, regardless of issuing authority";[214]

- Use "misleading or fraudulent practices during the recruitment of employees or offering of employment, such as failing to disclose, in a format and language accessible to the worker, basic information or making material misrepresentations during the recruitment of employees regarding the key terms and conditions of employment";[215]

- "Charge employees recruitment fees";[216]

- "Fail to provide return transportation or pay for the cost of return transportation upon the end of employment" for certain categories of workers;[217]

- "Provide or arrange housing that fails to meet the host country housing and safety standards";[218]

- "If required by law or contract, fail to provide an employment contract, recruitment agreement, or other required work document in writing."[219]

---

[212] Exec. Order No. 13627 (Sept. 25, 2012), 77 Fed. Reg. 60,029 (Oct. 2, 2012).
[213] 22 U.S.C.A. § 7104(g)(iv)(IV).
[214] FAR 52.222-50(b)(4).
[215] FAR 52.222-50(b)(5).
[216] FAR 52.222-50(b)(6).
[217] FAR 52.222-50(b)(7).
[218] FAR 52.222-50(b)(8).
[219] FAR 52.222-50(b)(9).

In addition, contractors with a contract that (1) is for supplies to be acquired outside the United States or services performed outside the United States and (2) has an estimated value above $500,000 must now create a compliance plan that "shall be appropriate to the size and complexity of the contract and the nature and scope of its activities, including the number of non-U.S. citizens expected to be employed and the risk that the contract or subcontract will involve services or supplies susceptible to trafficking in persons."[220] These contractors must also submit an annual certification that the compliance plan has been implemented.[221]

Contractors now also have an obligation to notify the contracting officer and the agency Inspector General of "[a]ny credible information it receives from any source (including host country law enforcement) that alleges a Contractor employee, subcontractor, subcontractor employee, or their agent has engaged" in trafficking behavior banned by FAR 52.222-50(b).[222] Contractors must also conduct due diligence to ensure that none of its agents, subcontractors, or sub-subcontractors are engaging in prohibited trafficking activities.[223] Besides these major changes, these amendments also revised and added defined terms and imposed other obligations on contractors.

Human trafficking is a problem that nearly every country in the world faces. Current estimates suggest that nearly 21 million people are victims of human trafficking with 68% of these individuals trapped in forced labor.[224] While the newly implemented Rule will create certain administrative burdens for contractors, the ultimate result of its implementation should help reduce the human trafficking statistics in the United States and abroad as those contractors working outside the United States must ensure that they are complying with these FAR amendments.

### [D] FCA and OSHA Civil Penalties Set to Increase in 2016

On November 2, 2015, President Obama signed the Bipartisan Budget Act of 2015, which includes the Federal Civil Penalties Inflation Adjustment Act Improvements Act of 2015. The Act requires federal agencies to increase the civil penalties they levy to account for inflation. Relevant to federal contractors, the Act will increase civil penalties for FCA and OSHA violations.

The FCA's penalty amounts were last updated in 1999, when they were increased to $5,500 to $11,000 per violation. The Act will significantly increase this range, allowing for a one-time "catch up adjustment" to account for inflation since 1999.[225] Per the Act, each government agency has until August 1, 2016 to

---

[220] FAR 22.1703(c).

[221] *Id.*

[222] FAR 52.222-50(d).

[223] *Id.*

[224] Polaris Project, The Facts, *available at* https://polarisproject.org/facts.

[225] Bipartisan Budget Act of 2015, Pub. L. No. 114-74, 129 Stat. 584 (Nov. 2, 2015).

decide on the "catch up adjustment" amount.[226] The Act caps the adjustment increase at 150% so the maximum possible range for an FCA violation is $13,750 to $28,750.[227] In addition, agencies must now update the penalty amount annually based on the Consumer Price Index's cost-of-living updates.[228]

These same changes apply to OSHA violations as well. OSHA's penalties were last updated under the Omnibus Budget Reconciliation Act of 1990, which set penalties for "Serious and Other-than-Serious" violations at $7,000 and penalties for "Willful and Repeat" violations at $70,000.[229] Since it has been 25 years since an update, these penalties will likely significantly increase due to the Act. Thus, government contractors should be on notice that future FCA and OSHA violations will subject them to much higher civil penalties.

FCA and OSHA penalties were significant prior to the increases that are set to occur in 2016. Agencies now have the ability to up the penalties each year ensuring that the penalties will continue to have teeth in the future. It is highly recommended that contractors consider reviewing their compliance plans to avoid these escalated penalties as failing to do so can have catastrophic consequences for ill-prepared contractors in 2016.

---

[226] *Id.*

[227] *Id.*

[228] *Id.*

[229] Omnibus Budget Reconciliation Act of 1990, Pub. L. No. 101-508, 104 Stat. 1388 (Nov. 5, 1990).

CHAPTER 7

# SOUTHEAST REGION

Alabama, Florida, Georgia, Kentucky, Mississippi, North Carolina, South Carolina, Tennessee, Virginia, West Virginia

Randall F. Hafer, Daniel B. Swaja*, Liza Akins, Jennifer S. Lowndes

---

* Special thanks to Daniel Johnson, Gautam Reddy, and Karen Bain for their contributions.

## § 7.01  INTRODUCTION

From the latter part of 2014 through 2015, the construction industry continues to recover from the economic downturn. This chapter explores some of the legal developments that occurred in the Southeastern United States during that timeframe. For example, this chapter examines developments in bond and lien law, arbitration, and various legislative developments. This chapter is not intended to address every legal issue that emerged throughout this period, but instead highlights some of the significant case law and legal developments that may impact the construction industry.

## § 7.02  PRINCIPLES OF CONTRACT FORMATION

At the heart of many construction disputes are the terms that make up the contractual relationships at issue. Parties negotiating contracts should remain conscious of what constitutes an offer and acceptance so each understands when an agreement is formed and the terms governing the parties' contractual obligations are established. In late 2013, the Alabama Supreme Court issued a decision in *Hardy Corp. v. Rayco Industrial, Inc.,*[1] reinforcing underlying principles of contract formation and what constitutes a true counteroffer. The case involved a dispute between a piping subcontractor, Hardy Corporation ("Hardy" or "Subcontractor"), and one of its suppliers, Rayco Industrial, Inc. ("Rayco" or "Supplier"). After Hardy was hired as a subcontractor by a general contractor constructing a facility for the production of kidney dialysis filters, it entered into negotiations with Absolute Welding Services, Inc. ("AWS"), a subsidiary of Rayco, to provide the specialized piping work on the project.

The Supplier's subsidiary, AWS, initially submitted an offer to the Subcontractor for a specific scope of work that expressly excluded passivation and the installation of pure-steam return piping. When the subsidiary supplier was unable to secure the performance bond the Subcontractor was requiring for the project, the subsidiary's parent corporation, Rayco, submitted the same offer on its own letterhead with a small write-up to cover the bond cost. The Supplier's offer also specifically excluded the passivation and installation of pure-steam return piping.[2] Two days later, Hardy submitted a subcontract for the Supplier's signature providing that Rayco would "install sanitary pharmaceutical piping that would meet the requirements of specification 15202."[3] Hardy's proposed subcontract did not explicitly state that the passivation and installation of pure-steam return was included in the scope. However, specification 15202 does

---

[1] 143 So. 3d 172 (Ala. 2013).
[2] *Id.*
[3] *Id.*

require such work.[4] Without seeking any clarification on the issue, the Supplier signed the subcontract.

The ensuing dispute centered around whether or not the Supplier was obligated to perform this specific passivation and installation scope. The Supplier took the position that it was not, as it had been purposefully carved out of both its offer and that of its subsidiary, AWS. The Subcontractor, therefore, purchased the installation services elsewhere and sued the Supplier for breach of the subcontract.[5] At trial, the court found that the Subcontractor rejected the Supplier's offer by specifically excluding the disputed scope and countered with the terms of the subcontract it provided. The court further found that although the subcontract did not speak expressly to the installation work, it referenced a specification that the Supplier's representatives understood to include such work.[6]

In its appeal, the Supplier sought a determination from the Court as to whether the subcontract was a counteroffer.[7] The Supplier's position was that negotiations had been completed and were reflected in the offer it extended to the Subcontractor, thereby creating a binding contract at that time.[8] The Supreme Court relied on the trial court's evaluation of the conflicting evidence of the negotiations at issue, holding that the record supported the conclusion that the Subcontractor did not accept the Supplier's attempt to relieve itself from the obligations of installing the passivation and pure-steam return piping and that the subcontract constituted a counteroffer.[9] While not express in highlighting the disputed work at issue, the Court held that the material terms of the executed subcontract were in fact different, and that "a response of a party that makes changes to the material terms of the offer is a counteroffer."[10] Thus, by signing the subcontract, the Supplier accepted those terms. This case provides an example of why a party should carefully review a contract to ensure the terms match expectations and services outlined in previous proposals.

## § 7.03 INSURANCE

Insurance plays an important role in any construction project, with heated coverage issues accompanied by prolonged litigation being common. Such issues can vary from the extent of the coverage of the policy to whom is even covered by a particular policy. Such issues are critically important in an industry where risk management is a major concern. There are numerous provisions in insurance policies that can give rise to complex questions involving coverage and liability,

---

[4] *Id.*
[5] *Id.* at 174-75.
[6] *Id.* at 176.
[7] *Id.* at 179.
[8] *Id.* at 180.
[9] *Id.* at 181.
[10] *Id.* (citing Hall v. Integon Life Ins., 454 So. 2d 1338 (Ala. 1984)).

especially in the additional-insured context. A recent Mississippi decision addressed the extent of coverage conferred by an additional-insured endorsement.

In *Noble v. Wellington Associates, Inc.*,[11] contractor hired a subcontractor to perform site preparation work. The contractor required the subcontractor to list it as an additional-insured on the subcontractor's commercial general liability ("CGL") policy. The subcontractor acquiesced and obtained an additional-insured endorsement. Critically, the endorsement limited the coverage provided to the additional-insured, stating that it only covered "liability . . . [c]aused in whole or in part by [subcontractor's] ongoing operations performed for that insured."[12]

The subcontractor performed its site preparation work by March 2006 and the contractor found that it met industry standards. The contractor then proceeded with construction of the property. In September 2007, the contractor sold the finished property to a homeowner. Soon after moving in, the homeowner discovered that there were defects in the foundation and sued the contractor.

The contractor first sought coverage for the dispute under its own CGL policy, but the insurer denied coverage. After a federal court ruled in favor of the insurer, the contractor amended a related state court action to add the subcontractor's insurer. In addition to claiming breach of contract and bad faith, the contractor also argued that the subcontractor's insurer was bound to provide coverage, even if there was no express coverage under the additional-insured endorsement, because the contractor reasonably believed there was coverage based on the insurer's actions in a lawsuit involving another home. The state court denied all of the contractor's claims, finding that there was no coverage under the additional-insured endorsement as it only covered liability for "ongoing operations" and the subcontractor had completed its work in March 2006.

On appeal, the Mississippi Court of Appeals agreed with the state trial court. The Court first considered how the phrase "ongoing operations" should be interpreted. As this issue was one of first impression in Mississippi, the court turned to other jurisdictions that had interpreted this phrase in the insurance arena. In doing so, the Court found that "in order for 'ongoing operations' to have any meaning, it cannot encompass liability arising after the subcontractor's work was completed."[13] Even if the damage was due to the subcontractor's work, the language of the endorsement was clear that only "ongoing" work was covered. As the Court explained: "[I]t is clear from the language of the endorsement that [contractor] was only an additional insured for liability caused by [subcontractor's] active work on the site. What this means is [contractor] was protected against lawsuits arising from accidents occurring during the time [subcontractor] performed dirt work. Had [subcontractor] accidentally knocked over a neighbor's tree with a bulldozer or cut a gas line while performing dirt work, [contractor] would be

---

[11] 145 So. 3d 714 (Miss. Ct. App. 2013).

[12] *Id.* at 717.

[13] *Id.* at 719.

covered for any resulting liability."[14] Thus, because active work was not at issue, the Court held that the subcontractor's insurer had no obligation to provide coverage to the contractor under the additional-insured endorsement.

This case illustrates the importance of understanding the breadth of coverage provided by the different policies under which a party is an insured. The extent of coverage may also differ based on how the jurisdiction interprets particular provisions. Parties should be aware of all of these interpretive issues to ensure that they are effectively managing their risk and to avoid a scenario such as in *Noble* where the contractor was left without coverage.

## § 7.04  LICENSING REQUIREMENTS

State licensing requirements can provide a plethora of potential fines, suspensions, and other undesirable consequences for those not educated in the requirements. Contractors, architects and engineers must remain educated on varying state licensing requirements to ensure compliance. In the case of design-build projects, it is critical for the general contractor to understand not only the statutory licensing and certification requirements as it pertains to contracting services, but to have a working knowledge of what it needs to provide for the design component as well. A recent opinion by the Florida District Court of Appeal for the Third District took up as a matter of first impression what the general contractor must provide in exactly such a design-build circumstance.[15]

*Diaz & Russell Corp. v. Department of Business & Professional Regulation*[16] involved an appeal taken from a final administrative order determining that the appellant—a licensed general contractor—violated the statutes pertaining to the practice of architecture in Florida by offering services for a design-build project.[17] As background, the general contractor at issue presented a design-build proposal for a small commercial job, but did not possess the certification or license needed to practice architecture in the State of Florida. The proposal failed to identify the architect that would be performing the work.[18]

The Board of Architecture and Interior Design ("Board") subsequently filed a complaint against the general contractor's president and his company for practicing architecture without the proper credentials as required by Florida Statutes Sections 481.219, 481.223 (2010).[19] The general contractor contended that the design-build proposal submitted was within the specific statutory exemption as outlined in Florida Statutes Section 481.229(3) (2010), which does not require a

---

[14] *Id.* at 720.

[15] Diaz & Russell Corp. v. Dep't of Bus. & Prof'l Regulation, 140 So. 3d 662, 663 (Fla. 3d Dist. Ct. App. 2014).

[16] *Diaz & Russell Corp.*, 140 So. 3d 662, 663.

[17] *Id.*

[18] *Id.*

[19] *Id.*

licensed general contractor to also be licensed as an architect when negotiating design-build services:[20]

> Notwithstanding the provisions of this part, *a general contractor who is certified or registered pursuant to the provisions of chapter 489 is not required to be licensed as an architect when negotiating or performing services under a design-build contract* as long as the architectural services offered or rendered in connection with the contract are offered and rendered by an architect licensed in accordance with this chapter.[21]

During the hearing before the administrative law judge, the Board offered testimony by a licensed architect and current Board member who testified that in any design-build contract, the Florida licensed architect must be specifically listed in the document.[22] The judge incorporated this testimony into the conclusions of law and held that "'the Florida licensed architect was not identified in the written proposal offering the architectural services' and thus that 'the design-build exception is not applicable to the instant case.'"[23] The Third District Court of Appeal rejected this position.

In its analysis, the Third District Court of Appeal noted that the Board's position appeared to be that a licensed general contractor providing a design-build contract must incorporate the name of the licensed architect at the time the proposal is made, and not when the architect is chosen to perform the work or when plans are prepared and submitted.[24] Such an interpretation, held the Court, "imposes requirements that are not found in the statutory design-build exemption."[25] The Court further pointed out that to read such a requirement into the statute would effectively render meaningless the express authorization for the general contractor to "negotiate" the design-build contract.[26] If the Board wished to require general contractors to name a licensed architect in the proposal or during negotiations, then the proper vehicle would be to amend the statute by legislative action.[27] While the Court ultimately upheld the contractor's right to enforce the exception to an architectural license requirement in *Diaz*, a similar contractor can further cover itself and prevent unnecessary litigation by adding language to its proposal that specifies it will not be performing the design work or, if known, who the licensed architect or engineer will be that will perform the services.

---

[20] *Id.*

[21] FLA. STAT. § 481.229(3) (2010) (emphasis added).

[22] *Diaz & Russell Corp.*, 140 So. 3d at 663-64.

[23] *Id.* at 664.

[24] *Id.*

[25] *Id.*

[26] *Id.* at 665.

[27] *Id.* at 666.

## § 7.05  LIENS

A state's mechanics' lien law may provide protection from a party's failure to pay by allowing a potential lien claimant to attach a lien onto the owner's property.[28] A lien is often a claimant's last means of receiving payment for its work and provides a potentially strong leverage tool in payment disputes; however, merely filing a lien does not mean the claimant will automatically receive payment. Contractors and suppliers must act carefully to fully satisfy all of the technical requirements of the mechanics' lien laws for every state in which they do business. It is important to remember that mechanics' lien law is generally strictly construed against the lien claimant in most states despite a public interest of ensuring that contractors and suppliers are paid for their work. Although lien law is generally strictly construed against the claimant, that does not mean that the claimant must always go above and beyond the minimum statutory requirements. Compliance is the key. The issue of whether strict versus substantial compliance with a lien statute is required can lead to heated court battles. If strict compliance is required, even a slight misstep can lead to invalidation of a lien, and the claimant, even when it is undisputedly owed money, may lose its last payment protection. As such, it is important for a potential lien claimant to be aware of the applicable laws of the state where it is working, especially those establishing the statutory period for a lien to be filed and any required actions to be taken prior to filing the lien in order for the lien to be considered perfected. Otherwise, a lien claimant may risk the entire lien being declared invalid, which could result in a range of consequences from losing the lien to liability for the defending party's attorneys' fees for a lien action on an invalid lien.

### [A]  Lien Amounts

A contractor or materialmen usually may file a lien against private property that it has improved or provided materials to in order to protect the claimant's entitlement to payment. A typical mechanic's lien requires the filing party to specify the lien amount that it is claiming. Jurisdictions differ in their laws on specifying this lien amount and what types of sums are subject to lien. Generally, the lien amount is the cost expended by the filing party on labor and/or materials. However, there are also ancillary costs such as interest and attorney's fees related to the lien. The Georgia Court of Appeals issued a recent decision clarifying whether such amounts can be included in the claim of lien.

In *Hill v. VNS Corp.,*[29] the plaintiff subcontractor was not fully paid by the general contractor for materials furnished. The subcontractor then filed a claim of lien against the property and sued the general contractor for breach of contract.

---

[28] The extent to which a party is defined as a lien claimant can vary by state.
[29] 329 Ga. App. 274, 764 S.E.2d 876 (2014).

Because the general contractor did not timely respond to the complaint, the trial court issued a default judgment against it for $43,408. The general contractor then partially satisfied this judgment with a $27,000 payment to the subcontractor. The subcontractor applied $18,798 of this amount towards its materials costs and the remaining $8,202 towards prejudgment interest and attorney's fees on the breach of contract claim.

Subsequently, the subcontractor reduced its lien amount and moved for summary judgment against the owner of the property on the claim of lien. The trial court granted the subcontractor's summary judgment motion and the owner appealed, claiming that fact issues remained regarding the amount of the lien. On appeal, the Georgia Court of Appeals first held that the state's lien statutes allow a materialman to secure a lien only for the work and materials that went into the property at issue.[30] In addition, the party filing the lien has the burden of proving the lien amount. The Court held that the subcontractor did not fully prove its claim amount as there were conflicting affidavits and other problems that presented a material issue of fact.[31] The Court then held that attorney's fees and interest are not lienable items under Georgia law and that the trial court should have credited the entire $27,000 paid by the contractor towards the lien amount.[32] In addition, the Court held that a party cannot claim prejudgment interest on a lien where there is no agreement fixing the amount of the lien.[33] The Court remanded to the trial court to apply these principles and ascertain the correct lien amount.

While the amount in controversy was relatively small in *Hill*, it provides a good example of what types of costs are generally considered lienable in Georgia.

## [B]  Excessive Liens

Due to either contractual or statutory requirements, prime contractors must worry about unjustified liens on a project by subcontractors and materialmen. In Kentucky, a contractor may file suit against any person filing an excessive lien against funds due to the contractor.[34] The contractor may recover for any damages caused by the excessive lien as well as reasonable court costs and attorneys' fees incurred by the contractor.[35] In *DCI Properties-DKY, LLC v. Coppage Construction Co., Inc.*,[36] the Kentucky Court of Appeals addressed whether a claim under the excessive lien statute was a mandatory counterclaim to an action to

---

[30] *Id.* at 276, 764 S.E.2d 876.
[31] *Id.*
[32] *Id.* at 277, 764 S.E.2d 876.
[33] *Id.*
[34] KY. REV. STAT. 376.220(3).
[35] *Id.*
[36] 465 S.W.3d 886 (Ky. 2015).

enforce a lien or could be brought after a lien was found to be excessive. The Contractor, after designing a sewer line funded with public funds, hired the Subcontractor to actually construct the sewer.[37] After the Contractor terminated the Subcontractor, the Subcontractor filed a lien against funds owed to the Contractor and the Contractor filed a notice of protest to the lien.[38] Because a lien was filed, the Owner was required to set aside the lien amount from funds to be paid to the Contractor.[39] The Subcontractor filed suit to enforce its lien, and the trial court found that nearly $3 million of the Subcontractor's lien was excessive.[40]

Six months later, the Contractor filed suit seeking damages caused by the excessive lien, and the Subcontractor filed a motion to dismiss, arguing that the Contractor should have brought its claim as a compulsory counterclaim.[41] In response to the motion to dismiss, the Contractor argued that its excessive lien claim did not accrue until the enforcement action was complete and the lien was declared excessive.[42] The trial court agreed with the Subcontractor and found that the Contractor was required to bring its claim as a compulsory counterclaim to the enforcement action and dismissed the Contractor's claim under *res judicata*.[43]

On appeal, the Kentucky Court of Appeals considered the issue of when the Contractor's claim accrued. The Contractor argued that until it knew that the Subcontractor's claim was excessive, the Contractor's claim was merely speculative and could not be brought as a counterclaim.[44] Considering several cases to which the Contractor drew parallels, the Court agreed that damages did not accrue until the trial court declared that the Subcontractor's lien was excessive.[45] As a result, the Court reversed the trial court's dismissal of the Contractor's claim and remanded to the trial court for further proceedings.[46] Thus, under Kentucky law, until a lien is declared to be excessive by a court, a contractor's claim for excessive lien does not accrue.

## [C] Lien Notification

The parties necessary to be notified of a lien are strictly construed in some jurisdictions. It is of utmost importance that a contractor or subcontractor asserting a lien on a property ensure that the applicable notice statute is complied with. In *Diaz Construction v. The Industrial Development Board of the Metropolitan*

---

[37] *Id.* at 887.
[38] *Id.* at 887–888.
[39] *Id.* at 888.
[40] *Id.*
[41] *Id.*
[42] *Id.*
[43] *Id.* at 888–889.
[44] *Id.* at 889.
[45] *Id.* at 891.
[46] *Id.*

*Government of Nashville & Davidson County*,[47] a subcontractor discovered that failure to substantively comply with the applicable lien statute could be fatal to its claim. The plaintiff was a third-tier subcontractor ("Subcontractor") hired to work on a convention center hotel.[48] The Subcontractor walked off the project when it was allegedly not paid and filed a lien.[49] When the Subcontractor filed a complaint against the Owner, Prime Contractor, and other subcontractors in the chain of privity, a motion to dismiss was filed, claiming that the Subcontractor failed to perfect its lien because it did not serve the lien on the Prime Contractor, but instead served the lien on the second-tier subcontractor in direct privity with Subcontractor.[50] The trial court granted the motion to dismiss and the Subcontractor appealed.[51]

The Tennessee Court of Appeal's decision hinged on the interpretation of the applicable lien statute:

> Every remote contractor with respect to an improvement, except one-family, two-family, three-family and four-family residential units, shall serve, within ninety (90) days of the last day of each month within which work or labor was provided or materials, service, equipment or machinery furnished and for which the remote contractor intends to claim a lien under this chapter, a notice of nonpayment for the work, labor, materials, service, machinery, or equipment to the owner and prime contractor in contractual privity with the remote contractor if its account is, in fact, unpaid.[52]

The Subcontractor argued that the "prime contractor in contractual privity with the remote contractor" was the second-tier subcontractor with which the Subcontractor had directly contracted and who Subcontractor had served with the lien.[53] The Defendants contended that the statute was instead referring to the Prime Contractor.[54]

The Court turned to the statute's definitions:

> A "remote contractor" is defined as an entity that "provides work or labor or who furnishes material, services, equipment or machinery in furtherance of any improvement under a contract with a person other than an owner." Tenn Code Ann. § 66-11-101(14). A "prime contractor" includes an entity "other than a remote contractor who supervises or performs work or labor or who furnishes material, services, equipment, or machinery in furtherance of any improvement, provided, that the person is in direct privity of contract with an

---

[47] No. M2014-00696-COA-R3-CV, 2015 WL 1059065 (Tenn. Ct. App. Mar. 6, 2015).
[48] *Id.* at *1.
[49] *Id.*
[50] *Id.* at *2.
[51] *Id.* at *3.
[52] TENN. CODE ANN. § 66-11-145(a).
[53] 2015 WL 1059065, at *2.
[54] *Id.*

owner, or the owner's agent, of the improvement." Tenn. Code Ann. § 66-11-101(12).[55]

The Court also considered the legislative history of the statute, noting that the prior version of the statute required a subcontractor to provide notice of the lien to the "owner and the contractor contracting with the owner," and that legislators stated during hearings on the current amendment that the purpose of the amendment was to clarify the terms used in the contract.[56] While noting that the statute was "not a model of clarity," the Court held that the legislature intended for remote contractors to give notice to the owner and the "prime contractor upstream from them."[57] As the Subcontractor had not provided notice to the Prime Contractor, it had not strictly complied with the requirements of the applicable statute.[58]

The Court then went on to reject the Subcontractor's argument that it had substantially complied with the statute's requirements,[59] stating that "[n]otification of proper parties goes right to the heart of the purpose of [the statute]."[60] As the Subcontractor's failure to comply with the statute was substantive, the Court upheld the trial court's dismissal of the lien enforcement action.[61] By failing to strictly comply with the essence of the lien statute, a potential lien claimant can allow entitlement to an otherwise meritorious claim slip away. A claimant should not only consult the lien statute to ensure compliance, but also confirm that its understanding of the statute's requirements are consistent with the prevailing interpretation of the jurisdiction.

## [D]  Lien Enforcement

The parties who are necessary to mechanic's lien enforcement actions are similarly strictly construed in some jurisdictions. The failure to timely serve a party who is a necessary party to a mechanic's lien claim can result in the dismissal of a claim with prejudice. Therefore, the identification of which parties are "necessary" to the enforcement action is crucially important to claimants seeking to enforce mechanic's liens. The Supreme Court of Virginia recently explored the identification of necessary parties in mechanic's lien enforcement actions in *Synchronized Construction Services, Inc. v. Prav Lodging, LLC.*[62]

---

[55] *Id.*

[56] *Id* at *5.

[57] *Id.* at *6.

[58] *Id.*

[59] TENN. CODE ANN. § 66-11-148 requires only substantial compliance with the requirements of the lien chapter.

[60] 2015 WL 1059065, at *6-7.

[61] *Id.*

[62] 764 S.E.2d 61 (Va. 2014).

In *Synchronized*, an owner set out to build a hotel. The owner secured a line of credit through a bank that provided financing. The owner then hired a construction manager who had the authority to enter into subcontracts with subcontractors to construct the project. The construction manager entered into several subcontracts, including the subcontract with the subcontractor at issue in the case, which was a cost-plus contract. A month after the job was deemed substantially complete, the subcontractor recorded a mechanic's lien for unpaid work on the project totaling over $200,000. The subcontractor later filed a breach of contract action against the construction manager, as well as a complaint to enforce its mechanic's lien, naming the owner, the construction manager, and the bank as defendants. However, the construction manager never entered an appearance in the case, ostensibly because the construction manager LLC entity was dissolved the day after the subcontractor recorded its lien and, as a result, was never served.[63] The owner and the bank filed motions to dismiss the subcontractor's complaint on the basis that the subcontractor failed to timely serve the construction manager, who they claimed was a necessary party to the mechanic's lien enforcement action. The lower court initially dismissed the subcontractor's breach of contract claim against the construction manager, finding that the construction manager was a necessary party that was not served in a timely manner, and then dismissed the subcontractor's mechanic's lien claim in its entirety with prejudice.[64] The subcontractor appealed.

On appeal, the Supreme Court of Virginia examined the law of mechanic's lien enforcement actions and necessary party jurisprudence. First, the Court determined that mechanic's liens are purely "creatures of statute," and therefore, a mechanic's lien enforcement action must strictly comply with statutory requirements and must name all necessary parties within the time set forth by the Virginia mechanic's lien statute. The Virginia statute did, in fact, require dismissal for the failure to name a necessary party as a defendant.[65] However, the Virginia mechanic's lien statute does not define which parties are considered a "necessary party," and therefore, the Court relied on an analysis of common law doctrines defining "necessary party" to determine whether the construction manager was, in fact, a necessary party.[66]

In its analysis, the Court first noted that a mechanic's lien enforcement action seeks to enforce the lien against "the property bound thereby" and, therefore, is related to real property rights. Therefore, the crux of a mechanic's lien enforcement action is real property, and a necessary party is one who has a real property interest in the real estate because that interest could be defeated or diminished by the enforcement claim.[67] Just being "interested" in the lien enforcement

---

[63] 764 S.E.2d at 64.
[64] *Id.*
[65] *Id.* at 65.
[66] *Id.*
[67] *Id.*

action does not make a party "necessary" to the enforcement action itself.[68] However, in this case, real property was no longer truly at issue, because the Virginia code allows for the defendants to a lien enforcement action to post a bond to release the real estate from the lien enforcement action, a provision which the owner and bank in this case utilized by posting a $237,906.80 bond.[69] Therefore, the Court had to make the further inquiry as to whether the subject matter of the suit, now being a bond and not real estate, changed the identity of the necessary parties to the lien enforcement action.

The Court ultimately determined that a necessary party is one that has a "pecuniary interest in the bond itself" (or interests due to potential financial gain or loss) that would likely be defeated or diminished by the claim against the bond.[70] Therefore, the Court determined that common law necessary party doctrines do not consider which parties "might be vital to proving the case," and "the controlling considerations of the necessary party doctrine are not issues of proof and issues as to which party may be best situated to provide proof."[71] A tangential interest to the pecuniary result of the property interest at stake in the lien enforcement action, which in this case was the bond posted by the owner and the bank, is not enough to establish a party as a necessary party to the lien enforcement action. The contract between the owner and the construction manager did not make the construction manager a necessary party, even though the terms of that contract could be contested during the course of the enforcement action.[72] Although the construction manager would have a "general pecuniary interest" in the outcome of the mechanic's lien enforcement action in this case, that interest was not a "pecuniary interest in the bond itself."

Based on this analysis, the Supreme Court of Virginia held that the construction manager was, in fact, not a necessary party to the lien enforcement action and reversed the lower court's dismissal in a 4-3 decision. The Court held that proof issues and the fact that the construction manager might be vital to proving the case still did not render the construction manager a necessary party, and because the lower court could "render complete relief" on the subcontractor's lien enforcement action, even in the construction manager's absence, the construction manager was not a necessary party.[73]

In conclusion, necessary party jurisprudence, a common law doctrine in Virginia, and lien enforcement actions, a creature of Virginia statute, will not always square in predictable ways. Contractors, owners, and sureties alike should be wary of which parties will be necessary to prove their claims and careful to check whether these parties are necessary to the action itself. It may not be enough to

---

[68] *Id.* at 65-66.
[69] *Id.* at 66.
[70] *Id.*
[71] *Id.* at 67.
[72] *Id.*
[73] *Id.* at 68.

dismiss a lien enforcement claim on the basis that an important party was left out of the action—the missing party must be strictly necessary as determined by their interest in the real property or other subject matter at issue in the lien enforcement action.

## § 7.06  BONDS

One of the ways an owner or a contractor can protect themselves from the possible default of its contractor or subcontractor is to require them to obtain payment and performance bonds from a viable surety for the project. Performance bonds can help protect an owner or general contractor from a lower tier contractor's default by providing assurance that a surety will step in the defaulting contractor's shoes and complete the work. Payment bonds can protect contractors and suppliers from the lack of payment by the owner or the general contractor.

## [A]  Applicable Law

In order to fully understand the requirements of a given bond, such as a notice requirement, all of the parties involved, including the sureties who provide the bond, should understand what law governs a particular bond. In many jurisdictions, bonds can be governed by either common law or by statute. This issue, determining whether a particular bond was a common law bond or a statutory bond, was recently discussed by the Supreme Court of South Carolina in *Hard Hat Workforce Solutions, LLC v. Mechanical HVAC Services, Inc.*[74]

In *Hard Hat*, a HVAC subcontractor was hired by a general contractor to perform mechanical and plumbing work for the construction of a new high school. The general contractor required the HVAC subcontractor to furnish a payment bond for those providing labor and material in the prosecution of the subcontractor's work. The HVAC subcontractor obtained a payment bond in the amount of $17,358,043 from a surety. The HVAC subcontractor then subcontracted some of the specific HVAC ductwork to a ductwork subcontractor, and that party subcontracted with a labor subcontractor to provide temporary skilled labor for that portion of the work.

The HVAC subcontractor paid to the ductwork subcontractor the full value of their contract, but that ductwork subcontractor failed to pay money it owed to the labor subcontractor for the labor it provided on the project. The labor subcontractor then filed a breach of contract claim against the ductwork subcontractor, and also filed a claim to collect on the HVAC subcontractor's original payment bond. The HVAC subcontractor's surety challenged the claim to collect on the payment bond, because the surety argued that the labor subcontractor did not meet

---

[74] 750 S.E.2d 921, 406 S.C. 294 (2013).

South Carolina's statutory bond claim notice requirement, Section 29-5-440 of the South Carolina Code, to provide a "notice of furnishing" that was (1) in writing; (2) to a bonded contractor; (3) sent via e-mail, fax, personal service or registered or certified mail; (4) to any place the bonded contractor maintains a permanent office or to its address on file at the Department of Labor.[75] The lower court granted summary judgment for the surety. The labor subcontractor appealed, challenging the lower court's ruling because the payment bond did not include a notice provision and did not include a reference to Section 29-5-440, the statutory notice provision. In the alternative, the labor subcontractor argued that it had in fact satisfied the Section 29-5-440 requirements.

The issue of whether a claim under this type of bond, which provided general coverage and did not reference the bond statute in South Carolina, must comply with Section 29-5-440 was a matter of first impression in South Carolina. The Supreme Court ultimately determined that the bond was in fact a common law bond and that the labor subcontractor was not required to comply with the bond statute notice requirements.

In its analysis, the Court found it persuasive that the bond at issue was not required by statute, but was required by the contract between the HVAC subcontractor and the general contractor.[76] The bond did not mention Section 29-5-440 or any of the statutory notice requirements. The Court believed that this decision was also consistent with South Carolina policy because the payment bond was to be enforced according to its terms, and because payment bonds issued by a surety for consideration are treated like insurance policies in South Carolina.[77] The Court determined that it was consistent with South Carolina policy to leave the door open for parties to freely contract and was hesitant to prohibit contractors and sureties from contracting for broader coverage or for less stringent notice requirements should they chose to do so.[78] Therefore, the Court reversed the lower court's summary judgment decision, and determined that the labor subcontractor was not required to comply with the South Carolina statutory bond notice requirements.

The Court also examined the labor subcontractor's claim that it technically complied with the notice requirements of the bond statute, assuming *arguendo* that the bond statute would apply. The Court determined that emails sent by the labor subcontractor to the original HVAC subcontractor at least created a material issue of fact as to whether adequate statutory notice had been provided, which provided an alternative basis to overturn the lower court's summary judgment in favor of the surety.[79]

---

[75] 720 S.E.2d at 923.

[76] *Id.* at 925.

[77] *Id.*

[78] *Id.* at 926.

[79] *Id.*

There is an important lesson to be found in *Hard Hat* for those including payment bond requirements as part of a contract: if a contractor or surety wants statutory notice requirements to apply in South Carolina, the notice requirements should be affirmatively stated in the bond, or at the very least, the bond should actually reference the state bond statute.

## [B]  Bond Claimants

While a contractor or materialman typically may assert a lien against a privately owned property where an improvement is being constructed, a lien may not be placed against public property. In order to protect contractors and materialmen on federal public projects, the federal government has enacted the Miller Act,[80] which requires an entity contracting with the federal government for a construction project to obtain payment and performance bonds.

Like most states, Alabama enacted its own version of the Miller Act in order to ensure that materialmen receive full compensation for labor or materials supplied to public works projects. Alabama's little Miller Act[81] requires that performance and payment bonds be executed to accompany contracts for the prosecution of any public works in the state. The payment bond carries an obligation that the contractor "shall promptly make payments to all persons supplying labor, materials, or supplies for or in the prosecution of the work provided in the contract. . . ."[82] Subsection (b) provides a statutory right for materialmen to file a claim on the bond for non-payment:

> (b) Any person that has furnished labor, materials, or supplies for or in the prosecution of a public work and payment has not been made may institute a civil action upon the payment bond and have their rights and claims adjudicated in a civil action and judgment entered thereon.[83]

Recently, the Alabama Supreme Court in *Johnson Controls, Inc. v. Liberty Mutual Insurance Co.,*[84] ruled on a case of first impression the issue of whether the "person that has furnished labor, materials, or supplies" needed to be in privity of contract with the contractor or subcontractor in order to invoke this statutory right and make a claim on the payment bond.[85] In 2010, Roanoke Healthcare Authority ("Roanoke Healthcare" or "Owner"), a public entity and owner, entered into a contract with Batson-Cook Company ("Batson-Cook" or "General

[80] 40 U.S.C. §§ 3131-3133.
[81] ALA. CODE § 39-1-1 *et seq.* (1975).
[82] ALA. CODE § 39-1-1(a) (1975).
[83] ALA. CODE § 39-1-1(b) (1975).
[84] 160 So. 3d 249 (Ala. 2014).
[85] *Id.* at 259-63.

Contractor"), a general contractor, to renovate the Randolph Medical Center.[86] In order to shelter the General Contractor and any subcontractors and suppliers from paying sales and use taxes, the Owner would pay for all equipment and materials necessary to prosecute the work, but the various subcontractors and suppliers would submit all invoices to the General Contractor which would then provide them to the Owner.[87]

Subsequent to entering into the contract with the Owner, the General Contractor executed a subcontract with Hardy Corporation ("Hardy" or "Subcontractor") to perform the mechanical work required by the contract. Pursuant to the terms of the subcontract, Hardy was to provide all material, labor, and equipment needed to complete the scope of work. In order to complete its obligations under the subcontract, the Subcontractor turned to a Supplier to furnish the materials and equipment. The Supplier was informed that the Owner would be paying all costs directly to the Supplier, but that the Supplier should submit its invoices to the Subcontractor which, in turn, would pass them up to the General Contractor to provide to the Owner.[88] Indeed, the purchase order the Subcontractor sent to the Supplier for the materials noted "P.O., Randolph County Medical Center, c/o Batson-Cook Company."[89]

In March 2011, the Owner notified the General Contractor that it had run out of funding and would be suspending the renovation project until a buyer for the facility emerged. The General Contractor in turn relayed this message to its subcontractors.[90] The General Contractor then sent the Subcontractor a change order removing the cost for all material items, including the materials and equipment the Supplier had furnished for the project. In accordance with Alabama's little Miller Act, the Supplier notified the Owner, the General Contractor, the Subcontractor, and the Surety at issue of its claim on the payment bond. After the Surety denied the claim, the Supplier sued to enforce its claim on the payment bond the surety had issued to the General Contractor.[91]

In a series of summary judgment motions and cross-motions between the Supplier and the Surety, the Surety's principal argument was that it could not be liable to pay the Supplier's claim if the General Contractor could not be liable to the Supplier. The terms of the payment bond expressly restricted the beneficiary class to "subcontractors, and persons, firms, and corporations having a direct contract with [Batson-Cook] or its subcontractor."[92] The Surety relied upon this exclusionary bond language and the project's payment structure to make the point that the equipment the Supplier furnished was provided at the Owner's request

---

[86] *Id.* at 250-51.
[87] *Id.* at 251, 252-53.
[88] *Id.* at 252-53.
[89] *Id.* at 253.
[90] *Id.* at 255.
[91] *Id.* at 256.
[92] *Id.* at 252.

because the Owner was to pay directly for it. Therefore, the Supplier's materials and equipment were furnished outside of the scope of the General Contractor's contract. To put it another way, the Surety contended that the Supplier had no direct contract with the General Contractor, the principal on the bond, and was not a proper claimant under the terms of the bond or the little Miller Act.[93]

The Supplier argued that the record showed the materials and equipment it supplied were included in the General Contractor's scope of work under the contract and were part of the total price of Hardy's subcontract with Batson-Cook. By accepting and filling the Subcontractor's purchase order, the Supplier entered into a direct contract with Hardy. Because the language of the payment bond defined beneficiaries as those "having a direct contract with the principal or subcontractor," the Supplier contended it was an eligible claimant.[94] The Supplier stressed to the circuit court that denying its claim would be against the fundamental purpose of Alabama's little Miller Act, which is "to shift the ultimate risk of nonpayment from workmen and suppliers to the surety."[95]

After consideration of the positions, the circuit court granted summary judgment on behalf of the Surety, agreeing with the surety that the equipment and materials were supplied outside the Batson-Cook contract. The circuit court also stated that the Alabama little Miller Act only applied to "labor, materials and supplies for or in prosecution of the work included in contracts between the owner and the contractor for public works projects."[96] The Supplier appealed to the Alabama Supreme Court.

In its discussion, the Court stressed that the purpose of the payment bond under the little Miller Act was " 'to provide security for those who furnish labor and material in performance of government contracts as a substitute for unavailable lien rights, and [the Act] is liberally construed to accomplish this purpose.' "[97] As a threshold matter, the Court noted that the circuit court's reliance on the Supplier selling the materials and equipment "directly" to the Owner was "immaterial to a determination whether [the Supplier] is a proper claimant under the payment bond."[98] The Court noted a critical difference between Alabama's little Miller Act and the wording of the federal act and those adopted by other states:

> As opposed to the federal Miller Act, supra, and the little Miller Act adopted by several of our sister states, § 39-1-1 is silent as to the issue of privity of contract. Rather, § 39-9-1(b) focuses exclusively on the intent for which the

---

[93] Id. at 256-57.

[94] Id. at 257.

[95] Id. (quoting Federal Ins. Co. v. I. Kruger, Inc., 829 So. 2d 732, 736 (Ala. 2002)).

[96] Id. at 258.

[97] Id. at 259 (quoting Headley v. Hous. Auth. of Prattville, 347 So. 2d 532, 535 (Ala. Civ. App. 1977)).

[98] Id. at 260.

labor, materials, or supplies are furnished by using the following broad language: "Any person that has furnished labor, materials, or supplies for or in the prosecution of a public work . . . may institute a civil action upon the payment bond. . . ."[99]

While the Court recognized the limitations in the payment bond restricting the claimants to those having a direct contract with either the General Contractor or one of its subcontractors, it went on to state that when a payment bond is issued to meet the requirements of the little Miller Act, the statute will be read into the payment bond.[100] Here, because the bond on its face noted it was executed in compliance with the little Miller Act, the Court was "authorized to read into it the provisions of the statute, 'and give it the form and effect the statute contemplated, regardless of its contents.'"[101] Finding no bar to the Supplier's ability to bring a claim under the little Miller Act based upon a lack of direct contract with the bond's principal (i.e., the General Contractor) or the express language of the bond, the Court held the Supplier was a proper claimant on the payment bond.[102] In doing so, the Alabama Supreme Court maintained the intent of Alabama's little Miller Act, which is to protect subcontractors and materialmen.

## § 7.07 STATUTES OF LIMITATION AND STATUTES OF REPOSE

It is not altogether uncommon for contractors and other entities operating in the construction industry to run against issues with statutes of limitation or statutes of repose. The statute of repose for construction projects provides an important limit on the liability of those designing or constructing improvements to real property, limiting the time to bring an action for defective construction against such persons after completion of the project. Sometimes these doctrines can operate to protect a contractor from liability, while on the other hand, the doctrines may preclude an otherwise valid claim.

### [A]  Statutes of Repose

A statute of repose could run from the date of substantial completion, thus it is important to calendar this date should a contractor have a potential claim. In *Ridenour v. Covenant Health,*[103] the plaintiff attempted to circumvent the applicable statute of repose by arguing that the absence of a key safety feature in the

---

[99] *Id.*

[100] *Id.*

[101] *Id.* at 261 (quoting Universal Elec. Constr. Co. of Ala. v. Robbins, 194 So. 194, 198 (Ala. 1940)).

[102] *Id.* at 263.

[103] No. E2014-01408-COA-R3-CV, 2015 WL 4736225 (Tenn. Ct. App. June 9, 2015). Similar orders regarding substantially the same facts were entered in: Lewellen v. Covenant Health, No.

construction meant the project could not be substantially complete. The case involved the construction of an emergency room at a hospital, which was in operation as intended by March 23, 2006.[104] Plaintiff filed suit on January 13, 2014, against the hospital's healthcare provider, the engineer and the architect for the project (the "Defendants"), alleging that the radiology facilities for the emergency room were constructed without all necessary lead shielding in the walls, exposing Plaintiff to excessive radiation.[105] After Plaintiff filed suit, the Defendants filed a motion for summary judgment on the grounds that the statute of repose had run.[106] Because the complaint was filed over seven years after the emergency room was in use, the trial court granted the Defendants' motion and dismissed the claim, and the Plaintiff appealed.[107]

The Tennessee Court of Appeals began its review by considering the applicable statute of repose.[108] Tennessee's statute of repose for construction states:

> All actions to recover damages for any deficiency in the design, planning, supervision, observation of construction, or construction of an improvement to real property, for injury to property, real or personal, arising out of any such deficiency, shall be brought against any person performing or furnishing the design, planning, supervision, observation of construction, construction of, or land surveying in connection with, such an improvement within four (4) years after substantial completion of such an improvement.[109]

Substantial completion is defined in the chapter as:

> "Substantial completion" means that degree of completion of a project, improvement, or a specified area or portion thereof (in accordance with the contract documents, as modified by any change orders agreed to by the parties) upon attainment of which the owner can use the same for the purpose for which it was intended; the date of substantial completion may be established by written agreement between the contractor and the owner.[110]

Plaintiff argued that the statute of repose did not apply because the absence of proper radiation shielding meant that the project was not substantially complete

---

E2014-01410-COA-R3-CV 2015, 2015 WL 3563046 (Tenn. Ct. App. June 9, 2015); Gillis v. Covenant Health, No. E2014-01409-COA-R3-CV, 2015 WL 3563034 (Tenn. Ct. App. June 9, 2015); Phillips v. Covenant Health, No. E2014-01405-COA, 2015 WL 3563108 (Tenn. Ct. App. June 9, 2015); and Raby v. Covenant Health, No. E2014–01399–COA–R3–CV, 2015 WL 3563134 (Tenn. Ct. App. June 9, 2015).

[104] 2015 WL 4736225, at *1-2.

[105] Id. at *1.

[106] Id.

[107] Id. at *4.

[108] Id. at *5.

[109] TENN. CODE ANN. § 28-3-202.

[110] TENN. CODE ANN. § 28-3-201 (2).

and thus the statute of repose never ran.[111] The Court rejected Plaintiff's interpretation of the phrase "substantial completion," as a requirement that the project be perfectly constructed in accordance with the project specifications would make the phrase "substantial" superfluous.[112] Further, the Plaintiff's interpretation would mean that "every defective construction project would be considered not substantially complete for purposes of the relevant statute of repose," circumventing the intent of the statute.[113] The Court upheld the trial court's grant of summary judgment and dismissed the Plaintiff's claim.[114] In the end, the statute of repose protected the hospital's designers from liability for a latent defect that had existed for years, and cut off a potential of never-ending liability for the parties.

## [B] Interaction with Other Legal Doctrines

While statutes of limitation and statutes of repose can provide an important protection to parties in the construction industry, how these legal doctrines interact with other legal doctrines can be complicated. An important case interpreting how express warranties impact statutes of limitation and statutes of repose in North Carolina, *Christie v. Hartley Construction, Inc.,*[115] was decided in December of 2014.

In *Christie,* the plaintiff homeowners contracted with a residential contractor to construct a new home and with a material supplier who provided a "stucco-like material" that was used as an exterior coating for their home. The contractor suggested using this specific product from the supplier as an exterior cladding system to protect their home from moisture intrusion. The homeowners conducted their own research before agreeing to the use of the product, which included research on the supplier's website. On the website, the homeowners noted that for the product at issue, the supplier promised that:

> "[p]roperly installed over [structural insulated panels], [the product] is fully warranted for twenty years not to crack, craze, fatigue or delaminate from the substrate. If maintained properly, [the product] could last forty or fifty years, even in salt air, freeze/thaw, or heavy rain or sun exposure."[116]

The homeowners decided to use the product, based in part on the representations found on the supplier's website. The home was finished and certified for occupancy in March of 2005. However, several years later, the exterior coating product began to crack and blister, allowing moisture intrusion. In March of 2011, six

---

[111] No. E2014-01408-COA-R3-CV, 2015 WL 4736225, at *5.
[112] *Id.*
[113] *Id.* at *6.
[114] *Id.* at *8.
[115] 766 S.E.2d 283, 367 N.C. 534 (2014).
[116] 766 S.E.2d at 285.

years after the home was certified for occupancy, the homeowners notified the supplier of their intent to make a warranty claim. The supplier responded that the product had been improperly applied and refused to compensate plaintiffs for the damage caused to their home by the moisture intrusion. In October of 2011, the homeowners filed suit in the Superior Court of Orange County, North Carolina against both the contractor and the supplier, alleging breach of contract, breach of implied warranty and various negligence counts against the contractor, and alleging breach of express and implied warranties and unfair practices on behalf of the supplier.

In the lower court, both defendants moved for summary judgment based on the six-year statute of repose for claims arising out of improvements to real property in North Carolina.[117] The statute of repose would not apply to willful or wanton fraudulent conduct, per North Carolina law, but would otherwise bar any claims not brought within the time bar.[118] Because the action was filed more than six years after issuance of the certificate of occupancy, the lower court granted all of the defendants' motions for summary judgment as to the claims against them. The homeowners appealed, but the Court of Appeals of North Carolina affirmed the trial court. The homeowners appealed again to the Supreme Court of North Carolina.

On appeal, the Court spent some time distinguishing the North Carolina statute of limitation from the statute of repose because of the fact that the "statutes exhibit significant differences in both form and function that have not always proved clear in practice."[119] On one hand, the statute of limitation is intended to require "diligent prosecution of known claims."[120] In North Carolina, statutes of limitation can serve as an affirmative defense, but could also be subject to equitable defenses, and as a result, statutes of limitation are procedural, not substantive.[121] On the other hand, statutes of repose are "intended to mitigate the risk of inherently uncertain and potentially limitless legal exposure," and as such, the statutes operate as of the "last act or omission" of a defendant and the time of occurrence or discovery of the plaintiff's injury is irrelevant to the time limit inquiry.[122] Statutes of repose operate automatically, in order to give potential defendants some degree of certainty and control over their potential legal exposure, and are not subject to equitable doctrines.[123]

However, regardless of the fact that the six year statute of repose period had passed for the homeowners, the Court nevertheless found an avenue for potential recovery. This was due to the importance the Court placed on the fact that "North

---

[117] *Id.*
[118] *Id.*
[119] *Id.* at 286.
[120] *Id.*
[121] *Id.*
[122] *Id.* at 287.
[123] *Id.*

Carolina has long recognized that parties generally are 'free to contract as they deem appropriate.'"[124] In this case, because the supplier was in the business of furnishing products to be used for real property improvements, the Court determined that the supplier had bargained away or waived their protection that would otherwise be afforded by the statute of repose by offering an express, affirmative 20-year warranty.[125] The Court would not allow the supplier to advertise its product as being "fully warranted for twenty years," but later claim that the warranty was limited to cover only the first six years after the product was applied and claim that the remaining 14 years were a "nullity," due to the operation of the North Carolina statute of repose for improvements to real property.[126] The Court found no reason to preclude sophisticated suppliers from bargaining away their own protections by offering express warranties and other benefits to potential consumers in order to make their products more attractive on the market. Due to these considerations, the Supreme Court of North Carolina reversed the lower courts' dismissal of the plaintiff homeowner's claims against the supplier.

The importance of the *Christie* holding is that even seemingly insurmountable bars, such as a statute of repose, can be overcome by affirmative conduct by a supplier or contractor. At least in North Carolina, an express warranty offered by a supplier may operate to override the statute of limitations or statute of repose and is an important consideration for those supplying real property improvements.

## § 7.08  ARBITRATION

Arbitration is a popular form of dispute resolution in the construction industry. By agreeing to arbitrate, the parties can select mutually agreeable arbitrators who are familiar with the construction industry or even the specific type of project at issue. As a result, the construction industry seems increasingly in favor of arbitrating disputes instead of proceeding through the expensive and cumbersome litigation process.

### [A]  Appeal

One of the touted benefits of arbitration is the general finality of the arbitration award—parties know that once the ruling is issued, it is very difficult to overturn. However, both the Federal Arbitration Act ("FAA") and many state statutes regarding arbitration allow for a party to appeal an arbitration award to a trial court. A recent Georgia case addressed the legality of an arbitration clause that barred either party from challenging the arbitration award.

---

[124] *Id.*
[125] *Id.*
[126] *Id.* at 288.

In *Atlanta Flooring Design Centers, Inc. v. R.G. Williams Construction, Inc.*,[127] the contractor and subcontractor agreed to a contract containing the following clause:

> The award rendered by the arbitrator[s] shall be final and binding on the parties and judgment upon the award may be entered in any court of competent jurisdiction. Contractor and Subcontractor hereby expressly agree not to challenge the validity of the arbitration or the award.[128]

The parties eventually submitted a dispute to arbitration wherein the arbitrator ruled in favor of the contractor. Per O.C.G.A. § 9-9-1,[129] the subcontractor then filed a motion seeking a court order vacating the award because it believed its rights were prejudiced in the arbitration. The trial court dismissed the motion, ruling that the contract language "unambiguously precluded any challenge to the arbitration or the award," and also held that this language was not unconscionable.[130]

The Georgia Court of Appeals reversed, holding that the Georgia Arbitration Code ("GAC") does not permit parties to waive their right to challenge the validity of an arbitration or the award. Because the GAC closely resembles the FAA, the court looked to analogous federal precedent for guidance. In *In re Wal-Mart Wage & Hour Employment Practices Litigation*,[131] the Ninth Circuit examined the exact same issue under the FAA—whether the right to appeal an arbitration award can be waived by contract. The Ninth Circuit held that "[p]ermitting parties to contractually eliminate all judicial review of arbitration awards would not only run counter to the text of the FAA, but would also frustrate Congress's attempt to ensure a minimum level of due process for parties to an arbitration."[132] By allowing a blanket waiver clause, an aggrieved party would have no recourse against arbitrator abuse.

The Georgia Court of Appeals applied this same reasoning, holding that a clause waiving the right to appeal an arbitration award "conflicts with and frustrates Georgia public policy as expressed in the GAC, and is void and unenforceable."[133] In light of this holding, parties should review their form arbitration clauses for any clauses restricting or barring either party from exercising its right to appeal. While parties may intend to allow this waiver of appeal, such clauses are now expressly barred in Georgia and may be looked at disfavorably in other states with statutes that track the FAA.

---

[127] 773 S.E.2d 868 (Ga. Ct. App. 2015), *recons. denied* (July 29, 2015).

[128] *Id.* at 869.

[129] Under this statute, a party can file an application with a trial court to vacate an arbitration award within three months of the award.

[130] *Atlanta Flooring Design Ctrs., Inc.*, 773 S.E.2d at 869.

[131] 737 F.3d 1262 (9th Cir. 2013).

[132] *Id.* at 1268.

[133] *Atlanta Flooring Design Ctrs., Inc.*, 773 S.E.2d at 870.

## [B]  Unconscionability

Enforcement of an arbitration agreement is sometimes met with resistance by the opposing party who strategically would prefer to be in court. As a result, the intersection of state law concerning the validity of specific arbitration agreements and the FAA is of special interest to construction litigators for parties involved with disputes over enforcing an arbitration agreement.

In *Berent v. CMH Homes, Inc.,*[134] the Tennessee Supreme Court considered whether the arbitration agreement at issue was unconscionable and unenforceable due to the non-mutuality of remedies based on a prior Tennessee Supreme Court ruling in *Taylor v. Butler,*[135] and, if so, whether the ruling in *Taylor* was preempted by the FAA under the U.S. Supreme Court's reasoning in *AT&T Mobility LLC v. Concepcion.*[136] In *Berent,* the Plaintiff had purchased a manufactured home from the Seller and filed suit after discovering that the home was improperly installed, resulting in issues with drainage and mold, among other things.[137] The Seller moved to compel arbitration based on an arbitration provision in the sales contract and the Plaintiff opposed. The Plaintiff's main argument was that the arbitration provision was void as unconscionable due to the non-mutuality of remedies.[138]

The arbitration agreement contained the following provisions:

*A. Agreement to Arbitrate:* Buyer and Seller . . . agree to mandatory, binding arbitration ("Arbitration) of all disputes . . . including, but not limited to, common law claims, contract and warranty claims, tort claims, statutory claims, and where applicable, administrative law claims and any other matter in question ("Claims" arising from or relating to this Contract, any products/ goods, service, insurance or real property . . . sold or financed under this Contract . . .

. . .

*G.Exceptions:* Notwithstanding any other provision of this Arbitration Agreement, Buyer agrees that Seller may use judicial process (filing a lawsuit): (a) to enforce the security interest granted in this Contract or any related mortgage or deed of trust, and (b) to seek preliminary relief, such as a restraining order or injunctive relief, in order to preserve the existence, location, condition or productive use of the Manufactured Home or other Collateral. Buyer and Seller also agree that this Arbitration Agreement does not apply to any

---

[134] No. E2013-01214-SC-R11-CV, 2015 WL 3526984 (Tenn. June 5, 2015).

[135] 142 S.W.3d 277 (Tenn. 2004) (holding that an arbitration agreement was unconscionable due to non-mutuality of remedies).

[136] ___ U.S. ___, 131 S. Ct. 1740, 179 L. Ed. 2d 742 (2011).

[137] *Berent,* 2015 WL 3526984, at *1-2.

[138] *Id.* at *2.

Claim where the amount in controversy is less than the jurisdictional limit of the small claims court in the jurisdiction where the Buyer resides. . . .[139]

The Plaintiff argued that because the Seller had access to the Courts in circumstances where the Buyer did not, the arbitration agreement was unconscionable under *Taylor*, which previously held an arbitration agreement unconscionable due to non-mutuality of remedies.[140] Both the trial court and the Tennessee Court of Appeals agreed with the Plaintiff and found that the arbitration agreement was unconscionable under *Taylor* and denied Seller's motion to compel.[141]

The Seller appealed to the Tennessee Supreme Court seeking to have *Taylor* overturned, arguing that *Taylor* adopted a *per se* rule regarding non-mutuality in arbitration agreements and that such a rule was preempted by the FAA under *Concepcion*, which held that any state rule specifically disfavoring arbitration agreements was preempted by the FAA.[142] In response, the Plaintiff argued that *Taylor* did not create a *per se* rule, but instead instructed courts to review arbitration agreements on a case-by-case basis.[143] Reviewing the ruling in *Taylor*, the Court determined that it did not establish a *per se* rule, but rather emphasized the consideration of "all facts and circumstances" in determining whether the agreement was unconscionable.[144] As this was consistent with the application of unconscionability to any contract reviewed under Tennessee law, *Taylor* was consistent with the holding in *Concepcion* and should not be overturned.[145]

Applying *Taylor* to the arbitration agreement at hand, the Court found that the agreement was not unconscionable due to non-mutuality.[146] Unlike *Taylor*, where the purchaser was required to arbitrate all claims but the seller had the right to litigate essentially all claims, here the Seller had a limited exception to seek judicial intervention to protect its security interest, along with both parties' access to small claims court.[147] The Court also noted that arbitrators do not necessarily have the authority to grant the relief necessary to protect security interests.[148] Given the overall context of the arbitration agreement, the Court found that it was not unconscionable and reversed the holdings of the trial court and Court of Appeals.[149] While the seller in this case was able to enforce the arbitration agreement, it is important when drafting arbitration clauses to be aware of the

---

[139] *Id.*
[140] *Id.*
[141] *Id.* at *3.
[142] *Id.*
[143] *Id.* at *4.
[144] *Id.* at *8.
[145] *Id.* at *9-10.
[146] *Id.* at *14.
[147] *Id.* at *13.
[148] *Id.*
[149] *Id.* at *14.

interaction of the FAA and applicable state law to ensure an intended arbitration agreement is enforceable.

## [C]   Delegation of Arbitrability

Another common issue in arbitration is whether a particular dispute is even subject to arbitration. Parties seeking to avoid arbitration often claim that the arbitration clause is unenforceable either in general or with regard to the dispute at issue. Arbitration clauses may then have a "delegation provision" explicitly stating that the parties agree that the arbitrator has the sole authority to decide whether the dispute is even arbitrable. In *Schumacher Homes of Circleville, Inc. v. Spencer*,[150] the West Virginia Supreme Court considered the enforceability of such a delegation provision.

In *Schumacher Homes*, a homeowner contracted with a contractor to build a home. The contract contained an arbitration clause with a delegation provision stating: "The arbitrator(s) shall determine all issues regarding the arbitrability of the dispute."[151] After finding defects in the construction, the homeowner sued the contractor in circuit court. The contractor moved to dismiss the lawsuit and to compel the homeowners to arbitrate. The homeowners replied that the arbitration clause was unconscionable and thus unenforceable. The homeowners argued that the contractor had unequal bargaining power and that the arbitration clause was unduly complex.

The contractor subsequently claimed that because of the delegation provision, the circuit court had no authority to rule on the validity of the arbitration clause. The circuit court held the arbitration clause unconscionable and unenforceable, but did not address the delegation provision.

On appeal, the West Virginia Supreme Court focused primarily on the delegation provision. Because the contract between the parties affected interstate commerce and thus implicated federal law, the Court looked first to the FAA for guidance. Under the FAA and the doctrine of severability, "arbitration clauses must be severed from the remainder of a contract, and must be tested separately under state contract law for validity and enforceability," including a delegation provision within the arbitration clause.[152] The Court considered the U.S. Supreme Court's ruling in *Rent-A-Center, Inc. v. Jackson*[153] that, when there is a valid delegation provision, the trial court cannot rule on the validity of the arbitration clause as a whole but can only consider a challenge to the validity of the delegation provision itself under state law. The Court commented that the "rule seem[ed]

---

[150] 235 W. Va. 335, 774 S.E.2d 1 (2015).
[151] *Id.* at 335.
[152] *Id.*
[153] 561 U.S. 63 (2010).

absurd"[154] and that it was "an ivory-tower interpretation of the FAA that is as dubious in principle as it is senseless in practice."[155]

Nevertheless, the Court deferred to the U.S. Supreme Court and, after examining *Rent-A-Center* and related FAA precedent, the Court surmised that under the FAA, there are two requirements for a delegation provision to be effective: (1) the delegation provision must "reflect a clear and unmistakable intent by the parties to delegate state contract law questions about the validity, revocability, or enforceability of the arbitration agreement to an arbitrator"; and (2) "the delegation provision itself must not be invalid, revocable or unenforceable under state contract law."[156]

The Court only reached the first requirement, holding that the phrase "all issues regarding the arbitrability of the dispute" did not "clearly and unmistakably" grant the arbitrator the authority to decide whether the arbitration clause is valid and enforceable. The Court reasoned that the term "arbitrability" was ambiguous and that the clause did not include any reference to "validity, revocability, or enforceability." The Court thus affirmed the trial court's decision refusing to compel arbitration.

This case illustrates the potentially convoluted precedent related to the FAA and the enforcement of arbitration clauses. Parties seeking to enforce arbitration clauses should include a clear and unambiguous delegation provision in accordance with the requirements set out in *Schumacher Homes*. Any ambiguity may be construed against the party seeking enforcement of the clause.

## § 7.09  SETTLEMENT AGREEMENTS

Although a party may not see the value of a claim, settlement can be a preferred method of ultimately deciding a dispute. By settling a case, parties can avoid the transaction costs associated with actually trying or arbitrating a case. However, parties in the construction industry should be careful when crafting their settlement agreements. In order for a settlement agreement to be enforceable in many states, it must be more than an "agreement to agree." This issue was examined in *77 Construction Co. v. UXB International, Inc.*,[157] a recent case in the United States District Court for the Western District of Virginia, where the Court applied Virginia contract law in denying a motion to enforce a settlement agreement.

---

[154] *Schumacher Homes*, 774 S.E.2d at 10 (citing *Rent-A-Center*, 561 U.S. at 85-87 (Stevens, J., dissenting)).

[155] *Id.* (citing Young v. United Parcel Servs., Inc., 135 S. Ct. 1338, 1361 (2015) (Scalia, J., dissenting)).

[156] *Id.*

[157] No. 7:13-cv-340, 2015 WL 926036 (W.D. Va. Mar. 4, 2015).

In *77 Construction*, the parties previously reached a settlement agreement during a settlement conference. The general contractor was seeking to enforce the settlement agreement against a subcontractor. The subcontractor, however, contended that the settlement was not complete, alleging it was merely an "agreement to negotiate at a later time."[158] Crucially, neither party contended that the settlement agreement actually resolved all of the disputed issues between the parties, as the terms of the agreement stated that the purpose was to "narrow the scope of disputed issues."[159] The Court undertook an examination to determine whether a settlement had been reached by looking "to the objectively manifested intentions of the parties."[160] The Court concluded that the agreement was actually "an agreement to attempt to settle their claims, or an agreement to negotiate at a later date, which is not an enforceable agreement under Virginia law."[161]

The Court stated that its conclusion was based on several factors, including the determination that the agreement was a "framework to settle their claims" that did not resolve all of the disputes at issue in the case or even all of the disputes as to the specific invoices that were the subject of the agreement. Furthermore, important reports that were submitted in order to meet the requirements of the settlement agreement, specifically the expert report of the subcontractor (the party attempting to avoid enforcement of the settlement agreement), were alleged by the general contractor to be "insufficient" for not complying with the requirements of the settlement agreement. Finally, it was again noted by the Court that the stated purpose of the settlement agreement was to "narrow the issues" and "facilitate the resumption" of settlement discussion.[162] Even though the general contractor accused the subcontractor of abusing the settlement process in order to stall the litigation for its own benefit, the Court would not "enforce an otherwise unenforceable agreement as a sanction for bad behavior."[163]

In conclusion, parties should be careful to craft their settlement agreements to completely resolve the issues at hand, or at least finally resolve the issues that it addresses. Settlement agreements must be more than an agreement to agree. Parties should carefully craft their settlement agreements to ensure enforceability if the parties do intend to fully and finally resolve the disputes at issue.

## § 7.10  DAMAGES

Jurisdictions vary in what types of damages are recoverable. When a property is harmed, the owner incurs direct damages of repair. However, the owner may also suffer a loss due to a decrease in property value, especially when the

---

[158] 2015 WL 926036, at *1.

[159] *Id.* at *3.

[160] *Id.* at *4.

[161] *Id.*

[162] *Id.* at *5.

[163] *Id.* at *6.

owner is unable to fully repair the property. In West Virginia, the long established rule was that an owner could recover either the repair costs or the loss to the property's fair market value, whichever was lower.[164] However, a November 2014 decision overturned this long-standing precedent.

In *Brooks v. City of Huntington*,[165] the West Virginia Supreme Court held that when an owner can establish that the property damage cannot be fully repaired such that there is a permanent decrease in fair market value, the owner may recover the full cost of repair *and* the loss to the fair market value.

The city of Huntington, West Virginia completed construction of a storm water management system in 2011. The plaintiffs in *Brooks* were residential homeowners that began experiencing flooding in their neighborhood in 2011, due allegedly to this new storm water system. The homeowners subsequently filed a negligence claim against the city. At trial, the homeowners' expert witness stated that the home had lost between 35% and 75% of its property value due to the flooding. The flooding also required the homes to be elevated two feet as they would otherwise now sit in the flood plain. Although the jury was instructed that the homeowners could only be awarded the lower of their loss in fair market value or cost of repair, the jury form contained lines for both measures of damages and the jury awarded damages for both.

The city then moved for a new trial and remittitur. The trial court denied the motion for a new trial, but granted remittitur and reduced the award such that the homeowners only recovered for the lower of the two damages amounts. The homeowners appealed, asking the West Virginia Supreme Court to overturn the long-standing precedent on this issue stated in *Jarrett v. E. L. Harper & Son, Inc.*:[166]

> When realty is injured the owner may recover the cost of repairing it, plus his expenses stemming from the injury, including loss of use during the repair period. If the injury cannot be repaired **or the cost of repair would exceed the property's market value**, then the owner may recover its lost value, plus his expenses stemming from the injury including loss of use during the time he has been deprived of his property. (emphasis added)

In closely examining the precedent, the Court noted that *Jarrett* imposes two requirements on damages to realty: (1) a ceiling on damages where cost of repairs are recoverable only to the extent that they not exceed the property's fair market value; and (2) the homeowner cannot recover both the cost of damages and the loss of value. Thus, where the cost of repairs exceeds the property's fair market

---

[164] Jarrett v. E. L. Harper & Son, Inc., 160 W. Va. 399, 235 S.E.2d 362 (1977).
[165] 234 W. Va. 607, 768 S.E.2d 97, 99 (2014).
[166] 160 W. Va. 399, 235 S.E.2d 362 (1977).

value and the loss in fair market value, a homeowner cannot recover the full cost of repair.

In its analysis, the Court first considered the goal of tort damages, reasoning that "[t]he law of torts attempts primarily to restore the injured party to as good a position as he held prior to the tort" and that "courts must be mindful of the fact that rules governing the proper measure of damages in a particular case are guides only and should not be applied in an arbitrary, formulaic, or inflexible manner, particularly where to do so would not do substantial justice."[167]

With this maxim in mind, the Court addressed the issue of limiting the cost of repair to the property's fair market value:

> [I]n instances where the cost of repair exceeds the property's pre-damage market value, *Jarrett* would compel the injured plaintiff to accept only the loss in value to the property. We find that this portion of our holding in *Jarrett* is no longer in accord with the modern recognition that cost of repair is often the only fair means of compensating the owner of damaged residential real property.[168]

Drawing from related jurisprudence in other states, the Court repudiated *Jarrett*, reasoning that "we find it abhorrent to the public policy of this State to craft a rule that would place its citizens in a ' 'take it or leave it' proposition'—sell the homes that they do not want to leave in order to make themselves whole again or continue to live with the consequences of the harm inflicted by a tortfeasor, which their damages are inadequate to repair."[169] The Court thus held that where residential real property is damaged, the homeowner may recover the cost of repair even if it exceeds the property's fair market value.[170]

The Court then turned to the second issue—the bar on recovering both cost of repair and loss of value. The Court first noted that in West Virginia, plaintiffs can recover both cost of repair and loss of value for damages to *personal* property.[171] In the context of real property, the Court was primarily concerned with the redundancy of awarding both types of damages. However, the Court reasoned that there are scenarios where there is a residual loss of value following repairs and that awarding both types of damages would not be redundant. The Court stated that "where the owner of residential real property which is damaged can establish that the pre-damage fair market value of the residential real property cannot be fully restored by repairs and that a permanent, appreciable residual diminution in value will exist even after such repairs are made, then the owner

---

[167] *Brooks*, 234 W. Va. at 612 (citing Myers v. Arnold, 83 Ill. App. 3d 1, 7, 403 N.E.2d 316, 321 (1980)).

[168] *Id.* at 614.

[169] *Id.* at 615.

[170] *Id.*

[171] *See* Ellis v. King, 184 W. Va. 227, 400 S.E.2d 235 (1990).

may recover both the cost of repair and for such remaining diminution in value."[172]

*Brooks* represents a major shift in how damages to residential real property are awarded in West Virginia. Contractors should be aware that the extent of their liability for defective work or other errors has increased. Indeed, this new framework must be accounted for in evaluating risk and may have far-reaching consequences with regards to insurance.

## § 7.11 PREMISES LIABILITY

One concern of owners is liability to third parties for damages sustained as a result of unsafe conditions caused by their independent contractors on their premises. In *Parker v. Holiday Hospitality Franchising, Inc.*,[173] a hotel owner faced liability for injuries sustained by a client when an improperly installed shower bench collapsed. The Plaintiff and his wife rented a handicapped accessible room at the Owner's hotel, and noticed upon entering that the shower bench was loose and pulling away from the wall.[174] While the Plaintiff was out of the room, the hotel's maintenance worker retightened the shower bench's bolts and tested the stability of the bench.[175] Upon returning to the room, the Plaintiff also tested the shower bench.[176] The following day, the bench collapsed while the Plaintiff was taking a shower, causing injury to the Plaintiff.[177]

The Plaintiff filed suit against the Owner seeking damages for medical expenses, loss of quality of life, and pain and suffering.[178] The Owner denied liability and raised the defense of comparative fault, arguing that its Contractor had negligently installed the shower bench.[179] The Owner moved for summary judgment, arguing that the shower bench's installation was a latent defect caused by the Contractor's negligence, that the Owner had no constructive notice of the defect, and that the Owner had no duty to inspect the Contractor's work and thus was not liable for Plaintiff's injuries.[180] It was undisputed that the shower bench failed due to Contractor's failure to use proper blocking during installation, that this defect would have been discovered if the shower bench was inspected during construction, and that the defect was hidden behind sheetrock at the time of the shower bench failure.[181]

---

[172] *Brooks*, 234 W. Va. at 618.
[173] 446 S.W.3d 341 (Tenn. 2014).
[174] *Id.* at 344.
[175] *Id.*
[176] *Id.*
[177] *Id.*
[178] *Id.* at 345.
[179] *Id.*
[180] *Id.*
[181] *Id.*

The trial court granted the Owner's motion, finding that property owners were generally not liable for the negligence of an independent contractor unless the property owner knew of and accepted the negligent work, and that property owners have no duty to inspect the work performed by independent contractors.[182] On appeal, the Court of Appeals agreed that property owners are not generally liable for injuries sustained due to an independent contractor's negligence, but found that there were disputes of material fact as to whether the Owner had constructive notice of the negligent installation and reversed the trial court's grant of summary judgment.[183] Both parties appealed to the Tennessee Supreme Court.[184]

The Court began its review by stating that as a general rule, a property owner is not vicariously liable for the negligent work of an independent contractor.[185] The Court rejected the Plaintiff's argument that the Owner became vicariously liable for the Contractor's negligence by accepting the Contractor's work (the "accepted work doctrine").[186] Although the Tennessee Supreme Court had at one time accepted this doctrine, it was rejected in 1975 in *Johnson v. Oman Construction Co.*[187] and had not been accepted since.[188] As the accepted work doctrine did not apply, the Owner was not automatically vicariously liable for the Contractor's negligence.[189]

The Court then turned to the Plaintiff's claim of premises liability. In order to prove the premises liability, the Plaintiff had to prove all elements of a negligence claim, as well as show either that the condition was caused by the Owner or its agent or that the Owner had actual or constructive knowledge of the condition prior to the accident.[190] The Court rejected the Plaintiff's argument that an independent contractor is an agent of a property owner, noting that such an argument would "obliterate the general rule that a property owner is not vicariously liable for the negligence of an independent contractor."[191] The Court also rejected the Plaintiff's argument that the Owner should have known of the defective condition because he was under an obligation to inspect the Contractor's work during construction.[192] The Court refused to impose a duty on the Owner to inspect the work of the Contractor during construction because the Owner "relied upon [the Contractor] to construct the Hotel in a reasonably safe manner."[193] As a

---

[182] *Id* at 346.
[183] *Id.*
[184] *Id.*
[185] *Id.* at 347.
[186] *Id.*
[187] 519 S.W.2d 782, 788 (Tenn. 1975).
[188] 446 S.W.3d at 348-49.
[189] *Id.* at 349.
[190] *Id.* at 350.
[191] *Id.* at 351.
[192] *Id.* at 352-53.
[193] *Id.* at 353.

result, the Court reinstated the trial court's grant of summary judgment in favor of the Owner and dismissed the case.[194]

*Parker v. Holiday* was a strong decision in favor of owners' rights, limiting the liability of owners who reasonably rely on their independent contractors to safely and prudently perform work.

## § 7.12   SOVEREIGN IMMUNITY

Sovereign immunity is an uncommon, but potentially important issue in construction law. The doctrine of sovereign immunity protects the state and other governmental entities from suit absent a waiver of that immunity. States generally have statutes waiving immunity for certain types of claims, but many others are strictly barred by the doctrine. Thus, a contractor or surety may be completely unable to prosecute a meritorious claim against a governmental entity because of sovereign immunity.

In *State Department of Corrections v. Developers Surety & Indemnity Co.*,[195] the Georgia Department of Corrections ("GDOC") argued that a surety's claims for payment were barred by sovereign immunity. GDOC contracted with a roofing contractor to perform work at a state prison. The contractor then obtained payment and performance bonds from a surety, as required by GDOC. The contractor and the surety also signed an indemnity agreement assigning the contractor's right to payment under its contracts with GDOC to the surety. GDOC was not a party to this indemnity agreement.

The contractor failed to complete the work on time so GDOC issued a formal notice of default, thus triggering the surety's obligations under the performance bond. The surety then gave GDOC the option to have another company complete the work, which GDOC accepted. Prior to the contractor's default, the surety had provided the contractor with over $500,000 in financial assistance.

The surety then sued GDOC for breach of contract and for a declaratory judgment that it had no obligation under the payment and performance bonds it issued to the contractor. GDOC filed a motion for summary judgment on the basis of sovereign immunity. The trial court held that the surety's claims were not barred by sovereign immunity and entered judgment in favor of the surety. GDOC unsuccessfully appealed to the Georgia Court of Appeals, resulting in further appeal by GDOC to the Georgia Supreme Court.

The Georgia Supreme Court began its analysis by examining sovereign immunity in Georgia. Sovereign immunity has constitutional status in Georgia, and thus can only be waived by an act of the General Assembly or by the Constitution itself.[196] Relevant to the surety's claims here, the Georgia Constitution

---

[194] *Id.*
[195] 295 Ga. 741, 763 S.E.2d 868 (2014).
[196] *Id.* at 744.

provides for the waiver of sovereign immunity "as to any action ex contractu for the breach of any written contract now existing or hereafter entered into by the state or its departments and agencies."[197] Thus, the Court held that GDOC waived its sovereign immunity for breach of contract claims when it initially contracted with the contractor.

After holding that that GDOC could be sued for breaching its contract with the contractor, the Court turned to whether the surety could stand in the place of the contractor and bring these claims. Under O.C.G.A. § 10–7–56 , "[a] surety who has paid the debt of his principal shall be subrogated, both at law and in equity, to all the rights of the creditor and, in a controversy with other creditors, shall rank in dignity the same as the creditor whose claim he paid."[198] Thus, having paid its bond obligation, the surety succeeded to the rights of the contractor as a subrogee.

In issuing its decision, the Court concluded on a practical note, stating "[i]nasmuch as a fundamental purpose of sovereign immunity is the protection of State funds, this Court will not sanction a result that is contrary to the constitutional and statutory text and would hamper the issuance of such payment and performance bonds, and thus, potentially cause greater exposure of the State's treasury and resources."[199] Indeed, the court's decision reflects the practical concerns of limiting the avenues of recourse private entities have against the government. This ruling is a positive development for contractors that perform work for the State of Georgia.

## § 7.13  FIDUCIARY DUTY

Joint ventures between two entities to develop or construct a project are commonplace in the construction industry. The joint venture arrangement is a convenient way for parties to pool resources, share in profits/losses and otherwise coordinate and manage the project. In terms of legal consequences, parties to a joint venture may owe a fiduciary duty to one another. This duty may give rise to a claim for the breach of fiduciary duty in the event of a dispute. A recent Georgia decision explored whether there is a fiduciary duty between members of a joint venture and, if so, the extent of that duty.

In *Inland Atlantic Old National. Phase I, LLC v. 6425 Old National, LLC*,[200] Inland Atlantic and Old National entered into a joint venture LLC to develop and construct a shopping center. The joint venture agreement gave Old National the right to either perform the site work or negotiate a contract for that work. After securing tenants for the shopping center, the parties planned to

---

[197] Ga. Const. of 1983, Art. I, Sec. II, Par. IX (c).
[198] *State Dept. of Corrections*, 295 Ga. at 745.
[199] *Id.* at 746-47.
[200] 329 Ga. App. 671, 766 S.E.2d 86 (2014).

develop the site in two phases. To that end, they entered into a two-phase site development agreement where Inland retained Old National to oversee Phase I.

Old National then hired a contractor to perform the site work involved in Phase I. There were numerous major issues with the contractor's work, including poor work quality, failure to pay subcontractors, and failure to complete items within its scope of work. Thus, after the completion of Phase I, Inland Atlantic chose not to retain Old National to oversee Phase II. Old National then brought suit against Inland Atlantic for breaching the site development agreement. In response, Inland Atlantic counterclaimed for breach of fiduciary duty, fraud and negligent misrepresentation. The trial court granted summary judgment to Old National on all three of these counterclaims.

On appeal, the Georgia Court of Appeals found that there were issues of fact precluding summary judgment on all three claims. Under Georgia law, a claim for breach of fiduciary duty has three elements: "(1) the existence of a fiduciary duty; (2) breach of that duty; and (3) damage proximately caused by the breach."[201] Inland Atlantic argued that Old National had a fiduciary obligation as a member of the joint venture (entered into pursuant to a LLC agreement) and had responsibility to oversee the joint venture's site work.

Thus, the Court looked to the statutory duties owed by a member of an LLC. A member of an LLC has a duty to act in a good faith manner and exercise ordinary care in the best interests of the company.[202] However, if the member is not managing the affairs of the LLC, no such duty applies.[203] Here, the Court held that the joint venture agreement delegated specific site development duties to Old National even though it did not expressly define Old National as a manager. Thus, there was a fact issue regarding whether Old National was "managing the affairs of the LLC" and thus bound by a fiduciary duty towards the other members of the LLC.

Next, the Court considered Inland Atlantic's fraud and negligent misrepresentation counterclaims. Inland Atlantic argued that Old National misrepresented the capability of its contractor to complete the Phase I work and withheld information regarding the contractor's poor financial condition. When a fiduciary relationship exists, that relationship "encompasses a duty to disclose so that suppression of a material fact which a party is under an obligation to communicate constitutes fraud."[204] Based on the record, the Court found that Old National knew that its contractor was having financial problems yet represented that the contractor was financially qualified and capable of completing the work. Thus, the Court held that there were issues of fact that precluded summary judgment and reversed the trial court's rulings on Old National's counterclaims for breach of

---

[201] *Inland Atl.*, 329 Ga. App. at 674, 766 S.E.2d at 90 (citing Ansley Marine Constr. v. Swanberg, 290 Ga. App. 388, 391(1), 660 S.E.2d 6 (2008)).

[202] *Id.* (citing O.C.G.A. § 14-11-305(1)).

[203] *Id.* (citing ULQ, LLC v. Meder, 293 Ga. App. 176, 184(7), 666 S.E.2d 713 (2008)).

[204] *Id.* (citing Goldston v. Bank of Am. Corp., 259 Ga. App. 690, 696, 577 S.E.2d 864 (2003)).

fiduciary duty, fraud and negligent misrepresentation. The Court then remanded the case to the trial court to resolve fact issues related to the site development agreement.

This case illustrates potential issues involved with a joint venture project organized as an LLC. If a party is "managing the affairs" of the LLC in its actions, then it owes a fiduciary duty to the other members. The existence of this duty may have legal consequences in the event of a dispute, as seen here. A joint venture partner may be obligated to disclose relevant information it has regarding potential contractors for the project.

## § 7.14   NEW STATUTE REGULATING UNDERGROUND UTILITIES

Contractors operating in North Carolina should be aware of recent legislation that came out of the state regarding the establishment of an underground utility "Notification Center." North Carolina House Bill 476, Session Law 2013-407 was enacted August 23, 2013. The new law provides for a "systematic, orderly, and uniform process to identify existing facilities in advance of any excavation or demolition" in the state.

Per the new bill, all "operators" in the state, which are people, utilities, municipalities, etc., that operate underground lines or infrastructures, are required to maintain a "Notification Center." This Notification Center, among other responsibilities,[205] tracks proposed excavations and reports of alleged violations of the law requiring notice before proposed excavations. The new legislation also states the responsibilities of excavators:

> Before commencing any excavation or demolition operation, the person responsible for the excavation or demolition shall provide or cause to be provided notice to the Notification Center of his or her intent to excavate or demolish. Notice for any excavation or demolition that does not involve a subaqueous[206] facility must be given within three to 12 full working days before the proposed commencement date of the excavation or demolition. Notice for any excavation or demolition in the vicinity of a subaqueous facility must be given with 10 to 20 full working days before the proposed commencement date of the excavation or demolition. Notice given pursuant to this subsection shall expire 15 full working days after the date notice was given.[207]

The notice that is required to be provided by the excavator has specific content and form requirements as well, which are stated in the bill. Excavators are

---

[205] The responsibilities of the "Notification Center" are defined in North Carolina House Bill 476, Session Law 2013-407, § 87-120: Notification Center; responsibilities.

[206] Subaqueous is defined as "a facility that is under a body of water, including rivers, streams, lakes, waterways, swamps, and bogs."

[207] North Carolina H.B. 476, Sess. Law 2013-407, § 87-122: Excavator responsibilities.

also required to provide the Notification Center with oral notice "as soon as practicable" in situations of an emergency excavation or demolition, and are required to provide notice when an excavation or demolition results in "any damage to a facility."

While the law specifically prohibits the Notification Center from imposing "any charge on any person giving notice to the Notification Center," operators and excavators are still liable for any damage or injury which they would otherwise be responsible for under applicable law.[208] Furthermore, the Notification Center can transmit reports of alleged violations of the notice requirements to the Underground Damage Prevention Review Board, which is a board established by the Notification Center with members appointed by the Governor.[209] The Underground Damage Prevention Review Board has the authority to enforce the provisions of the bill and the ability to assess civil penalties for violations.

## § 7.15 VIRGINIA PUBLIC PROCUREMENT ACT

The Virginia Public Procurement Act ("VPPA") governs public contracts in Virginia. When contracting with public bodies in the Commonwealth of Virginia, the VPPA applies to ensure that the public entities "obtain high quality goods and services at reasonable cost" and "that all procurement procedures be conducted in a fair and impartial manner."[210] The notice requirements associated with the VPPA can be strict, and it is therefore important for contractors who have contracted with public entities in Virginia to carefully follow the VPPA requirements.

Two recent federal court cases examined the VPPA requirements, applying Virginia law. The first is *Carnell Construction v. Danville Redevelopment & Housing Authority*.[211] In *Carnell*, the Court of Appeals for the Fourth Circuit examined several issues, including racial discrimination claims by a minority-owned contractor who worked on a public-housing project but was ultimately required to leave the project before the completion of the work. The Court primarily examined evidentiary issues with respect to the contractor's racial discrimination claims, but the Court also examined the amount of damages the contractor could recover based on the provisions of the VPPA.

To determine whether the contractor in *Carnell* had appropriately complied with the requirements of the VPPA, the Fourth Circuit examined (1) whether the contractor had provided sufficient notice per the VPPA's notice requirement; and

---

[208] North Carolina H.B. 476, Sess. Law 2013-407, § 87-119: Costs associated with compliance; effect of permit.

[209] North Carolina H.B. 476, Sess. Law 2013-407, § 87-129: Underground Damage Prevention Review Board; enforcement; civil penalties.

[210] Virginia Public Procurement Act, Va. Code Ann. § 2.2-4300(c) (2001).

[211] 745 F.3d 703 (4th Cir. 2014).

(2) whether the VPPA "monetary cap" on modifications to public contracts operated to limit the amount recoverable by the contractor on its contract claims.[212]

With respect to the VPPA notice requirement, the Court held that the VPPA written notice requirement is a "mandatory, procedural requirement . . . that must be met before a court can reach the merits of a claim."[213] In order to satisfy the VPPA requirements, notice must be specific, and must " 'conspicuously declar[e] that, at least in the contractor's view, a serious legal threshold has been crossed,' and that the contractor intends to claim reimbursement for the particular damages."[214] Based on the facts of the case, the Court determined that the contractor only satisfied the notice requirement with respect to the contract claims for which the contractor specifically requested reimbursement *and* signified an intent to file a claim.[215] Therefore, although the contractor alleged numerous claims for unpaid work in its pleadings, only claims that were specifically made for two discrete aspects of the work performed by the contractor survived due to the operation of the VPPA notice requirements.

The Fourth Circuit also examined the VPPA limitation of the amount by which public contracts can be increased. The VPPA provides that fixed price public contracts cannot be increased by "more than twenty-five percent of the amount of the contract or $50,000, whichever is greater, without the advance written approval of . . . the governing body."[216] While the contractor argued that its contract was not a fixed price contract, because it was subject to additions and deductions based on lump sum and unit prices, the Fourth Circuit determined that the site work was to be performed for a "firm, fixed price," and the contract mechanism for negotiating modifications did not transform the contract into a unit price contract. The Court also rejected the contractor's constitutional challenge that the VPPA "permits the government to obtain the benefit of a contractor's additional labor . . . without being required to pay fully for that work."[217] The Court held that the VPPA only affects the remedy available for certain breach of contract actions against public entities, and does not affect the validity of the underlying contractual obligations. The contractor had no "fundamental right . . . to a particular remedy in the contract," and the VPPA provisions are reasonably related to a legitimate government purpose.[218] Therefore, the monetary cap on damages from the VPPA applied, and the contractor could not recover for a contract modification increase of more than 25% of the amount of the contract.

---

[212] 745 F.3d at 721.

[213] *Id.* at 721-22.

[214] *Id.* at 722.

[215] *Id.*

[216] *Id.* at 723.

[217] *Id.* at 724.

[218] *Id.*

On the other hand, another recent case examining the VPPA did not interpret the requirements as strictly. In *Costello Construction Co. v. City of Charlottesville*,[219] the Western District Court of Virginia examined a City/owner motion to dismiss, alleging that a contractor who performed work for a new fire station had failed to submit timely notice of claims and failed to exhaust its administrative remedies under the VPPA. However, unlike in *Carnell*, the *Costello* court did not take as strict of an interpretation of the notice requirements of the statute. Instead, the court examined the notice that was provided by the contractor in the context of the "circumstances of [the] case."[220]

The Court determined that under Virginia law, notice did not need to be provided separately from a claim per the VPPA. Because the claims that were provided by the contractor stated that they were "Notice of Claims" and identified the specific damages that the contractor sought to recover, the Court held that the notice provided by the contractor was sufficient to withstand the City's motion to dismiss, because "[a]ny document can suffice if it clearly and timely states the contractor's intention to later file an administrative claim."[221] The fact that the contractor provided notice in the form of a claim against the City did not make the contractor's notice defective.

With respect to the City's motion to dismiss some of the contractor's claims based on the contractor's alleged failure to exhaust its administrative remedies, the VPPA states that public bodies may establish an administrative procedure for a hearing, but contractors do not necessarily have to utilize those administrative procedures if they are available.[222] However, if the contractor does invoke the administrative procedures provided by the public body, then the contractor is required to exhaust those procedures prior to bringing a legal action concerning the same procurement transaction, unless the public body agrees otherwise.[223] In *Costello*, the City did provide an administrative procedure to hear appeals arising from its contract decisions, and the contractor did invoke those procedures for some of its claims. The City therefore claimed that the contractor's other claims, which the contractor did not bring to the administrative appeal board and which the City claimed were related "ripple effects" from the claims that were heard by the administrative appeal board, should have been brought to the appeal board as well. The Court determined that the "same procurement transaction" language of the VPPA meant that the VPPA does not require all disputes arising out of a construction contract to be exhausted administratively once a contractor invokes the administrative procedure with respect to any dispute. The Court determined that it was possible, however, for the contractor's "cumulative impact" claims to be

---

[219] No. 3:14-CV-00034, 2015 WL 1274695 (W.D. Va. Mar. 19, 2015).
[220] 2015 WL 1274695, at *4 (internal citations omitted).
[221] *Id.*
[222] *Id.* at *5.
[223] *Id.*, citing the VPPA, VA. CODE § 2.2-4364(F).

"inextricably intertwined" with the claims that it presented to the appeals board, and therefore did not decide the issue.

Finally, the Court examined the City's argument that the contractor failed to state a valid claim under Virginia law based on the contractor's claim, which was based on the *Spearin* doctrine, that the City had breached the implied warranty of design adequacy. The City argued that (1) the contractor agreed in the contract to "review and evaluate the Construction Documents"; and (2) the *Spearin* doctrine is inconsistent with the VPPA and the construction contract at issue, because it attempts to "circumvent the contract's fixed price." The Court determined first of all that standard contract provisions, such as the "duty to review and evaluate" construction documents, do not amount to an express warranty whereby the contractor would affirmatively accept the burden of potential defects in the City's design documents.[224] The Court also rejected the City's argument that the *Spearin* doctrine was inconsistent with the VPPA. The Court held that while the VPPA may restrict and limit the damages available to the contractor (as was examined in *Carnell*, above), the VPPA damage limitations do not prevent contractors from alleging the claim in the first place.[225]

In conclusion, issues related to the impacts of the VPPA often lead to heated court disputes. In particular, courts in Virginia may have varied stances as to how strictly they interpret the notice requirements of the VPPA. It is therefore good practice for contractors to take the approach of the least possible resistance, and to make certain that their notices under the VPPA are technically compliant. Not only will this help their claims survive, it could help to reduce the transactional costs associated with disputes as to whether the notice provided was sufficient.

## § 7.16  CONSTRUCTION DEFECTS

In an effort to develop an alternative method to resolving construction disputes based on alleged defective work, the Florida Legislature enacted Chapter 558 in 2003. Sometimes referred to as Florida's Notice and Opportunity to Cure Statute, Chapter 558 has proven to be an effective vehicle to both protect construction professionals from lawsuits and, at the same time, protect the rights of property owners. In late 2014 and early 2015, both the Florida House of Representatives and the Senate proposed identical bills amending several provisions of Chapter 558.[226] House Bill 87 was approved by Governor Scott on June 16, 2105, with an effective date of October 1, 2015.

---

[224] *Costello*, 2015 WL 1274695, at *6.
[225] *Id.* at *7.
[226] 2015 Florida H.B. 87 (filed Dec. 9, 2014); 2015 Florida S.B. 418 (filed Jan. 21, 2015).

The newly enacted amendments include the following:

- Revision of Section 558.001, Legislative findings and declaration, to specifically note that the statute is also intended to provide the insurer of the contractor, subcontractor, supplier, or design professional with an opportunity to resolve the claim pre-suit, as well as adding language that such negotiations would be confidential settlement negotiations.[227]

- Revision of Section 558.002, Definitions, to include a temporary certificate of occupancy in the definition of "completion of building or improvement."[228]

- Revision of Section 558.004(1)(b), Notice and opportunity to repair, to add additional requirements for notice of a claim, including requiring the claimant to conduct a visual inspection and providing the location of every defect sufficiently to enable the responding parties to locate the alleged defect without undue burden.[229]

- Revision of Section 558.004(13), Notice and opportunity to repair, specifying that providing a copy of claimant's notice to the party's insurer shall not constitute a claim for insurance purposes, "unless the terms of the policy specify otherwise."[230]

- Revision of Section 558.004(15), Notice and opportunity to repair, amending the scope of documentation that can be requested to include "maintenance records and other documents related to the discovery, investigation, causation, and extent of the alleged defect identified in the notice of claim and any resulting damages." This revised Section further provides that "[a] party may assert any claim of privilege recognized under the laws of this state with respect to any of the disclosure obligations specified in this chapter."[231]

The purpose behind the amendments is to improve the already successful construction defect resolution procedure in Florida by ensuring recipients of Chapter 558 notices are provided with additional information so that alleged defects can be proactively and effectively handled while avoiding costly litigation. Contractors, subcontractors and design professionals, however, should pay close attention to the increased notification and documentation requirements for purposes of challenging Chapter 558 notices.

---

[227] FLA. STAT. § 558.001 (2015).

[228] Id. § 558.002.

[229] Id. § 558.004(1)(b).

[230] Id. § 558.004(13).

[231] Id. § 558.004(15).

Chapter 558, and in particular its legislative intent and the revisions to Section 558.004(13), was the focus of a recent federal decision by the United States District Court of the Southern District of Florida even before the Governor signed the bill into law. The case of *Altman Contractors, Inc. v. Crum & Forster Specialty Insurance Co.*[232] contained two separate issues of first impression.[233] The Insured at issue was the general contractor for a high-rise residential condominium building and carried insurance for the project with the Insurer. The condominium served the Insured with several Notice of Claims under Chapter 558 alleging construction defects in the project, to which it demanded its Insurer defend and indemnify the Insured. The Insurer denied that it had a duty to indemnify under Chapter 558 as the case was not "in suit" and the notice did not constitute a claim.[234]

The Insured filed a complaint seeking a declaration that the Insurer owes Insured a duty to defend and indemnify it relative to the Chapter 558 notice and that the Insurer was in breach of contract for failing to do so. On cross summary judgment motions, the Insurer argued that Florida Statutes Section 558.004(13) bars a notice under Chapter 558 from constituting a claim for insurance purposes and further that the Chapter 558 process does not constitute a suit under the terms of its policy with the Insured. The Insured contended that the purpose and intent of Chapter 558 supports the conclusion that a notice under its provisions rises to the level of a suit.[235]

The Court identified two issues—both matters of first impression—(1) whether Section 558.004(13) bars the Insured's claim; and (2) whether the mechanisms contained in Chapter 558 constitute civil proceedings. On the first issue, the Court disagreed with the Insurer.[236] The applicable language of Section 558.004(13) provides as follows: "However, notwithstanding the foregoing or any contractual provisions, the providing of a notice to the person's insurer, if applicable, shall not constitute a claim for insurance purposes."[237] The proposed (now enacted) amendment to this provision adds the language "unless provided for under the terms of the policy" at the end. As evidenced by the recent legislative comments accompanying the bill, the only purpose of this Section was to clarify that the statute was not supplanting any notice requirements under the insurance policy itself.[238] The Court held that "[n]othing in this language of the statute or the legislative history suggests that this provision acts as a bar to insurance coverage if the policy otherwise would provide for coverage."[239]

---

[232] 2015 WL 3539755 (S.D. Fla. June 4, 2015).

[233] *Id.* at *2, 5.

[234] *Id.* at *1.

[235] *Id.* at *2.

[236] *Id.*

[237] *Id.* at *3.

[238] *Id.* at *4.

[239] *Id.* at *5.

As there was no outright statutory bar to the Insurer providing coverage, the Court next turned to the Insurer's argument that the terms of the policy only required it to defend the insured against any "suit" and that Chapter 558 proceedings did not constitute a suit under the terms of the policy.[240] The policy defined suit as a "civil proceeding" and the Court turned to the recent edition of *Black's Law Dictionary* for guidance of this terminology.[241] *Black's* defined "civil proceeding" as "[a] judicial hearing, session, or lawsuit in which the purpose is to decide or delineate private rights and remedies, as in a dispute between litigants in a matter relating to torts, contracts, property, or family law."[242] Based on this definition, the Court concluded that "[n]othing about the Chapter 558 process satisfies this definition."[243]

According to the Court, a civil proceeding requires a forum where a decision maker is involved. The Florida Legislature, however, describes Chapter 558 as a "mechanism" not a proceeding.[244] In fact, noted the Court, "Chapter 558 is intended to avoid the commencement of an action."[245] Based on the foregoing, the Court held that the Chapter 558 mechanism does not constitute a civil proceeding and therefore it cannot be a "suit" under the Crum & Forster policy requiring the Insurer to defend the Insured.[246]

While *Altman Contractors, Inc.,* involved the interpretation of a specific insurance policy, the general holding of the Court that Chapter 558 does not describe civil proceedings, despite the legislative intent that it be a method of alternative dispute resolution, may have much broader implications in the insurance arena.

---

[240] *Id.*

[241] *Id.* at *6.

[242] *Id.*

[243] *Id.*

[244] *Id.* at *7.

[245] *Id.*

[246] *Id.* at *9.

CHAPTER 8

# NORTHEAST REGION

Connecticut, Delaware, Maine, Maryland, Massachusetts,
New Hampshire, New Jersey, New York, Pennsylvania,
Puerto Rico, Rhode Island, Vermont, Virgin Islands

Stanley A. Martin

## § 8.01  INTRODUCTION

This chapter covers cases and other developments from the Northeast Region of the United States, including Connecticut, Delaware, Maine, Maryland, Massachusetts, New Hampshire, New Jersey, New York, Pennsylvania, Rhode Island, and Vermont. No effort is made to report on all construction-related cases in those states. Rather, cases and other developments considered to be of interest to a broad section of the construction industry—whether due to developments in the law, or due to interesting or novel factual or legal issues—are included. Cases reported this year include a New York decision on insurance coverage for the tower crane with a boom left dangling over the Manhattan skyline after Hurricane Sandy, a Massachusetts decision on the interplay between the Construction Manager ("CM") at risk procurement law and the *Spearin* doctrine, and a Connecticut Supreme Court decision allowing liquidated damages to be assessed by a public authority after terminating the construction contract for convenience.

## § 8.02  PUBLIC CONSTRUCTION ISSUES

Public projects are a major part of the construction industry, and cases arising from those projects continue to aid in developing the body of case law surrounding the construction industry. This year we have occasion to review a decision by the Massachusetts Supreme Judicial Court on the (relatively new) CM at risk procurement law, and whether the public owner still impliedly warrants sufficiency of design in that setting, and another Massachusetts decision involving a subcontract that was too low for the subcontractor to pay prevailing wage rates.

### [A]  Subcontract Is Enforceable Even Though Too Low to Pay Prevailing Wage Rates

A subcontractor agreed to perform site clearing work for $5,000, and only later learned it was a public project requiring payment of prevailing wages. Instead of paying workers $13 and $14 per hour, the subcontractor would have to pay $36 and $43 for a chainsaw operator and bucket truck operator, respectively. Was the subcontractor entitled to more money, on the theory of an invalid contract, or alternatively in *quantum meruit*? A Massachusetts appellate court has said no.

The project paper trail left much to be desired. The original oral agreement, not disputed, was $5,000 to clear two sites. Only after starting work did the subcontractor learn that he would have to pay prevailing wages. He sought an increased price, but nothing was agreed upon. He also sought money for extra work; again, there was no documentation and no agreement. It appears from the decision that the workers were paid properly and the $5,000 estimate was inadequate to cover the labor cost for the original scope. The trial court found the subcontractor to be entitled to more money based on signed invoices, and under the theory of *quantum meruit*. But the appellate court reversed.

The appellate court noted that the law requiring prevailing wages to be explicitly stated applied to prime contracts but not to subcontracts. Thus, the lack of any reference to prevailing wages in the original estimate did not trouble the court. There was no consideration for the signed invoices, and so they were not enforceable against the contractor. The court also had no problem with the fact that the $5,000 quote was inadequate to cover the anticipated wage costs at prevailing rates. Its comments included:

- "courts are reluctant to protect someone from the effects of having made an unwise choice or a bad bargain."

- "[the subcontractor]'s failure to consider the consequences of his entering into a prevailing wage contract at a price well below the actual value of the work should not excuse his compliance with the law."

- "It is entirely possible that [the subcontractor] elected to take a loss on the initial $5,000 contract as a 'loss leader' in an attempt to secure an advantage over his competitors on future public contracts."

With comments like these, it was no surprise that the court ruled against the subcontractor. The case is *Cocchi v. Morais Concrete Service, Inc.*[1]

## [B]  CM at Risk—Owner Still Impliedly Warrants Design

A Massachusetts public authority argued that the CM's role of reviewing and commenting on the design in process meant that the authority did not impliedly warrant the sufficiency of the design. And thus the CM would have no claim against the public authority when a subcontractor pursued a claim based on improper design. But the Massachusetts Supreme Judicial Court has held[2] that the implied warranty remains intact in a CM at risk setting unless the authority expressly disclaims any such implied warranty.

The Massachusetts high court discussed the nature of CM pre-construction activities, including the CM providing input and feedback during the design phase. And it also addressed the fact that the CM may take into account, in establishing the GMP, risks arising from incomplete design. But it then noted:

> As significant as these differences in relationship are [from traditional design-bid-build], we are not persuaded that the relationships are so different that no implied warranty of the designer's plans and specifications should apply in construction management at risk contracts made pursuant to [the Mass. CM

---

[1] 2015 Mass. App. Div. 50, 2015 Mass. App. Div. LEXIS 14 (Mar. 17, 2015).

[2] Coughlin Elec. Contractors, Inc. v. Gilbane Bldg. Co., et al., 472 Mass. 549, 36 N.E.3d 505 (2015).

at risk law] and that the CMAR should bear all the additional costs caused by design defects.

More critically, the court noted that "the owner, through the designer, ultimately controls the design . . . " Since the implied warranty is based on the concept that responsibility for a problem rests on the one who controls (or represents that it can control) the issue giving rise to the problem, this ultimate control with owner and designer means that the CM can still pursue a claim based on this theory. Also, the court noted that the CM at risk procurement law provided that the CM "may" provide "consultation" concerning the design. Relying on Webster's dictionary definition of "consult," the court found that this did not translate into any guarantee by the CM against design defects.

But the court did note that the CM's role during design might affect the scope of the owner's implied warranty. It remains to be seen whether any of the major public authorities in Massachusetts will now seek to modify some of the contract terms going forward, to dilute the owner's implied warranty in a CM at risk setting.

### [C]    No Equitable Adjustment for Contractor with Penny Bid

Believing actual quantities of rock removal would be far less than the engineer's estimate, the contractor bid a penny per cubic yard of rock removal on a water main extension project. But the estimated 1,000 cy of rock turned out to be an actual amount of 2,524 cy. The contractor sought an "equitable adjustment" in the unit price, from \$.01/cy to \$220/cy. The contractor later reduced the request to a mere \$190/cy, but the town denied any adjustment. The lower court agreed.

The Massachusetts Appeals Court[3] was polite, taking eight pages to reach what most would consider a foregone conclusion. It held that the statutory differing site condition clause "is designed to protect contractors from unknown and unforeseen subsurface conditions, not from the consequences of their decisions to bid a unit price for the performance of the work that is wholly unrelated to their anticipated cost to perform the work. In such circumstances it defies logic to invoke 'equity' as a basis for adjustment to the contract price." So the contractor would receive \$25.24 for the rock removal, as it had bid.

### [D]    Subcontractors May Have Limited Relief Against Town
When Prime Contractor's Surety Fails

Subcontractors on a public project for the town of Darien, Connecticut found themselves on the short end of the stick when the prime contractor failed

---

[3] Celco Constr. Corp. v. Town of Avon, 87 Mass. App. Ct. 132 (2015).

to pay, apparently went out of business, and its surety turned out to be bogus. Subcontractor claims against the town were initially dismissed, but a Superior Court judge reinstated certain claims, at least allowing the subcontractors to seek unpaid amounts the town may still be holding against the prime.

The Superior Court noted[4] that there is Connecticut case law allowing a subcontractor to pursue a claim for unjust enrichment directly against a project owner in limited circumstances, "affording an equitable claim in the absence of a recognized legal claim." The court also distinguished the extent of available remedies for claims against the state—barred by principles of sovereign immunity except via contract or statute—from the realm of remedies available against municipalities. The municipality not enjoying the same defenses as the state, it could be subject to equitable claims for relief by the subcontractor.

This was not a decision on the merits, but was a decision that allows the subcontractors to attempt to demonstrate that the town gained a benefit (i.e., a finished project) for which it never fully paid, and thus allows the subcontractors the opportunity to try to recoup some of those unpaid funds. It appears from the decision that there is no dispute that the full contract amount was never paid to the now-absent general contractor.

### [E]  Does Pennsylvania Payment Statute Apply to Public Works Contracts?

Pennsylvania has a "Contractor and Subcontractor Payment Act"[5] ("CASPA") which provides certain obligations and rights among owners, contractors and subcontractors. Upon certification from the Third Circuit Court of Appeals, the Pennsylvania Supreme Court held that CASPA does not apply in the context of public works projects.[6]

The underlying project was a marine/navy reserve training center for the U.S. Navy. An unpaid subcontractor filed suit for money due, and included a cause of action under CASPA. One item of contention was whether CASPA or the Pennsylvania Prompt Pay Act[7] applied to the public project. A central issue in that dispute was the scope of the reference to "owner" in CASPA. The statutory definition is in two parts. First, "owner" is a "person who has an interest in the real property that is improved." Second, "person" is defined as a "corporation, partnership, business trust, other association, estate, trust foundation or a natural individual." The defense argued that a government entity was not included in the

---

[4] M&L Constr., Inc. v. Town of Darien, 2015 Conn. Super. LEXIS 497 (Mar. 5, 2015).
[5] 73 P.S. § 502.
[6] Clipper Pipe & Serv., Inc. v. The Ohio Cas. Ins. Co., 2015 Pa. LEXIS 1275 (June 15, 2015).
[7] 62 Pa. C.S. §§ 3931-3939.

CASPA definition of "owner," and further that the Prompt Pay Act governed public works, and it could not have been the legislative intent to have both statutes apply to a public works project.

The Pennsylvania high court found the defense arguments to be persuasive for a few reasons. First, the government is neither a "person" nor an "association" and did not come within the literal language of CASPA. Second, any statute in derogation of sovereign immunity is to be strictly construed in favor of the sovereign. Third, applying CASPA would be "too disharmonious with the statutory mechanics to support the extension" [referring to the interplay or inconsistency with the Prompt Pay Act].

## § 8.03  ARCHITECT'S STANDARD OF CARE FOR BALLPARK DESIGN

A spectator hit by a foul ball during a Mets game decided to sue for damages, and his suit included the architects of Citi Field as defendants. He was sitting inside a luxury box, with the window open, when hit by the errant ball. (Unfortunately for baseball fans, none of the critical information—batter, opposing team, or score—is identified.)

Per the New York Appellate Division,[8] the spectator/plaintiff struck out. The duty of care imposed on ballparks requires protection for spectators behind home plate "where the danger of being struck by a ball is the greatest," and the plaintiff's position in a luxury box did not place him in such an area. The defendants had met their duty of care by designing and installing screens to protect those who are behind home plate at the field level. Thus, motions by the architects (as well as other defendants) to dismiss the lawsuit against them were all allowed. Further, the spectator/plaintiff's proposed amended complaint, to try to get around the infirmities of his original complaint, "was palpably insufficient and patently devoid of merit," per the court. Turns out he wasn't even behind home plate.

## § 8.04  CONTRACTOR LIABLE FOR BREACH OF IMPLIED WARRANTY IN HOME CONSTRUCTION

Homeowners who had bought a house in early 2009 from the original owner discovered extensive mold a few months after moving in; the house had been completed in 2004. They subsequently learned that structural defects most likely causing the mold conditions would have to be addressed before any remediation could take place. A lawsuit against the original contractor resulted in a jury verdict on an implied warranty cause of action. The New Hampshire Supreme Court upheld that verdict, in *Murray v. McNamara*.[9]

---

[8] Tarantino v. Queens Ballpark Co., LLC, 2014 N.Y. App. Div. LEXIS 9035 (App. Div. 2d Dept. Dec. 31, 2014).

[9] 2015 N.H. LEXIS 23 (Mar. 20, 2015).

The contractor defended on the basis that the original homeowner would have been aware of the conditions, and his knowledge should be imputed to the plaintiffs. Alternatively, the contractor argued that construction "in accordance with a plan and specifications" should be a defense. But the New Hampshire high court noted that there was evidence that the defects were latent, and so the original owner would not necessarily have been on notice of the same. Also, the court noted evidence to the effect that there were no "plans and specifications" for the original construction, but only a rudimentary program of what was to be included in the house. In that situation, the court had no difficulty upholding the jury verdict on the implied warranty theory.

## § 8.05  MIND THE (PROCEDURAL) GAP—THIRD-PARTY CLAIMS LOST

A project owner sued the contractor, who filed third-party claims against subcontractors seeking only indemnity from them if the contractor was found liable to the owner. The contractor then moved to dismiss the owner's claim as barred by the statute of limitations. The court allowed that motion, and then noted that it would dismiss the third-party claims as moot unless any party took action; no one did. The owner filed an appeal, and the owner and contractor later settled as between them. The contractor sought subcontractor participation in the settlement kitty, but realized that the third-party claims had been dismissed, and under Vermont law this dismissal was with prejudice. The contractor's belated efforts to resurrect the third-party claims were turned down by the Vermont Supreme Court, in the case of *Stratton Corp. v. Engelberth Construction, Inc.*[10]

The contractor initially sought to have dismissal of the third-party claims re-characterized as without prejudice. It argued (prior to the owner-contractor settlement) that, should the owner's appeal be successful, it would need to be able to reinstate the third-party claims. But it did not argue that there was any independent basis for its claims against the subs. And the contractor and owner asked the court to stay all other action in light of settlement discussions. Several months later the contractor and owner reported the case settled between them, and the court dismissed the entire case. At which point the contractor discovered it was in a procedural pickle.

The contractor then argued that its third-party claims were based on express indemnity obligations of the subcontractors, independent of the claims the owner had made against it. The subcontractors noted in response that the original third-party claims as alleged were only derivative of the owner's claims. The lower court agreed, and the Vermont Supreme Court reviewed that decision on an "abuse of discretion" standard. The high court held that the contractor failed to alter the "law of the case" in terms of the basis of the third-party claims and how

---

[10] 2015 VT 75, 2015 Vt. LEXIS 55 (May 29, 2015).

they would be addressed, and the lower court was within its discretion to refuse to let the contractor take that step after the fact. So the contractor was left to fund the settlement on its own. A good reminder to pay attention to the procedural issues even when a settlement is pending.

## § 8.06  CONTRACT INTERPRETATION

Ordinarily a common source of friction in construction disputes, this past year has seen fewer reported decisions delving into the details of contract language. But one court did construe an indemnity obligation in the context of a rather unique construction accident.

### [A]  Apply Common Sense to Indemnity Claim

A mechanical subcontractor's employee was severely injured during a coffee break when an improperly fastened section of limestone façade came loose near where he was sitting. In the subsequent personal injury lawsuit, the prime contractor sought an indemnity from the mechanical sub, based on a standard subcontract indemnity. The Massachusetts Appeals Court, though, in the case of *Leahy v. Daniel O'Connell's Sons, Inc.*,[11] held that the mechanical sub did not owe any duty of indemnity to the prime contractor in that situation. It is hard to imagine a set of facts where the mechanical sub's indemnity obligation would arise for this sort of accident.

The Appeals Court decision is thorough, examining and reciting various terms of the prime contract, in addition to the sub's indemnity obligation. That indemnity, both in the subcontract itself and via the Massachusetts anti-indemnity law,[12] was limited to claims caused by the sub. The prime contractor's argument was that the injured worker's claim arose out of the mechanical sub's work, because otherwise the worker would not have been on the site. The appellate court politely declined to adopt that interpretation. The prime contractor had "overall responsibility" to protect the health and safety of workers on the project, and was also responsible for coordinating the work of the various subcontractors. If an area was unsafe, it had a duty to warn workers in that area. In short, the Appeals Court found that the prime contractor had a duty to prevent the façade subcontractor from performing work in a manner unreasonably dangerous to others.

The appellate decision includes some statements that many prime contractors may find troublesome, as to the scope of their duty to protect workers of the various trades when means and methods have been delegated to those trades. But that is to be expected when the prime contractor seeks to invoke an indemnity

---

[11] 2015 Mass. App. Unpub. LEXIS 777 (July 20, 2015).
[12] MASS. GEN. LAWS. ch. 149 § 29C.

obligation of a sub who had nothing to do with the injury or the conditions that caused it.

## [B]  Crane Operator's Claim of Gender Discrimination

A federal appeals court reviewed allegations of gender discrimination and related claims filed under the Labor Management Relations Act.[13] The plaintiff, a member of Operating Engineers Local 14-14B, claimed that her supervisor, her employer and the local business agent collaborated to establish a second shift (staffed by the son of her supervisor), and then one week later removed the plaintiff's shift and allowed the son to continue with the later shift. She argued that she should have been allowed to take the second shift or else be allowed to operate another machine. The trial court held that the employee did not sustain an allegation of gender bias, and the Second Circuit Court of Appeals affirmed.[14]

The court noted the burden-shifting framework applicable to gender discrimination claims: once the plaintiff demonstrates a prima facie case, the burden shifts to the employer to prove a legitimate, non-discriminatory reason for its decision. In this instance, the employer stated that "changes in workflow made a later shift better able to accommodate deliveries and coincide with certain construction operations." In contrast, the court described the employee's claim of pretext in that decision as "little more than speculation that her employer, her union, and her supervisor collaborated to take a coordinated series of actions culminating in her layoff."

The construction industry has often not been welcoming to women in the workplace, particularly on the jobsite. This case verifies, though, that gender discrimination standards will be applied in the same manner, even in an industry where women are a distinct minority.

## [C]  Malicious Prosecution Claim Based on Erroneous Expert Report

"This is a regrettable case." Thus begins the decision of the Delaware Supreme Court in the case of *Blue Hen Mechanical, Inc. v. Christian Brothers Risk Pooling Trust.*[15] The defendant in that case was an insurance trust, suing as subrogee for the Little Sisters of the Poor. Blue Hen had signed a maintenance agreement to service chillers for low-income housing owned and run by the Little Sisters of the Poor. A chiller pipe had frozen and burst during the wintertime, causing the unit to fail. The Little Sisters had obtained expert opinions on causation pointing the finger at Blue Hen, and a lawsuit was subsequently filed. During the course of the litigation, the Little Sisters came to the realization that the

---

[13] 29 U.S.C. § 185(a).

[14] Hoffman v. Schiavone Contracting Corp., 2015 U.S. App. LEXIS 19819 (2d Cir. Nov. 13, 2015).

[15] 2015 Del. LEXIS 291 (June 15, 2015).

timing of the maintenance agreement did not support imposition of liability against Blue Hen. Blue Hen then sought and obtained summary judgment in its favor. It did not seek any costs in conjunction with resolution of that case.

Nine months later, Blue Hen sued the Little Sisters for malicious prosecution. It argued that the Little Sisters should be liable for malicious prosecution if they failed to dismiss their original lawsuit upon learning that Blue Hen was not liable. But the trial court, and the Delaware Supreme Court, held that the applicable standard was whether the Little Sisters had a good faith belief in the cause of action at the time the lawsuit was started. Using that standard as the gauge, the Little Sisters' prior lawsuit had been brought in good faith, given the existence of expert opinions forming the basis of the original claims. Thus, the Little Sisters would not be liable for malicious prosecution.

## § 8.07  INSURANCE

Decisions concerning insurance coverage relative to construction projects emanate from many courts each year. We report on several of those decisions this year. Cases discussed include a Maine court decision concerning workers' compensation laws vis-à-vis worker classification (or mis-classification), a Massachusetts case where an insurance policy statute of limitations was the deciding factor, and the New York case addressing the builder's risk claim filed for damages arising from the tower crane damaged by Hurricane Sandy.

### [A]  Tower Crane Is Neither "Temporary Works" Nor "Incidental" to Construction; Damage Excluded from Builder's Risk Coverage

Many readers will remember seeing photos and videos of a dangling tower crane boom, high above the Manhattan skyline, resulting from Hurricane Sandy. A divided (3-2) New York appellate court[16] ruled against the One57 building owner and construction manager on a builder's risk claim seeking to recover costs for damage to the crane. The nub of the decision is that the tower crane did not fall within the definition of "temporary works" in that it was not "incidental" to construction. In fact, the appellate court stated that the crane "was integral, not 'incidental to the project,'" and thus did not come within the policy definition of "temporary works." Since it was not a "temporary work," the crane and resulting damage were not covered by the builder's risk policy. The difference between the majority and dissenting opinions was in how they defined and applied "temporary" and "incidental."

---

[16] Lend Lease (US) Constr. LMB Inc. v. Zurich Am. Ins. Co., 2015 N.Y. App. Div. LEXIS 9390 (Dec. 22, 2015).

With any insurance coverage dispute, policy language is paramount. The decision noted the following:

> The insuring agreement provides that the "[p]olicy, subject to [its] terms, exclusions, limitations and conditions . . . insures against all risks of direct physical loss of or damage to Covered Property while at the location of the INSURED PROJECT* and occurring during the Policy Term." Covered Property includes "Property Under Construction" and "Temporary Works."
> The policy defines "Temporary Works," as
> "[a]ll scaffolding (including scaffolding erection costs), formwork, falsework, shoring, fences and temporary buildings or structures, including office and job site trailers, all incidental to the project, the value of which has been included in the estimated TOTAL PROJECT VALUE* of the INSURED PROJECT* declared by the NAMED INSURED."
> The policy excludes coverage for
> "[c]ontractor's tools, machinery, plant and equipment [3] including spare parts and accessories, whether owned, loaned, borrowed, hired or leased, and property of a similar nature not destined to become a permanent part of the INSURED PROJECT*, unless specifically endorsed to the Policy."[17]

The owner and CM argued that the crane was a temporary structure to be used only during construction and then dismantled. By implication, they argued a much broader use of that term than the examples given in the policy. The owner and CM also argued that the word "incidental" could be used to connote something in a supporting role, although not necessarily an insignificant role.

The tower crane was obviously not "property under construction," and so the analysis was whether it was part of "temporary works." The majority examined the list of examples provided in the policy—scaffolding, formwork, job site trailers, etc.—and concluded that the tower crane did not fit into the type of items listed. Also, and more critically, the court focused on the phrase "all incidental to the project" in its assessment. Citing to numerous aspects of the tower crane design and construction, much less to its use during construction, the appellate court noted that the crane was specifically designed for the project, the building structure was also designed uniquely for the crane, and once erected the crane "was integral and indispensable, not incidental" to construction.

The dissent also focused on the nature of the term "temporary works," and would have applied that phrase more broadly than the majority. The dissent found, as well, the owner's and contractor's argument about the word "incidental" to be more persuasive. With a $7 million insurance claim at stake, this case may well be taken up to the New York Court of Appeal, which is the highest New York court. We may not yet have the final word.

---

[17] *Lend Lease (US) Constr.*, 2015 N.Y. App. Div. LEXIS 9390, at *2-3.

## [B]  Insurance Policy Statute of Limitations Upheld Even After Timely Notice

The insured sustained major water damage on December 19, 2009 (an unoccupied house under construction), and learned about the damage on December 28. He gave prompt notice to the carrier. The carrier investigated, and January 14, 2011—just over a year later—denied coverage. The insured inexplicably waited until December 28, 2011, to file suit against the carrier, just over two years after the damage occurred. He argued that the discovery rule should apply since he did not learn of the damage until December 28, 2009, and so that his lawsuit would be deemed filed within the two year statute of limitations.

Massachusetts laws governing insurance companies specify a number of clauses that must be included in certain insurance policies issued in the state. One clause[18] is a two-year statute of limitations for filing suit to pursue a claim against the carrier.

On these facts, the Massachusetts Appeals Court allowed summary judgment in favor of the carrier.[19] It held that the damage was not "inherently unknowable," which is the standard normally applied to invoke the discovery rule. The court also cited to federal court decisions, which had previously held that the discovery rule does not apply to the Massachusetts statute, since the trigger is the incident "causing the damage to the property." So the insured may have been only nine days late, but might as well have been a year late.

## [C]  Parsing the GL Exclusion of Coverage for "Your Work"

Another state has joined the group of states that parse a common GL exclusion to allow coverage to remedy non-defective work damaged by defective work. The Supreme Court of New Hampshire reached this conclusion in the case of *Cogswell Farm Condominium Ass'n v. Tower Group, Inc.*[20] The exclusion at issue bars coverage for property damage to "[t]hat particular part of any property that must be restored, repaired or replaced because 'your work' was incorrectly performed on it." The argument was whether "your work" applied to all work of the general contractor (whose insurance coverage was in contention), or only the defective work. The New Hampshire court came out on the side of applying the exclusion only to the defective portion of the work, thus allowing coverage for the non-defective work damaged by the defective work.

---

[18] Mass. Gen. Laws c. 175, § 99, cl. Twelfth.

[19] Nurse v. Omega US Ins. Co., No. 14-P-653 (Mass. App. Ct. Oct. 5, 2015).

[20] 2015 N.H. LEXIS 3 (Jan. 13, 2015).

Cases cited by the carrier—at least, those noted in the decision—to apply "your work" to all aspects of construction were from Colorado, Mississippi, and South Carolina. Cases cited by the condo association arguing a more narrow interpretation of "your work" were from Montana, Massachusetts, and Ohio.

### [D] Duty to Defend and Scope of Indemnity

After construction of one building caused collapse of a party wall with the abutter, the abutter filed suit against the developer/contractor whose subcontractor caused the collapse. The contractor, named as an additional insured on the subcontractor's policy, demanded a defense and indemnity from the subcontractor and its carrier. There are two parts of this story that, in hindsight, seem incredulous.

First, the carrier for the subcontractor failed to respond to repeated notices tendering to the carrier any claims that might arise from the collapse. Only when the abutter's own insurance carrier made payment on a property damage policy, and sought subrogation against the original contractor, was there any response. When the contractor sought a defense and indemnity from the subcontractor's carrier, that response was to deny coverage. The second incredulous part of the story is that the District Court[21] held that there was no coverage and duty to defend.

The Court of Appeals for the Fourth Circuit[22] reviewed the language of the policy and a pertinent endorsement. It noted: "the language is quite clear that coverage is provided for [the contractor], for 'property damage . . . caused in whole or in part by' [the subcontractor]." It noted that various commentators have construed the same language and found coverage when the insured party was at least partially negligent. It also stated: "We thus conclude that the plain language of the Endorsement provides for exactly what it says: coverage to [the contractor] for property damage caused by [the subcontractor], either in whole or in part."

The carrier also argued that coverage was limited to situations where the contractor would be vicariously liable for the subcontractor, to which the Court of Appeals noted: "there is no mention of vicarious or derivative liability in the Endorsement." And the carrier was not on solid ground to argue that the coverage granted by the endorsement was limited to a situation involving vicarious liability. The District Court decision was vacated, and the matter remanded to the District Court to determine whether the contractor was entitled to recover expenses and attorneys' fees.

---

[21] Capital City Real Estate, LLC v. Certain Underwriters at Lloyd's London, C.A. No. MJG-13-1384 (D. Md. Feb. 24, 2014).

[22] Capital City Real Estate, LLC v. Certain Underwriters at Lloyd's London, 788 F.3d 375 (4th Cir. 2015).

## [E] Consequential Damages from Defective Work Are "Property Damage"

Are damages to condominium common areas and units, arising from defective work on elements of the building, "property damage" and an "occurrence" under the terms of the contractor's general liability policy? That was the issue decided by a New Jersey Appellate Division court[23] this past year. The condominium association sued the original developer, who had served as the general contractor, and sought coverage for its claims against the contractor's general liability policy. The trial court held that the damage resulting from defective work was neither an "occurrence" nor "property damage" to trigger coverage. But the appellate court held otherwise.

The court noted that "[i]n relation to sharing the cost of risks as a matter of insurance underwriting, consequential damages flowing from defective work are vastly different than the costs associated with replacing defective work." Noting that the resulting damage (from defective work) clearly constituted "physical injury to tangible property," the court held that interior damage resulting from defective work would constitute "property damage." And the court also noted that it was not realistic that the contractor and its subcontractors "either expected or intended for their faulty workmanship to cause 'physical injury to tangible property.'" Thus, the resulting damage was also an "occurrence" as defined by the contractor's general liability policy. The case was remanded to the trial court to proceed per the appellate division decision.

## [F] Worker's Compensation and Alleged Misclassification of Workers

Misclassification of workers is a big issue among small—and even some medium-size—contractors. It is no secret that some contractors label workers as "subcontractors" when those workers are, in substance, employees of the contractor, and thus gain a competitive advantage on the cost of labor. The Supreme Court of Maine[24] this past year reviewed a dispute between a contractor and a worker's compensation investigative unit, coming out, in this instance, on the contractor's side.

The builder involved had, several years back, suffered the financial consequences of misclassification when it had been assessed a major premium surcharge. Since then, the builder had required of any person or company hired as a subcontractor or independent contractor to obtain, from the state workers' compensation board, a predetermination of independent contractor status. The present

---

[23] Cypress Point Condo. Ass'n, Inc. v. Adria Towers, LLC, 2015 N.J. Super. LEXIS 114 (July 9, 2015).

[24] Fn x Workers' Comp. Bd. Abuse Investigation Unit v. Nate Holyoke Builders, Inc., 2015 Me. 99 (Aug. 4, 2015).

dispute arose in that context, where the builder could demonstrate that any person or company engaged as a subcontractor had been required to obtain and provide this predetermination, and also that it had procured insurance that would cover any person entitled to workers' compensation benefits. But the crux of the dispute was whether the builder was obligated to have determined in advance which persons were employees and which were subcontractors (as the state board argued), or merely to have in place workers' compensation insurance that would cover all such persons (as the contractor argued). And so the court turned to the pertinent provisions of the Maine worker's compensation act.[25]

As discussed by the Maine high court, the language in pertinent provisions of the Maine worker's compensation law "does not require an employer to correctly classify workers for payroll purposes and to pay workers' compensation premiums based on those classifications." Rather, the Maine law "obligates an employer to make arrangements for the payment of workers' compensation benefits to its employees." These are subtle distinctions, but distinctions nonetheless. As the builder had procured insurance that would be available "to those persons who are entitled to receive [workers' compensation benefits]," the builder had complied with the law.

## § 8.08  ARBITRATION

With the U.S. Supreme Court upholding arbitration clauses in a variety of situations, under the Federal Arbitration Act ("FAA"), the amount of litigation over the scope of arbitration is surprising. This year we cover a case where the arbitrator awarded damages for defamation, and a New Jersey case where the court held that the arbitration clause was not an effective waiver of the right to a jury trial.

### [A]  An Arbitration Award for Defamation

Hell hath no fury like a homeowner scorned, particularly one with access to sophisticated IT professionals who will establish and optimize a website solely to criticize the contractor. But a cabinetry contractor—whose arbitration award including attorneys' fees was affirmed by a Connecticut appellate court[26] is having the last laugh. The arbitrator awarded damages and attorneys' fees for the homeowners' defamatory actions. And the appellate court confirmed that the arbitrator did not engage in "manifest disregard" for the law when he found the homeowners to have acted maliciously in conducting their war of words.

---

[25] 39-A M.R.S. §§ 401, *et seq.*
[26] SBD Kitchens, LLC. v. Jefferson, 2015 Conn. App. LEXIS 216 (June 16, 2015).

In an age of web-based commentary and criticism that forms the basis of sites such as Yelp, the homeowners' actions went well beyond the norm. The husband used his company's IT professionals to establish a website and take steps to ensure that anyone searching for the cabinetry business would find his site, with all its critical comments, first. But the original site (the site appears to have been modified) included statements that the arbitrator found not only defamatory, but also to have been issued with malice.

The homeowners argued to the appeals court that the award manifestly disregarded the pertinent legal standards. But the arbitrator had specifically rejected the homeowners' arguments that their statements were protected opinion, or were immunized by the doctrine of fair comment, or were true. The arbitrator also cited the prevailing legal standards in the award. The appellate court agreed that manifest disregard for the law would be a basis to overturn the award, if the arbitrator had exhibited such disregard. It found he had not.

Under Connecticut law, to award punitive damages in a defamation case requires proof of actual malice. In satisfaction of that standard, the court noted several instances where the homeowners had published statements about the contractor either with knowledge of their falsity or with reckless disregard for the truth. It found "ample support" for that decision. Thus, the arbitrator had followed Connecticut law in finding libel per se under Connecticut law, and actual malice by the homeowners.

## [B]  Non-Signatory Compels Arbitration by Signatory Party

Occasionally there are cases where one party to an arbitration agreement attempts to compel arbitration with a non-signatory party. The Massachusetts Supreme Judicial Court ("SJC") issued a decision[27] this past year, however, supporting the action of a *non-signatory party* to compel arbitration with parties who had signed the agreement, based on the theory of equitable estoppel.

The plaintiffs were System4 franchisees. They had entered into franchise agreements with NECCS, Inc., d/b/a System4 of Boston. Unhappy with the manner in which business had developed—or, more accurately, had allegedly not developed—they sued NECCS and System4 LLC, described as "regional 'subfranchisor'" and "master franchisor," respectively. The plaintiffs claimed that NECCS misclassified them as independent contractors, when they were in reality employees. And that System4 participated in this misclassification. (There were other claims, but the misclassification claim was central to the argument about the scope of arbitration.) When System4, which had not signed any of the franchise agreements, attempted to compel arbitration, the plaintiffs argued that System4 was not signatory to the arbitration agreements and could not force that process. They also argued that statutory wage act claims were not subject to arbitration,

---

[27] Machado v. System4 LLC, 471 Mass. 204 (2015).

based on a prior SJC decision holding that a release did not bar statutory wage claims unless the release specifically referenced such claims and/or the wage act.

The SJC, relying on U.S. Supreme Court precedent, held that System4 could compel the plaintiffs to arbitrate their claims against System4. The court noted that the wage act claims were intertwined with the terms of the franchise agreement. The decision states: "the plaintiffs here must rely, in part, on the terms of the franchise agreements in asserting that the provisions are unenforceable and that they were mischaracterized as independent contractors. The plaintiffs cannot avoid arbitration with System4 when the issues System4 is seeking to resolve in arbitration are intertwined with the agreements that the plaintiffs signed." Thus, the plaintiffs were equitably estopped to deny the validity and scope of the arbitration agreement as it pertained to the allegations they had made against System4.

Even the plaintiffs' argument that several franchise agreement terms were unconscionable, and rendered the agreement unenforceable, was addressed succinctly by the court. The Massachusetts high court stated first that "not all of these provisions are unconscionable." It noted that an arbitrator applying the statutory wage act could override a cost-splitting provision in the franchise agreement. And the plaintiffs "presented no evidence to suggest that the shortened statute of limitations at issue is unreasonable or contrary to public policy." Finally, although a confidentiality clause might be suspect, the SJC declared that if so it could be severed from the franchise agreement without affecting the validity of the rest of the agreement.

This decision reinforces the ability of companies to utilize arbitration to cover a broad range of prospective disputes. Fueled by Supreme Court decisions upholding broad arbitration clauses, courts in Massachusetts and other states are likely to read arbitration clauses broadly, to encompass many causes of action that have historically been fought mostly in the courts.

### [C]    Arbitration Award Stands Despite Apparent Error of Law

A federal appellate court reminded the business community this year that a mistake of law by an arbitration panel will not ordinarily be grounds to overturn the award. The arbitration concerned a terminated financial services consultant, who filed for arbitration almost two years after the termination. Initial claims were arguably based on the wrong state's laws, and proposed amendments to conform the pleadings with applicable (Florida) law were denied. Yet the arbitration panel appeared to apply the correct state law, just in a manner that the respondent thought was contrary to state law—specifically a one-year statute of limitations and a civil rights act that would apply to an employee but not an independent contractor. The district court had vacated the award on the grounds that the arbitrators exceeded their powers.

The federal Court of Appeals directed reinstatement and confirmation of the arbitration award. Its decision[28] notes a "high hurdle for finding reversible error by the arbitrators." It also discusses the standard of "manifest disregard of the law" sometimes invoked in an effort to vacate an arbitration award, but did not apply that standard here (and noted as an aside that standard would not have changed the outcome).

On the statute of limitations claim, the appellate court commented that Florida law had been in flux on that point. But more critically, "Given the legal uncertainty reflected in the certified question presented to the Florida Supreme Court, and the fact that even 'serious error' by arbitrators will not invalidate their award, any error by the panel in refusing to dismiss [the consultant]'s claims as untimely does not rise to the level necessary to justify vacatur." As for the civil rights claim, "the panel's unexplained reliance on the [Florida Civil Rights Act] leaves us perplexed, and may have been erroneous, [but] it does not render the award unsustainable."

The court ended with the critical message: "In opting for arbitration as its preferred mechanism for resolving employment disputes, [the financial services firm] 'trade[d] the procedures and opportunity for review of the courtroom for the simplicity, informality, and expedition of arbitration.' [citations omitted] Barring exceptions inapplicable here, our limited review of arbitral decisions requires us to uphold an award, regardless of its legal or factual correctness, if it 'draw[s] its essence from the contract' that underlies the arbitration proceeding." In other words, a simple error of law will not justify vacating an arbitration award. Remember that point.

## [D] Owner's Claim for Defective Work Not Barred by Prior Arbitration

A contractor who successfully pursued payment in arbitration objected when the public authority owner subsequently filed a lawsuit claiming defective work. The contractor argued that the lawsuit was barred by doctrines of res *judicata* or collateral estoppel, but the Appellate Court of Connecticut has ruled[29] in favor of the owner. Thus continues a lengthy battle. But there is more to the story.

The project for 22 buildings was started in 1991 and completed in 1996. Issues then arose concerning the construction and alleged defects. The contractor eventually filed for arbitration, seeking the contract balance. In that arbitration, the contractor attempted to assert a claim for declaratory judgment, in effect seeking a decision that the work was "free from defect." But the public authority objected, arguing that the attempted declaratory judgment action was barred by

---

[28] Raymond James Fin. Servs., Inc. v. Fenyk, 780 F.3d 59 (1st Cir. 2015).
[29] State v. Bacon Constr. Co., 160 Conn. App. 75 (2015).

Connecticut laws[30] in that the contractor had not given the proper notice to pursue this claim. The authority further stated that it was reserving the right to pursue claims concerning defects in a different forum.

The arbitration had focused on delays in the project, and ended with an award in favor of the contractor for $82,812.81. No claims for defective construction were advanced in the arbitration. In fact, the arbitrator had determined that he lacked jurisdiction to hear the contractor's attempted declaratory judgment claim.

On this record, the trial court in the subsequent lawsuit held:

> The conduct of the arbitration and its resolution by the arbitrator demonstrates that the [public authority] never asserted in arbitration the claim of defective construction it makes here. Furthermore, when the [contractor] attempted to force the issue by its proposed amendment of the arbitration complaint, the arbitrator refused to entertain the amendment because he lacked jurisdiction to do so. Finally, whether or not [the contractor]'s performance was in conformity with its contract with the state was never litigated in the arbitration, the arbitrator ordering payment of the retainage based on the state's admission of that allegation for purposes of the arbitration.

The appellate court noted, first, that Connecticut is a permissive counterclaim jurisdiction. So the public authority was not required to assert its counterclaim in the arbitration. The counterclaim not having been filed, the arbitrator had made no findings as to whether the contractor's work was without defect. Thus, the doctrine of *res judicata* did not apply. And since this issue was not "fully and fairly litigated" in the first action, the doctrine of collateral estoppel did not apply. Thus, the contractor's efforts to cut off that claim by motion did not succeed.

## [E]  Arbitration Clause May Not Be Effective Waiver of Right to Trial

A New Jersey Appellate Division court has held[31] that an arbitration clause must effectively spell out what court or litigation rights are being given up, in order for the parties to be required to arbitrate. The decision makes no mention of the FAA, and one can only wonder how this case would have come out had the parties focused on the FAA instead of the New Jersey arbitration law. (The lawsuit claimed violation of New York wage laws, but was filed in New Jersey.) The case arises in the context of a broker-dealer dispute, where the arbitration clause was based on FINRA regulations.

---

[30] CONN. GEN. STAT. § 4-61.

[31] Barr v. Bishop-Rosen & Co., Inc., No. A-2502-14T2 (N.J. App. Div. Oct. 26, 2015).

After the broker defended a customer claim in arbitration, the broker filed suit against his employer, claiming violation of New York wage laws and seeking reimbursement of costs incurred in the customer arbitration. The employer moved to compel arbitration with the broker, but the trial court refused to do so; the employer appealed.

The court cites to several New Jersey appellate decisions, requiring language in an arbitration clause that spells out what rights are being lost if a dispute must be arbitrated. The court stated that the arbitration clause must "convey that parties are giving up their right to bring their claims in court or have a jury resolve their dispute." It cited with approval other arbitration clauses that referenced waiver of jury trial or other court proceedings. The clauses in question, the court found, "failed to clearly and unambiguously inform plaintiff of his waiver of the right to pursue his claims in a judicial forum."

The FINRA regulations did not help the employer, as those regulations called for an explanation to be provided, each time the employee signed a form containing an arbitration clause, as to the meaning and effect of that clause. The employer had failed to provide this information each time the broker signed a form that included an arbitration clause.

## § 8.09  STATUTES OF LIMITATION AND REPOSE

We review this year a New Hampshire case that had to decide what constitutes "substantial completion" to trigger the statute of repose, and Massachusetts case where one party had sought arbitration within the limitations period but had otherwise taken no action.

### [A]  Statute of Repose Not Tolled by Builder's Occupancy of House

Is the New Hampshire eight-year statute of repose tolled when the original builder occupies a house for four years? The New Hampshire Supreme Court said no this past year.[32] Drouin Builders built the house in 2001 and conveyed it to sole shareholder Michael Drouin. He lived there and later sold the house in 2005. The new homeowners noticed problems in 2008 but did not file suit until 2011. The homeowner's lawsuit claimed defective work in the original construction. Faced with a motion for summary judgment, they argued that the statute of repose was tolled during the period of time Drouin occupied the house.

The New Hampshire law provides that an action to recover damages arising from the original construction must be brought within eight years after substantial completion. There is other language in the statute which provides that claims arising from negligence in the "repair, maintenance or upkeep" are not subject to

---

[32] Ingram v. Drouin, 2015 N.H. LEXIS 11 (Feb. 15, 2015).

the statute of repose. But the successor homeowners claimed that the problems arose from the original construction and not from any repair, maintenance or upkeep. The New Hampshire high court noted: "We agree with the majority of courts addressing the issue that, when a builder-owner is sued for his construction-related activities, the statute of repose applies. To interpret the statute of repose otherwise would be contrary to the legislature's intent in enacting it—which was to protect the building industry." Thus, there was no tolling in this situation, and the homeowners were simply too late to file suit.

## [B]  Reference to Arbitration Did Not Toll Statute of Limitations

Where homeowners sought to arbitrate an insurance coverage dispute within a two-year statute of limitations, but the carrier declined to do so, the homeowners' failure to file a lawsuit within that two-year period resulted in the claim being dismissed. The Massachusetts Appeals Court has held that "it was open to the [homeowners] to file their complaint timely" even while waiting for the carrier to respond to the request for arbitration. What appears to have factored into the court's decision was that the homeowners waited almost until the end of the two-year period to seek arbitration, and then waited another two years to file suit. Thus, not only did they fail to meet the literal deadline of the statute of limitations, but they also failed to file within "a reasonable period of time" afterward. And so their argument—that the carrier was estopped from defending on the statute of limitations basis due to the carrier's failure to promptly respond to the request for arbitration—was not persuasive. The case is *Hawley v. Preferred Mutual Insurance Co.*[33]

## § 8.10  DAMAGES

Cases addressed this year concerning damages include two Connecticut decisions, one where a public authority assessed liquidated damages after terminating the construction contract for convenience, and another decision concerning a worker claim for lost wages due to a contractor's negligence. Also, a federal appellate court considered the pertinent standard of damages where a condition for limiting the contractor's liability was not met by the contractor apparently for strategic reasons.

---

[33] 88 Mass. App. Ct. 360 (2015).

## [A]  Agreement for Specific Performance Precludes Actual Damages Claim

In settling an environmental contamination claim, the property owner agreed to accept a cash payment and the environmental company agreed to perform remediation work. The settlement documents provided that the owner's remedy was in specific performance, to require the remediation company to do its work. Unhappy with the remediation, the owner instead declined to demand or require specific performance, had the property demolished, and then sought money damages. The trial judge turned the owner down, and the Massachusetts Appeals Court agreed.

The appellate court quoted an argument made by the defendants, that the owner "cannot create a condition which prevents specific performance, and then demand monetary damages in its place." If the parties agreed that specific performance was the owner's remedy, the owner would be held to that agreement. Even if the owner believed the remediation to have been performed improperly, taking action to frustrate the agreed remedy was not the way to get redress. (From the relatively short opinion, it is clear that the court viewed the owner as his own worst enemy.) The case is *Abdella v. Hydro Environmental Technologies, Inc.*[34]

## [B]  Liquidated Damages Liability After Convenience Termination

A contractor and public authority struggled through much of a pump station replacement project. During the work, the town agreed to extend the completion date by five months. Many change orders were presented and agreed to. The extended completion date came and went, and the town considered terminating the contract for cause but did not do so. More than two years after the extended completion date, the town terminated the contract for convenience. It later sought to impose liquidated damages, to offset against the contractor's claim for payment made after termination. The contractor's defense was that the town could not impose liquidated damages after a termination for convenience. But the Connecticut Supreme Court has held that the town can impose liquidated damages in that situation.

The contract included a "time of the essence" clause, and also provided for liquidated damages of $400/day for late completion. An essential element of this decision was the language in the termination for convenience clause, which allowed termination for the town's convenience "without cause and without prejudice to any other right or remedy of [the town]." The Supreme Court noted that this reservation of rights "appears exceedingly broad." The contractor argued that termination for convenience made unavailable any default-based remedy. But

---

[34] 2015 Mass. App. Unpub. LEXIS 484 (May 22, 2015). It has been published as a case not to be cited as binding precedent, but "only for its persuasive value."

the court contrasted default-based remedies arising post-termination from such remedies existing at the time of termination. The town was entitled to more than two years' worth of liquidated damages at the time of the convenience termination. The court noted: "When a contract expressly preserves remedies following termination, such a reservation must be given full effect absent evidence of a more limited intent." So the right to liquidated damages existing at the time of termination could be imposed even with the convenience termination.

As with many construction-related cases, the facts are far more involved than the summary above can relate, and there were other issues although none with as much import. Readers wanting more information should refer to the decision, in *Old Colony Construction, LLC v. Town of Southington*.[35]

### [C] Warranty Limits Avoided by Contractor's Denial of Liability

A roofing contractor's warranty limitation, capping its liability at the original cost of the roofing services, applied only if the roofer determined that any leaks were caused by its own workmanship or the materials installed. Thus, when the roofer denied that roof leaks were due to its own workmanship, the court found that the limitation did not apply. Which meant that the roofer was liable for repair costs of $1.8 million as compared to the original installation contract of approximately $550,000. The decision was issued this past year by the Third Circuit Court of Appeals in the case of *Buddy's Plant Plus Corp. v. CentiMark Corp.*[36]

CentiMark had installed the original roof, and was later called back to address leaks. Multiple attempts to correct the leaks failed, and the last attempt by CentiMark involved ungasketed fasteners. When a lawsuit was filed, it appears that CentiMark defended primarily on the basis of a one-year contractual statute of limitations. In any event, CentiMark refused to acknowledge that any leaks were the result of its materials or its workmanship, or that the ungasketed fasteners were a cause of some problems, as the plaintiff's expert opined. The court noted:

> Under the plain language of the warranty, the limitation only applies if CentiMark itself "determines that the leaks in the roof are caused by defects in materials or workmanship supplied by CentiMark." CentiMark, however, has denied that its materials or workmanship caused the leaks.

Thus, the plaintiff was free to pursue a claim for breach of the warranty, and the contract limitation on warranty damages did not apply.

---

[35] 2015 Conn. LEXIS 94 (Apr. 21, 2015).
[36] 2015 U.S. App. LEXIS 3551 (3d Cir. Mar. 6, 2015).

## [D]  Lost Wage Claims Barred by Economic Loss Doctrine

The introductory sentence in the decision states the issue: "The sole issue in this appeal is whether construction companies owe a duty of care to workers employed on a jobsite who suffer purely economic harm, namely lost wages, as a result of an accident caused by the construction companies' negligence." The Connecticut Supreme Court answered that question in the negative this past year.[37]

In February 2010, a horrific explosion at a nearly completed power plant in Middletown, CT, killed and injured several workers, and construction activity was halted for a period of time. This lawsuit was not brought by workers with physical injuries, but rather by workers who claimed to have lost income as a result of the work stoppage. The court noted that its threshold inquiry for a legal duty involved—

> (1) a determination of whether an ordinary person in the defendant's position, knowing what the defendant knew or should have known, would anticipate that harm of the general nature of that suffered was likely to result, and (2) a determination, on the basis of a public policy analysis, of whether the defendant's responsibility for its negligent conduct should extend to the particular consequences or particular plaintiff in this case.

There was no dispute that the plaintiffs' injuries were foreseeable, so the analysis focused on the public policy issue. That analysis, in turn, involved the "totality" of four factors: (a) normal expectations of participants, (b) the public policy of encouraging participation in the action, (c) the avoidance of increased litigation, and (d) the decisions of various jurisdictions.

To review the parties' expectations, the court cited an 1856 decision.[38] It cited others, as well, for the general and continuing proposition that, in the absence of a privity relationship, economic harms caused by the negligence of others have typically been without redress. After citing a number of cases addressing a variety of circumstances where the Connecticut courts barred economic losses on tort claims, the Connecticut high court also noted the alternative redress afforded to the workers: unemployment benefits. It ended this part of its analysis by noting: "we conclude that the reasonable expectations of the participants, as informed by existing Connecticut law, favor the defendants in the present case."

Finding that the remaining three factors also were in favor of the defendants, the court refused to erode the economic loss doctrine any further. The alternative outcome would have sent a ripple through the industry, at least in Connecticut.

---

[37] Lawrence v. O&G Indus., 2015 Conn. LEXIS 373 (Nov. 24, 2015).

[38] Conn. Mut. Life Ins. Co. v. New York & New Haven R.R. Co., 25 Conn. 265 (1856). It seems likely that any court citing a 160-year-old case is probably not going to make new law.

CHAPTER 9

# NORTHWEST REGION

Alaska, Idaho, Montana, Nebraska, North Dakota,
Oregon, South Dakota, Washington, Wyoming

Meghan A. Douris, Erich C. Potter, Ashley J. Sherwood,
Melia A. Preedy, Alix K. Town, Shaun C. Kennedy,
Sean P. Dowell, Eric P. Forner, David C. Weaver,
Michael J. Schmidt

## § 9.01 ALASKA

### [A] Introduction

Recent case law may impact the construction industry in Alaska.

### [B] Recent Statutory Developments

No significant legislation impacting the construction industry was enacted into law during the 2015 legislative session.

### [C] Case Law

#### [1] Construction Company Denied Permit to Mine "Common Varieties" of Stone Which Are Not Subject to "Location" and Cannot Be Permitted Under Alaska Mining Laws

In *McGlinchy*,[1] the Supreme Court of Alaska affirmed the Department of Natural Resources ("DNR")'s denial of construction company's permit application to mine a mineral deposit for construction rock. The company held a lease on a mineral deposit it planned to develop to supply a nearby railroad project and submitted a plan and permit application, which was denied by DNR.

Under the 1872 Mining Law, 30 U.S.C. § 22, "all valuable mineral deposits in lands belonging to the United States . . . shall be free and open to exploration and purchase." But the minerals must be subject to "location," which was limited by the Common Varieties Act of 1955 to exclude deposits of "common varieties of sand, stone, gravel . . ." unless located and exploited with some other uncommon mineral. DNR performed a site inspection and concluded that the constituent materials were not valuable and denied the company's permit. The company appealed and DNR held a hearing in which it held that even if some of the minerals were considered valuable, the company had no plans to extract the valuable minerals from the common construction rock, and denied the appeal. The company then appealed to the Alaska Superior Court, which also upheld the DNR's decision. The Alaska Supreme Court upheld the prior decisions agreeing with DNR's reasoning.

---

[1] McGlinchy v. State, Dep't of Natural Resources, 354 P.3d 1025 (Alaska 2015).

### [2]  In Action Against Construction Company, Landowner Was Not Relieved of Joint and Several Liability Where Landowner Could Have Avoided Damages Related to Hazardous Waste Cleanup with Reasonable Effort

In *Oakley Enterprises,*[2] the Supreme Court of Alaska upheld a superior court's apportionment of damages following a jury's apportionment of harm.

In 2004, a logger leased wood chipping equipment from a construction and timber company, which was stored on leased property. In 2006, the Alaska Department of Environmental Conservations discovered several diesel spills near the chipper, and notified the logger and landowner. Shortly thereafter, the logger vacated the property, leaving the equipment behind. In 2009, the landowner and a neighbor sued the logger and the construction company that had leased the equipment seeking damages for the contamination of their properties and costs of cleanup. The logger never answered the complaint and a default judgment was entered.

Following a trial in which the jury apportioned harms caused by the diesel spill among the landowner and construction company, the superior court granted the construction company's motion to equitably allocate damages. The Court concluded "[t]he most equitable and fairest means of dividing responsibility for the diesel spill is to allocate fault based upon the amount of time each party had responsibility for and control over the leaking chipper." The landowner appealed, arguing that the jury's apportionment of harms rendered contribution unnecessary.

The Alaska Supreme Court upheld the trial court's apportionment, ruling that under Alaska statutes where a party has been found jointly and severally liable for a release of hazardous substances, the damages may be recast as a claim for contribution upon conclusion of the litigation.

## § 9.02  IDAHO

### [A]  Introduction

Recent statutory changes and case law may impact the construction industry in Idaho.

---

[2] Oakley Enters., LLC v. NPI, LLC, 354 P.3d 1073 (Alaska 2015).

**[B]  Recent Statutory Developments**

**[1]  Change in Duration of Mechanics' Liens**

The Idaho legislature changed the duration of Mechanic's Liens from five (5) years to ten (10) years after the judgment becomes final.[3]

**[2]  Change in Application of Mechanics' Liens**

The Idaho legislature amended the application of Mechanic's Liens to specify that "owner" does not include a trustee or deed of trust,[4] and specifying that a trustee or deed of trust not be included in a claim of lien.[5]

**[3]  Exception to Public Works Engineering Review Requirement for Ditch Projects**

The Idaho legislature revised the statute making it unlawful for state agencies that have the power to levy taxes to engage in the construction of public works projects absent a review by a professional engineer, in order to provide for an exception for projects involving the maintenance or repair of ditches.[6]

**[4]  Changes to Lateral Ditch Water Users' Associations**

The Idaho legislature revised the statutes pertaining to Lateral Ditch Water Users' Associations to provide that the operation, improvement, repair and maintenance of laterals and ditches are under the direction of the Associations Directors.[7] Costs associated with the same are to be assessed against each water user, either in proportion to water usage, or by lot when within a city.[8] Further, the legislature provided a new statute allowing for the cost assessments to be a lien against the water user's land entitled to receive water.[9] Liens are recorded pursuant to the statutes governing homeowner's association liens, except that the period of enforcement is three years, with a three-year extension.[10] Finally, the legislature provided a new statute allowing for withdrawal from an Association if the water user can establish that the land is no longer entitled to receive water.[11]

---

[3] I.C. § 45-510(1).
[4] I.C. § 45-507.
[5] I.C. § 45-510(2).
[6] I.C. § 54-1218(20), I.C. § 42-1201, *et seq.*
[7] I.C. § 42-1301.
[8] I.C. § 42-1303.
[9] I.C. § 42-1311.
[10] *Id.*
[11] I.C. § 42-1312.

### [5] Exception to Requirements for Certain Electrical Contractors' Industrial Equipment

The legislature added a new section that creates an exception to the approval and certification requirements for certain industrial equipment, unless the Idaho Electrical Board otherwise deems such requirements necessary.[12]

### [6] Addition of Inactive License Status for Plumbing Contractors

The legislature added an inactive license provision for plumbing contractors and journeymen, allowing for reinstatement of an active license after demonstrating proof of completing continuing education requirements for the inactive period and paying administrative fee.[13]

### [7] Expansion of Division of Building Safety's Power to Conduct Safety Inspections

The legislature added a provision allowing for the Division of Building Safety to conduct safety inspections, in addition to state-owned public buildings, to include buildings owned or maintained by other political subdivisions of the state, at the political subdivision's request and agreement to pay fees of inspection.[14]

## [C] Case Law

### [1] Statutory Attorney Fees Allowed in All Actions Involving Commercial Transactions, Even Where Party Is Only Seeking Injunctive Relief

In *Ascorp, Inc.*,[15] the Idaho Department of Transportation ("IDT") brought a declaratory relief action against a contractor regarding rights and obligations pertaining to a contract for highway construction services on a project in Twin Falls, Idaho. The contract called for an administrative claims review process before proceeding with binding arbitration. The contractor filed for arbitration, and IDT brought a declaratory relief action alleging that the administrative process had not been exhausted and arbitration was not proper. The contractor responded on a motion to dismiss that procedural arbitrability was a matter for the arbitrator. The court granted the motion and awarded the contractor attorneys'

---

[12] I.C. § 54-1016(5).
[13] I.C. § 54-2617.
[14] I.C. § 67-2312(4).
[15] Idaho Transp. Dep't v. Ascorp, Inc., 159 Idaho 138 (2015).

fees pursuant to statute allowing for attorneys' fees to the prevailing party in all commercial transactions.[16] IDT appealed the award of fees, claiming that injunctive relief is not an action to recover or collect on a debt arising from a commercial transaction.

The Idaho Supreme Court ruled that the award of attorneys' fees per statute is applicable in any commercial transaction, regardless of whether action involves injunctive relief or seeks monetary recovery.

### [2] Breach of Contract Claim Is Separate from Mechanic's Lien Foreclosure Claim, Giving Rise to Statutory Attorney Fees Arising from Commercial Transaction

In *Sims*,[17] the contractor timely filed a mechanic's lien and subsequent action for lien foreclosure, breach of contract, and quantum meruit claims against owner. Contractor then added the lenders who had an interest in the property as defendants on the same causes of action after the six (6) month statute of limitations for filing the lien. Lenders successfully had all causes of action dismissed, and were awarded statutory attorneys' fees for a commercial transaction for the breach of contract and quantum meruit claims.[18] Contractor appealed the fee award.

The Idaho Supreme Court acknowledged that actions arising out of lien foreclosures are not commercial transactions, but held that the breach of contract and *quantum meruit* claims are evaluated separately and thus arose out of a claimed commercial transaction, meriting a statutory attorneys' fee award.

### [3] Trustee Must Be Named for Purposes of Mechanic's Lien (Later Overruled by Statute)

In *ACI Northwest, Inc.*,[19] the Idaho Supreme Court re-affirmed its prior ruling in *Parkwest Homes, LLC v. Barnson* that per statute,[20] a mechanic's lien must include a trustee where a property is encumbered by a deed of trust, or the mechanic's lien is lost for purposes of the subsequent holder of legal title. The Idaho Supreme Court stated that any change to the statutory rule must come from the legislature. Subsequent to the Court's ruling, the legislature amended Idaho Code § 45-510 to specifically exclude the trustees or deeds of trusts from being named in mechanic's liens.

---

[16] I.C. § 12-120(3).
[17] Sims v. Jacobson, 157 Idaho 980 (2015).
[18] I.C. § 12-120(3).
[19] Sims v. ACI Northwest, Inc., 157 Idaho 906 (2015).
[20] I.C. § 45-510.

#### [4] Engineer Only Responsible for Duties Within Contract or Those Voluntarily Assumed; Engineer's Voluntary Assumption of Certain Discreet Duties Does Not Give Rise to Liability for All Related Duties

In *BRN Development*,[21] a bank brought a foreclosure action against a developer and a civil engineering/land use planning services provider for a failed golf course development. Developer cross-claimed against the engineer, alleging negligence. Developer spent over $7 million on unnecessary infrastructure to preserve a zone change for a planned unit development ("PUD"), which it claimed the engineer erroneously advised was necessary in order to preserve PUD rights prior to suspending the project. Developer relied upon "special relationship" exception to economic loss rule as basis for negligence claim. The district court determined the claim was not a matter of professional malpractice, as land use planning did not require application of engineering principles. The district court ruled on summary judgment that there was no special relationship between the engineer and the developer giving rise to an exception to the economic loss rule. The district court further determined at trial that there was no proof of an agreement to provide land use planning or that the engineer actually advised it was necessary to perform the work to preserve the PUD, thus not breaching any duty of care to developer.

The Idaho Supreme Court ruled that developer had failed to establish the engineer breached its duty of care. The court held that while the engineer had voluntarily assumed some land use planning activities, there was no evidence that it had assumed by contract responsibility for all land use planning, as such, the engineer was only responsible for the activities it actually undertook. Because the developer could not show a breach of duty, the court did not address whether the special relationship exception to the economic loss rule applied.

#### [5] Granting of Conditional Use Permit Overturned Where Commission Failed to Fully Vet Impact on Adjacent Property Owners

In *917 Lusk, LLC*,[22] an adjacent commercial property owner sought judicial review of the city council's granting a conditional use permit ("CUP") for the development of an apartment complex. The adjacent property owner argued that the property, intending to have 622 total bedrooms (intended to be leased individually to college students) and 280 parking space would place an undue burden on transportation and adversely affect neighboring properties. The Commission

[21] American Bank v. BRN Dev., Inc., 159 Idaho 201 (2015).
[22] 917 Lusk,LLC v. City of Boise, 158 Idaho 12 (2015).

granted the permit for the apartment complex, which was upheld by the City Council and affirmed by the district court.

On Appeal, the Idaho Supreme Court reversed the decision approving the CUP. The Court noted from the record that the Commission erroneously concluded that parking issues were not before the commission, and that the Commission had no power to enforce standards beyond those in the Code. The court noted that Commission could enforce conditions to more restrictive than those provided by ordinance.[23] As such, the Court determined that the Commission's lack of deliberation and failure to attach conditions amounted to a failure to properly consider whether the proposal would adversely affect other property in the vicinity.[24] Further, the Court ruled that the adjacent property owner had established a potential prejudice of its substantial rights,[25] because the failure to address parking would devalue the adjacent property, and cause the adjacent property owner extra expense related to parking at its own building.

### [6]  Statutory Prohibition of Union "Job Targeting" Deemed Preempted by National Labor Relations Act

The Ninth Circuit issued two opinions regarding the Trades Councils' challenges to the Open Access to Work Act ("OAA") and Fairness in Contracting Act ("FCA"). The Trades Councils argued that the OAA and FCA interfered with the Federal National Labor Relations Act ("NLRA"), and were thus preempted. The purpose of the statutes is to prohibit "job targeting," a/k/a "market recovery," programs developed by construction unions, which would use dues to subsidize union contractor's bids, allowing the union contractors to be more competitive with non-union contractor bids. The Trades Councils had been granted summary judgment by the district court enjoining the enforcement of both acts.

In the first opinion,[26] the Ninth Circuit held that the FCA was preempted by the NLRA.[27] The Court noted that the National Labor Relations Board has repeatedly held that job targeting programs are protected under the NLRA.[28] The state argued that the law could not be enjoined because there were select circumstances when the FCA would not be preempted by the NLRA, specifically citing

---

[23] I.C. § 67-6512(d)(7).

[24] BCC § 11-06-04.13.D.

[25] Hawkins v. Bonneville Cnty. Bd. of Comm'rs, 151 Idaho 228 (2011).

[26] Idaho Bldg. & Constr. Trades Council, AFL-CIO v. Inland Pac. Chapter of Associated Builders & Contractors, Inc., 801 F.3d 950, 956 (9th Cir. 2015).

[27] San Diego Bldg. Trades Council, Millmen's Union, Local 2020 v. Garmon, 359 U.S. 236 (1959).

[28] J.A. Croson Co., 359 N.L.R.B. No. 2, 2012 WL 5246914, at *5 (2012); Int'l Bhd. of Elec. Workers, Local 48, 332 N.L.R.B. 1492 (2000), *modified,* 333 N.L.R.B. No. 122, *enforced,* 345 F.3d 1049 (9th Cir.2003); Assoc'd Builders & Contractors, *Inc.,* 331 N.L.R.B. 132, 137 (2000), *modified as to remedy,* 333 N.L.R.B. 955 (2001); Manno Elec., Inc., 321 N.L.R.B. 278, 298 (1996).

case law holding on Federal contracts subject to the prevailing wage requirements of the Davis-Bacon Act, job targeting is prohibited.[29] The Court rejected
the state's argument, holding that any enforcement of the FCA as consistent with
the Davis-Bacon Act would necessarily be preempted by Davis-Bacon itself, as
it was not for the state to enforce penalties for violation of federal law. Further,
the Court noted that the NLRB decisions regarding job targeting and Davis-
Bacon established that the actions were arguably protected by the NLRA. Thus,
the Court concluded that there was no circumstance where the FCA would be
valid and the entirety of the FCA was preempted by the NLRA.

In the second opinion,[30] the Ninth Circuit dismissed the OAA claim based
on the fact that the Trade Councils had never sought a Project Labor Agreement
("PLA") with a state or local government entity, nor that they intended to do so
in the future. As such, the Trade Councils lacked standing to seek to enjoin
enforcement of the OAA.

## § 9.03  MONTANA

### [A]  Introduction

Recent statutory changes and case law may impact the construction industry
in Montana.

### [B]  Recent Statutory Developments

#### [1]  Procurement Laws for Montana Conservation Districts

Senate Bill 0088, which became law on March 30, 2015,[31] set forth requirements for the public procurement of services, materials, supplies, and construction contracts by Montana conservation districts. Under this statute, conservation
districts are authorized to enter into construction contracts utilizing competitive
bidding procedures that provide for award to the lowest responsible bidder.

#### [2]  Hiring Preferences for Veterans

Senate Bill 0196, which became law on March 30, 2015,[32] permits private
sector employers to adopt employment policies adopting hiring preferences for

---

[29] 40 U.S.C. § 3142(a)-(b).

[30] Idaho Bldg. & Constr. Trades Council, AFL-CIO v. Inland Pac. Chapter of Associated Builders & Contractors, Inc., 616 Fed. Appx. 319 (9th Cir. 2015).

[31] Mont. Code, tit. 76, ch. 15.

[32] Id., tit. 39, ch. 29.

veterans. For the purposes of this statute, "private sector employer" means any employer that is not a public employer.[33]

## [C]  Case Law

### [1]  Contract's Indemnity Clause Did Not Require "Negligence" or "Wrongful Conduct" by Subcontractor

In *A.M. Welles, Inc.,*[34] the Supreme Court of Montana considered the terms of an indemnification clause between a general contractor and its subcontractor. In 2000, the State of Montana contracted with Welles for a highway paving project near the town of Ennis. Welles subcontracted parts of the project, including the application of an oil primer and blotter. When a storm struck, the oil primer emulsified and splashed onto passing vehicles, causing significant damage. After Welles reimbursed the State of Montana for the damages, pursuant to its contract, it sought indemnification from its subcontractor.

At issue in this case was the Supreme Court's interpretation of the indemnity clause in the agreement between Welles and its subcontractor. In that agreement, the subcontractor agreed to indemnify Welles for losses "on account of *any* act or omission" caused by the subcontractor.[35] Accordingly, the Supreme Court of Montana rejected the subcontractor's argument that, in order to recover under the indemnification clause, Welles was required to demonstrate that the damage was caused by the subcontractor's "negligence" or "wrongful conduct."

### [2]  Montana Occupational Safety and Health Act Does Not Apply to Independent Contractors

In *McDonald,*[36] the Supreme Court of Montana considered an independent contractor's claim for damages against a general contractor and subcontractor pursuant to the Montana Occupational Safety and Health Act ("MOSHA"). The independent contractor, McDonald, suffered severe injuries while attempting to lift a 30-foot × 12-foot wall that collapsed. Upon settling his Workers' Compensation claim, McDonald sought additional damages pursuant to MOSHA.

The Supreme Court reviewed the language of MOSHA, which requires an employer to "furnish a place of employment that is safe for each of the employer's employees."[37] Although MOSHA does not expressly define the term "employee," the statute refers to the state's Workers' Compensation Act, codified

---

[33] *Id.*

[34] A.M. Welles, Inc. v. Montana Materials, Inc., 378 Mont. 173 (2015).

[35] *Id.* at 177 (emphasis in original).

[36] McDonald v. Ponderosa Enters., Inc., 379 Mont. 379 (2015).

[37] *McDonald,* 379 Mont. at 383 (quoting MONT. CODE ANN. § 50-71-201).

in Title 39, Chapter 71 of the Montana Code. Importantly, the Workers' Compensation Act expressly excludes independent contractors from the definition of "employee," defining the term "employee" as, "each person in this state, including a contractor *other than an independent contractor* who is in the service of an employer. . . ."[38] The Supreme Court concluded, therefore, that McDonald could not qualify for damages under MOSHA because he was an independent contractor.

In this case, McDonald argued further that he was a "loaned servant" to the general contractor, thus qualifying him for damages under MOSHA. Under the "loaned servant" doctrine, an employer may temporarily borrow or exercise control over another employee.[39] The Supreme Court rejected McDonald's argument, however, concluding that because McDonald was an independent contractor, there was "no employer to loan him."[40]

## § 9.04   NEBRASKA

### [A]   Introduction

The following is a summary of recent legislative changes and case law developments concerning the construction industry in the state of Nebraska.

### [B]   Recent Statutory Developments

#### [1]   Nebraska Department of Roads Contracts May Solicit Bids from Three Potential Bidders That Need Not Be Pre-Qualified

Legislative Bill (LB) 312, effective August 31, 2015, modified the public bidding requirements used by Nebraska Department of Roads (DOR) when seeking bids for projects that have an estimated cost of $100,000 or less. Additionally, LB 312 authorizes the DOR to allow federal agencies to let contracts for construction, repair and maintenance on state highways and bridges.

Prior to the adoption of LB 312, Nebraska Revised Statute § 39-1348 required the DOR to advertise for sealed bids to the public any contract for the "construction, reconstruction, improvement, maintenance or repair of roads, bridges, or their appurtenances," regardless of the amount of award.[41] Nebraska Revised Statute § 39.1349 also provided that the DOR was required to award such contracts to the "lowest responsible" *and* pre-qualified bidder.[42]

---

[38] *Id.* (emphasis in original).
[39] *Id.* at 385 (citing Devaney v. Lawler Corp., 101 Mont. 579, 56 P.2d 746 (1936)).
[40] *Id.*
[41] NEB. REV. STAT. § 39-1348(1).
[42] NEB. REV. STAT. § 39-1349(1).

LB 312 effectively broadens the DOR's authority in soliciting and awarding bids in three ways. First, for projects with an estimated cost of $100,000 or less, the DOR need no longer publish and solicit bids from the public, and may request bids from three potential bidders.[43] Second, for any project with an estimated cost of $100,000 or less, the DOR may grant an exemption from all prequalification requirements.[44] Finally, LB 312 authorizes the DOR to permit federal agencies to administer contracts for the construction or repair of state highways and bridges and to perform any other related services such as engineering, environmental clearance, and design.[45]

## [C]  Case Law

### [1]  Contract Language Providing That a Document Is Affixed "For General Reference Purposes" Is Not Sufficient to Incorporate the Terms of Such Document into the Contract

In *Facilities Cost Management*,[46] the Supreme Court of Nebraska considered whether a customized American Institute of Architects ("AIA") agreement between a school district and an architect was "ambiguous" with respect to the parties' intention that the architect's response to a request for proposal was incorporated into the parties' contract.[47] In this case, a school district entered into an agreement with an architect wherein the architect would provide architectural, representative, and management services in connection with the construction and renovation of three schools within the district. The parties utilized the 1987 version of the standard AIA contract, but customized some sections of the contract, including a section regarding the architect's response to the district's request for proposals (RFP). The parties amended this section to read as follows:

> The Architect's Response to the District's Request for Proposal is attached to this Agreement for general reference purposes including overviews of projects and services. [The District's] approvals following execution of this Agreement and related to the scope of work on the individual projects and corresponding portions of Project Budgets during the various Phases shall incorporate applicable adjustments through the projects [sic] development.

---

[43] Neb. Rev. Stat. § 39-1348(2).

[44] Neb. Rev. Stat. § 39-1351(2).

[45] Neb. Rev. Stat. § 39-1349(4).

[46] Facilities Cost Mgmt. Grp., LLC v. Otoe Cnty. Sch. Dist. 66-0111, 868 N.W.2d 67, 291 Neb. 642 (2015).

[47] The Court also considered and reversed the lower courts on the issue of whether the term "scope of work" was ambiguous, finding that the term was ambiguous such that parol evidence was admissible to interpret the provision.

With respect to rates on the project, the architect's response RFP stated that the firm utilizes "lump sum fees" and confirmed that the architect was proposing a guaranteed maximum price for the project. Other provisions of the parties' contract, however, provided that there would be "no fixed limit of Construction Costs," and that the project would be billed on a time and materials basis. Following execution of the contract, the architect proceeded with its work on the projects. The district made payments to the architect for several years until it learned that the projects were almost $2 million over budget, and stopped making payments on the basis that the billings exceeded the architect's guaranteed maximum price. The architect later sued for breach of contract arguing that the contract did not provide for a guaranteed maximum price, but rather the contract and the parties' course of dealing supported the conclusion that the parties' intended the contract be paid on a time and materials basis.

At the district court level, the district argued that the architect's response to its RFP was incorporated by reference and thereby the parties intended the contract to be a lump sum contract. The architect countered that its RFP response was *not* incorporated into the parties' contract and, as evidenced by the other language in the contract, the parties never agreed on a guaranteed maximum price. In essence, the Nebraska Supreme Court explained, the parties disagreed over whether the phrase "for general reference purposes" was sufficient to incorporate the response to the RFP into the parties' contract.

Ultimately, the Nebraska Supreme Court agreed with the district court's conclusion that "while the words 'for general reference purposes' are possibly ambiguous, they do not equate to incorporating [the architect's responses] into the terms of the contract." The court went on to explain that the phrase "for general reference purposes" contrasts too significantly with the recognized iterations on "deemed incorporated" to effectively incorporate a document by reference into a contract. The fact that the reference language was not sufficient and in light of the other, conflicting provisions, the court determined the response to the RFP was *not* incorporated into the parties' contract and therefore the parties did not agree on a guaranteed maximum price.

### [2] A Project May Be Deemed "Substantially Complete" for the Purposes of the Statute of Limitations Notwithstanding the Parties' Failure to Follow Contract Completion Requirements

In *Village of Doniphan*,[48] a municipal corporation brought a breach of contract action against a sewer system contractor, alleging the contractor failed to comply with the specifications for the design and construction of a sewer system

---

[48] Village of Doniphan v. Starostka Grp. Unlimited, Inc., 855 N.W.2d 598, 22 Neb. App. 464 (2014).

for a new residential development. At the district court level, the parties agreed that Nebraska's four-year statute of limitations for construction defects applied to the dispute and that the period commenced to run from the date of substantial completion of the contractor's work.[49] The parties disputed the issue of the date of substantial completion. The case proceeded to a jury trial on this issue, thereby determining whether the municipality's claims were barred by the statute of limitations. The jury returned a verdict in favor of the contractor, finding its work was substantially complete in December 2005, and thus the municipality's February 2010 complaint was barred by the four-year statute of limitations. The district court denied the municipality's subsequent motion for judgment notwithstanding the verdict, and the municipality appealed that decision to the court of appeals.

At the district court and appeal levels, the parties' primary disagreement was whether subsequent testing of the sewer system effectively extended the substantial completion date from December 2005 to May 2006. The municipality argued that the contractor's work was not substantially complete until May 2006 on the basis there was subsequent testing to be performed *and* that the project engineer had not issued a certificate of substantial completion as required by the parties' contract until that time. The contractor argued that the work was substantially complete in December 2005 on the basis that by that date, the municipality approved and made final payment to the contractor at that time (less a nominal amount for punch list work), that the sewer system was capable of being put to effective use, at least one home was already using the system by that date, and the remaining testing was not considered "primary" contract work. The contractor also argued that although the contract provided a process that could have been used for determining the substantial completion date, neither of the parties initiated that process, the municipality never issued a certificate of substantial completion, and thus the court should not use the procedures as the determining factor as to when its work was substantially complete.

In deciding whether there was "substantial and competent evidence" to support the jury's verdict, the court of appeals found the fact that the parties' contract provided for a process by which the substantial completion date would be determined was not dispositive. Rather, the court found the jury was properly permitted to consider other factors in rendering its verdict, including whether the additional sewer testing was primary or secondary contract work, whether the contractor had received final payment for its work, and whether the system was capable of being put to use. Having found that the contractor presented sufficient evidence relating to these factors, the court of appeals affirmed the jury's verdict and the district court's denial of the municipality's motion.

---

[49] *See* Neb. Rev. Stat. § 25-223.

[3] **Statute of Limitations for Construction Defects Runs from Date of Substantial Completion of the Project and Is Not Necessarily Extended by Warranties**

In *Adams*,[50] the Nebraska Supreme Court revisited the issue of when the four-year statute of limitations for actions arising out of defective construction is effectively "triggered." In that case, homeowners entered into an agreement with a contractor for construction of a new home. The home was substantially complete and a final inspection occurred on September 19, 2007. The following day, the contractor issued the homeowners a one-year limited warranty for material defects in the workmanship or materials. Six months later, the homeowners began noticing defects in the home, including cracks in the walls and a leaking roof. The contractor attempted to make repairs pursuant to the one-year warranty but was unable to resolve all defects, and the homeowners filed on September 22, 2011.

At the district court level, the contractor moved for summary judgment asserting the action was barred by the four-year statute of limitations set forth in Nebraska Revised Statute § 25-223, which provides in part that any action to recover damages based on construction defects "shall be commenced within four years after any alleged act or omission constituting such a breach of warranty or deficiency." The statute also provides a two-year "extension" of the statute of limitation if the defect is not discovered within the initial four-year period or within one year preceding the expiration of the four-year period. While the parties agreed the statute of limitation applied to their dispute, they disagreed as to the triggering event. The contractor argued that the "act or omission" giving rise to the homeowners' claims was improper compacting of soil which occurred in 2003, making homeowners' September 22, 2011 complaint untimely. In contrast, the homeowners argued that the triggering event was the expiration of the one-year warranty on September 20, 2008, making their September 22, 2011 complaint timely. The district court granted summary judgment in favor of the contractor, agreeing that the four-year limitations period began to run in 2003 when the soil was improperly compacted. The Court of Appeals reversed the district court's decision, agreeing with the homeowners that the statute of limitations began to run in 2008 at the expiration of the warranty.

The Nebraska Supreme Court disagreed with both lower courts' rationales, finding that where the basis of a claim is improper workmanship resulting in defective construction, the § 25-223 statute of limitations runs from the date of substantial completion of the project, and *not* the date of any specific act, which resulted in the defect. Accordingly, the court reasoned, the latest date the four-year limitation period was triggered was September 19, 2007, the date of substantial completion of the home. Agreeing with the district court's conclusion that the homeowners' claims were barred, the court held because the lawsuit was not filed

---

[50] Adams v. Manchester Park, LLC, ___ N.W.2d ___, 291 Neb. 978 (2015).

until September 22, 2011—i.e., three days past the four-year mark—the home-owners' claims were untimely and barred under the statute of limitations. The court also addressed at length its rejection of the homeowners' (and the Court of Appeals') rationale that the one-year warranty somehow extended the limitation period. The homeowners never claimed that the contractor failed to make repairs when requested to do so pursuant to the express warranty and, as such, the home-owners' claims did not arise from breach of the warranty. Rather, as the court explained, the "act or omission which served as the basis for all of the homeown-ers' claims was the defective construction itself."

## § 9.05 NORTH DAKOTA

### [A] Introduction

Recent statutory changes and case law may impact the construction industry in North Dakota.

### [B] Recent Statutory Developments

There are no statutory developments for 2015 impacting the construction industry.

### [C] Case Law

#### [1] Option Contract Valid, Contractor Required to Donate Private Toll Bridge to Cities After Expiration of 25-Year Contract

In *City of Moorhead v. Bridge Co.*,[51] the Company appealed from a district court judgment ordering it to donate a toll bridge to the cities of Fargo and Moor-head.

In May 1986, the cities and the Company agreed to the construction and operation of a private toll bridge over the Red River between Fargo and Moor-head. The Company would own and operate the bridge and pay all costs for its design, construction, maintenance, and repair. If after 25 years the Company's debts had been fully paid, "the Company shall donate the Bridge to the Cities free and clear from any liens, and the Cities shall accept the Bridge for public use to be operated by the Cities as they may determine." The agreement also had a clause suspending the Company's obligations for acts of God. The bridge started operations on June 1, 1988, and during those 25 years was closed 249 days because of flooding. In 2013, Moorhead brought this declaratory judgment action

---

[51] 867 N.W.2d 339 (N.D. 2015).

against the Company and Fargo to require the Company to turn the bridge over to the cities. The Company argued Fargo had already approved a five-year extension of the agreement and Moorhead had waived the early termination option. Following a trial, the district court ruled the agreement was extended 249 days to February 5, 2014, and because there was no qualifying debt existing as of that date, the Company was required to donate the bridge to the cities.

Among the issues on appeal, the Company argued the district court failed to recognize the agreement was automatically extended to allow it to operate the toll bridge for an additional five years. The Court concluded that the district court was correct and affirmed. With regard to the Contractor's argument that the toll bridge agreement had been extended because the cities failed to exercise their option to pay the outstanding indebtedness on June 1, 2013, the Court disagreed, finding that even if the agreement had created a franchise from the cities for the construction and operation of a toll bridge (as contractor argued), a franchise is a contract subject to the general rules of contract interpretation. Under those rules, the Court determined that requiring the cities to exercise their option before the 25-year term the Company was given to perform its obligations expired was an illogical and unreasonable interpretation of the agreement.

## § 9.06  OREGON

### [A]  Introduction

Recent statutory changes and case law may impact the construction industry in Oregon.

### [B]  Recent Statutory Developments

#### [1]  A Company Cannot Contract Around the Prevailing Wage

The Oregon Legislature passed SB 963 to protect the prevailing wage of employees. Pursuant to SB 963, no contractor, subcontractor, or agent of a contractor or subcontractor can enter into an agreement under the terms of which the employee receives less than the prevailing wage or fail to pay the prevailing rate of wage.

#### [2]  Construction Flagging Licenses Are Required

The Oregon Legislature passed SB 596 requiring a person employing, contracting with or leasing services of construction flaggers to obtain a construction flagging contractor license.

[C]   Case Law

[1]   Quasi-Contract Theory of Quantum Meruit Is a Valid Claim
      Against a Surety in a Little Miller Act Action

In *State v. Ross Bros. & Co., Inc.*,[52] the state awarded a contractor a contract to renovate a freeway bridge. The contractor subcontracted out the traffic control portion of the work. The project took two years longer to complete than contemplated in the contract. The subcontractor properly filed a "Little Miller Act" claim against the surety for additional costs for traffic control, in addition to filing a claim for breach of contract and quantum meruit against the contractor. However, the subcontractor failed to properly plead a quantum meruit claim against the surety. The trial court subsequently found for the subcontractor against the contractor in quantum meruit, but did not find against the surety specifically.

On appeal, the Court of Appeals determined that the subcontractor's failure to properly plead the quantum meruit claim against the surety did not prevent the subcontractor from recovering from the surety on that claim because to hold otherwise would deprive the Little Miller Act of its meaning. Whether a claimant prevails on a contract theory, or a quasi-contract theory, should not prevent the claimant from recovering against the surety.

[2]   Failure to Provide the Statutory Lien Notice Was Fatal to an
      Engineer's Claim

In *Multi/Tech Engineering Services, Inc.*,[53] an owner hired an engineer to design a commercial building. The owner failed to pay the last bill from the engineer, causing the engineer to lien on property. Unfortunately, the engineer did not follow the notice provisions required by ORS 87.021(1). While, ORS 87.021(1) includes an exception to providing the required notice for someone who provides "commercial improvements" as the site, the Court of Appeals determined that the contractor's contacts with the site (digging holes, taking measurements, field exploration work, and taking a soil sample) were incidental contacts that did not trigger the exception pursuant to *Teeny v. Haertl Constructors, Inc.*[54]

## § 9.07   SOUTH DAKOTA

[A]   Introduction

Recent statutory changes and case law may impact the construction industry in South Dakota.

---

[52] 268 Or. App. 438, 342 P.3d 1026 (2015).
[53] Multi/Tech Eng'g Servs., Inc. v. Innovative Design & Const., LLC, 274 Or. App. 389 (2015).
[54] 314 Or. 688, 842 P.2d 788 (1992).

## [B] Recent Statutory Developments

House Bill No. 1029, signed by the Governor on March 11, 2015, amended Section 5-14-32 to change update the requirements regarding high performance building design and construction standards for newly constructed or renovated state-owned buildings. The Bill updates the high performance green building definition to move to 2013 baselines. Additionally, the definition of "New construction" and "Renovation" under the chapter is updated to increase the cost requirement from five hundred thousand dollars to one million dollars and increase the square footage requirement from five thousand square feet to ten thousand square feet.

House Bill No. 1029 also amended 5-14-33 to require any state building project as defined in § 5-14-32 to meet or exceed a high-performance green building standard that was in effect when the project was registered with the rating system.

House Bill No. 1085, signed by the Governor on February 27, 2015, amended Section 5-21-1.1 to change the bid amount limit, which establishes when waiver of performance security is allowed, to be consistent with the limits established pursuant to § 5-18A-14 for public improvement. Section 5.18A-14 sets the limits at $50,000 for a contract for any public improvement and $25,000 for a contract for the purchase of supplies or services, other than professional services.

House Bill No. 1139, signed by the Governor on March 12, 2015, amended Chapter 5-18B. Specifically, a new section (§ 5-18B-46) was included to provide for the option to waive the 30-day award requirement in § 5-18A-5(7) and § 5-18B-9 for invitations to bid airport improvements.

Senate Bill 126, signed by the Governor on March 13, 2015, revised certain publication date citation for reference to the International Building Code and international Property Maintenance Code from the 2012 edition to the 2015 edition.

## [C] Case Law

### [1] Actual Notice of the Specific Facts Constituting a Cause of Action Is Not Required to Start the Statute of Limitations

In *Gades v. Meyer Modernizing Co., Inc.*,[55] the Supreme Court held that the property owners had sufficient notice to trigger the statute of limitations period upon the discovery of water intrusion and not upon the eventual discovery that defects in the siding were causeing of the water intrusion. Consequently, their suit was time barred under SDCL 15-2-13(1) which provides for a six-year statute of limitations.

---

[55] 865 N.W.2d 155 (S.D. 2015).

In this case, the property owners filed a Complaint against the Contractor in April 2010. The Contractor filed a motion for summary judgment, arguing that the six-year statute of limitations had expired. There was no question, the property owners had actual notice of water infiltration by at least 2002 and would therefore have been required to bring suit by 2008. However, the question was whether the actual notice of water infiltration was sufficient, as a matter of law, to put the property owners on notice of its cause of action. The lower court found that it did and the Supreme Court affirmed, determining that actual knowledge of the water intrusion started the statute of limitations for any claim with sufficient relationship to the water intrusion issue. The Supreme Court distinguished its holding in an eerily similar case, *East Side Lutheran Church of Sioux Falls v. NEXT, Inc.*,[56] stating that structural design error and construction error claims are potentially distinguishable from the water intrusion claims and issues of material fact existed about whether actual notice of water intrusion put an owner on notice of those structural design error and construction error claims. In the present case, and in contrast to the plaintiff in East Side Lutheran Church, the property owner here only asserted claims that relate to the water intrusion and actual knowledge of water intrusion started the six-year statute of limitations period and barred the property owner's suit.

### [2] Settlement and Execution of a "Full and Final Release of All Claims" with SDDOT Released Claim Against Other Potential Defendants

In *Aggregate Construction, Inc. v. Aaron Swan & Associates, Inc.*,[57] the Supreme Court held that a full and final release of all claims "arising from any act, occurrence or omission up to the present time" on a specific project extended to a third-party soil testing company that provided services for the project. Therefore, the construction company's suit against the soil testing company was barred by the South Dakota Department of Transportation ("SDDOT") release.

In this case, the soil testing company provided pre-construction services for the contractor to test the soil for sodium-sulfate content for its eventual use on SDDOT projects. Issues arose with the testing of both the soil testing company and SDDOT which caused the soil to mistakenly violate the SDDOT requirements. The contractor was required to perform additional work to correct the soil, which was later determined to have been unnecessary. SDDOT and the contractor entered into a settlement and release barring all "causes of action . . . arising from any act, occurrence or omission" by SDDOT "and all others directly or indirectly liable . . . up to the present time[.]" However, the release also stated that it barred "incidents that occurred during construction season 2008-2009." The

---

[56] 852 N.W.2d 434 (S.D. 2014).
[57] 871 N.W.2d 508 (S.D. 2015).

contractor argued because the soil testing company performed its work prior to the 2008-2009 construction season, its claim against them was not barred by the release with SDDOT. The Supreme Court found the 2008-2009 restriction was a part of the broader language releasing all claims associated with the SDDOT projects, finding that a specific reading of the 2008-2009 restriction would render the "any act, occurrence or omission up to the present time" language meaningless. Therefore, contractor's claims were barred under the terms of the SDDOT release.

### [3] Contractor Breached Agreement to Deliver Turn-Key Hotel and Owner's Actions Did Not Violate Its Duty to Mitigate Damages

In *Casper Lodging, LLC v. Akers*,[58] the Supreme Court affirmed a jury verdict that, among other things, the contractor breached its agreement to deliver a turn-key hotel to the owner and that the owner had not violated its duty to mitigate damages

The contractor agreed to deliver to the owner a turn-key hotel "built pursuant to the plans and specifications," to "complete the construction of the improvements in compliance with all city, county, state, and federal government requirements." The owner and the contractor later changed the agreement by addendum, but the addendum reiterated that the contractor "shall have a continuing obligation to construct and finish the [i]mprovements in accordance with all government requirements and the standards and specification of the [larger hotel chain]." The Supreme Court held the language of the agreement and addendum was sufficient to require a specific quality of construction, which the contractor did not provide.

The contractor also argued in a motion for directed verdict that the owner failed to mitigate damages because issues with the hotel were observable in 2004, but not addressed or repaired until 2009-2010. At the trial court, both parties presented evidence relating to the reasonableness of the efforts to mitigate the issues. The jury found that the owner's actions to address the issues as they arose were reasonable under the circumstances and sufficient to deny the contractors motion for a directed verdict.

### [4] Construction Management At-Risk Services Are Subject to Contractor's Excise Tax

In *Puetz Corp. v. South Dakota Department of Revenue*,[59] the Supreme Court held the nature of the construction management at-risk services provided subjected the company to contractor's excise tax.

---

[58] 871 N.W.2d 477 (S.D. 2015).
[59] 871 N.W.2d 632 (S.D. 2015).

The South Dakota Department of Revenue issued a certificate of assessment against a company asserting that the company's services were subject to contractor's excise tax under SDCL 10-46A-1. The company challenged the assessment on the grounds that it was not a prime contractor engaged in a realty improvement contract when it provided construction management at-risk services. The company claimed that its only services on the public projects were to streamline the construction process and protect government entities from cost overruns, construction delays, and unsatisfactory work. Additionally, the company argued that the payments made to subcontractors were simply being passed through and all contractor's excise taxes were paid by the owner. Finally, the company argued that because it was an architect on the project it could not legally also be a contractor on the project under SDCL 5-18B-15. The Supreme Court determined that the company performed construction manager services which fit the definition of a general contractor for excise tax purposes even though it did not perform any actual construction work on the project. Additionally, the Supreme Court rejected the company's argument that it cannot be liable for contractor's excise tax because it was also the architect, finding instead that the restrictions on architects acting as contractors under SDCL 5-18B-15 did not impact its classification of the services rendered by the company for excise tax purposes.

## § 9.08  WASHINGTON

### [A]  Introduction

The following provides recent legislative changes and case law developments concerning the construction industry in the State of Washington.

### [B]  Recent Statutory Developments

#### [1]  Scope of Apprentice Hours Counted as "Labor Hours" for Minimum Apprenticeship Requirements Is Expanded

House Bill No. 1595, effective July 24, 2015, revises the definition of "labor hours" in the apprenticeship utilization statutes to include hours that workers are employed "upon" a project, instead of limiting the hours to those that workers are employed "on the site" of the project. The broader employed "upon" language aligns with Washington's prevailing wage requirements, and extends beyond work performed directly on the site of the project.

### [2]  Public Body No Longer Allowed to Refuse Contractor's Retainage Bond for Good Cause

Substitute House Bill 1575, effective July 24, 2015, eliminates the option given to public bodies in RCW 60.28.011 to reject a contractor's retainage bond "for good cause." RCW 60.28.011 is revised to eliminate the good cause exception, and now provides that if the contractor submits a retainage bond in a form acceptable to the public body and from an authorized surety insurer (the public body can require a minimum A.M. Best financial strength rating so long as such minimum does not exceed A-), the public body must accept the bond.

### [3]  Counties Prevented from Contractually Restricting Venue to the Superior Court of the County in Public Works Contracts

House Bill No. 1601, effective July 24, 2015, makes clauses in county public works contracts that require suit be brought in the superior court of that county for actions arising under the contract void and unenforceable. The bill prevents counties from contracting around the effects of RCW 36.01.050, which allows suits against a county to be brought in either that county's superior court, or the superior court of either of the two nearest judicial districts.

### [4]  Expanded Use of Recycled Construction Aggregates and Recycled Concrete

Engrossed Substitute House Bill 1695, effective January 1, 2016, requires the Washington State Department of Transportation's ("WSDOT") to use at least 25% recycled aggregate and concrete materials, cumulatively, across all of its projects (if available and cost effective). Additionally, any local government with 100,000 or more residents must give a bid preference to bidders proposing to use the highest percentage of "construction aggregate and recycled concrete materials." However, the bill establishes that the preference will be given only if it is at "no additional cost." Thus, it appears this preference would only operate if two bids are submitted at the same price.

The bill also requires local governments with less than 100,000 residents to review their capacities for utilizing recycled construction content, establish strategies for meeting that capacity, and implement those strategies. Local governments with less than 100,000 residents, or any local government constructing a transportation or public works project, must also adopt the WSDOT standards for the use of recycled materials as contained in its Standard Specifications for Road, Bridge, and Municipal Construction.

### [5] Property Owners Not Required to Be Registered Contractors to Sell Improved Property Less Than One Year After Substantial Completion if Registered Contractor Performed the Work

Substitute House Bill 1749, effective July 24, 2015, modifies the Contractor Registration Act to allow a property owner who is not a registered contractor to sell improved property in the pursuit of an independent business without having occupied or used the improved property for more than one year. To do so, the owner must have contracted with a registered general contractor to perform the work, and could not have superintended any part of the work. The Contractor Registration Act previously defined owners selling improved property in the pursuit of a business as contractors (thereby requiring them to register) if the owner offered the property for sale without occupying or using the improvements for more than one year following substantial completion, regardless of whether the owner actually performed or superintended any of the work. The legislative history suggest this modification was intended to allow "house flippers" to not be required to register as a contractor and obtain the requisite bond if they use a registered contractor to perform the work. However, the modification also applies with equal effect to commercial property owners.

### [6] WSDOT Authorized to Utilize Design-Build Delivery on Projects over $2 Million

The Legislation passed Second Engrossed Substitute Senate Bill 5997, effective July 6, 2015, which revised RCW 47.20.780 and expanded the WSDOT authorization to contract for projects using the design-build delivery method. WSDOT was previously authorized to utilize design-build on projects greater than $10 million, and on five "pilot projects" between $2 million and $10 million. The bill eliminates the pilot project section, and reduces the project cost threshold to $2 million.

To be eligible for a design-build contract, the project must still involve highly specialized construction activities, present an opportunity for innovation and efficiencies between the designer and builder, or allow for a significant savings in project delivery time if the design-build delivery method is utilized. The bill also tasks the Joint Transportation Committee with reviewing the WSDOT's implementation of design-build contracts, and directs WSDOT to develop a construction program business plan to incorporate the findings of the Committee.

## [C]  Case Law

### [1]  Statute of Limitations for Construction Defect Suit Runs from Termination of Services if Any Nexus Exists Between Post-Substantial Completion Work and the Cause of Action

In *Dania, Inc. v. Skanska USA Building Inc.*,[60] a warehouse owner sued its contractor and roofing subcontractor for leaks in the warehouse roof. The contractor moved for summary judgment, arguing that the suit, filed in April 2012, was time-barred because the warehouse was substantially complete in January, 2006. The contractor argued that the suit was barred by the statute of repose, RCW 4.16.310, which bars any action for construction defects that fail to accrue within six years of substantial completion or termination of services. The owner argued that the final work on the roofing did not occur until June, 2006, when the roofing subcontractor installed the final layer of roofing—the mineral cap sheet.

In its motion for summary judgment, the contractor introduced deposition testimony, establishing that the roof was watertight without the mineral cap sheet, which was installed only to provide UV protection. The trial court granted summary judgment for the contractor after determining that the owner failed to produce any evidence that the mineral cap sheet caused the leaks.

On appeal, Division II of the Court of Appeals clarified that the statute of repose in RCW 4.16.310 only requires a claim to accrue within six years; once the claim accrues the applicable statute of limitations determines whether a suit is timely. RCW 4.1.326(1)(g), however, provides an affirmative defense to cut off contractor liability on any claim for breach of a written construction contract that is not filed within six years of substantial completion or the termination of services, whichever is later. For the six-year period to run from the termination of services date instead of substantial completion, the court held that a "nexus" between the post-substantial completion services and the cause of action was required (work unrelated to the cause of action would not extend the time to file suit).

During the appeal, the owner again failed to introduce any evidence that this nexus existed. However, the court appeared to adopt the owner's argument that the nexus is established if there is "some kind of connection between the final services and the cause of action"—that the roof leaked and the roofing subcontractor had performed work on it (even though the only offered evidence established that the work was unconnected to the waterproof integrity of the roof). Therefore, the court held that because the roofing subcontractor performed work on the roof in June 2006, this was the termination of services date, and the suit was timely filed in April 2012.

---

[60] 185 Wn. App. 359, 340 P.3d 984 (2014).

## [2] Award of Attorneys' Fees for Actions Brought Under the Underground Utility Damage Prevent Act—Chapter 19.122 RCW—Is Mandatory

In *Hayfield v. Ruffier*,[61] a landowner using a backhoe damaged an underground drainage pipe that extended onto his property from his neighbor's basement. The neighbor's basement flooded as a result of the damage, and the neighbor brought suit for damages under chapter 19.122 RCW—the "Underground Utility Damage Prevention Act." The neighbor prevailed at trial, but the trial court judge refused to grant the neighbor attorneys' fees because the judge determined that even though the landowner's actions "technically violated the terms of RCW 19.122.040, notice to the [neighbor] of the excavation and/or calls to '811' would not have prevented the damage that occurred."

Division II of the Court of Appeals reversed the trial court's denial of attorney fees. It held that RCW 19.122.40(4), which provides that: "In any action brought under this section, the prevailing party is entitled to reasonable attorneys' fees," provides no discretion to the trial court and requires the court to award attorneys' fees to the prevailing party. The appellate court also granted the neighbor's request for attorneys' fees on appeal because of the statutory fee provision.

## [3] Termination for Convenience Clause in Private Construction Subcontract Is Valid When Supported by Consideration, and Is Not Limited by Implied Duty of Good Faith and Fair Dealing

In *SAK & Associates v. Ferguson Construction, Inc.*,[62] a contractor terminated its subcontractor's contract pursuant to a subcontract provision allowing the contractor to terminate the subcontract "for its own convenience and require Subcontractor to immediately stop work." Division I of the Court of Appeals recognized that, while prevalent in government contracts, there is very little authority addressing this type of termination for convenience clause in private contracts.

The subcontractor argued that the termination for convenience clause was an unenforceable illusory promise because it allowed the contractor to terminate the contract at its discretion—it lacked consideration. However, the court held that because the contractor terminated the subcontract after the subcontractor had performed some of the subcontract work (24%), and had been paid a proportionate amount of the subcontract value, this partial performance provided adequate consideration, validating the clause. The court also alluded to the fact that if the contractor had terminated the subcontractor when either no work or a nominal amount of work had been performed, there may have been a different outcome.

---

[61] 187 Wn. App. 914, 351 P.3d 231 (2015).
[62] 189 Wn. App. 405, 357 P.3d 671 (2015).

The subcontractor also argued that the contractor terminated its subcontract only to increase its own profits on the job, and therefore did not terminate the subcontract in good faith. However, the court held that not even the covenants of good faith and fair dealing trump express contract terms.

### [4]   Lien Releases Do Not Extinguish the Contractor's Ability to Re-file a New Lien for Unpaid Work That Was Covered in the Original Lien

In *Shelcon Construction Group, LLC v. Haymond*,[63] an earthwork contractor provided site development services to a landowner, who failed to pay the contractor. The contractor recorded a mechanic's lien on the property. The Landowner then sought to obtain additional financing on the project, and the lender informed him that it would not lend to him unless the Contractor's lien was released. The Developer then asked the Contractor to release the lien, and promised to pay the Contractor with the loan proceeds. The Contractor released the lien; the lien release contained no language addressing whether the Contractor had in fact been paid or whether the release was limited or conditional. The Bank took no further steps to verify the contractor had been paid, and proceeded to lend money to the Landowner.

The Contractor continued to work on the project, and eventually recorded a second lien, which included work that was initially included in the first lien. When the Contractor sought to foreclose the lien, the Bank argued that the contractor was not entitled to include work in the second lien that it had previously included in the first lien, which it had released.

On appeal, Division II of the Court of Appeals held that a lien release does not prevent the lien claimant from later recording a second lien when the underlying work is not fully paid. In so holding, the court determined that the statutory scheme providing for mechanic's liens is silent as to the effect of a lien release. Under RCW 60.04.071, the mechanic's lien statute merely requires that a lien be released upon request when full payment is made.

The Bank also argued that the contractor was equitably estopped from including the earlier released amounts in the second lien. The court held that this argument failed, however, because the Bank's reliance on the lien release as a statement that the contractor had been paid for the previous work was unreasonable. The court based this holding on the fact that the Bank could have inquired the contractor as to whether it had actually been paid for the work. Additionally, the court did not believe that it was plausible for the Bank to believe that the landowner, who was seeking additional funds for his project, would suddenly being able to pay off the Contractor in full.

---

[63] 187 Wn. App. 878, 351 P.3d 895 (2015).

## § 9.09  WYOMING

### [A]  Introduction

Recent case law may impact the construction industry in Wyoming.

### [B]  Recent Statutory Developments

No significant legislation impacting the construction industry was enacted into law during the 2015 portion of the Wyoming Legislature's 2014-2015 session.

### [C]  Case Law

#### [1]  County Commissioner's Utilization of Known and Unannounced Criteria of Residence in Awarding Contract Opened for Competitive Bid Constituted an Illegal Exercise of Discretion

In *Western Wyoming Construction Co. Inc. v. Board of County Commissioners of County of Sublette*,[64] Sublette County issued an invitation to bid on a highway reconstruction project. Western Wyoming Construction Co. ("WWC"), a company based out of Lander, Wyoming, submitted the low bid of $4,232,854.50. R.S. Bennett, a firm based out of Sublette County, submitted the next lowest bid of $4,241,074.10, approximately $8,000 higher than the WWC bid. The Commissioners awarded the contract to R.S. Bennett despite the fact R.S. Bennett was not the low bidder.

WWC filed a complaint in district court alleging that by not awarding the contract to WWC, the Commissioners violated Wyoming law and that the Commissioners were obligated to enter into the contract with WWC. In a series of rulings and without trial, the district court found in favor of the Commissioners, concluding that the Commissioners were not statutorily required to accept the lowest bid and they made a legitimate executive decision to award the contract to a company other than WWC. WWC appealed and the Wyoming Supreme Court subsequently remanded the case to the district court for a presentation of evidence and determination of whether the award was appropriate.

At trial, the evidence presented illustrated that the Commissioners' decision to award the contract to R.S. Bennett was motivated by a known and undisclosed local preference. According to the Chairman of the Board of County Commissioners, the Commissioners awarded the contract on the basis that R.S. Bennett was a local contractor, and because the difference in the bids was negligible, a contract award to R.S. Bennett was in the best interest of the local economy. The

---

[64] 351 P.3d. 250 (Wyo. 2015).

Chairman further testified that the Board chose not to notify bidders of the potential for local preference because the Board would likely not receive any bids from companies residing outside the county if it did so. He explained that this would limit the information the Board could use to evaluate and compare its options.

The district court again ruled in favor of the Commissioners, finding that it did not have the authority to compel the Commissioners to contract with any other party. Further, it found that WWC failed to prove the Commissioners' award to R.S. Bennett was an illegal exercise of discretion. WWC timely appealed the district court's judgment.

On appeal, the Supreme Court held that the utilization of known and unannounced criteria of residence in awarding a public contract opened for competitive bid constituted an illegal exercise of discretion. In so holding, the Court first reaffirmed its previous decision in *State v. Weisz & Sons*[65] that it is the responsibility of a public agency to accept a bid which, in its judgment, would provide the best project for the money, even if—but also placed limits on the considerable discretion the *Weisz & Sons* decision granted to a public agency. The Court reasoned that while the Commissioners were not statutorily obligated to put the Project up for competitive bidding, by making such an election, the Commissioners became bound by the principles of competitive bidding requiring that each bidder be placed upon the same footing and in fair competition with each other. The Court found that in making their decision to award the Project to R.S. Bennett, the Commissioners not only utilized an undisclosed preference for Sublette County contractors, but also intentionally concealed the preference in order to obtain an advantage in evaluating the bids. The Court held that if the Commissioners wished to use a local preference in deciding whom to award the contract, they must disclose the nature of the preference to bidders.

---

[65] 713 P.2d 176 (Wyo. 1986).

# CHAPTER 10

# MIDWEST REGION

Illinois, Indiana, Iowa, Michigan, Minnesota,
Missouri, Ohio, Wisconsin

David P. Muth, Kevin M. Long, Charles E. Harper Jr.,
Daniel B. Lewin, Eric Van Schyndle, Michael A. Rogers,
Larissa E. Koshatka, Lucy R. Dollens

## § 10.01   ILLINOIS

### [A]   Introduction

On the legislative front, Illinois has now joined the majority of states that include a statutory bonding provision to enable persons interested in real property to post a bond in lieu of the property against which a mechanics lien has been asserted. The Illinois courts have clarified under what factual scenarios the statutes of limitations and repose for construction-related claims apply, reinforced the scope of lienable work under the Mechanics Lien Act to include pre-construction activities even if the construction project is not ultimately completed, and limited the ability of residential developers to enforce waivers of the warranty of habitability against subsequent purchasers.

### [B]   Recent Statutory Developments—Illinois Joins the Majority of States to Include a Bonding Provision in Its Mechanics Lien Act

The Illinois Mechanics Lien Act has been amended to add a new provision permitting an owner, developer, lender, other lien claimant or another contractor to bond off (also known in some states as "bonding over") a lien claim.[1] Essentially any interested party in the real estate field may now post a surety bond in place of the real property. Under the new section to the Lien Act, the substitute bond must satisfy certain prerequisites, such as being issued by a financially strong surety company (as detailed by the new section) which submits to the court's jurisdiction and is authorized to issue surety bonds by the Department of Insurance. The amount of the bond must be 175% of the lien claim.

If no action is pending, an interested party may file a petition for the bonding off of a lien, or if an action to enforce the lien is already pending, the interested party, within five months after the filing of the complaint, may petition to substitute the bond for the subject property. The new section prescribes the necessary contents of the petition, including a verification; the name and address of the petitioner's attorney, the lien claimant, the owner and any condo association, if applicable; a description of the property; a copy of the lien to be bonded off; a copy of the proposed bond; the surety's certificate of authority from the Department of Insurance; and the petitioner's undertaking that it will replace the bond in the event the surety later becomes ineligible.

The new section also requires notice to all persons named in the petition and prescribes the precise language that must be contained in the notice. As with all aspects of the Mechanics Lien Act, Illinois courts will likely strictly construe the

---

[1] 770 ILCS 60/38.1

statute and thus will require bond petitioners to follow all requirements of the petition and notice to the letter in order to successfully bond off a lien claim.

Under the new section, the principal and the surety shall be jointly and severally liable to the lien claimant for any amount it would have been entitled to recover under the Act had no bond been furnished, subject only to the limitation of the face amount of the bond as to the surety.

The new section also includes a fee-shifting provision, providing attorneys' fees to the prevailing party. Unlike many statutes that leave the definition of prevailing party to the courts, the Illinois legislature included a specific definition here. The prevailing party is the lien claimant if it recovers at least 75% of its lien claim or the principal if the lien claimant recovers 25% or less. Any recovery in between 25% and 75% results in no prevailing party.

### [C]  Recent Case Law Developments

#### [1]  Case Law Developments Relating to Statutes of Limitations and Repose

##### [a]  *Ten-Year Limitation for Breach of Written Contract, Not the Four-Year Construction Limitation, Applies to Express Indemnity Claims Even in The Construction Context, and Claim Accrual Provisions in Construction Contracts Are Permissible*

In *15th Place Condominium Ass'n*,[2] the plaintiff condo association discovered latent defects after the developer had turned over the building to the association, which then sued for breach of the warranty of habitability, breach of fiduciary duty and negligence. Three years later, the developer sued its general contractor and architect through a third-party complaint in the association's action for breach of contract and implied indemnity for the association's claims.

The developer's contracts with its general contractor and architect both contained claim accrual provisions, by which the parties agreed that the accrual of any action (the trigger for the running of any applicable statute of limitations) was to be the date of substantial completion of the project as defined in the contract. The appellate court affirmed the trial court's holding that the accrual provision applied to the developer's claims for breach of contract and for implied indemnity, and held that the statutes of limitations began to run both claims as of the date of substantial completion as defined by the contracts, despite the developer's argument that the accrual clauses should be declared void as against public policy. The court found that these sophisticated parties were free to, and indeed did, contract the accrual date for all claims.

---

[2] 15th Place Condo. Ass'n v. South Campus Dev. Team, LLC, 2014 IL App (1st) 122292.

The court then addressed the question of which statute of limitations would apply to each of the developer's claims. With respect to the implied indemnity claim, the court relied on the two-year indemnification statute, which requires the action to be brought two years from the date the party knew or reasonably should have known of the act or omission giving rise to the indemnity.[3] But in this case, because of the *contractual* accrual provision, the court held that the statute expired two years from substantial completion and held the claim time-barred. The contracts also stated that all breach of contract actions would be governed by the four-year statute for construction-related cases,[4] and so the court held that the breach of contract claims expired four years after substantial completion.

However, this did not result in total defeat for the developer, which had also brought a claim under the express indemnity provisions of the contract with its general contractor. The appellate court, following the Illinois Supreme Court's holding in *Travelers Casualty & Surety v. Bowman*,[5] held that a written agreement to indemnify is subject to the ten-year statute of limitations for breach of written contracts and that the act of agreeing to indemnify is not a construction activity protected by the four-year construction statute. Since ten years had not passed since either substantial completion or the timely filing of the association's claims against the developer, the court held that the developer's express indemnity claim was timely.

### [b]   Statute of Limitations for Construction Cases Applies to Claims in the Construction Context for Breach of Fiduciary Duty and Ordinance Violations

In *Henderson Square Condominium Ass'n v. LAB Townhomes, LLC*,[6] a condominium association sued the developer and contractor for breach of the implied warranty of habitability, negligence, fraud, violation of the Chicago Municipal Code, and breach of fiduciary duty. The suit was filed 15 years after construction of the building was completed and four years after the discovery of the defects. The trial court dismissed the plaintiff's claims, finding that they were barred by the ten-year statute of repose for construction cases.[7]

The appellate court reversed, finding that not all the claims were necessarily time-barred given plaintiff's allegations of fraudulent concealment. The appellate court held that the ten-year repose period could not apply because defendants fraudulently concealed the latent defects in the building, and thus section

---

[3] 735 ILCS 5/13-204(b).

[4] 735 ILCS 5/13-214(a).

[5] 229 Ill. 2d 461 (2008).

[6] 2014 IL App (1st) 130764.

[7] 735 ILCS 5/13-214.

13-214(e)[8] precluded the application of the ten-year repose period to plaintiff's claim. Accordingly, the appellate court reversed and remanded the case to the trial court for determination of whether there was a fraudulent concealment under the facts of this case.

The appellate court also held that with respect to the code violation and breach of fiduciary duty claims, the four-year statute of limitations for real estate construction claims applied, rather than the statute of limitations applicable to unwritten contracts. The court held that the four-year construction statute of limitations would apply because in the case at bar, the material misrepresentations giving rise to the claims were related to the construction project. Because the court had determined that the fraud exception potentially applied based on the pleadings, the court did not make a determination as to when the limitations period began to run.

### [c]  Four-Year Construction Statute of Limitations Applies to Insurer Subrogation Action Against HVAC Contractor for Negligent Installation of Ventilation System

In *Fireman's Fund Insurance Co. v. Rockford Heating & Air Conditioning, Inc.*,[9] the appellate court held that the installation of a ventilation system constituted "improvement to real property," and thus the four-year statute of limitations for construction cases[10] applied to the plaintiff-insurer's subrogation action for negligence against the HVAC contractor who installed a ventilation system that caused a fire at the property. As a result, the insurer's action, filed more than four years after the fire, was time-barred. The insurer argued that the five-year statute of limitations for actions to recover damages to real property should apply.[11] The appellate court noted that whether an action constitutes an improvement to real property is a question of law, the resolution of which is grounded in fact.[12]

The court found that even though the ventilation system was not a permanent part of the building, its temporary nature was not dispositive of the issue of whether its construction and installation constituted an improvement as required by the statute of limitations for construction cases. Because in this case the entire building was new construction, where the nature and scope of the work unquestionably enhanced the value of the real estate, the HVAC contractor's work at the property should be considered part of the overall construction project, because the ventilation system in question was necessary in order to complete the construction of the building. Consequently, the court held as a matter of law that the

---

[8] 735 ILCS 5/13-214(e).
[9] 214 IL App (2d) 130566.
[10] 735 ILCS 5/13-214.
[11] 735 ILCS 5/13-205.
[12] Citing St. Louis v. Rockwell Graphic Sys., Inc., 153 Ill. 2d 1, 3 (1992).

installation of the ventilation system was subject to the four-year statute of limitations applicable in construction cases. One dissenting judge found otherwise, concluding that the defendant's installation of the temporary ventilation system did not constitute "the construction of an improvement to real property" as that term is used in the statute of limitations applicable to construction cases.

### [d]   The Construction Statute of Repose Does Not Resurrect Lapsed Claims Against Dissolved Corporations

In *Michigan Indiana Condominium Ass'n v. Michigan Place, LLC*,[13] a condominium association brought an action against a general contractor for latent defects in a condominium complex built nine years earlier. The general contractor then asserted third-party claims against two corporate subcontractors that had been dissolved more than five years before. The court held in the first instance that the general contractor could not bring claims against the dissolved corporate entities, because more than five years had passed since their dissolution. On appeal, plaintiff argued that the ten-year statute of repose for construction cases should apply in lieu of the five-year limitation provided by the Illinois Business Corporations Act. The appellate court rejected this argument, and held that despite the ten-year repose period provided by 735 ILCS 5/13-214(b), the five-year limitation on actions against dissolved corporations still controlled regardless of whether a longer statute of repose might also apply. The court said, "We fail to see how the repose period, or any limitations period, trumps or nullifies the statutory five-year period after which a corporation ceases to exist."

### [e]   Five-Year Statute of Limitations Applies to Fraudulent Misrepresentations Made in a Construction Context

In *Gillespie Community Municipal District No. 7 v. White & Co.*,[14] the Illinois Supreme Court held that the five-year statute of limitations applicable to claims for damage to property applied to the fraudulent misrepresentations made by an architect regarding the subsidence of a coal mine beneath plaintiff's school building, rather than the four-year statute of limitations for construction cases.[15] The court found that subsection (e) of the statute for construction cases regarding fraudulent misrepresentations[16] applied, and therefore the fraudulent misrepresentations were subject only to the five-year statute of limitations for injury to property.[17]

---

[13] 2014 IL App (1st) 123764.
[14] 2014 IL 115330.
[15] 735 ILCS 5/13-214.
[16] 735 ILCS 5/13-214(e).
[17] 735 ILCS 5/13-205.

## [2] Case Law Developments Relating to Mechanics Liens

### [a] *Illinois Supreme Court Reinforces That Pre-Construction Engineering Services Is Lienable Work Even If the Project Is Not Completed*

In *Christopher B. Burke Engineering, Ltd. v. Heritage Bank of Central Illinois*,[18] the Illinois Supreme Court reversed the appellate and trial courts to hold that the survey services provided by plaintiff in drafting and recording a plat of subdivision was lienable work under the Illinois Mechanics Lien Act.[19] Plaintiff performed the surveying for the entity that eventually purchased the property, but who was not the owner at the time the work was started. However, the plaintiff continued to perform work relating to the property after its client had purchased the property. The trial and appellate courts had held that because the construction project never materialized, plaintiff's survey work did not constitute an improvement to the property as defined by section 1 of the Illinois Mechanics Lien Act.[20] The Illinois Supreme Court reversed, holding that the plaintiff's engineering services constituted an improvement to the property even though there was no physical improvement that resulted from plaintiff's work.

The court held that the plaintiff's work, which included creating a plat of subdivision, surveying the property and planning out roads and sewers, was done in an effort to develop a neighborhood on the property and thus was done for the purpose of improvement and that there was no convincing evidence that the engineering services were done for any other purpose. The court noted "if a physical improvement is required in order for an engineer to secure a lien for their work, then these professionals would be subject to the whims of the parties with whom they contract, who may decide to complete the project or not. Such an outcome is contrary to the protective purpose of the Act."[21] The court also noted that the requirement of a physical improvement or calculable increase in property value is contrary to long-standing Illinois case law.

The court found that there was sufficient evidence in the record to establish that the owner before plaintiff's client was aware of and knowingly consented to plaintiff's work on the property. However, the court also found that there was insufficient evidence to determine whether or not the previous owner knew the details of the contract between the subsequent property purchaser and the plaintiff, and therefore remanded the case to the circuit court to determine whether the first owner knowingly permitted the subsequent purchaser to enter into the contract with plaintiff. If the first owner did authorize the work, the court concluded that the work could not be said to have commenced under a contract with the

---

[18] 2015 IL 118955.

[19] 770 ILCS 60/1 *et seq.*

[20] 770 ILCS 60/1.

[21] Citing Contract Dev. Corp. v. Beck, 255 Ill. App. 3d 660, 669 (1994).

owner until the plaintiff's client purchased the property. Ultimately, the question of when the lienable work began was important, because it was determinative of the priority position of the plaintiff versus the defendant mortgage lienholder.

### [b]   The Illinois Appellate Court Reinforces Lienability of Pre-Construction Services

In the unpublished opinion of *Young v. CES, Inc.,*[22] the appellate court reached a similar conclusion, holding that the engineering firm lien claimant's preparatory survey and construction drawing services were lienable, even though the properties were not developed. Similar to the Illinois Supreme Court's holding in *Christopher B. Burke*, the court in *CES* noted that "the proper focus in determining the validity of a mechanics lien is whether the work actually enhanced the value of the land or benefitted the land-owner."[23] The court also noted that "any person who does improvement work on the land under a contract with the owner can assert a mechanics lien."[24] The court held that even though the engineering firm never submitted final plats for permitting, at a minimum a sanitary main was completed on part of the project based on the preliminary plans. Additionally, testimony at trial was presented that the plans added value to the property. The court concluded that even though the engineering firm's work was preliminary development work, and even though the real estate market crisis ultimately contributed to the development's failure, the engineering firm's work constituted improvements to the subject properties.

### [c]   Releases of Mechanics Liens Are Final and Binding on Lien Claimants

In *Oxford 127 Huron Hotel Venture, LLC v. CMC Organization, LLC,*[25] the court held that a mechanics lien claimant who had released its liens as part of a settlement agreement with the owner was prohibited from re-recording those liens after the owner failed to honor the terms of the settlement agreement. The court held that under section 35 of the Illinois Mechanics Lien Act,[26] the unconditional lien releases recorded by the claimant operated as a complete release of the lien claims as asserted. Even though the lien claimant never received the payment promised to it by the owner under the settlement agreement, the liens against the property had nonetheless been released and the court determined that the

---

[22] 2014 IL App (2d) 131090-U.

[23] *Id.* ¶ 131, citing Mostardi-Platt Assocs., Inc. v. Czerniejewski, 399 Ill. App. 3d 1205, 1211 (2010).

[24] *Id.* ¶ 131.

[25] 2014 IL App (1st) 130265.

[26] 770 ILCS 60/35.

re-recorded liens could not be enforced against the property. The court did note that the outcome might be different had this been a situation where the lien claimant never recorded its liens in the first place and instead had contractually agreed to waive its right to enforce any lien it might have, but had then received only part of the payment promised in exchange for the waiver. Here, however, because of the recording of unconditional lien waivers, the lien claimant was barred from any subsequent lien claim for the same work.

### [3]   Other Case Law Developments

#### [a]   *Homeowner Who Purchased Home from Seller Without Knowledge the Seller Waived Implied Warranties Was Not Bound by the Waiver*

In *Fattah v. Bim*,[27] the court held that a subsequent purchaser would not be bound by a prior waiver of the implied warranty of habitability, and that an "as-is" addendum to a real estate contract was not a knowing waiver of such warranty. In *Fattah*, the patio of plaintiff's single-family home collapsed four months after he moved in. Plaintiff bought the house "as-is" from its original purchaser, who had given the developer a waiver of the implied warranty of habitability when she purchased the home new three years earlier. Plaintiff filed suit against the developer, alleging a breach of the implied warranty of habitability. The trial court determined that the waiver of the implied warranty made by the prior owner was binding on plaintiff and dismissed the case. The appellate court reversed.

The appellate court relied on the existing Illinois Supreme Court precedent stating that the implied warranty of habitability protecting the original purchaser of the new home extends to subsequent purchasers.[28] The court noted the strong public policy reasons expressed by the Illinois Supreme Court in *Redarowicz* behind the implied warranty of habitability and the purpose of extending it to subsequent purchasers. The court also noted the long history that any waiver of the implied warranty of habitability must be knowing and voluntary. The appellate court held that the waiver made by the previous owner was not a knowing and voluntary waiver made by the subsequent purchaser, and therefore not binding on the plaintiff. Additionally, the court held that the "as-is" language in the rider of the contract between the plaintiff and the initial purchaser was not sufficient to constitute a waiver of the implied warranty of habitability. The court relied on other Illinois precedent holding that an as-is clause standing alone cannot be an effective waiver of an implied warranty of habitability.[29] For that reason, the court

---

[27] 2015 IL App (1st) 140171.

[28] Redarowicz v. Ohlendorf, 92 Ill. 2d 171 (1982).

[29] 2015 IL App (1st) 140171, ¶ 36, citing Schoeneweis v. Herrin, 110 Ill. App. 3d 800, 805-07 (1982).

found that the defendants had failed to meet their burden to establish that plaintiff had knowingly waived the implied warranty of habitability on the house. This case has been accepted for review by the Illinois Supreme Court.

### [b]   Home Inspector's Limitation of Liability Clause in Contract Upheld

In *Boshyan v. Private I. Home Inspections, Inc.,*[30] the court affirmed the dismissal of claims against a home inspector because the contract between the parties contained express limitations of the inspector's liability. Specifically, the contract limited the homeowner's remedy to the cost of the $500 inspection. In bold, capitalized font, the contract stated that the homeowners agreed that their sole damages to which they may be entitled are limited to the amount paid for the inspection services. The appellate court found that it was the intention of the parties to create a liquidated damages clause and limit the inspector's potential liability. The court also found that there was no ambiguity in the liquidated damages clause, and therefore held that the potential liability of the inspector was limited to the $500 paid for the inspection.

## § 10.02   INDIANA

### [A]   Introduction

The most significant Indiana statutory update in 2015 was the Indiana General Assembly's repeal of Indiana's Common Construction Wage Act in 2015 and the legislature's replacement of it with a law imposing a number of responsibilities on contractors.[31]

Indiana courts also addressed Indiana's mechanic's lien statute, decided a number of construction contract interpretation issues, and addressed the scope of discretionary functions under which Indiana Department of Transportation (INDOT) may validly claim immunity from liability.

### [B]   Recent Statutory Developments.

#### [1]   Indiana Repealed the Common Construction Wage Act and Imposed Other Requirements on Contractors for Public Works Projects

Through a bill codified as 2015 Indiana Legislative Services P.L. 213-2015 (West), the Indiana General Assembly repealed Indiana's Common Construction

---

[30] 2014 IL App (1st) 287715-U.
[31] IND. CODE § 5-16-13-(9-11) (2015).

Wage Act ("CCWA"), effective July 1, 2015. Indiana Code § 5-16-13-11 replaced the CCWA with a law mandating contractors comply with certain responsibilities. As a result of the repeal, unless federal or state law provides otherwise, a public agency may not establish, mandate or require a wage scale or schedule for public works contracts awarded after June 30, 2015.[32] However, contracts entered into *prior to July 1, 2015*, must remain in full compliance with the CCWA as if it was still in effect.[33]

For contracts entered into after June 30, 2015, on the other hand, the General Assembly mandates several requirements be met in the absence of the CCWA. General and prime contractors on public works projects must: (1) be directly responsible for contributing at least 15% of the total contract price, via work performed by the contractor's employees, materials supplied directly by the contractor, services supplied directly by the contractor's employees, or any combination thereof; (2) maintain general liability insurance; (3) submit the E-Verify case verification number for each employee; (4) not pay in cash; and (5) be in compliance with the Fair Labor Standards Act.[34] Contractors that employ ten or more employees must provide access to a training program applicable to the tasks to be performed, and contractors employing 50 or more journeymen must participate in an apprenticeship or training program.[35]

For public works projects awarded after June 30, 2016, the law also imposes upon contractors the duty to preserve its payroll and records for three years after completion of the project, and such records must remain open for inspection by the department of workforce development.[36]

## [C]   Recent Case Law Developments

### [1]   The Indiana Supreme Court Held, Under Indiana's Mechanic's Lien Statute, That Subcontractors Are Entitled to Recover Attorney Fees Against a General Contractor That Posts a Surety Bond to Eliminate A Lien

In *Goodrich Quality Theaters, Inc.*, the Indiana Supreme Court held that Indiana's mechanic's lien statute permits subcontractors to collect attorney fees from a general contractor who posts a surety bond to secure and release the mechanic's liens during the pendency of the litigation.[37] In *Goodrich*, construction of a movie theater was completed months behind schedule, and the general

---

[32] IND. CODE § 5-16-7.2-5 (2015).

[33] IND. CODE § 5-16-7.1-2 (2015).

[34] IND. CODE § 5-16-13-11 (2015).

[35] IND. CODE § 5-16-13-12 (2015).

[36] IND. CODE § 5-16-13-13 (2015).

[37] Goodrich Quality Theaters, Inc. v. Fostcorp Heating & Cooling, Inc., 39 N.E.3d 660 (Ind. 2015).

contractor did not pay three subcontractors due to disputes over the cause of the delay. The subcontractors timely recorded mechanic's liens, then sued the property owner and the general contractor to foreclose those liens, as permitted by Indiana Code § 32-28-3-1(a). In addition to the contractual payments due, the subcontractors sought attorney fees under Indiana Code § 32-28-3-14(a).

When the litigation was pending, the general contractor posted a surety bond requiring itself and its surety company to pay any judgment. The court approved the bond and released the mechanic's lien pursuant to Indiana Code § 32-28-3-11. Having a bond in place to ensure payment of any judgment, the property owner then paid the general contractor the total amount due. And litigation continued between the general contractor and the three subcontractor lienholders. After a long trial, the court awarded contractual damages and attorney fees to all three subcontractors. The general contractor appealed numerous issues, but the propriety of the attorney fee award was the only issue considered by the Indiana Supreme Court.

Attorney fees are typically recoverable in mechanic lien foreclosure cases, but the *Goodrich* disputed hinged on the exception in Indiana Code § 32-28-3-14(b), which provides that "a plaintiff may not recover attorney's fees as part of the judgment against a property owner in an action in which the contract consideration for the labor, material, or machinery has been paid by the property owner or party for whom the improvement has been constructed." The general contractor argued the subcontractors could not collect attorney fees because the property owner had paid the general contractor in full once it posted the bond, fulfilling the purpose of Indiana's lien statute—to prevent a property owner from enjoying the fruits of the labor without paying for it. The subcontractors countered that attorney fees awards are mandatory in lien foreclosure cases, and the above-cited exception applies only to subcontractors seeking to recover damages and fees from a "property owner" who has already paid—not to subcontractors seeking to recover against a general contractor and its surety.

The court agreed with the subcontractors, but based its decision primarily on the portion of the lien statute permitting a party to post a surety bond to obtain release of a lien during the pendency of the litigation. That statute provides, in relevant part, that the person filing the surety bond will pay any judgment "including costs and attorney's fees allowed by the court." The bond at issue in *Goodrich* contained similar language. The court thus held that this statutory and contractual language unambiguously obligated the general contractor—as principal on the bond—to pay any attorney fee award. The court noted it would be "an unfair and certainly unintended result if . . . a general contractor could post a surety bond and avoid paying the attorney's fees that it would otherwise have to pay if a subcontractor foreclosed on a lien, thereby leaving the subcontractor in a worse position than if it had foreclosed—especially when the subcontractor cannot object to the posting of a surety bond."

The court went on to note, however, that the subcontractors would have been entitled to recover attorney's fees even if the general contractor had not posted a bond. The court reasoned that the exception upon which the general contractor relied only prohibits attorney fee recoveries against a "property owner" who has already paid the contract consideration. Because the general contractor was not the "property owner," it was not immune from an attorney fee award. The take-away from this decision is that general contractors addressing mechanic's lien claims (and property owners who have not paid the contract balance) should expect to face the risk of an attorney fee award and should plan their defense and litigation strategy accordingly.

### [2] Under Indiana's Mechanic's Lien Statute, Parking Lots May Qualify as "Buildings" That Can Be Severed and Sold to Satisfy a Lien, Even If a Mortgagee Holds a Mortgage on the Building Itself

In *Wells Fargo Bank*, a contractor paved a parking lot, and Wells Fargo held a mortgage on the property.[38] Upon completion of the project, the property owner failed to pay the contractor, who recorded a mechanic's lien and filed a lawsuit to foreclose the lien. The contractor named the mortgagee as a defendant. The court held the contractor could assert priority over the mortgagee by removing and selling only the parking lot. Despite the impracticality of this remedy, the court held it was the only method to secure priority for the contractor.

In an effort to prevent this partition, the mortgagee argued the parking lot was not a "building" under the mechanic's lien statute and, as a result, its removal would be unauthorized because Indiana's mechanic's lien statute provides: "buildings may be sold to satisfy the lien."[39] The court disagreed and construed "buildings" to include parking lots that can be removed, whenever practical. Under this holding, it is unnecessary for a "building" to have walls and a roof, meaning "building"—as applied under the statute—may hinge on the removability of the improvements at issue.

### [3] INDOT Is Not Entitled to Immunity from Liability for Discretionary Functions When It Used Professional Judgment In Failing to Close a Median Crossover

In *Indiana Dept. of Transp.*, INDOT failed to temporarily close or block a median crossover as a safety measure during construction road work.[40] A road worker was struck by a car and killed, and the road worker's personal representative filed a wrongful death action against INDOT. In response, INDOT claimed

---

[38] Wells Fargo Bank, N.A. v. Rieth-Riley Constr. Co., Inc., 38 N.E.3d 666 (Ind. Ct. App. 2015).
[39] IND. CODE § 32-28-3-2(b).
[40] Indiana Dept. of Transp. v. Sadler, 33 N.E.3d 1187 (Ind. Ct. App. 2015).

immunity under the section of the Indiana Tort Claims Act (Indiana Code § 34-13-3-3(7)) that provides immunity to governmental entities from losses resulting from the performance of a discretionary function. INDOT argued it exercised its discretionary function when it: (1) conducted a risk-benefit analysis; and (2) deferred to engineers to weigh the safety of keeping the crossovers open. The court rejected both arguments, finding INDOT employees were exercising professional judgment—not creating policy decisions that receive immunity under Indiana's Tort Claims Act. The court held that the exercise of professional judgment does not receive immunity, whereas policy decisions do. The court deemed INDOT's decision here to have been the product of professional judgment and held that INDOT was not entitled to discretionary function immunity for failing to close the median crossover to protect citizens during a construction project.

### [4]  The Indiana Supreme Court Held That the American Institute of Architects' Standard Waiver of Subrogation Clause Includes All Property Unless Otherwise Agreed to Within the Contract

In *Board of Commissioners of County of Jefferson*, the contracting parties agreed to waive subrogation rights for damages, by incorporating an American Institute of Architects ("AIA") standard form into their contract for the repair of a courthouse.[41] The AIA contract waives subrogation rights for all "*damages caused by fire or other perils to the extent covered by property insurance.*"[42] After a fire destroyed the entire courthouse, Jefferson County recovered the entirety of its damages under its insurance policy. Jefferson County then filed a subrogation claim seeking to recover damages caused to the portion of the courthouse that was outside the scope of the contractor's work. The county argued the waiver of subrogation clause applies only to construction-related damages, so the county may subrogate for damages to non-work property. Conversely, the contractor argued that subrogation rights for *all damages* covered by the owner's insurance policy were waived.

In a matter of first impression, the Indiana Supreme Court ruled in favor of the contractor, holding under the standard form agreement of AIA, the waiver of subrogation rights extended to damages to non-work property. The court ruled so long as a property owner's damages are covered by an "*any property* insurance policy" used to insure construction-related damages, the waiver applies to all damages. Parties incorporating the AIA contract into construction agreements are free to restrict the scope of subrogation waivers, but the contract must expressly limit the waiver to work-related damages alone.

---

[41] Board of Comm'rs of Cnty. of Jefferson v. Teton Corp., 30 N.E.3d 711 (Ind. 2015).
[42] 30 N.E.3d at 715.

### [5] A Construction Manager Does Not Assume a Duty of Care When Its Contractual Obligations Consist of Correcting Safety Problems Through the Implementation of Safety Programs

In *Lee*, the defendant contracted with Ivy Tech to act as a construction manager for the building of a new facility.[43] The construction manager was responsible for providing "recommendations and information to the Owner regarding the allocation of responsibilities for safety programs among the Contractors," but the agreement created no relationship between the construction manager and any third party. The court held the contract language unambiguously stated that the construction manager was not responsible for other contractors' performance relating to the project. Rather, the construction manager was responsible for reviewing other contractors' safety programs and coordination of the programs.

The plaintiff—an independent contractor performing air tests to detect leaks in gas lines—was severely injured by an explosion. The court that the construction manager contractually disclaimed any responsibility for the safety of other contractors' employees. The construction manager was only responsible to Ivy Tech, and only owed a duty to act if it became aware of hazardous or unsafe practices. Consequently, the construction manager did not assume a duty of care to the independent contract employee to correct safety problems where the construction manager was only contractually obligated to fix unsafe conditions if, and when, it became aware of them.

### [6] Irrespective of a No Oral Modification Clause, Parties May Still Orally Modify a Contract if the Agreeing Party Consents to the Modification Then Witnesses and Approves the Implementation of the Modification

In *Ambrose,* a husband and wife contracted with a contractor to build an in-ground swimming pool.[44] The contract was silent as to the location of the pool. After the contractor demarcated the boundaries of the pool with metal stakes, the wife asked to move the pool to a different location, but wanted to first wait for the husband's approval. The contractor agreed. When the contractor returned the next day, the wife informed the contractor that her husband approved new location and the project should resume accordingly in the new location. The husband witnessed the construction project in its new location until its completion and never disapproved. After the project's completion, the husband began paying the contract balance but later became upset with the location and refused the balance due until the contractor reconstructed the pool. The contractor filed a mechanic's

---

[43] Lee v. GDH, LLC, 25 N.E.3d 761 (Ind. Ct. App. 2015).

[44] Ambrose v. Dalton Constr., Inc., No. 29A02-1407-CC-479, 2015 WL 5320346 (Ind. Ct. App. Sept. 14, 2015).

lien against the property and filed suit. The court held even though the contract had a "no oral modification" clause, such clauses may themselves be orally modified. On the facts presented, the court concluded the parties effectively orally modified the agreement when the wife requested the pool be moved to a new location then observed the pool being constructed in that location.

### [7] Despite the Applicability of the Economic Loss Doctrine to Damages on the Project Property, a Subcontractor May Still Be Liable for Claims That Plausibly Include "Other Property"

In *City of Whiting*, the city contracted with a general contractor to revitalize a waterfront area.[45] The general contractor sought design and construction services from a subcontractor. The subcontractor designed a retaining wall to provide shoreline protection for the area. The subcontractor's design relied on a specific elevation level determination that the subcontractor had received. Prior to construction, however, the general contractor notified the subcontractor that the elevation level was actually 11 feet lower than the level on which the subcontractor had relied. Despite this notice, the subcontractor moved forward with construction using its original elevation level determination. The retaining wall failed, causing significant delays in the waterfront project and imposing significant repair costs related to the project.

The city sued the subcontractor for negligence seeking "*subsequent damage to the City's property at the Project.*"[46] The subcontractor sought dismissal under the economic loss doctrine, which generally prohibits a party from recovering tort damages or proceeding on tort theories for contractual breaches. The court recognized the economic loss doctrine, but held the property damaged alleged in the complaint—"the City's property at the Project"—could plausibly include "other property" outside of the project to which the economic loss doctrine would not apply. Reading the language of the complaint broadly, the court declined—at the pleadings stage—to dismiss the city's negligence claim.

## § 10.03 IOWA

### [A] Introduction

Iowa recently revised its competitive bid process for public improvement contracts. Iowa also modified its immunity statute to protect municipalities from claims of negligent design or construction at public facilities for various recreational activities. Specifically, the revised legislation exempts cities from liability

---

[45] City of Whiting, Ind. v. Whitney, Bailey, Cox & Magnani, LLC, No. 2:14-CV-440-TLS-PRC, 2015 WL 6756857 (N.D. Ind. Nov. 5, 2015).

[46] *City of Whiting*, 2015 WL 6756857, at *8.

if the affected person knew or should have known of the risk created by the rec-reational activity.

The Iowa Appellate Court held that installation of defective product before notice to the material supplier is not a *per se* failure to give timely notice, but remanded the matter for a determination at what portion of the damages arose *after* the contractor knew or should have known of the defect. The Court also held that damages caused in a defective product must be foreseeable. Additionally, the Courts held that expert testimony was required to prove a purported "standard" negligence claim against a contractor for damages caused by the contractor's allegedly defective system. Finally, the Eighth Circuit affirmed a decision that granted summary judgment to an insurer under a contractor's claim to a subro-gated interest in policies issues after the building had been constructed.

## [B]   Recent Statutory Developments

### [1]   Changes to Iowa's Law Involving Competitive Bids for Public Improvement Contracts

Effective July 1, 2015, Iowa required that a government entity shall have an engineer, landscape architect, or architect prepare plans and specifications and calculate the estimated total cost of a proposed public improvement.

A government entity is also required to ensure that a sufficient number of paper copies, and if available, electronic and digital copies of the project's con-tract documents, including all drawings, plans, specifications and estimated total costs of the proposed public improvement are made available for distribution at no charge to prospective bidders, subcontractor bidders, suppliers and plan room services.

The statute also requires if a deposit is required as part of a paper contract documents distribution policy by the public owner, the deposit shall not exceed $250 per set. The deposit must be refunded upon return of the contract docu-ments within 14 days after award of the project. If the contract documents are not returned in a timely manner in a reusable condition, the deposit shall be forfeited. The governmental agency is also required to reimburse the landscape architect, architect, or professional engineer for the actual costs of preparation and distri-bution of plans and specifications.

### [2]   Changes to Municipal Exemptions to Liability

Also effective on July 1, 2015, the Iowa legislature modified the scope of liability municipalities are subject to under I.C.A. § 670.2 by amending I.C.A. § 670.4.

The amendments, at § 670.4(n) and (o), make clear that except for liability imposed by the express statute dealing with such claims, the municipality shall be immune from liability for the following:

(n)Any claim based upon or arising out of a claim of negligent design or specification, negligent adoption of design or specification, or negligent construction or reconstruction of a public facility designed for recreational activities that was constructed or reconstructed, reasonably and in good faith, in accordance with generally recognized engineering or safety standards or designed theories in existence at the time of the construction or reconstruction; and

(o)Any claim for injuries or damages based upon or arising out of an act or omission of an officer or employee of the municipality or the municipality's governing body and arising out of a recreational activity occurring on public property or the claimed injuries or damages resulted from the normal and expected risks inherent in the recreational activity and the person engaging in the recreational activity was voluntary on the public property where the injuries or damages occurred and knew or reasonably should have known that the recreational activity created a substantial risk of injuries or damages.

To date, there are no published decisions analyzing the extended immunity afforded by the above modifications to I.C.A. § 670.4. That said, care must be taken to make sure that there is no liability imposed from any other statutory provision expressing dealing with such claims.

## [C]  Recent Case Law Developments

### [1]  Iowa Appellate Court Upholds Contractor's Claim for Defective Product Even When Installed and That Consequential Damages Asserted by Contractor Against Product Supplier Were Not Speculative or Unreasonable

In *Trustees of the Iowa Labors District Council Health & Welfare Trust v. Ankeny Community School District*,[47] the Iowa Appellate Court ("Court") found that a subcontractor may be entitled to recover for defective concrete masonry units ("CMUs") even after installing the product, but remanded the matter to determine if notice had been reasonable. The Court also held that contractor's lost profits damages of approximately $1 million were neither speculative nor unreasonable.

In *Ankeny*, the school district undertook two simultaneous building projects, a high school and a middle school. The contractor won the mason bid for both projects. It contracted with a materials supplier to provide the CMUs it would

---

[47] 865 N.W.2d 270 (Iowa Ct. App. 2014).

need to complete the work. After beginning work, the contractor noticed some of the blocks were defective. First, some the blocks were pitted and chipped on their surfaces; a patent defect. Second, some of the blocks had a slight outward protrusion on their surfaces, a latent defect not noticeable until after the blocks had been installed.

The trial court noted the record was unclear as to when the contractor first noticed the defects in the CMU. Specifically, one witness testified they first noticed the problem in approximately January or February 2010. Another witness stated that the product supplier was on site within a few days of noticing the defects in April or May 2010. Nonetheless, the trial court found the contractor properly notified the product supplier, who came to the construction site to review the product and troubleshoot with the contractor.

Problems with the defective blocks required very costly corrective measures, which the contractor initially bore. During this remedial phase, the contractor continued to receive and install multiple deliveries of additional CMU's from the product supplier but stopped paying for the product.

The trial court found the record supported a finding that the schools' projects had been a pivotal one for the contractor. After trouble with the CMUs on the two school projects, the contractor fell into serious economic hardships and was unable to obtain bonding on its projects and struggled to win contracts. The contractor also provided evidence that it had been left out of calls for bids in its area.

Eventually, the product supplier and the contractor were co-defendants in an action filed as a result of the defects to the project which included, *inter alia*, the defective CMUs. The product supplier filed a cross-claim for payment against the contractor for deliveries of the CMU for which the contractor still refused to pay. The product supplier also filed a cross-claim for an open account against the contractor. The contractor filed cross-claims against the product supplier, alleging the CMUs violated an implied warranty of merchantability and an implied warranty of fitness for particular purpose.

The case went to a bench trial. The trial court held that the product supplier's relationship with the contractor was not an open account and denied any claim for payment under that theory. The trial court also entered judgment in favor of the contractor, finding that the product had violated the implied warranty of merchantability. The contractor received an award of approximately $785,000 in direct economic damages and just over $1 million in consequential lost profit damages.

The product supplier appealed. The Court held that, under the Uniform Commercial Code, a buyer must, within a reasonable time after he discovered or should have discovered any breach, notify the seller of the breach or be barred from any remedy. First, the products supplier asserted the contractor's claim was barred because it failed to plead in its cross-complaint that it provided notice of the defective CMUs to the products supplier. Second, the products supplier argued that in as far as the contractor did provide notice, it was not within a reasonable time after it discovered or should have discovered the defects.

The Court rejected the products supplier's procedural arguments. The Court noted that in 1976, the Iowa Rules of Civil Procedure were amended to substantially lower the burden on plaintiffs as to the technical requirements in pleading. The Court acknowledged that there was, based upon precedent, a potential gap in the notice pleading jurisprudence as to dealing with conditions precedent. However, the Court held it was not persuaded that a pre-amendment formalistic pleading requirement survived Iowa's adoption of its current notice pleading system, which merely required only a general statement of the claim. Accordingly, the Court held that the contractor's lack of pleading a condition precedent did not preclude recovery.

However, the Court found that the sufficiency and reasonableness of notice were fact questions. Nonetheless, the product supplier cited cases from other jurisdictions which explicitly or implicitly found notice untimely as a matter of law when construction materials were installed.

The Court rejected the product supplier's arguments for a *per se* violation. The Court instead held that the trial court's determination that notice was provided within a reasonable time was not supported by substantial evidence. Specifically, the Court found there was a fluctuating time frame as to when notice actually occurred. The Court held that the trial court failed to account for the testimony indicating the defective CMUs were continually installed after the defects were initially discovered or reasonably should have been discovered. Because of that imprecise evidence concerning the dates of discovery and notification, in addition to the continued installation of CMUs in spite of defects, the Court concluded it could not say the evidence was sufficient for a neutral, detached person to conclude notice was timely.

The Court therefore reversed the trial court's finding of timely notice and remanded for a determination of what portion of the damages arose from the installation of block the contractor knew or should have known was defective.

At trial, the contractor claimed three categories of consequential damages: damages arising from loss of goodwill, damages arising from loss of business reputation, and damages arising from loss of profits. The trial court held that the contractor could not recover on the first two categories because any calculation as to the economic value would be purely speculative. However, the trial court found that the contractor's loss of profits were measurable, foreseeable and proximately caused by the product supplier's breach.

The product supplier appealed, claiming that the lost profits were speculative and should have been rejected as were the first two categories of requested consequential damages. The Court disagreed. Specifically, the Court held that the trial court did not hold that the injury to the contractor's goodwill or business reputation itself was speculative; it simply held any dollar amount assigned to those injuries would be speculative. Conversely, the Court found the measure of lost profits was not guesswork—it was supported by trial testimony and calculations asserted by the parties. Those lost profits directly flowed from the immeasurable injuries to the contractor's goodwill and business representation. But it does not follow that the lost profits therefore are likewise speculative.

The Court also found that the lost profits were foreseeable. The Court agreed with the trial court that it was reasonably foreseeable at the time of contracting that a breach of warranty of merchantability would result in lost profits. The Court noted the record demonstrated that the school projects were of such a size and profile that the contractor's performance on those jobs could foreseeably have affected its future business prospects. The Court therefore held it was not only reasonably foreseeable at the time of contracting that the quality of work product and the product it received from its product suppliers could impact a contractor's future profits, but also that the evidence supported the finding that these types of profits ultimately lost were reasonably foreseeable to the parties at the time of contract.

Lastly, the product supplier appealed the trial court's denial of its claim as to an open account between itself and the contractor. The product supplier established at trial that the contractor continued to accept delivery of product, did not pay for that product, and the amount owed for the product was accepted. The trial court denied the claim because it held those transactions fell out of the technical definition of an open account. The Court found that the controversy arose from the parties competing interpretations of the Iowa Supreme Court decision in *Rogers's Backhoe Service, Inc. v. Nichols*.[48] In *Roger's Backhoe*, the Court held:

> [i]n a general sense, [an account] encompasses any claim or demand based on a transaction creating a debtor/creditor relationship . . . [W]hen the evidence fails to establish the elements of account stated, the creditor may nevertheless recover by proving a contractual obligation for individual terms in the account and the fair and reasonable value of the amounts claimed.

The trial court accepted the contractor's reliance upon a 1931 case in which Iowa's Supreme Court held that a series of independent express contracts for services to be performed for an agreed compensation did not constitute an open continuous current account.[49]

The Court found that case to be distinguishable. It found that the *Sammon* case dealt with the *quantum meruit* claim which the individual contracts had been paid in full as they became due. Thus, the *Sammon* court statement about open accounts related only to the *quantum meruit* claim before it, as the language of the decision as a whole makes clear.

The Court agreed with the products supplier that the trial court's interpretation was improperly constrained by its reading of *Sammon*. The Court found

---

[48] 681 N.W.2d 647, 650 (Iowa 2004).
[49] Sammon v. Roach, 211 Iowa 1104, 235 N.W. 78, 79 (1931).

that the transactions spanned multiple overlapping, unbroken contractual obligations creating an account that was never settled. The products supplier proved the contractor had not paid for the CMUs it accepted, and should have prevailed on this claim. The Court therefore reversed the trial court's findings as against the product supplier for its open account, and awarded it approximately $155,000.

The *Ankeny* decision makes clear that one must provide credible evidence in terms of the timing and reasonableness of the timing of the defect notice to recover damages. The case also provides a good explanation as to the current existing law of an open account as another basis for seeking to recover on a continuous delivery of product that was not paid for when the amounts can be adequately proven.

### [2] Iowa Federal Court Finds Plaintiff's Negligence Claim Against Professional Engineering Firm Required Expert Testimony to Establish Liability and No Evidence was Established as to What Caused System to be Defective

In *Johnson Co. v. Johnson Controls, Inc.,*[50] the plaintiff filed a claim against the contractor as a result of a water line freezing and bursting, causing damages. The owner alleged the contractor was negligent in installing and programming the system.

The contractor's system was programmed to automatically open and close roof vents and run exhaust fans to control the temperature and CO levels in the building. The system included a CO monitor and two temperature sensors in each part of the building. When a temperature sensor signaled a high temperature, the system opened the vents and ran the fans until the temperature lowered to a specified level. The system would automatically shut down the fans and close the vents once the temperature cooled. In a low temperature situation, the vents and fans would not activate unless there was a CO alarm or manual override.

In commissioning the system, the contractor tested the sensors and controls and insured the system was performing in line with the specified order of operations. After completing the system in October 2009, the contractor turned over control of the system to the plaintiff. The plaintiff did not retain the contractor to maintain, inspect or calibrate the system. The contractor provided a one-year warranty on the system. There was no evidence in the record that there were any problems with the system until late December 2012, more than three years after it had been installed.

On December 31, 2012, the plaintiff discovered a water pipe had broken. Water was bursting from the pipe, causing damage. Evidence at trial established that when the broken pipe was discovered, the system's exhaust fans were running and the roof vents were open.

---

[50] 96 F. Supp. 3d 912 (S.D. Iowa 2015).

It is undisputed that the parties were uncertain as to why the vents and fans activated sometime between December 27 and December 31. Although the system had an alarm log, it had a limited storage capacity with no override protection. Unfortunately, the alarm log was not viewed until all relevant data was no longer available.

Plaintiff's technical expert opined that the vents should not have been open and the fans should not have been running at the time the frozen pipe was discovered. Therefore, the plaintiff's technical expert concluded the system malfunctioned. However, the plaintiff's technical expert did not test the system and was therefore unable to identify why or how the system malfunctioned, or explain how the contractor was negligent in installing and programming the system.

Conversely, the contractor's employee who had extensive experience servicing, troubleshooting, and supervising the service of similar systems, opined it was impossible the system malfunction because of any error on the contractor. For example, if an alarm signaled on December 27 and the condition was not discovered until December 31, he concluded the system operated as intended. The contractor also pointed out that the vents and fans could be manually activated by an override. Barring either a specific type of alarm or manual activation, the contractor expert offered that the system may have malfunctioned, but he could not opine as to the nature or reason for the malfunction. However, contractor noted that the CO sensors were supposed to be calibrated yearly and the plaintiff had failed to do so the past three years.

The plaintiff brought the action against the contractor on a single claim for common law negligence. Based on the evidence, the contractor moved for summary judgment. Plaintiff claimed its evidence was supported through the testimony of its technical expert. However, the plaintiff's technical expert had acknowledged he did not test the system and was unable explain why the system malfunctioned or what contractor did or failed to do to cause the system malfunction.

The plaintiff relied upon *Schlader v. Interstate Power Co.*,[51] for the broad proposition is not required to provide expert testimony to establish the contractor's negligence in installing and programming the system. In *Schlader*, dairy farmers brought claims alleging stray voltage harmed their cow herd. The Iowa Supreme Court found expert testimony was not necessary in stray voltage claims, because the nature of electricity and its results of contact with it by humans and animals is not beyond a common person's understanding. In that instance, the Court held the record contained sufficient evidence to survive summary judgment, i.e., presented evidence stray voltage was on their farm, that after the energy company installed isolator blocks, the voltage on the farm decreased, and a veterinarian testified that the herd's health problems were related to voltage.

---

[51] 591 N.W.2d 10 (Iowa 1999).

Here, the Court found the plaintiffs' claim was readily distinguishable from *Schlader*. Although it asserted a cause of action for simple negligence, the Court found the record established the claim was more in the nature of a professional negligence claim. Accordingly, the applicable standard of care should be measured by the degree of skill and care ordinarily possessed by members of that profession in similar circumstances. Moreover, the system records were not preserved, precluding any ability to determine what caused the vents and fans to activate. Thus, the record contained no evidence explaining how and why the contractor was negligent in installing and program the system, or how that alleged negligence caused the system to malfunction and caused damages to the plaintiff. Therefore, the Court found that no reasonable juror could find that the contractor negligent either on a professional negligence or simple negligence theory, and granted the contractor's motion for summary judgment.

### [3] Eighth Circuit Denies Construction Companies' Subrogation Claim Against Property Owners' Post Construction Insurance Policies

In *White Co., LLC v. Lexington Insurance Co.*,[52] the contractor contracted with Hyatt to build an assisted living facility in Florida.

The facility was completed in July 2003. In November 2003, Hyatt obtained certain post-construction insurance policies. These policies did not come into being until after completion of the construction work performed by the contractor. The contractor was neither a party to these insurance contracts nor a third-party beneficiary. Equally as important, the policies excluded from coverage damages due to faulty workmanship and mold, except to the extent that another covered loss results from the faulty workmanship—for instance, business interruption losses.

The completed construction was defective in numerous ways. The defective construction resulted in moisture, mold growth and cracked stucco. While Hyatt initially gave notice of this loss to its post-construction insurers, it chose to sue the contractor and the architects directly in federal court. The contractor in turn sued its subcontractors and their insurers as well as its own insurers. Eventually, defendants settled with Hyatt for $53 million, a small part of which was paid by the project's architects. The contractor contributed over $51 million. The contractor was then indemnified by its contract liability insurers and the subcontractor's insurance, in amounts exceeding $55 million.

Via subrogation, the contractor attempted to obtain coverage for itself under Hyatt's post-construction insurance policies. Specifically, the contractor asserted theories of equitable subrogation or unjust enrichment. The Court rejected both of these arguments.

---

[52] 786 F.3d 641 (8th Cir. 2015).

The trial court found that the contractor's suit was barred by the statute of limitations. The trial court also found that in addition to defective notice and the statute of limitations, the contractor had already collected $55.8 million from other parties, several million more than it paid to settle with Hyatt. Thus, the trial court failed to see any basis in equity for a double recovery. Further, the trial court was unconvinced that the contractor paid a liability for which the defendant insurers were primarily liable, a requirement of equitable subrogation. Finally, the trial court rejected the contractor's unjust enrichment claim because the subrogation claim failed, the unjust enrichment claim could not survive as a stand-alone claim. The contractor appealed.

The Eighth Circuit first noted that the premise of equitable subrogation is that one party has paid a debt for which another is primarily liable. The Eighth Circuit held that the contractor could not establish that the insurers were primary liable, or liable in any measure, for the damages for which it reimbursed or should have reimbursed Hyatt. The Eighth Circuit held the insurers were post-construction insurers and their insurance contracts excluded losses caused by the contractor's faulty workmanship, and the resulting mold, from its coverage.

However, the contractor's expert provided testimony that some of the resulting damages, while created by faulty workmanship, also included business interruption claims. Thus, the expert opined these business interruption damages could properly be recovered by the post-construction insurance policies.

However, the Eighth Circuit noted that the expert relied on certain provisions found in the construction related insurance policies as opposed to the post-construction insurance policies. The Eighth Circuit also held that construction of insurance policies is an issue law for the trial court to determine, not for experts. The Eighth Circuit recognized that because the record appeared to indicate that the trial court essentially ignored the expert's report, the Eighth Circuit opined it was clear that the Court correctly recognized the serious deficiencies in the validity of the contractor's legal claims concerning the insurance policies at issue in rendering its decision.

Additionally, the Eighth Circuit held that the contractor was the initial source of the negligence and poor workmanship. Accordingly, equitable subrogation failed because the contractor was primarily liable for damages.

The Eighth Circuit also held that a party claiming equitable subrogation stands in the shoes of person whose claims been discharged, and acquires the rights and defenses of that person, but no more. The Eighth Circuit held that Hyatt received over $51 million from the contractor and chose to compromise and release the rest of its claim in return for settlement. Thus, wearing Hyatt's shoes, the contractor would be entitled to that amount but nothing more. Since the contractor received more than this amount from its insurers and subcontractors, it could not seek a double recovery.

The Eighth Circuit also held the contractor's unjust enrichment claim failed for the same reasons. In order to succeed on a claim of unjust enrichment, a party must allege that another has received a benefit, the retention of which would be an inequitable. The Eighth Circuit held that contractor failed to establish that the defendant insurers unjustly retained a benefit. Because the only possible benefit contractor could allege is not paying insurance claims that the contractor's experts allege were covered under the contracts between the defendant insurers and Hyatt, the relative positions of the parties with regard to the equities were fatal to the contractor's unjust enrichment claim.

The Eighth Circuit also found the contractor's arguments circular. Had Hyatt made a claim against the defendant insurers and the claim paid, the defendant insurers could have, and undoubtedly would have, exercised a contractual right of subrogation to seek compensation from the contractor and presumably the sub-contractors. The fact that Hyatt chose to circumvent this route and proceed directly against the general contractor and subcontractors did not confer an unjustly retained benefit upon the defendant insurers. The Eighth Circuit held that perhaps it did benefit the defendant insurers to not have to pay the claim and proceed to litigation via subrogation, but benefit was not inequitable in comparison to the tortfeasor's negligence. To hold otherwise would unreasonably stretch the bounds of the doctrine. Accordingly, the Eighth Circuit held that the defendant insurers, as a matter of law, had not enriched themselves unjustly at the expense of the contractor and dismissed the claim.

## § 10.04  MICHIGAN

### [A]  Introduction

In 2015, several statutes, regulations, published and unpublished federal and state cases addressed Michigan construction law issues worthy of attention, ranging from application of "pay if paid" clauses in construction subcontracts to the constitutionality of city building department fees. Even though the unpublished state court decisions and federal court decisions are not precedentially binding,[53] they provide valuable guidance in interpreting noteworthy construction topics in Michigan.

Although it is not an all-inclusive overview of construction law in Michigan, this chapter identifies several significant recent legal developments in the state. For example, the U.S. District Courts for the Eastern and Western Districts of Michigan recently clarified and interpreted Michigan's application of the economic loss doctrine in two unpublished opinions.[54] The doctrine generally

---

[53] Michigan Court Rule (MCR) 7.215(C)(1) currently provides that "[a]n unpublished opinion is not precedentially binding under the rule of stare decisis. A party who cites an unpublished opinion must provide a copy of the opinion to the court and to the opposing parties with the brief or other paper in which the citation appears."

[54] Farm Bureau Mut. Ins. Co. of Michigan v. Borkholder Bldg. & Supply, LLC, No. 1:14-CV-1118, 2015 WL 5682729 (W.D. Mich. Sept. 25, 2015); Home Owners Ins. Co. v. ADT LLC, No. 15-CV-11262, 2015 WL 3763489 (E.D. Mich. May 21, 2015).

prevents recovery in tort where a purchaser's expectations in a sale are frustrated because the product is not working properly.[55] The doctrine hinges on a distinction between transactions involving the sale of goods for commercial purposes where economic expectations are protected by commercial and contract law, and those involving the sale of defective products to individual consumers who are injured in a manner which has traditionally been remedied by resort to the law of torts.[56] However, the economic loss doctrine in Michigan is broader than other jurisdictions, in that it not only includes damage to the product itself, but may also include damage to other property when the damage was within the contemplation of the parties to the agreement.[57]

Surprisingly, construction law intersected with constitutional challenges in several recent Michigan state and federal cases. For example, the Sixth Circuit in *Borman, LLC v. 18779 Borman, LLC*[58] found that Michigan's Nonrecourse Mortgage Loan Act, which rendered solvency covenants in nonrecourse loans unenforceable, did not violate the Contract or Due Process Clauses of the United States and Michigan Constitutions. Additionally, in *Ming Kuo Yang v. City of Wyoming, Michigan*,[59] the Sixth Circuit concluded that the city's demolition notices prior to razing plaintiffs' commercial building comported with the Due Process Clause. Moreover, in *Michigan Ass'n of Home Builders v. City of Troy*,[60] the Michigan Supreme Court concluded that a group of associations representing builders, contractors, and plumbers did not need to exhaust administrative remedies prior to filing suit against the City of Troy claiming that the city building department fees violated the Single State Construction Code Act and Michigan State Constitution, and it remanded for further proceedings.

## [B]   Recent Statutory and Regulatory Developments

### [1]   Personal Protective Equipment[61]

Effective March 24, 2015, the Michigan Department of Licensing and Regulatory Affairs enacted specifications for personal protective equipment for the employee's head, face, eyes, hands, feet, and body when the equipment is necessary to protect against hazards during construction operations. Included in these specifications, all face and eye protection devices must include a certification by the manufacturer that the device has been produced according to ANSI

---

[55] *Farm Bureau Mut. Ins. Co. of Michigan*, 2015 WL 5682729, at *5.

[56] *Id.*

[57] *Id.*

[58] 777 F.3d 816 (6th Cir. 2015).

[59] 793 F.3d 599, 601 (6th Cir. 2015).

[60] 497 Mich. 281 (2015).

[61] MI ADC R 408.40601, *et seq.*

standard Z-87.1, "Practice for Occupational and Educational Eye and Face Protection," 1991 edition. Safety toe footwear must show the manufacturer's name or trademark and a certification of compliance with ANSI standard Z-41 "Personal Protection—Protective Footwear," 1991 edition.

### [2]  Mobile Home Parks[62]

Effective September 1, 2015, the Michigan legislature enacted additional rules with regard to the licensure, regulation, construction, operation, and management of mobile home parks. The amendments include penalties for violation of the act and require the owner of a distressed mobile home park to post financial assurance to ensure repair of the mobile home park.

### [3]  Accident Prevention Programs[63]

Effective October 28, 2015, except where preempted in another rule, every employer performing construction operations must develop an accident prevention program that provides instructions to each employee regarding operating procedures, hazards, and safeguards of tools and equipment when necessary to perform the job.

### [4]  Employment of Minors at Construction Sites[64]

Effective March 6, 2015, minors less than 16-years-old cannot be employed in occupations in a construction operation, which includes repair or cleanup of a construction site. The rule does not apply to employment of a student minor who is at least 14-years-old with the student's school board's agreement, employment by a parent or guardian of a minor, domestic work or chores for private residences, selling or distributing newspapers, shoe shining, services related to youth organizations, and farm work.

### [5]  Construction Safety Standards[65]

The Michigan Department of Licensing and Regulatory Affairs adopted various construction safety standards that became effective on February 24, 2015. The standards include requirements for employers related to work in hazardous

---

[62] 2015 Mich. Legis. Serv. P.A. 40.
[63] MI ADC R 408.40114.
[64] MI ADC R 408.6203, *et seq.*
[65] MI ADC R 408.40105, *et seq.*; MI ADC R 408.41001a, *et seq.*

spaces; confined spaces; boilers and pressure vessels; guarding, belts, gears, pulleys, sprockets, and moving parts; sanitation; food handling; medical services and first aid; illumination; and lifting and digging equipment. Additionally, the standards require employers to identify unsafe machines or power tools and either make them inoperable or physically remove them from the jobsite. Employers may not permit the use of damaged or defective machinery or equipment that could create a hazard.

### [6] Construction Code for Electrical Systems or Material[66]

Effective June 18, 2015, the Michigan Bureau of Construction Codes amended the Construction Code Rules, Part 8. All units of government that administer and enforce the electrical code shall enforce the amended state electrical code effective June 18, 2015. The rules adopt by reference the National Electrical Code, 2014 edition, and include deletions, additions, and amendments to the national code. A copy of the Part 8 rules are available to be downloaded for free from the bureau's website at www.michigan.gov/bcc.

## [C] Recent State Case Law Developments

### [1] The Michigan Court of Appeals Determines That "Pay if Paid" Clauses Do Not Apply to Work Performed Outside the Scope of the Contract

The Michigan Court of Appeals recently examined the scope of "pay if paid" clauses. Often inserted in construction subcontracts, these clauses trigger the contractor's obligation to pay the subcontractor only if the contractor receives payment from the owner, and "pay if paid" clauses are designed to shift the credit risk to the subcontractor. In *Macomb Mechanical, Inc. v. LaSalle Group, Inc.,*[67] an unpublished opinion per curiam, the Michigan Court of Appeals reversed in part the trial court's decision, holding that there may be limits to the applicability of "pay if paid" clauses when applied to extracontractual work.

In *Macomb Mechanical*, the general contractor engaged a subcontractor to provide plumbing and mechanical work for the construction of a dining facility. The work was originally planned to be completed in six months, but unforeseen circumstances extended the work for an additional nine months. The subcontractor claimed that a change in the scope of the project caused the delay, but the contractor refused to sign change orders necessary to secure the subcontractor payment, claiming that the subcontract prohibited any additional funds for an increase in the duration of the project.

---

[66] MI ADC R 408.30801, *et seq.*
[67] No. 319357, 2015 WL 1880189 (Mich. Ct. App. Apr. 23, 2015).

The subcontractor filed suit and then appealed the trial court's entry of summary judgment for the contractor. The Michigan Court of Appeals reversed in part, holding there was a genuine issue of material fact as to whether the work was outside the scope of the subcontract and therefore not subject to the pay-if-paid clause. Additionally, despite a clause in the subcontract specifying that no damages were available in the event of a delay, the court held that if the delays involved work outside the scope of the contract, damages for delay were not barred until the contractor was paid. The court remanded for further proceedings on whether the contractor changed the project drawings after the subcontractor bid on the project, thereby requiring the subcontractor to provide extracontractual work.

If a general contractor or subcontractor is engaged in commercial or residential construction, *Macomb Mechanical,* reveals the importance of reviewing the "pay if paid" clause and the scope of the work specified in the subcontract to avoid the unfortunate surprise experienced by the general contractor in *Macomb Mechanical.* If the subcontractor's work is outside the scope of the subcontract, the "pay if paid" clause may not apply, and the general contractor may be responsible for payment even if the general contractor has not received payment from the owner.

### [2] The Michigan Court of Appeals Addresses Unjust Enrichment Claims Based on Construction Contracts

In *Lawrence M. Clarke, Inc. v. Draeger,*[68] the Michigan Court of Appeals held that damages are not recoverable under a theory of unjust enrichment when the disputed matter is covered by a valid express or implied contract. The case involved a contract for work on a portion of a sanitary system. After encountering a variety of problems during the project, the parties sued each other, both making breach of contract and unjust enrichment claims. The Michigan Court of Appeals reviewed the contracts between the parties and determined that actual performance was based on both an express and implied contracts. The court remanded the case to the trial court to analyze what aspects of the parties' claims cam under contract, express or implied, and resort to unjust enrichment "only to the extent that justice requires operation of that equitable [theory] where no valid contract was in place."

### [3] A Group of Associations Challenge the City of Troy's Building Department Fees as Unconstitutional

In *Michigan Ass'n of Home Builders v. City of Troy,*[69] a group of associations representing builders, contractors, and plumbers filed suit against the

---

[68] No. 316194, 2015 WL 205182 (Mich. Ct. App. Jan. 15, 2015).
[69] 497 Mich. 281 (2015).

City of Troy claiming that the city building department fees violated the Single State Construction Code Act ("CCA") and Headlee Amendment, Const. 1963 art. 9, § 31. The City of Troy privatized the building department in July 2010 after several years of operating at a deficit. It entered into a contract with SafeBuilt Michigan, Inc., and the plaintiff claimed that the contractual arrangement produced significant monthly surpluses that were used to augment the city's general fund in violation of the CCA and constituted an unlawful tax increase in violation of the state constitution. The trial court granted summary judgment to the city and the Court of Appeals affirmed because plaintiff had not pursued administrative remedies. Because the administrative proceedings in the CCA do not provide the director with the authority to evaluate the city's legislative body, the Michigan Supreme Court reversed the judgment and held that the associations were not required to exhaust administrative remedies with the Director of Department of Licensing and Regulatory Affairs before bringing suit.

### [D]   Recent Federal Case Law Developments

#### [1]   The Nonrecourse Mortgage Loan Act Renders "Solvency Covenants" in Commercial Mortgage-Backed Securities Loans Unenforceable

In *Borman, LLC v. 18779 Borman, LLC*,[70] the Sixth Circuit reviewed the structure of Commercial Mortgage-Backed Securities ("CMBS") loans and their recent history in Michigan. The court explained that CMBS loans are nonrecourse loans, and they often included covenants by the borrower to remain solvent. However, if insolvency in the covenant was interpreted to mean simply a loss of cash flow resulting in default, then a default would expose the borrower to personal liability, effectively obviating the bedrock principle of nonrecourse liability.

The Nonrecourse Mortgage Loan Act ("NMLA"), passed by the Michigan legislature in March 2012, rendered solvency covenants in nonrecourse loans unenforceable, and it was applied retroactively. The Borrower in this case obtained an 8.7 million CMBS loan from Morgan Stanley Mortgage Capital, Inc., in 2005, secured by the commercial property. The Borrower's principal, Joseph Schwebel, guaranteed all the obligations on the loan for which the Borrower might become personally liable. After a grocery chain that leased the property filed for bankruptcy, and the Borrower could not find a replacement tenant, Morgan Stanley's servicer foreclosed on the property in 2011. In 2012, the loan servicer sold the property to a Purchaser, who filed for deficiency judgment against the Borrower.

---

[70] 777 F.3d 816 (6th Cir. 2015).

Each party moved for summary judgment, and the district court granted it to Borrower and Schwebel. The Sixth Circuit affirmed the district court's findings that the NMLA: (1) rendered the solvency covenant in the Borrower's CMBS loan unenforceable; (2) violated neither the Contract nor Due Process Clauses of the United States and Michigan Constitutions; and (3) comported with Michigan's constitutional provision mandating the separation of governmental powers.

### [2] The Sixth Circuit Interprets the Term "Decay" in an Insurance Policy to Include Both "Organic Rot" and "Gradual and Progressive Decline"

In *Joy Tabernacle-The New Testament Church v. State Farm Fire & Casualty Co.*,[71] the ceiling of a church constructed in 1927 partially collapsed 85 years later in 2012. The policy in effect at the time of the collapse covered "accidental direct physical loss" to the premises. Exclusions to the coverage included wear and tear; decay; settling, cracking, shrinking, or expansion; and losses caused by faulty, inadequate or defective designs, construction, and repair. The policy further provided that it would cover accidental direct physical loss caused by "decay that is hidden from view" even if use of defective material or methods in construction contributes to the loss. State Farm denied the church's claim after an inspector determined that there was no wood decay due to roof leaks or insect or vermin damage. The church argued that decay should be defined broadly to include "gradual and progressive decline," while State Farm argued that it should be restricted to "organic rot."

After turning to the dictionary and prior case law for interpretation of "decay," the Sixth Circuit Court of Appeals adopted a broader definition of the word. The court concluded that State Farm could not carry its burden of proving that the general exclusions in the policy apply, and reversed summary judgment for State Farm and remanded for further proceedings.

### [3] The Sixth Circuit Evaluates Whether a City's Demolition Notice Satisfies Due Process

In *Ming Kuo Yang v. City of Wyoming, Michigan*,[72] commercial property owners brought a § 1983 action against the City of Wyoming, Michigan, alleging that the city violated their due process rights by failing to give them proper notice before demolishing their building. The city posted two notices on the building for abandonment and demolition, sent a letter about the demolition hearing to the owners, forwarded a copy of the hearing notice to the owners' realtor, and sent a final notice prior to demolition to the owners' address. The Sixth Circuit Court of

---

[71] 616 Fed. Appx. 802 (6th Cir. 2015).
[72] 793 F.3d 599, 601 (6th Cir. 2015).

Appeals found that the city provided notice reasonably calculated, under all the circumstances, to give sufficient notice to satisfy due process. The Sixth Circuit affirmed the summary judgment in favor of the city.

### [4] The District Courts Evaluate the Application of the Economic Loss Doctrine to Insurance Policies

In *Farm Bureau Mutual Insurance Co. of Michigan v. Borkholder Buildings & Supply, LLC*,[73] plaintiff's claims arose out of the collapse of trusses in an insured hog building approximately six years after construction. After paying the insured's claim, Farm Bureau Mutual Insurance Co., filed a complaint against the truss manufacturer for breach of implied warranty based on manufacturing defects. The court reviewed the economic loss doctrine in Michigan, which provides that "where a purchaser's expectations in a sale are frustrated because the product he bought is not working properly, his remedy is said to be in contract alone, for he has suffered only 'economic' losses."[74] After conducting a thorough analysis of the economic loss doctrine, the District Court for the Western District of Michigan determined that plaintiff could not recover its alleged damages in the realm of tort law. Because the plaintiff's insured suffered damage to property that was within the contemplation of the parties to the agreement, the exclusive remedy of Michigan's Uniform Commercial Code applied, including the four-year statute of limitations, which barred plaintiff's recovery.

In *Home Owners Insurance Co. v. ADT LLC*,[75] the homeowner's insurer, as subrogee of the insured homeowners, brought an action against a contractor hired to install temperature sensors at the homeowners' home, alleging that the contractor breached the contract, committed fraud, acted negligently, and violated the Michigan Consumer Protection Act when it failed to install the sensors. After contracting with ADT to install thermal sensors, the homeowners' thermocouple on a furnace broke or malfunctioned, and a pipe on the property froze and burst, releasing water into the residence. The Eastern District of Michigan dismissed all claims against the defendant for the following reasons: (1) the breach of contract claim failed because it was brought outside of the statute of limitations period; (2) the plaintiff could not bring a negligence and fraud tort claims against defendants for failure to perform under the contract; (3) plaintiff did not plead its claim under the Michigan Consumer Protection Act with particularity as required by Federal Rule of Civil Procedure 9(b).

---

[73] No. 1:14-CV-1118, 2015 WL 5682729 (W.D. Mich. Sept. 25, 2015).

[74] *Farm Bureau Mut. Ins.*, 2015 WL 5682729, at *4 (internal citations omitted).

[75] No. 15-CV-11262, 2015 WL 3763489 (E.D. Mich. May 21, 2015).

### [5] The Home Affordable Modification Program Does Not Impose a Legal Duty on a Lender to Evaluate Mortgagors for Loan Modification

*Rush v. Freddie Mac*[76] is another appeal in a long line of cases arising from the home mortgage crisis. Plaintiffs defaulted on their note and mortgage, and Bank of America foreclosed under Michigan's foreclosure-by-advertisement statute. Plaintiffs did not exercise their statutory right to redeem the foreclosed property, which extinguished the plaintiffs' right, title and interest in the property. Plaintiffs contended that the foreclosing party must be the assignee of both the mortgage and the promissory note in order to foreclose. But the Sixth Circuit Court of Appeals held that under Michigan law, it is lawful for the holder of the mortgage to be different than the holder of the debt, and Bank of America had standing to foreclose on the property. The court further held that plaintiffs' negligence claim, based on a failure to evaluate loan modification under the federal Home Affordable Modification Program, also failed because the program did not impose a legal duty on the lender to evaluate the mortgagors for loan modification. The Sixth Circuit affirmed the Eastern District of Michigan's entry of judgment on the pleadings in favor of Freddie Mac.

## § 10.05   MINNESOTA

### [A]   Introduction

Minnesota saw several published cases in 2015 in construction law. Additionally, the legislature enacted revisions to its new statute enumerating requirements for a "responsible contractor" in state procurement for projects in excess of $50,000.

### [B]   Recent Statutory and Regulatory Developments

### [1]   Requirements for a "Responsible Contractor"

Effective January 1, 2015, Minnesota implemented a statewide procurement statute for publicly funded procurements. Specifically, the statute mandated that only a "responsible contractor" can be awarded government contracts on projects with a projected value in excess of $50,000.

Effective July 1, 2015, Minnesota clarified certain provisions to expressly exclude design professionals from the "responsible contractor" requirements.[77]

---

[76] 792 F.2d 600, 601 (6th Cir. 2015).
[77] MINN. STAT. § 16C.285 Subd. 1(c).

Pursuant to Minn. Stat. § 16C.285, all government projects with a projected value in excess of $50,000 can only be awarded to a "responsible contractor." Responsibility is defined as a contractor that conforms to the responsibility requirements in the statute. Further, amongst other changes, the session law now mandates that, prior to execution of the prime contract, the prime contractor must submit to the government, under oath, a verification confirming the prime contractor, and all subcontractors, are "responsible contractors" as defined by the statute.

As stated in last year's update, the general requirements of a "responsible contractor" include the following:

- The contractor:
    - Is in compliance with workers' compensation and unemployment insurance requirements;
    - Has registered with the Minnesota Department of Revenue and Department of Employment and Economic Development;
    - Has a valid federal tax id or social security number; and
    - Has filed a certificate of authority to transact business in Minnesota.
- Has not had the following occur:
    - Failing to pay prevailing wages for a total underpayment of $25,000 or more in a three-year period;
    - Been issued a final order to comply by the commissioner of labor and industry;
    - Been issued at least two determination letters within the three-year period by the Minnesota DOT finding an underpayment by the contractor to its employees;
    - Been found by the commissioner of labor and industry to have repeatedly or willfully violated labor and industry rules;
    - Been issued a ruling or finding of underpayment by the US Department of Labor, and the determination has become final; or
    - Been found liable for underpayment of wages or penalties or misrepresenting a construction worker as an independent contractor in an action brought in a court having jurisdiction.
- Has not violated section 181.723 or chapter 326B;
- Has not, more than twice during the previous three-year period had a certificate of compliance under section 363A.36 revoked or suspended;
- Has not received a final determination assessing a monetary sanction from the Minnesota DOA or DOT for failure to meet, or comply in good faith in obtaining DBE goals;

- Is not currently suspended or debarred by the federal government, Minnesota or any subdivision thereof; and

- All subcontractors the contractor intends to use have verified their compliance with the above requirements.

## [C] Recent Case Law Developments

### [1] Minnesota Supreme Court Sets the Standard for Review of a Best Value Public Procurement

The issues reviewed by the Minnesota Supreme Court in *Rochester City Lines, Co. v. City of Rochester*[78] was (1) the applicable standard of review of a "best value" competitive bidding process; and (2) whether the district court erred in granting summary judgment on bid-protest claims.

As to the first question, the Court held that the unreasonable, arbitrary, or capricious standard is the appropriate standard for reviewing a city or county's decision to award a government contract after a "best value" bidding process. As to the second question, the Court categorized the challenges into four general groups: (1) challenges to the terms of the Request for Proposals ("RFP"); (2) procedures in addressing a bid protest; (3) whether an organizational conflict of interest existed; and (4) whether the cumulative irregularities rendered the procurement arbitrary, capricious, or unreasonable.

For more than 30 years Rochester City Lines, Co. ("RCL") operated all municipal bus services in Rochester, paid through state and federal grants. In 2011 the City of Rochester, upon advice from the Federal Transit Administration ("FTA") issued a RFP using a "best value" bidding process to award a contract to the winning transit operator. Before proposals were due, RCL filed a formal bid protest claiming that the RFP constituted an unconstitutional taking of RCL's property. The bid protest was denied, and RCL filed suit against the City.

RCL unsuccessfully moved for a temporary injunction to stop the bidding process, and the City eventually awarded the contract to a competitor, First Transit. RCL filed another formal bid protest to the selection of First Transit. The subsequent protest was also denied, and, per the terms of the RFP, the denial was upheld by the Rochester City Counsel. RCL then amended its complaint to add claims against the City, members of the City Council, and First Transit. In the meantime, First Transit began operations on July 2, 2012, and RCL ended its fixed-route service the following day.

In November 2012, the district court granted summary judgment to the defendants on each of RCL's claims, and this decision was affirmed by the court of appeals.

---

[78] 868 N.W.2d 655 (Minn. 2015).

The first claim by RCL, that the RFP terms were unfair, was easily dispensed with by the Court because RCL never timely protested this issue before submitting a proposal. The Court reiterated the maxim that contractors cannot sit on their rights and therefore forfeit their challenge on this ground.

As to the second claim, RCL claimed that the reviewer of the bid-protests, the City Attorney, was biased because he wore two hats. The City Attorney counseled the City on the RFP and bidding process, and also reviewed and decided bid protests. The Court found that the bid-protest determinations were quasi-judicial, and therefore could only be reviewed by writ of certiorari in the court of appeals, which RCL failed to do. Because RCL did not seek a writ of certiorari, the claim was dismissed.

As to the third claim that First Transit had an organizational conflict of interest ("OCI"), the Court used federal OCI standards looking for either an unfair advantage, or biased ground rules towards First Transit. The Court found neither and upheld the dismissal of this claim.

As to the fourth and final claim, that the numerous irregularities suggest an arbitrary, capricious, or unreasonable decision, the district court granted summary judgment on this issue. So, the Court reviewed the issue as to whether genuine issues of material fact exist. Because RCL presented some evidence, that if viewed in the light most favorable to RCL would permit a fact-finder to reasonably conclude that the City's decision was arbitrary, capricious, or unreasonable, the Court remanded this claim for trial.

As of November 17, 2015, RCL filed a petition for certiorari with the U.S. Supreme Court.

### [2] Minnesota Court of Appeals Rules That Whether a Pre-Lien Notice Is Required Depends Upon the Nature of the Improvement

In a many-layered malpractice action, the Court of Appeals in *Ryan Contracting Co. v. O'Neill & Murphy, LLP*,[79] provided greater clarity on when a pre-lien notice is required. The issue was whether or not a pre-lien notice was or was not required to be filed based upon the real property as it existed prior to improvement, or based upon the improvement to be constructed.

The statute, Minn. Stat. § 514.011, states in relevant part:

> Every person who enters into a contract with the owner for the improvement of real property and who has contracted or will contract with any subcontractors or material suppliers to provide labor, skill or materials for the improvement shall include in any written contract with the owner the notice required in this subdivision and shall provide the owner with a copy of the written

---

[79] 868 N.W.2d 473 (Minn. Ct. App. 2015).

contract . . . A person who fails to provide the notice shall not have a lien and remedy provided by this chapter. Minn. Stat. § 514.011, subd. 1.

The notice required by this section shall not be required to be given in connection with an improvement to real property which is not in agricultural use and which is wholly or partially nonresidential in use if the work or improvement [meets one of three conditions.] Minn. Stat. § 514.011, subd. 4c.

The real property was undeveloped before construction commenced on a mixed used project. The contractor did not provide notice, but did file a lien claim which led to a foreclosure action. For other reasons the foreclosure action failed, and the contractor sued its attorneys for malpractice.

The defense raised by the defendant attorneys was that the contractor failed to provide the pre-lien notice, and therefore any malpractice did not matter as to the validity of the lien.

As stated above, the requirement for a pre-lien notice in this case turned upon whether the exception stated above considers the improvement, or state of the real property before improvement. The Court of Appeals ruled the statute ambiguous, and construed in the ambiguity in favor of the contractor by ruling the intended improvement controls the need for a pre-lien notice.

### [3] Flooding Twice for Only a Day Is Not a Taking

In *Blaine v. City of Sartell*,[80] the Court of Appeals held that, as a matter of law, private property which is flooded, on only two occasions, does not constitute a taking even assuming that a public entity is responsible for the flooding.

### [4] Minnesota Supreme Court Rules That the Two-Year Statute of Limitations for Construction Defects Begins to Run Upon Discovery, Regardless of When the Defect Is Discovered

In *328 Barry Avenue, LLC v. Nolan Properties Group, LLC*,[81] the Minnesota Supreme Court reviewed two questions concerning Minn. Stat. § 541.051, subd. 1(a)—two-year statute of limitations for actions arising out of the defective and unsafe condition of an improvement to real property: (1) when the limitations period begins to run; and (2) whether a defect has been discovered.

In *328 Barry Avenue*, the owner of property under construction was first made aware of a potential leak in October 2009. To all parties understanding, the leak went away a month later, and the project was substantially completed in May 2010. In August 2010, the owner noticed water on the floor, and the leak was determined to be substantially the same as that found in October 2009.

---

[80] 865 N.W.2d 723 (Minn. Ct. App. 2015).
[81] A14-0724, 2015 WL 7566613 (Minn. Nov. 25, 2015).

Throughout 2011 and 2012, the general contractor and owner investigated the extent and cause of water damage, and in the process found numerous defects related to water leaks. Subsequently the owner brought suit for negligence against the general contractor and subcontractors in June 2012.

Both the district court and court of appeals concluded that the negligence action was untimely as the limitations began to run upon discovery, which was determined to be October 2009. The owner appealed to the Minnesota Supreme Court arguing that the statute cannot begin to run until substantial completion, and that, there was a genuine issue of material fact as to when the defect was discovered.

As to whether the limitations period begins to run, the Court looked to the statute which states, in relevant part: "no action by any person in contract, tort, or otherwise to recover damages for any injury to property . . . arising out of the defective and unsafe condition of an improvement to real property, shall be brought . . . more than two years after discovery of the injury." The owner argued that, during construction, any defect found is a circumstance whereby some piece of work has yet to be completed, and therefore discovery of a defect cannot take place until after substantial completion. The contractors argued that the plain language of the statute says discovery, regardless of the state of construction.

The Court held to the plain language of the statute holding that discovery of a defect, and the running of the applicable statute of limitations, does not depend upon when substantial completion takes place. Discovery is the trigger whenever it happens.

As to the second question, whether a "discovery" is sufficient to trigger the statute of limitations, the Court held that whether discovery was made is a factual question, not appropriate for resolution on summary judgment when reasonable minds can differ about the timing of the discovery of the injury. Therefore, the Court applies an objective standard as to whether an owner "knew or should have known, through the exercise of due diligence, of the injury."

As to whether the owner in *328 Barry Avenue* "knew or should have known," the fact that construction was ongoing when the leaks were first found created a genuine issue of material fact maintaining a fact issue for trial.

### [5] The Court of Appeals, in an Unpublished Decision, Affirmed the Application of Prevailing Wage Standards to Material Suppliers in Limited Circumstances

In *J.D. Donovan, Inc. v. Minnesota DOT*,[82] the Court of Appeals affirmed two lower court decisions determining that work conducted by materials suppliers on state highway projects were subject to prevailing wage standards. This was the case especially since the prime contract received DBE credit for the material suppliers.

---

[82] 2015 WL 404666 (Minn. Ct. App. 2015).

## [6] The Court of Appeals Extends Common Law Immunity to Independent Contracting Engineer

In *Kariniemi v. City of Rockford*,[83] the Court of Appeals was faced with the issue of whether official immunity can extend to a contracted entity. The plaintiffs' property flooded allegedly due to negligent design of the drainage system which was approved by a private entity contracted to act as the city engineer.

Acting as city engineer, Bonestroo designed and approved the storm-drainage improvements for the development which was the subject of the lawsuit. Bonestroo claimed the defense of official immunity since it was acting as the city engineer through a contract with the City. The plaintiff homeowner's argued that Bonestroo simply did not qualify as "a public official" eligible for immunity protection because it was an independent contractor, despite performing functions typically assigned to government employees.

After a short history of common law immunity protections the court held that "a city should not lose vicarious official immunity merely because it chooses [to] outsource some of its functions." The court was careful though to limit this application to design, and likely closed the door to immunity for construction contractors executing a design.

Review by the Minnesota Supreme Court was granted in August 2015.

## § 10.06 MISSOURI

### [A] Introduction

In the past year, Missouri case law expounded on several of construction law doctrines. A Missouri federal court, for example, held that a builder's risk policy did not cover damages caused by a design defect. Another Missouri federal court held that First Amendment protections do not extend to bidding on municipal construction contracts. Missouri state court cases discussed mechanic's liens, the effect of a homeowner's disregard of the contractors' right to cure on their right to sue for defective work, and a utility company's duties of care to construction workers.

### [B] Recent Statutory Developments

In 2015, there were no significant statutory or regulatory changes to construction law.

---

[83] 863 N.W.2d 430 (Minn. Ct. App. 2015).

## [C]  Recent Case Law Developments

### [1]  First Amendment Protections Do Not Extend to Bidding on Municipal Construction Contracts

In *Demien Construction Co. v. O'Fallon Fire Protection District*, an unsuccessful bidder on a municipal construction project sued under 42 U.S.C. § 1983, alleging the bidding procedure did not permit all bidders to compete on equal terms and, therefore, violated the First Amendment of the Federal Constitution.[84] The bidder argued the municipality, which held the responsibility of awarding the contract, deprived the bidder of First Amendment rights by failing to present objective data supporting its decision not to award the contract to the bidder. In response, the municipality argued the act of bidding on a municipal construction contract does not qualify as activity protected by the First Amendment and therefore, there could be no First Amendment violation. The municipality highlighted that the bidder brought his claims in the capacity of a general contractor seeking employment from a government entity—not as a citizen voicing a public concern.

The court agreed with the municipality and determined that First Amendment protections do not extend to bidding on a municipal construction contract, where the underlying action constitutes a private business interest as opposed to a matter of public concern. The court reasoned that the bidder's claim failed on the merits because the activity at issue—bidding on a municipal construction contract and failing to obtain the contract—was a private business interest and not a matter of public concern. The Court cautioned that extending First Amendment protection to activities involving private business and self-interest would "diminish" the applicability of the First Amendment to retaliation protection for public employees and government contractors with regard to activity involving matters of public concern. Therefore, in the interest of maintaining the appropriate application of First Amendment protections, the court concluded First Amendment protections do not extend to bidding on municipal contracts where, as here, the underlying action does not constitute a matter of public concern.

### [2]  The Missouri Court of Appeals Rejected A Contractor's Argument That a Single Mechanic's Lien on an Entire Subdivision Results in Separately Enforceable Liens on the Lots Within the Subdivision

In *Medlin v. RLC, Inc.*, a subcontractor who performed work on an entire subdivision filed a blanket mechanic's lien against the entire subdivision, then

---

[84] Demien Constr. Co. v. O'Fallon Fire Protection Dist., 72 F. Supp. 3d 967 (E.D. Mo. 2014).

filed a petition to enforce it.[85] At the trial court, the subcontractor obtained a default judgment that referenced at least 13 specified lots within the subdivision. The trial court granted the subcontractor a judgment, secured by its mechanic's lien, against the entire subdivision for $34,508. Citing the default judgment, the subcontractor argued the court's recitation of the 13 individual lots in its judgment created 13 lot-specific liens. In other words, the contractor was lobbying for separate enforceable liens on each of the thirteen lots, instead of a single lien on the entire subdivision.

The Missouri Court of Appeals disagreed with the contractor. The court held the entry of default judgment mentioning 13 individual lots within a subdivision did not automatically give rise to 13 distinct mechanic's liens. Focusing on the subcontractor's single lien statement and single action to enforce it, the court held that the subcontractor claimed and protected only one lien. The Missouri Court of Appeals, therefore, concluded that the subcontractor's multi-lien theory was wrong and affirmed the lower's court decision enforcing and perfecting only one $34,508 mechanic's lien against the entire subdivision.

### [3]  A Homeowner's Refusal to Honor a Contractor's Right to Cure Can Constitute Anticipatory Repudiation of the Contract by the Homeowner

In *Consolidated Service Group, LLC v. Maxey,* a roofing contractor agreed to install a new roof on a home.[86] Before completion of the project, a dispute arose between the homeowners and contractor about defective tile shingles on the roof. The contractor offered to replace and cure the defective shingles at no additional cost to the homeowners, but the homeowners refused to allow the contractor to do so—a fact the court determined was undisputed. The homeowners then sued the contractor, seeking damages for the defective work. The trial court granted summary judgment to the contractor, and the homeowners appealed.

The contract at issue contained a right-to-cure provision, which expressly prohibited the homeowners from suing for damages if the contractor had agreed, at no additional cost, to perform repairs but the homeowner had refused the repairs. In the case at hand, the court concluded the roofing contractor did not abandon the project but, rather, was prevented from performing after the dispute with the homeowners arose. Thus, the court concluded the roofing contractor did not breach the contract by its defective shingle installation. The court cited case law holding that if a party is seeking to recover for breach of contract, there cannot be evidence that same party prevented the contractor from performing work. Where there is such evidence, the contractor may sue for the value of the labor and materials provided. The court held that the homeowners' refusal to permit the

---

[85] Medlin v. RLC, Inc., 2015 WL 5577159 (Mo. Ct. App. Sept. 21, 2015).
[86] Consolidated Serv. Grp., LLC v. Maxey, 452 S.W.3d 768 (Mo. Ct. App. 2015).

contractor to install a new roof at no cost to the homeowner, as offered, was fatal to the homeowner's claim, since the contract at issue contained an express right-to-cure provision.

### [4]  Electric Utility Companies Are Subject to the Highest Standard of Care to Prevent Injuries It Could Anticipate

In *Basta v. Kansas City Power & Light Co.*, a roofer was installing a metal rubber boot around a two-inch galvanized pipe extending from a home's electric meter through the roof (often called a "meter mast" or "service mast").[87] The roofer was electrocuted and died of cardiac arrest after touching an uninsulated wire connector.

The roofer's parents sued the electric utility for wrongful death. After presentation of evidence at trial, the court instructed the jury that the utility service was negligent, as a matter of law, if it failed to insulate the connectors, failed to inspect the connectors, *or* failed to maintain the service drop lines 18 inches above the roof. The court defined "negligent" to mean the failure to use the highest degree of care.

On appeal, the utility service provider argued that the court's jury instructions improperly defined negligence as failure to use the highest degree of care. The utility service provider pointed to Missouri law and public policy which, it argued, require a utility service provider be subject to an ordinary standard of care where an anticipated injury would be caused by low voltage (i.e., the current in a home) rather than by high voltage (i.e., power lines). In response, the decedent's parents relied primarily on undisputed expert testimony they offered at trial—that low-voltage currents are dangerous and, often, more dangerous than high voltage currents.

The Missouri Court of Appeals disagreed with the utility service provider's application of the standard of care. Instead, the court relied on case law holding that a supplier of electricity is required to exercise the highest degree of care to prevent injury. Specifically, the court explained "that while a generator and transmitter of electricity is not an insurer of the safety of all persons, it is nonetheless required to use the highest degree of care to prevent injury which it could anticipate. . . ." Accordingly, the Missouri Court of Appeals held that the lower court did not err in its jury instructions, imposing the highest level of care on the utility service provider.

### [5]  Design Defect Damages Are Not Covered by a Builder's Risk Policy

In *Performing Arts Community Improvement District v. Ace American Insurance Co.*, a structural design servicer was contractually required to obtain a

---

[87] Basta v. Kansas City Power & Light Co., 456 S.W.3d 447 (Mo. Ct. App. 2014).

builder's risk policy that listed the project's financier as an additional insured.[88]
The project required installation of a 50 foot tall concrete retaining wall between
a garage and a limestone rock face, including placement of flowable concrete fill
in the area between the retaining wall and the limestone embankment. During the
installation of the concrete fill, the wall began to crack and deflect. The wall ultimately bulged, requiring significant investigation, repair, and replacement costs.
The financier sought to recover those costs under the builder's risk policy and
sued when the insurer denied coverage.

The insurance policy at issue provided that, subject to certain exclusions, it
"insures against risks of direct physical loss or damage to property of every kind
and description intended to become a permanent part of the project." It was undisputed that the retaining wall qualified as insured property, but the policy excluded
coverage for loss or damage caused by deficiency in design, plans, specifications,
engineering or surveying. The insurer argued the wall's failure was a result of the
defective design and that no insurable cause occurred thereafter. In response, the
financer argued that a subsequent event—a build-up of lateral pressure—caused
the wall to fail.

The district court agreed and granted judgment in favor of the insurer, holding that the retaining wall failed as a result of defective design. The court determined that the financer's attempt to identify the build-up of lateral pressures as
an ensuing event was simply another way of saying the wall was defectively
designed (i.e., that it was insufficient to withstand that pressure). The court reasoned that if a defectively designed building collapses, the court would not char-
acterize the effect of gravitational forces as a distinct and separate event. In such
example, like here, the collapsed building is not a covered loss. The court drew
this parallel and reasoned because losses due to defective design were expressly
excluded from coverage, the loss incurred by the collapsed wall was not covered.
An appeal is currently pending.

## § 10.07   OHIO

### [A]   Introduction

In 2015, the Ohio legislature passed a law that will give preference to
"veteran-friendly business enterprises" when awarding state contracts. The Ohio
judiciary also handed down several notable cases. The Ohio Supreme Court bol-
stered its longstanding rule that government entities will not be equitably
estopped, ruling that a contractor cannot rely on inaccurate information on a local
building commissioner's website. The Supreme Court also held that tenants suing

---

[88] Performing Arts Cmty. Improvement Dist. v. Ace Am. Ins. Co., 2015 WL 3491292 (W.D. Mo.
June 3, 2015).

a developer and manager for faulty wiring are tort actions, notwithstanding a contractual arrangement, thus subjecting them to punitive-damages caps. The appellate court also issued noteworthy decisions on exhaustion of administrative appeals, when causes of action accrue, workers-compensation immunity, and economic loss doctrine.

This section is not meant to serve as a comprehensive update; rather, it should serve as a useful summary of the most significant cases of the year.

## [B]  Statutory Developments

The Ohio General Assembly passed an omnibus bill that, among other things, requires the director of administrative services and the director of transportation to create procedures that give preference to "veteran-friendly business enterprises" in awarding state contracts.[89] The law requires the directors to define standards for determining which businesses are "veteran-friendly business enterprises," and establish procedures to provide preferences or bonus points for bids from such entities. To date, the directors of administrative services and transportation have not yet promulgated regulations implementing these standards and procedures.

## [C]  Developments in Ohio Case Law

### [1]  Appellate Court Rules That Parties Cannot Rely on Incorrect Information on Building Department Website

In *Union Township-Clermont County, C.I.C., Inc. v. Lamping*,[90] the Ohio Supreme Court ruled that parties cannot rely upon a mistake on a county's website in interpreting the Ohio Building Code. Union Township-Clermont County, C.I.C ("CIC") engaged a contractor to perform roofing repairs on a building CIC owned, including removing felt and reshingling on certain portions of the roof. CIC searched the building department's website to determine whether CIC would need permits for the roofing project. The website incorrectly stated that permits were needed for new roofs, but not new shingles only.[91] In reliance on this incorrect information, CIC did not draw permits for the project. The building department found CIC in violation of the Ohio Building Code, and the Board of Building Appeals affirmed.

A divided panel of the Ohio Court of Appeals affirmed. First, the court rejected CIC's argument that the building department should be equitably estopped from finding CIC in violation of the building code, because CIC acted

---

[89] Am. Sub. H.B. 64., 2015 Ohio Laws File 11.
[90] 31 N.E.3d 116 (Ohio 2015).
[91] *Union Township-Clermont County, C.I.C.*, 31 N.E.3d at 121.

in reliance on the department's own website. The court cited the longstanding rule that equitable estoppel cannot be used against the state, and that a private party assumes the risk that the advice of a government agent (here, the department's website) is inaccurate. The court also rejected CIC's argument that the building department's website should be used to interpret the Ohio Building Code. The court ruled that the code unambiguously required permits for reshingling projects.

### [2]  Ohio Supreme Court Rules That Action Against Developer and Property Manager with Tort and Contract Elements Sounded in Tort, Resulting in a Statutory Cap on Punitive Damages

In *Sivit v. Village Green of Beachwood LP*,[92] the Ohio Supreme Court held that an action against a developer and property manager for property damage from a fire caused by faulty workmanship sounded in tort. The case concerned a fire that broke out in an apartment building in 2007 and caused extensive property damage. An investigator determined that the fire originated in the space between the second and third floors due to faulty electrical wiring in between units. Four years earlier, a similar fire had damaged another building in the same complex, also caused by construction defects.[93] Several unit owners and subrogated insurers brought suit against the developer, claiming that the building had been negligently constructed. The plaintiffs were awarded $582,146 in compensatory damages and $2,000,000 in punitive damages after a jury trial.

Before the Ohio Supreme Court, the developer urged that the suit sounded in tort, and was therefore subject to R.C. 2315.21, which caps punitive damages for tort actions at twice the compensatory award. The Supreme Court agreed, holding that the property manager and plaintiffs, "have a contractual agreement, but the harm caused . . . is not the result of a contractual breach; it is the result of a violation of [the Ohio Landlord-Tenant Law], which constitutes negligence per se."[94] Moreover, plaintiffs' counsel conceded in oral argument that the action sounded in tort.[95] As a result, the action was subject to R.C. § 2315.21(D)(2)(a), which prohibits courts from entering judgment for punitive damages in excess of twice the amount of compensatory damages.[96] The Ohio Supreme Court then ordered a reduction in the amount of punitive damages.[97]

---

[92] 35 N.E.3d 508 (Ohio 2015).
[93] *Sivit*, 35 N.E.3d at 168.
[94] *Id.* at 170.
[95] *Id.*
[96] *Id.*
[97] *Id.* at 171.

[3]   Appellate Court Excuses Building Owner's Failure to Exhaust
      Administrative Remedies Where Building Owner Lost Lessee
      Because of Zoning Denial and Sought Compensation for a
      Regulatory Taking

In *Rural Building of Cincinnati, LLC v. Village of Evendale*,[98] Rural Building won a bid to use its building as a new office for the federal Immigration and Customs Enforcement ("ICE") agency. A small part of the lease with ICE required that rooms be available for temporary holding areas to interview detainees. A competitor falsely told the village building commissioner that ICE intended to use the premises as a detention facility, which was a prohibited use for the building under the village zoning code. The village building commissioner denied Rural Building a certificate of zoning approval. ICE then revoked the lease for nonperformance, and Rural Building had to sell the building at a loss.

Rural Building sued the village for a writ of mandamus to force the village to start appropriation proceedings, arguing that the commissioner's denial was a regulatory taking and that Rural Building was entitled to just compensation. The trial court dismissed the complaint for failure to exhaust administrative remedies, because Rural Building could have appealed the denial to the village council.

The appellate court reversed, holding that further administrative appeal would have been "vain and futile."[99] The court recognized that normally, a party must exhaust administrative remedies before seeking relief from an administrative decision. But the court also recognized an exception for where the further administrative review would be "vain and futile." The court held that this case fell within the "vain and futile" exception, because the village council could have reversed the denial of zoning approval, but could not have awarded compensation to Rural Building for a Regulatory Taking.


[4]   Appellate Court Holds That Implied Warranty Claim Accrued
      When the Plaintiff Discovered the Product Was Defective,
      Rather Than When Plaintiff Submitted a Formal Warranty Claim,
      Resulting in Application of Earlier, Plaintiff-Friendly Statutes

In *Quill v. Albert M Higley Co.*,[100] a late-2014 case, the Ohio appellate court took up several issues related to construction law. In 1994, the Ohio Department of Transportation ("ODOT") engaged a contractor to construct a new ODOT headquarters. The manufacturer of the roofing panels (Butler) issued an express warranty. After years of progressing corrosion and rust on the roofing panels, an ODOT employee submitted a formal warranty claim with respect to the roof on

---

[98] 32 N.E.3d 983 (Ohio Ct. App. 2015).
[99] *Rural Bldg.*, 32 N.E.3d at 987.
[100] 26 N.E.3d 1187 (Ohio Ct. App. 2014).

June 7, 2004. ODOT brought suit against several parties involved with the construction of the roof, including Butler. All parties but Butler settled with the plaintiff. After a jury returned a verdict in favor of the plaintiff, the court offset the amount ODOT received in settlement with the other defendants from the judgment.

Both Butler and ODOT appealed. Butler argued, *inter alia*, that ODOT's implied-warranty claim was barred by the economic loss doctrine. The court rejected this argument, noting that the economic loss rule for products-liability cases in Ohio changed effective April 7, 2005. In *Carrel v. Allied Products Corp.*,[101] the Ohio Supreme Court held that the Ohio Product Liability Act ("OPLA") did not abrogate common-law claims for purely economic loss (i.e., damage to the product itself). In response to *Carrel*, the Ohio General Assembly amended the OPLA to expressly abrogate common-law claims, effective April 7, 2005. In this case, the court found that the common-law cause of action clearly accrued before April 7, 2005.

ODOT argued that its judgment against Butler should not have been offset by the amount it received in settlement with the other defendants. The appellate court agreed. The court first held that the implied-warranty cause of action accrued when an inspector noticed the rust and corrosion on the roof (starting in 1997), rather than when the formal warranty claim was submitted (in 2004). Thus, the pre-2003 setoff statute applied, which only permitted a setoff where a co-defendant was "liable in tort."[102] Because the settling defendants were not found liable, nor did they stipulate to liability in the settlement, Butler was not entitled to the setoff. The court further held that, in any event, the settlement proceeds, which settled claims for faulty workmanship, did not concern the "same injury or loss" as the rusted roof panels.[103]

### [5] Federal District Court in Ohio Permits Subcontractor's Injured Employee Who Received Workers' Compensation to Sue Other Subcontractors, But Not General Contractor

In *Stolz v. J & B Steel Erectors, Inc.*,[104] a late-2014 case, the U.S. District Court for the Southern District of Ohio considered the effect of workers' compensation on an injured subcontractor's employee's claims against a general contractor and other subcontractors. Plaintiff was injured while working as a concrete finisher for Jostin, a subcontractor on a casino construction project. Messer, the general contractor, obtained approval from the Ohio Bureau of Workers' Compensation to self-insure the project, which allowed employees of enrolled

---

[101] 677 N.E.2d 795 (Ohio 1997).
[102] *Quill*, 26 N.E.3d at 1201–02.
[103] *Id.* at 1202.
[104] 76 F. Supp. 3d 696 (S.D. Ohio 2014).

subcontractors (including Jostin and the subcontractor defendants in the case) to participate in Messer's workers' compensation program. Plaintiff obtained benefits from Messer's workers' compensation program, but thereafter sued Messer and several other subcontractors for negligence. All defendants claimed they enjoyed workers' compensation immunity and moved for summary judgment.

The court ruled that Messer was entitled to workers' compensation immunity, since Jostin enrolled in Messer's workers' compensation program and Plaintiff accepted benefits from the program. The court rejected Plaintiff's argument that Messer had not strictly complied with the statutory requirements for general contractors to self-insure. Specifically, the court ruled that the Ohio Bureau of Workers' Compensation had already found Messer to be in full statutory compliance.

However, the court ruled that the remaining subcontractor-defendants were not entitled to workers' compensation immunity. The court found that the statute authorizing general contractors to offer workers' compensation plans for enrolled subcontractors did not permit subcontractors *other than the injured worker's employer* to enjoy the benefits of immunity. The court reasoned, "The words 'contractor*'s*' and 'subcontractor*'s*' are written in the singular possessive form. . . . As the statute is written, each subcontractor is protected from liability for injuries to one of the subcontractor's employees—its own."[105] Additionally, the court explained that granting the other subcontractors immunity would not comport with the policy behind workers' compensation, as the other subcontractors did not directly compensate Plaintiff for his injuries, and thus conferred no benefit that would entitle them to immunity.

### [6] Appellate Court Rules That Owner's Affiliate-Tenants Cannot Obtain Relief Against Subcontractor Under Economic Loss Doctrine and Third-Party Beneficiary Principles

In *Federal Insurance Co v. Fredericks*,[106] the appellate court affirmed a defense judgment in favor of subcontractors against a property owner and its affiliate tenants. Pasco purchased land in Vandalia to build a facility where its affiliates, Express and Logistics, would be tenants. Pasco's principal was friendly with a local contractor, Fredericks, and engaged Fredericks to construct the property on a handshake deal, without a written contract. Fredericks then engaged Skiles to erect a steel framework pursuant to a written subcontract. The subcontract identified a prime contract between Fredericks and Pasco, but made no mention of Express or Logistics. Skiles inadequately braced the structure and the framework collapsed in a windstorm.

---

[105] *Stolz,* 76 F. Supp. 3d at 704-05.
[106] 29 N.E.3d 313 (Ohio Ct. App. 2015).

Pasco, Express, and Logistics' subrogated insurers brought suit against Fredericks and the subcontractor. After a bench trial, the court found that damages for economic losses were only available to Pasco, because the economic loss doctrine barred any remedies other than contract, and Pasco was the only third-party beneficiary to the Fredericks/Skiles contract entitled to sue Skiles in contract. Logistics and Express, on the other hand, could not recover against Skiles at all because they were neither third-party beneficiaries nor owners of the property.

The appellate court affirmed, rejecting Express and Logistics' arguments that their claims fell in the narrow "sufficient nexus" exception to the economic loss doctrine. The court examined the Ohio Supreme Court's *Corporex* decision,[107] which held that an owner may not file a tort action against a subcontractor for economic losses, because the owner must instead sue the contractor, with whom it has a contract. The *Corporex* court further explained that while it was possible for a subcontractor to have a "sufficient nexus" to the property owner, such that the owner could claim against the subcontractor for economic damages, the owner must show more than that the subcontractor knew who the owner was. In general, courts have held that this "sufficient nexus" test can be met where the subcontractor has "excessive control" over the project, such as design professionals.[108]

In this case, the appellate court first held that *Corporex*'s "sufficient nexus" test can be applied to any subcontractor, not merely design professionals, rejecting the trial court's contrary interpretation. But the court went on to hold that Logistics and Express failed to prove a sufficient nexus to avoid the application of the economic loss doctrine. Skiles did not have any direct contact with Logistics or Express.[109] The court then further rejected Logistics and Express' argument that they were entitled to sue under the subcontract as third-party beneficiaries. The court found that the subcontract unambiguously identified only Pasco as a third-party beneficiary.[110]

## § 10.08 WISCONSIN

### [A] Introduction

The most interesting and impactful Wisconsin Construction case law in 2015 came out of the federal system, where two district court decisions provide insight for practitioners on some of the most prevalent construction issues. Though those

---

[107] Corporex Dev. & Constr. Mgmt., Inc. v. Shook, Inc., 835 N.E.2d 701 (Ohio 2005).

[108] *Fredericks*, 29 N.E.3d at 321 (citing Ohio Plaza Assoc., Inc. v. Hillsboro Assoc., 835 N.E.2d 701).

[109] *Id.* at 322–23.

[110] *Id.* at 326.

cases are only of persuasive value (and one remains on appeal in the Seventh Circuit), they are certainly worth a read for construction counsel and clients.

Though this chapter is not a comprehensive review of the State of Wisconsin construction law, for context purposes, a few baseline points are noteworthy. Wisconsin has adopted a form of the economic loss rule barring tort claims where a contract existed or could have existed. However, Wisconsin also has a services exception to that economic loss rule.[111] Thus, service providers (such as architects, engineers and owners' representatives) are subject to liability under both tort and contract theories while theoretically contractors (who provide only a product) are subject to liability only under contract. In Wisconsin, tort claims are subject to a discovery rule, meaning the cause of action accrues upon discovery of the injury. However, a contract cause of action accrues at the moment the contract is breached, meaning that most construction-related contract claims are barred six years after the certificate of substantial completion of the project.[112]

As noted in *Linden v. Cascade Stone Co.*[113] courts "use the predominant purpose test to determine whether a mixed contract for products and services is predominantly a sale of a product and therefore subject to the economic loss doctrine, or predominantly a contract for services and therefore not subject to the economic loss doctrine."

Wisconsin also has a consumer protection statute (Wis. Stat. § 100.18) which could provide remedies to purchasers where a defendant made an untrue, deceptive or misleading statement to induce a sale. Many construction companies have begun to rely on that statute. Claims under that statute must be brought within three years of the statement at issue.

Wisconsin also has a statute of repose, Wis. Stat. § 893.89. The statute prohibits, with many exceptions, actions or injury to a person, injury to property, or a wrongful death resulting from improvements to a property brought within 10 years after substantial completion of the improvement, regardless of when the injuries are discovered or the cause of action accrues. Exceptions include (1) fraud or misrepresentation; (2) an express warranty for a longer period; (3) claims against an owner or occupier resulting from negligence of a maintenance operation or inspection of property; and (4) damages that were sustained before the effective date of the statute (1994).

---

[111] Insurance Co. of N. Am. v. Cease Elec. Inc., 2004 WI 139, 276 Wis. 2d 361, 688 N.W.2d 462.

[112] CLL Assocs. Ltd. P'ship v. Arrowhead Pac. Corp.,174 Wis. 2d 604, 607, 497 N.W.2d 115 (1993).

[113] 2005 WI 113, 283 Wis. 2d 606, 699 N.W.2d 189, ¶ 8 (citations omitted).

## [B]  Recent Statutory and Regulatory Developments

### [1]  Right to Work Legislation

The most significant Wisconsin piece of legislation affecting the construction industry was 2015 Wisconsin Act 1, which creates what is commonly referred to as a "right-to-work" law for private sector employers and employees in that the Act prohibits an employer and labor organization from entering into an agreement that requires membership in a labor organization as a condition of employment. That law was enacted on March 9, 2015, and took effect the next day.

Under the Act, a private sector employer may not enter into an all-union agreement with a labor organization. In addition, the Act prohibits a person from requiring an individual to do any of the following as a condition of obtaining or continuing employment:

- Refrain or resign from membership in, voluntary affiliation with, or voluntary financial support of a labor organization.

- Become or remain a member of a labor organization.

- Pay any dues, fees, assessment, or other charges or expenses of any kind or amount, or provide anything of value, to a labor organization.

- Pay to any third party an amount that is in place of, equivalent to, or any portion of dues, fees, assessments, or other charges or expenses required of members of, or employees represented by, a labor organization.

This legislation remains subject to court challenge, but a Dane County Circuit Court Judge declined to block the law while several unions challenge it. The challenge remains pending.[114]

### [2]  Limits on Local Regulation of Professionals

Senate Bill 81 limits the authority of political subdivisions to regulate professions. Specifically, the bill prohibits a city, village, town, or county from imposing occupational fees or licensing requirements on any additional professions, but allows them to continue imposing fees and licensing requirements on professions subject to such regulation on the effective date of the bill.

---

[114] Dane Cnty. Circuit Ct. Case No. 15-cv-628.

### [3]  Potential Tax-Exemption for Materials Purchases

Near the end of 2015, legislation exempting contractors from having to pay sales and use taxes on material bought for certain otherwise tax-exempt projects was close to passage, but had not yet been enacted.

## [C]  Recent Case Law Developments

### [1]  U.S. District Court Rejects Breach of Contract and Promissory Estoppel Claims Where Curtain Wall Subcontractor Disengages After General Contractor Awards Bid but Parties Cannot Come to Agreement on Subcontract Terms

In *CG Schmidt, Inc. v. Permasteelisa North America*,[115] the U.S. District Court, applying Wisconsin law, analyzed the applicability of the Uniform Commercial Code ("UCC") while dismissing on summary judgment breach of contract and promissory estoppel claims brought by the general contractor against a curtainwall subcontractor.

The general contractor issued a comprehensive bid package that required subcontractors to agree to the GCs form of subcontract, allowed for several alternative bids, but required that subcontractors not withdraw their base bid for 120 days after bid opening. After award of the bid to curtain wall subcontractor, the subcontract was not executed because (1) the general contractor had not yet entered into either the general contract or the Guarantee Maximum Price Amendment with the owner; and (2) the parties actively engaged in refining various aspects of their agreement in a value engineering process. The parties exchanged nonbinding letters of intent and subcontract forms, none of which were signed and each of which included prices, which changed. Ultimately, the curtainwall subcontractor disengaged for reasons related to its production capacity and the general contractor sued for damages under both breach of contract and promissory estoppel theories.

The subcontractor moved for summary judgment. The Court first looked to *Linden* and concluded that because the thrust of the parties' negotiations related to the sale of goods, the UCC applied. The Court acknowledged that under the UCC (and common law) parties may become bound by contract in the absence of a "mirror image" response, and that the key question of the parties' intent to contract is often factually based and thus not appropriate for summary judgment. However, the Court concluded that the parties through their own words and actions, expressly manifested an intention not to be bound by any bids, agreements, proposals, or negotiations until they signed a written subcontract with the complete terms of their agreement. Accordingly, it found that the undisputed facts

---

[115] No. 14-CV-1553-JPS, 2015 WL 6442634 (E.D. Wis. Oct. 23, 2015).

made clear that the parties lack the requisite intention to be bound and the breach of contract action was subject to summary judgment dismissal.

The Court also dismissed the GC's claim under promissory estoppel, an equitable doctrine intended to protect parties that have not entered into a contract, but nonetheless incurred damages acting in reliance on a promise made by another party. The Court noted the four elements of such a claim: (1) a promise; (2) on which the promisor should reasonably expect to induce action or forbearance; (3) which does induce such action or forbearance; and (4) that injustice can be avoided only by enforcement of that promise. For largely the same reasons stated above with respect to the contract claim, the Court found that no reasonable fact-finder could conclude that the subcontractor's bid was a promise that the subcontractor should expect to induce action or forbearance, in light of the parties' manifest intent to be bound to a fully integrated and superseding subcontract, which was never signed. Moreover, it found that any reliance by the general contractor on the sub's bid was unreasonable under the circumstances and that the general contractor has established no damages. The Court last found that justice did not require the bid's enforcement in part because both the general contractor and subcontractor were experienced actors in the commercial real estate industry.

The general contractor has filed an appeal of the decision, which remains pending in the U.S. Court of Appeals for the Seventh Circuit.

### [2] Federal Court Decision Dismissing Claims of Subcontractor Provides Insights into "Total Cost Method" and "Measured Mile" Damage-Calculation Methods as well as "No Damages for Delay" Clauses

In *North American Mechanical v. Walsh Construction Co. II, LLC,*[116] the Court rejected all but $7,320.64 of the subcontractors' multi-million claim, largely because the subcontractor was contractually barred from seek delay damages and the Court found the impact claim it presented was a delay damage claim. In doing so in a decision to be published, the Court addressed a number of issues common to construction disputes, including the Total Cost Method and the effect of short claim deadlines in construction contracts.

### [a] Rejection of Delay Damage Claim

The case's most significant ruling was the dismissal of a labor inefficiency or delay claim. The Court found (1) that the claim however characterized, fell within the scope of the "delay, hindrance, interference or other similar event"

---

[116] No. 12-CV-598, 2015 WL 5530190 (E.D. Wis. Sept. 18, 2015).

language within section 4.4 of the GC-Sub contract (a no-damage for delay pro-vision); (2) much of the claim was likely barred by a failure of the sub to comply with a requirement that it bring claims within seven (7) days of the occurrence of the event giving rise to such claim; and (3) the subs' total cost method damages calculation was not appropriate.

The Court noted that under Wisconsin law, there are only three instances where a claim otherwise barred by a "no damages for delay" clause can go for-ward: (1) delays caused by fraudulent conduct, (2) delays caused by orders made in bad faith, and (3) orders that are unnecessary and the result of inexcusable ignorance or incompetence.[117] The Court found none of these to apply and enforced the limiting clause.

The Court also found that the GC's 21-day claim deadline (imposed in its contract with the Owner), made the seven-day deadline for the sub reasonable, and general letters by the Subcontractor reserving rights to later bring claims were not sufficient, to meet this requirement.

The Court then rejected the subs' total cost method damages calculation. The Court cited a Federal Circuit case, *Propellex Corp. v. Brownlee*,[118] for the rule that before a contractor can obtain the benefit of the total cost method, it must prove (1) the impracticability of proving its actual losses directly; (2) the reason-ableness of its bid; (3) the reasonableness of its actual costs; and (4) lack of responsibility for the added costs. The Court found that the sub could not utilize this method because it failed to analyze or account for its own responsibility for the added costs. The Court briefly discussed a complementary "measured mile" analysis done by the subs' expert, but concluded (as had the expert) that the analy-sis could not stand on its own. The Court similarly rejected the expert's rudimen-tary analysis based on Mechanical Contractors Association of America (MCAA) Factors.

### [b]   GC Need Not Sue Owner for Unwarranted COs Forwarded by Sub

The Court rejected some of the subs' claims (related to extra cost attribut-able to BIM issues) after the GC concluded that it could not in good faith certify the extra work claims to the Owner. The GC-Sub contract provided that the sub was bound to the GC to the same extent that the GC was bound to the Owner. The contract provided that should the GC be unable to in good faith certify claims submitted by the sub, it shall not be required to do so, the subs' claims against the GC (or its surety) are waived, but the GC has the option of allowing the sub to

---

[117] 2015 WL 5530190, at *10 (citing John R. Gregory & Son, Inc. v. A. Guenther & Sons Co., 147 Wis. 2d 298, 304, 432 N.W.2d 584, 586 (1988)).

[118] 342 F.3d 1335, 1339 (Fed. Cir. 2003).

present the claims directly to the Owner. The GC submitted the first BIM-related change order request to the Owner and set up a meeting among the sub, GC, and Owner. The Owner rejected the request after that meeting. The GC also passed on two additional CO requests, though it contended the sub did not provide sufficient substantiation for the requests. The Owner rejected those rejects and the GC did not forward on a fourth related CO request. The Sub contended that the GC did not do enough to pursue the CO requests. The Court disagreed, finding that the GC did enough, that the Contract did not require the GC to sue the Owner over the request, and, in any event, the sub was unable to prove it was damaged by any work done outside its original scope.

The Court also rejected the subs' claim for extended general conditions where the subs' expert merely calculated an increased general conditions amount by multiplying the extras days by a daily general conditions average rather than analyzing the actual expenses incurred.

### [c]   Lien Waivers Did Not Waive Claims

Prior to dismissing the claims as noted above, the Court preserved them by rejecting overbroad language in a contractually required lien waiver that the general contractor contended limited the subs' claim. The lien form, which was contractually required, was very comprehensive, waiving any remedy of any sort in exchange for the draw. While the sub used this form for the first four draws, in subsequent requests it added the phrase "with the exception of all previously made claims in writing," and later even more expansive claim reservation language. The sub issued several claim letters throughout construction. The GC contended that the sub breached the contract by altering the form, and as a consequence, the Court should excise the reservation language and enforced the waiver as originally written. The Court rejected the GCs argument, going so far as to say that applying the principles of the cases relied upon by the GC would render the entire waiver void in its entirety. While the Court did not so rule, it concluded that the lien waivers had no impact on the vitality of the subs' claims.

### [3]   Title Insurance Coverage Case Give Insurance Duty to Defend, but Not Indemnify

In *BB Syndication Services, Inc. v. First American Title Insurance Co.,*[119] a construction lender brought an action title insurer, seeking defense and indemnification in an adversary bankruptcy proceeding after the lender cut off loan disbursement to a construction project and the project's developer declared bankruptcy. After removal to federal court, both the district court and the Seventh

---

[119] 780 F.3d 825 (7th Cir. 2015).

Circuit found that the title insurer owed a duty of defense, but not a duty to indemnify. The court's rationale was that the lender had created or suffered the mechanics liens at issue, thus triggering an exclusion in the policy, and the title insurer's agreement not to invoke a different exclusion did not bar it from raising the exclusion at issue.

The decision includes a helpful background on how title insurance functions in the construction context as well as an intriguing footnote from the author, Judge Diane Sykes stating that within the realm of title insurance policies, there is reason to doubt the application of the general rule in Wisconsin that ambiguities in policy language are construed against the insurer.[120]

Exclusion 3(a) of the policy excludes from coverage any liens that are "created, suffered, assumed or agreed to" by the insured [Lender]. The court concluded that if the lender in some way caused the costs overrun, or had control over when the project was aborted, then it could be deemed at fault for any resulting mechanics' liens. The court addressed a split in authority among the federal circuits, and sided with the Eighth and Tenth circuit in holding that the exclusion excludes coverage for liens that arise as a result of insufficient funds (as opposed to liens that arise because a lender is being asked to pay twice). The court noted that only the lender has the ability—and thus duty—to investigate and monitor the construction project's economic viability. When liens arise from insufficient funds, the insured lender has "created" them by failing to discover and prevent costs overruns. Thus, the court found, there is no duty to indemnify.

### [4] Debtor Contractors Theft by Contractor Debt Is Non-Dischargeable

Both the Seventh Circuit, in *Stoughton Lumber v. Sveum*,[121] and the district court thereafter in *Sveum v. Stoughton Lumber*,[122] held that officer and shareholder of corporate contractor had acted with at least willful blindness to fiduciary obligation imposed on him by statute when he failed to take any action to ensure that contractor was complying with its trust obligations under the Wisconsin theft-by-contractor statute. Accordingly, his debts were non-dischargeable in bankruptcy.

---

[120] 780 F.3d at 830 n.4.
[121] 787 F.3d 1174 (7th Cir. 2015).
[122] 534 B.R. 771 (W.D. Wis. 2015).

### [5] State's Claim for Falsification of Education Qualifications and Overbilling by DBE Contractor Is Non-Dischargeable

Similarly, in *Burse v. Gottlieb,*[123] the Bankruptcy, District and Seventh Circuit Courts agreed that $822,000 owed to the state by a Contractor in the Disadvantaged Business Enterprise ("DBE") Program were not dischargeable in bankruptcy. While the DBE contractor also falsified his resume to gain admittance to the program, the debt at issue was related to overbilling as the State did not seek return of every dollar received from the contractor, just the amounts overbilled. To prove a debt is non-dischargeable because of fraud, a creditor must prove by a preponderance of evidence that "(1) the debtor made a false representation or omission, (2) that the debtor (a) knew was false or made with reckless disregard for the truth and (b) was made with the intent to deceive, and (3) upon which the creditor justifiably relied."[124] The debtor challenged the second element contending that no direct evidence made him responsible for the "mistakes" that lead to the overbilling. However, the Seventh Circuit concluded that the bankruptcy judge was entitled to rely on circumstantial evidence, which showed that, by signing inflated timesheets and overseeing a billing system that regularly overcharged the state, the debtor knew about the falsehoods and intended to deceive the state.

## [D] Unpublished Case Law

While Wisconsin State Courts has actually no published opinions on construction-related issues in 2015, a few unpublished decisions confirmed the direction of the courts and merit brief discussion here.

### [1] Governmental Immunity Shields Contractor from Damages Caused While Working for Wisconsin Department of Transportation

In *Melchert v. Pro Electric Contractors,*[125] an electrical contractor who damaged a sewer lateral while installing a traffic light was sued by nearby businesses, and claimed municipal immunity. The Court of Appeals in an unpublished decision applied precedent from *Estate of Lyons v. CNA Ins. Cos.*[126] and *Showers Appraisals LLC v. Musson Bros., Inc.*[127] and dismissed the claims. The Court concluded that in order to claims immunity, the governmental contract must prove

---

[123] No. 14-3492, 2015 WL 5235659 (7th Cir. Sept. 9, 2015).

[124] Ojeda v. Goldberg, 599 F.3d 712, 716-17 (7th Cir. 2010).

[125] 2015 WI App 37, 862 N.W.2d 902, 2015 WL 1034756 (unpublished).

[126] 207 Wis. 2d 446, 558 N.W.2d 658 (Ct. App. 1996).

[127] 2013 WI 79, 350 Wis. 2d 509, 835 N.W.2d 226.

both that it meets the definition of "Agent" as set forth in Lyons and that the contractor's act is one for which immunity is available under § 893.80(4). That is, the contractor must show that the relevant decision of the government entity that the contractor implements is itself, entitled to immunity.

Here, it was clear that the engineering plan, detailing where and how to install a traffic light, i.e., how deep and wide and with an auger, was part of the governmental design selection which is a legislative or quasi-legislative decision entitled to immunity. However, the plaintiffs argued that the contractor must have realized that the sewer lateral had been severed and the contractor was negligent in backfilling the hole without first repairing the damage, and that such action was not protected by any governmental immunity. The Court rejected the argument, finding that there is nothing in the record to support a causal connection between these specific allegations and the alleged negligence.

### [2] Jury And Court Find That Property Insurance Coverage Triggers Exclusion in Builders Risk Policy After Fire Destroys Project After Owner Occupies It, but Before Substantial Completion

In *Fontana Builders v. Assurance*,[128] a homebuilder purchased builder's risk insurance policy on the home it was building. Before it was completed, the builder's owner and his family moved into the house, still titled to the Builder. Because the builder's mortgagee required the owner to purchase homeowner's insurance before it would close on a loan with them , the Owner did. A week after the policy went into effect, a fire destroyed much of the home and its contents.

The Builder filed a claim under the builder's risk policy and the owner made a claim under the homeowner's policy. Pointing to Section E.3 of the builder's risk policy, which provides that coverage would terminate "when permanent property insurance applies," the Builders' Risk insurer denied coverage on grounds that the homeowner's policy constituted "permanent property insurance" that "applied." Without admitting liability, the homeowner's policy paid $1.5 million pursuant to a settlement agreement.

The builder filed suit and the circuit court determined that the builder's risk policy provided coverage as a matter of law. That ruling was overturned on appeal.[129] The Court said that on remand the jury would have to determine whether permanent property insurance applied at the time of the fire, and that the court could not "preclude the jury from considering the Chubb policy or any other extrinsic evidence that is relevant to Section E.3 of the builder's risk policy."[130]

---

[128] 2015 WI App 43.

[129] Fontana Builders, Inc. v. Assurance Co. of Am., No. 2010AP2074, unpublished slip op. ¶ 11 (Dec. 7, 2011).

[130] *Id.*

During the remand trial, the jury heard that the Homeowner's policy had paid $1.5 million. On appeal, it was argued that this was inadmissible settlement evidence. The Court of Appeals affirmed, noting that evidentiary decisions are discretionary decisions for the trial court and that the Court gave a instruction that the jury was not to use the settlement evidence to show liability or proved the invalidity of the claim at issue.

This unpublished decision was appealed to the Wisconsin Supreme Court, who accepted review of the case and framed the issues as follows: (1) whether the "fact, purpose and amounts of settlement" payments a homeowner policy made to buyers should have been barred by application of Wis. Stat. § 904.08; (2) whether the trial court's ruling that the policy was not "other insurance" as a matter of law required the trial court to remove the issues presented to the jury from jury consideration; (3) whether the interpretation of the provisions of an insurance policy can ever be an issue of fact for the jury; and (4) does a builder's risk insurance coverage obtained by a builder/owner terminate when a potential purchaser obtains property insurance to cover the potential purchaser's separate insurable interest in the property?

# CHAPTER 11

# SOUTHWEST REGION

Arkansas, Colorado, Kansas, Louisiana, New Mexico, Oklahoma, Texas

Michael Cortez, Michael F. Albers

## § 11.01  INTRODUCTION

This chapter is intended to update the recent major developments (not cumulative or exhaustive) in construction law in the Southwest Region. Also, the authors' commentary contained herein is not meant as legal advice. While 2015 was a tumultuous economic year in the region relating to the energy industry, there was no slowdown in developments of interest to the construction law practitioner. The trends of interest are the "usual suspects," but with some interesting twists and turns, with some outcomes expected, and some not.

## § 11.02  LIEN LAW

In *Pham v. Harris County Rentals, L.L.C.*, an appellate court in Texas held that a general contractor's lien waiver could not serve as a basis for waiving a subcontractor's lien rights.[1] The owner argued that he relied on the general contractor's waiver and affidavit that all subcontractor payments had been made.[2] There was no evidence that the subcontractor executed such a waiver and release and the owners did not provide any authority for its argument that these releases by other entities somehow serve to also waive the subcontractor's right to file a lien.[3] Therefore, because the subcontractor is not "the undersigned" on any of the releases in the record executed by the general contractor, the releases cannot be construed as a waiver of its right to file a lien.[4] While the general contractor might be liable to the owners for damages arising out of any false statement in its signed lien releases, including its statement that "any and all payment due to third parties on said project for services and/or materials have been paid in full," the court of appeals concluded that any misstatement by the general contractor in its own lien waiver could not serve as a basis for waiving the subcontractor's lien rights.[5]

Also on appeal, the owners contended that subcontractor did not perfect its lien against the property as a matter of law since the subcontractor failed to comply with the statutory notice provision of § 53.103 the Texas Property Code. According to the subcontractor, however, it was not required to prove that it complied with § 53.103 because, pursuant to Texas Rule of Civil Procedure 54, it pleaded that all conditions precedent had been performed or had occurred. Rule 54 provides:

> In pleading the performance or occurrence of conditions precedent, it shall be sufficient to aver generally that all conditions precedent have been performed or have occurred. When such performances or occurrences have been so

---

[1] 455 S.W.3d 702 (Tex. App.—Houston [1st Dist.] 2014, no pet.).

[2] *Id.* at 709.

[3] *Id.* at 710.

[4] *Id.*

[5] *Id.* (quoting Tex. Prop. Code § 53.085(e)).

plead, the party so pleading same shall be required to prove only such of them as are specifically denied by the opposite party.

The court of appeals stated that the language in the subcontractor's pleading sufficiently placed the owner on notice of the subcontractor's claim that all conditions precedent had occurred. Because the lien claimant pleaded that all conditions precedent had "been performed or occurred," it was required to only prove the conditions precedent that the owner specifically denied. In its responsive pleadings filed with the trial court, the owner did not specifically deny that subcontractor had timely filed its affidavit. In the owner's *pro se* answer, he asserted that he had paid the general contractor in full and argued that there had to be some way to protect consumers, and that the matter should be between the subcontractor and the general contractor. Pursuant to the appeals court, that general rather than specific denial, however, was not sufficient. Texas Rule of Civil Procedure 54 requires the opposing party to specifically deny which conditions precedent have not been performed or have not occurred. By failing to specifically deny that the subcontractor failed to timely file its lien affidavit, according to the court, the owner waived his right to complain of such failure or invalidity of the lien on appeal.

**Authors' Commentary**: This is what we commonly refer to as "bad facts make bad law." Please note that the owner of the property was, at first, representing himself or herself and filed a less than "formal" pleading with the court. The court of appeals took that "general" rather than "specific" denial of the lien validity under the Texas Property Code for the subcontractor's failure to send the required pre-lien notices. The lesson (other than to hire an experienced construction attorney rather than to represent yourself) is to always review the validity of lien foreclosure lawsuits, and if there is, or could be a specific lien validity defect or issue, it must be specifically denied in the answer to the lawsuit. Otherwise, this case might be used to argue the resuscitation of an otherwise defective lien. In the authors' opinion, the lien statute could not have meant for court rules of procedure to trump the meaning and intent of the lien statutes in Texas, however, this case could be seen otherwise.

In a case regarding lien priority in Arkansas,[6] on September 17, 2007, a bank and the owner of the property executed a promissory note and loan agreement for $8,606,250 to finance construction of a residential subdivision in Arkansas. The project was commenced by the contractor on the morning of October 1, 2007, and the bank filed its mortgage that afternoon.

An engineering firm subsequently began working on the project for the owner. On September 25, 2009, the engineering firm filed an "Architect's and Engineer's Account and Affidavit of Account" stating that the owner owed the engineering firm $37,239.45.

---

[6] Crafton, Tull, Sparks & Assocs., Inc. v. Ruskin Heights, LLC, 2015 Ark. 1, 453 S.W.3d 667 (2015).

The engineer subsequently filed suit and requested, among other causes of action, that its lien and the contractor's lien be declared superior to any lien or claims by the bank and the owner. The engineer filed a motion for summary judgment as to its lien claims. After hearings, the court ruled that: (1) the engineer had an engineering and architectural lien against the property at issue; (2) the engineer's lien did not have priority over the bank's mortgage lien; and (3) the engineer's lien did not relate back to the date of commencement of the construction. Then, the court issued a partial judgment and decree, finding that: (1) the owner had defaulted and owed the bank damages; (2) the bank's mortgage lien was valid and enforceable; (3) the bank had first priority as to any lien claim by contractor or engineer; and (4) the engineer had a second lien on the property.

The engineer appealed, and the lower appellate court ruled that the "Architect's and Engineer's Liens are not given the same priority under [Arkansas Code Annotated section] 18-44-105 as Materialmen's [sic] and Laborer's Liens," and further found that "Engineering Firm's Architect's and Engineer's Lien did not attach to the property until August 25, 2009, which [was] the date Engineering Firm's lien was filed of record." Several appeals, motions, and judgments were made. Ultimately, the engineer appealed to the Supreme Court of Arkansas.

On appeal to the Supreme Court of Arkansas, the engineer argued two points. The court addressed them together as they were related. First, the engineer contended that it was error when the lower court failed to grant the engineer's lien priority over a mortgage filed after construction had commenced. They asserted that the lower court incorrectly interpreted the engineer's lien statute, Arkansas Code Annotated § 18-44-105 (Supp. 2013), in connection with Arkansas Code Annotated § 18-44-110 (Repl. 2003). Furthermore, the engineer maintained that its September 25, 2009 lien should have related back to the *morning* of October 1, 2007, when construction was commenced by the contractor, thereby giving it priority over the bank's mortgage lien, which was filed in the *afternoon* of October 1, 2007 (emphasis added). For the second point on appeal, the engineer argued that § 18-44-110 removes any distinction between an engineer's lien and a materialman's lien and reiterated that its' lien should have related back to the commencement of construction and should have had priority over bank's mortgage.

The court stated that the statute was clear and so the plain meaning of the language was used. The sole issue on appeal involved the court's statutory interpretation of §§ 18-44-105 and 18-44-110. Section 18-44-105, the engineer's lien statute, provides as follows:

> (a) Every architect, engineer, surveyor, appraiser, landscaper, abstractor, or title insurance agent who shall do or perform any architectural, engineering, surveying, appraisal, landscaping, or abstracting services upon any land, or who shall issue a title insurance policy or provide landscaping supplies upon any land, building, erection, or improvement upon land, under or by virtue of any written agreement for the performance of the work with the owner thereof, or his or her agent, shall have a lien upon the land, building,

erection, or improvement upon land to the extent of the agreed contract price
or a reasonable price for those services.

(b)(1) However, the lien does not attach to the land, building, erection,
or improvement upon land unless and until the lien is duly filed of record with
the circuit clerk and recorder in the county in which the land, building, erection, or improvement is located.

(2) The lien shall be:

(A) Subject to the notice requirements of §§ 18-44-114 and
18-44-115;

(B) Filed under § 18-44-117; and

(C) Enforced under this subchapter.

The court said the plain meaning of this statute says that engineers shall
have a lien, but that the lien "does not attach to the land, building, erection, or
improvement upon [the] land unless and until the lien is duly filed of record."
Here, the engineer filed its lien on September 25, 2009. Thus, the court held that
the engineer's lien was attached on September 25, 2009, when it was "duly filed
of record" as noted in (b)(1) above.

Next, the court addressed the engineer's argument that its engineer's lien
related back to the date the construction commenced. Pursuant to § 18-44-105, the
engineer argued that its engineer's lien related back to the date that the construction commenced under a relate-back provision contained in § 18-44-110. Section
18-44-110 provides in its entirety as follows:

(a)(1) The liens for labor performed or material or fixtures furnished, as
provided for in this subchapter, shall have equal priority toward each other
without regard to the date of filing the account or lien or the date when the
particular labor or material was performed or furnished. All such liens shall
date from the time that the construction or repair first commenced.

(2) Construction or repair commences when there is a visible mani-
festation of activity on real estate that would lead a reasonable person to
believe that construction or repair of an improvement to the real estate has
begun or will soon begin, including, but not limited to, the following:

(A) Delivery of a significant amount of lumber, bricks, pipe, tile,
or other building material to the site;

(B) Grading or excavating the site;

(C) Laying out lines or grade stakes; or

(D) Demolition in an existing structure.

(3) In all cases in which a sale shall be ordered and the property sold,
and the proceeds arising from the sale are not sufficient to discharge in full all
the liens against the property without reference to the date of filing the
account or lien, the proceeds shall be paid pro rata on the respective liens.

(b)(1) (A) The liens for labor performed or materials or fixtures furnished, as provided for in this subchapter, shall attach to the improvement on
which the labor was performed or the materials or fixtures were furnished in

preference to any encumbrance existing on the real estate prior to the commencement of construction or repair of the improvement.

(B) In all cases in which the prior encumbrance was given for the purpose of funding construction or repair of the improvement, that lien shall have priority over all liens given by this subchapter.

(2) The liens, as provided for in this subchapter, shall be enforced by foreclosure, as further provided for in this subchapter, and the property ordered sold subject to the lien of the prior encumbrance on the real estate.

(c) The lien for labor performed and materials or fixtures furnished, as provided for in this subchapter, shall have priority over all other encumbrances that attach to the real estate or improvements thereon subsequent to commencement of construction or repair.

However, contrary to the engineer's assertions, the court did not read § 18-44-110 to expand the priority-lien privilege to include the engineer's liens. Section 18-44-110(a)(1) contains the sentence, "All such liens shall date from the time that the construction or repair first commenced," but the court said that the sentence does not apply to all liens contained in the code's subchapter entitled, "Mechanics' and Materialmen's Liens" as the engineer suggested. Rather, the court said "all such liens" in § 18-44-110(a)(1) specifically modifies "[t]he liens for labor performed or material or fixtures furnished" contained in the first sentence of section 18-44-110(a)(1). In other words, the plain "such liens" language in § 18-44-110(a)(1) refers to materialmen's, laborer's, and mechanics' liens contained in the subchapter but not an engineer's lien, which the legislature set forth separately in § 18-44-105.

Further, the court explained that § 18-44-110(a)(1) expressly gives equal priority to materialmen's, laborer's, and mechanics' liens "without regard to the date of filing," while § 18-44-105(b)(1) specifically states that engineer's liens attach upon filing. Thus, given a strict construction of § 18-44-110, the court concluded that any relate-back provisions in § 18-44-110 do not apply to engineer's liens and that § 18-44-1.10 does not allow for an engineer's lien to relate back to the date of construction. The court held that the lower court properly granted summary judgment as a matter of law by finding that the bank's lien, filed on October 1, 2007, had priority over the engineer's lien filed on September 25, 2009.

For those reasons, the Supreme Court of Arkansas affirmed. The court ruled that the statute allowing materialmen's, laborer's, and mechanics' liens to relate back to the date on which construction or repair first commenced does not allow for an engineer's lien to relate back to the date of initial construction by the contractor.

**Authors' Commentary**: Contrary to the Texas case in this chapter, this case from Arkansas illustrates the strict interpretation of lien statutes rather than the liberal construction in favor of the lien claimants. The language of the statute was clear as to the different commencement and priority of an engineer's and materialman's lien in Arkansas.

## § 11.03  PAY-IF-PAID

A general contractor and subcontractor entered into a subcontract to perform excavation work on a project in Arkansas.[7] The subcontract contained what
is commonly known in the construction industry as a "pay-if-paid" clause. The
pay-if-paid clause in this case specified that contractor's receipt of payment from
the project owner for work performed by the subcontractor was an absolute condition precedent to the contractor's obligation to pay the subcontractor for that
work. The contractor was not fully paid by the owner for the subcontractor's
work. After a dispute arose regarding how much compensation was owed under
the subcontract, the subcontractor filed a materialmen's lien against the project,
and the contractor filed a bond in contest of the lien. A surety company issued a
lien-release bond as surety on behalf of its principal, the contractor.

The subcontract between the contractor and the subcontractor contained the
following provisions:

> Subcontractor will receive payment from the contractor once the contractor
> has been paid by the owner. No monies are owed to the subcontractor until
> Contractor has received payment from the owner for the subcontractor's
> work.
>
>     The parties hereto agree and acknowledge, that as an absolute condition
> precedent to Progress Payments to the SUBCONTRACTOR, the CONTRAC-
> TOR must receive corresponding payment from the OWNER for SUBCON-
> TRACTOR's Work. In the event of nonpayment by OWNER,
> SUBCONTRACTOR's remedies are against the OWNER.
>
>     [N]o payment from CONTRACTOR SUBCONTRACTOR shall be due
> unless the CONTRACTOR receives payment from OWNER for the Work of
> the SUBCONTRACTOR. In the event of nonpayment by OWNER,
> SUBCONTRACTOR's remedies are against the OWNER.

The subcontractor filed suit against the contractor and surety seeking
recovery against contractor for breach of contract and against both contractor and
surety under the lien-release bond. The circuit court directed a verdict in favor of
contractor, ruling that the pay-if-paid clause in the subcontract barred recovery
from contractor because there was no evidence that contractor had been paid by
the owner for the work the subcontractor alleged it had performed. The case
against surety on the lien-release bond was submitted to the jury. The jury
reached a verdict in favor of the subcontractor and awarded damages against the
surety in the amount of $25,478.20 (less than the full amount requested by the
subcontractor).

---

[7] Travelers Cas. & Sur. Co. of Am. v. Sweet's Contracting, Inc., 2014 Ark. 484, 450 S.W.3d 229
(2014).

The subcontractor appealed to the Supreme Court of Arkansas. The surety argued that a surety's liability on a lien-release bond cannot exceed the liability of its principal (the contractor). A suretyship as a contractual relation whereby one party engages to be answerable for the debt or default of another. Because a surety's liability is derivative, it ordinarily does not exceed that of the principal. Generally, a surety may invoke all defenses available to the principal. In a suretyship, the principal's contract and the bond or undertaking of the surety are to be construed together as one instrument.

Under the terms of the subcontract, the contractor and the subcontractor agreed that contractor would pay sub for performance of "the Work," *if* the owner paid the contractor for the subcontractor's performance of the work (see clause above). Surety's obligation on the bond was coextensive with and measured by the promises of the contractor to the subcontractor contained in the subcontract. In other words, the surety, by the bond, bound itself *only* to the performance of the acts that the contractor had promised to perform as part of the subcontract. The contractor expressly agreed in the subcontract to pay the subcontractor only if the owner paid the contractor for the subcontractor's work. Because the owner did not pay the contractor for the subcontractor's work, the contractor was entitled to invoke the pay-if-paid clause as a defense. As such, the surety, as the contractor's surety, was entitled to invoke the same defense.

The subcontractor contended that, even if the pay-if-paid clause allowed the contractor to avoid liability, the pay-if-paid clause did not absolve the surety because the surety had an independent obligation to the subcontractor under the surety bond issued pursuant to the materialmen's lien statute. The Supreme Court of Arkansas disagreed.

The law states that if the bond is filed and approved by the circuit clerk, and the claimant, after notice, does not question its sufficiency or form, the lien is discharged and the claimant shall have recourse only against the principal and surety upon the bond.[8] If an action to enforce the lien is filed within the time prescribed for enforcement of a lien against the surety, "the surety shall be liable in like manner as the principal."[9] Because the contractor was not liable under the subcontract, then it follows that surety was also not liable, concluded the court.

For those reasons, the Supreme Court of Arkansas affirmed in part, reversed in part. The surety was entitled to rely upon pay-if-paid clause as a defense to the subcontractor's claim against surety under lien-release bond.

**Authors' Commentary**: First, beware of jury verdicts in construction cases. The subcontract language was clear; however, the jury still awarded part of the subcontractor's claim under the surety bond. Also, if you represent subcontractors, beware of pay-if-paid clauses, as they create a large legal obstacle to payment in

---

[8] ARK. CODE ANN. § 18-44-118(b).
[9] *Id.* § 18-14-118(c)(2).

many states and cannot be circumvented through a payment bond claim as this case illustrates.

## § 11.04   PAYMENT BOND CLAIMS

In February 2011, a metal building, roofing, and siding subcontractor entered into a contract with a construction company ("Contractor") and developer ("Developer") to perform part of the construction of a gymnasium at a public school in Oklahoma.[10] Pursuant to Oklahoma's Bonding Statute, 61 O.S.2011 §§ 1 and 2, Contractor obtained the required statutory bond from a surety to cover any payments due to subcontractors if the main contractor defaulted.

Contractor paid the subcontractor regular progress payments, but withheld 10% for retainage. The total withheld as retainage was $37,600. The subcontractor completed its portion of the work on January 20, 2012, and invoiced Developer for the remaining $37,600 as final payment. Developer replied that it was not required to make a final payment to the subcontractor until final payment was made by the school, which was due only on "substantial completion" of the project. Developer told the subcontractor that the school had not yet made this payment. The subcontractor checked periodically with Developer in the following months, but received a similar response. The subcontractor then asked the school about the delay in payment. The school informed the subcontractor that all sums owed to Contractor had been paid. The subcontractor later learned that Contractor had received a final payment from the school some four months earlier, on May 31, 2012.

On October 3, 2012, the subcontractor notified the surety that Developer had defaulted, and demanded payment of the $37,600 as a final payment. The surety contacted Contractor regarding the default. Contractor replied that it disputed the claim for return of the $37,600 retainage because subcontractor had "gone over its allotted time" during several phases of construction, and that the subcontractor was liable for a "charge back" due to alleged damage to the school's gymnasium floor.

Eleven weeks after the initial notification to the surety, the dispute as to whether Contractor was required to make the payment to the subcontractor still had not been resolved. The subcontractor states that, during this period, the surety represented that it would eventually pay, but that it could not do so until the contractor determined the final amount owed to the subcontractor However, on February 4, 2013, one year and fifteen days after the subcontractor last performed work at the school, the surety denied the claim on the bond.

---

[10] Vanguard Builders, Inc. v. Granite Re, Inc., 2015 OK CIV APP 35, 348 P.3d 1093 (Div. 2 2014), *cert. denied* (Mar. 30, 2015).

On March 21, 2013, the sub filed suit against the Surety and Contractor ("Defendants"). The subcontractor's petition included a claim against surety for payment of the $37,600, plus interest. On July 12, 2013, the surety filed a motion for summary judgment, alleging that the subcontractor had failed to file suit to recover on the bond within the one-year statute of limitation provided by the bonding statute. The district court granted the surety's motion.

The subcontractor appealed to the Court of Civil Appeals of Oklahoma.

The statutory language in question is found in 61 O.S.2011 § 2(A), which states in relevant part:

> Any person to whom there is due any sum for labor, material or repair to machinery or equipment, furnished as stated in Section 1 of this title, the heirs or assigns of such person, may bring an action on the bond for the recovery of the indebtedness, provided that no action shall be brought on the bond after one (1) year from the day on which the last of the labor was performed or material or parts furnished for which the claim is made.

The court said the language of the statute, without further inquiry, appears to show a statute of repose. A statute of repose "restricts potential liability by limiting the time during which a cause of action can arise," and may bar a cause of action before it accrues.

Further inquiry by the court regarding the period in which a claim against the bond may be filed revealed that in *Phillips Petroleum Co. v. U.S. Fidelity & Guaranty Co.*,[11] the Oklahoma Supreme Court held:

> [T]he limitation provision for bringing the action referred to in 61 O.S.1961, §§ 1 and 2 [previous bonding statute], **is subject to waiver and estoppel** where the necessary facts are established as in other instances of the application of waiver and estoppel to a statute of limitation. (Emphasis added.)

The court held that *Phillips Petroleum* is still good law, and its rule that "the limitation provision for bringing the action referred to in 61 O.S. [ ] §§ 1 and 2, is subject to waiver and estoppel where the necessary facts are established as in other instances of the application of waiver and estoppel to a statute of limitation"[12] controls in this case.

However, the court noted that the factual record in this case was very limited, and many significant questions remain unanswered. The subcontractor's right to payment or any amount due was not yet established, nor was Developer's exact status as the main contractor. However, the subcontractor alleged that it attempted to call on the bond well within the limitation period; that it waited a substantial period before calling on the bond because of misrepresentation by

---

[11] 1968 OK 23, 442 P.2d 303.
[12] 1968 OK 23, ¶ 15, 442 P.2d 303.

Developer; that it relied on assurances by surety that payment was merely delayed by questions as to the amount of a chargeback or a delay penalty; and that the contractor and surety delayed decision by 11 weeks before deciding, immediately after the limitation period expired, that the subcontractor was owed no money. The court also noted that the bonding contract required this decision be made "[w]ithin a reasonable period of time." Those disputed facts alone could have supported a waiver or estoppel argument, declared the court.

Allegedly, the contractor in this case concealed the fact of payment by the school, and failed to inform the subcontractor that it disputed the subcontractor's right to a final payment. It raised a defense to payment only when demand was made on the bond. The surety then failed to admit or deny liability for more than 11 weeks, until the statute of limitations had run. The court concluded that if those allegations were true, the stated purpose of the statute appears ill-served by denying recovery on the bond.

For those reasons, the Court of Civil Appeals of Oklahoma vacated and remanded the grant of summary judgment in favor of surety on the basis of the statute of limitations was "improvidently made at this time." The one-year limitations period for the subcontractor's claim against the surety to collect bond proceeds, due to Contractor's alleged failure to pay fully for the subcontractor's work on the school's gymnasium, began to run on the day the subcontractor performed the last of its labor on the project, rather than when the amount due was finally decided or when the project was substantially complete.

**Authors' Commentary**: This case illustrates the lessons to not rely on the "check is in the mail" type statements when pursuing payment rights and the courts, usually do not "reward bad behavior." First, as the court did in this case, the authors had many unanswered questions regarding the facts surrounding this case. It is unclear of the contractual relationships involved and whether the language of the contract at issue would have been helpful to circumvent some of the quasi-contractual claims needed by the subcontractor. Unfortunately for those with payment rights on construction projects, you must be diligent and not rely on the "run around" because ultimately you may be losing your rights under the law. In this situation, the subcontractor was fortunate to ultimately prevail, although it was only after a long legal (and probably expensive) process.

### § 11.05  UNJUST ENRICHMENT

A general contractor was bonded by a surety company and subcontracted with an electrical subcontractor for installation and electrical work on the Armed Forces Reserve Center project in Arkansas.[13] The subcontractor purchased a generator from a supplier. The subcontractor was terminated from the project before

---

[13] Travelers Cas. & Sur. Co. of Am. v. Cummins Mid-South, LLC, 2015 Ark. App. 229, 460 S.W.3d 308 (2015).

the work was completed, and the general contractor assumed the liabilities of the subcontractor.

On August 3, 2011, the general contractor contacted the supplier to ascertain if any money was owed for supplies relating to the project. Initially, the supplier told the general contractor that the supplier was paid in full. However, on September 20, 2011, the supplier contacted the general contractor and explained that it had made a mistake and their records showed that the general contractor actually owed $59,115.14 for the generator. The general contractor took no action.

In November 2011, the general contractor received written notice that a $2,748.16 bill from a September 2, 2011 service call on the generator had gone into collection. On December 1, 2011, the general contractor paid the bill with a check dated December 1, 2011, and wrote *"Paid in Full"* (emphasis added). The general contractor prepared the release, which was dated December 13, 2011 and was entitled "SUBCONTRACTOR/MATERIALMAN UNCONDITIONAL WAIVER AND RELEASE UPON FINAL PAYMENT," and was signed by the supplier's chief financial officer ("Supplier's CFO"). Supplier's CFO testified that he handled unpaid accounts as a part of his job, regularly signing lien waivers and that he signed the release drafted by the general contractor. He explained that he did not contact the general contractor to discuss the release. Supplier's CFO testified that he knew what a final lien waiver was, and he knew that if he signed it, the supplier was not going to get paid any more on that project. He testified that he did not check to see if any money was owed by the general contractor on the project.

Three more times in January 2012, the generator required repair, which the supplier provided, and for which the general contractor paid. However, for these repairs, the supplier prepared its own lien release, specifically noting that the generator had not been paid for as previously discussed with the general contractor. On March 28, 2012, the supplier submitted a notice of subcontractors claim against the general contractor's bond for the amount of the generator, transfer switch, and start-up materials. The surety denied the claim based on the execution of the previous lien release.

On July 2, 2012, the supplier filed a complaint against the general contractor and surety, asking for payment for the generator, interest, and attorney's fees. The circuit court entered an order finding that the supplier did not waive its bond claim on the grounds that the language of the first release was ambiguous and did not indicate it was payment for anything other than the service call. The circuit court found that "supplier provided the generator and was never paid for it" and hence, the general contractor was unjustly enriched. The circuit court also found that the supplier could recover under the bond based on the general contractor's unjust enrichment. The circuit court denied the general contractor's defensive claims of detrimental reliance, estoppel, and payment on the ground that the general contractor did not meet its burden to assert the defenses. In its final finding, the circuit court found that the bond should have covered the generator: "The purpose of the statute requiring a bond for public works projects is to provide for payment of subcontractors of materialmen in cases such as this." The circuit court awarded supplier $59,115.14 plus costs, 12% penalty, prejudgment and post-judgment interest, and attorney's fees. The general contractor and surety appealed to the Court of Appeals of Arkansas.

On appeal, the court said the language of the first lien release was not ambiguous. The release was entitled at the top of the document: "SUBCONTRACTOR/MATERIALMAN UNCONDITIONAL WAIVER AND RELEASE UPON FINAL PAYMENT." It contained the statements that the release "covers the full and final payment of the contract amount for labor, services and equipment, or material furnished on the job. . . ." The release clearly set forth that the person who signs the document waives any bond right he or she may have: "[T]he undersigned hereby releases and waives any mechanics' lien, stop notice, or bond right he/she/it has on the said job." The language was clear that the supplier releases any bond right "it may have" against general contractor concerning the project. There was no ambiguity, and therefore no call to look beyond the plain language of the contract, declared the court. The court held that the circuit court erred in finding the language of the release ambiguous, and on this point, reversed.

The terms of the release were unambiguous, and the document was signed by Supplier's CFO, an experienced professional who was a long-term employee and familiar with release forms. Supplier's CFO testified that he read the waiver and release before he signed it, but did not contact anyone at the general contractor before he signed it. Furthermore, the supplier put on no evidence that the general contractor defrauded the supplier into signing the release. Thus, the court held that the circuit court erred in finding that supplier did not waive its right to recover on the bond, and on this point, reversed.

The general contractor asserted on appeal that the circuit court erred in finding that the supplier was able to recover under the doctrine of unjust enrichment. Unjust enrichment is an equitable doctrine. It is the principle that one person should not be permitted unjustly to enrich himself at the expense of another, but should be required to make restitution of or for property or benefits received, retained, or appropriated, where it is just and equitable that such restitution be made, and where such action involves no violation or frustration of law or opposition to public policy, either directly or indirectly. However, the concept of unjust enrichment has no application when an express written contract exists. The general rule is that one cannot recover in quasi-contract when an express contract exists, and governs the matter in the present case. Here, a written contract for the purchase and installation of the generator existed between the subcontractor and the supplier; therefore, the supplier was barred from asserting the doctrine of unjust enrichment. Therefore, as a matter of law, the court held that the circuit court erred in applying the equitable remedy of unjust enrichment in light of the existing contract, and it reversed on this point.

For those reasons, the Court of Appeals of Arkansas reversed. The court held that the lien release was not ambiguous, and the supplier's CFO had read the waiver and knew what he was signing. Based on the facts of the case, the supplier was not entitled to relief from the release on the basis of unilateral mistake, and there was no fraud to excuse the signing of the release. Thus, the supplier could not recover the cost of the generator because it signed the release. Finally, because there was a written contract, the supplier could not recover the cost of the generator on the basis of unjust enrichment.

**Authors' Commentary**: Be careful what you sign. Simply put, if you have not been paid in full, do not, under any circumstances sign a document that can be construed otherwise. The supplier's CFO should have known better and did not check if other money was owed by the general contractor or specify in the first release that it was not "unconditional." Also, be careful of endorsements on checks. The authors understand the necessity of payment and temptation of payment of money now, albeit less than the full amount owed, however, as this case illustrates "haste makes waste"—i.e., in the rush to get cash sooner rather than later, a supplier forfeited payment that it was duly owed.

## § 11.06 ARBITRATION

Pursuant to a construction contract executed in 2006, a contractor remodeled and performed repairs to an owner's facility. The owner then subsequently claimed that certain aspects of the construction were deficient or otherwise noncompliant with the contract and applicable building codes. In 2013, the owner sued the contractor for breach of contract, breach of warranty, negligence, and negligent representation.[14]

In response to the lawsuit filed by the owner, the contractor filed a "Motion to Compel Binding Arbitration and Abate Proceedings" under the Texas General Arbitration Act (the "Act").[15] After a hearing, the trial court signed an order denying the motion to compel arbitration, and the contractor appealed to the Court of Appeals of Texas, Houston (14th Dist.).

Under the Act, a court must stay proceedings and compel arbitration if the applicant demonstrates (1) an agreement to arbitrate, and (2) the opposing party's refusal to arbitrate.[16] If the opposing party denies the existence of an arbitration agreement, the trial court shall summarily determine that issue.[17] If the trial court finds a valid arbitration agreement, the burden shifts to the party opposing arbitration to raise an affirmative defense to its enforcement.

---

[14] LDF Constr., Inc. v. Texas Friends of Chabad Lubavitch, Inc., 459 S.W.3d 720 (Tex. App.—Houston [14th Dist.] 2015).

[15] *See generally* Tex. Civ. Prac. & Rem. Code Ann. §§ 171.001-.098 (West, Westlaw through 2013 3d C.S.).

[16] *See* Tex. Civ. Prac. & Rem. Code Ann. § 171.021.

[17] *Id.* § 171.021(b).

Here, to support its motion to compel arbitration, the contractor presented the contract between the parties, which was a standard construction-industry form published by the American Institute of Architects (AIA). The form was entitled "AIA Document A101™-1997" and was described thereon as "Standard Form of Agreement Between Owner and Contractor where the basis of payment is a STIPULATED SUM" ("A101 Form of Agreement"). The A101 Form of Agreement was completed with the specifics for this project, and both parties signed the contract. There was no arbitration agreement expressly included as part of that document.

The contractor presented another contract document—another AIA form entitled "AIA Document A201™-1997" ("A201 General Conditions"), and was described as "General Conditions of the Contract for Construction." The detailed document contained 37 pages, with an identical note at the bottom of each page demonstrating that the page was part of A201 General Conditions. The document contained numerous provisions applicable to a construction contract, including an arbitration clause in §4.6 which, among other things, stated:

§ 4.6 ARBITRATION

§ 4.6.1 Any Claim arising out of or related to the Contract, except Claims relating to aesthetic effect and except those waived as provided for in Sections 4.3.10, 9.10.4 and 9.10.5, shall, after decision by the Architect or 30 days after submission of the Claim to the Architect, be subject to arbitration. Prior to arbitration, the parties shall endeavor to resolve disputes by mediation in accordance with the provisions of Section 4.5.

§ 4.6.2 Claims not resolved by mediation shall be decided by arbitration which, unless the parties mutually agree otherwise, shall be in accordance with the Construction Industry Arbitration Rules of the American Arbitration Association currently in effect. The demand for arbitration shall be filed in writing with the other party to the Contract and with the American Arbitration Association, and a copy shall be filed with the Architect. . . .

The A201 General Conditions was not completed with any information independently showing it was applicable to the project at issue. The form included sections to be completed to identify the project, but they were left blank on this document. Further, it was not signed by either party (nor is there a place for such signature). However, the contractor asserted the A201 General Conditions was expressly incorporated into the contract in the A101 Form of Agreement. On the face of the A101 Form of Agreement was the following language:

*AIA Document A201-1997, General Conditions of the Contract for Construction, is adopted in this document by reference. . . .*

On the second page of the A101 Form of Agreement was Article 1, entitled "The Contract Documents," which provided:

> The Contract Documents consist of this Agreement, Conditions of the Contract (General, Supplementary and other Conditions), Drawings, Specifications, Addenda issued prior to execution of this Agreement, other documents listed in this Agreement and Modifications issued after execution of this Agreement; these form the Contract, and are as fully a part of the Contract as if attached to this Agreement or repeated herein. The Contract represents the entire and integrated agreement between the parties hereto and supersedes prior negotiations, representations or agreements, either written or oral. An enumeration of the Contract Documents, other than Modifications, appears in Article 8.

Then, Article 8 of the A101 Form of Agreement, entitled "Enumeration of Contract Documents," stated:

> § 8.1 The Contract Documents, except for Modifications issued after execution of this Agreement, are enumerated as follows:
>
> § 8.1.1 The Agreement is this executed 1997 edition of the Standard Form of Agreement Between Owner and Contractor, MA Document A101-1997.
>
> § 8.1.2 The General Conditions are the 1997 edition of the General Conditions of the Contract for Construction, AIA Document A201-1997.

. . .

Furthermore, the A101 Form of Agreement included multiple other references to A201 General Conditions when setting forth various terms, such as rules for calculating progress payments and terminating or suspending the contract.

In response to the motion to compel, the owner acknowledged that the A201 General Conditions attached to the contractor's motion contained a clear and express arbitration clause and the owner did not dispute that its claims fell within the scope of the clause. However, the owner contended that it did not agree to the clause. In support, the owner presented affidavits from two of its representatives who were involved in negotiating the contract. Both made the following essentially identical averments:

- A201 General Conditions was neither signed nor assented to by Owner
- Owner's witnesses neither saw, nor knew of the existence of A201 General Conditions at the time of contracting with the contractor
- Owner's witnesses had never seen or received A201 General Conditions until after filing this lawsuit
- Owner's witnesses were not put on notice by the contractor that an arbitration clause might govern problems arising out of the contract. Nor did the owner's witnesses bargain for or agree to this clause

In the order denying the motion to compel, the trial court recited that it considered the following to make its decision:

> (1) lack of sophistication on the part of the owner in construction matters/contracts,
> (2) contract was drafted by the contractor,
> (3) lack of a binding arbitration clause within the contract itself, and the lack of specific incorporation by reference of such clause as well as the lack of inclusion of such clause in any documents attached to the signed contract,
> (4) rules referencing the arbitration agreement were not attached to the signed contract, and
> (5) compelling the owner to go to arbitration would constitute a denial of its fundamental constitutional rights including: the right to Trial By Jury, requirement of adherence to the Texas Rules of Civil Procedure and the Texas Rules of Evidence, respectively, at an arbitration subject to appellate review and the right of appeal, without specific agreement of the parties or conspicuous notice in the signed contract or any attachments thereto that the rights described above would be waived by the parties.

It was clear to the court that the trial court refused to compel arbitration because it concluded that the owner did not agree to arbitrate. Additionally, the findings indicated the trial court determined that enforcing any arbitration agreement would be procedurally unconscionable although the trial court did not expressly use that term, commented the court.

The trial court ruled that there was no arbitration agreement. It relied on the following facts when making that conclusion: (1) there was no arbitration clause in the contract itself; (2) the contract did not specifically incorporate by reference an arbitration clause in any other document; and (3) no document containing an arbitration clause was attached to the signed contract.

However, the appeals court noted that the contract not only specifically incorporated A201 General Conditions, which contained an arbitration clause, and identified it as one of the contract documents, but also reference to A201 General Conditions was necessary to determine some terms of the contract not expressly set forth in the A101 Form of Agreement. A valid agreement to arbitrate exists when a signed contract incorporates by reference another document containing the arbitration clause, explained the court. Additionally, the court noted that A201 General Conditions does not even include a space for signatures, so parties are not expected to sign it.

Contrary to the trial court's conclusion, the court said there was no requirement that the signed contract had to specifically refer to the arbitration clause for the clause to be enforceable. Also contrary to the trial court's conclusion, there was no requirement that the incorporated document containing the arbitration clause must necessarily be attached to the contract for the clause to be enforceable. Thus, under the circumstances of the present case, the A201 General

Conditions was incorporated into the A101 Form of Agreement even if the document was not physically attached when the parties signed the contract.

In particular, the court explained, the law presumes that a party knows and accepts the terms of the contract being signed, and the law does not excuse a party's failure to read the contract when there was an opportunity to do so. Owner presented no evidence that it lacked the opportunity to read either the contract or A201-1997 before signing the contract. In sum, the court concluded as a matter of law that the parties agreed to arbitrate their dispute.

Since it concluded there was an agreement, the court next had to determine if it was unconscionable, excusing the owner from compliance. On appeal, the owner asserted that the contractor engaged in the "sharp" business practice of hiding the existence of an arbitration agreement from a less sophisticated party. A court may not enforce an agreement to arbitrate if the court finds the agreement was unconscionable at the time it was made.[18] There were two factors cited by the trial court for refusing to compel arbitration suggest a procedural-unconscionability finding because they concerned the circumstances under which the contract was executed: (1) the owner's lack of sophistication in "construction matters/contracts"; and (2) the contract was drafted by the contractor. However, the court found that there was no evidence supporting the trial court's findings or the owner's contentions that the arbitration clause was procedurally unconscionable.

For those reasons, the Court of Appeals of Texas, Houston (14th Dist.) reversed the trial court's order denying the contractor's motion to compel arbitration, and remanded with instructions that the trial court sign an order compelling arbitration and staying the present proceedings. The court held that there was no requirement that the signed contract specifically refer to the arbitration provision of the incorporated document or that the incorporated document be physically attached to the signed contract.

**Authors' Commentary**: The phrase "litigation is often paved with standard forms" comes to mind. While the construction industry commonly uses the AIA form of construction contracts, it is not surprising to see this fact pattern. In using the AIA forms, many parties "overlook," whether intentional or not, the inclusion of the A201 General Conditions. Also, it is interesting to note that the more recent form of A101 Form of Agreement updated in 2007, includes an express reference to the "binding dispute resolution" mechanism (see § 6.2 of the agreement), as well as an express reference to the A201 General Conditions. However, in reading this case, it could be read to also include other matters (like warranty and indemnity) that are not included in the A101 Form of Agreement (or other AIA forms of agreement), but rather in the A201 General Conditions. Bottom line is if a document is referenced in an agreement, it should be reviewed, read and negotiated as if part of the agreement.

---

[18] TEX. CIV. PRAC. & REM. CODE ANN. § 171.022.

CHAPTER 12

# WEST REGION

Arizona, California, Hawaii, Nevada, Utah

Peter J. Ippolito, Laurence R. Phillips

§ 12.06  Hawaii Cases
    [A]   Indemnity—Lower-Tiered Contractors' Duty to Defend
          [1]   Opinion
          [2]   Background
               [a]  Background on Decedent's Death
               [b]  Defendant Parties' Contractual Relationships
               [c]  Expert Testimonies
               [d]  Procedural History
          [3]   Discussion
               [a]  Arthur's Appeal
                    [i]   Summary Judgment on Arthur's Negligence Claims Was Improper
                    [ii]  Summary Judgment for KIC on Arthur's Punitive Damages Claim Was Proper
               [b]  Sato's Appeal
                [c]  Pacific Fence's Contentions on Appeal
                    [i]   Pacific Fence Had a Duty to Defend
                    [ii]  KIC Did Not Waive Its Claim to the Defense and Indemnification from Pacific Fence
                    [iii] The Contracts Did Not State That Duties to Defend "Pass-Through" to Subsequent Contractors
                    [iv] The Pacific Fence Subcontract Is Not Void Under HRS § 431:10-222
                    [v]  Joint and Several Provisions in the Pacific Fence Subcontract Required Contribution from Other Parties
               [d]  Coastal's Cross-Appeal
                      [i]   Coastal Owed a Duty to Defend KIC and DHHL up Until the Circuit Court Granted Summary Judgment in Favor of Coastal on February 25, 2010
                    [ii]  Coastal's Obligation to Defend Extended to Claims Potentially Arising Under the Coastal Contract
          [4]   Conclusion

## § 12.01  INTRODUCTION

This chapter focuses on construction law developments in the West Region during the past year. Section 12.02 addresses Nevada cases relating to: (1) the enforcement of subordination agreement in the context of mechanic's lien claims and (2) immunity under the Nevada Industrial Insurance Act. Section 12.03 addresses Arizona cases discussing: (1) enforcement of a settlement agreement against a non-party title insurance carrier and (2) enforcement of notice provisions under Arizona's Little Miller Act. Section 12.04 addresses California cases regarding: (1) application of the *Eichleay* method to measure damages resulting from project delays; (2) enforceability of contract provisions requiring disputes between contractors and California subcontractors to be litigated outside California; and (3) the substantial compliance exception to contract licensing requirements. Section 12.05 addresses a Utah case relating to owners' right to recover attorney fees following successful challenge of mechanic's liens. Section 12.06 addresses a Hawaii case relating to lower-tiered contractors' right to indemnity.

## § 12.02  NEVADA CASES

### [A]  Mechanic's Lien—Enforcement of Subordination Agreements

In *In re Manhattan West Mechanic's Lien Litigation,*[1] a contractor, with second-priority mechanics' liens, brought action against a real estate developer and developer's lender, which had entered into an agreement to subordinate lender's first-priority deeds of trust to lender's third-priority deed of trust. The trial court granted summary judgment to lender, concluding that the contractor's liens remained in second-priority position. The contractor appealed and the Supreme Court of Nevada ruled as follows: (1) the subordination agreement resulted in partial, rather than complete, subordination; and (2) partial subordination was not statutorily precluded.

The court determined whether a subordination agreement that subordinates a lien for original land financing to a new construction deed of trust affects the priority of a mechanic's lien for work performed after the date of the original loan but before the date of the construction deed of trust. Because contractual partial subordination differs from complete subordination, the court agreed that a contractual partial subordination by creditors of a common debtor do not subordinate a first priority lien to a mechanic's lien. Further, nothing in NRS 108.225 changes the priority of a mechanic's lien to a partially subordinated lien recorded before the mechanic's lien became effective. Thus, the priority of the mechanic's lien remains junior to the amount secured by the original senior lien.

---

[1] 359 P.3d 125 (Nev. 2015).

## [1]   Procedural and Factual History

Gemstone Apache, LLC ("Apache") intended to develop a mixed-use property (Manhattan West) in Las Vegas. Real party in interest Scott Financial Corporation ("SFC") made multiple loans to Apache for this purpose. The first three loans, which were recorded in July 2006, totaled $38 million ("the Mezzanine Deeds of Trust") and financed the purchase of the property. In April 2007, petitioner APCO Construction ("APCO"), the contractor hired by Apache, began construction on Manhattan West, setting the priority date for mechanic's lien services. In May and October of 2007, the Mezzanine Deeds of Trust were amended to secure additional funds for the project.

In early 2008, Gemstone Development West, LLC ("GDW") purchased Manhattan West from Apache, assuming Apache's loan obligations. To obtain financing for construction, GDW borrowed an additional $110 million from SFC ("the Construction Deed of Trust"), recording the deed of trust on February 7, 2008. As part of the overall transaction, SFC and GDW entered into a subordination agreement subordinating the Mezzanine Deeds of Trust to the Construction Deed of Trust. SFC indicated that its intent for the subordination agreement was for SFC to determine "in what order SFC's debts would be satisfied." The subordination agreement did not state whether the subordination was complete or partial, nor did it address the priority of any potential mechanic's liens.

The relationship between APCO and GDW deteriorated. APCO stopped work on Manhattan West and filed suit against GDW, SFC, and others. SFC and APCO both moved for summary judgment on the issue of lien priority. SFC argued that the subordination agreement partially subordinated the Mezzanine Deeds of Trust to the Construction Deed of Trust, giving the Construction Deed of Trust senior priority for $38 million and leaving APCO's mechanic's liens unaffected. APCO argued that the subordination agreement completely subordinated the Mezzanine Deeds of Trust to the Construction Deed of Trust, prioritizing the Mezzanine Deeds of Trust after APCO's mechanic's liens and the Construction Deed of Trust. It further argued that NRS 108.225 precluded the Construction Deed of Trust from taking priority over APCO's mechanic's liens.

The district court initially granted summary judgment in favor of APCO, but, after SFC filed a motion for reconsideration, the district court granted summary judgment in favor of SFC. The district court determined that the subordination agreement only partially subordinated the Mezzanine Deeds of Trust to the Construction Deed of Trust and left the mechanic's liens in the second-priority position. APCO petitioned for a writ of mandamus to compel the district court to vacate its order and recognize APCO's mechanic's liens as holding a first priority.

## [2] Discussion

"A writ of mandamus is available to compel the performance of an act that the law requires as a duty resulting from an office, trust, or station or to control an arbitrary or capricious exercise of discretion."[2] The court exercised its discretion to entertain this writ petition because an important issue of law requires clarification—whether a mechanic's lien takes priority over a contractually subordinated debt by creditors of a common debtor either because (1) the subordination agreement constitutes a complete subordination or (2) NRS 108.225 (Nevada's mechanic's lien statute) precludes the partial subordination of an existing lien.

Contractual subordination allows creditors of a common debtor to contractually rearrange the priority of their enduring liens or debt positions.[3] Central to this case is the distinction between complete and partial contractual subordination, which differ on their rearrangements of the priorities of lienholders.

In a complete subordination, the agreement subordinating the senior lien to a junior lien effectively also subordinates the senior lien to intervening liens.[4] Here, for example, the Mezzanine Deeds of Trust would simply become junior to the Construction Deed of Trust, which would remain junior to the mechanic's liens, thus moving the mechanic's liens to first priority. In contrast, partial subordination gives a junior lien priority over a senior lien to the extent that it does not affect the priority of the intervening lien; thus, the junior lien only has priority over the intervening lien in the amount of the senior lien.[5] In other words, in partial subordination, the priority of liens is contractually rearranged without affecting the position of any intervening lien.[6] Here, the Construction Deed of Trust would partially subordinate the Mezzanine Deeds of Trust, giving the Construction Deed of Trust $38 million in first priority, leaving the mechanic's liens in second priority, and placing the remainder of the Construction Deed of Trust in third priority over the Mezzanine Deeds of Trust.

At issue is whether the subordination agreement effected a complete subordination and whether Nevada case law and statutes preclude partial subordination.

---

[2] Int'l Game Tech., Inc. v. Second Judicial Dist. Ct., 124 Nev. 193, 197, 179 P.3d 556, 558 (2008) (internal citation omitted); *see* NRS 34.160.

[3] *See* Robin Russell, *Distinction Between Contractual and Equitable Subordination*, 2 Tex. Prac. Guide: Fin. Transactions § 10:10 (Robin Russell & J. Scott Sheehan eds., 2014); *see also* George A. Nation, III, *Circuity of Liens Arising From Subordination Agreements: Comforting Unanimity No More*, 83 B.U. L. Rev. 591, 591-92 (2003) (describing subordination).

[4] *See* Nation, III, *Circuity of Liens Arising From Subordination Agreements: Comforting Unanimity No More*, 83 B.U. L. Rev. 591, 593 (2003).

[5] *See* Nation, III, *Circuity of Liens Arising From Subordination Agreements: Comforting Unanimity No More*, 83 B.U. L. Rev. at 593-94; Caterpillar Fin. Servs. Corp. v. Peoples Nat'l Bank, N.A., 710 F.3d 691, 693-94 (7th Cir. 2013).

[6] *Caterpillar*, 710 F.3d at 693-94.

### [a] The Subordination Agreement Effected a Partial Subordination

APCO argues that the district court erred when, in granting summary judgment in favor of SFC, it determined that the subordination agreement was intended to create a partial subordination, not a complete subordination. The court reviewed an order granting summary judgment de novo, viewing all evidence "in a light most favorable to the nonmoving party."[7] The court had held that "[s]ummary judgment is appropriate under NRCP 56 when the pleadings, depositions, answers to interrogatories, admissions, and affidavits, if any, that are properly before the court demonstrate that no genuine issue of material fact exists, and the moving party is entitled to judgment as a matter of law."[8] Additionally, "[w]hen the facts in a case are not in dispute, contract interpretation is a question of law, which this court reviews de novo."[9]

Different courts have reached different conclusions about whether a general subordination agreement effects complete or partial subordination.[10] The minority view concludes that a general subordination agreement results in complete subordination.[11] Relying on Black's Law Dictionary 's definition of "subordination agreement," this view contends that "[b]y definition, 'subordination' contemplates a reduction in priority. Nothing in the definition contemplates raising a lower priority lienholder up to the position of the subordinating party."[12] Thus, this view holds that lienholders can only step into the shoes of another lienholder when the agreement explicitly indicates that there is a transfer of priority rights.[13]

In contrast, the United States Court of Appeals for the Seventh Circuit adopted the majority approach and held in favor of partial subordination when the subordination agreement was silent on the issue.[14] This approach holds that nonparties are unaffected by the subordination agreement and "simply swaps the priorities of the parties to the subordination agreement."[15] It reasoned that the party agreeing to subordinate its higher-priority lien surely wants the subsequent loan to occur so that the debtor would be strengthened, but that complete subordination would "drop the subordinating creditor to the bottom of the priority ladder,"

---

[7] Wood v. Safeway, Inc., 121 Nev. 724, 729, 121 P.3d 1026, 1029 (2005).
[8] *Wood*, 121 Nev. at 731, 121 P.3d at 1031.
[9] Lehrer McGovern Bovis, Inc. v. Bullock Insulation, Inc., 124 Nev. 1102, 1115, 197 P.3d 1032, 1041 (2008).
[10] See *Caterpillar*, 710 F.3d at 693-94; *In re* Price Waterhouse Ltd., 202 Ariz. 397, 46 P.3d 408, 410 (2002); *see also* George A. Nation, III, *Circuity of Liens Arising from Subordination Agreements: Comforting Unanimity No More*, 83 B.U. L. Rev. 591, 592-93 (2003).
[11] *See, e.g.*, AmSouth Bank, N.A. v. J & D Fin. Corp., 679 So. 2d 695, 698 (Ala. 1996).
[12] *See, e.g.*, AmSouth Bank, N.A. v. J & D Fin. Corp., 679 So. 2d 695, 698 (Ala. 1996).
[13] *See, e.g.*, AmSouth Bank, N.A. v. J & D Fin. Corp., 679 So. 2d 695, 698 (Ala. 1996).
[14] *Caterpillar*, 710 F.3d at 693-94.
[15] *Caterpillar*, 710 F.3d at 693-94.

thus benefiting "a nonparty to the subordination agreement."[16] Therefore, as a practical matter, the court "c[ould]n't think why [the subordinating party] would have insisted on complete subordination."[17]

The court agreed with the reasoning in *Caterpillar*. In the instant case, complete subordination would move APCO's mechanic's liens (nonparties to the subordination agreement) into the first-priority position and leave SFC's liens junior to all mechanic's liens. Partial subordination, however, would leave $38 million of the Construction Deed of Trust in first priority and the mechanic's liens in the same position they were in prior to the subordination agreement. The court could not determine any reason SFC would have intended to completely subordinate the Mezzanine Deeds of Trust, only for APCO's mechanic's liens to then take the first-priority position. Moreover, this aligns with SFC's claimed intent for the subordination agreement—that it should be "allowed to freely contract the order of payment as between" itself. The subordination agreement neither stated it intended to create complete subordination nor mentioned the mechanic's lien. Absent this clear intent, the court concluded that a commonsense approach weighs in favor of partial subordination.

APCO argues that, while parties may contractually subordinate the priorities of their liens, NRS 108.225 does not permit partial subordination, only complete subordination. Specifically, APCO asserts that NRS 108.225 prevents SFC from partially subordinating the Mezzanine Deeds of Trust in favor of the Construction Deed of Trust. That statute, which protects the right to payment for those who have worked to improve property, states, in pertinent part, that mechanic's and materialmen's liens are senior to "[a]ny lien, mortgage or other encumbrance which may have attached to the property after the commencement of construction of a work of improvement."[18] SFC argues that NRS 108.225 does not preclude other lienholders from contracting for a partial subordination with respect to their lien priorities. This court reviews questions of statutory construction de novo.[19]

The statute gives priority to mechanic's liens over liens that attach after the commencement of the work of improvement. It does not, however, address subordination agreements between other lienholders. This court does not "fill in alleged legislative omissions based on conjecture as to what the [L]egislature would or should have done."[20] Therefore, the court concluded that NRS 108.225 does not prohibit negotiations between lienholders with priority over mechanics' liens and those with lesser priority in situations where the mechanic's liens will

---

[16] *Caterpillar*, 710 F.3d at 693-94.

[17] *Caterpillar*, 710 F.3d at 694.

[18] NRS 108.225(1)(a); *see In re* Fontainebleau Las Vegas Holdings, LLC, ___Nev. ___, ___, 289 P.3d 1199, 1211 (2012); Hardy Cos., Inc. v. SNMARK, LLC, 126 Nev. 528, 538, 245 P.3d 1149, 1156 (2010).

[19] I. Cox Constr. Co. v. CH2 Invs., LLC, ___ Nev. ___, ___, 296 P.3d 1202, 1203 (2013).

[20] Falcke v. Cnty. of Douglas, 116 Nev. 583, 589, 3 P.3d 661, 665 (2000) (internal quotations omitted).

be left in exactly the same position as if the subordination agreement had never occurred. In other words, the statute does not preclude partial subordination.

Here, when APCO began work on Manhattan West, it did so with notice of SFC's Mezzanine Deeds of Trust and knowledge that its mechanic's liens would be in second priority to those liens. Crucially, nothing about the subordination agreement alters the amount of debt that APCO was junior to, and thus, the subordination agreement does not violate NRS 108.225. To read the statute in a way that would grant APCO first priority even though the subordination agreement did not prejudice APCO's lien position—or change APCO's status whatsoever—would be an over-reading of the statute.

### [3] Conclusion

The district court did not improperly determine that the subordination contract effected a partial subordination. Further, NRS 108.225 does not preclude parties from contracting for a partial subordination.

Accordingly, the court denied APCO's petition for a writ of mandamus and prohibition.

### [B] Personal Injury—Immunity Under Nevada Industrial Insurance Act

In *D&D Tire, Inc. v. Jack R. Ouellette*,[21] an injured worker brought personal injury action against the employer's independent contractor, after its employee pinned the worker against a dumpster with a truck he was driving after making repairs to it. Following jury verdict in favor of the worker, the Second Judicial District Court denied the independent contractor's motion for judgment as a matter of law, or alternatively a new trial. The independent contractor appealed.

The Nevada Supreme Court held that:

> 1. The independent contractor did not have immunity from civil liability as a statutory employer or coemployee under Nevada Industrial Insurance Act (NIIA), and
> 2. The court did not abuse its discretion by refusing to give proffered "mere happening" jury instruction.

In Nevada, employers and co-employees of a person injured in the course of employment are immune from liability for the injury under the exclusive remedy provision of the workers' compensation statutes. Additionally, some subcontractors and independent contractors are accorded the same status as employers or co-employees of the injured employee and are thus immune from liability.

---

[21] 352 P.3d 32 (Nev. 2015).

However, a subcontractor or independent contractor is not considered to be a statutory employee when it is performing a major or specialized repair that the injured worker's employer is not equipped to handle with its own work force. This opinion addresses when an independent contractor's actions are within the scope of a major or specialized repair so as to prevent it from claiming immunity as a statutory employer or co-employee.

The court held that when evaluating whether an independent contractor's actions are within the scope of a major or specialized repair, a district court must consider the act giving rise to the injury within the entire context of the overall specialized repair and not in isolation. Thus, factors such as whether the presence of the contractor at the job site was for the purpose of the specialized repair or whether the activity was in furtherance of the specialized repair can help guide the court's analysis. The court further held that where, as in this case, the jury is instructed on negligence, proximate cause, and the essentiality of a finding of the defendant's negligence, an incomplete "mere happening" jury instruction may be duplicative and/or confusing, and thus the district court's failure to give such an instruction was not an abuse of discretion.

### [1]  Factual and Procedural History

Respondent Jack R. Ouellette was employed by Allied Nevada Gold Corporation (Allied) to perform tire service work, including the installation, removal, repair, and replacement of tires on various pieces of mining equipment. Appellant Purcell Tire & Rubber Company is a commercial tire retailer. Among other things, it provides tire changing and repair services to mining companies.

As part of his job, Ouellette drove and operated a tire-changing boom truck owned by Purcell and leased to Allied. When a problem developed with the boom truck's power take off unit (PTO), Purcell contacted an independent repair company, Dakota Diesel, who sent repairman Scott Durick to make specialized repairs to the PTO. Purcell, as owner of the truck, also sent Ryan Wintle, a tire technician for Purcell with responsibilities similar to those of Ouellette, to assist with the repairs.

After the initial repairs were completed, Wintle and Durick filled the truck with hydraulic oil. Wintle then got into the truck to move it to another area before testing the PTO. While backing up the truck, Wintle struck and pinned Ouellette against a dumpster, causing Ouellette to suffer a shoulder injury.

Ouellette filed a personal injury claim against Purcell. At trial, Purcell moved for a judgment as a matter of law on the grounds that it was a statutory employee of Allied and was thus immune from liability under the Nevada Industrial Insurance Act (NIIA). The district court denied Purcell's motion. Purcell also requested a mere happening jury instruction, which the district court declined to give.

The jury returned a verdict in favor of Ouellette. Purcell then renewed its motion for judgment as a matter of law on the ground that it was a statutory employee of Allied. Alternatively, it moved for a new trial, arguing that the district court's error in refusing to give Purcell's mere happening jury instruction materially affected its substantial rights. The district court denied Purcell's motion. Purcell appealed.

### [2]  Discussion

Purcell argues that the district court erred in denying its motion for judgment as a matter of law because Purcell was a statutory employee of Allied at the time of Ouellette's injury and would thus be immune from liability for the injury under the NIIA. Purcell also argues that the district court abused its discretion by refusing to give a mere happening jury instruction.

Ouellette argues that the district court did not err in denying Purcell's motion for judgment as a matter of law because Purcell was performing a specialized repair at the time of Ouellette's injury and thus was not a statutory employee of Allied. Ouellette also argues that the district court did not err in refusing to give Purcell's proffered jury instruction because it misstated Nevada law and was adequately covered by other instructions given to the jury.

### [a]  The District Court Did Not Err by Denying Purcell's Motion for Judgment as a Matter of Law

NRCP 50(a)(1) provides that a district court may grant judgment as a matter of law "with respect to a claim or defense that cannot under the controlling law be maintained or defeated." In deciding a motion for judgment as a matter of law, "[t]he [district] court must view all evidence and inferences in favor of the non-moving party."[22] Thus, a nonmoving party can defeat a motion for judgment as a matter of law if it "present[s] sufficient evidence such that the jury could grant relief to that party."[23]

The court reviewed a district court's order granting or denying judgment as a matter of law and its interpretation of a statute de novo.[24]

---

[22] FGA, Inc. v. Giglio, ___Nev. ___, ___, 278 P.3d 490, 500 (2012).

[23] Bielar v. Washoe Health Sys., Inc., ___ Nev. ___, ___, 306 P.3d 360, 368 (2013) (internal quotations omitted).

[24] Wyeth v. Rowatt, 126 Nev. 446, 460, 244 P.3d 765, 775 (2010) (reviewing judgment as a matter of law de novo); Int'l Game Tech., Inc. v. Second Judicial Dist. Ct., 124 Nev. 193, 198, 179 P.3d 556, 559 (2008) (reviewing statutory interpretation de novo).

### [b]   An Independent Contractor Is Not Immune from Liability When Performing Specialized Repairs

In Nevada, employers and co-employees of a person injured in the course of employment are immune from liability under the NIIA.[25] Additionally, the NIIA is "uniquely different from industrial insurance acts of some states in that subcontractors and independent contractors are accorded the same status as employees" and are immune from liability.[26]

However, not all types of subcontractors and independent contractors are considered to be statutory employees under NRS 616A.210.[27] A subcontractor or independent contractor is not a statutory employee if it "is not in the same trade, business, profession or occupation as the [employer of the injured worker]."[28]

The "normal work" test, first articulated in *Meers*, guides courts as to whether a subcontractor or independent contractor is considered to be in the same trade, business, profession, or occupation as the employer of an injured worker.[29] The *Meers* normal work test is not one of whether the subcontractor's activity is useful, necessary, or even absolutely indispensable to the statutory employer's business, since, after all, this could be said of practically any repair, construction or transportation service. The test (except in cases where the work is obviously a subcontracted fraction of a main contract) is whether that indispensable activity is, in that business, normally carried on through employees rather than independent contractors.[30]

With regard to subcontracted maintenance activities, "[t]he general rule is that major repairs, or specialized repairs of the sort which the employer is not

---

[25] NRS 616B.612; Lipps v. S. Nev. Paving, 116 Nev. 497, 501, 998 P.2d 1183, 1186 (2000) (noting that co-employees are immune from liability for injuries incurred by other employees during the course of employment under NRS 616B.612(3), NRS 616A.020(1), and NRS 616C.215(2)(a)).

[26] Meers v. Haughton Elevator, 101 Nev. 283, 285, 701 P.2d 1006, 1007 (1985) (internal quotations omitted) (interpreting a prior version of NRS 616C.215); *see also* NRS 616A.210(1) ("[S]ubcontractors, independent contractors and the employees of either [are] deemed to be employees of the principal contractor for the purposes of [the NIIA].").

[27] Meers v. Haughton Elevator, 101 Nev. 283, 285, 701 P.2d 1006, 1007 (1985) (internal quotations omitted) (interpreting a prior version of NRS 616C.215); *see also* NRS 616A.210(1) ("[S]ubcontractors, independent contractors and the employees of either [are] deemed to be employees of the principal contractor for the purposes of [the NIIA].").

[28] *See* NRS 616B.603(1)(b); Hays Home Delivery, Inc. v. Emp'rs Ins. Co. of Nev., 117 Nev. 678, 682, 31 P.3d 367, 369-70 (2001) (noting that NRS 616B.603 codifies the *Meers* test, discussed below, which is used to "determine[ ] whether independent contractors are 'employees' under the NIIA").

[29] *See* Hays Home Delivery, Inc., 117 Nev. at 682-83, 31 P.3d at 369-70 (2001).

[30] *Meers*, 101 Nev. at 286, 701 P.2d at 1007 (internal quotations omitted); *see also* Oliver v. Barrick Goldstrike Mines, 111 Nev. 1338, 1349, 905 P.2d 168, 175 (1995) (holding that the "same trade" language in NRS 616.262, replaced by NRS 616B.603, refers to the *Meers* test).

equipped to handle with his own force, are held to be outside his regular business."[31]

The court noted that Purcell's interpretation of the *Meers* normal work test was incorrect. Purcell conceded that the job of repairing the truck's PTO would be considered a specialized repair under *Meers*. However, it argued that Dakota Diesel performed the specialized repair, while Wintle was merely there to "monitor the repair process." Purcell further argued that even if Wintle was performing a specialized repair on the day of Ouellette's injury, Wintle was not performing a specialized repair at the time Ouellette was actually injured.

In making its argument, Purcell contended that the focus of the normal work test is on the work being performed at the time the injury occurred. Therefore, because Wintle was moving the tire changing boom truck at the time of Ouellette's injury, which was work normally performed by employees of Allied, Purcell argued that Wintle was not performing a specialized repair at the time of Ouellette's injury. In support of its argument, Purcell relied on *State Industrial Insurance System v. Ortega Concrete Pumping, Inc.*, which held that under the normal work test, "the relevant factual inquiry . . . is whether [the contractor who caused the accident] was in the 'same trade, business, profession or occupation' as [the injured employee] *at the time of the accident*."[32] Purcell also relies on *Employers Insurance Co. of Nevada v. United States*, which held that a principal contractor was immune under the NIIA as the statutory employee of the subcontractor because the work that the subcontractor "was performing *at the time of his injury*" was normally carried out by the principal contractor.[33]

The court rejected Purcell's narrow interpretation of the *Meers* normal work test. Purcell effectively argued that the relevant inquiry under *Meers* is whether, at the exact moment of an employee's injury, the activity being performed by the subcontractor or independent contractor was normally performed by the injured worker's employer. Purcell misstated the holdings of *Ortega* and *Employers Insurance Co.*. In *Ortega*, the court found the district court's failure to apply the *Meers* test was in error, and the court reversed and remanded so that it could apply the proper analysis.[34] Because the *Ortega* court did not actually apply the *Meers* normal work test, its holding is inapposite to the current case.[35] And in *Employers Insurance Co.*, the district court examined whether the defendant was the statutory employer "at the time of the accident" by examining the circumstances surrounding the employment, not the acts at the exact moment of the injury.[36] Thus, nothing in the reasoning of either case supports Purcell's contention.

---

[31] *Meers*, 101 Nev. at 286, 701 P.2d at 1007-08 (internal quotations omitted).

[32] *Ortega*, 113 Nev. 1359, 1363-64, 951 P.2d 1033, 1036 (1997) (emphasis added).

[33] *Employers Ins. Co.*, 322 F. Supp. 2d 1116, 1118 (D. Nev. 2004) (emphasis added).

[34] *Ortega*, 113 Nev. at 1364, 951 P.2d at 1036.

[35] *Ortega*, 113 Nev. at 1364, 951 P.2d at 1036.

[36] 322 F. Supp. 2d at 1118.

Furthermore, Purcell's narrow interpretation could readily create absurd results. Under Purcell's reasoning, the status of a worker performing specialized repairs would change from moment to moment depending on whether that particular task is normally performed by employees of the primary contractor. For instance, repairing an engine valve on a vehicle might be considered a specialized repair, but checking the oil level afterwards would not be if the primary contractor's employees normally check the oil level of the vehicles they are driving. Thus, the status of the work that an independent contractor is performing could repeatedly alternate between a specialized repair and something else during the same overall repair.

The court held that Wintle was performing a specialized repair at the time of Ouellette's injury. In rejecting Purcell's narrow interpretation of *Meers*, the court held that in order to determine whether a subcontractor or independent contractor was engaged in a specialized repair under the *Meers* test, and therefore whether that subcontractor or independent contractor is liable for any injuries caused to workers during the course of that specialized repair, the court must consider the subcontractor or independent contractor's activity leading to a worker's injury within the context of their other actions, both before and after the injury, and not in isolation. In this case, the court held that Wintle's presence at the mine for the purpose of a specialized repair was sufficient to establish that he was not acting as an employee of Allied at the time of the injury.

Wintle was at the mine on the day of Ouellette's injury because the truck's PTO required specialized repair. Purcell sent Wintle to the site specifically to accompany Durick, who was hired to make those specialized repairs. Even if Wintle's only purpose at the mine that day was to "monitor the repair process" of the truck, as Purcell claims, Wintle was nonetheless there for the sole purpose of the specialized repair. To put it another way, Wintle would not have been at the mine that day but for the specialized repair. Because Wintle was at the mine on the day of Ouellette's injury for the purpose of a specialized repair, the court held that there was sufficient evidence for the jury to find that Wintle and Purcell were performing a specialized repair under *Meers* at the time of Ouellette's injury, and were therefore not statutory employees of Allied under NRS 616B.603 and NRS 616A.210.

Even under Purcell's narrow interpretation of *Meers*, the court held that, when looked at in context, Wintle would still have been acting in furtherance of the specialized repair at the time of Ouellette's injury and thus be considered to be performing a specialized repair under *Meers*. Wintle arrived at the mine with Durick, the Dakota Diesel repairman Purcell had engaged to perform the specialized repair work. Both Durick and Wintle testified that Wintle actively assisted Durick in the specialized repair. Wintle testified that "[he] was going out to assist and facilitate . . . Durick in repairs to the 508 boom truck." Durick testified that Wintle assisted him in his work on the truck, stating that:

[Wintle and I] had to drain all of the hydraulic oil. Wintle drained the transmission fluid out, removed the hydraulic pump, and the power takeoff unit, mounted the new one on, had to do some setup procedure on it, got that all mounted, filled the tranny back full of oil, and remounted the hydraulic pump.

After Durick and Wintle performed the initial repairs, they "got to a point where [they] needed hydraulic oil" and drove the truck from the tire pad to the shop where the hydraulic oil was kept. After filling the truck with hydraulic oil, Durick testified that he and Wintle were next going to "take pressure checks and . . . were going to operate the crane to make sure it was operating and functioning properly." Ouellette testified that this was to see if the repairs were successful. Wintle then asked Durick if he "wanted to do the pressure checks and the function checks right there," but Durick wanted to first move the truck to the tire pad because the shop area was congested. Wintle then got into the truck to move it to the tire pad, a move that led to Ouellette's injury.

Thus, while employees of Allied may usually drive the truck and fill it with hydraulic oil, in the context of Wintle's other actions, it is clear that in this case he was acting in furtherance of the overall specialized repair at the time of Ouellette's injury. Therefore, even had evidence not been presented that Wintle was at the mine solely for the purpose of the specialized repair, there was sufficient evidence demonstrating that Wintle was still in the process of performing a specialized repair at the time of Ouellette's accident. Accordingly, Purcell was not a statutory employee of Allied under NRS 616B.603 and NRS 616A.210, and the court held that the district court did not err in denying Purcell's motion for judgment as a matter of law regarding NRS 616B.612's application.

The court also held that the district court did not improperly reject Purcell's jury instruction. The court reviewed a decision to admit or refuse jury instructions for an abuse of discretion or judicial error.[37] The court reviewed de novo whether a jury instruction accurately states Nevada law.[38] Although "a party is entitled to jury instructions on every theory of [its] case that is supported by the evidence,"[39] the offering party must demonstrate that the proffered jury instruction is warranted by Nevada law.[40]

At trial, the district court rejected the following jury instruction offered by Purcell:

The mere fact that there was an accident or other event where someone was injured is not in and of itself a sufficient basis for negligence.

---

[37] Ins. Co. of the W. v. Gibson Tile Co., 122 Nev. 455, 463, 134 P.3d 698, 702-03 (2006).

[38] Cook v. Sunrise Hosp. & Med. Ctr., LLC, 124 Nev. 997, 1003, 194 P.3d 1214, 1217 (2008).

[39] Johnson v. Egtedar, 112 Nev. 428, 432, 915 P.2d 271, 273 (1996).

[40] NRCP 51(a)(1).

The instruction was based on *Gunlock v. New Frontier Hotel Corp.*, which held, in relevant part, that "[t]he mere fact that there was an accident or other event and someone was injured is not of itself sufficient to predicate liability. Negligence is never presumed but must be established by substantial evidence."[41]

### [c] The Omitted Portions of Purcell's Jury Instruction Were Adequately Covered by Other Instructions

While Purcell's proffered jury instruction accurately reflects the first part of the *Gunlock* mere happening instruction, it omits the second part, stating that "[n]egligence is never presumed but must be established by substantial evidence."[42] Therefore, Purcell's proffered jury instruction, by itself, is an inaccurate statement of Nevada law. However, in civil cases, "if an instruction is not technically correct, the instruction should be examined in the context of all instructions given to the jury" in deciding whether "the jury was sufficiently and fairly instructed."[43]

Here, the statement that "[n]egligence is never presumed" is merely a restatement of the first part of the Gunlock reasoning presented above,[44] and the concept that negligence "must be established by substantial evidence" was adequately covered by other jury instructions stating the burden of proof for a claim of negligence.[45] Thus, when taken as a whole with the other jury instructions given by the court, the court found that Purcell's proposed jury instruction would have sufficiently and fairly instructed the jury on Gunlock's holding.[46]

### [d] Purcell's Proposed Jury Instruction Was Adequately Covered by Other Instructions

"[T]he number of instructions to be given is discretionary with the court."[47] "If one instruction adequately covers a given theory of liability or defense, it is preferable that the court refuse additional instructions relating to the same theory, though couched in different language."[48]

---

[41] *Gunlock*, 78 Nev. 182, 185, 370 P.2d 682, 684 (1962), *abrogated on other grounds by* Foster v. Costco Wholesale Corp., ___ Nev. ___, ___, 291 P.3d 150, 156 (2012).

[42] *Gunlock*, 78 Nev. at 185, 370 P.2d at 684.

[43] Gordon v. Hurtado, 96 Nev. 375, 380, 609 P.2d 327, 330 (1980).

[44] *Gunlock*, 78 Nev. at 185, 370 P.2d at 684 ("The mere fact that there was an accident . . . is not of itself sufficient to predicate liability.").

[45] *See, e.g.*, Jury Instruction No. 20 (stating the elements that Ouellette must prove to prevail on a negligence theory and that those elements must be proven by a preponderance of the evidence).

[46] *See Gordon*, 96 Nev. at 380, 609 P.2d at 330.

[47] Duran v. Mueller, 79 Nev. 453, 460, 386 P.2d 733, 737 (1963).

[48] Duran v. Mueller, 79 Nev. 453, 460, 386 P.2d 733, 737 (1963).

Where other jury instructions "adequately cover[ ] negligence, proximate cause, and the essentiality of a finding of defendants' negligence to permit a verdict for [the] plaintiff," a mere happening instruction is duplicative or confusing.[49]

Here, the district court's jury instructions covered the issues of negligence, proximate cause, and the essentiality of a finding of Purcell's negligence.[50] Therefore, the district court did not abuse its discretion by refusing to give Purcell's incomplete mere happening jury instruction.[51]

### [3]  Conclusion

Because there was sufficient evidence demonstrating that Wintle was present at the mine for the purpose of a specialized repair and acting in furtherance of the specialized repair when he caused Ouellette's injury, Purcell was not immune from liability for Ouellette's injury under NRS 616B.612. Thus, the district court did not err in denying Purcell's motion for judgment as a matter of law. Furthermore, the district court did not abuse its discretion in refusing to give an incomplete mere happening jury instruction because to do so would have been duplicative and/or confusing.

### § 12.03  ARIZONA CASES

### [A]  Mechanic's Liens—Enforcement of Settlement Agreement Against Non-Party Title Insurance Carrier

In *Fidelity National Title Insurance Co. v. Centerpoint Mechanic Lien Claims, LLC,*[52] mechanic's lien claimants brought foreclosure action claiming priority over insureds' deed of trust for a development project, which the insureds later purchased. As part of a global settlement and sale of development, the

---

[49] Gagosian v. Burdick's Television & Appliances, 254 Cal. App. 2d 316, 62 Cal. Rptr. 70, 73 (1967); *see also* Kennelly v. Burgess, 337 Md. 562, 654 A.2d 1335, 1341 (1995) ("Even the use of a proper 'mere happening' instruction can lead to confusion in the minds of jurors. . . ."); Simmons v. Monarch Mach. Tool Co., 413 Mass. 205, 596 N.E.2d 318, 324 (1992) (holding that a mere happening instruction was redundant to an instruction which stated that "if the defendant acted with reasonable care under the circumstances, then it is not negligent and not liable to the plaintiff even though the plaintiff might have been injured"), *abrogated on other grounds by* Vassallo v. Baxter Healthcare Corp., 428 Mass. 1, 696 N.E.2d 909, 910 (1998).

[50] *See* Jury Instruction No. 18 (stating that Ouellette had the burden to prove that his injury was caused by Purcell's negligence); Jury Instruction No. 20 (stating the elements that Ouellette must prove to prevail on a negligence theory and that those elements must be proven by a preponderance of the evidence); Jury Instruction Nos. 21-26 (defining negligence, contributory negligence, proximate cause, and duty of care).

[51] *See Gagosian*, 62 Cal. Rptr. at 73.

[52] 238 Ariz. 135 (Ariz. Ct. App. 2015).

insureds formed a wholly owned and controlled entity that purchased the lien claims and settled with insureds over the objection of the title insurer, which had accepted the defense of the mechanic's lien claims but reserved its right to contest coverage. The superior court held the settlement agreement was valid, and dismissed a companion case by the title insurer the against wholly owned entity for intentional interference with the contract. The title insurer appealed, and insureds and insureds' wholly owned entity cross-appealed.

The court of appeals held that settlement agreement between insureds and wholly owned entity was not enforceable.

In this case, the court addressed whether a title insurance company is liable under *United Services Automobile Ass'n v. Morris*,[53] for damages agreed to by its insureds in a settlement agreement resolving third-party mechanic's lien claims against the insureds' interest in a real estate development. Under *Morris*, when an insurer agrees to defend its insured against a third-party liability claim, but reserves the right to challenge coverage under the insured's policy, the insured may independently settle with the third-party claimant without violating the insured's duty of cooperation under the insurance contract; this settlement may assign to the claimant the insured's rights against the insurer, subject to the insurer's retained right to contest coverage.

Here, the settlement agreement was not between the insureds and the third-party mechanics' lien claimants, but was rather an agreement between the insureds and an entity they controlled that had purchased the mechanic's lien claims. Moreover, the settlement agreement was for an amount significantly greater than the amount paid to purchase the mechanic's lien claims. Accordingly, and for reasons discussed below, the court concluded that the settlement agreement between the insureds and the entity that purchased the mechanic's lien claims was not a compliant Morris agreement, and the court accordingly reversed the superior court's ruling that the amount of the insurer's liability (if it loses the yet-to-be-litigated coverage dispute) is the negotiated settlement amount.

## [1]  Facts and Procedural Background

### [a]  *Parties and Title Insurance Policies*

In March 2007 and early April 2008, Mortgages, Ltd., a private lender, agreed to loan a developer additional funds to build Centerpoint, a high-rise residential condominium development in Tempe. Construction on the project had begun in December 2005, and a portion of the loan was used to pay off an earlier loan from Freemont Investment and Loan ("Freemont") secured by a deed of trust, with the balance used to fund construction. The loan was secured by a deed of trust against Centerpoint. A predecessor to Fidelity National Title Insurance

---

[53] 154 Ariz. 113, 741 P.2d 246 (1987).

Company ("Fidelity") issued a title insurance policy insuring priority of Mortgages, Ltd.'s deed of trust for a face amount of $165.2 million (the "ML Policy").

Two months after issuing the loan, Mortgages, Ltd. went into bankruptcy. As part of its bankruptcy reorganization plan, Mortgages, Ltd.'s Centerpoint deed of trust interests were transferred to two investors—Centerpoint I Loan, LLC ("CPI") and Centerpoint II Loan, LLC ("CPII")—and eight individual fractional interest holders. ML Manager, LLC acted as manager of CPI and CPII, as well as agent and attorney-in-fact for the fractional interest holders. The court referred to ML Manger, CPI, CPII, and the fractional interest holders collectively as "ML Investors."

In April 2010, ML Investors purchased Centerpoint at a trustee's sale for a credit bid of $8 million. Soon thereafter, CPI and CPII purchased a parking lot adjacent to Centerpoint. Fidelity issued a title insurance policy to CPI and CPII for the parking lot (the "Parking Lot Policy") for the amount of the purchase price, $875,000.

Universal–SCP 1, LP ("Universal") contemporaneously provided CPI and CPII a bankruptcy exit loan of $20 million, secured in part by CPI and CPII's Centerpoint assets. Commonwealth Land Title Insurance Company ("Commonwealth") issued Universal a $5 million exit lender title policy insuring priority of its security interest in Centerpoint (the "Universal Policy").

CPI and CPII also obtained a $5 million loan from VRCP Funding, LP ("VRCP"), used in part to purchase the parking lot. The VRCP loan was secured by a deed of trust on Centerpoint and the parking lot, and Commonwealth issued VRCP a $5 million lender title policy insuring priority of its deed of trust (the "VRCP Policy").

### [b]   Mechanics' Lien Litigation

Funding for the Centerpoint project became erratic during construction, which eventually stalled. Starting in April 2008, subcontractors and suppliers began to record mechanic's liens and notices of lis pendens against Centerpoint. The first of eventually dozens of mechanic's lien foreclosure claims was filed in October 2008, asserting that the mechanic's liens had priority over Mortgages, Ltd.'s (subsequently ML Investors) security interest in Centerpoint.

ML Investors tendered the defense of the mechanic's lien claims to Fidelity, and in September 2009, Fidelity accepted the defense with a general reservation of rights and engaged counsel to represent ML Investors. Counsel asserted that ML Investors, as Mortgages, Ltd.'s assignees, were entitled to be equitably subrogated to the priority position held by Freemont, whose loan Mortgages, Ltd.'s initial loan had been paid off and whose deed of trust undisputedly had priority over the mechanic's liens. In September 2010, the superior court denied summary judgment on equitable subrogation, finding issues of fact as to whether there was an agreement to subrogate at the time of Mortgages, Ltd.'s loan and whether

Mortgages, Ltd. was at fault for failing to fund the loan while encouraging continued construction and representing that funding was forthcoming. The ruling further determined the validity and amount of several mechanic's liens, although it left the issue of priority for trial.

After the summary judgment ruling, Fidelity reaffirmed its general reservation of rights under the ML Policy. In December 2010, Fidelity accepted the defense of CPI and CPII under the Parking Lot Policy, again with a reservation of rights. Universal and VRCP tendered their defense against the mechanic's lien claims to Commonwealth, which was accepted with a reservation of rights in December 2010.

Meanwhile, ML Investors were considering selling the Centerpoint property, which was incurring ongoing security, maintenance, and other expenses during the pendency of the lawsuit. In addition to attempting to recoup at least part of their investment, ML Investors were also under pressure to liquidate Centerpoint to fund payments on the Universal exit loan, which risked substantial default penalties if not cured.

In September 2010, ML Investors contracted to sell Centerpoint for $30 million. The sale failed to close in October as planned, at least in part due to Fidelity's decision, in the wake of the summary judgment ruling, not to provide a title policy to the buyer that would insure priority over the mechanic's liens.

ML Investors concurrently pursued settlement negotiations with the mechanic's lien claimants. After the summary judgment ruling, the claimants insisted on a cash settlement, rather than an assignment of ML Investors' title insurance claims. ML Investors needed money from the potential sale of Centerpoint to fund the settlement, but the sale could not be completed without first settling the mechanic's lien claims to enable the buyer to receive clear title. Beginning in October 2010 and continuing until the eventual sale of Centerpoint in January and February 2011, ML Investors informed Fidelity that they were seeking a potential Morris settlement directly with the mechanic's lien claimants.

### [c]  Sale and Settlement

After extensive negotiations, ML Investors, Universal, VRCP, the buyer, and the mechanic's lien claimants reached a global agreement in February 2011 (as memorialized in November 2011) to sell Centerpoint and settle the mechanic's lien claims. Concerned that Fidelity would deny coverage if ML Investors simply paid the liens (thus clearing title) or if ML Investors—rather than a third party—purchased the liens (under the merger doctrine), the investors created a new entity, Centerpoint Mechanic Lien Claims, LLC ("CMLC"), which was wholly owned and controlled by CPII, to acquire the mechanic's lien claims and, later, to pursue the title insurance claims against Fidelity.

Under the global agreement, the buyer purchased Centerpoint for $30 million. To provide clear title to the buyer, CMLC purchased the mechanic's liens for $13.65 million and agreed to subordinate its interest in Centerpoint to the buyer's fee interest. Additionally, Universal and VRCP subordinated their interests in Centerpoint to that of the buyer. As a failsafe, CMLC agreed to a liquidated damages provision requiring it to pay $38 million to the buyer if CMLC failed to release the mechanic's liens within three years.

ML Investors waived $13.5 million of their proceeds from the sale for CMLC to use to purchase the mechanic's liens. They further set aside $3 million from the sale as CMLC's litigation reserve to pursue title insurance claims. ML Investors also waived their right to proceeds from the sale of the parking lot. Additionally, CPII purchased VRCP, and Universal and VRCP waived their claims to $5 million each from the sale proceeds and subordinated their interests in Centerpoint to that of the buyer.

The global agreement provided that once CMLC had been substituted for the mechanic's lien claimants, CMLC and ML Investors would enter a stipulated judgment for $38 million and a declaration that the mechanic's liens had priority over ML Investors' interest in Centerpoint. CMLC would accept assignment of ML Investors' claims against Fidelity, would agree not to execute against ML Investors, and would pursue title insurance claims directly against Fidelity. The agreement included a plan to distribute any money recovered from Fidelity to ML Investors.

### [d]  Intervention and Judgment

In the wake of the February 2011 agreement, CMLC substituted itself for the mechanic's lien claimants in the ongoing litigation. Fidelity and Commonwealth intervened to challenge the settlement agreement. After a five-day hearing, the superior court ruled that: (1) the settlement agreement was valid under *Morris*, (2) the agreement was neither fraudulent nor collusive, (3) Fidelity had received proper notice of the settlement, and (4) the settlement amount was reasonable. The court thus found the settlements of the claims against Fidelity's ML Policy ($24,583,799.38 + $1,880,994.51 in mechanic's lien attorney fees) and Parking Lot Policy ($875,000) and on Commonwealth's Universal Policy ($5 million) and VRCP Policy ($5 million) "were reasonable, prudent, and fully supported by the evidence produced at the hearing" and entered judgment in favor of ML Investors, Universal, VRCP, and CMLC.

The superior court thereafter denied Fidelity's motion for new trial. The court also denied as premature CMLC and ML Investors' requests for attorney fees, concluding that they were not yet successful parties within the meaning of Arizona Revised Statutes ("A.R.S.") § 12-341.01 because the insurance coverage issue remained pending. Fidelity, but not Commonwealth, timely appealed, and CMLC and ML Investors timely cross-appealed.

## *[e]   Companion Intentional Interference Case*

In a companion case, Fidelity and Commonwealth sued CMLC for intentional interference with contract, alleging that CMLC had intentionally interfered with the title insurance contracts by entering into the *Morris*-type agreement. The superior court dismissed the case on the basis that it had previously found that the insureds did not breach the insurance contracts by entering into the settlement agreement. Fidelity and Commonwealth timely appealed.

## [2]   Discussion

Fidelity argues that, as a matter of law, a title insurance policy holder may not enter a *Morris* agreement. Fidelity and amicus curiae American Land Title Association assert that, unlike the third-party insurance claim at issue in *Morris*, the policies here provide insurance for a first-party property loss, meaning loss caused by alleged defects that, if established, could lessen the value of the insureds' property. The court indicated it need not address this argument, however, because even assuming *Morris* applies to title insurance claims, under the circumstances presented here, the settlement agreement is not a compliant *Morris* agreement.

## *[a]   Settlement Agreements Under* Morris

As a general rule, an indemnitor with a duty to defend its indemnitee has the right and obligation to provide a defense against any third-party claim potentially within its indemnity obligation.[54] "[B]y defending all claims the [indemnitor] obtains the advantage of exclusively controlling the litigation," including settlement with the third-party claimant.[55] Under these circumstances, the indemnitee is contractually bound by a cooperation clause to participate and aid the indemnitor in the defense, and may not independently settle with the claimant without breaching this contractual duty.[56]

The situation changes if the indemnitor accepts the defense, but reserves its right to contest coverage. An indemnitor may "appropriately perform its contractual duty to defend while simultaneously reserving the right to later assert the defense," provided the indemnitor asserts the potential coverage defense in good faith.[57]

---

[54] *See Morris*, 154 Ariz. at 117, 741 P.2d at 250.

[55] *See Morris*, 154 Ariz. at 117, 741 P.2d at 250.

[56] *See Morris*, 154 Ariz. at 117, 741 P.2d at 250.

[57] Parking Concepts, Inc. v. Tenney, 207 Ariz. 19, 22, ¶ 12, 83 P.3d 19, 22 (2004).

In *Morris*, the court noted that an insurer's reservation of rights places an insured in a "precarious position."[58] The insureds in that case faced "the possibility of a jury verdict greater than their [ ] policy limit or, even if within the limit, one that might not be covered."[59] The insureds were thus entitled "to act reasonably to protect themselves from 'the sharp thrust of personal liability.' "[60] *Morris* thus held that "[t]he [indemnitor]'s reservation of the privilege to deny the duty to pay relinquishes to the [indemnitee] control of the litigation."[61] And an indemnitee may then independently settle with a third-party claimant without breaching the indemnitee's contractual cooperation obligation.[62]

Under a typical *Morris* agreement, the insured agrees to allow judgment to be entered against it in exchange for a covenant not to execute, and assigns its rights under the policy to the claimant, who then pursues the insurer.[63] Because this type of covenant not to execute insulates the indemnitee from potential liability, neither party to the settlement has an incentive to minimize the stipulated judgment amount.[64] In fact, by contemporaneously assigning its right to sue the insurer for bad faith, the insured can potentially bind the insurer to a stipulated judgment in excess of policy limits.[65]

To protect the indemnitor, *Morris* announced several limitations on an insured's right to enter into such an agreement. The insured must: (1) "provide notice to the insurer," (2) "demonstrate that the settlement was free from fraud and collusion," and (3) "prove that the settlement amount is reasonable."[66] Reasonableness turns on "what a reasonably prudent person in the [indemnitee's] position would have settled for on the merits of the claimant's case" in light of the circumstances affecting liability, defense, and coverage.[67] This inquiry attempts to recreate "what would have occurred if there had been an arm's-length negotiation between interested parties."[68]

---

[58] 154 Ariz. at 118, 741 P.2d at 251.

[59] 154 Ariz. at 118, 741 P.2d at 251.

[60] 154 Ariz. at 118, 741 P.2d at 251(quoting Ariz. Prop. & Cas. Ins. Guar. Fund v. Helme, 153 Ariz. 129, 137, 735 P.2d 451, 459 (1987)); *see also* Damron v. Sledge, 105 Ariz. 151, 153, 460 P.2d 997, 999 (1969) (quoting Critz v. Farmers Ins. Grp., 230 Cal. App. 2d 788, 41 Cal. Rptr. 401, 408 (1964)); *Tenney*, 207 Ariz. at 22, ¶ 13, 83 P.3d at 22.

[61] 154 Ariz. at 119, 741 P.2d at 252.

[62] 154 Ariz. at 119, 741 P.2d at 252; *see also Tenney*, 207 Ariz. at 22, ¶ 13, 83 P.3d at 22.

[63] *Tenney*, 207 Ariz. at 22, ¶¶ 14, 15, 83 P.3d at 22.

[64] *Id.* ¶ 14.

[65] Leflet v. Redwood Fire & Cas. Ins. Co., 226 Ariz. 297, 300, ¶ 13, 247 P.3d 180, 183 (Ct. App. 2011).

[66] *Leflet*, 226 Ariz. at 300, ¶ 14, 247 P.3d at 183 (citing *Morris*, 154 Ariz. at 119-20, 741 P.2d at 252-54).

[67] *Tenney*, 207 Ariz. at 23, ¶ 15, 83 P.3d at 23 (quoting *Morris*, 154 Ariz. at 121, 741 P.2d at 254).

[68] Himes v. Safeway Ins. Co., 205 Ariz. 31, 38-39, ¶¶ 22-23, 66 P.3d 74, 81-82 (Ct. App. 2003).

"The overarching goal of Morris is to permit the insured and the insurer to balance their competing interests in an atmosphere of fairness and defined risk— not to promote the transformation of underlying contract and tort claims into bad faith claims at inflated values."[69] Thus, a *Morris* agreement that falls "outside the permitted parameters" is unenforceable.[70]

Here, the court concluded that the settlement agreement between the insured and the entity that purchased the lien claims fell outside the permitted parameters of *Morris*. Rather than representing an arm's length settlement between lien claimants and insureds, the purported *Morris* agreement in this case was between the insureds and an entity they controlled. The lien claimants—the parties whose claims created the insureds' potential liability—were not parties to the agreement. Instead, ML Investors interposed CMLC, which was wholly owned and controlled by CPII, as a purported proxy for the lien claimants. Thus, the interests of the parties to the settlement agreement, CMLC and ML Investors, were aligned, not divergent.[71]

Moreover, by assigning their claims to the insureds' entity, the lien claimants effectively settled their claims unconditionally for a fixed sum, leaving no risk of excess liability for the insureds. This is particularly significant because the insureds no longer faced the risk of personal liability that motivates a *Morris* agreement. And having settled with the lien claimants, ML Investors' remedy against Fidelity was instead to seek reimbursement under the insurance contract, and, if appropriate, to pursue a potential bad faith claim based on Fidelity's allegedly improper reservation of rights. Given these circumstances, the settlement agreement—even if economically prudent from ML Investors' perspective—was not a compliant *Morris* agreement.

The circumstances in this case are in stark contrast to those in cases in which *Morris* agreements have been upheld, where such agreements resolve outstanding adverse claims by third-party claimants who accept an assignment of the insured's claims against the insurer and/or partial payment for stipulated liability.[72] In those cases, the *Morris*-type agreement with third-party claimants operated to protect the insured against the "sharp thrust of personal liability." In contrast, here, the agreement at issue was not a protection against potential liability; that liability had already been resolved through a settlement with the lien claimants.

The unity of parties and lack of remaining risk of liability were further reflected in the artificially inflated judgment—$38 million despite the underlying

---

[69] *Leflet*, 226 Ariz. at 301, ¶ 15, 247 P.3d at 184.

[70] Safeway Ins. Co. v. Guerrero, 210 Ariz. 5, 15, ¶ 34, 106 P.3d 1020, 1030 (2005).

[71] *Compare Leflet*, 226 Ariz. at 301, ¶ 17, 247 P.3d at 184 (noting that a *Morris* agreement generally settles a dispute between opposing parties).

[72] *See, e.g., Morris*, 154 Ariz. at 118, 741 P.2d at 251; *Tenney*, 207 Ariz. at 22, ¶¶ 11-15, 83 P.3d at 22.

settlement with the lien claimants for $13.65 million—entered pursuant to the purported *Morris* agreement. CMLC and ML Investors argued that although the lien claimants settled their claims in their entirety, ML Investors still faced greater economic risk. But this argument conflates *Morris*'s discussion of "personal liability" with overall economic or financial risk, which here included ML Investors' potential loss of their investment due to foreclosure of the mechanic's liens.

As relevant here, Fidelity's title policies insured only against loss stemming from the priority of the mechanic's liens over ML Investors' interest in Centerpoint. The policies did not otherwise guaranty the value of the property or that the insureds could complete the sale of Centerpoint in February 2011 (even accepting that it was in the insureds' interests generally to do so).

Because a *Morris* agreement cannot expand the insured's rights under the insurance contract,[73] the only loss for which Fidelity was potentially liable was the cost to the insureds of the mechanic's liens' priority, i.e., the $13.65 million paid to acquire the mechanic's lien claims. Thus, the relevant "arm's-length negotiation" occurred in this case between the mechanic's lien claimants and the insureds,[74] and the subsequent agreement between CMLC and ML Investors for a judgment in an amount almost three times what was paid for the liens goes beyond ML Investors' established liability and beyond Fidelity's potential liability under the insurance contract.

Moreover, the stipulated judgment exceeded ML Investors' liability in scope as well as amount. The judgment's award to the insureds of the mechanics' lien claimant's attorney fees illustrates this point. Because the insureds did not pay the mechanics' lien claimants any sum for attorney fees, those fees could not reasonably be considered a loss incurred due to a defect in title. The insureds could not, by using CMLC as a proxy, artificially inflate Fidelity's indemnity obligation to nearly three times the price actually paid.

In sum, the purported *Morris* agreement bound parties whose interests aligned, after the actual opposing party had settled for a fixed sum and stipulated to a judgment that exceeded actual liability both in scope and in amount. The court thus concluded that the agreement did not fit within the parameters of a Morris agreement.

Because of the court's resolution of this issue, the court indicated it need not address Fidelity's alternative arguments attacking the agreement and stipulated judgment. Similarly, this conclusion rendered moot CMLC and ML Investors' cross-appeal from the superior court's order denying their requests for attorney fees as premature.

---

[73] *Tenney*, 207 Ariz. at 24, ¶ 25, 83 P.3d at 24.
[74] *See Himes*, 205 Ariz. at 39, ¶ 23, 66 P.3d at 82.

### [b] Intentional Interference Claims

Fidelity and Commonwealth appealed the superior court's dismissal of their companion case, asserting a claim that CMLC intentionally interfered with Fidelity's insurance contracts and induced the insureds to breach their contracts by improperly entering a *Morris* agreement. The superior court dismissed this claim on the basis of issue preclusion, ruling that, because the purported *Morris* agreement was found to be reasonable and not fraudulent or collusive, the insureds did not breach the insurance contracts by entering the agreement.

Because the court vacated the judgment as against Fidelity, issue preclusion no longer barred the intentional interference claim. Accordingly, the court reversed the judgment dismissing Fidelity's claim in CV 2011-015738 and remanded for further proceedings. Because the stipulated judgment remained in effect as against Commonwealth, however, and because Commonwealth had stated no alternative grounds for reversing dismissal, the court affirmed the judgment dismissing Commonwealth's intentional interference claim.

### [c] Attorney Fees on Appeal

All parties sought awards of attorney fees expended on appeal pursuant to A.R.S. § 12-341.01. In an exercise of the court's discretion, the court declined to award fees to any party.

### [3] Conclusion

Based on the foregoing, the court reversed the decision of the superior court and remanded for further proceedings consistent with this opinion.

## [B] Little Miller Act—Notice Provisions

In *Cemex Construction Materials South, LLC v. Falcone Brother & Associates, Inc.*,[75] a materialman filed suit against a general contractor, alleging it had not been paid for materials it had supplied to a public works improvement project. Contractor moved for summary judgment, claiming it had not received the statutorily required 20-day notices and that the notices were insufficient to satisfy the statutory requirements of Little Miller Act. The Superior Court, Pima County, No. C20121949, Carmine Cornelio, J., denied the motion, concluding that materialman's certificates of mailing and affidavits were sufficient to meet the purposes of the Act. Contractor appealed.

---

[75] 237 Ariz. 236 (Ct. App. 2015).

The court of appeals held that:

1. Act notices are required to be sent by registered or certified mail, and

2. The genuine issue of material fact as to whether contractor had received the notices precluded summary judgment.

Although statutes such as the Little Miller Act are to be construed liberally in favor of the materialman, such construction must give way to express limitations imposed by the legislature. A.R.S. § 34-223(A).

Falcone Brothers & Associates, Inc. ("Falcone") appealed the trial court's judgment awarding damages to Cemex Construction Materials South, LLC ("Cemex") for materials and labor Cemex provided to a public works construction project for which Falcone was the general contractor. Falcone argued that the court erred in concluding that notices sent by Cemex to Falcone regarding amounts Cemex was owed satisfied the requirements of Arizona's "Little Miller Act."[76] Falcone contends Cemex's notices, which were sent by first class mail with a certificate of mailing, did not comply with section 34-223(A), and Cemex therefore was precluded from bringing its action. For the following reasons, the court vacated the judgment and remanded for a new trial.

### [1]   Factual and Procedural Background

The record supports the following facts and procedural history. Falcone was the general contractor for a city of Tucson public works improvement project. The project was bonded and guaranteed by The Guarantee Company of North America ("GCNA"). Falcone subcontracted with J & S Commercial Concrete Contractors, Inc. ("J & S") for concrete work on the project and J & S, in turn, subcontracted with Cemex to provide construction materials.

In 2011, Cemex filed a complaint against J & S, Falcone, and GCNA, alleging it had not been paid for the materials it had supplied to the project. J & S did not answer the complaint, and Cemex obtained a default judgment against it. Cemex then moved for summary judgment against Falcone and GCNA, claiming it was entitled to recover against the statutory payment bond. In its motion, Cemex asserted that it had filed four preliminary 20-day notices to Falcone pursuant to A.R.S. § 34-223(A) before filing suit, and that each notice had been mailed separately via first class mail, postage prepaid, with a certificate of mailing.

In its response to Cemex's motion, Falcone asserted that "[a]t no time before, during or after The Project did [it] receive a Preliminary Twenty–Day Notice from [Cemex] for materials" Cemex had supplied to J & S, as is required

---

[76] *See* A.R.S. § 34-223(A) (requiring materialman to provide estimate of costs within 20 days of supplying labor or materials and notice of any unpaid balance within 90 days of completion).

by section 34-223(A). This claim was supported by a declaration from Falcone's owner, who asserted Falcone had not received any 20-day notices. Falcone also contended that genuine issues of material fact existed regarding whether Cemex had delivered any concrete to the project and the amount of concrete delivered. Subsequently, the trial court granted Cemex's request to withdraw its motion for summary judgment, allowing the parties additional time for disclosure and discovery.

In December 2012, Cemex renewed in part its motion for summary judgment on the issue of damages, urging that Falcone's discovery responses indicated Cemex had "supplied at least 837 cubic yards of concrete to the project." Falcone agreed the project had required 837 cubic yards of concrete but maintained that a genuine issue of material fact existed regarding "how much concrete Cemex actually provided to J & S" for the project.

Falcone then filed a motion for summary judgment, claiming it had not received the statutorily required 20-day notices and Cemex therefore was precluded from bringing its action. It further contended the notices were insufficient to satisfy the statutory requirements because they were sent by first class, rather than by registered or certified mail. Cemex maintained that the four preliminary 20-day notices it had sent by first class mail with certificates of mailing satisfied the statute's requirements.

In March 2013, the trial court denied Cemex's motion for partial summary judgment on the issue of damages. After a hearing, the court also denied Falcone's motion for summary judgment, concluding that Cemex's certificates of mailing and affidavits were "sufficient to meet the purposes of" section 34-223(A). After a bench trial on the sole issue of damages, the court entered judgment in favor of Cemex, awarding it $81,913.04 in damages along with prejudgment interest, costs, and attorney fees. Falcone timely appealed. The court indicated it had jurisdiction pursuant to A.R.S. § 12-2101(A).

### [2]  Discussion

Falcone argues that the trial court erred by concluding that the 20-day notices Cemex sent to Falcone by first class mail satisfied section 34-223(A) as a matter of law. Falcone asserts the statute specifies that both 20- and 90-day notices must be sent only by registered or certified mail, as provided for in the last sentence of that section.[77] Cemex, by contrast, claims that because this sentence contains the singular form ("[s]uch notice"), it applies only to 90-day notices; this, according to Cemex, leaves an "unfilled statutory gap," which the court should fill by applying the mailing provision found in A.R.S. § 33-992.01(F) (the mechanic's lien law). Because section 33-992.01 allows for

---

[77] See A.R.S. § 34-223(A) ("Such notice shall be served by registered or certified mail, postage prepaid. . . .").

service by first class mail with a certificate of mailing, Cemex maintains its notices were sufficient. The court reviewed issues of statutory interpretation and application de novo.[78]

"The primary rule of statutory construction is to find and give effect to legislative intent."[79] To determine that intent, the court looked first to the plain language of the statute.[80] "When a statute is clear, the Court did not 'resort to other methods of statutory interpretation to determine the legislature's intent because its intent is readily discernible from the face of the statute.'"[81] But when a statute's language is ambiguous, the court resorted to principles of statutory interpretation to discern the legislature's intent.[82] Although statutes such as the LMA are to be construed liberally in favor of the materialman, such construction "must give way to express limitations imposed by the legislature."[83]

Both Cemex and Falcone conceded at argument that the notice provision of the statute was ambiguous. Because the term "such notice" was susceptible to both parties' interpretations, the court agreed. The court therefore looked to the language of the statute as well as principles of statutory interpretation to discern the legislature's intent.[84]

Arizona's "Little Miller Act" (LMA), 4 A.R.S. §§ 34-221 through 34-227, requires a general contractor on a public project to post a bond to ensure that all who supply labor or materials to the project are paid.[85] section 34-222. Both a payment bond and a performance bond, executed by a surety company, must be posted before public work begins.[86] The LMA provides a materialman with a right to recover from the payment bond when it has not been paid for material or labor it has provided.[87] To maintain an action on the bond, a claimant must comply with the notice requirements of section 34-223(A), which provides in pertinent part:

> [A]ny such claimant having a direct contractual relationship with a subcontractor of the contractor furnishing such payment bond but no contractual relationship express or implied with such contractor shall have a right of action upon such payment bond upon giving the contractor only a written preliminary twenty day notice, as provided for in § 33–992.01,

---

[78] Schwarz v. City of Glendale, 190 Ariz. 508, 510, 950 P.2d 167, 169 (Ct. App. 1997).

[79] Mail Boxes, Etc., U.S.A. v. Indus. Comm'n, 181 Ariz. 119, 121, 888 P.2d 777, 779 (1995).

[80] Canon Sch. Dist. No. 50 v. W.E.S. Constr. Co., 177 Ariz. 526, 529, 869 P.2d 500, 503 (1994).

[81] *In re* Estate of Wyatt, 235 Ariz. 138, ¶ 5, 329 P.3d 1040, 1041 (2014), quoting State v. Christian, 205 Ariz. 64, ¶ 6, 66 P.3d 1241, 1243 (2003).

[82] Bentley v. Building Our Future, 217 Ariz. 265, ¶ 13, 172 P.3d 860, 865 (Ct. App. 2007).

[83] Maricopa Turf, Inc. v. Sunmaster, Inc., 173 Ariz. 357, 361, 842 P.2d 1370, 1374 (Ct. App. 1992); Coast to Coast Mfg. v. Carnes Constr., Inc., 145 Ariz. 112, 113, 700 P.2d 499, 500 (Ct. App. 1985).

[84] *See Bentley*, 217 Ariz. 265, ¶ 13, 172 P.3d at 865.

[85] A.R.S. § 34-222.

[86] A.R.S. § 34-222.

[87] A.R.S. § 34-223.

subsection C, paragraphs 1, 2, 3 and 4 and subsections E and H, and upon giving written notice to such contractor within ninety days from the date on which such claimant performed the last of the labor or furnished or supplied the last of the material for which such claim is made, stating with substantial accuracy the amount claimed and the name of the party to whom the material was furnished or supplied for whom the labor was done or performed. Such notice shall be served by registered or certified mail, postage prepaid, in an envelope addressed to the contractor at any place the contractor maintains an office or conducts business, or at the contractor's residence.

The statute requires a materialman claimant to send both a preliminary 20-day notice and a final 90-day notice, and neither notice may substitute for the other.[88]

The purpose of these notice requirements is " 'to fix a time limit after which the prime contractor could make payment to the subcontractor with certainty that he would not thereafter be faced by claims of those who had supplied labor and materials to the subcontractor,' "[89] and to "protect those who furnish labor or materials in the construction setting,"[90] A.R.S. § 34223(A) also "relieve[s] a prime contractor of liability to sub-subcontractors or materialmen (who have no contractual relation to the prime contractor) after ninety days so that the prime contractor may safely pay his subcontractor without the fear of being subject to 'double payments' to sub-subcontractors."[91]

Section 34-223(A) requires 20-day notices to conform to certain provisions contained in section 33-992.01, which establishes requirements for persons seeking to pursue a claim against a mechanic's or materialman's lien. Specifically, section 34-223(A) states that 20-day notices shall be prepared "as provided for" by section 33-992.01(C) (1), (2), (3), and (4), as well as section 33-992.01(E) and (H). Those subsections, respectively, specify the information that must be included in a 20-day notice, section 33-992.01(C), permit materialmen to file 20-day notices for subsequent work or materials even if a preliminary 20-day notice for earlier work or deliveries was not mailed, section 33-992.01(E), and state the effect on payment when a materialman provides labor or services exceeding the description in a 20-day notice, section 33-992.01(H). Pertinent to this opinion, subsection (F) of that statute, which is not included in section 34-223(A), also states:

---

[88] Westburne Supply, Inc. v. Diversified Design & Constr., Inc., 170 Ariz. 598, 600, 826 P.2d 1224, 1226 (Ct. App. 1992).

[89] United States ex rel. Blue Circle W., Inc. v. Tucson Mech. Contracting Inc., 921 F.2d 911, 914 (9th Cir. 1990), quoting Bowden v. United States ex rel. Malloy, 239 F.2d 572, 577-78 (9th Cir. 1956).

[90] W. Asbestos Co. v. TGK Constr. Co., 121 Ariz. 388, 391, 590 P.2d 927, 930 (1979).

[91] *Coast to Coast Mfg.*, 145 Ariz. at 113, 700 P.2d at 500.

The notice or notices required by [§ 33–992.01] may be given by mailing the notice by first class mail sent with a certificate of mailing, registered or certified mail, postage prepaid in all cases, addressed to the person to whom notice is to be given at the person's residence or business address. Service is complete at the time of the deposit of notice in the mail.

### [a]  Applicability of § 33–992.01(F) to the LMA

Falcone maintains that section 34-223(A) requires LMA notices to be sent by registered or certified mail and does not authorize service of 20-day notices by first class mail with certificates of mailing. It contends the legislature "expressly excluded" section 33-992.01(F)—the mechanic's lien provision permitting its 20-day notices to be sent by first class mail with a certificate of mailing—from section 34-223(A) of the LMA. Cemex, by contrast, urges that section 33-992.01(F) is "implicitly incorporated" into section 34-223(A), and that notices sent by first class mail with a certificate of mailing therefore are proper.

To determine whether the mailing provision in section 33-992.01(F) applies to 20-day notices sent pursuant to section 34-223(A) of the LMA, the court applied the doctrine of *expressio unius est exclusio alterius*, an established rule of statutory construction meaning " 'the expression of one or more items of a class indicates an intent to exclude all items of the same class which are not expressed.' "[92] When the court applied this doctrine to the plain language of section 34-223(A), it was clear the legislature did not intend the mailing provision of section 33-992.01(F) to apply to the notices required by section 34-223(A). Section 34-223(A) specifically refers to subsections (C)(1), (2), (3), and (4), and subsections (E) and (H). As noted above, subsections (C), (E), and (H) refer to the content and treatment of 20-day notices. By excluding subsection (F) from the list of provisions applicable to 20-day notices under the LMA, the legislature indicated it did not intend subsection (F)'s mailing provisions to apply.[93]

Nothing in the legislative history of these statutes contradicts this conclusion.[94] When the LMA was enacted in 1969, it only required a claimant to provide a 90-day notice to the contractor.[95] Section 34-223(A) was amended in 1984 to include the requirement that a claimant also provide a written preliminary estimate within 20 days of furnishing services or materials.[96] In doing so, section

---

[92] *See* Boynton v. Anderson, 205 Ariz. 45, ¶ 8, 66 P.3d 88, 90-91 (Ct. App. 2003), quoting State v. Fell, 203 Ariz. 186, ¶ 11, 52 P.3d 218, 221 (Ct. App. 2002).

[93] *Cf.* PAM Transp. v. Freightliner Corp., 182 Ariz. 132, 133, 893 P.2d 1295, 1296 (1995) ("[I]f a statute specifies under what conditions it is effective, the Court indicated it could ordinarily infer that it excludes all others.").

[94] *See* Carrow Co. v. Lusby, 167 Ariz. 18, 20, 804 P.2d 747, 749 (1990) ("Legislative intent often can be discovered by examining the development of a particular statute.").

[95] 1969 Ariz. Sess. Laws, ch. 52, § 11.

[96] 1984 Ariz. Sess. Laws, ch. 242, § 1.

34-223(A) incorporated by reference certain subsections of the mechanic's lien law: specifically, section 33-992.01(C)(1), (2), (3), and (4), as well as subsections (D), (E), and (I).[97]

The LMA was amended again in 1992 to account for section 33-992.01 having been renumbered that same year.[98] In pertinent part, section 33-992.01(I) was renumbered as subsection (H) and subsection (G) was renumbered as subsection (F) following the deletion of section 33-992.01(D).[99] Accordingly, section 34-223(A) removed the reference to section 33-992.01(D) and renumbered its reference to section 33-992.01(I) as subsection (H).[100] The act was amended again in 1992 to remove gender-specific references, but the pertinent language was not altered.[101]

Although the legislature could have incorporated the mailing requirements of subsection (F) into section 34-223(A) while making any of these amendments, it did not, creating a strong inference it did not intend to allow LMA notices to be mailed via first class mail.[102] The court presumed that "'what the Legislature means, it will say.'"[103]

### [b]  Implicit Incorporation

In an amicus brief filed with the court, the Arizona Rock Products Association (ARPA) notes that section 34-223(A) expressly refers to section 33-992.01(C), which in turn refers to section 33-992.01(B) ("The preliminary twenty day notice referred to in subsection B of this section shall be given not later than twenty days after the claimant has first furnished labor"); subsection (B), in turn, refers to the requirement that a claimant file a "written preliminary twenty day notice as prescribed by this section." ARPA contends that "[t]he express reference to providing notice 'as prescribed by this section' refers to the entire section 33–992.01, and not just subsection B." And because section 33-992.01 relies on subsection (F) to prescribe acceptable methods of notice, including notice by first class mail with a certificate of service, ARPA maintains that subsection (F)'s mailing provision implicitly applies to section 34-223(A).

---

[97] 1984 Ariz. Sess. Laws, ch. 242, § 1.

[98] 1992 Ariz. Sess. Laws, ch. 353, § 8.

[99] 1992 Ariz. Sess. Laws, ch. 353, § 1.

[100] 1992 Ariz. Sess. Laws, ch. 353, § 8.

[101] 1992 Ariz. Sess. Laws, ch. 227, § 4.

[102] *See Boynton*, 205 Ariz. 45, ¶¶ 10-11, 66 P.3d at 91 (concluding legislature did not intend to incorporate statutory provision into a related statute when it "could have . . . but decided not to" amend statutory language to include such provision).

[103] *Canon Sch. Dist. No. 50*, 177 Ariz. at 529, 869 P.2d at 503, quoting Padilla v. Indus. Comm'n, 113 Ariz. 104, 106, 546 P.2d 1135, 1137 (1976).

But this is a strained reading of the statute that contradicts its plain language. First, ARPA's argument would appear to incorporate every provision of section 33-992.01 into the LMA. Such a reading would render meaningless the legislature's express intent to include certain provisions and exclude others, leaving section 33-223(A)'s specific references to section 33-992.01 irrelevant.[104]

This interpretation also would incorporate into the LMA certain provisions of the mechanic's lien law that expressly conflict with the LMA's own requirements. For example, the mechanic's lien law requires a claimant to serve 20-day notices on the project owner, the original contractor, the construction lender, if any, and to the person the claimant contracted with to provide labor or materials.[105] The LMA, by contrast, requires its 20- and 90-day notices be served on "the contractor only."[106] Similarly, a claimant under the mechanic's lien law must bring an action to enforce the lien within six months after the lien is recorded.[107] The LMA allows an action to be brought within one year from the date a materialman last provided labor or materials.[108]

Additionally, to preserve a claim under the mechanic's lien law, a lien claimant must state under oath, inter alia, that it gave section 33-992.01's preliminary 20-day notice, and must attach "the proof of mailing required by § 33-992.02."[109] The LMA has no such requirement, and reading into section 34-223(A) the additional provisions of the mechanic's lien law would effectively alter how an LMA claimant may perfect and pursue its claim.

The results would be equally untenable if ARPA's argument could somehow be construed as urging only that subsection (F)'s mailing provision be implicitly incorporated into section 34-223(A). That subsection of the mechanic's lien law states that service of any notice required under that section "is complete at the time of the deposit of notice in the mail."[110] This provision, known as the "mailbox rule," has been determined not to apply to section 34-223(A). In *Maricopa Turf*, the court examined whether the mailbox rule contained in section 33-992.01(F)6 could be read into section 34–223(A).[111] After noting that the LMA only "incorporates the form of notice set out in the" lien statute, the court

---

[104] *See* Weitekamp v. Fireman's Fund Ins. Co., 147 Ariz. 274, 275, 709 P.2d 908, 909 (Ct. App. 1985) (when interpreting statutes, no part of statute may be "rendered void, superfluous, contradictory or insignificant").

[105] A.R.S. § 33-992.01(G).

[106] A.R.S. § 34-223(A).

[107] A.R.S. § 33-998(A).

[108] A.R.S. § 34-223(B).

[109] A.R.S. § 33-993(A); *see also* A.R.S. § 33-981(D) ("A person required to give preliminary twenty day notice pursuant to § 33-992.01 is entitled to enforce the lien rights . . . only if he has given such notice and has made proof of service pursuant to § 33-992.02."); Allstate Util. Constr., LLC v. Towne Bank of Ariz., 228 Ariz. 145, ¶ 13, 263 P.3d 694, 696-97 (Ct. App. 2011).

[110] A.R.S. § 33-992.01(F).

[111] 173 Ariz. at 362-63, 842 P.2d at 1375-76.

concluded the legislature had "excluded those provisions not mentioned" by section 34-223(A), including section 33-992.01(F)'s mailing requirements.[112]

In doing so, the court pointed out that the "timely filing of a written claim with the contractor before the expiration of ninety days is a condition precedent to recovery under a Little Miller Act bond."[113] To incorporate the mailbox rule into the LMA would effectively alter the stringent time requirements within which a claimant must file its notices.[114] Although, as Cemex had pointed out, this analysis was discussed in dicta, the court nonetheless found this logic persuasive. To incorporate subsection (F) into section 34-223(A) would effectively allow both 20- and 90-day notices to be mailed on the day the LMA requires the notices to be received, in violation of both the express terms of the LMA and its stated policy to protect contractors from late-filed claims.[115]

For these reasons, ARPA's argument had to fail. The court could not expand the language of the LMA so drastically as to incorporate all provisions of the mechanic's lien law without producing contradictory and confusing results. And the court could not, absent express statutory language, selectively choose which provisions may have been implicitly incorporated into section 34-223(A)'s language. The court therefore concluded that section 34-223(A) of the LMA did not incorporate the mailing provision found in section 33-992.01(F).

## [c] Section 34-223(A)'s Mailing Requirements

The court indicated it must next resolve how the notices required by section 34-223(A) are to be mailed. To determine whether the last sentence of section 34-223(A) applies to both the 20- and 90-day notices, the court looked first to the statute's language.[116] Unless a word was otherwise defined, the court indicated it would construe statutory language pursuant to its ordinary and common meaning.[117] In doing so, the court sought to avoid "impossible or absurd consequences."[118] If the statute's language did not disclose the legislative intent,

---

[112] 173 Ariz. at 362, 842 P.2d at 1375.

[113] 173 Ariz. at 363, 842 P.2d at 1376, citing *Coast to Coast Mfg.*, 145 Ariz. at 113, 700 P.2d at 500; Greaig v. Park W. Constr. Co., 130 Ariz. 576, 579, 637 P.2d 1079, 1082 (Ct. App. 1981); *see also W. Asbestos*, 121 Ariz. at 390, 590 P.2d at 929.

[114] *Maricopa Turf*, 173 Ariz. at 362-63, 842 P.2d at 1375-76.

[115] *See* United States *ex rel.* Blue Circle W., Inc. v. Tucson Mech. Contracting Inc., 921 F.2d 911, 914 (9th Cir. 1990); *Coast to Coast Mfg.*, 145 Ariz. at 113, 700 P.2d at 500.

[116] *See* Citadel Care Ctr. v. Ariz. Dep't of Revenue, 200 Ariz. 286, ¶ 11, 25 P.3d 1158, 1161 (Ct. App. 2001).

[117] *See* Citadel Care Ctr. v. Ariz. Dep't of Revenue, 200 Ariz. 286, ¶ 11, 25 P.3d 1158, 1161 (Ct. App. 2001); A.R.S. § 1-213; *accord* Beatie v. Beatie, 235 Ariz. 427, ¶ 19, 333 P.3d 754, 758 (Ct. App. 2014).

[118] *Boynton*, 205 Ariz. 45, 49 n.2, 66 P.3d at 92 n.2.

"the Court scrutinized the statute as a whole and give it a fair and sensible meaning."[119]

The language of the statute contradicted Cemex's argument. First, the meaning of the word "such" encompasses a plural construction. "Such" is defined as "[o]f this or that kind," or "[t]hat or those; having just been mentioned."[120] This indicates that the term "such notice" is applicable to both the 20- and 90-day notices. Because the rest of the sentence is written in the singular, the term "such notice" likewise is applicable to each individual notice sent by an LMA claimant.

Second, even if the last sentence of section 34-223(A) was written solely in the singular form, it would not compel Cemex's proposed interpretation that it applies only to the 90-day notices. It is an established rule of statutory construction that "[w]ords in the singular number include the plural, and words in the plural number include the singular,"[121] "unless the legislature expresses 'manifest intent' to the contrary,"[122] The legislature did not indicate a "manifest intent" that the last sentence of section 34-223(A) apply only to the 90-day notices; rather, as the sentence is the only provision in the LMA that addresses notice mailing requirements, the court concluded that the legislature intended it to apply to both the 20-and 90-day notices.[123] Had the legislature intended this sentence to apply to only the 90-day notice, the court presumed it would have said so.[124]

Moreover, the court's "scrutin[y of] the statute as a whole [to] give it a fair and sensible meaning" compels the same conclusion.[125] Applying the last sentence to only the 90-day notice would, as Cemex has pointed out, result in a gap in the statute, depriving a claimant of guidance regarding how to mail a 20-day notice. This is an absurd result, which the court indicated it would neither presume nor give effect.[126] The more logical construction is to conclude that the legislature intended the last sentence to apply to both the 20- and 90-day notices, requiring that each be sent by registered or certified mail.

---

[119] *Citadel Care Ctr.*, 200 Ariz. 286, ¶ 11, 25 P.3d at 1161.

[120] Black's Law Dictionary 1661 (10th ed. 2014).

[121] A.R.S. § 1-214(B).

[122] N. Valley Emergency Specialists, L.L.C. v. Santana, 208 Ariz. 301, ¶ 18, 93 P.3d 501, 505 (2004), quoting Homebuilders Ass'n of Cent. Ariz. v. City of Scottsdale, 186 Ariz. 642, 649, 925 P.2d 1359, 1366 (Ct. App. 1996).

[123] *See Homebuilders Ass'n of Cent. Ariz.*, 186 Ariz. at 649, 925 P.2d at 1366 (the court presumed legislature "meant what it said" when it enacted rules of statutory construction and was aware of those rules when enacting statutes).

[124] *See, e.g.*, 1992 Ariz. Sess. Laws, ch. 353, § 2 (amending A.R.S. § 33-992.02 to replace the term "[s]uch affidavit" with the term "[t]he affidavit" when referring to one specific form).

[125] *See Citadel Care Ctr.*, 200 Ariz. 286, ¶ 11, 25 P.3d at 1161.

[126] *See* State v. Medrano–Barraza, 190 Ariz. 472, 474, 949 P.2d 561, 563 (Ct. App. 1997) ("The Court presumed the framers of the statute did not intend an absurd result and the Court's construction must avoid such a consequence."); Ariz. Health Care Cost Containment Sys. v. Bentley, 187 Ariz. 229, 233, 928 P.2d 653, 657 (Ct. App. 1996) (courts must give statutes sensible constructions and avoid absurd results).

Cemex and ARPA have pointed out that "requir[ing] certified or registered mail for twenty day notices would increase the cost of construction for both public and private jobs with no real benefit" and will "deprive contractors of payment who relied upon first class mail pursuant to industry understanding." ARPA maintains that the "industry has relied upon first class mail in conjunction with sending all preliminary twenty day notices for more than thirty years, since 1984, [and] the Court's ruling could undermine all of the notices that have been sent in reliance upon this industry practice that are currently pending." It further urges that reading the LMA to require the 20-day notices to be sent via registered or certified mail would "increase the costs of construction for both public and private jobs with no real benefit" and "makes [no] legislative sense."

The court acknowledged that this opinion may have a negative impact on an apparently longstanding industry practice. But "it is well-settled that 'the Court indicated it could not legislate,'" and that "'[o]ur province is to construe the law as written.'"[127] Although the legislature could have taken the approach urged by Cemex and ARPA, specifying first class mail as a method of delivering LMA notices, it did not.[128] If the legislature so intends, it can amend the statute accordingly.[129]

### [d]  Actual Notice

Arizona and federal courts have, to an extent, mitigated the stringency of the notice requirements by determining that the requirements are satisfied when the contractor receives actual notice of a materialman's claim. In *Western Asbestos*,[130] the Arizona Supreme Court addressed whether section 34-223(A)'s notice requirements were satisfied when a materialman sent a letter to the general contractor via a method other than the required registered or certified mail. In holding that the materialman's deviation in the method of mailing was not fatal to its claim, the court quoted with approval the United States Supreme Court's rationale in *Fleisher Engineering & Construction Co. v. United States*,[131] that the purpose of the statutory registered mail provision was to assure receipt of the notice, not to make the described method mandatory so as to deny right of suit when the required written notice within the specified time had actually been given and received. In the face of such receipt, the reason for a particular mode of service

---

[127] *Westburne Supply*, 170 Ariz. at 601, 826 P.2d at 1227, quoting Reichenberger v. Salt River Project, 61 Ariz. 465, 471, 150 P.2d 758, 760 (1944) (alteration in *Westburne*).

[128] *See Westburne Supply*, 170 Ariz. at 601, 826 P.2d at 1227, quoting Reichenberger v. Salt River Project, 61 Ariz. 465, 471, 150 P.2d 758, 760 (1944) (alteration in *Westburne*).

[129] *See* Galloway v. Vanderpool, 205 Ariz. 252, ¶ 17, 69 P.3d 23, 27 (2003) ("[I]f the court interprets the statute other than as the legislature intended, the legislature retains the power to correct us.").

[130] Western Asbestos Co. v. TGK Constr. Co., 121 Ariz. 388, 390, 590 P.2d 927, 929 (1979).

[131] 311 U.S. 15, 19, 61 S. Ct. 81, 85 L. Ed. 12 (1940).

fails. It is not reasonable to suppose that Congress intended to insist upon an idle form. Rather, the Court thought that Congress intended to provide a method, which would afford sufficient proof of service when receipt of the required written notice was not shown.[132]

The *Western Asbestos* court concluded that its decision was "supported by the great weight of case law to the effect that this statute is remedial in nature and must be interpreted so as to effectuate its intent to protect those who furnish labor or materials in the construction setting."[133]

Federal cases similarly have deemed the notice requirements satisfied when the contractor received actual notice.[134] Thus, if a notice sent pursuant to the LMA is actually received by a contractor, the fact that it was sent by a method other than registered or certified mail will not preclude a materialman's action on the bond.

### [e]  *Remedy*

In light of this conclusion, the court indicated that its final task was to determine the appropriate remedy in this case. Falcone, urging the "trial court committed reversible error in ruling that Cemex's 20–day notices were valid," asked the court to enter "summary judgment against Cemex as a matter of law." It claimed the record contained a declaration from Falcone's owner stating Falcone did not receive the notices and, consequently, there was no genuine issue of fact regarding actual notice that would preclude entry of summary judgment. Cemex contended that "the appropriate remedy is a remand for trial on the factual issue of actual receipt of the preliminary twenty-day notices."

Summary judgment is appropriate only if "there is no genuine dispute as to any material fact and the moving party is entitled to judgment as a matter of law."[135] On appeal, "the Court determined de novo whether any genuine issues of material fact exist and whether the trial court properly applied the law."[136]

---

[132] 121 Ariz. at 390, 590 P.2d at 929.

[133] 121 Ariz. at 391, 590 P.2d at 930; *see also* Norman S. Wright & Co. v. Slaysman, 124 Ariz. 321, 324, 604 P.2d 252, 254 (1979); *Maricopa Turf*, 173 Ariz. at 362, 842 P.2d at 1375; *Greaig*, 130 Ariz. at 578-79, 637 P.2d at 1081-82.

[134] *See* United States ex rel. Moody v. Am. Ins. Co., 835 F.2d 745, 747-48 (10th Cir. 1987) (noting most circuit courts found notice not sent by prescribed means sufficient when contractor had actual notice of claim against him); *see also* United States ex rel. Water Works Supply Corp. v. George Hyman Constr. Co., 131 F.3d 28, 32 (1st Cir. 1997); United States ex rel. Hillsdale Rock Co. v. Cortelyou & Cole, Inc., 581 F.2d 239, 243 (9th Cir. 1978).

[135] Ariz. R. Civ. P. 56(a).

[136] Best Choice Fund, LLC v. Low & Childers, P.C., 228 Ariz. 502, ¶ 10, 269 P.3d 678, 682 (Ct. App. 2011); *see also* Ray Scottsdale Lumber Co. v. First Fed. Sav. & Loan Ass'n of Phoenix, 3 Ariz.App. 366, 368, 414 P.2d 754, 756 (1966) (appellate court examines record to determine existence of dispute of material fact).

The court's review of the record revealed a genuine dispute of material fact. In its motion for summary judgment, Falcone asserted that it had not received any of Cemex's 20-day notices. It supported this contention with a declaration prepared by Falcone's owner, Gaetano "Tom" Falcone, who stated without further explanation that Falcone did not receive any of the notices Cemex had mailed. Cemex replied that it had sent four 20-day notices to Falcone on four separate occasions, each with an affidavit of service and certificate of mailing. It supported this contention with a declaration from the person who had mailed the notices, as well as copies of the certificates of mailing, which had been stamped, dated, and initialed by a postal employee. Falcone did not dispute that the notices were mailed.

At the hearing on the summary judgment motions, Cemex stated that it had no evidence Falcone had received the notice aside from "pro[of] that the notice went into the mail." It argued, however, that it would be unlikely for a general contractor "on the job" to be completely unaware of the source of its materials for that project. The court responded that it did not "have facts as to this" and that it was "not going to make any rulings based on" the factual issue of actual notice. The court then concluded that the 20-day notices did not need to be mailed via registered or certified mail and that Cemex's affidavits and notices were "sufficient to meet the purposes of the statute."

In so ruling, the trial court purposefully did not make findings as to whether Falcone actually had received Cemex's 20-day notices. Although Falcone urged that Mr. Falcone's declaration conclusively resolved this issue, the court disagreed. His declaration was an insufficient basis upon which a court could make a determination, as a motion for summary judgment could not be granted or denied when supported solely by a self-serving and conclusory affidavit.[137]

Mr. Falcone's declaration stated that "Falcone has never received any communication" from Cemex and "[a]t no time did Falcone receive a Preliminary Twenty–Day Notice" from Cemex. But it provided no evidence that Mr. Falcone was the person designated to receive such notices or specify any steps Falcone took to verify it had not, in fact, received them; nor did it suggest any possible reason—such as an incorrect address or missing postage—that might explain why each of four separate notices might not have reached Falcone. Mr. Falcone's declaration did not conclusively demonstrate that Falcone did not receive the notices, nor establish the absence of a genuine issue of material fact. Accordingly, the court vacated the judgment and remanded the case to the trial court for a new trial.

---

[137] *See* Florez v. Sargeant, 185 Ariz. 521, 526-27, 917 P.2d 250, 255-56 (1996) (self-serving affidavits or affidavits setting forth ultimate facts or legal conclusions lack "relevant foundation" and "can neither support nor defeat a motion for summary judgment").

### [f]  Attorney Fees

Cemex had requested its reasonable attorney fees pursuant to the terms of the bond, which provided that "[t]he prevailing party or any party which recovers judgment on this bond shall be entitled to such reasonable attorney's fees as may be fixed by the court or a judge thereof." Because neither party had prevailed on appeal, the court made no award at that time. If Cemex ultimately is the prevailing party, the trial court may consider an award to Cemex for attorney fees incurred during this appeal.[138]

### [3]  Conclusion

For the foregoing reasons, the court vacated the judgment and remanded for a new trial.

## § 12.04  CALIFORNIA CASES

### [A]  Delay Claims—*Eichleay* Method Approved by California Appellate Court (Sixth District)

In *JMR Construction Corp. v. Environmental Assessment & Remediation Management, Inc.,*[139] a dispute arose from a public works project involving the construction of a dental clinic at the Presidio of Monterey (the "Project"). The owner, the United States Army Corps of Engineers (the "Corps"), retained JMR Construction Corp. ("JMR") as general contractor for the Project. JMR, in turn, entered into various subcontracts, including separate electrical and plumbing subcontracts, with Environmental Assessment and Remediation Management, Inc. (EAR). SureTec Insurance Company ("SureTec") issued separate bonds guaranteeing EAR's performance under the two subcontracts.

While the Project was ongoing, JMR (1) communicated with EAR about alleged delays, deficient and late submittals, and improper plumbing work, and (2) retained certain funds otherwise due to EAR under the subcontracts. After the Project was completed, JMR filed suit against EAR and SureTec (collectively, defendants) for breach of contract and for foreclosure of the performance bonds. JMR alleged it was damaged as a result of EAR's failure to perform under the two subcontracts. EAR filed a cross-complaint for recovery of retention funds withheld under the subcontracts.

---

[138] *See* Tierra Ranchos Homeowners Ass'n v. Kitchukov, 216 Ariz. 195,. ¶ 37, 165 P.3d 173, 182 (Ct. App. 2007) (deferring party's request for attorney fees on appeal "to the trial court's discretion pending resolution of the matter on the merits").

[139] No. H039055 (Cal. Ct. App. Dec 30, 2015).

After a court trial, JMR was awarded the net amount of $315,631, which included an offset for the retention funds JMR withheld under the subcontracts. In post-trial proceedings, the court issued an order determining JMR was entitled to recover attorney fees in an amount to be determined for its successful defense of the cross-complaint. The court also awarded JMR $90,644.07 in expert witness fees pursuant to Code of Civil Procedure § 998 by concluding that JMR's total monetary recovery ($315,631 plus an undetermined amount of attorney fees) had exceeded the $375,000 amount of its pretrial settlement offers. SureTec and EAR filed separate appeals.

EAR made seven arguments on appeal. First, it asserted that there was no substantial evidence to support the trial court's finding that it was liable to JMR for delays on the Project. Second, it argued that the court erred by using the *Eichleay* method of calculating extended home office overhead damages. Third, it asserted that the court erred by utilizing the modified total cost method of calculating disruption and delay damages. Fourth, it argued that the court, in its statement of decision, failed to address essential matters of fact and law. Fifth, it contended that the court erred in determining JMR was entitled to attorney fees in defending the cross-complaint. Sixth, it asserted that JMR was not entitled to recover its expert witness fees pursuant to section 998. And seventh, it contended that the court erred by denying its motion for new trial.

SureTec contended that JMR could not prevail against SureTec because JMR failed to declare EAR in default under the subcontracts, and JMR failed to notify SureTec of any such default. It also contended that the order finding JMR entitled to attorney fees on EAR's cross-complaint was improper as to SureTec. Further, it contested the award to JMR of expert witness fees under section 998. And it argued that SureTec's liability must be limited to a maximum of $471,881, the ceiling of its liability under the performance bond on the plumbing subcontract.

In the published portion of this opinion, the court concluded that the court did not err in its utilization of the *Eichleay* method to calculate extended home office overhead damages and in its use of the modified total cost method of calculating JMR's disruption and delay damages. The court also held that the court did not err in finding SureTec liable under the performance bonds, concluding that formal notice of EAR's default was not a condition precedent to JMR's recovery under the bonds. In the unpublished portion of this opinion, the court concluded that: (1) there was substantial evidence supporting the court's finding that EAR was liable to JMR for Project delays; (2) the court's statement of decision was not defective; (3) defendants' challenges to the interim, non-final, post-judgment order determining that JMR was entitled to recover attorney fees in defending the cross-complaint are not cognizable at this time; (4) defendants' challenges to the award of JMR's expert witness fees under section 998 are meritorious; (5) EAR's claim that the court abused its discretion in denying EAR's motion for new trial had no merit; and (6) SureTec's request for an order that its maximum liability is $471,881 was not cognizable because it was a request for an advisory opinion.

Accordingly, the court affirmed the judgment, reversed the order awarding expert witness fees, and remanded the case for further post-judgment proceedings consistent with this opinion.

### [1] Procedural Background

On April 29, 2010, JMR filed its complaint against EAR and SureTec. JMR alleged four causes of action: (1) breach of the plumbing subcontract; (2) enforcement and foreclosure on the performance bond for the plumbing subcontract; (3) breach of the electrical subcontract; and (4) enforcement and foreclosure on the performance bond for the electrical subcontract. The first and third causes of action were alleged against EAR, while the second and fourth causes of action were alleged against SureTec. JMR alleged that EAR's failure or refusal to perform its work under the two subcontracts in accordance with the Project's schedule "caused project delay, acceleration, and related damages to JMR." The alleged damages included "offset of JMR claims against the Owner, increased cost of JMR on-site performance costs and other loss of cost recovery and overhead on the Project." In each of the four causes of action, JMR claimed its damages were in an amount "not less than $200,000.00."

EAR filed a cross-complaint against JMR alleging breach of contract and common counts. It alleged in separate causes of action that JMR had breached the electrical subcontract and plumbing subcontract, and that as a result of these breaches, EAR had been damaged in an amount in excess of $108,913.31.

A five-day court trial took place in January 2012. After the parties submitted post-trial briefs in lieu of final argument, the court issued a ruling on April 30, 2012, finding in favor of JMR in the total amount of $379,318, which amount included a deduction of $121,893 that had been previously withheld from EAR under the subcontracts. The court further ordered that EAR take nothing on its cross-complaint.

Pursuant to the court's request, JMR submitted a proposed statement of decision in which it withdrew one of its claims and adjusted the amount of another claim, resulting in revised damages award of $315,631. The damages were derived by (1) adding five damage figures in amounts of $29,249 (air compressor), $132,168 (field overhead for delay), $15,440 (field overhead for Project closeout), $14,244 (markup for field overhead), $60,693 (*Eichleay* home office overhead), and $185,730 (damages during framing and drywall phase); and (2) subtracting from this amount $121,893 previously withheld under the subcontracts. On July 19, 2012, the court signed the statement of decision. On August 14, 2012, the court entered judgment in favor of JMR and against defendants in the amount of $315,631. The court also ordered that EAR and SureTec take nothing on the cross-complaint and that defendants were liable for JMR's costs, including attorney fees in defending the cross-complaint, in an amount to be determined after appropriate filings by JMR.

In post-judgment proceedings (discussed in greater detail, *post*), the court issued an order on November 13, 2012, granting JMR's request for recovery of expert fees of $90,644.07. In the same order, the court reaffirmed a prior tentative ruling that it would award attorney fees to JMR for its successful defense of EAR's cross-complaint in an amount to be determined at a later time.

## [2]  Discussion

### [a]  *EAR's Appeal of the Judgment*

EAR asserts four challenges to the court's judgment. First, it contends that there is no substantial evidence to support the court's finding that EAR breached its subcontracts with JMR. Second, it argues that the court erred in using the *Eichleay* formula of calculating home office overhead damages. Third, it claims that the court erred in applying the modified total cost method of damages in connection with alleged delay damages associated with the interior installation of metal studs and drywall (hereafter, the "framing and drywall phase"). And fourth, it argues that the court's statement of decision was defective in that it failed to take into consideration essential matters of fact and law. The court addresses each of these contentions below.

**[i]  Challenges to the Calculation of Contract Damages.**  In the alternative to its sufficiency-of-the evidence challenge, EAR contests the court's acceptance of the *Eichleay* formula of recovering home office overhead damages. EAR also contends that the court erred in applying the modified total cost method of calculating the cost associated with delays in the framing and drywall phase of the Project. The court will address these two challenges after first identifying the appropriate standards of review. At the outset, however, the court will present a summary of the evidence concerning JMR's claims of damages.

**[ii]  Evidence Concerning Damages.**  JMR presented evidence of damages that involved four categories: (1) field overhead delay damages; (2) home office overhead (*Eichleay* delay damages); (3) delay damages associated with the framing and drywall phase of the Project, utilizing the modified total cost method; and (4) costs associated with EAR's failure to supply an approved air compressor. The court will not summarize the air compressor damages, since they are not at issue in this appeal. But given their interrelationship with the *Eichleay* delay damages, the court will review the evidence of field overhead damages even though those damages are not directly challenged by EAR.

**[iii]  Field Overhead Damages.**  Daniel Spade, JMR's project manager, testified that the Corps had rejected JMR's recovery of any extended overhead damages resulting from delays in the Project's completion. The Corps rejected these damages because there were concurrent delays caused by parties other than the Corps. At trial, JMR's construction management expert, John Elmer, explained that when the owner of a public works project causes delay, and a subcontractor or subcontractors concurrently cause delay, the owner may grant the general contractor an extension of time to complete the project, but it will not grant the general contractor compensable time (i.e., delay damages payable by the owner). Elmer testified that under such circumstances, the general contractor will typically seek delay damages from the subcontractor, under the theory that the general contractor "should have recovered compensable time, but . . . was precluded from [doing so] because of [the subcontractor's] delay."

Juan Perez, a construction expert retained by JMR, provided extensive testimony regarding JMR's delay damages attributable to EAR. Defendants did not challenge Perez's qualifications as an expert. Perez testified that he has had experience in presenting disruption claims on behalf of contractors. A disruption claim is based upon a contractor's intended performance or method of performance being impacted by another contractor or by an event, resulting in the contractor's performance being more costly because it is either done out of sequence or for an extended duration.

Perez calculated JMR's damages based upon (1) his review of the project documents and (2) his reliance upon the opinions of John Elmer, JMR's construction management expert. Specifically, Perez relied upon Elmer's opinions that: (1) there was a critical path delay that extended the Project's completion by 180 days; (2) 180 days is reflected in change orders issued by the Corps extending the Project's completion date; (3) the parties responsible for the delays were the Corps and three subcontractors (EAR, Countywide Mechanical, and Del Monte Glass); (4) EAR and Countywide were each concurrently responsible for 142 days of the 180 days of delay; (5) within the 142-day period, Del Monte Glass was concurrently responsible for 28 days of delay.

Perez opined that, under the two subcontracts combined, EAR was responsible for at least 75 percent of the delay damages sustained by JMR during the 142-day concurrent delay period identified by Elmer. Perez arrived at this percentage allocation after considering (a) Elmer's allocation of EAR's responsibility for concurrent delays (63%); (b) a determination of EAR's percentage of the total contract value of the mechanical, electrical, and plumbing trades (67%); and (c) the percentage of punch list items for the 142-day concurrent delay period (83%).

Perez also rendered the opinion that JMR sustained field overhead damages associated with EAR's concurrent delay. Field overhead costs are the costs a contractor incurs in maintaining its field operations, including cost items such as storage trailers, office trailers, and a job superintendent's salary. Perez concluded that JMR's total field overhead damages for which EAR was responsible was $161,851.33.

**[iv]  Home Office Overhead Damages.**  Perez testified that he calculated damages for JMR's home office costs (otherwise known as unabsorbed overhead costs) using the *Eichleay* formula. Perez explained that this formula "is a method of allocating those home office overhead costs to a project that [has] been extended or delayed." According to Perez, the *Eichley* formula is the "exclusive method approved by the Federal Government to arrive at the fair compensation amount for unabsorbed overhead costs." He testified that "[b]ut for the concurrent delays on the project, the *Eichleay* [f]ormula would have been used by both JMR and the Government to arrive at the fair compensation amount for unabsorbed overhead costs that belonged to JMR."

**[v]  Framing and Drywall Phase Damages.**  JMR qualified its vice president, Ron Rivard, as an expert witness in estimating interior framing and drywall work. Rivard had over 30 years' experience as a licensed general contractor, and approximately 35 years as an estimator in which he had estimated at least 300 jobs.

Rivard testified that he prepared the bid for the framing and drywall phase of the project. In doing so, he utilized the plans in an electronic format and used computer software to perform a detailed cost takeoff. The takeoff yielded a bill of materials, and the software automatically assigned a labor factor indicating the number of labor hours associated with the particular area of work. The labor factor was based upon historical data, i.e., JMR's experience in constructing buildings similar to the building in the project. The total bid for the framing and drywall phase was $220,000, an amount JMR assumed would be sufficient to perform the work in an orderly fashion and with a reasonable crew size. Rivard testified he was unaware of any mistakes in the bid, and opined that $220,000 was a reasonable cost for that phase of the project.

Craig Connerty, a certified public accountant with 27 years of experience, testified as an expert on JMR's behalf. JMR had been a client of Connerty's accounting firm for over 15 years. Connerty reviewed the costs posted in JMR's books allocated to the framing and drywall phase of the Project. He testified that the total cost allocated to this phase was $461,535, and he reviewed the subcategories of those costs. Connerty "did a lot of testing with regard to the accounts for reasonableness" by selecting a number of different invoices for review before arriving at the $461,535 figure. Connerty also noted that this figure should be reduced by approximately $48,200 to account for costs that, based upon his conversation with Rivard, were erroneously posted to the framing and drywall phase.

Perez offered testimony relating to disruption damages for the framing and drywall phase. In forming his opinion, Perez spoke with job superintendent Steven Hupaylo, project manager Daniel Spade, and JMR's vice president Ron Rivard. Perez also reviewed documents identifying the costs of the framing and drywall phase; certified payroll figures indicating the number of workers on the job site during that phase; and other correspondence. Perez relied on Hupaylo's testimony to the effect "that every wall was impacted by EAR's performance, meaning that the impacts and the costs [were] intrinsically intertwined [and it was] difficult if not impractical or impossible to segregate [the] individual impacts." In calculating disruption damages, Perez performed a "modified total cost analysis." He described this approach as follows: "[Y]ou would take a selected portion of the contractor's costs that he incurred and subtract from that the contractor's budget for those items, removing . . . items which were not part of the original budget . . . to ensure you're comparing apples to apples."

Thus, one component of Perez's calculation was the original bid. Perez did an independent analysis of JMR's bid for the framing and drywall phase. He found that Rivard's bid contained the kind of detail indicative of a good estimate, the bid used methods that were "consistent with other contractors," and the bid was "based on historic[al] information[,] which is also important." Perez testified that he "was satisfied" with Rivard's bid and that the numbers within it "appeared reasonable." He noted that in comparing the material costs in the bid with the actual material costs, "the material estimate was almost dead on." He also noted that because labor estimates are based upon the material scheduled, the fact that the actual cost of materials was consistent with the estimate for those materials was "a good indication of a good estimate." He concluded that "if your material estimate is off, your labor estimate would be off. And Mr. Rivard's material estimate was on, was accurate."

Perez also reviewed the "logged" costs that related to the framing and drywall phase of the Project. This amount totaled $461,534. Perez subtracted the costs that had been incorrectly allocated to the framing and drywall phase. These were the same figures identified in the testimony of JMR's accounting expert, Craig Connerty. Perez also subtracted a per diem figure associated with the erroneously posted costs. Perez then calculated the total amount of disruption damages allocable to EAR relating to the framing and drywall phase, which he determined to be $185,729.

### [b]    Standards of Review

An appellant's challenge to damages, depending upon its specific nature, may be subject to a substantial evidence, abuse of discretion, or de novo standard of review. The question of whether a plaintiff was, in fact, damaged by the defendant's breach of contract is reviewed for substantial evidence.[140] The question of whether "a certain measure of damages is permissible given the legal right the defendant has breached, is a matter of law, subject to de novo review.

---

[140] *See* GHK Assoc's v. Mayer Grp., Inc., 224 Cal. App. 3d 856, 873 (1990) (*GHK*).

[Citation.]"[141] But where the measure of damages is legally permissible, a trial court's choice of that measure, among other legally permissible measures of damages, is reviewed for abuse of discretion.[142]

EAR contends that neither the *Eichleay* formula nor the modified total cost method was legally authorized in this case. EAR does not make the further argument that, assuming the legal validity of these damage calculations, the court abused its discretion by selecting them over other legally permissible methods of computing damages. Accordingly, the court reviewed the legal propriety of the court's use of the two damages calculations de novo. In addition, EAR contends that, even assuming the legal validity of the *Eichleay* formula, JMR failed to establish the requisite elements for its application, a question the court reviewed under the substantial evidence standard of review.

### [c]   Challenges to the Eichleay *Formula*

**[i]   The *Eichleay* Formula.**   As explained by JMR's expert, Juan Perez, the *Eichleay* formula "is a method of allocating those home office overhead costs to a project that [have] been extended or delayed." It originated from a case before the Armed Services Board of Contract Appeals[143] and is typically used in federal litigation involving federal public works projects.[144] The Federal Circuit has held that "the *Eichleay* formula is the *only* means for calculating recovery for unabsorbed home office overhead."[145]

As explained by the *Altmayer* court:

> "Home office overhead costs are those that are expended for the benefit of the whole business, which by their nature cannot be attributed or charged to any particular contract. [Citation.] In contracting with the government, a company necessarily includes a portion of home office overhead expenses, which it calculates based on the contract's duration, in its estimate of costs to perform the contract. [Citation.] When the government delays or disrupts contract performance, ultimately requiring that it be extended, the contractor's stream of income from the government for the direct costs it has incurred under the contract is reduced or interrupted. [Citation.] However, home office overhead continues to accrue throughout both the original and extended performance periods, regardless of direct contract activity. [Citations.] This, of course, results in a reduction or interruption of payments for overhead, especially

---

[141] New West Charter Middle Sch. v. Los Angeles Unified Sch. Dist., 187 Cal. App. 4th 831, 843 (2010) (*New West*); *see also* Hurtado v. Superior Ct., 11 Cal. 3d 574, 579 (1974).

[142] *New West*, 187 Cal. App. 4th at 843, citing *GHK*, 224 Cal. App. 3d at 873.

[143] *See* Eichleay Corp., 60-2 BCA (CCH) 2688 (A.S.B.C.A. 1960).

[144] *See, e.g.*, P.J. Dick Inc. v. Principi, 324 F.3d 1364, 1370 (Fed. Cir. 2003); Altmayer v. Johnson, 79 F.3d 1129, 1132-1133 (Fed. Cir. 1996) (*Altmayer*).

[145] E.R. Mitchell Constr. Co. v. Danzig, 175 F.3d 1369, 1372 (Fed. Cir. 1999) (italics original); *see also* Nicon, Inc. v. United States, 331 F.3d 878, 884 (Fed. Cir. 2003).

when, as here, the contractor has prepared a critical path schedule, for any delay along the critical path results in the delay of the overall project."[146]

There are three steps in the calculation of extended overhead using the *Eichleay* formula. They are (1) "to find [the] allocable contract overhead [by] multiply[ing] the total overhead cost incurred during the contract period times the ratio of billings from the delayed contract to total billings of the firm during the contract period; [(2)] to get the daily contract overhead rate, divide allocable contract overhead by days of contract performance; and [(3)] to get the amount recoverable, multiply the daily contract overhead rate times days of government-caused delay. [Citation.]"[147]

**[ii]  Legal Propriety of Using *Eichleay* Formula.**  EAR argues it was improper for the court to accept JMR's proffer of the *Eichleay* formula to establish its unabsorbed overhead damages caused by EAR's concurrent delay. EAR asserts there is no legal precedent for applying the formula because (1) there have been no published California decisions endorsing its use and (2) there is no legal authority authorizing its use in situations, such as here, where the defendant causing the delay was not the government. EAR also urges that Perez, JMR's expert, "admitted application of the *Eichleay* formula is 'debated.' "

Under Civil Code § 3300, a party may recover for a breach of contract a sum that will compensate it "for all the detriment proximately caused thereby, or which, in the ordinary course of things, will be likely to result therefrom." "[I]n the law of contracts the theory is that the party injured by a breach should receive as nearly as possible the equivalent of the benefits of performance. [Citations.] The aim is to put the injured party in as good a position as [it] would have been had performance been rendered as promised. This aim can never be exactly attained yet that is the problem the trial court is required to resolve. [Citation.]"[148] "Where the *fact* of damages is certain . . . the *amount* of damages need not be calculated with absolute certainty. The law requires only that some reasonable basis of computation be used, and the result reached can be a reasonable approximation."[149]

---

[146] *Altmayer*, 79 F.3d at 1132.

[147] Wickham Contracting Co., Inc. v. Fischer, 12 F.3d 1574, 1577, n.3 (Fed. Cir. 1994) (*Wickham Contracting*).

[148] Brandon & Tibbs v. George Kevorkian Accountancy Corp., 226 Cal. App. 3d 442, 454 (1990); *see also* Lewis Jorge Constr. Mgmt., Inc. v. Pomona Unified Sch. Dist., 34 Cal. 4th 960, 967-68 (2004) (*Lewis Jorge*).

[149] Acree v. General Acceptance Corp., 92 Cal. App. 4th 385, 398, (2001) (footnotes omitted, italics in original) (*Acree*); *see also* SCI Cal. Funeral Servs., Inc. v. Five Bridges Found., 203 Cal. App. 4th 549, 570 (2012) (*SCI Cal. Funeral Servs.*).

Delay damages are a common element recoverable by a party aggrieved by the breach of a construction contract.[150] A subcontractor who is responsible for delaying the progress of a construction project may be held liable for delay damages incurred by the general contractor or by another subcontractor.[151] Increased overhead expenses incurred by a general contractor as a result of the subcontractor's breach may be an item of recoverable damages.[152]

As explained in one treatise: "A building contractor whose performance is delayed by the owner may have increased overhead and fixed costs resulting from a delay and may suffer labor and material cost increases or loss of labor productivity due to delays for all of which he or she would be entitled to damages."[153] Extended home office overhead is one type of delay damages for which a contractor may seek recovery.[154]

The court acknowledged that there are no reported California appellate decisions approving the use of the *Eichleay* formula. In the only reported California case addressing the formula, the appellate court did not decide the legal propriety of its use because the municipality against which such damages were sought did not dispute the formula's general applicability to construction delay claims.[155]

The court did not infer from the absence of California authority that the *Eichleay* formula is unavailable as proof of delay damages in this state. As has been observed in one treatise: "The federal government developed the *Eichleay* formula to compute the amount of home office overhead expense for which a government contractor should be reimbursed for a period of delay. Although the formula has not been discussed in a reported California case, it is frequently used at the trial court level and in arbitration proceedings to compute damages."[156]

That the circumstances of this case are different from those in which *Eichleay* damages are typically discussed in reported decisions—i.e., the general contractor seeking delay damages *from a subcontractor*, rather than *from a governmental agency/owner*—does not preclude use of the formula. JMR presented

[150] *See, e.g.*, Coughlin v. Blair, 41 Cal. 2d 587, 603-04 (1953) (plaintiffs entitled to damages for increased building costs and loss of use of property resulting from defendants' delay in performance of contract to pave road and install utilities); State of Cal. ex rel. Dep't of Transp. v. Guy F. Atkinson Co., 187 Cal. App. 3d 25, 32-34 (1986) (*Guy F. Atkinson*) (contractor entitled to disruption and delay damages caused by material changes to contract ordered by state); Bird v. American Sur. Co., 175 Cal. 625, 631 (1917) (delay damages incurred by owner, including rental losses, recoverable).

[151] 10 Miller & Starr, Cal. Real Estate, § 27:39, p. 109 (3d ed. 2001).

[152] *See* Allen v. Gardner, 126 Cal. App. 2d 335, 344 (1954).

[153] Cal. Attorney's Guide to Damages, § 1.49, p. 1-50 (Cont. Ed. Bar 2d ed. 2014).

[154] *See* Cal. Construction Contracts, Defects, and Litigation, §§ 5.107, 6.86, pp. 394, 537 (Cont. Ed. Bar 2013) ; Gibbs & Hunt, Cal. Construction Law,*Construction Claims*, § 6.07[F], p. 441 (17th ed. 2011).

[155] *See* Howard Contracting, Inc. v. G.A. MacDonald Constr. Co., Inc., 71 Cal. App. 4th 38, 53 (1998).

[156] Cal. Constr. Contracts, Defects, and Litig., *supra*, § 5.107, p. 394.

unrebutted testimony from Daniel Spade that because there were concurrent delays, the Corps rejected JMR's effort to recover extended overhead damages from the Corps. And JMR's construction management expert, John Elmer, testified that when the owner of a public works project causes delay, but a subcontractor or subcontractors concurrently cause delay, the owner may grant the general contractor additional time but it will not grant the general contractor compensable time (i.e., delay damages). Elmer testified that under such circumstances, the general contractor will typically seek delay damages from the subcontractor under the theory that the general contractor "should have recovered compensable time, but . . . was precluded from [doing so] because of [the subcontractor's] delay."[157] EAR presented no expert testimony of its own to rebut JMR's expert testimony concerning *Eichleay* damages.

The court concluded the trial court did not err in applying the *Eichleay* formula as a legally permissible method of determining JMR's home office overhead damages. The court based this conclusion upon the expert evidence presented at trial, the general recoverability of extended home office overhead as an element of delay damages, and the federal courts' general acceptance of the *Eichleay* formula. In other words, the calculation of extended home office overhead damages using the *Eichleay* formula was an appropriate method to compensate JMR "for all the detriment proximately caused" by EAR's breach of contract.[158] That recovery facilitates "[t]he goal [of placing] the plaintiff 'in as good a position as he or she would have occupied' if the defendant had not breached the contract. [Citation.]"[159] Indeed, it would be anomalous to allow recovery to JMR for *Eichleay* extended home office overhead damages in a claim against the government-owner—had there been no concurrent delay and where, as here, JMR had established the fact of such damages and causation—while denying such recovery from EAR where EAR was concurrently responsible for the delay.

**[iii]  Proof of Elements of *Eichleay* Formula.**   EAR also challenges the use of the *Eichleay* formula on the basis that JMR did not establish the requisite elements for its application. The federal courts have identified three *Eichleay*

---

[157] *See* William F. Klingensmith, Inc. v. United States, 731 F.2d 805, 809 (Fed. Cir. 1984) (contractor generally denied recovery for government-caused delays where there are concurrent delays and absent "'proof a clear apportionment of the delay and expense attributable to each . . . '"); Gibbs & Hunt, *supra*, Construction Claims, § 6.07[E], p. 440 (where owner causing project delays shows that "simultaneous cause of delay was the contractor's own mismanagement of the project," and delays "contributed to or overlapped the owner caused delays, then they may be considered concurrent and may be treated as noncompensable delays").

[158] Cal. Civ. Code § 3300.

[159] *Lewis Jorge*, 34 Cal. 4th at 967, quoting 24 WILLISTON ON CONTRACTS § 64:1, p. 7 (4th ed. 2002).

requirements. "[T]he contractor [must] establish: (1) a government-caused delay; (2) that [the contractor] was on 'standby'; and (3) that [the contractor] was unable to take on other work. [Citation.]"[160] EAR asserts there was no evidence JMR was unable to take on other work.

JMR presented evidence, through Perez, concerning JMR's inability to obtain other work. Perez's expert testimony was based in large part upon his conversations with Rivard and JMR's bonding agent, Sharon Rusconi. Perez testified that JMR was a woman-owned business that received work on Small Business Administration Section 8A projects. Such projects are not strictly bid competitively; contract awards are largely dependent on the contractor's ratings. Perez testified that as a result of Project delays during the 142-day concurrent delay period, JMR's rating was downgraded to marginal. This rating downgrade negatively impacted JMR's ability to obtain new work. Rivard informed Perez that during the period of November 2007 through sometime in 2008, JMR could not obtain a bid bond. JMR was thus precluded from bidding on public projects and could not get other work.

This evidence constituted substantial evidence of the third *Eichleay* prerequisite, i.e., "that [JMR] was unable to take on other work. [Citation.]"[161] Accordingly, EAR's claim that there was insufficient evidence supporting application of the *Eichleay* formula fails.

### [d]   Challenges to Modified Total Cost Method

EAR contends the court erred in several respects in using the modified total cost method in its award of delay damages relating to the framing and drywall phase. "The total cost method derives damages as the difference between a contractor's actual costs and its original bid."[162] In the event some of the costs of the contractor are deemed unreasonable or were the result of "its own errors or omissions, then those costs are subtracted from the damages to arrive at a modified total cost. [Citation.]"[163] As explained by the California Supreme Court, to invoke the total cost method for recovering damages, a contractor must establish: "(1) the impracticality of proving actual losses directly; (2) [its] bid was reasonable;

---

[160] *Altmayer*, 79 F.3d at 1133.

[161] *Altmayer*, 79 F.3d at 1133.

[162] Servidone Constr. Corp. v. United States, 931 F.2d 860, 861(Fed. Cir. 1991).

[163] Dillingham-Ray Wilson v. City of Los Angeles, 182 Cal. App. 4th 1396, 1408 (2010) (*Dillingham-Ray Wilson*); *see* Annot., "Total Cost Method (or Approach)" and "Modified Total Cost Method (or Approach)" to *Proving Damages in State Contract Cases*, 124 A.L.R. 5th 375, 389 (2004) (modified total cost approach may be utilized where most damages are attributable to defendant and "contractor can isolate and quantify those damages that arose due to causes for which the contractor is responsible").

(3) its actual costs were reasonable; and (4) it was not responsible for the added costs. [Citation.]"[164]

EAR, citing *Amelco*,[165] contends the total cost method of computing damages "is generally disfavored" under the law. Although not favored, the total cost method—along with its subcategory, the modified total cost method—has been recognized in California as an appropriate way of computing damages.[166] Further, although the court's high court in *Amelco*—because the municipality did not contest the issue—declined to decide whether the total cost formula was an appropriate method of calculating damages in a breach of a public contract case,[167] the Second District Court of Appeal, Division Two, concluded that the *Amelco* court in fact upheld common law principles "permit[ting] a public contractor to pursue either a total cost theory or a modified total cost theory."[168] The court reached this conclusion because *Amelco* cited *Guy F. Atkinson*,[169] and did not disapprove of the result in that case.[170]

The California Supreme Court has emphasized that one of the major concerns in the use of the total cost method is that it not be used as "'a substitute for proof of causation.' [Citation.]"[171] Here, there was substantial evidence of a causal connection between the extra cost JMR incurred in the Project's framing and drywall phase and EAR's breach of contract. Moreover, the cautionary statement in *Amelco* that the total cost method "'should be applied only to the smallest affected portion of the contractual relationship that can be clearly identified' [citation]" was heeded: JMR used the modified total cost method to calculate damages related only to the framing and drywall phase of the Project, not to damages related to the entire Project.

EAR also contends there was a lack of evidence to support a finding of the four prerequisites recited in *Amelco* (hereinafter the "*Amelco* elements") for use of the modified total cost method. As the court discussed below, the trial court specifically addressed each of the *Amelco* elements in its statement of decision, and substantial evidence supported the court's conclusions that JMR established each element.

---

[164] Amelco Elec. v. City of Thousand Oaks, 27 Cal. 4th 228, 243 (2002) (*Amelco*); *see also* *Amelco* 27 Cal. 4th at 243-44 ("trial court bears the initial responsibility of determining that each element of the four-part test" is satisfied).

[165] 27 Cal. 4th at 243, *supra.*

[166] *See, e.g., Guy F. Atkinson Co.*, 187 Cal. App. 3d at 32; C. Norman Peterson C. v. Container Corp. of Am., 172 Cal. App. 3d 628, 646-47 (1985); *see also* California Civil Jury Instruction (CACI) No. 4541.

[167] *Amelco*, 27 Cal 4th at 242.

[168] *Dillingham-Ray Wilson*, 182 Cal. App. 4th at 1408.

[169] 172 Cal. App. 3d 25, *supra.*

[170] *Dillingham-Ray Wilson*, 182 Cal. App. 4th at 1408.

[171] *Amelco*, 27 Cal. 4th at 244.

The trial court specifically found JMR had established the first *Amelco* element—"the impracticality of proving actual losses directly."[172] In so concluding, the court cited the testimony of JMR's job superintendent, Steven Hupaylo, which it found credible. As the court stated, Hupaylo had testified that JMR had a good design for performing the framing and drywall work, but he (Hupaylo) "had to wait for EAR to complete its rough-in work before he could complete the walls, and, because of EAR's delays, he never had all four walls and a ceiling in any room to work with." The trial court concluded: "Consequently, the disruption occurred throughout the entire period of that work, was not confined to one particular section or time, so [it] could not be tracked specifically as the disruption occurred." Furthermore, Perez testified, based upon Hupaylo's testimony, that because "every wall was impacted by EAR's performance, [this] mean[t] that the impacts and the costs are intrinsically intertwined [and it is] difficult if not impractical or impossible to segregate [the] individual impacts."

The trial court also found JMR had established the second *Amelco* element, i.e., the reasonableness of its bid.[173] The court noted that: (1) Rivard, as an expert experienced in estimating, testified concerning his methodology for preparing his bid, and opined that the bid for the framing and drywall phase was reasonable; (2) Perez reviewed the bid, noted that Rivard's methodology was consistent with other contractors and was based upon historical information, and was satisfied it was accurate; (3) Perez opined the $220,000 stated in the bid was a reasonable cost for the framing and drywall phase; and (4) EAR offered no expert testimony to rebut or contradict the reasonableness of the framing and drywall bid.

Likewise, the court concluded JMR's actual costs for the framing and drywall phase were reasonable—the third *Amelco* element.[174] In concluding that "the actual costs were reasonable and accurately recorded," the trial court cited to the testimony of JMR's experts, Connerty and Perez. It noted that Connerty reviewed JMR's costs associated with the framing and drywall phase, and that Connerty's work was "substantial." The trial court indicated that Connerty "did not just accept JMR's numbers; he [']did a lot of testing['] of the accounts for reasonableness by actually reviewing a number of invoices, and conducted an independent analysis."

Finally, the trial court found JMR was not responsible for the added costs— the fourth *Amelco* element.[175] It concluded EAR was solely at fault for the disruption in the completion of the framing and drywall phase. The court cited the testimony of Hupaylo that because of EAR's delays in "not having materials, not having skilled people, and sometimes not having any people working at all, JMR's crews had to work piecemeal" and in an inefficient manner to complete

---

[172] *Amelco*, 27 Cal. 4th at 243.
[173] *Amelco*, 27 Cal. 4th at 243; *see* Gibbs & Hunt, *Construction Claims*, § 6.14[A], p. 471 (stressing the importance of accuracy of bid estimate to contractor's claim under total cost method).
[174] *Amelco*, 27 Cal. 4th at 243.
[175] *Amelco*, 27 Cal. 4th at 243.

the work. The court "accept[ed] the testimony of Steve Hupaylo as accurate." It also relied on Perez's testimony that, based upon his review of certified payroll records, "the number of [EAR] workers reported on the certified payroll corresponded with the low percentage of completion." Perez also testified that EAR's rough-in work took four months to complete, notwithstanding that EAR had scheduled 34 days for the work. The trial court agreed with Perez's "conclusion that . . . JMR was confronted with the incomplete work and stacking of trades, which disrupted its efficiency."

EAR points to testimony it presented to suggest that JMR's cost overruns were due to its hiring of expensive out-of-town labor and the high level of quality required for the drywall finish. But the trial court rejected these arguments. The court indicated in its statement of decision that "Pendurthi's contrary conclusory explanations [regarding the framing and drywall disruption we]re not credible," and the court found Pendurthi's "testimony weak and unreliable." Moreover—as was the case with JMR's presentation of *Eichleay* damages—EAR offered no expert testimony to contradict JMR's showing that the modified total cost method was appropriate for calculating its damages associated with the framing and drywall phase.

As a variant of its contention that the court erred in concluding JMR was not responsible for the added cost, EAR argues, quoting from *Amelco*[176] that damages were not recoverable under this method because JMR did not " 'distinguish between those inefficiencies that were [JMR's] and those believed to be the responsibility of the [Army] (and presumably other prime contractors and subcontractors).' " But the court rejected EAR's contention that JMR was responsible for inefficiencies in the framing and drywall phase, and there was substantial evidence to support the court's conclusion.

Lastly, EAR contends that the disruption damages awarded by the court were "admittedly inaccurately calculated" because they failed to account for a $90,000 miscoding error about which Rivard testified. This argument relates to cross-examination in which defendants' counsel asked if Rivard had given prior deposition testimony to the effect that there was an approximate $90,000 miscoding of costs that were not related to the framing and drywall phase of the Project. Defendants raised this issue twice in their post-trial briefing. The trial court addressed this contention in its statement of decision. The court concluded that Rivard's deposition testimony concerning the "$90,000 coding overcharge" was essentially superseded by testimony from Perez and Connerty that, shortly before trial, Rivard advised them that the adjustment for miscoded items was approximately $48,200. The trial court thus characterized the $90,000 coding error as a "relatively unfocused pre-trial examination estimate" that did not warrant further consideration in its award of damages. Giving deference to the court's role as trier

---

[176] 27 Cal. 4th at 246.

of fact, the court concluded there was no error in disregarding the purported $90,000 coding error in determining JMR's disruption damages.

The court thus concluded there was no legal impediment to JMR's use of the modified total cost method of calculating its damages associated with the framing and drywall phase of the project. The trial court was justified in concluding that JMR had established each of the four *Amelco* elements required for utilizing this method.[177] The fact that the damages claimed using this formula may have only been a reasonable approximation of JMR's loss associated with this phase of the Project is not an obstacle to its use, since the fact of such damages was established by substantial evidence.[178]

### [e] SureTec's Challenge to the Judgment Due to Lack of Default Notice

SureTec contends that the trial court erred in finding it liable under the performance bonds because JMR failed to give it (SureTec) notice of EAR's default under the subcontracts. SureTec argues that a "declaration of default was a condition precedent to SureTec's liability." It also argues that, looking at the language of the bonds as a whole, there was an implied requirement that JMR provide a notice of default to SureTec as a condition precedent to SureTec's liability under the bonds.

There was undisputed evidence, based upon Rivard's testimony, that JMR did not formally declare EAR in default under either subcontract. Nor did JMR ask SureTec to complete the bonded work under either subcontract. At trial, Cynthia Vincent, a SureTec vice president, testified that SureTec received no notice of any default under the plumbing or electrical subcontracts. She also testified that SureTec was not given the opportunity to complete work under either subcontract, and that JMR never asked SureTec to obtain new plumbing or electrical subcontractors.

### [f] Contractual Conditions Generally

A conditional obligation is one in which "the rights or duties of any party thereto depend upon the occurrence of an uncertain event."[179] "[P]arties may expressly agree that a right or duty is conditional upon the occurrence or nonoccurrence of an act or event."[180] A condition in a contract may be a

---

[177] *Amelco*, 27 Cal. 4th at 243.

[178] *Acree*, 92 Cal. App. 4th at 398.

[179] Cal. Civ. Code § 1434; *see also* Restatement (Second) of Contracts § 224: "A condition is an event, not certain to occur, which must occur, unless its non-occurrence is excused, before performance under a contract becomes due."

[180] Platt Pac., Inc. v. Andelson, 6 Cal. 4th 307, 313 (1993) (*Platt Pacific*).

condition precedent, concurrent, or subsequent.[181] "[A] condition precedent is either an act of a party that must be performed or an uncertain event that must happen before the contractual right accrues or the contractual duty arises."[182]

"The existence of a condition precedent normally depends upon the intent of the parties as determined from the words they have employed in the contract. [Citation.]"[183] But "stipulations in an agreement are not to be construed as conditions precedent unless such construction is required by clear, unambiguous language; and particularly so where a forfeiture would be involved or inequitable consequences would result. [Citations.]"[184] Because "such conditions are not favored by the law, [they] are to be strictly construed against one seeking to avail [it]self of them. [Citation.]"[185]

### [g]  *Interpretation of the Contract Language*

Resolution of SureTec's contention that a notice of default was a condition precedent to its liability requires an independent review of the trial court's interpretation of the bonds, since no extrinsic evidence was introduced by the parties on that question.[186]

"A surety bond is a 'written instrument executed by the principal and surety in which the surety agrees to answer for the debt, default, or miscarriage of the principal.' [Citation.]"[187] In the suretyship context, "the risk of loss remains with the principal, while the surety merely lends its credit so as to guarantee payment or performance in the event that the principal defaults. [Citation.] In the absence of default, the surety has no obligation. [Citation.]"[188] A performance bond, a species of a surety bond, is one in which the surety "guarantee[s] that obligations undertaken by the principal will be completed under the terms of the bonded contract."[189] When the principal breaches its contract with the bond's beneficiary (i.e., the owner, or, in this case, the general contractor), "generally the surety's

---

[181] Cal. Civ. Code § 1435.

[182] *Platt Pacific*, 6 Cal. 4th at 313; *see also* Cal. Civ. Code § 1436.

[183] Realmuto v. Gagnard, 110 Cal. App. 4th 193, 199 (2003).

[184] Alpha Beta Food Mkts. v. Retail Clerks Union Local 770, 45 Cal. 2d 764, 771 (1955) (*Alpha Beta Food*); *see also* Rubin v. Fuchs, 1 Cal. 3d 50, 53 (1969) (contract provisions are not construed as conditions precedent in the absence of language plainly requiring such construction); City of San Diego v. Haas, 207 Cal. App. 4th 472, 493 (2012).

[185] Antonelle v. Kennedy & Shaw Lumber Co., 140 Cal. 309, 315 (1903).

[186] Campbell v. Scripps Bank, 78 Cal. App. 4th 1328, 1336 (2000); *see also* Airlines Reporting Corp. v. United States Fid. & Guar. Co., 31 Cal. App. 4th 1458, 1461(1995) (appellate court reviews interpretation of bonds de novo).

[187] American Contractors Indem. Co. v. Saladino, 115 Cal. App. 4th 1262, 1268 (2004).

[188] Cates Constr., Inc. v. Talbot Partners, 21 Cal. 4th 28, 38 (1999) (*Cates Constr.*).

[189] 1 Baier et al., Cal. Mechanics Liens and Related Construction Remedies,*Private Works Remedies*, § 2.115, p. 145 (Cont. Ed. Bar 4th ed. 2014).

liability has been found to be coextensive with that of its principal. If the principal is liable under the contract, the surety is liable under the performance bond. [Citation.]"[190] This may include, in the event of the principal's default, the surety's liability under the bond for "damages attributable to [its] principal['s] delay in performing [a] construction contract."[191]

A surety contract is interpreted pursuant to the same rules that govern the interpretation of contracts generally.[192] To determine the surety's liability, "the Court looks first to the express terms of the performance bond. [Citations.]"[193] Performance bonds typically incorporate by reference the general contract or subcontract for which the bond was issued. As such, "'the bond and the contract should be read together and construed fairly and reasonably as a whole according to the intention of the parties.' [Citations.]"[194]

Each subcontract here requires EAR to furnish JMR, as the named obligee, a performance bond and a payment bond "to secure the faithful performance of the Subcontract Work and to satisfy all Subcontractor payment obligations related to the Subcontract Work." On November 10, 2006, SureTec issued separate performance bonds for EAR's electrical subcontract and its plumbing subcontract, listing the penal amounts of the bonds as $732,500 and $471,881, respectively. Each performance bond specifically incorporates by reference the respective subcontract for which the bond was issued.

The one-page "Articles" of the two performance bonds contain identical language. Article 1, containing the heading "SCOPE OF BOND" (emphasis omitted), states: "The Principal [EAR] and the Surety [SureTec], jointly and severally, bind themselves . . . to the Obligee [JMR] for the performance of the Subcontract." Under the heading "EFFECT OF OBLIGATION" (emphasis omitted), Article 2 provides: "If the Principal performs the Subcontract, then this bond shall be null and void; otherwise it shall remain in full force and effect." Article 4, under the heading "PRINCIPAL DEFAULT" (emphasis omitted), provides: "Whenever the Principal shall be, and is declared by the Obligee to be in default under the Subcontract, with the Obligee having performed its obligations in the Subcontract, the Surety may promptly remedy the default, or shall promptly" (1) "[c]omplete the Subcontract in accordance with its terms and conditions"; (2) retain a new subcontractor to complete the Principal's work

---

[190] 1 Baier et al., Cal. Mechanics Liens and Related Construction Remedies, *Private Works Remedies*, § 2.115, p. 145 (Cont. Ed. Bar 4th ed. 2014).

[191] *Cates Constr.*, 21 Cal. 4th at 41.

[192] Pacific Emp'rs Ins. Co. v. City of Berkeley, 158 Cal. App. 3d 145, 150 (1984)(*Pacific Emp'rs*), citing United States Leasing Corp. v. DuPont, 69 Cal. 2d 275, 284(1968); Cal. Civ. Code § 2837.

[193] *Cates Constr.,* 21 Cal. 4th at 39.

[194] *Cates Constr.*, 21 Cal. 4th at 39-40; *see also Pacific Emp'rs*, 158 Cal. App. 3d at 150 (generally, "contract performance bond will be read with the contract").

under the subcontract; (3) pay the Obligee the amount for which the Surety is liable; or (4) deny liability in whole or in part, providing an explanation for doing so.

Each subcontract details JMR's right to deduct or withhold payments to EAR, and JMR's rights in the event of EAR's breach. Furthermore, each subcontract specifically requires JMR to provide written notice to EAR in a number of circumstances. Those circumstances include where: (1) JMR elects to deduct from amounts otherwise due to EAR any sums EAR owes JMR; (2) JMR "deems it necessary and desirable to [withhold payments due to EAR to] protect itself against possible loss or damages"; (3) JMR concludes EAR has failed to (a) supply sufficient skilled workers, (b) adhere to the work schedule, (c) pay workers or suppliers, (d) follow the law, or (e) has otherwise materially breached the subcontract, requiring JMR to give EAR notice to cure the default; (4) JMR elects to suspend EAR's work under the subcontract; (5) the owner suspends its agreement with JMR; (6) JMR elects to terminate the subcontract due to EAR's material default of its obligations under the subcontract, after having given EAR written notice to cure; and (7) the owner terminates its agreement with JMR. None of these notice provisions requires JMR to give written notice *to the surety, SureTec.* Furthermore, each subcontract provides that the surety need not be advised of any changes, additions, or omissions to the subcontract.

### [h]  Discussion

SureTec implicitly acknowledges that neither performance bond *expressly* provides that JMR must give notice to SureTec of EAR's default as a condition precedent to SureTec's liability. But it asserts that "[a] contractual provision need not be expressly labeled 'condition precedent' to be treated as such. Rather, whether a provision is a condition precedent is to be determined from the whole contract, its purpose, and the intention of the parties." Quoting from *Wal-Noon Corp. v. Hill*,[195] SureTec contends the default notice as a condition precedent 'may be necessarily implied in the language of [the] contract. . . .'" Applying principles of contract interpretation, the court conclude that JMR was not required to give SureTec notice of EAR's default as a condition precedent to SureTec's liability on the bonds.

The only notice language in the bonds is found in Article 3, where SureTec expressly "waive[d] notice of any alteration or extension of the Subcontract, including but not limited to the Subcontract price and/or time, made by the Obligee [JMR]." (Italics added.) And the default provisions in the subcontracts— incorporated by reference into the bonds—include requirements in several instances that JMR give notice to EAR without any similar requirement of giving

---

[195] 45 Cal. App. 3d 605, 611 (1975) (*Wal-Noon*).

notice to SureTec. Thus, the bonds do not contain the requisite "clear, unambiguous language"[196] that would support a finding that JMR was required to provide a notice of default to SureTec as a condition precedent to liability under the bonds.

*Pacific Allied v. Century Steel Products*,[197] is instructive. There, the defendant ("Century") agreed to fabricate and sell steel forms to plaintiff ("Pacific") for the purpose of using them to install storm drains.[198] Century also guaranteed that Pacific's labor costs, through its use of Century's steel forms, would not exceed four cents per square foot, and that Century would, upon completion of the job and Pacific's submission of an itemized cost breakdown, pay Pacific's labor costs in excess of four cents per square foot.[199] Pacific agreed to keep a detailed account of labor costs and give Century a "continuous report."[200] Pacific kept Century apprised of costs during the project and gave it periodic oral reports, but it did not provide a detailed cost breakdown upon the project's completion.[201] The court rejected Century's contention that Pacific was required to provide a detailed cost breakdown as a condition precedent to its recovery under the contract.[202] The appellate court held that: (1) conditions precedent are not favored in the law; (2) neither the express terms of the contract nor a reasonable implication drawn from them compelled a finding that providing the cost breakdown was condition precedent to Pacific's recovery; and (3) the interpretation advanced by Century was particularly disfavored because it would result in a forfeiture.[203]

Here, as in *Pacific Allied*, there was no language expressly conditioning SureTec's performance under the bonds upon receipt of a notice of default from JMR. In *Pacific Allied*, there was an express agreement by the plaintiff to provide some level of notification (a detailed cost breakdown) to the defendant. Here, there was no such express covenant requiring JMR to provide any notice to SureTec.

The court concluded that SureTec's receipt of a declaration of default by JMR was not a condition precedent to triggering SureTec's liability under the bonds. This interpretation necessarily defeats SureTec's argument that a condition precedent should be implied from the language of the bonds. This interpretation is also consistent with the statutory mandate that courts, in construing an

---

[196] *Alpha Beta Food*, 45 Cal. 2d at 771.
[197] 162 Cal. App. 2d 70 (1958) (*Pacific Allied*).
[198] 162 Cal. App. 2d at 72.
[199] 162 Cal. App. 2d at 73.
[200] 162 Cal. App. 2d at 73.
[201] 162 Cal. App. 2d at 78.
[202] 162 Cal. App. 2d at 79-80.
[203] 162 Cal. App. 2d at 79-80.

instrument, shall "'not [] insert what has been omitted, or [] omit what has been inserted.'"[204]

Likewise, the court's construction comports with the law governing surety-ships. "A suretyship obligation is to be deemed unconditional unless its terms import some condition precedent to the liability of the surety."[205] Here, Article 1 of each bond creates the unconditional obligation to the effect that EAR and SureTec "jointly and severally, bind themselves . . . to [JMR] for the performance of the Subcontract."

SureTec contends that, notwithstanding Article 1, its obligation here was dis-charged under Article 2 of the performance bonds, which reads: "If the Principal performs the Subcontract, then this bond shall be null and void; otherwise it shall remain in full force and effect." SureTec asserts that because EAR performed its obligations by completing its work under the subcontracts, the bonds became "null and void" under Article 2. This contention has no merit.

As discussed in detail, *ante*, the trial court found, based upon substantial evi-dence, that EAR breached the plumbing and electrical subcontracts by, among other things, delayed performance under the contracts and by disrupting the effi-cient completion of the framing and drywall phase of the Project. EAR's breach gave JMR the option to terminate the subcontracts, but it was not required to do so.[206] That JMR did not terminate the subcontracts as a result of EAR's breach does not absolve EAR of responsibility for breaching the contracts. "[Breach of contract d]amages for delay can result from either a total or partial failure of per-formance. In both cases, delay damages are an extra item of recovery in addition to the normal measure of damages. However, even when there has been complete performance of a contract, damages for delay can result when performance was not completed on time."[207]

Furthermore, under general suretyship law, Cal. Civil Code § 2807 provides that "[a] surety who has assumed liability for payment or performance is liable to the creditor immediately upon the default of the principal, *and without demand or notice.*[208]

---

[204] Edwards v. Arthur Andersen LLP, 44 Cal. 4th 937, 954 (2008), quoting § 1858; *see also* Safeco Ins. Co. of Am. v. Robert S., 26 Cal. 4th 758, 763 (2001) (applying § 1858 to reject insurer's contention that illegal act exclusion in homeowner's insurance policy should be construed as a "criminal act" exclusion, observing that if insurer had "wanted to exclude criminal acts from cov-erage, it could have easily done so").

[205] Cal. Civ. Code § 2806; *see* Bank of Am. v. McRae, 81 Cal. App. 2d 1, 7 (1947) ("guaranty is unconditional unless its terms import some condition precedent to the liability of the guarantor").

[206] *See* Whitney Inv. Co. v. Westview Dev. Co., 273 Cal. App. 2d 594, 602 (1969).

[207] Cal. Attorney's Guide to Damages, § 1.49, pp. 1-49 to 1-50.

[208] Italics added; *see* Croskey et al., Cal. Practice Guide: Insurance Litigation ¶ 6:3436, pp. 6I-72 to 6I-73 (The Rutter Group 2015) ("if the bond is silent, the obligee is not required to give the surety notice of the principal's default or make demand upon the surety for payment").

Thus, for instance, in *State Bd. of Equalization v. Balboa Ins. Co.,*[209] the surety was held liable on sales tax surety bonds after the principal's default, not-withstanding the obligee's (State Board of Equalization's) failure to make demand for payment or its failure to include the surety on a notice of lien.[210] The court explained that when the surety executed the surety bonds, "it did not put conditions of special or separate notice" upon its "agreement to stand good for [the principal's] tax liability."[211] Citing Civil Code § 2807, the court held the surety was liable under the bonds because neither the law nor the agreement required notice as a condition to the surety's liability.[212]

SureTec relies on several out-of-state cases to support its contention that a declaration of EAR's default by JMR to SureTec was a condition precedent to JMR's recovery under the bonds. Several of these cases were based upon the courts' interpretation of the relevant contracts under applicable Florida law.[213] In *L&A Contracting*—a case relied upon by a number of the authorities cited by SureTec—the Fifth Circuit Court of Appeals concluded that a contractor's unequivocal declaration of the subcontractor's default was "a necessary precon-dition" to the surety's liability under a performance bond.[214] But *L&A Contract-ing*, and other cases relied on by SureTec, did not involve a contractual interpretation of performance bonds under California law. And none of those authorities considered the appropriateness of implying a condition precedent relating to default notice in light of decisional authority prohibiting such a con-struction unless the contractual language plainly requires it.[215] Indeed, *L&A Con-tracting* does not discuss conditions precedent generally or the appropriateness of implying a condition not expressly stated in a contract. The court therefore decline to follow the out-of-state authorities relied upon by SureTec.[216]

---

[209] 89 Cal. App. 3d 499 (1978).

[210] 89 Cal. App. 3d at 503-04.

[211] 89 Cal. App. 3d at 504.

[212] 89 Cal. App. 3d at 504.

[213] *See, e.g.,* L&A Contracting v. Southern Concrete Servs., 17 F.3d 106 (5th Cir. 1994) (*L&A Contracting*); School Bd. of Escambia Cnty. v. TIG Premier Ins., Co., 110 F. Supp. 2d 1351 (N.D. Fla. 2000); DCC Constructors, Inc. v. Randall Mech., Inc., 791 So. 2d 575 (Fla. Ct. App. 2001).

[214] *L&A Contracting,* at 111; *cf* Colorado Structures Inc. v. Ins. Co. of the West, 167 P.3d 1125, 1134 (Wash. 2007) (disagreeing with *L&A Contracting,* concluding that a proper interpretation of the bond's language in that case is that it created "liability, subject to a single express condition sub-sequent (the principal's prompt and faithful performance"); Walter Concrete Constr. Corp. v. Led-erle Labs., 788 N.E.2d 609, 610 (N.Y. 2003) (rejecting surety's claim that default notice was required, holding that had parties wished to make liability conditioned on default notice, they could have expressly so provided in performance bond).

[215] *See Rubin,* 1 Cal. 3d at 53; *Alpha Beta Food,* 45 Cal. 2d at 771.

[216] *See* People v. Uribe, 199 Cal. App. 4th 836, 865, n.15 (2011) (California courts not bound by out-of-state decisional authority).

The court read the performance bonds together with the subcontracts to which they relate in ascertaining the intentions of the parties.[217] A number of provisions in the EAR subcontracts require JMR to give notice to EAR; none of these provisions requires notice to SureTec. The performance bonds themselves contain no express requirement of any notice to the surety. The only mention of notice in either bond is a provision under which SureTec waives notice of any alteration or extension of the referenced subcontract. Reading Article 1 together with Article 2 of each bond—in conjunction with the language of the subcontracts incorporated by reference— yields the conclusion that SureTec's obligation to JMR in the event of EAR's breach of the underlying subcontract is unconditional.[218]

The court concluded that the performance bonds did not require JMR to give notice of default to SureTec as a condition precedent to recovery under the bonds. Any interpretation of the bonds as implying such a condition precedent would be contrary to (1) suretyship principles[219] and (2) the principle that conditions precedent should not be implied unless the construction is compelled by the clear language of the agreement, particularly here, where such an implied condition would result in a forfeiture.[220]

### [B]   Forum Selection Clause—Unenforceability of Contract Provisions Requiring Disputes Between Contractors and California Subcontractors to Be Litigated Outside California Enforced in Favor of Design Professional

In *Vita Planning & Landscape v. HKS Architects*,[221] the California Court of Appeal refused to affirm a trial court's order to dismiss an action where, although defendant established the existence of a contract between the parties containing a forum selection clause, its enforcement is prevented by Civil Procedure Code § 410.42, which prohibits enforcement of construction contract provisions requiring disputes between contractors and California subcontractors to be litigated outside California.

---

[217] *Cates Constr.*, 21 Cal. 4th at 39-40.

[218] *See Cates Constr.*, 21 Cal. 4th at 41 (considering the documents "as a whole, the bond and underlying construction contract are fairly and reasonably read as requiring" surety to answer for principal's failure to perform under contract).

[219] *See* Cal. Civ. Code §§ 2806, 2807.

[220] *Alpha Beta Food*, 45 Cal. 2d at 771.

[221] A141010 (Cal. Ct. App. Sep 25, 2015).

## [1]   Factual and Procedural Background

### [a]   *The Project*

HKS is an architecture firm and a Texas corporation. C.E. Mammoth LLC ("Owner") planned to develop a luxury hotel in Mammoth Lakes ("Project"). Owner hired HKS to provide architectural services for the Project pursuant to an "Agreement Between Owner and Architect" ("Prime Agreement"). Among other things, the Prime Agreement contained a Texas forum selection clause providing: "[a]s a condition precedent to the institution of any action [or] lawsuit[,]" that "all disputes shall be submitted to mediation" and that "[a]ll claims, disputes, and other matters in question between the parties arising out of or relating to [the Prime] Agreement be resolved by the courts in Texas." The Prime Agreement also contained a Texas choice of law provision. Additionally, the Prime Agreement authorized HKS to obtain proposals and hire "[c]onsultants" to perform certain work in connection with the Project. The Prime Agreement was revised as of September 11, 2007, but not signed by Owner and HKS until October 2008.

InSite is a landscape design firm with offices in Berkeley and Napa. In October 2007, InSite sent HKS a proposal to provide landscape architecture design services for the Project ("Proposal").The "Scope of Basic Services" section of the Proposal stated InSite would: (1) "support [HKS] and other design consultants in the preparation of design and construction documentation[;]" (2) "conduct a series of reviews of landscape construction[;]" (3) collaborate with HKS "for hardscape design of the outdoor environment[;]" and (4) have "primary responsibility for design and construction documentation of all planting, irrigation and associated landscape architectural features." According to the Proposal, InSite would "[w]ork with the selected contractor and their sub-contractors to clarify the landscape architecture issues and assist the contractor in understanding the design." Neither InSite nor HKS signed the Proposal, apparently because it contained provisions unacceptable to HKS.

In November 2007, InSite and HKS signed an "Architect and Consultant Agreement and Release" ("Release") wherein InSite agreed: (1) HKS "is or will be in the process of negotiating an agreement with [ ] Owner[;]" (2) "it is not certain that [ ] Owner will execute such an agreement[;]" (3) "Owner may not pay for any invoices submitted by [HKS], including those invoices for services provided by [InSite].In the event [ ] Owner does not pay [HKS] for amounts due to [InSite] for services rendered and expenses incurred, [InSite] hereby agrees not to take any legal action against [HKS] relative to such amounts and agrees to release [HKS] for any and all liability arising out of non-payment to [InSite] for any amounts of money due [InSite] and/or for the services rendered by [InSite]." InSite also agreed "once a proposed architect-consultant agreement is received by [InSite] from [HKS], [InSite] will have thirty days to review and execute [it].In the event that the [a]greement is not executed by [InSite] within 30 days of receipt, all payments that may otherwise be due and payable to [InSite] will be held by [HKS] until the [a]greement is executed by [InSite]."

Around this time, Vita acquired InSite. Vita is a California corporation with a main office in Marin County. HKS sent Vita a "Standard Form of Agreement Between Architect and Consultant" ("Contract").The Contract states Vita is to perform "[l]andscape architectural services" for the Project. The Contract attaches the Proposal as an exhibit and incorporates it to describe the scope of Vita's services. Sections 1.1 and 1.3 of the Contract incorporate the terms of the Prime Agreement. Section 8.1 provides in relevant part, "[s]ubject to Section 8.2, any claim, dispute or other matter in question arising out of or related to [the Contract] shall be subject to the same dispute resolution provisions as set forth in the Prime Agreement." Section 8.2 provides, "If the claim, dispute or other matter in question arising out of or related to [the Contract] is unrelated to a dispute between [HKS] and Owner, or if [Vita] is legally precluded from being a party to the dispute resolution procedures set forth in the Prime Agreement, then claims, disputes or other matters in question shall be resolved in accordance with this Section 8.2. Any such claim, dispute or matter in question shall be subject to mediation as a condition precedent to binding dispute resolution." Pursuant to section 10.1, the Contract "shall be governed by the law provided in the Prime Agreement."

Neither Vita nor HKS signed the Contract, but Vita performed work in 2008 while the Project was in the "design phase" and sent invoices to HKS. Owner began having financial problems before construction commenced; in 2008, work on the Project was "placed on hold." Owner "ceased paying for any work," leaving HKS "with extensive unpaid bills" for its own services, and those provided by its "consultants." HKS obtained a judgment against Owner in 2010 in Texas for $1,617,073.70 but was "unable to recover anything on that judgment, despite diligent efforts to do so."

### [b]   The Operative Complaint

In 2013, Vita filed a complaint against HKS, which HKS answered. Vita's operative first amended complaint (complaint) alleged claims for: (1) breach of contract; (2) unjust enrichment; (3) quantum meruit; and (4) breach of the implied covenant of good faith and fair dealing. In its breach of contract cause of action, Vita alleged "[o]n or about September 11, 2007, [Vita] and [HKS] entered into [a] contractual agreement, evidenced by a writing, a true and correct copy of which is attached hereto as Exhibit A. whereby [HKS] agreed to pay for services rendered by [Vita], in connection with the work of improvement known as the '[Project].'" According to the complaint, HKS breached that contract "by failing and refusing to satisfy its obligation to pay" Vita for its performance, and "[a]s a direct and proximate result of [HKS's] breach of the Contract," Vita had "been damaged in the amount of $370,650.53, which includes costs for labor, expenses, and interest." HKS answered the complaint, responded to written discovery propounded by Vita, and attended a court-ordered mediation. HKS also appeared by telephone at two case management conferences.

### [c]  HKS's Motion to Dismiss and Vita's Opposition

Approximately seven months after answering the complaint, HKS moved to enforce the forum selection clause and dismiss or stay the action pursuant to section 410.30. HKS argued "the contract upon which [Vita] has filed suit incorporates the terms of [the Prime Agreement], which in turn contains forum selection clauses requiring any action to be filed in Texas." HKS also argued the forum selection clause was "valid, enforceable, applicable to the dispute, and mandatory[.]"

In a supporting declaration, HKS principal Donald Harrier averred Owner hired HKS pursuant to the Prime Agreement, which "provides that any lawsuits must be filed in Texas." In turn, HKS hired Vita as one of its "consultants" on the project "to provide landscaping architectural services[.]"  Harrier sent the Contract to Vita. According to Harrier, while Vita "never signed the [C]ontract, it performed services thereafter, and the parties adopted its provisions by performance thereunder[.]" Harrier explained that HKS had InSite sign the Release—which contained a "pay-if-paid" clause—because HKS did "not want to be in a situation in which it must pay for work performed by consultants, when the [O]wner is not paying [HKS] for that work." Harrier's declaration attached the Prime Agreement, the Contract, and the Release.

Vita raised several arguments in opposition. First, it characterized HKS as a "general contractor" and itself as a "subcontractor" and claimed the forum selection clause in the Contract was unenforceable under section 410.42.Vita also argued the case implicated "fundamental public policy concerning pay provisions in subcontractor-contractor contracts," and suggested enforcing the forum selection clause would violate California public policy, under which "pay-if-paid" provisions are unenforceable. Next, Vita argued the motion was untimely and HKS "procedurally waived" its right to enforce the forum selection clause by litigating the case in California. Vita also contended "enforcing the forum selection clause in the unsigned" Contract—which it described as a "contract of adhesion"—would be unreasonable. Finally, Vita claimed there was no contract containing a forum selection clause because the Release did not contain such a clause and because the Contract was "unsigned and the parties intended their final agreement to be reduced to a signed writing[.]" In a supporting declaration, Vita's office manager averred HKS acted "as a general contractor" on the Project and the Contract "called for Vita to provide subcontractor professional design services." The office manager also stated Vita performed the work required by HKS and "Vita had no interactions, negotiations, or communications with [Owner] concerning Vita's work for the Project. Vita's agreement was with HKS."

In reply, HKS argued section 410.42 did not apply because HKS is not a contractor and Vita is not a subcontractor. As HKS explained, "[t]his is not a contract for construction. Rather, HKS and Vita are both design professionals, a category of entity very distinct from contractors and subcontractors and this is a design services contract[.]" HKS also claimed it had not waived its right to enforce the forum selection clause and that Vita could not demonstrate it would be unreasonable to enforce the clause. Finally, HKS argued Vita's arguments regarding the execution of the Contract had "no effect" because the complaint attached the Contract and Vita alleged "the [C]ontract memorializes its agreement with HKS."

### [d]  The Order Granting the Motion to Dismiss

Following a hearing, the court granted the motion to dismiss and concluded HKS was "entitled to have the action filed in the state selected" in the Prime Agreement. The court determined Vita and HKS signed "a contract with a forum selection clause. The contract is attached to the complaint as Exhibit A, and [Vita] is suing on the contract. The contract designates Texas as the forum for litigation." Rejecting Vita's waiver argument, the court concluded HKS did not engage in "'profound and extensive' litigation in California." The court also declined to apply section 410.42, concluding "[t]his is not an action between a contractor and a subcontractor for construction, but a contract between design professionals—a landscape architecture firm and an architecture firm." The court entered judgment for HKS.

### [2]  Discussion

### [a]  HKS Established the Existence of a Contract Between HKS and Vita Containing a Forum Selection Clause

Vita contends that the court erred by granting HKS's motion to dismiss because there is no contract containing a forum selection clause. The parties disagree on the standard of review. Vita urges the court to review the court's order de novo, claiming the threshold issue is the existence of a contract containing a forum selection clause. HKS contends that the court made a factual determination that the parties formed a contract, which the court reviews for substantial evidence.

"'[W]hether a certain or undisputed state of facts establishes a contract is one of law for the court. On the other hand, where the existence of a contract or the terms thereof is the point in issue, and the evidence is conflicting or admits of more than one inference, it is for the trier of the facts to determine whether the contract did in fact exist," [Citations.]' "[222] "Mutual assent or consent is necessary to the formation of a contract" and "[m]utual assent is a question of fact."[223] Here, the evidence regarding contract formation is conflicting because Vita claims there was no mutual assent and the parties merely had an agreement to "negotiate a more complete contract in the future."

As a result, the existence of the contract is a question of fact, and the court must uphold the trial court's finding if supported by substantial evidence.[224] Substantial evidence is evidence of "'ponderable legal significance,'" "reasonable in nature, credible, and of solid value.' [Citations.]"[225] "The ultimate determination is whether a reasonable trier of fact could have found for the respondent based on the whole record. [Citation.]"[226]

The court is not persuaded by Vita's claim that there is no contract containing a forum selection clause. In the complaint, Vita alleged it "entered into [a] contractual agreement, evidenced by a writing," and attached a "true and correct copy[.]" As the court has explained, the Contract incorporated the terms of the Prime Agreement, including the forum selection clause requiring disputes to be litigated in Texas. "The admission of fact in a pleading is a 'judicial admission.' It is a waiver of proof of a fact by conceding its truth, and it has the effect of removing the matter from the issues. Under the doctrine of "conclusiveness of pleadings," a pleader is bound by well pleaded material allegations. [Citations.]' [Citation.]"[227]

Vita's judicial admissions regarding the existence of the contract are binding.[228] Vita attempts to avoid the consequences of its judicial admission by claiming it attached the contract to the complaint merely "as a convenience to illustrate the nature and scope of the work involved in the [Project], to show that the Parties had an understanding as to the scope of the work, and to provide support for Vita's damages claim." Vita also contends it is "entitled to clarify its allegations

---

[222] Alexander v. Codemasters Grp. Ltd., 104 Cal. App. 4th 129, 141 (2002) (*Alexander*), disapproved on another ground in Reid v. Google, Inc., 50 Cal. 4th 512, 524; *see also* Bustamante v. Intuit, Inc., 141 Cal. App. 4th 199, 208 (2006) (*Bustamante*).

[223] *Alexander*, 104 Cal. App. 4th at 141.

[224] *Bustamante*, 141 Cal. App. 4th at 208; Winograd v. American Broad. Co., 68 Cal. App. 4th 624, 632 (1998).

[225] Howard v. Owens Corning, 72 Cal. App. 4th 621, 631 (1999).

[226] Kuhn v. Dep't of Gen. Servs., 22 Cal. App. 4th 1627, 1633 (1994) (italics omitted).

[227] Valerio v. Andrew Youngquist Constr., 103 Cal. App. 4th 1264, 1271 (2002).

[228] Toro Enters., Inc. v. Pavement Recycling Solutions, Inc., 205 Cal. App. 4th 954, 957 (2012) (complaint's allegations established existence of subcontract); Faigin v. Signature Grp. Holdings, Inc., 211 Cal. App. 4th 726, 737 (2012) (plaintiff "admitted the existence of the written contract by alleging it" in his unverified complaint); *see also* Food Safety Net Servs. v. Eco Safe Sys. USA, Inc., 209 Cal. App. 4th 1118, 1127 (2012) (allegation in unverified cross-complaint "constituted a binding admission" regarding the terms of a contract).

by filing an amended complaint[.]" The court rejected these arguments because Vita did not raise them in the trial court.[229]

The absence of signatures does not render the contract unenforceable. On appeal, Vita concedes the parties "conducted themselves as though they had an agreement[.]" There is no dispute Vita performed pursuant to the Contract, and HKS accepted Vita's performance. A "*voluntary* acceptance of the benefit of a transaction is equivalent to a consent to all the obligations arising from it, so far as the facts are known, or ought to be known, to the person accepting."[230] Here, substantial evidence supports the court's conclusion regarding the existence of a contract memorialized by a writing.[231]

Vita's reliance on *Banner Entertainment, Inc. v. Superior Court*[232] does not alter the court's conclusion. *Banner* held there is no binding contract when "it is clear, both from a provision that the proposed written contract would become operative only when signed by the parties as well as from any other evidence presented by the parties that both parties contemplated that acceptance of the contract's terms would be signified by signing it[.]"[233] Here and in contrast to *Banner*, there is no such condition precedent in the Contract, nor any evidence the parties contemplated acceptance of the contract "would be signified by signing it[.]"[234]

Vita contended that there is no contract containing a forum selection clause because the release demonstrates the parties intended to "negotiate a more complete contract in the future." The court disagreed for two reasons. First, this interpretation of the Release is completely inconsistent with the allegations of the complaint. Second, the Release states HKS has no obligation to pay Vita if Owner does not pay HKS, and it authorizes HKS to withhold payment for Vita's services until Vita signs the contract. The release's reference to the contract does not—as Vita suggests—"provide[ ] assurances" the parties "would negotiate a more complete contract in the future." It simply states Vita will not get paid until it signs the contract. This situation is unlike *Copeland v. Baskin Robbins U.S.A.*[235] where the parties signed a contract providing they would eventually negotiate a "separate [ ] agreement."[236] Nothing in the record suggests Vita and HKS entered into a contract to negotiate like the one at issue in Copeland. To the contrary, Vita

---

[229] Sea & Sage Audubon Soc'y, Inc. v. Planning Comm'n, 34 Cal. 3d 412, 417 (1983).

[230] Cal. Civ. Code § 1589 (italics added); *see also* Cal. Civ. Code § 1584 ("acceptance of the consideration offered with a proposal, is an acceptance of the proposal"); Grant v. Long, 33 Cal. App. 2d 725, 736 (1939) ("[w]hile an express contract is one, the terms of which are stated in words., one party may use the words and the other may accept, either in words or by his actions or conduct").

[231] Bohman v. Berg, 54 Cal. 2d 787, 794-95 (1960).

[232] 62 Cal. App. 4th 348 (1998) (*Banner*).

[233] 62 Cal. App. 4th at 358.

[234] 62 Cal. App. 4th at 358.

[235] 96 Cal. App. 4th 1251 (2002) (*Copeland*).

[236] 96 Cal. App. 4th at 1254.

acknowledged in the release it would not be paid if it failed to timely execute the contract.

The court concluded that substantial evidence supports the existence of a contract between HKS and Vita containing a forum selection clause.

### [b] Section 410.42 Bars Enforcement of the Forum Selection Clause

Vita contends section 410.42 bars enforcement of the forum selection clause. "California favors contractual forum selection clauses so long as they are entered into freely and voluntarily, and their enforcement would not be unreasonable. [Citation.] This favorable treatment is attributed to the Court's law's devotion to the concept of one's free right to contract, and flows from the important practical effect such contractual rights have on commerce generally."[237] Nonetheless, "California courts will refuse to defer to the selected forum if to do so would substantially diminish the rights of California residents in a way that violates the Court's state's public policy."[238]

Section 410.42 precludes out-of-state contractors from requiring California subcontractors to litigate certain contract disputes in the contractor's home state. It renders "void and unenforceable" a "provision[ ] of a contract between the contractor and a subcontractor with principal offices in this state, for the construction of a public or private work of improvement in this state" that "purports to require any dispute between the parties to be litigated, arbitrated, or otherwise determined outside this state" or that "purports to preclude a party from commencing such a proceeding or obtaining a judgment or other resolution in this state or the courts of this state."[239] Section 410.42, subdivision (b) defines "construction" as "work or services performed on, or materials provided for, a work of improvement, as defined in Section 8050 of the Civil Code, and for which a lien may be claimed pursuant to Section 8400 of the Civil Code[.]"

Section 410.42 is intended to "provide California subcontractors with the protection of California courts and law to which they are entitled" "including 'the prompt pay laws.'"[240] According to the statute's legislative history, "large out-of-state general contractors have an unfair bargaining advantage when negotiating with California subcontractors." This advantage, they argue, is evident when the subcontractors are forced to sign contract provisions that waive their right to have

---

[237] America Online, Inc. v. Superior Ct., 90 Cal. App. 4th 1, 11 (2001).

[238] *America Online, Inc.*, 90 Cal. App. 4th at 12; Intershop Commc'ns v. Superior Ct., 104 Cal. App. 4th 191, 200 (2002) ("a forum selection clause will not be enforced if to do so would bring about a result contrary to the public policy of this state").

[239] Cal. Civ. Proc. Code § 410.42, subds.(a)(1), (2); Templeton Dev. Corp. v. Superior Ct., 144 Cal. App. 4th 1073, 1081 (2006) (*Templeton*).

[240] *Templeton*, 144 Cal. App. 4th at 1083.

disputes resolved in California or lose the contract. Further, they argue that permitting general contractors to choose their home state as the site to resolve all contract disputes is unfair "when all the work was done in California and all witnesses and evidence are available in this state." They suggest that "subcontractors often are forced to [forgo] attempts to resolve disputes in the general contractor's home state for economic reasons even when they have a meritorious case. [Citation.]"[241] At least 24 states have similar statutes voiding forum selection clauses requiring construction disputes to be adjudicated outside the state where the project is located.[242]

Section 410.42 does not define "contractor" or "subcontractor" and the courts are aware of no cases interpreting these terms. The court applies a de novo standard of review to issues of statutory construction.[243] " 'The objective of statutory construction is to determine the intent of the enacting body so that the law may receive the interpretation that best effectuates that intent.[Citation.] "The Court first examine[s] the words themselves because the statutory language is generally the most reliable indicator of legislative intent.[Citation.] The words of the statute should be given their ordinary and usual meaning and should be construed in their statutory context." [Citation.] If the plain, commonsense meaning of a statute's words is unambiguous, the plain meaning controls. [Citation.]' [Citation.]"[244]

Black's Law Dictionary defines a contractor generally as "[a] party to a contract" or more specifically as "one who contracts to do work or provide supplies for another."[245] Here, HKS is a contractor, because it contracted with Owner to design the Project.[246] The court was not persuaded by HKS's contention that section 410.42 does not apply because it is not a "general contractor," which "construct[s] improvements," but rather a "design professional." In industry parlance, a " 'contractor' " may be "synonymous with 'builder'[.]"[247] But the term "contractor" in section 410.42 is not limited to builders, nor does it exclude an architect or design professional.

[241] *Templeton*, 144 Cal. App. 4th at 1083.

[242] *See* Travers et al., *Forum–Selection Clauses after Atlantic Marine* 34 Construction Law. 6 (Summer 2014).

[243] Nguyen v. Western Digital Corp., 229 Cal. App. 4th 1522, 1543 (2014).

[244] *Templeton*, 144 Cal. App. 4th at 1081.

[245] Black's Law Dictionary 375 (9th ed. 2009).

[246] *See* Chapman v. Edwards, 133 Cal. App. 72, 76 (1933) ("[a] contractor, obviously, is one party to a contract or one who has contracted to do or perform certain work"); *see also* Cal. Civ. Code § 8012 (broadly defining a " '[c]ontractor' " as "a direct contractor, subcontractor, or both").

[247] *See* Cal. Bus. & Prof. Code § 7026; *see also Templeton*, 144 Cal. App. 4th at 1076 ("electrical contractor" sued "general building contractor").

Black's Law Dictionary defines a subcontractor as "[o]ne who is awarded a portion of an existing contract by a contractor, esp[ecially] a general contractor."[248] Civil Code section 8046 also broadly defines a subcontractor as "a contractor that does not have a direct contractual relationship with an owner. [It] includes a contractor that has a contractual relationship with a direct contractor or with another subcontractor." Here, Vita is unquestionably a subcontractor because it was "awarded a portion" of HKS's contract with Owner and because it did "not have a direct contractual relationship" with Owner. There is no dispute that Vita did not interact, communicate, or negotiate with Owner concerning Vita's work for the Project.[249] HKS argues that the legislature was aware of the difference between contractors and subcontractors on the one hand and architects and design professionals on the other, and intentionally excluded architects and design professionals from section 410.42. To support this argument, HKS refers the court to numerous statutes, including Civil Code § 8400, which lists the entities entitled to a mechanic's lien as including direct contractors, subcontractors, and design professionals.[250] The court is not persuaded. Civil Code § 8400 does not—as HKS contends—distinguish between contractors, subcontractors, and design professionals. The statute simply lists entities entitled to a lien.

Nor does HKS's reliance on section 8404 alter the court's conclusion. Under section 8404, a "work of improvement" is "authorized" when "provided or authorized by a direct contractor, subcontractor, architect, project manager, or other person having charge of all or part of the work of improvement or site improvement."[251] That "design professional" is listed in this statute and in various other Civil Code sections does not mean architects and design professionals cannot also be contractors or subcontractors under section 410.42 and the authority discussed above.[252]

This case presents the very situation section 410.42 was designed to prevent: one where a California subcontractor performs work in California but is forced to litigate its dispute out of state, in a forum with laws unfavorable to the subcontractor. "In interpreting statutes, the Court must presume the Court's Legislature intended reasonable results. Where there are two possible constructions, one leading to mischief or absurdity and the other to a result consistent with

---

[248] Black's Law Dictionary, *supra*, at 1560.

[249] Black's Law Dictionary, *supra*, at 1560; Cal. Civ. Code § 8046; *see also* Union Asphalt, Inc. v. Planet Ins. Co., 21 Cal. App. 4th 1762, 1767 (1994) (*Union Asphalt*) (broadly construing " 'subcontractor' " in former Civ. Code § 3104 as including "all persons who agree with the original contractor").

[250] Cal. Civ. Code § 8400, subds.(a), (b), (f).

[251] Cal. Civ. Code § 8404, subd. (b).

[252] *See* D'Orsay Int'l Partners v. Superior Ct., 123 Cal. App. 4th 836, 838 (2004) ("licensed general contractor provided design related services, both by performing design and planning services, and by hiring design professionals").

justice and common sense, the choice is self-evident."[253] The court's interpretation of section 410.42 leads "to a result consistent with justice and common sense[.]"[254] The court concluded section 410.42 precludes enforcement of the forum selection clause requiring Vita to litigate its dispute against HKS in Texas.

Having reached this result, the court need not consider Vita's argument that the motion to dismiss was untimely and HKS waived its right to move to enforce the forum selection clause. The court also declined to consider whether the "pay-if-paid" provisions in the Contract provided an additional basis to invalidate the forum selection clause.

### [C]  Contractor Licensing—Substantial Compliance

In *Judicial Council of California v. Jacobs Facilities, Inc.*,[255] plaintiff Judicial Council of California, Administrative Office of the Courts ("JCC") entered into a contract with defendant Jacobs Facilities, Inc. ("Facilities"), a wholly owned subsidiary of defendant Jacobs Engineering Group Inc. ("Jacobs"). Performance of the contract required a license issued pursuant to the Contractors' State License Law[256] ("CSLL"), and Facilities was properly licensed when it commenced work. In the ensuing months, Jacobs, as part of a corporate reorganization, transferred the employees responsible for performing the JCC contract to another wholly owned subsidiary. In the process, Jacobs caused the new subsidiary to obtain a contractor's license, while permitting the Facilities license to expire. Notwithstanding the lapse of its license, Facilities remained the signatory on the JCC contract until nearly a year later, when the parties entered into an assignment of the contract to the new, licensed subsidiary.

JCC sued Jacobs and the two subsidiaries under section 7031, subdivision (b), which requires an unlicensed contractor to disgorge its compensation. JCC sought return of all monies paid to Facilities under the contract, some $18 million. In response, the defendants contended: (1) Facilities had complied with the CSLL, (2) Facilities had "internally" assigned the contract to the new subsidiary prior to expiration of its license, (3) JCC ratified the internal assignment when it consented to the assignment to the new subsidiary, and (4) Facilities had "substantially complied" with the CSLL under the provisions of section 7031, subdivision (e).

When the matter was called for trial, defendants requested a hearing on the issue of substantial compliance. The trial court deferred that hearing until after a jury trial on defendants' other defenses to JCC's claim. After the jury found for defendants, the substantial compliance hearing was never held.

---

[253] *Union Asphalt*, 21 Cal. App. 4th at 1765.
[254] *Union Asphalt*, 21 Cal. App. 4th at 1765.
[255] A140890 (Cal. Ct. App. Aug 20, 2015).
[256] Cal. Bus. & Prof. Code § 7000 *et seq.*

JCC appeals the denial of its motion for judgment notwithstanding the verdict and the trial court's award of attorney fees to defendants. The court reversed the judgment and attorney fees award entered on the jury's verdict, concluding Facilities violated the CSLL when it continued to act as the contracting party after its contractor's license expired. The court declined to order entry of judgment for JCC, however, because defendants remained entitled to an opportunity to prove their substantial compliance under the statute. The court remanded for a hearing pursuant to section 7031, subdivision (e).

## [1]  Background

JCC is the administrative agency of California's judicial branch. In 2005, JCC issued a request for proposals (RFP) for the provision of maintenance and repair services to courthouses and other judicial branch buildings throughout Southern California. The successful respondent was Facilities, a wholly owned subsidiary of Jacobs, which is a publicly traded corporation.

JCC and Facilities entered into a three-year facilities maintenance and repair agreement (the contract) in April 2006. The contract anticipated Facilities would organize, supervise, and bill for building repair and maintenance, while retaining subcontractors to perform some or all of the actual repair work. Among the provisions pertinent to this lawsuit, the contract precluded its assignment by Facilities, "in whole or in part," without JCC's written consent. Facilities also represented and warranted it held a class B contractor's license and agreed it would secure and maintain all licenses required for the performance of work under the contract.

Facilities commenced work under the contract, which covered a total of 121 buildings, in April 2006. In performing the contract, Facilities employees provided only administrative and oversight services, while retaining subcontractors to perform actual maintenance and repair work. When work was completed, Facilities recorded its completion in a dedicated computer system and generated an invoice. The invoices called for payment to Facilities, but the account to which JCC was directed to remit payment was a general Jacobs account from which Jacobs allocated payments among its subsidiaries.

In December 2006, Jacobs undertook a "branding initiative" designed, among other things, to reduce the costs associated with maintaining its many subsidiaries. As part of this initiative, Jacobs decided to dissolve Facilities and transfer its employees to Jacobs. Although the liquidation of Facilities into Jacobs was accomplished pursuant to a document effective December 2006, Facilities was not actually dissolved as a corporate entity until September 2010. The change in corporate structure did not affect performance of work under the contract, which was carried on in the same way by the same persons, but those persons appear to have become employees of Jacobs in January 2007. Throughout the reorganization, Facilities continued to invoice for payment and execute contractual amendments as necessary, and insurance and bonds required under the contract continued to be maintained in the name of Facilities.

Defendant Jacobs Project Management Co. ("Management") was formed in January 2008, as a wholly owned subsidiary of Jacobs. Under a written agreement, Jacobs transferred 713 employees, including some former Facilities employees, to Management, as well as the "fixed assets use[d] by those employees." It appears all employees providing services to JCC under the contract became employees of Management in February 2008, although the record is not wholly clear on this point. Throughout 2008, Jacobs allocated compensation received from JCC under the contract to Management, rather than Facilities. As before, actual work under the contract was unaffected, and invoices sent to JCC continued to instruct it to remit payment to "Jacobs Facilities Inc."

When a corporation applies for a contractor's license, it must designate a "qualifying individual," a corporate officer or employee who is qualified for the same license classification for which the corporation is applying.[257] Once the license issues, the qualifying individual is "responsible for exercising that direct supervision and control of his or her employer's or principal's construction operations to secure compliance with this chapter and the rules and regulations of the board."[258] The qualifying individual for the Facilities license was Scott McCallister. He remained in that position until August 12, 2008, at which time he voluntarily withdrew. Three days later, Management was issued a class B contractor's license, on which McCallister was the qualifying individual. Because Facilities failed to designate another qualifying individual, its contractor's license was suspended, and the license expired by operation of law in November 2008.[259] McCallister's withdrawal as the qualifying individual on the Facilities license was not legally necessary to permit him to serve in that role for Management, since the Business and Professions Code permits such overlap.[260]

At trial, Jacobs claimed to have performed an "internal assignment" of the contract from Facilities to Management on the date the new license was issued to Management, but the internal assignment was not documented by a written contract or, it appears, any other writing. In explaining the internal assignment, Jacobs's witnesses said the company assigned performance of the "business functions" of Facilities to Management—essentially, transferring responsibility for performing "the work" under the contract—as of the date of Management's licensure. If the Jacobs entities told JCC of the internal assignment, it was not until much later.

Although Facilities had begun divesting itself of assets and employees in December 2006, the Jacobs entities' first documented mention of the reorganization to JCC is an e-mail from April 2008, sent in connection with the negotiation

---

[257] Cal. Bus. & Prof. Code § 7068, subd. (b)(3).
[258] Cal. Bus. & Prof. Code § 7068.1, subd. (a).
[259] Cal. Bus & Prof. Code § 7068.2, subd. (c).
[260] Cal. Bus. & Prof. Code § 7068.1, subds. (a), (b).

of a different contract. At that time, a Jacobs employee told JCC that, as a result of a corporate reorganization, Facilities would not be the contracting entity on the new contract. During a subsequent exchange of e-mails, the employee explained that Jacobs intended to "novate" existing Facilities contracts to Management, once Management acquired the necessary contractor's license. In response, a JCC employee confirmed his understanding that Jacobs intended to transfer the contract to a new operating entity.

Jacobs did nothing to implement the intended novation of the contract until December 2008, when a Jacobs employee sent a copy of a proposed novation agreement to JCC under a "to whom it may concern" cover letter. Although JCC directed the letter to a responsible JCC employee, neither he nor anyone else at JCC responded to it, and Jacobs did nothing to follow up until eight months later, in August 2009, when the same Jacobs employee sent the same proposed novation agreement again, this time addressing the cover letter to a particular JCC employee. In the meantime, in February 2009, JCC exercised the first of three discretionary one-year extensions of the contract. McCallister executed the agreement extending the contract on behalf of Facilities.

Jacobs's August 2009 letter seeking consent to a novation did raise a response from JCC, but the parties displayed no urgency in transferring the contract until JCC learned in October 2009 that Facilities had allowed its contractor's license to lapse nearly a year earlier. JCC was particularly concerned about appearances that the "Administrative Office for the Courts, which represents the justice system, had a contractor who was not in compliance with the law." As a cure, the parties entered into an agreement assigning the contract to Management in November 2009.Hereafter, the court referred to this agreement as the "assignment," distinguishing it from Jacobs's earlier internal reassignment of duties to Management, which the court referred to as the "internal assignment."

JCC filed this action in December 2009 against Facilities and Management. The operative complaint, JCC's second amended complaint (complaint), joined Jacobs as well. The complaint alleges three causes of action: (1) breach of contract growing out of the expiration of Facilities' contractor's license; (2) disgorgement under section 7031, subdivision (b), which allows a person who has employed an unlicensed contractor to obtain "all compensation paid" to the contractor; and (3) breach of guaranty against Jacobs. Management cross-claimed against JCC for compensation payable under the contract that JCC began to withhold after it learned the Facilities license had expired.

JCC's statutory and contract claims were bifurcated, and the statutory claims proceeded to trial in April 2012. Prior to trial, defendants requested a "substantial compliance" hearing from the trial court. Under section 7031, subdivision (e), a contractor who has failed strictly to comply with the CSLL can avoid disgorgement if the "court" determines that the contractor substantially complied, as defined in subdivision (e). Among other elements, the contractor must show that it "acted reasonably and in good faith to maintain proper licensure."[261] The court granted defendants' request, but it deferred the hearing until "after the case went to the jury."

Responding to a special verdict, the jury found Facilities had maintained a contractor's license at all times while performing the contract; Facilities had "internally assign[ed]" the contract to Management prior to the expiration of the Facilities license; JCC was not "adversely affect[ed]" by the internal assignment; and Management was owed $4,669,376. The jury also found that Facilities had been paid $18,331,911 by JCC for its work under the contract, but the jury declined to require Facilities to disgorge that amount. The deferred substantial compliance hearing was never held.

In November 2013, JCC dismissed with prejudice its contract cause of action, and Management dismissed the claims in its cross-complaint seeking relief other than recovery under the unpaid invoices. On motion of the Jacobs entities, the trial court entered a defense judgment on JCC's statutory claim and Management's counterclaim for unpaid invoices, requiring JCC to pay Management the $4.7 million found by the jury. The court thereafter summarily denied JCC's motion for judgment notwithstanding the verdict (JNOV). In February 2014, the trial court granted the Jacobs entities' motion for contractual attorney fees.

JCC appeals the denial of its motion for JNOV and the award of attorney fees.

### [2]  Discussion

#### [a]  Denial of JCC's JNOV Motion

The evidence is essentially undisputed that Facilities contracted to deliver services requiring a contractor's license, allowed its license to expire, and continued to deliver the services while unlicensed. On its face, this would appear to constitute a violation of the CSLL, entitling JCC to the remedies specified in section 7031. While it might be argued that the violation was merely a technical one, given Management's licensure, this is an argument for substantial compliance, an issue deferred by the trial court. Accordingly, the question before the jury, and now before us, was whether defendants strictly complied with the statute. Any failure of compliance, whether or not technical or de minimis, requires reversal of the jury's verdict.

Defendants argue that the court can affirm the jury's conclusion that the requirements of the CSLL were met because: (1) they did not violate the CSLL because the statute does not penalize changes in a contractor's form of business; (2) the internal assignment of the contract from Facilities to Management prevented a violation; or (3) in executing the assignment, JCC retroactively ratified

---

[261] Cal. Bus. & Prof. Code § 7031, subd. (e)(2).

an assignment from Facilities to Management as of the time Management acquired its license, thereby avoiding a violation. The court found none of these arguments sufficient to uphold the verdict.

[i] **Applicable Law.** The CSLL provides "a comprehensive scheme which governs contractors doing business in California."[262] "The purpose of the licensing law is to protect the public from incompetence and dishonesty in those who provide building and construction services. [Citation.] The licensing requirements provide minimal assurance that all persons offering such services in California have the requisite skill and character, understand applicable local laws and codes, and know the rudiments of administering a contracting business."[263] For purposes of the CSLL, "a contractor is any person who undertakes to or offers to undertake to, or does himself or herself or by or through others, construct, alter, [or] repair any structure, project, development or improvement, or to do any part thereof."[264] There is no dispute the work undertaken by Facilities in the contract required a contractor's license.

The two provisions of the CSLL of concern here are designed to enforce compliance with the CSLL's licensing requirements. Section 7031, subdivision (a) provides that no person "engaged in the business or acting in the capacity of a contractor" can bring an action for compensation for work requiring a contractor's license if the person was not properly licensed at all times during the performance of the work. Section 7031, subdivision (b) goes further, permitting a person "who utilizes the services of an unlicensed contractor" to bring an action for disgorgement of "all compensation paid to the unlicensed contractor." Although the language of the two provisions is somewhat different, they are interpreted "in a consistent manner, resulting in the same remedy regardless of whether the unlicensed contractor is the plaintiff or the defendant."[265] The statutory intent behind subdivisions (a) and (b) is "to discourage persons who have failed to comply with the licensing law from offering or providing their unlicensed services for pay."[266] Because the remedies of subdivisions (a) and (b) of section 7031 are essentially two sides of the same coin in denying compensation to an unlicensed contractor, the Court will refer to the remedies jointly as "forfeiture." Both aspects of forfeiture are involved here, since JCC seeks disgorgement of compensation paid under subdivision (b), while the Jacobs entities were awarded a judgment for compensation withheld by JCC, which subdivision (a) would preclude them from recovering if a CSLL violation were found.

---

[262] Asdourian v. Araj, 38 Cal. 3d 276, 282 (1985) (*Asdourian*).

[263] Hydrotech Sys., Ltd. v. Oasis Waterpark, 52 Cal. 3d 988, 995 (1991) (*Hydrotech*).

[264] Cal. Bus. & Prof. Code § 7026.

[265] Alatriste v. Cesar's Exterior Designs, Inc., 183 Cal. App. 4th 656, 666 (2010) (*Alatriste*).

[266] *Hydrotech*, 25 Cal. 3d at 995.

Because it denies all compensation for a contractor's work, regardless of the quality of the work or the reasons for the failure of licensure, section 7031 can have harsh and seemingly unfair effects. To mitigate these effects, the courts developed, in the decades prior to 1990, the doctrine of "substantial compliance," which was applied "in exceptional circumstances [when] the purposes of the [CSLL] are not furthered by strict enforcement of section 7031."[267] Recognizing "the severity of th[e] sanction" imposed by section 7031, the courts did not "insist[ ] on literal compliance [with the CSLL] in the situation in which the party seeking to escape his obligation has received the full protection which the statute contemplates."[268] To excuse a failure of strict compliance with the CSLL by invoking the doctrine of substantial compliance, "the test [was] whether the contractor's 'substantial compliance with the licensing requirements satisfies the policy of the statute.'"[269]

Judicial discretion in the enforcement of section 7031 came to an end in 1989, when the legislature amended section 7031 to abolish the doctrine of substantial compliance. The new language stated unequivocally: "The judicial doctrine of substantial compliance shall not apply to this section."[270] In an extensive discussion of the amendment, MW Erectors characterized the statutory history as making clear the legislature intended "to narrow a 'loophole' created by the courts' use of the substantial compliance doctrine to avoid 'apply[ing] the licensing law strictly.'"[271] The unequivocal language of the amendment communicates unambiguously the legislature's insistence on strict enforcement of section 7031.Although statutory amendments since 1989 have reintroduced a limited defense of substantial compliance, via subdivision (e) of section 7031, compliance with the terms of subdivision (e) is the exclusive means for avoiding forfeiture in the event of a violation of CSLL.[272]

Courts have taken their cue from the legislature in enforcing the letter of the law, consoled by the legislature's "determination that the importance of deterring unlicensed persons from engaging in the contracting business outweighs any harshness between the parties."[273] Accordingly, if a contractor is unlicensed for any period of time while delivering construction services, the contractor forfeits all compensation for the work, not merely compensation for the period when the

---

[267] *Asdourian*, 38 Cal. 3d at 282.

[268] *Asdourian*, 38 Cal. 3d at 282-83.

[269] Latipac, Inc. v. Superior Ct., 64 Cal. 2d 278, 281(1966).

[270] Stats. 1989, ch. 368, § 1, p. 1509; *see* MW Erectors, Inc. v. Niederhauser Ornamental & Metal Works Co., Inc., 36 Cal. 4th 412, 429 (2005) (*MW Erectors*).

[271] *MW Erectors,* 36 Cal. 4th at 430.

[272] *MW Erectors*, 36 Cal. 4th at 429, 432-34; Pacific Caisson & Shoring, Inc. v. Bernards Bros. Inc., 198 Cal. App. 4th 681, 694 (2011).

[273] *MW Erectors*, 36 Cal. 4th at 423 (italics omitted).

contractor was unlicensed.[274] Although construction contractors often make substantial payments to others for materials and labor, an unlicensed contractor forfeits all money paid, without offsets for such payments to third parties.[275] Because section 7031 is held to apply "[r]egardless of the equities,"[276] unlicensed contractors are prohibited from asserting equitable defenses, such as estoppel, to forfeiture.[277] On the contrary, "[c]ourts may not resort to equitable considerations in defiance of section 7031."[278] As a result, an unlicensed contractor is subject to forfeiture even if the other contracting party was aware of the contractor's lack of a license, and the other party's bad faith or unjust enrichment cannot be asserted by the contractor as a defense to forfeiture.[279]  For a contractor failing to qualify under the statutory safe harbor of subdivision (e), section 7031 is truly a strict liability statute.

"The trial court's power to grant a motion for JNOV is the same as its power to grant a directed verdict. [Citation.]  The court must accept as true the evidence supporting the jury's verdict, disregarding all conflicting evidence and indulging in every legitimate inference that may be drawn in support of the judgment. The court may grant the motion only if there is no substantial evidence to support the verdict. [Citations.]  On appeal from the denial of a motion for JNOV, the Court determine whether there is any substantial evidence, contradicted or uncontradicted, supporting the jury's verdict."[280] Where, however, the trial court's denial of JNOV is based on an issue of law, the court's review is de novo.[281]

**[ii]   Penalizing Changes in Business Form Under the CSLL.**   As suggested above, the court agreed with JCC that, on the basis of what is materially undisputed evidence, the Jacobs entities failed to comply with the CSLL. The analysis is straightforward. Facilities contracted with JCC to supply services requiring a contractor's license. Although Facilities was licensed at the time the contract was made, its license expired in November 2008. Yet Facilities continued to deliver services and accept compensation from JCC as the signatory under the contract until November 2009, when the assignment was executed. Because Facilities was unlicensed for a portion of the period of its contract performance, its compensation under the contract is subject to forfeiture under subdivisions (a) and (b) of section 7031.

---

[274] *Alatriste*, 183 Cal. App. 4th at 665.

[275] Ahdout v. Hekmatjah, 213 Cal. App. 4th 21, 31 (2013) (*Ahdout*).

[276] *MW Erectors*, 36 Cal. 4th at 423.

[277] Twenty-Nine Palms Enters. Corp. v. Bardos, 210 Cal. App. 4th 1435, 1455 (2012) (*Twenty-Nine Palms*).

[278] *Ahdout*, 213 Cal. App. 4th at 31.

[279] *MW Erectors*, 36 Cal. 4th at 424.

[280] Taylor v. Nabors Drilling USA, LP, 222 Cal. App. 4th 1228, 1237 (2014).

[281] Wolf v. Walt Disney Pictures & Television, 162 Cal. App. 4th 1107, 1138 (2008).

Defendants argue that section 7031 was not intended to penalize a violation resulting from a mere change in business form, citing language to similar effect from *E.J. Franks Construction, Inc. v. Sahota*.[282] In *Franks*, the sole shareholder of the plaintiff corporation entered into a home construction contract as a sole proprietorship. During performance of the contract, he incorporated the business, creating the plaintiff corporation, and the contractor's license that had been issued to him in his personal capacity was reissued to his corporation.[283] The corporation then took over work on the residence.[284]   The defendants sought to avoid payment for the corporation's work under section 7031, arguing it was not licensed at all times during the performance of the contract.[285]   The court held section 7031 inapplicable because at no time was work on the home provided by an unlicensed contractor; rather, the court found, the circumstances involved a mere change in business entity by a licensed contractor, thereby maintaining proper licensure throughout. Section 7031, the court concluded, "is not intended to deter licensed contractors from changing a business entity's status and obtaining a reissuance of the license to the new entity during a contract period."[286]

While Franks may have reached the correct result on its facts, the broad interpretation of its language urged by defendants cannot be justified, and the decision should only cautiously be applied beyond the precise situation before that court. Franks never mentions the doctrine of substantial compliance, but to the extent the court purported to approve the delivery of services under a construction contract by an entity that was not licensed at the time work on the construction began, the court was necessarily invoking the now defunct doctrine. While it may be true that section 7031 was not intended to deter licensed contractors from changing the form of a business entity, there is nothing in the statute to suggest that a violation of the CSLL occurring during or as a result of such a change is excused. On the contrary, by restricting the doctrine of substantial compliance to the circumstances established in section 7031, subdivision (e), the legislature implicitly ruled that any CSLL violation not satisfying subdivision (e), regardless of its cause, is subject to section 7031.

For purposes of this decision, however, the court need not decide whether Franks was correctly reasoned. It is sufficient to note the decision's rationale rested heavily on the continuity of licensure resulting from reissuance of the license of the sole proprietorship to the corporation, in effect perpetuating the license. As the court held, the CSLL was not intended to deter a contractor from changing its business form and "obtaining a reissuance of the license to the new entity."[287]   That is not what happened here. Facilities did not change its business

---

[282] 226 Cal. App. 4th 1123 (2014) (*Franks*).
[283] *Franks*, Cal. App. 4th at 1126.
[284] *Franks*, Cal. App. 4th at 1126, 1131.
[285] *Franks*, Cal. App. 4th at 1126.
[286] *Franks*, Cal. App. 4th at 1129.
[287] *Franks*, Cal. App. 4th at 1129.

form, nor did it transfer its license to another entity. Rather, an entirely new entity was created, and a new contractor's license was issued to Management. Following the licensure of Management, Facilities retained both its corporate existence and its license, although the license was suspended and eventually expired. Unlike the hand-off of both license and business form that occurred in *Franks*, Jacobs maintained two separate business entities and two licenses for a significant period of time. The continuity of license and business entity that was central to the rationale of *Franks* was not present here.

Defendants do their best to analogize the circumstances here to those in *Franks*, but their situation is different in critical ways. Defendants argue that during the "challenged period," which they define as the time between the expiration of Facilities' license and the execution of the assignment, a licensed contractor, Management, was performing the contract, and all payments made under the contract during that time were allocated to Management, thereby preventing an unlicensed entity from receiving compensation. The statute, however, requires licensure throughout a period of "work," not merely during a selected time period during the performance of the contract[288] and the circumstances prevailing throughout the contract period diverge significantly from defendants' characterization. First, because the employees of Facilities appear to have been transferred to the employment of Jacobs in 2007, and then to Management in February 2008, well before its licensure, services under the contract were actually performed by unlicensed entities for over 18 months, from January 2007 to mid-August 2008. Second, Management was allocated compensation received under the contract for the entirety of 2008, not merely after November. To the extent, the internal allocation of funds is relevant, funds were credited to an unlicensed entity for the first seven months of 2008. Finally, while the compensation after 2007 may have been allocated to Management by Jacobs, it was Facilities that collected the money by placing its name on the invoices. An unlicensed entity therefore received the compensation after October 2008. In short, this was not a seamless situation, like Franks, in which both license and performance were transferred from one entity to another at precisely the same time, thereby preventing a period of noncompliance.

In arguing their corporate reorganization did not result in a violation of the CSLL, defendants contend disgorgement in these circumstances does not serve the statutory purposes. Part of the legislature's purpose, however, was to impose "strict and harsh penalties"[289] in order to ensure contractor compliance with the statute. As the California Supreme Court noted in *Hydrotech*: "The purpose of the licensing law is to protect the public from incompetence and dishonesty in those who provide building and construction services. [Citation.] . . . [¶] Section

---

[288] *Alatriste*, 183 Cal. App. 4th at 665.
[289] *MW Erectors*, 36 Cal. 4th at 418.

7031 advances this purpose by withholding judicial aid from those who seek compensation for unlicensed contract work. The obvious statutory intent is to discourage persons who have failed to comply with the licensing law from offering or providing their unlicensed services for pay. [¶] Because of the strength and clarity of this policy, it is well settled that section 7031 applies despite injustice to the unlicensed contractor. 'Section 7031 represents a legislative determination that the importance of deterring unlicensed persons from engaging in the contracting business outweighs any harshness between the parties, and that such deterrence can best be realized by denying violators the right to maintain any action for compensation in the courts of this state.' "[290] To the extent of serving that deterrent purpose, loss of compensation by the Jacobs entities was fully within the legislature's intent.

Yet the court acknowledged penalizing the Jacobs entities for these technical transgressions only indirectly serves the CSLL's larger purpose of preventing the delivery of services by unqualified contractors, since the Jacobs entities were neither dishonest nor incompetent. For better or worse, however, this is beside the point. The doctrine of substantial compliance, as developed by the courts, attempted to limit the forfeiture remedy to circumstances in which that remedy served the larger statutory purpose. In that form, the doctrine was rejected by the legislature. It is preserved in a restricted statutory form; thus, courts can no longer exercise discretion in the application of the doctrine. To avoid forfeiture for a CSLL violation, a contractor must now satisfy the terms of section 7031, subdivision (e).[291] To the extent the contractor fails to satisfy that exception, the courts have no choice but to allow forfeiture, regardless of the nature of the violation or its relation to the larger ends of the CSLL. "The Court's function is to ascertain and give effect to legislative intent, and 'not to determine whether the Legislature's policy choices were right or wrong.' [Citation.] Courts may not evaluate the desirability of the policies embodied in legislation." "[T]he choice among competing policy considerations in enacting laws is a legislative function."[292] While the court appreciates the potentially great harshness of this legislation in these circumstances, any argument for expansion of the substantial compliance doctrine must be directed to the legislature.

**[iii]  The Effect of the Internal Assignment.** Defendants argue that Facilities internally assigned the contract to Management after its acquisition of a license in August 2008, thereby avoiding a violation upon the expiration of Facilities' license. The court concluded that the internal assignment was irrelevant to the issue of CSLL compliance because Facilities continued to act in the capacity of a contractor until November 2009, when it was relieved of that role by the

---

[290] *Hydrotech*, 52 Cal. 3d at 995.
[291] *See generally MW Erectors*, 36 Cal. 4th at 432-34.
[292] *Alatriste*, 183 Cal. App. 4th at 672.

assignment. Facilities was therefore required by the CSLL to maintain a contractor's license until that time.

As a practical matter, the internal assignment shifted responsibility for providing services under the contract from Facilities to Management. The requirement of licensure under section 7031, however, does not necessarily adhere to the person who is performing services under a construction contract. Rather, a license is required for any person who is "engaged in the business or acting in the capacity of a contractor."[293]  Following the internal assignment, Facilities did not cease its involvement in the contract. On the contrary, Facilities continued as the signatory on the contract, executed amendments to it, issued invoices and received payments, and maintained in its own name the insurance and bond required under the contract. Because JCC was given no formal notification of the change, it continued to look to Facilities for performance. By continuing to serve after the internal assignment as the contracting entity in connection with work requiring a contractor's license, Facilities continued to act "in the capacity of" a contractor, notwithstanding Jacobs's delegation of performance to Management. Facilities therefore was required to be licensed until the time it was relieved of this role by the assignment.

Controlling in this regard is *Opp v. St. Paul Fire & Marine Ins. Co.*,[294] The plaintiff in *Opp*, an individual, was a licensed contractor who served as the president of an unlicensed corporation. Opp's corporation executed a subcontract for construction services under his individual license number. When Opp brought an action for payment, the defendant asserted the bar of section 7031, subdivision (a), arguing the corporate signatory to the contract was unlicensed.[295] Opp claimed section 7031 was inapplicable because he used his personal license number in executing the contract, personally supervised the work, and dealt with the general contractor as a sole proprietor.[296] The court rejected the argument, distinguishing between Opp's performance of work under the subcontract and his corporation's agreement to deliver that performance. As the court reasoned, the CSLL does not necessarily require "the person who 'does the work'" to possess a license, but rather the person who qualifies as a contractor under the statute by acting in the capacity of a contractor.[297] Such a person, the statute recognizes, can perform construction services "himself or herself or by or through others."[298] As the court concluded, "The issue, then, is not who 'did the work,' but who was 'engaged in the business or acting in the capacity of a contractor.'"[299] Because Opp's corporation undertook to provide construction services by executing the

---

[293] Cal. Bus. & Prof. Code § 7031, subd. (a).

[294] 154 Cal. App. 4th 71 (2007) (*Opp*).

[295] *Opp*, 154 Cal. App. 4th at 72-73.

[296] *Opp*, 154 Cal. App. 4th at 74.

[297] *Opp*, 154 Cal. App. 4th at 74-75.

[298] Cal. Bus. & Prof. Code § 7026.

[299] *Opp*, 154 Cal. App. 4th at 75.

contract, the court held that, the corporation was required by the CSLL to possess a license, and its failure to possess a license precluded its recovery of compensation for the work.[300]

Putting aside the issue of ratification, considered below, there is no evidence to suggest JCC gave its written consent to a transfer of responsibilities, required by the contract to effect a valid assignment, prior to November 2009. Without the consent of the obligee, the delegation of a duty by an obligor under a contract does not extinguish the obligor's duty.[301] Accordingly, even if Facilities unilaterally delegated its duties under the contract through an internal assignment to Management in August 2008, Facilities remained responsible to JCC for the delivery of services. Further, as noted above, Facilities continued to act as the contracting party vis-à-vis JCC, executing contract amendments, maintaining insurance, and sending invoices in its own name. Under the rule of Opp, Facilities' delegation of performance under the contract to Management did not relieve Facilities of its obligation under the CSLL to remain licensed so long as it was obligated to deliver services under the contract.

For this reason, the court concluded that the jury's finding that Facilities maintained a contractor's license "at all times while engaged in the business or acting in the capacity of a contractor in connection with" the contract is not supported by substantial evidence. The evidence is undisputed that Facilities continued to act as a contractor by remaining the signatory on the contract and accepting compensation even after its license expired in November 2008. Defendants contend that Management's assumption of day-to-day work under the contract provided evidence to support the jury's finding but Management's performance of such work did not preclude Facilities from continuing to act as a contractor. In remaining the signatory on the contract, continuing to secure bonding and insurance, executing contract amendments, and soliciting and receiving payments, Facilities continued to act as a contractor after the lapse of its license. Management's assumption of day-to-day duties is not evidence to the contrary.

Defendants argue that following the internal assignment, Facilities was merely a surety of Management's performance and therefore did not require a license.[302] Neither case relieves Facilities of its responsibilities here. In a sentence quoted only partially by Facilities in its brief, the Wiseman court explained the effect of an unconsented assignment: "The obligations of an assignor of a contract continue to rest upon him and he will be required to respond to the other party to the contract in the event of a default on the part of the assignee."[303] As a result, "irrespective of the legality or lack of legality of the assignment, [the

---

[300] *Opp*, 154 Cal. App. 4th at 75; *see similarly* Montgomery Sansome LP v. Rezai, 204 Cal. App. 4th 786, 797 (2012); *Twenty–Nine Palms*, 210 Cal. App. 4th at 1449-50.

[301] Restatment (Second) of Contracts, § 318, p.19.

[302] Citing Wiseman v. Sklar, 104 Cal. App. 369 (1930) and Cutting Packing Co. v. Packers' Exch., 86 Cal. 574, 577 (1890).

[303] *Wiseman*, 104 Cal. App. at 374.

assignor] was at all times responsible to [the other parties] under the contract."[304] As this demonstrates, Wiseman does not suggest that, following an unconsented assignment, the obligor under a contract is relegated to the role of surety. Cutting Packing is similar. While the decision refers to the assignor as a surety, the term is used only to describe the assignor's relationship to the assignee; that is, if the assignee failed to pay, the assignor would be required to pay. With respect to the obligee under the contract, "the burden of the obligation that rested upon the [assignor] could not be transferred without the consent of [the obligee]. [Citation.] And as he refused to consent the relations of himself and the plaintiff as to such burden were not affected by the assignment of the contract."[305] Accordingly, as to JCC, the internal assignment did not alter Facilities' duties under the contract.

Yet even if Facilities became a common law surety, it would not have been relieved of the duty of licensure under the CSLL, given its continued status as the contracting party after the internal assignment. Section 7044.2, the exception for sureties cited by Facilities, applies only to an "admitted surety insurer," and only when it "engages a contractor to undertake the completion of a contract on which a performance or completion bond was issued by the surety insurer." There is no evidence Facilities was an admitted surety insurer or had issued a bond to guarantee performance.[306] Nothing in the Business and Professions Code outside section 7044.2 exempts a surety from the requirement of licensure while acting in the capacity of a contractor.

Defendants also argue that the internal assignment did not require JCC's approval because it resulted from a corporate reorganization. The principle was first suggested in *Trubowitch v. Riverbank Canning Co.*,[307] in which the plaintiff, an assignee, sought to arbitrate a dispute over non-delivery of fruit under a contract containing a non-assignment clause. After the contract was made, the original party, a corporation, was dissolved, and its assets were distributed to its shareholders, who carried on the business.[308] The defendant resisted arbitration over its nondelivery because it had not consented to an assignment to the shareholders.[309] In considering the issue, the court held, "if an assignment results merely from a change in the legal form of ownership of a business, its validity depends upon whether it affects the interests of the parties protected by the non-assignability of the contract."[310] In finding the assignment valid under this principle, Trubowitch reasoned the "seller's financial interests were fully protected"

---

[304] *Wiseman*, 104 Cal. App. at 374-75.

[305] *Wiseman*, 104 Cal. App. at p. 576.

[306] *See* Cal. Civ. Proc. Code § 995.120, subd. (a) [defining admitted surety insurer as "a corporate insurer or a reciprocal or interinsurance exchange" licensed under the Ins. Code).

[307] 30 Cal. 2d 335 (1947) (*Trubowitch*).

[308] *Trubowitch*, 30 Cal. 2d at 337-38.

[309] *Trubowitch*, 30 Cal. 2d at 338.

[310] *Trubowitch*, 30 Cal. 2d at 344-45.

because the contract involved only the delivery of goods and contained provisions ensuring payment would be made.[311] The court distinguished such a contract from one for the provision of "services requiring special skill, capacity or taste."[312]

In the second decision cited by defendants,[313] the defendant corporation was granted a state construction contract. Following its entry into the contract, the defendant assigned its interest in the contract to its wholly owned subsidiary without obtaining the state's consent.[314] After performance of the contract was "brought to satisfactory completion,"[315] the state defended against a claim for payment, in part, by contending the contract was rendered unenforceable as a result of the lack of consent. While the court quoted *Trubowitch* in reaching its conclusion, it ultimately held that the assignment did not render the contract unenforceable because the unconsented assignment was ineffective. Because the parent corporation remained responsible to the state under the contract, the court held, to deny enforcement "would be to exalt form above substance."[316]

Accordingly, neither *Trubowitch* nor *McNamara* holds that contracts are freely assignable among the wholly owned subsidiaries of a corporate parent, notwithstanding the presence of a non-assignment clause. The holding in *Trubowitch* was actually quite narrow. The contract was merely for the delivery of goods, and there were provisions in the contract to ensure the defendant would receive payment for the goods.[317] The court expressly noted that a different result was likely if the contract required, as here, "services requiring special skill, capacity or taste."[318] *McNamara*, in turn, appears to have based its holding on the ineffective nature of an unconsented assignment. Just as the court has held with respect to Facilities, *McNamara* found that the defendant, the putative assignor, continued to have an "unaltered duty to perform the contract notwithstanding the assignment, since, in the absence of state consent, the assignment was ineffective to shift the defendant's obligation to the state to perform.[319] Both decisions are therefore consistent with the court's conclusion that the internal assignment did not relieve Facilities of its status of obligor under the contract.

The essence of defendants' argument is that there was no CSLL violation because Management, following its licensure, began performing day-to-day work under the contract well before the lapse of Facilities' license. Indeed, Facilities

---

[311] *Trubowitch*, 30 Cal. 2d at 346.

[312] *Trubowitch*, 30 Cal. 2d at 346.

[313] People ex rel. Dep't Pub. Wks. v. McNamara Corp. Ltd., 28 Cal. App. 3d 641 (1972) (*McNamara*).

[314] *McNamara*, 28 Cal. App. 3d at 645.

[315] *McNamara*, 28 Cal. App. 3d at 645.

[316] *McNamara*, 28 Cal. App. 3d at 649.

[317] *Trubowitch*, 30 Cal. 2d at 346.

[318] *Trubowitch*, 30 Cal. 2d at 346.

[319] *McNamara*, 28 Cal. App. 3d at 649.

was incapable of such work, because the necessary employees and assets had been transferred to Management. The CSLL is not necessarily satisfied merely because the person or entity actually performing services under a contract is licensed.[320] Rather, a license is required for any person who is "engaged in the business or acting in the capacity of a contractor."[321] In remaining the responsible party on the contract, Facilities continued to act as a contractor well past the lapse of its license. Further, while Facilities may not have maintained the employees necessary to perform day-to-day work, it continued in corporate existence and retained officers, thereby permitting it to carry out such administrative duties as securing insurance and bonding, soliciting and accepting payment, and executing contract amendments. Because these activities were in the capacity of a contractor, Facilities was required to be licensed until execution of the assignment relieved it of that responsibility.

[iv] **Ratification Through the Assignment.** Even if the internal assignment was ineffective in avoiding a forfeiture, defendants argue that (1) JCC ratified the internal assignment in executing the assignment and (2) the assignment itself was retroactive or related back to the date of the internal assignment. It is by no means clear that a violation of the CSLL can be cured after the fact in this manner, but the court assumed its effectiveness for purpose of argument.

The parties to the assignment are JCC and the three Jacobs entities. The recitals of the assignment state: (1) Jacobs, at some unspecified time, notified JCC that due to a corporate consolidation Facilities would no longer enter into contracts for the type of services provided under the contract and that such services "are" being performed by Management; (2) in furtherance of Jacobs's corporate consolidation, the assignment "is intended to evidence [Facilities'] assignment of the Contract to [Management], and [Management's] assumption of the Contract"; (3) Facilities "desires to memorialize its assignment of the Contract to [Management]"; (4) Management "desires to memorialize its assumption of the Contract"; and (5) Management possesses the qualifications to perform under the contract. The covenants of the assignment include an assignment of the contract from Facilities to Management, a ratification by Management of "all actions taken by [Facilities] under or with respect to the Contract," a warrant by Management of its suitability, a consent by JCC to the assignment, and a guaranty by Jacobs of Management's performance. The covenant of assignment states Management assumes the contract "as if [Management] was the original party to the Contract." JCC's consent states: "The State hereby executes and enters into this Agreement solely for the purpose of consenting to, and the State hereby consents to, the

---

[320] *See, e.g.,* Vallejo Dev. Co. v. Beck Dev. Co., 24 Cal. App. 4th 929, 940 (1994) (unlicensed entity that entered into contract and claimed merely to be the "administrator" of work barred from recovery).

[321] Cal. Bus. & Prof. Code § 7031, subd. (a).

Assignment and Assumption of the Contract on and subject to the terms and conditions set forth in this Agreement."

Defendants argue that the jury could have relied on the assignment as evidence in finding a ratification of the internal assignment. In making this argument, defendants seek to convert what would appear to be an issue of contract interpretation into an issue of fact, thereby invoking the deferential standard of review applicable to appellate review of findings of fact. The court might agree with defendants if there were some other evidence to support a finding of ratification. That is not the case. There is no indication the parties even discussed JCC's ratification of the internal assignment. Instead, Facilities' only evidence of a ratification is the effect of the assignment. The issue is therefore one of contract interpretation, to which the court applied de novo review.[322]

The court finds little or nothing in the assignment to support a conclusion JCC ratified the internal assignment. Most importantly, there is no express covenant of ratification. If the parties had intended for JCC to ratify the internal assignment, it would have been simple for them to include such a covenant. To the contrary, in the places in the agreement where one might expect confirmation of a ratification by JCC, it is absent. Most obviously, the provision entitled "Ratification" refers only to Management's ratification of actions taken by Facilities under the contract; there is no mention of ratification by JCC of the internal assignment. In addition, the covenant relating to JCC's consent to the assignment, another logical place to insert a provision relating to ratification by JCC, makes no mention of it. That provision states only that JCC consents to the assignment itself, not to any earlier internal assignment.

As discussed above, the assignment contained a series of recitals that referred indirectly to the internal assignment. One of these constituted an acknowledgement by JCC that, at some unspecified date prior to the execution of the assignment, Facilities had notified JCC that Management was actually performing the services being delivered under the contract. Defendants argue from this and the other recitals that the assignment should be interpreted as effecting the internal assignment, which occurred over a year earlier. The language of the covenants suggests otherwise. The language of the assignment covenant states Facilities "hereby assigns and transfers the Contract" and Management "hereby assumes the Contract." Both are phrased in the present tense, implying the transfer of rights and duties occurred by means of the assignment itself, at the time of execution of the assignment. There is no reason to construe this language to ratify or recognize an earlier transfer.

Defendants also argue the language in the assignment covenant stating Management assumes the contract "as if [Management] was the original party to the Contract" is evidence of a ratification. The meaning and legal implications of this

---

[322] Pittsburg Unified Sch. Dist. v. S.J. Amoroso Constr. Co., Inc., 232 Cal. App. 4th 808, 826 (2014).

phrase are unclear, but there is no reason to construe it as a ratification of the internal assignment, which did not occur until two years after the execution of the contract. If the language were taken literally, it would substitute one CSLL violation for another, since Management did not possess a license until two years after performance of the contract began.

Defendants also argue JCC "relinquished its right to object to the [internal] assignment because a subsequent consent to a prior assignment 'relates back to the time of the assignment.'"[323] As part of its acquisition of real property, the plaintiff in *Transamerica* was assigned a fire insurance policy covering the property, issued by the defendants. No change in use occurred as a result of the acquisition, since the lessee of the property was the same before and after. One month later, the property burned, and the defendants were not notified of the assignment of their policy until after the fire.[324] They attempted to cancel the policy, citing a clause requiring the insurers' consent to any assignment.[325]

In denying cancellation, the court noted the purpose of the non-assignment provision was to prevent an increase of risk of loss due to a change of ownership without the knowledge of the insurer.[326] The court explained: "In this case, had notice been promptly given prior to the loss, defendants would have routinely approved the assignment of the policy to plaintiff. There is no evidence that the change of ownership in any way increased the risk to defendants. Since the change of ownership did not increase the risk to defendants, and they would have routinely approved the assignment, they cannot claim they suffered any prejudice from the late notice. [Citation.] The language of the provision is consistent with plaintiff's theory that defendants should be deemed to have consented to the assignment, and that such consent relates back to the time of the assignment. To avoid a forfeiture, plaintiff may, in lieu of express approval, show that the assignment would have been routinely approved."[327] The holding of Transamerica is an exception to the general rule of law, which enforces non-assignment clauses in insurance contracts.[328]

The court concluded that *Transamerica*'s finding of deemed approval and relation back must be restricted to the assignment of standard property insurance policies, the situation before the *Transamerica* court. It seems likely, as the court believed that property insurers routinely approve the assignment of their policies from the seller to the purchaser of covered property when the underlying use of the property does not change. In the absence of a change in use, there is unlikely to be a good faith reason to refuse. Further, if an assignment is approved, the

---

[323] Quoting University of Judaism v. Transamerica Ins. Co., 61 Cal. App. 3d 937, 942 (1976) (*Transamerica*).

[324] *Transamerica*, 61 Cal. App. 3d at 939.

[325] *Transamerica*, 61 Cal. App. 3d at 940.

[326] *Transamerica*, 61 Cal. App. 3d at 940.

[327] *Transamerica*, 61 Cal. App. 3d at 942 (footnote omitted).

[328] *E.g.*, Henkel Corp. v. Hartford Accident & Indem. Co., 29 Cal. 4th 934, 943-45 (2003).

approval necessarily relates back to the date of the sale in order to avoid a lapse in insurance coverage. There is no basis, however, for applying this rule to the assignment of other, less standardized contracts. To do so would cause the enforceability of non-assignment clauses to depend upon an after-the-fact evaluation of the likelihood of routine approval of a typical assignment, an entirely impractical standard.

In any event, there was no evidence to suggest JCC would "routinely" consent to the type of assignment sought by Facilities, as required by *Transamerica*. JCC engaged in a formal RFP process in order to find a suitable service provider. Any change in provider, even if due to a corporate reorganization, would require similar due diligence. JCC would necessarily have wanted to satisfy itself the assignment posed no business risk, even if the assignment merely recognized a change in corporate structure. Simply as a matter of fact, JCC delayed when first approached for a novation, and it refused to sign an assent to novation and would not consent to the assignment without a guarantee of performance by Jacobs. There was nothing routine about its consent.

Nor is there any justification for finding that JCC's consent relates back to the time of the internal assignment. As noted above, such consent is necessary in the insurance context to avoid a lapse in coverage. While defendants argue relation back was necessary here to avoid the lapse in licensure, there is no reason to conclude JCC's duty of good faith required it to absolve Facilities of its lapse in licensure, in the same way the insurer's duty of good faith required it to maintain coverage. As noted by *Transamerica*, the insurers accepted premium payments made after the assignment; providing coverage was simply delivering the services for which they had already accepted compensation. There is no parallel circumstance here.

Defendants once again raise *Trubowitch* and *McNamara* in this context, arguing, in effect, that even if the internal assignment was not effective at the time it was entered into, given JCC's right of consent, the court should view JCC's eventual consent as retroactive because the assignment was the result of a mere corporate reorganization and, as the jury found, did not harm JCC's interests.[329] At this point, the court ran into the abolished doctrine of substantial compliance. As discussed above, JCC's interest in the prospective performance of the contract was sufficient to preclude its free assignment among wholly owned subsidiaries of Jacobs. JCC had the contractual right to approve such a change, even if it was merely the result of a corporate reorganization. To find that the assignment had a retroactive effect merely because Facilities' breach of the assignment clause did not harm JCC, when the ordinary principles of law discussed above provide no grounds for finding the assignment to be effective prior to its effective date, would be to invoke a special rule excusing a section 7031 remedy because a violation of

---

[329] *Trubowitch*, 30 Cal. 2d at 345-46.

the CSLL was harmless. This is just the type of rule-bending precluded by the legislature when it abolished the substantial compliance doctrine.

Defendants also argue JCC waived its right to object to the internal assignment by dealing with Management at a time when it had knowledge of the assignment, citing *Trubowitch*.[330] Assuming the applicability of the principle in this context, the record does not support a finding that the Jacobs entities informed JCC of the internal assignment prior to execution of the assignment. The initial notification, in April 2008, merely informed JCC that Jacobs intended to execute a novation transferring the contract from Facilities to another subsidiary at some point in the future. Thereafter, Jacobs sent proposals to JCC seeking its consent to a novation, and it continued to send invoices and execute contractual documents in the name of Facilities. There is no evidence Jacobs informed JCC it had unilaterally assigned the contract to Management, and Jacobs's continued attempts to negotiate a formal assignment of the contract suggested otherwise.

Defendants additionally contend that the internal assignment was not void but voidable,[331] and argue that JCC effectively affirmed the internal assignment when it entered into the assignment. In *Klopstock*, a party's claim of right in property derived from the assignment of a lease, which had occurred without the consent of the lessor. After the lessor learned of the assignment, it objected but "served no notice terminating or declaring a forfeiture of the lease."[332] The court held that the lessor's objection to the assignment, in the absence of a formal declaration of forfeiture, was ineffective to prevent the vesting of property rights in the assignee. As the court explained, the assignments of the lease "though made without the written consent of the lessor, were merely voidable, not void; there was no ipso facto termination of the lease by reason of the lessee's failure to obtain the lessor's written consent to assignment."[333] Because the lessor did not "take advantage of the exclusive remedy available to it for termination of the lease" by "declaration of a forfeiture upon proper notice," the court held, the lessor did not prevent the passing of property rights through assignment.[334]

As the foregoing account suggests, the principle announced by *Klopstock* is unique to lease law: the unconsented assignment of a lease can be voided by the lessor's declaration of forfeiture, but it is valid unless and until such a declaration has been made.[335] *Klopstock* does not purport to make this principle applicable outside lease law, in which there are no comparable procedural requirements for the rejection of an assignment, and subsequent decisions have applied the

---

[330] *Trubowitch*, 30 Cal. 2d at 342.
[331] Citing People v. Klopstock, 24 Cal. 2d 897 (1944) (*Klopstock*),
[332] *Klopstock*, 24 Cal. 2d at 899.
[333] *Klopstock*, 24 Cal. 2d at 901.
[334] *Klopstock*, 24 Cal. 2d at 902 (italics omitted).
[335] *Klopstock,* 24 Cal. 2d at 901-02.

decision solely within that framework.[336] With respect to an ordinary contract containing a non-assignment clause, an unconsented assignment, rather than effective until voided, is simply ineffective. Taking the present situation as an example, it is inconsistent with contract law to claim, following the internal assignment, that JCC was required to accept performance from Management unless or until it voided the contract. On the contrary, JCC had the right to insist on performance by Facilities until or unless it had consented to the assignment. To hold otherwise would, in effect, permit Jacobs to force JCC to accept the internal assignment or forfeit the contract, a choice inconsistent with JCC's contractual right to approve any assignment. Accordingly, JCC's act in entering into the assignment did not affirm the earlier internal assignment; rather, it effected an assignment as of the effective date of the assignment.

[v]  **Conclusion.**  The court viewed the jury's verdict as an attempt to reach an equitable resolution, given the harsh consequences to defendants from the strict application of section 7031.The Jacobs entities' violation of the statute, clear as it is, appears to have resulted from the manner of execution of their corporate reorganization, rather than any attempt to evade licensure requirements. But though the jury was unwilling to give its imprimatur to the forfeiture of income, that is the remedy the legislature has prescribed, and the court's task is to implement the legislature's prescription. Accordingly, the court reversed the judgment.

### [b]  *Substantial Compliance*

Defendants requested that, in the event the judgment was reversed, the matter be remanded for the conduct of a substantial compliance hearing. The court found such a remand appropriate.

[i]  **Waiver of Hearing.**  As discussed above, section 7031, subdivision (e) codifies the substantial compliance defense to enforcement of the forfeiture remedy. Defendants asserted a substantial compliance defense in their answer to the complaint and requested a substantial compliance hearing when the parties appeared for trial. The court granted the request "with the understanding that the hearing would take place after the case went to the jury and that the type [sic] would rely on trade testimony as the evidentiary hearing that's required by statute and that counsel could offer more evidence especially for that hearing if they needed or wanted to do so." Counsel clarified with the court that the hearing would occur "at the conclusion of the trial," which the court confirmed. Defendants never thereafter requested a substantial compliance hearing, either at the close of evidence or after judgment.

---

[336] *E.g.*, Guerin v. Blair, 33 Cal. 2d 744, 746-47 (1949); Weisman v. Clark, 232 Cal. App. 2d 764, 767 (1965).

JCC contends defendants forfeited such a hearing when they failed to request it after submission of the case to the jury and before the jury returned with its verdict. The court did not understand the trial court's ruling to have anticipated that the hearing would occur immediately after the matter was sent to the jury. On the contrary, because there would be no way of knowing how long the jury's deliberations would require, it would make no sense to hold a hearing immediately after submission. Rather, the court interpreted the court as deferring the substantial compliance hearing until after trial, as defendants' counsel suggested.

Further, the court found no forfeiture. Defendants timely requested a substantial compliance hearing. The trial court granted the request but deferred the hearing until after the jury rendered its verdict. Once the defense judgment was entered, a substantial compliance hearing became superfluous. Defendants should not be deprived of their right to prove compliance with section 7031, subdivision (e) merely because the trial court chose to defer the matter and they prevailed at trial.[337] The sole case cited by JCC in support,[338] is wholly inapposite.

The court also declined JCC's invitation to find as a matter of law that the Jacobs entities failed to comply with section 7031, subdivision (e).To demonstrate substantial compliance, a contractor must show it was licensed prior to performing, acted reasonably and in good faith to maintain its license, was unaware of any failure of licensure upon commencement of performance, and acted promptly and in good faith to reinstate its license upon learning it was invalid.[339] As the trial court anticipated in its ruling, this demonstration may require the presentation of evidence on matters that were not directly relevant to the issues before the jury. Defendants are entitled to a full evidentiary hearing on the issues relevant to the elements of substantial compliance under subdivision (e).

**[ii]  Nature of Hearing on Remand.**  In ruling that defendants have not waived their right to a substantial evidence hearing, the court assumed that section 7031, subdivision (e) requires resolution of the issue by a judge, rather than jury. That appears to have been defendants' assumption in seeking such a hearing from the trial court. Rather than rely on an unexamined assumption, however, the court asked the parties for supplemental briefing regarding the nature of the hearing to be conducted on remand. Reviewing the issue de novo,[340] the court concluded that the court's assumption was correct. On remand, the substantial evidence hearing must be conducted by the court.

Section 7031, subdivision (e) states that "the court may determine that there has been substantial compliance with licensure requirements under this section if

---

[337] *See Pacific Caisson & Shoring*, 198 Cal. App. 4th at 681, 693-96 (where court failed to address issue of substantial compliance in granting summary judgment, contractor was entitled to remand for a trial on the issue).

[338] Maxwell v. Powers, 22 Cal. App. 4th 1596 (1994).

[339] Maxwell v. Powers, 22 Cal. App. 4th 1596 (1994).

[340] Hopkins v. Kedzierski, 225 Cal. App. 4th 736, 744 (2014).

it is shown at an evidentiary hearing" that the contractor satisfied the statutory requirements. Based on this language, there is little room for doubt that the legislature intended the determination of substantial compliance to be made by a judge, rather than a jury. The language of the legislature's instruction, that "the court" make the determination after an "evidentiary hearing," is ordinarily used to indicate resolution by a judge.[341] Reflecting trial courts' similar understanding of this language, the statutory substantial compliance determinations reviewed in reported appellate decisions have been made by judges, rather than juries.[342]

This conclusion is reinforced by the equitable nature of the substantial compliance doctrine. Equitable matters are traditionally reserved for resolution by the court.[343] Substantial compliance, a doctrine established long before its adoption in the context of the CSLL, is considered to arise in equity.[344] Given the equitable nature of the substantial compliance doctrine, it is unsurprising that the legislature would assign its determination to the court, rather than a jury.

Defendants contend that, regardless of the legislature's intent, they have a constitutional right to the jury determination of substantial compliance. "[T]he state constitutional right to a jury trial 'is the right as it existed at common law in 1850, when the Constitution was first adopted.' [Citations.] [¶] 'As a general proposition, "[T]he jury trial is a matter of right in a civil action at law, but not in equity." [Citations.]' [Citation.] '[I]f the action is essentially one in equity and the relief sought "depends upon the application of equitable doctrines," the parties are not entitled to a jury trial.' [Citation.] And 'if a proceeding otherwise identifiable in some sense as a "civil action at law" did not entail a right to jury trial under the common law of 1850, then the modern California counterpart of that proceeding will not entail a constitutional right to trial by jury.'"[345]

Defendants' counterclaim for payments withheld under the contract was asserted under section 7031, but it was premised on the contract. The court therefore assumed for purposes of argument that it was legal in nature. Although disgorgement is ordinarily viewed as an equitable remedy,[346] when, as here, "liability

---

[341] Mendoza v. Ruesga, 169 Cal. App. 4th 270, 285 (2008); *e.g.*, Evid. Code § 402 (preliminary determinations of evidence admissibility to be made by "court" out of the presence of jury); Cal Civ. Proc. Code §§ 116.520, 116.610 ("court" to hear matters in small claims court).

[342] *E.g.*, Oceguera v. Cohen, 172 Cal. App. 4th 783, 788-89 (2009); Construction Fin. v. Perlite Plastering Co., 53 Cal. App. 4th 170, 174 (1997).

[343] *See generally* Hoopes v. Dolan, 168 Cal. App. 4th 146, 155-56 (2008) (*Hoopes*).

[344] *See, e.g.*, Knapp Dev. & Design v. Pal-Mal Props., Ltd., 173 Cal. App. 3d 423, 436 (1985) (referring to "equitable considerations" in connection with § 7031 substantial compliance); Roth v. Morton's Chef Servs., Inc., 173 Cal. App. 3d 380, 387 (1985) (substantial compliance is an "equitable defense" in a wrongful detainer action); Hill v. Newkirk, 26 Cal. App. 4th 1047, 1059 (1994) (labeling substantial compliance an "equitable doctrine" as a defense to failure to comply with California Tort Claims Act); Knight v. Black, 19 Cal. App. 518, 525-26 (1912) (substantial compliance, asserted to avoid forfeiture of a lease, "appeals to the equity side of the court").

[345] Franchise Tax Bd. v. Superior Ct., 51 Cal. 4th 1006, 1010 (2011).

[346] Cruz v. PacifiCare Health Sys., Inc., 30 Cal. 4th 303, 307, 317-18 (2003).

is definite and damages may be calculated without an accounting, the action is legal," even though the relief is in the nature of disgorgement.[347] JCC's cause of action is therefore likely legal, as well.

That is not the end of the issue. As *Hoopes* noted, "Complications arise when legal and equitable issues (causes of action, requested remedies, or defenses) are asserted in a single lawsuit."[348] In that situation, "The lawsuit is rarely treated as a single unit for purposes of determining the right to a jury trial. [Citations.] In most instances, separate equitable and legal issues are 'kept distinct and separate,' with legal issues triable by a jury and equitable issues triable by the court."[349]

When equitable defenses are interposed to a legal cause of action, the "proper rule" is for the court to hear and dispose of the equitable defenses first, before submitting the legal claim to a jury.[350] Alternatively, the court may try all issues in one proceeding, with the jury sitting in an advisory role with respect to factual issues applicable to the equitable issue.[351] In that circumstance, it remains "the duty of the trial court to make its own independent findings. [Citation.]There is no authority for asking a jury's advice as to 'whether injustice can only be avoided by enforcing the promise' or, more generally, whether the equitable doctrines of promissory estoppel or unclean hands should be applied."[352] Whichever approach is adopted, equitable issues retain their character, despite being raised in the context of a legal claim. A litigant has no constitutional right to a jury determination of an equitable issue merely because it is raised in the context of a claim at law.

Defendants argue the substantial compliance doctrine should be viewed as arising at law in these circumstances because the doctrine "goes to [Management's] capacity to recover under the contract." In making their argument, defendants equate "capacity to recover" with "capacity to contract" and argue the latter is an element of their cause of action at law for breach of contract. Contrary to defendants' premise, however, capacity to contract and capacity to recover are quite different concepts. Capacity to contract refers to a party's power to enter into a binding contract, and it ordinarily depends upon an individual's age and mental soundness.[353] Defendants suggest no reason why a contractor lacking a

---

[347] American Master Lease LLC v. Idanta Partners, Ltd., 225 Cal. App. 4th 1451, 1483 (2014).

[348] *Hoopes,* 168 Cal. App. 4th at 156.

[349] *Hoopes,* 168 Cal. App. 4th at 156.

[350] Swasey v. Adair, 88 Cal. 179, 180 (1891) (*Swasey*); *Hoopes,* 168 Cal. App. 4th at 157 ("better practice" is for the court to decide equitable issues first); Stephen Slesinger, Inc. v. Walt Disney Co., 155 Cal. App. 4th 736, 763 (2007).

[351] A-C Co. v. Security Pac. Nat'l Bank, 173 Cal. App. 3d 462, 473 (1985); *but see Swasey*, 88 Cal. at 181 (equitable defense that could be asserted in independent suit against the plaintiff must be heard first).

[352] *A-C Co.,* 173 Cal. App. 3d at 474.

[353] Restatement (Second) of Contracts § 12, p.30; Cal. Civ. Code §§ 38, 39, 1556, 1557.

license is legally unable to contract. While, as a result of section 7031, the contractor cannot use the courts to enforce payment if performance of its contract requires a license, the contract itself is not void or voidable for lack of capacity. The argument therefore provides no basis for concluding substantial compliance is a legal doctrine as asserted in Management's counterclaim.

Compliance with the CSLL can fairly be characterized as an element of defendants' cause of action for breach,[354] but that alone does not make substantial compliance a legal doctrine. Rather, in that context, substantial compliance is an equitable doctrine asserted by defendants to permit recovery in spite of their inability to prove CSLL compliance, in much the same way the doctrine can be asserted to excuse a failure to comply with the Tort Claims Act.[355] Alternatively, as asserted by defendants in response to JCC's claim for disgorgement, substantial compliance is an equitable defense to JCC's claim. Either way, the doctrine is equitable in nature. Accordingly, defendants have no constitutional right to its determination by a jury.

### [c]   Attorney Fees

The Jacobs entities are not entitled to attorney fees because they are no longer the prevailing party, but the court would have reversed the award anyway as unauthorized by the contractual provisions relied upon by defendants. The court reviewed the legal basis for the attorney fee award de novo.[356]

There is no prevailing party attorney fees clause in any of the parties' contractual documents.Defendants sought attorney fees under a standard indemnity clause in the contract, under which Facilities agreed to indemnify JCC against claims arising from, among other things, Facilities' breach of the contract or its violation of law.The clause included attorney fees as one of the costs that Facilities agreed to indemnify. Although the indemnity clause imposed a duty only on Facilities, defendants argued it should be found to impose a mutual attorney fees obligation under Civil Code section 1717, subdivision (a).

In addition, defendants sought attorney fees under the guaranty executed by Jacobs at the time of the assignment, which provided that Jacobs guaranteed the payment of "obligations" by Facilities and Management. The term "obligations" was defined to include "any and all costs and expenses, including attorney fees and costs, incurred by [JCC] in enforcing the Contract or this Parent Guaranty." Again, defendants argued the reference to attorney fees imposed a mutual obligation.

---

[354] Cal. Bus. & Prof. Code § 7031, subd. (a)).

[355] *See* Hill v. Newkirk, 26 Cal. App. 4th at 1059.

[356] California Wholesale Material Supply, Inc. v. Norm Wilson & Sons, Inc., 96 Cal. App. 4th 598, 604 (2002).

The indemnity provision in the contract is an ordinary indemnity clause. The general rule is "the inclusion of attorney fees as an item of loss in a third-party claim-indemnity provision does not constitute a provision for the award of attorney fees in an action on the contract" because "an indemnity clause generally obligates the indemnitor to reimburse the indemnitee for any damages the indemnitee becomes obligated to pay third persons.[357] To find a right to attorney fees in a direct action under an ordinary indemnity clause, such as the clause in the contract, would invest every agreement containing an indemnity clause with an attorney fees clause, even if, as occurred here, the parties omitted such a clause. This is particularly inappropriate because Civil Code section 1717, which governs the award of contractual attorney fees, applies only when the contract "*specifically* provides that attorney's fees and costs, which are incurred to enforce that contract, shall be awarded either to one of the parties or to the prevailing party."[358] The indemnity clause in the contract does not "specifically" refer either to actions to enforce the contract or to the prevailing party.

Defendants cite two decisions in which attorney fees were awarded in direct actions under indemnity clauses, *Zalkind v. Ceradyne, Inc.*[359] and *Wilshire–Doheny Associates, Ltd. v. Shapiro.*[360] Both decisions recognized that indemnity clauses generally cover only third-party claims, but they also held each clause must be interpreted individually to determine whether direct actions were intended to be included as well.[361] In both decisions, the court described at length the unique contractual terms indicating an intent to permit recovery in the particular direct action at issue.[362] There is no similar language here. The contract's indemnity clause is a garden variety clause that must be interpreted according to the ordinary rule.

Similarly, the guaranty contained no clause "specifically provid[ing] that attorney's fees and costs, which are incurred to enforce that contract, shall be awarded either to one of the parties or to the prevailing party."[363] The guaranty merely provided that Jacobs would pay any obligation incurred by the other Jacobs entities under the contract. There is no reason to believe the guaranty, the purpose of which was merely to ensure the payment of any debts to JCC of the other two Jacobs entities, was intended to expand their obligations under the contract by creating a right to attorney fees not otherwise available under the contract—in other words, to permit an award of attorney fees under circumstances in which the contract itself did not permit such an award. On the

---

[357] Carr Bus. Enters., Inc. v. City of Chowchilla, 166 Cal. App. 4th 14, 20 (2008) (denying direct action attorney fees under a standard indemnity clause).

[358] Cal. Civ. Code § 1717, subd. (a) (italics added).

[359] 194 Cal. App. 4th 1010 (2011).

[360] 83 Cal. App. 4th 1380 (2000).

[361] *Zalkind*, 194 Cal. App. 4th at 1023-24; *Wilshire–Doheny*, 83 Cal. App. 4th 1396.

[362] *Zalkind*, 194 Cal. App. 4th at 1027-29; *Wilshire–Doheny*, 83 Cal. App. 4th at 1397.

[363] Cal. Civ. Code § 1717, subd. (a).

contrary, the guaranty specifically provided that Jacobs's liability under the guaranty was not to be greater or less than Facilities' and Management's liability under the contract. The court declined to construe the guaranty to create an independent right to attorney fees beyond the rights created by the contract.

## [D]   Disposition

The judgment of the trial court is reversed. The matter is remanded to the trial court for an evidentiary hearing on substantial compliance pursuant to section 7031, subdivision (e).If the Jacobs entities are successful in demonstrating statutory substantial compliance, the trial court shall reinstate the judgment. If defendants are unsuccessful, the trial court shall enter judgment against defendants in the amount of $18,331,911, plus taxable costs and interest, if appropriate. Unless the prevailing party can demonstrate a valid basis for an award of attorney fees other than those already asserted by the Jacobs entities, it shall not be awarded attorney fees. JCC shall recover its costs on appeal.

## § 12.05   UTAH CASES

### [A]   Mechanic's Liens—Owner's Right to Recover Attorney Fees Following Successful Challenge of Lien

In *Reev & Associates, Inc. v. Kye Tanner*,[364] a contractor, who was retained by developer with plan to create residential subdivision, filed two mechanics' liens on real property, seeking payment from landowners for completed work. The Second District Court, Ogden Department ruled that liens were invalid and that contractor's unjust enrichment claim failed and denied landowners' claim for attorney fees. Landowners appealed and contractor cross-appealed.

The court of appeals held that:

(1)   Landowners were entitled to attorney fees;
(2)   Landowners were not entitled to statutory damages;
(3)   Evidence supported findings that developer was not landowners' agent and that landowners did not directly authorize contractor's work; and
(4)   Agency relationship between developer and landowners was required before property could have been subject to liens.

### [1]   Opinion

The owners of real property contracted to sell their land to a developer with a plan to create a residential subdivision. The developer retained a third-party

---

[364] 2015 UT App 166.

contractor to undertake the tasks necessary for the project to receive county approval. While the contractor was completing its work, the developer's financiers got cold feet. The developer then sought a reduction in the price of the land to appease them. During this time, the developer failed to pay the contractor, but the contractor continued working on the project, in apparent hope that the landowners and developer would reach an agreement. The financiers eventually backed out, the land sale fell through, and the project ground to a halt. The contractor then filed two mechanics' liens on the real property, seeking payment from the landowners for the completed work. After a bench trial, the district court ruled that (1) the liens were invalid because the contractor had worked only for the developer, who was not an agent of the landowners and (2) the contractor's unjust-enrichment claim failed because the contractor had not shown the value of the benefit conferred. The district court also denied the landowners' claim for attorney fees after determining that, while the liens were invalid, they were neither brought in bad faith nor abusive.

Despite largely prevailing at trial, the landowners appealed. They contended that they defeated the lien and were therefore statutorily entitled to an award of attorney fees. They also contended that the unjust-enrichment claim should have failed on more grounds than those the district court found. The contractor cross-appealed, arguing that the liens were valid because the landowners consented to or authorized the work the contractor performed. The court reversed in part and affirmed in part and remanded the case to the district court to calculate and award attorney fees.

## [2]  Background

Helen and Ralph Hansen ("Landowners") own parcels of land in Weber County via a revocable trust. In 2006, a real estate developer ("Developer") approached Landowners with a proposal to buy the land and turn it into a residential subdivision. In 2007, Landowners and Developer entered into a real estate purchase contract (the "REPC"). As part of that deal, Landowners would keep three lots in the subdivision for themselves. Shortly thereafter, Developer sought bids from contractors to test the soil, plan the subdivision, and obtain the proper permitting from the county. After selecting a bid from Reeve & Associates, Inc. ("Contractor") to perform this work, Developer gave Contractor a $4,000 retainer.

By September 2007, Contractor was working on the project. That month, Landowners met with Contractor to discuss the test holes that needed to be dug. Landowners and Contractor also discussed several of Landowners' requests for the lots they would keep. In October, Weber County approved the preliminary plans for the subdivision. Throughout the winter, Contractor continued the preparatory work and permitting processes.

The deadline for closing the transaction expired on March 10, 2008. In May 2008, Landowners and Developer agreed to extend the REPC closing deadline to June 13, 2008. This deadline also expired without the deal closing.

Throughout this time, Contractor continued working on the project and sent monthly invoices to Developer, all of which went unpaid. In February 2009, Contractor submitted plat revisions and construction plans to Weber County for final approval. By May 2009, after Developer failed to meet certain bond requirements, Contractor realized the project was dead. In June 2009, Weber County informed Landowners that the plat-approval recommendation had expired and that, if the project were to proceed, a new application process would have to begin essentially from scratch.

Contractor filed two mechanics' liens on the property, totaling $71,105.97 plus interest and fees. Contractor filed a complaint, seeking to foreclose on those liens and asserting an unjust-enrichment claim. The complaint sought the same amount, but at trial, Contractor stated that the correct amount owed was $59,891.88 plus interest and fees. Contractor attempted to explain this discrepancy by noting that it had not originally applied the $4,000 retainer to the amount owed. As the district court noted, "How application of the $4,000 retainer fee resulted in a reduction of approximately $11,000 is unclear."

The district court held a bench trial on the lien-foreclosure and unjust-enrichment claims. The court found that Developer had not acted as Landowners' agent in his dealings with Contractor and that, as a result, Contractor had performed work only for Developer. The court concluded that the mechanics' liens claim therefore failed. The court also denied Landowners' request for attorney fees. With respect to the unjust-enrichment claim, the court found that Contractor had conferred a benefit on Landowners and that Landowners had inequitably retained that benefit. However, because there was no reliable testimony of the amount of the benefit conferred, the court was "unable to award the damages requested." After the decision was issued, Landowners filed a motion asking the court to amend the judgment, seeking an award of attorney fees. The district court denied that motion.

### [3]  Issues

First, Landowners contend that the district court erred in denying their request for an award of attorney fees, because the relevant statute mandated such an award. Second, Landowners contend that the district court erred by finding that the filing of the mechanics' liens was not abusive.

Third, Landowners contend that the district court erred by finding that Contractor had conferred a benefit on them and that they inequitably retained it. Fourth, Landowners contend that the district court erred by failing to find that the mechanics' liens were untimely filed. Fifth, Landowners contend that the district court's "findings of fact on several material issues are against the weight of the evidence, clearly erroneous, and must be corrected."

Contractor cross-appeals, contending that the district court erred in determining that the mechanics' liens statute required Developer to be Landowners' agent in order for Contractor to lien Landowners' property.

## [4] Analysis

### [a] The Attorney Fee Statute

Landowners contend that the district court applied the wrong standard for determining whether they were entitled to an award of attorney fees. They assert that under the correct standard, an award was mandatory.

Utah Code section 38-1-18 (the "Attorney Fee Statute") provided that, subject to two restrictions not pertinent here, "in any action brought to enforce any lien under [the mechanics' liens] chapter the successful party *shall* be entitled to recover a reasonable attorneys' fee."[365] The district court denied Landowners' request for attorney fees, reasoning, "As there was not a valid mechanic's lien in this case, [Landowners] cannot now seek to apply [the Attorney Fee Statute]."

The court reviewed a district court's interpretation of a statute for correctness and its factual findings for clear error.[366] When interpreting a statute, the court looked first to its plain language.[367] The plain language of the Attorney Fee Statute does not distinguish between successful and unsuccessful lien-enforcement actions. The Utah Supreme Court has recognized that the Attorney Fee Statute cuts both ways, simultaneously enabling rightful lienors to recover without bearing the costs of litigation and "discouraging abuse of the lien process by creating a strong disincentive for a would-be litigant to wrongly inflict a mechanic's lien."[368] Specifically, "a mechanic's lien plaintiff who is not successful must pay the defendant's attorney fees."[369] In short, the Attorney Fee Statute's use of the phrase "any action brought to enforce any lien" contemplates actions that are ultimately unsuccessful due to the invalidity of the mechanics' lien at issue. The court therefore concluded that the district court erred in ruling that the absence of a valid mechanics' lien precluded an award of attorney fees under that statute.

Contractor responds by asserting that, in the district court, Landowners sought relief only in the form of statutory damages under Utah Code section

---

[365] Utah Code Ann. § 38-1-18(1) (LexisNexis 2010) (emphasis added).

[366] Town of Leeds v. Prisbrey, 2008 UT 11, ¶ 5, 179 P.3d 757.

[367] Salt Lake City v. Miles, 2014 UT 47, ¶ 13, 342 P.3d 212.

[368] A.K. & R. Whipple Plumbing & Heating v. Guy, 2004 UT 47, ¶ 24, 94 P.3d 270.

[369] A.K. & R. Whipple Plumbing & Heating v. Guy, 2004 UT 47, ¶ 24, 94 P.3d 270.

38-1-25 (the "Abusive Lien Statute").[370] Contractor argues that "[Landowners] attempt on appeal to change their claim and focus on [the Attorney Fee Statute]—a statutory remedy that was only mentioned in passing at the trial." Contractor urges that Landowners "should not be allowed to argue for a remedy that was not at issue at trial." This is essentially a preservation claim. Under the court's preservation rule, issues that are not raised at trial in such a way as to give the district court an opportunity to address them are generally deemed waived on appeal.[371]

Here, however, Landowners raised the issue below, and the district court explicitly addressed the Attorney Fee Statute claim. The district court's order notes that, at trial, Landowners "argued for fees and costs under both Utah Code Annotated §§ 38-1-18 and 38-1-25," i.e., the Attorney Fee Statute and the Abusive Lien Statute. Moreover, the district court referred to the Attorney Fee Statute in its ruling: "As there was not a valid mechanic's lien in this case, [Landowners] cannot now seek to apply *the statute for an award of attorneys' fees*." (Emphasis added.) Contractor urges the court to read this as a reference to the Abusive Lien Statute. But the district court considered in a separate part of the ruling whether statutory damages could be awarded under the Abusive Lien Statute. It therefore appears that the quoted portion of the order constituted the district court's ruling on the Attorney Fee Statute claim. This is reinforced by the district court's subsequent order, clarifying that "the [Landowners'] basis for requesting relief [was] two sections of the Utah Code Annotated, namely sections 38-1-18 and 38-1-25." The court therefore concluded that the issue of whether the Attorney Fee Statute applied was properly preserved for appeal.

Contractor next contends that the district court had the discretion to decline to award attorney fees, that the district court did so, and that the court acted within its discretion. In its order denying an award of attorney fees and statutory damages, the district court ruled that Landowners were not the successful party:

> [Landowners were] not the prevailing party. The court determined [Landowners] prevailed on a legal technicality, but lost on the equity of the case. [Landowners] also lost on the issue of the abusive lien. Based on the facts and equities presented, the court determined that [Landowners] were not the prevailing party.

Contractor argued that this ruling was within the district court's discretion under the "flexible and reasoned approach" to attorney fee awards that the Utah Supreme Court has extended from contract to statutory-lien cases.[372]

---

[370] *See* Utah Code Ann. § 38-1-25 (LexisNexis 2010) (current version at Utah Code Ann. § 38-1a-308 (LexisNexis 2014).

[371] Wohnoutka v. Kelley, 2014 UT App 154, ¶ 3, 330 P.3d 762.

[372] *See Whipple Plumbing*, 2004 UT 47, ¶¶ 16-26, 94 P.3d 270 (citing Mountain States Broad. Co. v. Neale, 783 P.2d 551, 557 (Utah Ct. App. 1989)).

In *Whipple Plumbing*, a homeowner hired Aspen Construction to coordinate construction projects on several of his properties.[373] Aspen hired Whipple to perform some of the tasks. Id. A dispute arose between Aspen and Whipple, and Aspen refused to pay Whipple.[374] Whipple then placed a mechanics' lien for $30,641.35 on one of the homeowner's properties.[375] Aspen counterclaimed, alleging that it had been damaged by Whipple's deficient work to the tune of $25,000.[376] The district court "calculat[ed] the consequences of the parties' respective wins and losses on their competing claims" and "awarded a net judgment to Aspen in the amount of $527."[377] Nevertheless, the district court determined that Aspen was not a "successful party" and thus not entitled to an award of attorney fees under the Attorney Fee Statute.[378] The Utah Supreme Court affirmed, noting the magnitude of the competing claims and the fact that Whipple and Aspen each enjoyed only partial success on the mechanics' lien issue before concluding that "[t]he mere fact that, once the dust had settled, Aspen walked away with a net judgment of $527, does not convince us that Aspen was the 'successful party'" under the Attorney Fee Statute.[379] However, while a district court has discretion to determine whether a party is "successful" under the "flexible and reasoned approach" formulated by this court in *Mountain States Broadcasting*, and adopted by the Utah Supreme Court in *Whipple Plumbing*, that discretion is not unfettered. "This approach requires not only consideration of the significance of the net judgment in the case, but also looking at the amounts actually sought and then balancing them proportionally with what was recovered."[380] *Whipple Plumbing* balanced the amount a subcontractor recovered under a valid lien against the amount a contractor recovered pursuant to a counterclaim.[381] The Utah

---

[373] *See Whipple Plumbing*, 2004 UT 47, ¶ 2, 94 P.3d 270 (citing Mountain States Broad. Co. v. Neale, 783 P.2d 551, 557 (Utah Ct. App. 1989)).

[374] *See Whipple Plumbing*, 2004 UT 47, ¶ 2, 94 P.3d 270 (citing Mountain States Broad. Co. v. Neale, 783 P.2d 551, 557 (Utah Ct. App. 1989)).

[375] *See Whipple Plumbing*, 2004 UT 47, ¶¶ 2-3, 94 P.3d 270 (citing Mountain States Broad. Co. v. Neale, 783 P.2d 551, 557 (Utah Ct. App. 1989)).

[376] *See Whipple Plumbing*, 2004 UT 47, ¶ 3, 94 P.3d 270 (citing Mountain States Broad. Co. v. Neale, 783 P.2d 551, 557 (Utah Ct. App. 1989)).

[377] *See Whipple Plumbing*, 2004 UT 47, ¶ 3, 94 P.3d 270 (citing Mountain States Broad. Co. v. Neale, 783 P.2d 551, 557 (Utah Ct. App. 1989)).

[378] *See Whipple Plumbing*, 2004 UT 47, ¶ 4, 94 P.3d 270 (citing Mountain States Broad. Co. v. Neale, 783 P.2d 551, 557 (Utah Ct. App. 1989)).

[379] *See Whipple Plumbing*, 2004 UT 47, ¶ 30, 94 P.3d 270 (citing Mountain States Broad. Co. v. Neale, 783 P.2d 551, 557 (Utah Ct. App. 1989)).

[380] *See Whipple Plumbing*, 2004 UT 47, ¶ 26, 94 P.3d 270 (citing Mountain States Broad. Co. v. Neale, 783 P.2d 551, 557 (Utah Ct. App. 1989)).

[381] *See Whipple Plumbing*, 2004 UT 47, ¶ 3, 94 P.3d 270 (citing Mountain States Broad. Co. v. Neale, 783 P.2d 551, 557 (Utah Ct. App. 1989)).

Supreme Court held that receiving a net judgment for $527 after counterclaiming for $25,000 did not make Aspen a "successful party."[382]

Here, in contrast, there is no indication that the district court weighed the amount sought by Contractor (either $71,105.97 or $59,891.88) against the amount actually recovered (nothing).[383] Indeed, the case currently before the court centers not on the amount recovered by each side but on the validity of the underlying liens. Landowners sought to have the two mechanics' liens encumbering their property declared invalid. They achieved that goal fully. Contractor, on the other hand, sought to enforce the liens only to have the liens declared entirely invalid. The court concluded that, at least with respect to the issue of the validity of the mechanics' liens, Landowners are the successful party under the "flexible and reasoned approach."

The Attorney Fee Statute's use of the word "shall" mandates an award of attorney fees to the prevailing party in any mechanics' lien action, including actions in which the lien is found invalid.[384] Landowners preserved a claim in the district court for such an award. To the extent that the district court determined that they were not the prevailing party, such a determination was an abuse of its discretion. Accordingly, the court remanded to the district court to calculate the reasonable amount of the attorney fees Landowners incurred in staving off the mechanics' lien claim and to award that amount to them, pursuant to the Attorney Fee Statute.

### [b]   The Abusive Lien Statute

Landowners also contended that the district court erred by concluding that the mechanics' liens were not abusive and therefore did not entitle them to an award of statutory damages under the Abusive Lien Statute. They argued that the evidence did not support the district court's finding that Contractor had a good-faith belief that it was entitled to liens in the amounts sought.

The Abusive Lien Statute criminalizes the intentional filing of "a claim of lien against any property containing a greater demand than the sum due to be recorded or filed" with the intent to cloud title, to use the lien to mulct an amount greater than that actually owed, or to procure an unjustified advantage.[385] It also

---

[382] See Whipple Plumbing, 2004 UT 47, ¶ 30, 94 P.3d 270 (citing Mountain States Broad. Co. v. Neale, 783 P.2d 551, 557 (Utah Ct. App. 1989)).

[383] See Stonecreek Landscaping, LLC v. Bell, 2008 UT App 144U, ¶ 7, 2008 WL 1822192 (explaining that, under the "flexible and reasoned approach" the district court must consider, at a minimum, the significance of the net judgment in the case and the amounts actually sought and recovered).

[384] See Utah Code Ann. § 38-1-18 (LexisNexis 2010).

[385] See Utah Code Ann. § 38-1-25(1) (LexisNexis 2010); Utah Code Ann. § 38-1a-308(1) (LexisNexis 2014).

provides that an abusive lienor is liable to the property owner for statutory damages.[386]

The court would only disturb a district court's findings of fact if they are "against the clear weight of the evidence, or if [we] otherwise reach[ ] a definite and firm conviction that a mistake has been made."[387] A district court's findings of fact "are clearly erroneous if the appellant can show that they are without adequate evidentiary foundation."[388]

Here, the district court was "not convinced that [Contractor's] actions were abusive." It found that Contractor "was acting under a good faith belief that [it was] entitled to a mechanics' lien in the amount sought." On appeal, Landowners assert that Contractor "knew [it] sought more than was actually due." The only evidence Landowners identify on this point is the fact that the filed liens totaled $71,105.97 while one of Contractor's employees testified that the amount due was only $59,891.88. Although the district court did not understand how Contractor arrived at the incorrect amount, it found that after litigation began, Contractor "realized that [its] request was for too much money, and [it] adjusted [its] demands to reflect a more accurate amount of the sum owing." This finding is at least somewhat supported by Contractor's explanation to the district court that Contractor had misapplied the $4,000 retainer in its original lien amount calculations.

There is simply no evidence in the record that Contractor inflated the amount of the lien with the intent to cloud title, to extract more from Landowners than was due, or to procure an unjustified advantage.[389] The court stated it could not agree with Landowners that the mere existence of a discrepancy between the lien amounts and the amount allegedly due renders the court's finding of good faith "without adequate evidentiary foundation."[390] Indeed, the only evidence Landowners cite is no more likely to prove bad faith than it is to prove good faith marred by bad math skills. Where the evidence is susceptible to two equally plausible interpretations, the court stated it could not say that the district court's election to believe one of those interpretations over the other is "against the clear weight of the evidence."[391] And the court was not convinced, let alone firmly or definitely, that a mistake has been made here.[392] The court indicated it would not disturb the district court's findings that the overage was a good-faith mistake.

---

[386] *See* Utah Code Ann. § 38-1-25(2) (LexisNexis 2010); Utah Code Ann. § 38-1a-308(2)(b) (LexisNexis 2014).

[387] Western Capital & Sec., Inc. v. Knudsvig, 768 P.2d 989, 991 (Utah Ct. App. 1989) (citation and internal quotation marks omitted).

[388] Western Capital & Sec., Inc. v. Knudsvig, 768 P.2d 989, 991 (Utah Ct. App. 1989) (citation and internal quotation marks omitted).

[389] *See* Utah Code Ann. § 38-1-25.

[390] *See Western Capital*, 768 P.2d at 991.

[391] *See Western Capital*, 768 P.2d at 991 (citation and internal quotation marks omitted).

[392] *See Western Capital*, 768 P.2d at 991 (citation and internal quotation marks omitted).

Consequently, the court saw no error in the district court's denial of an award under the Abusive Lien Statute.

### [c]   Unjust-Enrichment Claim

Landowners contend that the district court's "dismissal of [Contractor's] cause of action for unjust enrichment was correct, but the articulated reasons are insufficient." The district court found that Contractor had conferred a benefit on Landowners and that Landowners' retention of that benefit was inequitable but also that Contractor had failed to prove the amount of that benefit. The district court therefore determined that it was "unable to award the damages requested." Landowners argue that the district court's findings—that Contractor had conferred a benefit on them and that they had inequitably retained it—were clearly erroneous.

Although Landowners extensively analyze these claims, they do not explain how the allegedly erroneous findings affect their substantial rights. After all, the claim they argue should have been dismissed was dismissed.

"The court at every stage of the proceeding must disregard any error or defect in the proceeding which does not affect the substantial rights of the parties."[393] To succeed on appeal, appellants must show that an error occurred and that the error somehow affected their substantial rights.[394] Carrying this burden is particularly important where, as here, the appellant prevailed on the primary issue at trial yet seeks appellate review with an eye toward securing the same legal result on different grounds.

Here, Landowners do not assert that the result would have differed in the absence of the alleged errors. Nor do they explain how the alleged errors affected their substantial rights. Accordingly, the court declined to further address this contention.[395]

---

[393] Utah R. Civ. P. 61.

[394] *See* Wardell v. Jerman, 18 Utah 2d 359, 423 P.2d 485, 487 (1967) (affirming after explaining that the appellant failed to show an error whose absence would have resulted in a "reasonable likelihood that there would have been a contrary result"); Hales v. Peterson, 11 Utah 2d 411, 360 P.2d 822, 825 (1961) ("[T]he judgment should not be disturbed unless it is shown that there is error which is substantial and prejudicial in the sense that it appears there is a reasonable likelihood that the result would have been different in the absence of such error. . . ."); *see also* ProMax Dev. Corp. v. Mattson, 943 P.2d 247, 256 (Utah Ct. App. 1997) ("[A]n appellant must show not only that an error occurred, but [also] that it was substantial and prejudicial in that the appellant was deprived in some manner of a full and fair consideration of the disputed issues." (citation and internal quotation marks omitted)).

[395] *See* Utah R. Civ. P. 61.

### [d]    Lien-Timeliness Claim

Landowners further contend that the district court erred by failing to enter findings regarding the timeliness of the mechanics' liens notices. Landowners argue that Contractor failed to file the liens within 180 days of completing the preparatory work. The liens were filed on May 8, 2009. Contractor points to trial evidence that it had performed 57 hours of work in the 90 days prior to May 8, 2009. It also refers to the plat it submitted to the county on February 24, 2009. Landowners dismiss these pieces of evidence as "trivialities" and claim that their alleged ignorance of this preparatory work at the time it was performed precludes the use of that work to toll the 180-day period. Regardless of the merits of this claim, Landowners do not even attempt to explain how the district court's alleged failure to enter findings regarding timeliness affected their substantial rights, especially in light of the fact that the district court ultimately found the liens invalid for other reasons.[396] Thus, the court did not further address this contention.

### [e]    Miscellaneous Findings of Fact

Landowners contend that the district court's "findings of fact on several material issues are against the clear weight of the evidence, clearly erroneous, and must be corrected." Specifically, they argued that the existence of conflicting evidence relating to the court's findings renders the evidence supporting those findings insufficient. But the existence of a conflict in the evidence does not render the totality of the evidence insufficient to support a finding.[397] Rather, it is the role of the factfinder to examine and resolve such conflicts.[398] Here, the district court functioned as the factfinder, and it was therefore proper for the court to resolve those conflicts. In any event, Landowners do not explain the significance of the court's findings of fact or how they impact any of the district court's legal rulings. Nor do Landowners claim that the court would have reached a different result in the absence of the alleged errors.[399] The court therefore declined to address this contention.

### [f]    Contractor's Cross-Appeal

Contractor cross-appeals, contending that the district court clearly erred by finding that Developer was not Landowners' agent or authorized representative and by finding that Landowners did not authorize Contractor's work directly. Contractor further contends that the court erred by determining that the law

---

[396] See § 12.05[A][4][c], supra.
[397] State v. Black, 2015 UT App 30, ¶ 19, 344 P.3d 644.
[398] State v. Black, 2015 UT App 30, ¶ 19, 344 P.3d 644.
[399] See § 12.05[A][4][c], supra.

required an agency relationship between Developer and Landowners in order for Landowners to be subject to a lien for work Developer requested. The court reviewed a district court's interpretation of a statute for correctness and its factual findings for clear error.[400]

**[i]  The District Court's Findings.**  Contractor asserts that the district court made two clearly erroneous findings: first, that Developer was not Landowners' agent or other authorized representative and second, that Landowners did not directly authorize Contractor's work. A district court's "findings of fact are clearly erroneous if the appellant can show that they are without adequate evidentiary foundation."[401] The court indicated it would only disturb those findings of fact if they are "against the clear weight of the evidence, or if [we] otherwise reach[ ] a definite and firm conviction that a mistake has been made."[402] Logically, to show that a factual finding is against the clear weight of the evidence, an appellant must candidly recount all of the evidence supporting the finding and explain why it is outweighed by the competing evidence.[403]

Here, Contractor fails to identify the evidence supporting the district court's finding that Developer was not acting as an agent or other authorized representative. For example, the court considered subdivision applications listing the owners as Developer and Contractor, rather than Landowners. Similarly, Contractor does not mention the evidence supporting the district court's finding that Landowners had not directly authorized Contractor's work, such as the facts that Developer had to grant permission for Contractor to communicate with Landowners and that Contractor had to seek Developer's approval to undertake any modifications requested by Landowners. Instead, Contractor merely highlights and reargues the evidence it presented at trial. But the factfinder—the district court—already weighed Contractor's evidence and found it wanting. Without recounting and addressing the evidence the district court found persuasive, Contractor cannot demonstrate that the evidence relied upon by the district court was inadequate or clearly outweighed by competing evidence. The court therefore rejected Contractor's claim that the district court's findings were clearly erroneous.

**[ii]  The District Court's Conclusions of Law.**  Contractor also contends that the district court erroneously read the law to require an agency relationship

---

[400] Town of Leeds v. Prisbrey, 2008 UT 11, ¶ 5, 179 P.3d 757.

[401] *Western Capital*, 768 P.2d 989, 991.

[402] *Western Capital*, 768 P.2d 989, 991 (citation and internal quotation marks omitted).

[403] *See* Dillon v. Southern Mgmt. Corp. Ret. Trust, 2014 UT 14, ¶ 59, 326 P.3d 656; State v. Mitchell, 2013 UT App 289, ¶ 31, 318 P.3d 238 ("Formal briefing requirements aside, an argument that does not fully acknowledge the evidence supporting a finding of fact has little chance, as a matter of logic, of demonstrating that the finding lacked adequate factual support." (citation and internal quotation marks omitted)).

between Developer and Landowners before Landowners' property could be subject to a lien for work requested by Developer.

Utah Code section 38-1-3 provided that "all persons performing [qualifying work] shall have a lien upon the property upon or concerning which they have rendered service . . . whether at the instance of the owner or any other person acting by his authority as agent, contractor, or otherwise."[404] Contractor asserts that the district court erroneously determined that "in order for [Contractor's] lien claim to be valid, [Developer] had to be an express 'agent' of [Landowners]." Contractor points the court to a case in which the Utah Supreme Court noted that "the interest of the vendor cannot be subjected to mechanic's liens unless the vendor consents either through ratification or by giving the vendee implied or express authority to bind him."[405] Contractor urges the court to hold that Developer fell within the statutory category of "or otherwise" because such a reading would comport with *Burton Walker.*

The court noted that under a plain reading of the statute anyone falling into the category of "or otherwise" under Utah Code section 38-1-3 must still satisfy the requirement of "acting by [the owner's] authority."[406] But here, the district court found that Developer was not acting under Landowners' authority. The court indicated it has explained that Contractor has failed to demonstrate clear error in that finding.[407] As a result, Contractor cannot show that Developer qualifies as a person "acting by [an owner's] authority" whether that be as an "agent, contractor, or otherwise."[408] Additionally, because Contractor has not shown that the district court clearly erred in finding that Landowners did not authorize Contractor's work, the court stated it could not conclude that the district court erred in determining that Contractor's work was not performed "at the instance of the owner."[409]

### [g]   Attorney Fees on Appeal

Landowners contend that they are entitled to an award of their attorney fees incurred on appeal. The general rule is that when a party who received attorney fees below prevails on appeal, that party is also entitled to fees reasonably incurred on appeal.[410] Here, Landowners did not receive attorney fees below. However, the court indicated it had determined that the district court erred in not

---

[404] *See* Utah Code Ann. § 38-1-3 (LexisNexis 2010) (current version at Utah Code Ann. § 38-1a-301 (LexisNexis 2014)).

[405] *See* Burton Walker Lumber Co. v. Howard, 92 Utah 92, 66 P.2d 134, 136 (1937).

[406] *See* Utah Code Ann. § 38-1-3 (LexisNexis 2010).

[407] *See* § 12.05[A][4][f][i], *supra.*

[408] *See* Utah Code Ann. § 38-1-3.

[409] *See* Utah Code Ann. § 38-1-3.

[410] *See* Valcarce v. Fitzgerald, 961 P.2d 305, 319 (Utah 1998).

awarding attorney fees to Landowners under the Attorney Fee Statute. Landowners will therefore receive an award of attorney fees incurred below and have prevailed on this issue on appeal. Accordingly, they are entitled to an award of the attorney fees incurred on appeal, insofar as allocable to the mechanics' lien issue.[411] Specifically, the court awarded Landowners their attorney fees incurred on appeal relating to the issues discussed in § 12.05[A][4][a] and [f] but denied any attorney fees incurred on appeal for the issues discussed in § 12.05[A][4][b]–[e].

### [5]  Conclusion

The court affirmed the district court's finding that Developer was not Landowners' agent or other authorized representative. The court reversed the district court's denial of attorney fees to Landowners under the Attorney Fee Statute but affirmed the denial of statutory damages under the Abusive Lien Statute. The court declined to address the numerous issues Landowners prevailed upon at trial yet nevertheless elected to raise on appeal. The court remanded to the district court to calculate and enter an award to Landowners of the attorney fees they reasonably incurred below. The court directed the district court on remand to calculate and enter an award to Landowners of the attorney fees they reasonably incurred on appeal relating to the mechanics' lien issue on which they prevailed.

## § 12.06  HAWAII CASES

### [A]  Indemnity—Lower-Tiered Contractors' Duty to Defend

In *William A. Arthur v. State of Hawaii, et al.*,[412] a husband brought negligence action against Department of Hawaiian Home Lands (DHHL), real estate developer, general housing contractor, architects, civil engineers, and housing association after his wife died from head injuries sustained in a fall on land owned by DHHL. DHHL and general housing contractor filed third-party complaint against general site development contractor, and general site development contractor filed fourth-party complaint against fencing subcontractor. The First Circuit Court, Karen T. Nakasone, J., entered summary judgment against husband and addressed specific claims of contribution, equitable indemnity, and contractual defense amongst the parties. Husband appealed.

---

[411] *See* Holladay v. Storey, 2013 UT App 158, ¶¶ 49-50, 307 P.3d 584; *see also* Gardner v. Madsen, 949 P.2d 785, 792 (Utah Ct. App. 1997) (remanding for an award of attorney fees "for the issues upon which plaintiff has prevailed on appeal").

[412] 135 Haw. 149 (2015).

The court of appeals held that:

(1) Expert testimony submitted by husband to support causation element of claim against housing association was not merely speculation or conjecture and thus could create fact issue precluding summary judgment;

(2) The decision by developer's project manager to reduce height of fence on housing development property did not amount to conscious wrongdoing, as could support award of punitive damages against developer;

(3) The trial court acted within its discretion in denying husband leave to amend complaint to add general site development contractor as defendant;

(4) The civil engineering firm's duty to defend developer, pursuant to indemnity contract, was triggered at outset of litigation against developer;

(5) Under "pass-through" indemnity provision of contract between general contractor and fencing subcontractor, subcontractor had duty to defend parties indemnified by general contractor in separate contract; and

(6) Indemnity provision of contract between general housing contractor and developer did not constitute assumption of developer's obligations to DHHL under separate contract between developer and DHHL.

## [1]  Opinion

This case arises out of an incident that occurred on or about November 10, 2003, and resulted in an alleged wrongful death, at the Kalawahine Streamside Housing Development ("Project"). The Project is located in Honolulu on 27 acres of land owned by Defendant/Appellee/Third Party Plaintiff/Cross-Appellee State of Hawai'i Department of Hawaiian Home Lands ("DHHL"). Plaintiffs/Appellees/ Appellants/Cross-Appellees William A. Arthur, Sr. (William Arthur), individually and the Estate of Mona Arthur, through William A. Arthur, as Personal Representative (collectively, "Arthur") brought suit against DHHL, the developer Defendant/ Appellee/Third Party Plaintiff/Cross-Appellee Kamehameha Investment Corporation ("KIC"), the general housing contractor Defendant/Appellee/Cross-Appellant Coastal Construction Co., Inc. ("Coastal"), the architecture firm Defendant/Appellee/Cross-Appellee/Appellant Design Partners, Inc. ("Design Partners"), the civil engineers Defendants/Appellees/Cross-Appellants Sato and Associates, Inc. and Daniel S. Miyasato (collectively, "Sato"), and Defendant/ Appellee Association of Kalawahine Streamside Association (AOAO) (collectively, "Defendants"). KIC and DHHL each filed a third-party complaint for indemnification and contribution against the general site development contractor, Third-Party Defendant/Appellee/Fourth-Party Plaintiff/Cross-Appellee Kiewit Pacific Company ("Kiewit") Kiewit filed a fourth-party complaint against the subcontractor who furnished and installed a chain-link fence, Fourth-Party Defendant/Appellant/Appellee/Cross-Appellee Pacific Fence Inc. ("Pacific Fence"). DHHL, KIC, Design Partners, Coastal, AOAO, Sato, Kiewit, and Pacific Fence ("Defendant Parties") also filed counterclaims or cross-claims for indemnification and contribution.

On April 2, 2013, the Amended Final Judgment ("Amended Final Judgment") and underlying orders were entered in the Circuit Court of the First Circuit ("circuit court"). The Amended Final Judgment superseded the Judgment filed on January 9, 2012, and was entered in favor of DHHL, KIC, Design Partners, Coastal, AOAO, and Sato and against Arthur. The Amended Final Judgment was also entered in favor of Kiewit and against KIC in the third-party complaint, and in favor of Pacific Fence and against Kiewit in the fourth-party complaint. The Amended Final Judgment provided judgment on specific claims of contribution, equitable indemnity, and contractual defense amongst the parties. Three appeals and two cross-appeals resulted from the complaint filed by Arthur on November 4, 2005 ("Arthur's complaint") On June 4, 2013, this court filed an order consolidating appeal case nos.[413]

On appeal, Arthur contends the circuit court erred by:

(1) Granting AOAO's motion for summary judgment on any and all claims asserted by plaintiffs due to lack of causation;
(2) Granting KIC's motion for partial summary judgment as to plaintiff's claim for punitive damages; and
(3) Denying Arthur's motion for leave to file a complaint against Kiewit.

On appeal, Pacific Fence contends the circuit court erred by:

(1) Granting Kiewit's motion for partial summary judgment in 2007, which included the holding, "[a]ny obligation Kiewit has to defend KIC and [Sato] passes through Kiewit, as a matter of law, to Pacific Fence."
(2) Granting KIC's motion for partial summary judgment in 2010, which included the holding that Pacific Fence had a joint and several duty to defend KIC from February 9, 2006;
(3) Granting KIC's motion regarding Coastal in 2010;
(4) Granting KIC's motion regarding Design Partners;
(5) Granting KIC's motion for partial summary judgment regarding Kiewit and Sato in 2010;
(6) Granting Kiewit's motion in 2010, which included the holding that Kiewit's obligation to reimburse KIC and/or make future payments for KIC's defense fees and costs passed through Kiewit as a matter of law to Pacific Fence; and
(7) Holding that Pacific Fence was required to pay KIC fees and costs incurred for periods and in percentages set forth in an exhibit to the Amended Final Judgment.

---

[413] CAAP-13-0000531, CAAP-13-0000551, and CAAP-13-0000615 under case no. CAAP-13-0000531.

On cross-appeal, Sato contends the circuit court erred by:

(1) Holding that Sato had a joint and several duty to defend KIC as of December 15, 2005;

(2) Finding that Sato was obligated to pay KIC fees or costs; and

(3) Finding that Sato had a contractual duty to indemnify and defend KIC and a joint and several duty to defend KIC.

On cross-appeal, Coastal contends the circuit court erred by holding that:

(1) Coastal and Kiewit assumed KIC's contractual duty to defend DHHL in litigation and thus relieved KIC from obligations to defend DHHL;

(2) KIC's contractual duty to defend DHHL included defense of claims regarding the negligence or willful acts, omissions, failure to act, or misconduct of DHHL;

(3) Coastal was bound to defend DHHL against all claims asserted in litigation and not only against claims attributable to work by Coastal or its subcontractors; and

(4) Coastal had a contractual duty to defend DHHL in litigation brought by Arthur under a contract between KIC and Coastal.


## [2]  Background

### [a]  *Background on Decedent's Death*

On October 31, 2000, DHHL executed an Assignment of Lease and Consent with William Arthur and his wife, Mona Arthur ("Mona"), for their residence, located at 2273 Kapahu Street in Honolulu, Hawai'i ("Residence").

A hillside was separated from the Residence by an open concrete drainage ditch and a chain link fence. Mona accessed the hillside from the Arthurs' backyard by walking across a four-foot by eight-foot wooden board to cross the drainage ditch and then William Arthur would help her over the fence. There was no gate on the fence that allowed access onto the hillside. William Arthur and Mona went onto the hillside about three times a week, where Mona would wear sneakers with snow spikes attached to prevent her from sliding down the hill. Four or five months after moving into the Residence, the Arthurs hired someone to clear bamboo from the hillside and thereafter the Arthurs planted ti leaves and flowers, then vines and grass, allegedly to prevent erosion. William Arthur installed stepping stones on the hillside.

On the afternoon of November 10, 2003, Mona, age 66, and William Arthur, age 68, were gardening on the hillside. William Arthur left Mona on the hillside, spent five to 15 minutes getting her ice water, returned and did not see Mona. He spent two or three minutes sitting on a swing and then saw Mona's "head pop up from the ditch." Mona was lying in the ditch and asking for help. William Arthur asked his neighbors, Allen Bird ("Bird") and Mark Gilbert ("Gilbert") for help.

Bird testified that he did not see how Mona entered the ditch nor was he aware of anyone else who saw her. He also testified that the fence on the upslope side of the ditch was not damaged and that Mona's clothing was not torn. William Arthur was not aware of Mona ever slipping or falling down the hillside prior to this incident.

Mona was treated for severe head injuries, lapsed into a coma, and died on March 9, 2004. Mona was unable to provide an account of the way she fell into the ditch.

### *[b]* Defendant Parties' Contractual Relationships

By a Development Agreement dated January 16, 1998 ("KIC Contract"), DHHL engaged KIC to develop 26.5 acres of land for the Project. The KIC Contract provided: "[KIC] will be responsible for all on-site grading, fill and compaction work necessary for the Project in accordance with the plans and specifications approved by [DHHL]."

Section 17, "Indemnification" of the KIC Contract provided that KIC shall:

> Notwithstanding other provisions in this Agreement, [KIC] agrees to pay, defend, indemnify, and hold harmless [DHHL] from any and all claims of any person . . . which arise out of or in connection with the construction of any unit of the Project, the sale of the units in the Project or any design or construction defects which arise or are made within one (1) year after completion.
>
> [KIC] accepts all risks with respect to which [KIC] will be responsible for disclosing to purchasers and defend, indemnify, hold harmless [DHHL] against all claims made by any homeowner or other person arising out of damage resulting from such risk or from non-disclosure or. inadequate disclosure.
>
> [KIC] shall be developing and constructing the Project in [KIC's] own behalf and shall pay, indemnify, defend, and hold [DHHL] harmless from all claims, demands, lawsuits, judgments deficiencies, damages (whether paid by [DHHL] as part of a settlement or as a result of a judgment) and expenses, including attorney's fees and all costs of suit, made against [DHHL] or incurred or paid by [DHHL] arising out of or in connection with [KIC's] development and construction of the Project.
>
> Section 17 shall not cover the negligence or willful acts, omissions, failure to act, or misconduct of [the Hawaiian Homes Commission], [DHHL], or its employees and agents either related to the development of this Project or related to the completion of [DHHL's] authorized mission.

The KIC Contract also required KIC to draft or provide documents, including a declaration of covenants, conditions, and restrictions that would run with the Project land and be "legally binding upon all owners of units in the Project." Arthur would later claim that DHHL and AOAO advised homesteaders, including himself and Mona, to landscape hillsides behind their homes.

The "Declaration of Covenants, Conditions, and Restrictions for Kalawahine Streamside" ("Project DCCR") includes the following provisions:

5.02 RESIDENTIAL LOTS: USES AND RESTRICTIONS. Each Residential Lot shall be for the exclusive use and benefit of its Owner, subject, however, to the following covenants, conditions and restrictions:

. . . .

(d) Each Owner shall landscape and plant ground covering on such Owner's Residential Lot to prevent erosion and runoff. Each Owner shall maintain all Improvements erected on such Owner's Residential Lot and all landscaping and vegetation planted on such Residential Lot in good, clean and neat condition and repair. . . .

. . . .

5.09 SPECIAL CONDITIONS. The Owner of each Residential Lot, by acceptance of a Lease for such Residential Lot, shall be deemed to acknowledge, accept and agree to the-following:

. . . .

(d) STEEP SLOPES. Each Owner acknowledges and understands that such Owner's Residential Lot will have a steep slope, either uphill or downhill. Each Owner acknowledges and understands that such Owner will be responsible for maintaining and landscaping such Owner's Residential Lot in a manner that (1) will not prevent proper drainage. . . . (2) will not promote soils erosion. . . . Each Owner understands and agrees that such Owner will be responsible for maintaining such Owner's Residential Lot so that rocks and other debris do not slide or fall into any Improvements or any other portion of the Project. Each Owner understands and agrees that such Owner will be responsible for all damage and injury caused by such sliding or falling rocks and other debris, or as a result of the improper maintenance or landscaping of such Owner's Residential Lot, and agrees to indemnify, defend, and hold [KIC], [DHHL], and [AOAO] harmless from and against any claim for loss resulting from such circumstances.

In addition to hiring KIC as the Project developer, DHHL also employed its own Project manager and at least two land development engineers.

By a Project Consultant Agreement dated February 24, 1998 ("Design Partners Contract"), KIC hired Design Partners to design houses for the Project. Paragraph 7 of the Design Partners Contract provided:

7. INDEMNITY BY CONSULTANT. [Design Partners] hereby agrees to indemnify, defend and hold harmless Developer, and each of its officers, directors and employees, from and against any and all claims, demands, losses, liabilities, actions, lawsuits, proceedings, judgments, awards, costs and expenses (including reasonable attorneys' fees), arising directly or indirectly, in whole or in part, out of work undertaken by [Design Partners] outside the scope of this Agreement and/or out of the negligence or any willful act or omission of [Design Partners], or any of its officers, directors, agents or

employees, in connection with this Agreement or [Design Partner's] services or work hereunder, whether within or beyond the scope of its duties or authority hereunder. The provisions of this Section shall survive completion of [Design Partner's] services hereunder and/or the termination of this Agreement.

By a Project Consultant Agreement dated March 10, 1998 ("Sato Contract"), KIC engaged Sato as the civil engineering firm for the Project. Paragraph 7 of the Sato Contract was identical to that of the Design Partners Contract.

By a Standard Form of Agreement Between Owner and Contractor dated April 16, 1999 ("Kiewit Contract"), KIC engaged Kiewit to complete all grading and site improvements. The Kiewit Contract was executed between the owner ("KIC") and the contractor ("Kiewit"), and specified that Sato would be the architect. Under the Kiewit Contract, KIC would pay Kiewit $5,263,381.50 for work performed. Section 3.18.1 of the Kiewit Contract provided:

> [t]o the fullest extent permitted by law, [Kiewit] shall indemnify, defend, and hold harmless [KIC], [Sato], [DHHL] . . . from and against all claims, damages, losses, costs, and expenses, including but not limited to attorney's fees, arising out of or resulting from performance of the Work, provided that such claim, damage, loss or expense is attributable to bodily injury, sickness, disease or death, or to injury to or destruction of tangible property (other than the Work itself) including loss of use resulting therefrom, but only to the extent caused in whole or in part by any negligent acts or omission of the Contractor, a Subcontractor, . . . or anyone for whose acts they may be liable, regardless of whether such claim, damage, loss, or expenses is caused in part by a party indemnified hereunder.

By a Standard Form of Agreement Between Owners and Contractor dated July 26, 1999 ("Coastal Contract"), KIC engaged Coastal to build houses for the Project. The Coastal Contract contained an indemnity clause under paragraph 3.18.1 of Amendments to the General Conditions of the Contract For Construction that was essentially the same indemnity clause as in the Kiewit Contract.

By a subcontract dated October 15, 1999, Kiewit subcontracted construction of the chain link fence to Pacific Fence ("Pacific Fence Subcontract") for approximately $18,235.74. Section 11 of the Pacific Fence Subcontract contained an indemnity clause in favor of Kiewit, KIC, and DHHL, providing in pertinent part:

> Section 11. INDEMNIFICATION. To the fullest extent permitted by law, [Pacific Fence] specifically obligates itself to [Kiewit], [Kiewit's] surety, and [KIC] and any other party required to be indemnified under the [Kiewit Contract], jointly and severally, in the following respects, to-wit:
> . . . .
> (b) To defend and indemnify them against and save them harmless from any and all claims, suits, liability for damages to property including loss of

use thereof, injuries to persons, including death, and from any other claims, suits or liability on account of acts or omissions of [Pacific Fence] . . . whether or not caused in part by the active or passive negligence or other fault of a party indemnified hereunder; provided however, [Pacific Fence's] duty hereunder shall not arise if such claims, suits, or liability, injuries or death or other claims or suits are caused by the sole negligence of [Kiewit], unless otherwise provided in the [Kiewit Contract].

. . . .

(f) To assume toward [Kiewit] all obligations and responsibilities that [Kiewit] assumes toward [KIC] and others, as set forth in the [Kiewit Contract], insofar as applicable, generally or specifically, to [Pacific Fence's] work.

To the fullest extent permitted by law, [Pacific Fence] shall defend and indemnify [Kiewit], [Kiewit's] surety, [KIC], and other indemnified parties against, and save them harmless from, any and all loss, damage, costs, expenses and attorneys' fees suffered or incurred on account of any breach of the aforesaid obligations and covenants, and any other provision or covenant of this Subcontract. Notwithstanding the above, [Kiewit] at is sole discretion reserves the right to defend any one or all of the following, [KIC], other indemnified parties, . . . and itself. Such election to defend by [Kiewit] shall not in any way limit [Pacific Fence's] responsibility to indemnify and hold harmless as provided herein.

According to KIC's project manager for the Project, Elton Wong ("Wong"), "[b]ased on the input from the design professionals, it was decided that the steeply sloped portions of the higher elevations of the [Project] would be left in the natural condition." Sato's design for the Project's drainage system included:

a series of shallow (2 ft. deep) surface drainage ditches that were intended to capture the sheet flow of water from the higher elevations and divert the water around the homes. The drainage ditches are located in an eight foot wide drainage easement that runs across the backyards of the uphill properties.

Sato's plan also included a single, unbroken debris fence on the upslope side of two-foot deep surface drainage ditches, allegedly pursuant to their understanding that the fences were intended solely for the collection of debris. The height of the debris fence as originally specified by Sato was to be four feet.

Prior to 1998, Sato's plans were presented to DHHL for review and comment, as well as to the City and County of Honolulu's Department of Planning and Permitting. By facsimile dated September 2, 1998, DHHL's project manager Michele Otake ("Otake") sent handwritten comments from a DHHL land development engineer, Gerald Lee ("Lee") that included a concern regarding the four-foot height of the debris fence. On or about September 9, 1998, Wong discussed Lee's concern with Richard Fujita ("Fujita"), another DHHL land development engineer, and they "concurred that the debris fence would be reduced in height from four (4) feet to two (2) feet in order to facilitate access to the hillside and for ease of maintenance of the ditch and the associate [sic] easement." These plans, Drainage Ditch Detail for Ditches A, B, C, and D, which were Sheet C-14 of Sato's Construction Plan, were approved by DHHL and Sato.

By letter dated January 5, 1999, Wong wrote to Sato instructing him to provide comments on the construction plans revised in December 1998, including reference to "0. Sheet C–15: Change 4' high chain link fence and post to 2'." Because KIC's initial construction contractor withdrew their bid, KIC prepared a new bid package on February 24, 1999, which included plans that depicted a two-foot high fence on the upslope side of the drainage ditches. According to Wong, the change from a four-foot to a two-foot fence "was not made in order to reduce the cost of the site work contract, but rather to implement a design that was perceived to be better than the prior design in light of the purpose of the debris fence."

### [c]   Expert Testimonies

Arthur introduced expert testimonies and reports by Richard Gill, Ph.D. ("Dr. Gill") of Applied Cognitive Sciences, dated January 2, 2009 ("Dr. Gill's Report"), and by Laura L. Liptai, Ph.D. ("Dr. Liptai") of Biomedical Forensics, dated December 19, 2008 ("Dr. Liptai's Report"). Dr. Gill's Report stated the following:

> [I]t was the Court's opinion that the concrete drainage canal, its associated approximately 2 foot high fence, and the surrounding terrain . . . created an unreasonably dangerous condition at the time of [Mona's] falling incident. It was foreseeable that an incident similar to [Mona's] would occur if this defective and hazardous condition was not corrected.

Dr. Gill's Report opined the record was "replete with examples that demonstrate . . . [Defendants'] failure to conduct any meaningful safety or hazard analysis" of the drainage canal.

Dr. Liptai's Report set forth a biomedical and mechanical engineering analysis of Mona's November 10, 2003 incident based on "information provided to date . . . literature review, analysis, and [Dr. Liptai's] knowledge, experience, and education." Her report stated, "[Mona's] general orientation at impact was inverted cranial (head leading). This is consistent with the short fence acting as a trip mechanism which caused [Mona's] center of gravity to rotate over the 21" fence in an inverted cranial (head leading) posterior/lateral (backwards/side) orientation."

Dr. Liptai's Report concluded that "the short fence likely generated the tripping mechanism that lead [sic] to the inverted cranial (head leading) orientation with impact to the posterior lateral (back/side) of the cranium. The unforgiving nature of the concrete impact surface, as well as the increased fall height generated by the uncovered ditch, further contribute to the possibility of head injury."

A report by Douglas E. Young, Ph.D. ("Dr. Young"), of Exponent Failure Analysis Associates, dated November 23, 2009 ("Dr. Young's Report") was attached to KIC's motion for partial summary judgment on Arthur's claim for punitive damages, filed on March 2, 2010. Dr. Young's Report concluded that the design of the ditch and fence did not pose an undue risk to individuals who behave prudently and with proper care and warnings would not have prevented the subject accident.

In Dr. Young's March 31, 2010 deposition, he stated that by his use of the phrase "potential hazard associated with the subject hillside fence and ditch[,]" he was "referring to the inherent characteristics of these objects and structures that may cause harm to an individual or has the potential to cause harm." In his deposition, Dr. Young was asked, "with regard to the potential hazard associated with the hillside fence and ditch collectively, what were the inherent characteristics that may cause harm to an individual or has the potential to cause harm to an individual?" Dr. Young responded, "it's their proximity in terms of their locations and the kinds of interactions that individuals would use to move in those areas."

Dr. Young's Report concluded that "[t]he subject accident was not foreseeable to the [Defendant Parties]" and "[t]he potential hazard associated with the subject hillside fence and ditch was open and obvious to those who interacted with the subject hillside."

In her March 5, 2009 deposition, Dr. Liptai stated that she was asked to do a biomedical engineering analysis and affirmed that she was not asked to do an accident reconstruction. When asked, "how is it that you can say that it was a fence that was the likely tripping mechanism?" Dr. Liptai stated, "I know based on the physical evidence [of] how she landed, and I know that there's evidence, forceful evidence, in a given direction, and that is most likely consistent with the tripping mechanism of the fence."

By letter dated March 5, 2009, KIC's expert witness, Donald M. Schultz ("Schultz"), a Hawai'i developer and engineer, provided a report of his February 9, 2009 site visit and review of information related to Mona's incident at the Project. Schultz evaluated conditions of the Project and provided his opinion regarding the standard of care to be exercised by a developer in Hawai'i for a residential development. Schultz noted that KIC was responsible for providing the Project DCCR and concluded that KIC "provided reasonable, appropriate and sufficient notice, disclosure and guidance related to the existence of steel [sic] slopes and of the concrete drainage culvert, easements, and hillside rear yards of the individual lots." In regard to Section 5.09, "Special Conditions," Schultz commented that "[t]his section identifies not only that lots will have steep slopes, but that the owner is responsible for the lot's maintenance. In addition, the owners are specifically advised of their responsibility and liability in the event of the owner's improper maintenance or landscaping of the owner's residential lot." In regard to the drainage culvert and debris barrier, Schultz stated the following:

> [t]he continuity of the [debris] barrier appears appropriate as breaks in the barrier would compromise its functionality as debris could easily pass through discontinuities. Additionally, the continuous nature of the debris barrier would discourage unnecessary access into the sloping natural areas beyond. The two-foot height of the debris barrier also facilitates cleanout of debris buildup without having to enter upon the sloping lot area beyond as maintenance could be accomplished by standing in the culvert and simply reaching over the barrier. . . . A higher continuous fence on one side of the culvert presents risks mitigated by the short debris barrier.

Schultz's report was attached to KIC's motion for partial summary judgment, filed March 2, 2010.

In their response to DHHL's interrogatories, dated March 9, 2009, Arthur stated, "[n]o one was present at the time of the accident, so the manner in which [Mona] ended up in the concrete ditch is unknown."

Gary T. Yamaguchi, PH.D., P.E. ("Dr. Yamaguchi"), another KIC expert witness, submitted a report dated November 30, 2009, which provided the results of his biomedical injury analysis of Mona's accident to KIC's counsel. Dr. Yamaguchi concluded that "[t]here are an infinite number of possible ways that [Mona] could have received her injuries and fallen into the channel. It is unlikely, however, that she could have fallen backwards over the fence and struck her head on the channel, because she did not have any scratches, abrasions, or lacerations on her posterior legs."

During his deposition, Wong said that he had discussed with Sato "how [residents] would get above that property to maintain it. And if [the chain link fence] was four feet, it would be very difficult and maybe unsafe to try and climb over it. Whereas a two-foot fence would have been easier to get over and still serve the purpose of catching the debris." Wong clarified his earlier deposition by saying that he had become "aware that homeowners [in the Project] were crossing the ditch to get to the upper part of their property." Wong did not recall discussing an "alternative of placing breaks in the fence so people could travel from the lower portion of the property or the property below the drainage ditch to the property above the drainage ditch."

At Wong's deposition, Arthur's counsel asked Wong to examine Sheet C-14 of the construction plan. Wong stated, "[t]he sheet that you show on C–14 refers to a culvert, the drainage culvert, the side embankments that retains the wall, and there's a good sized [sic] drop into the side walls. So it protects people [from falling] into that area and get[ting] hurt."

[Arthur's Counsel:] So you're saying that the chain link fence shown on C-14 was four feet to protect people from falling into the ditch and getting hurt?

[Wong:] That's not a ditch.

[Arthur's Counsel:] I'm sorry. From falling into the culvert and getting hurt?

[Wong:] It's a culvert. Yes.

[Arthur's Counsel:] Is that correct?

[Wong:] Yes.

In his deposition on February 18, 2010, Kiewit's superintendent, Craig Oshimo ("Oshimo") stated that he had "asked what the intent of the fence was. And it was indicated [to Kiewit] that it was a debris barrier." In response to an inquiry into whether he asked about "the fence being two feet high because it was related to [Kiewit Contract section] 10.2.1[,]" Oshimo said, "[i]t was related to make changes to the fence design, the ditch, you know, as a whole structure. It wasn't just one issue. But knowing what the intent of the fence was, you needed to kind of have that—you need to know what the design intent of that structure is for, so you could make the appropriate changes." Oshimo also stated the following:

> When we asked the question about that drainage ditch and the fence and what the intent was, when we're [sic] told that the fence is going to be used for that, if we were told the fence was going to be used for something else and the we feel that's not a safe application for the fence, of course we're going to say something.
>
> But that's why we asked the question. We asked the question so the [sic] we can understand what we're building, and then the we build it right.

On March 4, 2010, Arthur's counsel deposed Corey Yamashita (Yamashita), a Kiewit engineer and Yamashita stated that Kiewit was "involved in reviewing designs now."

Arthur introduced "Exhibit 29," a photograph, as evidence that the two-foot-high fence was later replaced with a four-foot-high fence. Schultz, KIC's expert witness, described the four foot chain-link fence as part of the "rock fall mitigation effort" undertaken by DHHL in 2003. According to Schultz, "[s]ite observations confirm this four-foot intermittent chain link fence does not function as intended by the original design of the debris barrier" and was "not nearly as effective as the original [two foot continuous] debris barrier. . . ." Arthur argued that its reference to the installation of a new, higher fence, was not inadmissible because "measures that are taken after an event but that are predetermined *before* the event are not 'remedial' under [Hawai'i Rules of Evidence] Rule 407, because they are not intended to address the event."[414] Arthur argued that Exhibit 29 would not constitute inadmissible evidence of subsequent remedial measures because Defendant Parties did not submit evidence that this was the intent of the alleged increased height of the fence.

---

[414] Ranches v. City & Cnty. of Honolulu, 115 Haw. 462, 467-68, 168 P.3d 592, 597-98 (2007) (emphasis in original).

### [d]  Procedural History

On November 8, 2005, Arthur filed a First Amended Complaint ("First Amended Complaint") against DHHL as the fee owner of the property, KIC as the developer for the Project within which the Residence was located, Design Partners as the architect of the Project, Coastal as the general contractor for the Project housing, AOAO who reviewed and controlled the design and development of each property, and Sato as the licensed engineer who prepared the construction plan for the Project. Kiewit, the general contractor for the Project site development, and Pacific Fence were not named in the First Amended Complaint.

By letters dated December 1, 2005 and December 15, 2005, KIC tendered claims to Kiewit and Sato. KIC's letters stated that KIC fully expected Kiewit, Sato, "and/or its insurer(s) to defend and fully indemnify KIC with respect to the allegations in the [First Amended Complaint]."

Similar cross-claims were filed as follows:

(1) December 5, 2005 by Design Partners against DHHL, KIC, AOAO, Coastal, and Sato, alleging that any injuries or damages to Arthur were the result of cross-claim Defendants' negligence or legal fault and, if Design Partners were found liable to Arthur, that cross-claim Defendants owed Design Partners indemnity and/or contribution;

(2) December 9, 2005 by AOAO against DHHL, KIC, Design Partners, Coastal, and Sato;

(3) December 9, 2005 by Sato against DHHL, KIC, Design Partners, Coastal, and AOAO;

(4) December 20, 2005 by Coastal against DHHL, KIC, Design Partners, AOAO, and Sato; [JROA doc 71 at 174]

(5) December 21, 2005 by KIC against DHHL, Design Partners, Coastal, AOAO and Sato;

(6) January 12, 2006 by DHHL against KIC, Design Partners, Coastal, AOAO, and Sato;

(7) January 31, 2006 by Kiewit against DHHL, Design Partners, Coastal, AOAO, and Sato;

(8) February 7, 2006 by AOAO against Kiewit and Pacific Fence;

(9) February 9, 2006 by KIC against Pacific Fence, which KIC later contended constituted sufficient notice of Pacific Fence's duty to defend. KIC requested the circuit court declare that Pacific Fence owed a joint and several duty to defend DHHL and KIC with respect to Arthur's allegations; and

(10) February 16, 2006 by Pacific Fence against DHHL, KIC, Coastal, Design Partners, AOAO, and Sato.

On December 21, 2005, KIC filed a third-party complaint against Kiewit, claiming Kiewit owed a contractual duty to defend and indemnify KIC. KIC alleged that Kiewit had "agreed to and did perform site work and infrastructure construction relating to the Project, including but not limited to the construction of improvements which [Arthur] allege[s] herein was negligently performed."

On January 12, 2006, DHHL filed a third-party complaint against Kiewit alleging negligence in performing work on the Project in 1999.

On January 31, 2006, Kiewit filed a counterclaim against KIC and a fourth-party complaint against Pacific Fence.

By letter dated February 9, 2006, Kiewit tendered the defense and indemnity of claims against Kiewit to Pacific Fence.

On February 16, 2006, Pacific Fence filed counterclaims against Kiewit.

By letter dated March 1, 2006, KIC tendered their claims to Kiewit to Pacific Fence.

By letter dated March 6, 20,06, DHHL tendered defense and indemnification of DHHL to KIC.

By letter dated March 29, 2006, KIC tendered the defense of DHHL, previously tendered to KIC, over to Kiewit.

By letter dated April 18, 2006, Kiewit tendered KIC's tender of DHHL's tender of its defense and indemnification to Pacific Fence.

By letters dated April 24, 2006, Kiewit and Sato separately responded to KIC's tender of its defense and, according to KIC's counsel, agreed to participate on a pro-rata basis in KIC's defense subject to conditions.

By separate letters dated May 4, 2006 and July 26, 2006, Pacific Fence's insurer, Island Insurance Co. (Island Insurance) agreed to provide a defense to Kiewit and a defense to KIC and DHHL.

On January 10, 2007, DHHL moved for partial summary judgment against KIC, requesting the circuit court find that KIC was contractually obligated to indemnify and defend DHHL under Section 17 of the KIC Contract.

On February 3, 2007, Arthur filed responses to KIC's interrogatories. Arthur noted that DHHL had "requested that the area [behind their residence] be maintained and cleaned" and referred to AOAO guidelines.

On March 5, 2007, KIC filed its own motion for partial summary judgment, requesting the circuit court find that Coastal and Design Partners each owed a duty to defend and indemnify KIC under the Coastal Contract and Design Partners Contract. KIC further requested the circuit court find that Design Partners, Kiewit, Sato, and Coastal had a duty to defend DHHL. KIC argued that the intent of the indemnification provisions in its contracts with these other parties was to pass the duty to indemnify and defend against any third-party claims, including but not limited to claims of [Arthur] and DHHL, to the persons or entities performing the actual design and construction work from which a claim might be made. KIC was in a "sandwich" position between DHHL and KIC's consultants and contractors. By contract, KIC ensured that it would not be held "holding the bag," including the "defense bag," for the parties that actually performed the design and construction work.

On March 23, 2007, oppositions to KIC's motion for partial summary judgment were filed by Sato, Design Partners, and Coastal. Sato argued that it was already participating in the defense of KIC on a conditional basis and, based on correspondence between Sato's counsel and KIC's counsel, Sato did not owe the other party any duty to defend or indemnify. Design Partners cited Arthur's inter-rogatory responses in support of its argument that the architectural services that Design Partners provided for the Project were unrelated to Arthur's claims of neg-ligent design, construction, and maintenance of the hillside, debris fence, and cul-vert. On March 23, 2007, Coastal filed its opposition to KIC's motion for partial summary judgment.

On March 29, 2007, Coastal filed its motion for summary judgment on KIC's cross-claim, in which Coastal sought a determination that it did not owe duties of defense or indemnification under the Coastal Contract.

On March 30, 2007, Coastal filed its motion for summary judgment on Arthur's First Amended Complaint. Coastal stated that under the Coastal Con-tract it had been responsible for only the construction of the Arthurs' Residence and not the grading, site work, civil engineering work, or fence or culvert con-struction where Mona was found. Coastal argued that it was not liable under any of the claims alleged by Arthur.

On April 27, 2007, the circuit court granted in part and denied in part KIC's motion for partial summary judgment. The circuit court found that, because there were genuine issues of material fact regarding the cause and circumstances of Mona's accident, summary judgment was precluded at that time as to any party's right to indemnity from another party. The circuit court concluded that:

> 1. Based upon the allegations in [Arthur's] First Amended Complaint and the terms of their respective contracts with [KIC],[Design Partners] and Coastal have a joint and several duty, as a matter of law, to defend KIC with respect to the claims asserted herein against KIC;
> 2. Based upon the terms of their respective contracts with [KIC], [KIC's] duty to defend [DHHL] passes through, jointly and severally, to [Coastal] and [Kiewit] as a matter of law;
> 3. Based upon the terms of their respective contracts with [KIC], [KIC's] duty to defend [DHHL] does not, as a matter of law, pass through to [Design Partners] and Sato.

The circuit court further provided that its findings were without prejudice to Coastal's motion for summary judgment on Arthur's First Amended Complaint, and Coastal's motion for summary judgment on KIC's cross-claim.

By letter dated May 1, 2007, Sato tendered the defense of Sato to Kiewit. And Kiewit in turn tendered Sato's defense to Pacific Fence in a letter dated May 4, 2007.

By letter dated May 8, 2007, Island Insurance asserted that "Kiewit and KIC have independent duties to defend and indemnify [DHHL] which were neither delegable nor delegated to Pacific Fence" and that "Kiewit has an independent duty to defend and indemnify KIC which was neither delegable nor delegated to Pacific Fence." Island Insurance further asserted that, "Kiewit's subcontract with

Pacific Fence requires Pacific Fence to indemnify KIC against liability because of Pacific Fence's performance of work under the subcontract. The subcontract does not require that Pacific Fence indemnify KIC against liability for Kiewit's performance of work which was not subcontracted to Pacific Fence." Island Insurance made a similar assertion in regard to the tender of DHHL's defense and indemnification.

On May 22, 2007, the circuit court granted in part and denied in part DHHL's motion for partial summary judgment. The circuit court found that KIC was obligated to defend DHHL, found a genuine issue of material fact as to DHHL's contractual right to indemnification from KIC for Arthur's Complaint against DHHL, and denied DHHL's motion as to the issue of KIC's duty to indemnify DHHL.

On May 22, 2007, the circuit court denied Coastal's motion for summary judgment on the First Amended Complaint.

On June 8, 2007, Kiewit filed a motion for partial summary judgment against Pacific Fence and asked the circuit court to find that Pacific Fence had a duty to defend Kiewit in the lawsuit, to assume Kiewit's duty to defend KIC and DHHL, and to assume the duty to defend DHHL that had passed through KIC to Kiewit. Kiewit argued that under Sections 11(b) and (f) of the Pacific Fence Subcontract, Pacific Fence agreed to assume Kiewit's defense obligations to KIC and others in regard to Pacific Fence's work, even though Arthur's complaints alleged claims outside of the indemnity provisions.

On July 18, 2007, the circuit court held a hearing on Kiewit's motion for partial summary judgment. Pacific Fence argued that the circuit court's April 27, 2007 order granting in part and denying in part KIC's motion for partial summary judgment did not establish the law of the case in regard to Pacific Fence's obligations. The circuit court responded "I understand that, and I'm assuming that's why [Kiewit] brought their motion, is [sic] because it was an outstanding issue." The circuit court stated that cases Pacific Fence cited in opposition to Kiewit's arguments, which relied on *Pancakes of Hawaii, Inc. v. Pomare Properties Corp.*,[415] were "clearly distinguishable" and orally granted Kiewit's motion for partial summary judgment. Pacific Fence argued further that Kiewit's duty to defend Sato under the Kiewit Contract could not be "passed on" to Pacific Fence unless and until Kiewit acknowledged that it had a duty to defend Sato. The circuit court stated that it did not see how Kiewit could refuse to recognize its duty to defend Sato under the Kiewit Contract.

On August 8, 2007, the circuit court granted Kiewit's motion for partial summary judgment against Pacific Fence. The circuit court found that Pacific Fence had a duty to defend Kiewit, KIC, DHHL, and Sato; that any duty to defend DHHL that had passed to Kiewit, passed through to Pacific Fence as a matter of

---

[415] 85 Haw. 286, 944 P.2d 83 (Haw Ct. App. 1997)

law; and any obligation that Kiewit had to defend KIC and Sato also passed through to Pacific Fence.

On September 22, 2009, Coastal filed its renewed motion for summary judgment on the First Amended Complaint. Coastal argued that new facts had come to light since the circuit court's May 22, 2007 order denying their motion for summary judgment.

On December 3, 2009, Arthur filed a Second Amended Complaint, stating "[o]n or around November 10, 2003, [Mona] was gardening on the hillside when she slipped and fell, rolled down the slope of the hillside over a fence, fell into a drainage embankment and hit her head against the concrete walling." Arthur alleged DHHL, KIC, Coastal, Sato, and Design Partners were negligent with respect to the design, construction, and supervision of the construction of the hillside area; and that AOAO was additionally negligent with respect to inspection, maintenance, and warning regarding the hillside area, including the fence and culvert. Arthur alleged that Wong, KIC's Project manager, ordered Sato to lower the height of the chain link fence along the concrete drainage ditch from four feet to two feet thus reducing construction costs and increasing profits, and that Wong knew the fence was intended to protect people from falling into the drainage culvert. The Second Amended Complaint added a claim for punitive damages against KIC.

On February 25, 2010, the circuit court entered its "Order Granting [Coastal's] Renewed Motion for Summary Judgment on the First Amended Complaint (Filed November 8, 2005), Including Any Pending Amendment and [KIC's] Conditional Substantive Joinder,"[416] The circuit court's order provided:

> 1. Summary judgment is hereby granted and entered in favor of [Coastal] and against [Arthur].
>
> 2. Partial summary judgment is hereby granted and entered in favor of [KIC] and against [Arthur] and all other parties hereto with respect to any and all claims by [Arthur] and any other party hereto against KIC arising out of, resulting from, attributed to, connected with, or otherwise premised upon the work contracted to and/or performed by [Coastal].
>
> 3. This order, summary judgment, and partial summary judgment shall apply to, among other things, [Arthur's] claims asserted in the [First Amended Complaint] and/or the [Second Amended Complaint].
>
> 4. The foregoing summary judgment and partial summary judgment is without prejudice to and shall not effect [sic ] KIC's rights and Coastal's duties pursuant to Order Granting in Part and Denying in Part [KIC's] Motion for Partial Summary Judgment Filed on March 5, 2007, filed on April 27, 2007, except that said summary judgments extinguish [Coastal's] duty to defend KIC beyond the date of the entry of this order, summary judgment, and partial summary judgment.

---

[416] Order Granting Coastal's Renewed Motion for Summary Judgment.

On March 9, 2010, Arthur filed its motion for leave to file a third amended complaint naming Kiewit as a defendant. Arthur's proposed third amended complaint: (1) alleged Kiewit was negligent and should be subject to punitive damages because Kiewit constructed a two-foot high fence and knew it was dangerous and would naturally and probably result in injury; (2) "state[d] and summarize[d] facts adduced at" Oshimo's February 18, 2010 deposition; and (3) considered the testimony of Yamashita, Kiewit's engineer who was assigned to the Project.

On March 16, 2010, Kiewit filed its opposition to Arthur's motion for leave to file an amended complaint. On March 15, 2010, Pacific Fence filed its opposition and Sato filed its joinder to Pacific Fence's opposition on March 18, 2010. On August 26, 2010, the circuit court denied Arthur's motion for leave to file a third amended complaint, specifying that it "agree[d] with the arguments and authorities advanced by [Kiewit] in its Memorandum in Opposition filed on March 16, 2010."

On April 7, 2010, Arthur filed its opposition to KIC's motion for summary judgment as to punitive damages. Arthur attached Dr. Gill's Report, dated January 2, 2009 as "Exhibit 17," and Dr. Liptai's Report, dated December 19, 2008 as "Exhibit 18."

On April 8, 2010, AOAO filed its "Motion for Summary Judgment on Any and All Claims Asserted by Plaintiffs Due to Lack of Causation" ("AOAO MSJ"). On June 9, 2010, Arthur filed their opposition to the AOAO MSJ.

On April 15, 2010, the circuit court held a hearing on KIC's motion for partial summary judgment on Arthur's claim for punitive damages and Coastal's motion for summary judgment.

On April 26, 2010, KIC filed another cross-claim against Pacific Fence, adding claims for defense and indemnification against allegations in Arthur's Second Amended Complaint.

On May 6, 2010, (1) KIC filed a substantive joinder to the AOAO MSJ and attached the accident reconstruction report from Dr. Yamaguchi as an exhibit; (2) KIC filed a motion for enforcement of the order granting in part and denying in part KIC's March 25, 2007 motion for partial summary judgment against Coastal, and (3) Pacific Fence filed a motion for partial summary judgment on all claims asserted against it in Kiewit's fourth-party complaint and cross-claims.

On May 11, 2010, KIC filed a motion for enforcement of the April 27, 2007 order granting in part and denying in part KIC's March 25, 2007 motion for partial summary judgment as against Design Partners.

On May 24, 2010, the circuit court granted KIC's motion for partial summary judgment as to Arthur's claim for punitive damages.

On May 28, 2010, KIC filed two motions. One motion requested partial summary judgment against Sato and Kiewit and for enforcement of an order granting its motion. The other motion requested partial summary judgment against Pacific Fence.

On June 17, 2010, the circuit court held a hearing on the AOAO MSJ and motions for substantive joinder filed by Sato, Design Partners, Kiewit, and KIC to the AOAO MSJ. The circuit court found there was "no genuine issue of material fact . . . that Dr. Liptai's opinion [was] based essentially on certain assumptions" and "[o]ther than what Dr. Liptai says, there's absolutely no other forensic evidence, for example, to explain how [Mona] got from where she was up to the point in time where Dr. Liptai's opinions take over."

On August 11, 2010, Sato filed its opposition to KIC's motion for partial summary judgment against Sato and Kiewit and for enforcement of the order granting the motion, which had been filed on May 28, 2010.

On August 26, 2010, the circuit court denied Arthur's motion for leave to file a third amended complaint.

On August 26, 2010, the circuit court held a hearing on the parties' various motions. The circuit court noted the parties had not agreed upon an allocation of KIC's defense costs and therefore ordered a pro rata allocation, which did not assign KIC a share of its own defense costs.

On September 8, 2010, the circuit court granted summary judgment against Arthur and in favor of AOAO on any and all claims asserted by Arthur due to lack of causation, and granted substantive joinders by KIC, Design Partners, Sato, DHHL, Coastal, Kiewit, and Pacific Fence.

On September 16, 2010, the circuit court granted Pacific Fence's motion for partial summary judgment.

On December 28, 2010, the circuit court granted Coastal's motion for summary judgment on cross-claims for contribution and implied indemnity, which extended to all cross-claims for contribution and for equitable and implied indemnity filed since the December 3, 2009 Second Amended Complaint. This order, together with the Order Granting Coastal's Renewed Motion for Summary Judgment, relieved Coastal of tort claims and cross-claims of contribution and indemnity.

On May 27, 2011, the circuit court granted KIC's motion for partial summary judgment against Sato and Kiewit. The circuit court found that Sato had a joint and several duty to defend KIC from December 15, 2005; Kiewit had a joint and several duty to defend KIC from December 1, 2005; KIC would furnish statements for fees and costs incurred in this matter for the period from December 1, 2005 through April 30, 2011; and that Sato and Kiewit were required to pay KIC's fees and costs for specified periods and in specified percentages. Kiewit and Sato were also required to pay their respective pro rata share of KIC's legal fees and costs from May 1, 2011 until such time as KIC's exposure to Arthur "arising out of or related to the work contracted to and/or performed by [Sato] and [Kiewit], respectfully [sic] is extinguished[.]"

On May 27, 2011, the circuit court granted KIC's March 25, 2007 motion for enforcement requiring Coastal to submit pro rata payment of KIC's defense costs according to specified periods and percentages. Coastal was to pay 50 percent of KIC's defense from December 1–14, 2005 (shared with Kiewit); 25 percent of KIC's defense from December 15, 2005 through February 8, 2006; and

20 percent of KIC's defense from February 9, 2006 through February 25, 2010 (with contributions from Sato, Kiewit, Pacific Fence, and Design Partners).

On May 27, 2011, the circuit court granted KIC's May 11, 2010 motion for enforcement against Design Partners.

On July 1, 2011, Kiewit filed a motion for enforcement of the August 8, 2007 order granting Kiewit's June 8, 2007 motion for partial summary judgment.

On August 31, 2011, the circuit court held a hearing on the various motions. Counsel for Kiewit stated that Kiewit was asking for enforcement of the circuit court's August 8, 2007 order, which decided that any obligation that Kiewit had to reimburse KIC's defense costs passed through to Pacific Fence. The circuit court determined it would grant the motion "for the same reasons that were previously the basis for its ruling relative to the [KIC] motions and more or less adopts the rationale in the Pancakes case[,] at 85 Hawai'i 286, 944 P.2d 83, a 1997 decision, regarding the duty to defend and that timely enforcement in this court's mind is appropriate."

On October 3, 2011, the circuit court granted Kiewit's July 1, 2011 motion for an enforcement of the August 8, 2007 order granting Kiewit partial summary judgment against Pacific Fence. This order found that Kiewit's obligation to reimburse KIC and to make future payments for KIC's defense fees and costs passed through Kiewit as a matter of law to Pacific Fence. The circuit court required Pacific Fence to reimburse KIC for the pro rata share of defense fees and costs allocated to Kiewit within the time period specified in the May 27, 2011 order granting KIC partial summary judgment against Sato and Kiewit.

On November 17, 2011, the circuit court granted Coastal's petition for a determination of a good faith settlement. The petition found the $47,500 settlement between Coastal and KIC was executed in good faith, the settlement did not apply to claims of Coastal's obligation to defend DHHL, and that $49,459.35 would be credited against KIC's defense costs through February 25, 2010 for purposes of determining obligations of co-obligors in KIC's defense obligation.

On February 1, 2012, Arthur filed a notice of appeal from the January 9, 2012 Final Judgment in CAAP-12-0000064. On July 27, 2012, the court granted a motion to dismiss CAAP-12-0000064 for lack of jurisdiction because the January 9, 2012 Final Judgment did not specifically identify the claims on which the circuit court intended to enter judgment as required under *Jenkins v. Cades Schutte Fleming & Wright*.[417]

On April 2, 2013, the circuit court entered its Amended Final Judgment.

On April 30, 2013, Pacific Fence filed its notice of appeal in case no. CAAP-13-0000531 from the Amended Final Judgment and eight underlying orders.

On April 30, 2013, Arthur filed its notice of appeal in case no. CAAP-13-0000551 from the Amended Final Judgment and 33 underlying orders.

---

[417] 76 Haw. 115, 119, 869 P.2d 1334, 1338 (1994).

On May 1, 2013, Coastal filed a notice of cross-appeal in case no. CAAP-13-0000551 from the Amended Final Judgment insofar as judgment was granted (1) to DHHL by virtue of the "Order Granting in Part and Denying In Part [DHHL's] Motion for Partial Summary Judgment Filed on January 10, 2007, which order was filed on May 22, 2007" and the "Order Granting in Part and Denying In Part [KIC's] Motion for Partial Summary Judgment Filed on March 5, 2007, which order was filed on April 27, 2007"; and (2) to KIC by virtue of "Order Granting in Part and Denying In Part [KIC's] Motion for Partial Summary Judgment Filed on March 5, 2007, which order was filed on April 27, 2007" and "the Order Granting [KIC's] Motion for Enforcement of Order Granting in Part and Denying In Part [KIC's] Motion for Partial Summary Judgment Filed on March 5, 2007, which order was filed on April 27, 2007. . . ."

On May 2, 2013, Sato filed a notice of cross-appeal in case no. CAAP-13-0000551 from the Amended Final Judgment and orders underlying that judgment, including but not limited to the "Order Granting [KIC's] Motion for Partial Summary Judgment Against [Sato] and [Kiewit], and for Enforcement of Order Granting Motion, filed on May 27, 2011."

On May 2, 2013, Design Partners filed its notice of appeal in case no. CAAP-13-0000615 from the Amended Final Judgment, the "Order Granting In Part and Denying In Part [KIC's] Motion For Partial Summary Judgment Filed On March 5, 2007," and the "Order Granting [KIC's] Motion For Enforcement Of Order Granting In Part And Denying In [KIC's] Motion For Partial Summary Judgment Filed On March 5, 2007, As Against [Design Partners.]"

On June 4, 2013, case nos. CAAP-3-0000531, CAAP-13-0000551, and CAAP-13-0000615 were consolidated under CAAP-13-0000531 by order of this court.

### [3]  Discussion

### [a]  *Arthur's Appeal*

**[i]  Summary Judgment on Arthur's Negligence Claims Was Improper.**   Arthur contended the circuit court erred by granting AOAO's MSJ in regard to Arthur's claims of negligent construction, maintenance, construction supervision, and lack of warning.

A moving party is entitled to summary judgment if:

> the pleadings, depositions, answers to interrogatories, and admissions on file, together with the affidavits, if any, show that there is no genuine issue as to any material fact and that the moving party is entitled to a judgment as a matter of law.

Hawai'i Rules of Civil Procedure (HRCP) Rule 56(c). To survive summary judgment, a party adverse to summary judgment "may not rest upon the mere allegations or denials of the adverse party's pleading, [and] the adverse party's response, by affidavits or as otherwise provided in this rule, must set forth specific facts showing that there is a genuine issue for trial."[418] "[S]ummary judgment is proper when the nonmoving party-plaintiff 'fails to make a showing sufficient to establish the existence of an element essential to that party's case, and on which that party will bear the burden of proof at trial.'"[419]

Arthur alleged DHHL, KIC, Design Partners, Coastal, and Sato were negligent in the design, construction, and supervision of the construction of the hillside area, and that AOAO was additionally negligent with respect to "inspection, maintenance and warning regarding the hillside area, including the fence and culvert." In order to prevail in their negligence claim, Arthur would have to establish that: (1) AOAO had a duty "to conform to a-certain standard of conduct [ ] for the protection of others against unreasonable risks"; (2) AOAO breached that duty; (3) there was "[a] reasonably close causal connection between the conduct and the resulting injury"; and (4) there was actual loss or damage as a result.[420]

Arthur contends AOAO and Defendant Parties did not establish a lack of causation because they did not assert a set of facts indicating that a connection cannot be made between their breach of duties and Arthur's alleged injuries.

AOAO and Defendant Parties argued to the circuit court that Arthur would be unable to prove the causation element of his negligence claim because Arthur had admitted that the manner in which Mona fell into the ditch was "unknown." According to AOAO, because Arthur "admitted" to not knowing how Mona fell into the ditch, Arthur's causation claims require speculation or conjecture. AOAO thus argues that there is "no circumstantial evidence in this particular case, even if looked at in the light most favorable to [Arthur], that would create genuine issues of material fact." This conclusion is unwarranted for several reasons.

The court noted that causation is established when it is "more likely than not [that the defendant's conduct was] a substantial factor in causing the harm complained of. . . ."[421] This determination "is normally a question for the jury. . . ."[422] Causation may be proven through circumstantial evidence.[423] In addition, a causal

[418] HRCP Rule 56(e).

[419] Miyashiro v. Roehrig, Roehrig, Wilson & Hara, 122 Haw. 461, 475, 228 P.3d 341, 355 (Haw. Ct. App. 2010) (citing Exotics Hawai'i–Kona, Inc. v. E.I. Du Pont de Nemours & Co., 116 Haw. 277, 302, 172 P.3d 1021, 1046 (2007)) (format altered).

[420] Knodle v. Waikiki Gateway Hotel, Inc., 69 Haw. 376, 385, 742 P.2d 377, 383 (1987) (quoting W.P. Keeton, Prosser & Keeton on the Law of Torts § 30, at 164-65 (5th ed. 1984) (format altered)).

[421] Knodle, 69 Haw. at 385, 742 P.2d at 383 (quoting Bidar v. Amfac, Inc., 66 Haw. 547, 553, 669 P.2d 154, 159 (1983)).

[422] Knodle, 69 Haw. at 385, 742 P.2d at 383 (brackets, citation, and internal quotation mark omitted).

[423] Wagatsuma v. Patch, 10 Haw. App. 547, 565, 879 P.2d 572, 583 (1994).

link may be inferred from an expert's testimony in light of the evidence admitted at trial.

Arthur submitted expert testimony from which a trier of fact could reasonably infer a causal link between Defendant Parties alleged negligence and Mona's injuries.[424] Dr. Liptai analyzed the event from the point when Mona was standing next to the fence. Dr. Liptai's Report concluded that "the short fence likely generated the tripping mechanism" that led to her fatal head injuries. Her report was based on site inspection photographs, medical records, expert reports, and depositions. Because it was unlikely that Mona would have sustained a brain injury from the fall if she landed onto grass, Dr. Liptai opined "even if [Mona] had slipped on the hill, been tripped by the fence and fallen onto grass, it would be unlikely that a brain injury would have been sustained." Dr. Liptai opined "[t]he short fence is responsible for altering the kinematics that caused the inverted cranial (head leading) orientation."

The court concluded the circuit court erred by granting partial summary judgment to AOAO, KIC, Sato, and Design Partners.

**[ii]  Summary Judgment for KIC on Arthur's Punitive Damages Claim Was Proper.** Arthur contends that the circuit court erred by granting KIC's motion for partial summary judgment as to Arthur's claim for punitive damages. Arthur's Second Amended Complaint alleged that Wong, acting as KIC's agent, "ordered the fence lowered simply to increase [KIC's] profits, without consideration to the safety of persons such as [Mona]. He reduced the height of the fence knowing that residents, such as [Mona], were required to maintain the steep hillside." Arthur alleges that KIC's "overriding concern was for a minimum-expense operation[ ] regardless of the peril involved." Arthur further alleges KIC "acted wantonly or oppressively or with such malice as implies a spirit of mischief or criminal indifference" so as to warrant punitive damages.

"[P]unitive damages are recoverable in tort action based on negligence."[425] "[T]o justify an award of punitive damages, 'a positive element of conscious wrongdoing is always required.' Thus, punitive damages are not awarded for mere inadvertence, mistake, or errors of judgment."[426] To prevail in a punitive damages claim, "[a] plaintiff must prove by clear and convincing evidence that the defendant has acted wantonly or oppressively or with such malice as implies a spirit of mischief or criminal indifference to civil obligations, or where there has been some willful misconduct or that entire want of care which would raise the presumption of a conscious indifference to consequences."[427]

The court noted that clear and convincing evidence must "produce in the mind of the trier of fact a firm belief or conviction as to the allegations sought to

---

[424] Rapoza v. Parnell, 83 Haw. 78, 86, 924 P.2d 572, 580 (Ct. App. 1996).
[425] Masaki v. Gen. Motors Corp., 71 Haw. 1, 10, 780 P.2d 566, 572 (1989).
[426] *Masaki*, 71 Haw. at 7, 780 P.2d at 571 (citation omitted).
[427] *Masaki*, 71 Haw. at 16-17, 780 P.2d at 575.

be established, and requires the existence of a fact be highly probable."[428] Arthur contends that KIC's failure to issue warnings and alleviate the hazard, in combination with its alleged knowledge of the "inherent risks" of the fence, constitutes conscious indifference to consequences in support of Arthur's claim for punitive damages.

The factual allegations underlying Arthur's complaint fail to raise a genuine issue of material fact as to punitive damages. Wong's instruction to reduce the height of the fence and knowledge that residents, including Mona, would access the hillside by climbing over the fence fails to establish KIC's conscious wrongdoing.[429] Even if KIC's decision to lower the height of the debris fence to two feet was "motivated by a desire to cut costs and boost profits[,]" such a decision would not amount to a conscious element of wrongdoing necessary to support an award of punitive damages.[430]

The circuit court did not abuse its discretion by denying Arthur leave to file their third amended complaint against Kiewit.

Arthur contends the circuit court erred by denying their March 9, 2010 motion to amend their complaint to add Kiewit as a defendant.

Under HRCP Rule 15(a)(2), "a party may amend the party's pleading only by leave of court or by written consent of the adverse party; and leave shall be freely given when justice so requires." The "grant or denial of leave to amend under [HRCP] Rule 15(a) is within the discretion of the trial court and is subject to reversal on appeal only for an abuse of discretion."[431] Reasons to deny leave to amend include "undue delay, bad faith or dilatory motive on the part of the movant, repeated failure to cure deficiencies by amendments previously allowed, undue prejudice to the opposing party by virtue of allowance of the amendment, [and] futility of amendment[.]"[432]

Arthur offers no reasonable explanation for their undue delay of more than four years in seeking to file a complaint against Kiewit. Arthur was served with KIC's third-party complaint, which identified Kiewit as a party, on December 21, 2005. KIC's complaint alleged that Kiewit had performed site work and infrastructure construction on the Project, including construction of improvements that Arthur alleged were negligently performed.

---

[428] *Masaki*, 71 Haw. at 15, 780 P.2d at 574.

[429] *See* Iddings v. Mee-Lee, 82 Haw. 1, 11, 919 P.2d 263, 273 (1996) (providing the three-part test for conduct rising to the level of "wanton neglect").

[430] Ass'n of Apt. Owners of Newtown Meadows ex rel. its Bd. of Dirs. v. Venture 15, Inc., 115 Haw- 232, 296-98, 167 P.3d 225, 289-91 (2007), as corrected on denial of reconsideration (Sept. 20, 2007).

[431] Keathe Cnty. Hawaiian Elec. Co., Inc., 65 Haw. 232, 239, 649 P.2d 1149, 1154 (1982) (citation and internal quotation mark omitted).

[432] Bishop Trust Co., Ltd. v. Kamokila Dev. Corp., 57 Haw. 330, 337, 555 P.2d 1193, 1198 (1976) (quoting Foman v. Davis, 371 U.S. 178, 182, 83 S. Ct. 227, 9 L. Ed. 2d 222 (1962) (applying Federal Rules of Civil Procedure Rule 15(a)).

Kiewit contended it would have suffered delay and prejudice if the circuit court had granted Arthur leave to amend their complaint nearly five years after KIC filed their third-party complaint against Kiewit. Kiewit contends it would have to "expend additional resources to re-depose witnesses, re-depose expert witnesses both in Hawai'i and on the mainland, and retain new expert witnesses to address the direct claims of [Arthur]." The end date for discovery was April 1, 2010, three weeks after Arthur's March 9, 2010 motion for leave to amend, and would likely have to be reopened to allow for parties to conduct further discovery in light of new claims against Kiewit. Therefore, the circuit court did not abuse its discretion in denying Arthur's belated attempt to add Kiewit as a defendant.

### [b]   Sato's Appeal

Sato's appeal included the contention that *Pancakes* was wrongly decided and resulted in a "flawed" holding and conclusion. Sato urged the court to depart from precedent. The court declined to "depart from the doctrine of stare decisis in the absence of some compelling justification."[433] *Pancakes* was correctly decided. Sato contends that the circuit court erred by concluding that Sato had a joint and several duty to defend KIC as of December 15, 2005, when KIC tendered its defense to Sato. The circuit court set forth this conclusion in its May 27, 2011 order granting KIC's May 28, 2010 motion for partial summary judgment, which required Sato and Kiewit to pay KIC's fees and costs related to the Arthur case for specific periods and in specific percentages dating from KIC's tender of its defense to Sato. Sato contends that the circuit court's ruling was erroneous, among other reasons, because *Pancakes* itself was "wrongly decided." In its motion for summary judgment, KIC argued that Sato and Kiewit had a joint and several duty to defend KIC as a matter of law and that their duty to defend KIC must be determined at the outset of the litigation using the "complaint allegation rule."[434] The "complaint allegation rule" refers to the principle that "the duty to defend is limited to situations where the pleadings have alleged claims for relief that fall within the terms for coverage of the insurance contract. Where pleadings fail to allege any basis for recovery within the coverage clause, the insurer has no obligation to defend."[435] According to Sato, the Sato Contract did not require Sato to either defend or indemnify KIC and was void to the extent that it required KIC to be indemnified for its own negligent or willful misconduct. Sato contends its duty to defend and indemnify KIC, pursuant to the indemnity clause in Sato Contract, extends only to claims:

---

[433] State v. Claunch, 111 Haw. 59, 67, 137 P.3d 373, 381 (Ct. App. 2006) (internal quotation marks and emphasis omitted) (citing Hilton v. South Carolina Pub. Ry. Comm'n, 502 U.S. 197, 202, 112 S. Ct. 560, 116 L. Ed. 2d 560 (1991)).

[434] *See Pancakes*, 85 Haw. at 291, 944 P.2d at 88.

[435] *See Pancakes*, 85 Haw. at 291, 944 P.2d at 88 (citations, internal quotation marks and brackets omitted).

1. Arising directly or indirectly, in whole or in part, out of work undertaken by [Sato] outside the scope of the [Sato Contract], and/or

2. Arising out of negligence or any willful act or omission of Sato in connection with the [Sato Contract] or [Sato's] work, whether within or beyond the scope of its duties or authority hereunder.

(Emphases in original.)

Sato argues that they cannot be held liable for defense costs or indemnity obligations to KIC until wrongful conduct on the part of Sato "is shown to have occurred, and be causally related to claims asserted by [Arthur]," because the Sato Contract indemnity provision would not apply until that time.

Sato's conclusion relies on their argument that the court's holding in Pancakes was wrongly decided. In Pancakes, the court interpreted a clause in a management agreement (Responsibility Clause) between a managing agent, Pomare Properties Corporation (indemnitor-defendant), and a realty corporation manager, Sofos Realty Corporation (indemnified-defendant), which provided:

> except for the willful misconduct or gross negligence of [indemnified-defendant], [indemnitor-defendant] shall indemnify, defend and hold [indemnified-defendant] harmless from and against any and all claims, demands, losses, liabilities and damages of every kind and nature arising from any cause whatsoever when [indemnified-defendant] is acting under this Agreement or the instructions of [indemnitor-defendant] or its designated representative. . . .[436]

Pancakes held that the law governing the duty of an insurer to defend its insured under indemnity provisions of an insurance contract applied to an indemnitor's duty to defend an indemnitee under a general indemnity contract. The Pancakes appeals court decided the indemnitor-defendants' duty to defend indemnified-defendant arose when the Pancakes plaintiff (*Pancakes of Hawai'i, Inc.*) filed its complaint because: (1) some of *Pancakes'* claims did not involve "willful misconduct or gross negligence" that was excluded from the subject Responsibility Clause and (2) "portions of [the indemnified-defendant's] alleged conduct were unquestionably leasing activities that fell within the parameters of the management agreement."[437]

Expanding an insurer's duty to defend based on the "complaint allegation rule" to general indemnity contracts makes sense "because if the duty to defend was determined only after the ultimate issue of liability on each claim has been made, the case would be fully resolved before the duty [to defend] was triggered, and there would be nothing left to defend."[438] The timing and trigger of a duty to

---

[436] *Pancakes*, 85 Haw. at 289 n.2, 944 P.2d at 86 n.2.

[437] *Pancakes*, 85 Haw. at 295, 944 P.2d at 92.

[438] *Pancakes*, 85 Haw. at 291, 944 P.2d at 88 (quotation marks omitted).

defend differs from those of a duty to indemnify. In the case of indemnity agreements that limit the liability of the indemnitor with a sole negligence exception, such as the Sato Contract, "the duty to indemnify cannot be determined initially, and sometimes it cannot be determined until a verdict is rendered. Therefore, the duty to indemnify cannot be used as the standard for the duty to defend."[439]

In light of such reasoning and the lack of a competing argument in *Pancakes*, the court "discern[ed] no logical reason why the duty to defend based on indemnity contracts should not follow the same philosophy [of imposing a duty to defend at the outset of litigation] used in the insurance context."[440]

The court stated that, in its opinion, the procedure used to determine the duty to defend based on indemnity contracts can follow the same procedure used in the insurance context. If a complaint alleges claims that fall within the coverage of the indemnity provision, then, according to the complaint allegation rule, the duty to defend begins. This is separate and distinct from the duty to indemnify. Once the trier of fact makes a determination on the claims in the lawsuit, the duty to indemnify will either arise or lie dormant. Claims falling within the indemnity provision will trigger the duty to indemnify, while claims falling outside the provision will relieve the indemnitor of his or her duty to indemnify. In the court's view, this was the only equitable interpretation that gives life to non-insurance indemnity clauses and prevents indemnitors from benumbing the duty to defend until after a case has been litigated.[441]

Once an indemnitor is found to have a duty to defend, "[t]he indemnitor must bear the cost of a defense whenever any of the claims asserted may potentially come within the scope of an indemnity agreement, and the defense must continue until it is clear that the liability cannot possibly come within the scope of the indemnity."[442] Contrary to Sato's contention that its duty to defend would not be triggered until wrongful conduct on the part of Sato "is shown to have occurred, and be causally related to claims asserted by [Arthur]," Sato's duty to defend KIC was triggered upon the filing of the complaint and/or the tender of KIC's defense to Sato and that duty encompassed all claims that could potentially come within the scope of the indemnity.

The indemnity provision was valid to the extent it required KIC to be indemnified for wrongful conduct that was partly the fault of KIC.

---

[439] James E. Joseph, *Indemnification and Insurance: The Risk Shifting Tools (Part I)*, 79 Pa. B. Ass'n Q. 156, 177-78 (2008) (footnote omitted).

[440] *Pancakes*, 85 Haw. at 291-92, 944 P.2d at 88-89.

[441] *Pancakes*, 85 Haw. at 292, 944 P.2d at 89 (emphases added).

[442] *Indemnification and Insurance*, 79 Pa. B.A. Q. at 178 (citing Jacobs Constructors, Inc. v. NPS Energy Servs., Inc., 264 F.3d 365, 376 (3d Cir. 2001)); Kiewit E. Co. v. L & R Constr. Co., 44 F.3d 1194 (3d Cir. 1995); Bituminous Ins. Cos. v. Pa. Manufacturers' Ass'n Ins. Co., 427 F. Supp. 539, 548-49 (E.D. Pa. 1976).

Sato also contends that, to obligate Sato to assume KIC's entire defense would be contrary to public policy and Hawai'i law, as set forth in HRS § 431:10-222, which provides:

§ 431:10–222 Construction industry; indemnity agreements invalid. Any covenant, promise, agreement or understanding in, or in connection with or collateral to, a contract or agreement relative to the construction, alteration, repair or maintenance of a building, structure, appurtenance or appliance, including moving, demolition or excavation connected therewith, purporting to indemnify the promisee against liability for bodily injury to persons or damage to property caused by or resulting from the sole negligence or willful misconduct of the promisee, the promisee's agents or employees, or indemnitee, *is invalid as against public policy*, and is void and unenforceable; provided that this section shall not affect any valid workers' compensation claim under chapter 386 or any other insurance contract or agreement issued by an admitted insurer upon any insurable interest under this code.

(Emphasis added.)

In the first instance, KIC countered that HRS § 431:10-222 is inapposite because it concerns contracts related to "construction, alteration, repair or maintenance of a building, structure, appurtenance or appliance, including moving, demolition or excavation connected therewith" and not "professional design services." The Sato Contract, however, included preparation of plans for grading, drainage, roadways, sewage, electricity, construction cost estimates, and site work civil drawings in Sato's scope of work. Sato's work was "relative to the construction, alteration, repair or maintenance of a building, structure, appurtenance or appliance, including moving, demolition or excavation connected therewith," and thus fell under the provisions of HRS § 431:10-222.

Interpreting language in HRS § 431-453 (1970), which was nearly identical to that of its superseding statute, HRS § 431:10-222, the Hawai'i Supreme Court stated: "[n]othing on [HRS § 431–453's] face suggests a subcontractor's promise to indemnify the general contractor against liability resulting from the subcontractor's negligence may be void[.]"[443] Rather, the statute declares invalid a promisor's agreement to indemnify against liability flowing from the negligence or misconduct of persons other than the promisor, his agents or employees. And a departure from the plain and unambiguous language of the statute cannot be justified without a clear showing that the legislature intended some other meaning would be given the language.[444]

---

[443] Espaniola v. Cawdrey Mars Joint Venture, 68 Haw. 171, 178, 707 P.2d 365, 370 (1985).

[444] *Espaniola*, 68 Haw. at 179, 707 P.2d at 370 (citing Kaiama v. Aguilar, 67 Haw. 549, 553, 696 P.2d 839, 842 (1985)); *see also* Kole v. Amfac, Inc., 665 F. Supp. 1460, 1465 (D. Haw. 1987) certified question answered, 69 Haw. 530, 750 P.2d 929 (1988) ("In construction contracts, [HRS] § 431-435[sic] prohibits an indemnitor from indemnifying an indemnitee for the sole negligence of the indemnitee.").

Under *Espaniola* and *Kole*, HRS § 431:10-222 would invalidate Sato's promise to indemnify KIC against the "sole negligence or willful misconduct" of any entities other than Sato.[445] HRS § 431:10-222 does not invalidate the indemnification provision in the Sato Contract, under the circumstances of this case, because Arthur's complaint did not allege that Mona's injuries were solely the result of KIC's negligence.

HRS § 431:10-222 establishes that Sato could not be held liable for the sole negligence or willful misconduct of KIC, but it does not bar Sato's duty to defend, and possibly to indemnify, in this case because Sato, as well as the other defendants, were alleged to have been negligent. Thus, this application of HRS § 431:10-222 does not conflict with the circuit court's determination : (1) that Sato's duty to defend KIC includes all claims potentially arising under the Sato Contract and not only for those arising from Sato's negligence or willful misconduct and (2) as discussed in the prior section, that Sato was liable for defense costs when KIC tendered its defense rather than after a judicial determination of Sato's fault.

In sum, HRS § 431:10-222 restricts the scope of indemnification provisions in construction contracts, but it does not invalidate the application of the provision in the Sato Contract to Arthur's claims here, and Sato's duty to ultimately indemnify KIC and/or others is separate from its duty to defend. Under Pancakes, Sato's obligation to defend KIC extended to claims that fell outside the scope of Sato's duty to indemnify KIC.[446] For these reasons, the court concluded that the indemnification provision in the Sato Contract was not void under HRS § 431:10-222.

### [c]   *Pacific Fence's Contentions on Appeal*

Pacific Fence appeals from the following orders:

(1) April 27, 2007 "Order Granting in Part and Denying in Part Defendant and Third–Party Plaintiff [KIC's] Motion for Partial Summary Judgment Filed on March 5, 2007";

(2) May 22, 2007 "Order Granting in Part and Denying in Part Defendant [DHHL's] Motion for Partial Summary Judgment Filed January 10, 2007";

(3) August 8, 2007 "Order Granting Third–Party Defendant and Fourth–Party Plaintiff [Kiewit's] Motion for Partial Summary Judgment, Filed Herein on June 8, 2007";

(4) May 27, 2011 "Order Granting Defendant and Third–Party Plaintiff [KIC's] Motion for Partial Summary Judgment Against Fourth–Party Defendant [Pacific Fence] and for Enforcement of Order Granting Motion";

---

[445] *Espaniola*, 68 Haw. at 178, 707 P.2d at 370-71; *Kole*, 665 F. Supp. at 1464-65.
[446] *Pancakes*, 85 Haw. at 291, 944 P.2d at 88.

(5) May 27, 2011 "Order Granting Defendant and Third–Party Plaintiff [KIC's] Motion for Partial Summary Judgment Against Defendant [Sato] and Third–Party Defendant [Kiewit] and for Enforcement Order Granting Motion";

(6) May 27, 2011 "Order Granting Defendant and Third–Party Plaintiff [KIC's] Motion for Enforcement of Order Granting in Part and Denying in Part Defendant and Third–Party Plaintiff [KIC's] Motion for Partial Summary Judgment Filed March 25, 2007, as Against Defendant [Design Partners]";

(7) May 27, 2011 "Order Granting Defendant and Third–Party Plaintiff [KIC's] Motion for Enforcement of Order Granting in Part and Denying in Part Defendant and Third–Party Plaintiff [KIC's] Motion for Partial Summary Judgment Filed March 25, 2007, as Against Defendant [Coastal]"; and

(8) October 3, 2011 "Order Granting Third–Party Defendant and Fourth–Party Plaintiff [Kiewit's] Motion for Enforcement Of Order Granting Third–Party Defendant and Fourth–Party Plaintiff [Kiewit's] Motion for Partial Summary Judgment Filed On July 1, 2011."

Pacific Fence's appeal presents three contentions: (1) that the language of the Pacific Fence Subcontract was not sufficient for Kiewit to "pass through" its duties to defend third parties; (2) that multiple indemnitors had an independent, concurrent duty to defend the indemnitee and must each be allocated defense costs equally on a pro-rata basis; and (3) that an indemnitee, such as Kiewit, should be allocated an independent share of the defense costs where negligence on the part of the indemnitee was alleged.

**[i] Pacific Fence Had a Duty to Defend.** Pacific Fence's contentions primarily concern the circuit court's grant of Kiewit's June 8, 2007 motion for partial summary judgment, in which the circuit court ordered that "[a]ny obligation Kiewit has to defend KIC and [Sato] passes through Kiewit, as a matter of law, to Pacific Fence." In its motion for partial summary judgment, Kiewit argued that, under the Kiewit Contract, Pacific Fence was responsible for Kiewit's entire defense obligations to KIC, DHHL, and Sato, including defense obligations for work not subcontracted to Pacific Fence, under the complaint allegation rule as interpreted by Pancakes. Kiewit further cited Pancakes for the proposition that Pacific Fence's duty to defend Kiewit, and including parties Kiewit was obligated to defend under the Kiewit Contract, commenced with the filing of Arthur's First Amended Complaint. Kiewit argued that because Arthur's First Amended Complaint made direct allegations of negligent construction of the fence constructed by Pacific Fence, such negligence claims fell within the Pacific Fence Subcontract, and therefore, "any party Kiewit is obligated to defend pursuant to the [KIC] Contract, commenced with the filing of the First Amended Complaint."

Section 11 of the Pacific Fence Subcontract obligated Pacific Fence to KIC, Kiewit, Kiewit's sureties, and:

> any other party required to be indemnified under the [KIC] Contract, jointly
> and severally, . . .
>
> . . . .
>
> (b) To defend and indemnify them against and save them harmless from
> any and all claims, suits, or liability for damages to property including loss of
> use thereof, injuries to persons, including death, and from any other claims,
> suits or liability on account of acts or omissions of [Pacific Fence]
> . . . whether or not caused in part by the active or passive negligence or other
> fault of a party indemnified hereunder[.]

Pacific Fence contends that the express terms of the Pacific Fence Subcontract restricts the scope of their duty to defend their acts or omissions. Pacific Fence relies on case law from other jurisdictions that rejects a general contractor's attempts to "pass through" liability for its own negligence to a third party. According to Pacific Fence, insurance law on the timing and trigger of the duty to defend under the complaint allegation rule may be properly considered in limited circumstances. Pacific Fence does not contest the circuit court's application of the complaint allegation rule to determine the duty to defend at the outset of litigation. Pacific Fence's contention in regard to this point of appeal is that it is improper "to require a private indemnitor to defend both covered and non-covered claims like an insurer."

Pacific Fence's duty to defend extends to claims that allege negligence "in part" by Kiewit, KIC, and Sato. Pacific Fence states the only claims excluded "from the scope of Pacific Fence's defense obligation are those 'caused by the sole negligence' of Kiewit."[447]

The First Amended Complaint against DHHL, KIC, Design Partners, Coastal, and Sato alleged "[n]egligent design of the hillside area, including the fence and culvert; [n]egligent construction of the hillside area, including the fence and culvert; and [n]egligent supervision of the construction of the hillside area, including the fence and culvert." The scope of Pacific Fence's work under its subcontract included furnishing supervision, labor, tools, equipment, materials, and supplies necessary to construct and install a box culvert and four fences in the Project. Pacific Fence's duty to defend extended to Arthur's claims against DHHL, KIC, and Sato because Arthur alleged acts or omissions that fell within the scope of Pacific Fence's contracted work.[448]

**[ii]   KIC Did Not Waive Its Claim to the Defense and Indemnification from Pacific Fence.**   Pacific Fence contends that KIC "waived" its claim to a defense or indemnification from Pacific Fence because it did not send a tender of defense letter to Pacific Fence and instead relied on its filing of a cross-claim to

---

[447] *See* HRS § 431:10-222.

[448] *Pancakes*, 85 Haw. at 292, 944 P.2d at 89 ("If a complaint alleges claims that fall within the coverage of the indemnity provision, then, according to the complaint allegation rule, the duty to defend begins.").

give Pacific Fence notice of the tender of the defense. Pacific Fence received KIC's cross-claim on February 9, 2006, nine days after Kiewit filed their fourth-party complaint against Pacific Fence on January 31, 2006. The earliest KIC could have tendered its defense to Pacific Fence was on November 21, 2005, when it was served with Arthur's Complaint. Pacific Fence provided no evidence of prejudice caused by alleged delay in receiving notice of claims that it was obliged to defend KIC. The court concluded that KIC did not waive its rights to reimbursement of defense costs.

**[iii]   The Contracts Did Not State That Duties to Defend "Pass-Through" to Subsequent Contractors.** The circuit court held that "pass-through" provisions in the KIC Contract, Kiewit Contract, and Pacific Fence Subcontract required Pacific Fence to defend Kiewit, KIC, DHHL, and Sato, to the exclusion of Kiewit's obligation to defend KIC, DHHL, and Sato. Pacific Fence contended that all indemnitees, including DHHL, "must participate in their own defense for their own independent negligence." This contention is consistent with the result in Pancakes, which required a defendant-indemnitor and a defendant-indemnitee to share the cost of the indemnitee's reasonable attorney fees and costs as determined by the trial court.[449] Requiring contribution from multiple defendants is even more appropriate in the instant case, which unlike Pancakes, involves a chain of indemnitee and indemnitor parties.

Pacific Fence contended that Pancakes did not require that an indemnitor be solely responsible for the defense of an indemnitee where there are other indemnitors with concurrent obligations to defend or where the indemnitee itself is independently negligent.

The circuit court's finding that KIC's duty to defend DHHL passed through KIC to Kiewit was based on the Kiewit Contract, which provided: "To the fullest extent permitted by law, [Kiewit] shall indemnify, defend, and hold harmless [KIC], . . . [Sato], . . . [and DHHL] . . . from and against all claims, damages, losses, and expenses . . . resulting from or attributable to . . . the performance of the Work and [Kiewit's] duties under the Contract Documents [.]" The circuit court also considered the terms of contracts KIC made with Kiewit, Coastal, Design Partners, and Sato to determine whether duties to defend "pass[ed] through" to subsequent contractors.

> 2. Based upon the allegations in [Arthur's] First Amended Complaint and the terms of their respective contracts with [KIC], [Design Partners] and Coastal have a joint and several duty, as a matter of law, to defend KIC with respect to the claims asserted herein against KIC;
> 3. Based upon the terms of their respective contracts with [KIC], [KIC's] duty to defend [DHHL] passes through, jointly and severally, to . . . Coastal and [Kiewit] as a matter of law;

---

[449] See Pancakes, 85 Haw. at 289-90, 944 P.2d at 86-87.

4. Based upon the terms of their respective contracts with [KIC], [KIC's] duty to defend [DHHL] *does* not, as a matter of law, pass through to [Design Partners] and Sato.

(Emphasis added.)

Under provisions in the Sato Contract and Design Partners Contract with KIC respectively, Sato and Design Partners "agree[d] to indemnify, defend, and hold harmless [KIC] and its officers, directors and employees[.]" By contrast, indemnity provisions in the Coastal Contract and Kiewit Contract with KIC required Kiewit and Coastal to "indemnify, defend, and hold harmless [KIC], . . . [Sato], . . . [and DHHL.]" The circuit court's consideration of contractual language was proper "[b]ecause the insurer's duty to defend its insured is contractual in nature, we must look to the language of the policy involved to determine the scope of that duty."[450]

Pacific Fence concedes that it had an obligation to defend Kiewit, but contends that Kiewit had an independent duty to defend itself, KIC, Sato, and DHHL that did not "pass through" to Pacific Fence. Under section 3.18.1 of the Kiewit Contract, Kiewit had a duty to indemnify, defend, and hold harmless KIC, Sato, and DHHL "from and against claims, damages, losses, and expenses, including but not limited to attorney's fees, arising out of or resulting from [work contracted to Kiewit.]" In granting Kiewit's motion for enforcement of the order granting its motion for partial summary judgment, the circuit court ordered that "Kiewit's obligation to reimburse [KIC] and/or make future payments for KIC's defense fees and costs . . . passes through Kiewit as a matter of law to Pacific Fence"; and required Pacific Fence to "reimburse KIC for the pro rata share of defense fees and costs allocated to Kiewit within the time period requirement under the [May 27, 2011 "Order Granting [KIC's] Motion for Partial Summary Judgment Against [Sato and Kiewit] and for Enforcement of Order Granting Motion"].

Section 11 of the Pacific Fence Subcontract required Pacific Fence to defend and indemnify indemnitees "from any and all claims, suits or liability for damages to property including loss of use thereof, injuries to persons, including death, and from any other claims, suits or liability on account of acts or omissions of [Pacific Fence] . . . whether or not caused in part by the active or passive negligence or other fault of a party indemnified hereunder [.]" Pacific Fence's duties to defend encompassed conduct alleged in the complaint that potentially arose under the agreement.[451] Pacific Fence's duty to defend was "limited to situations where the pleadings have alleged claims for relief that fall within the terms for

---

[450] Hawaiian Holiday Macadamia Nut Co. v. Indus. Indem. Co., 76 Haw. 166, 169, 872 P.2d 230, 233 (1994).

[451] *See Pancakes*, 85 Haw. at 293, 944 P.2d at 91.

coverage of the insurance contract. Where pleadings fail to allege any basis for recovery within the coverage clause, the insurer has no obligation to defend."[452]

Hawai'i requires contracts of indemnity be "strictly construed, particularly where the indemnitee claims that it should be held safe from its own negligence."[453] Hawai'i has scrutinized contracts that allegedly hold safe an indemnitee from its own negligence for "a clear and unequivocal assumption of liability by [the indemnitor] for [the indemnitee's] negligence."[454] Strictly construing the Pacific Fence Subcontract indemnity provision, the court concluded that it did not extend to Kiewit's liability unless it arose at least in part from Pacific Fence's work under their subcontract.

Pacific Fence's obligations were not coextensive with KIC's obligations to DHHL under Section 17 of the KIC Contract and were not coextensive with Kiewit's obligations to KIC under Section 3.18.1 of the Kiewit Contract. Section 11 of the Pacific Fence Subcontract obligated Pacific Fence "[t]o assume towards [Kiewit] all obligations and responsibilities that [Kiewit] assumes toward [KIC] and others, as set forth in the [Kiewit] Contract, insofar as applicable, generally or specifically, to [Pacific Fence's] Work." The court interpreted this clause to mean that Pacific Fence assumed a duty to defend those whom Kiewit was obligated to defend under the Kiewit Contract, but only insofar as applicable to Pacific Fence's work.

Pacific Fence's alleged acts or omissions, as set forth in Arthur's complaint, were the basis for its duties to defend itself as well as portions of the defense of its contractors insofar as their liabilities potentially arose from Pacific Fence's acts or omissions. Pacific Fence is not liable for portions of Kiewit's independent contractual obligation to defend DHHL, Sato, and KIC that arose from its decision to enter the Kiewit Contract and those obligations do not "pass through" to Pacific Fence. The lack of clear language in the Pacific Fence Subcontract expressly stating that Pacific Fence would assume all liabilities for Kiewit's duties to defend KIC, DHHL, and Sato against omissions or acts arising out of Kiewit's work indicates that Kiewit retained an independent duty to defend Kiewit, KIC, DHHL, and Sato, and that this duty did not exclusively pass through to Pacific Fence. Therefore, Kiewit has an independent duty to defend DHHL and KIC and should contribute to defense costs of DHHL and KIC, as well as the cost of its own defense in the Arthur litigation.

For these reasons, and those discussed elsewhere in this opinion, the court concluded that Pacific Fence did not assume duties to defend Kiewit, KIC, Sato, and DHHL to the exclusion of these other parties' independent obligations to also contribute to defense costs.

---

[452] *Pancakes*, 85 Haw. at 291, 944 P.2d at 88 (citation, internal quotation marks, and brackets omitted).

[453] Keathe Ct. v. Hawaiian Elec. Co., 65 Haw. 232, 237, 649 P.2d 1149, 1153 (1982) (citing Kamali v. Hawaiian Elec. Co., 54 Haw. 153, 161, 504 P.2d 861, 866 (1972)).

[454] *Kamali*, 54 Haw. at 162, 504 P.2d at 866.

**[iv] The Pacific Fence Subcontract Is Not Void Under HRS § 431:10-222.** Pacific Fence contends that Kiewit and the circuit court interpreted subcontract indemnity provisions to require Pacific Fence to indemnify Kiewit and other indemnified parties against their own negligence. This, Pacific Fence contends, is a violation of public policy and other case law that prohibits indemnification of an indemnitee's own negligence.

Pacific Fence contends that agreements, which require subcontractors to indemnify general contractors against the general contractor's "sole negligence" are void as against public policy. The Pacific Fence Subcontract excluded Pacific Fence from its duty to defend and indemnify acts or omissions caused by the "sole negligence" of Kiewit. However, Pacific Fence does not contend that the alleged acts or omissions in Arthur's complaints were solely attributable to Kiewit and therefore the Pacific Fence Subcontract was not void under HRS § 431:10-222.

**[v] Joint and Several Provisions in the Pacific Fence Subcontract Required Contribution from Other Parties.** The court's conclusion that Kiewit had an independent duty to defend KIC and DHHL that did not pass through to Pacific Fence accords with the express language of the Pacific Fence Subcontract. The Pacific Fence Subcontract provides that Kiewit, Kiewit's surety, KIC, and "any other party required to be indemnified under the Kiewit Contract" would be liable, "jointly and severally . . . [t]o defend and indemnify. . . ."

Under the Pacific Fence Subcontract, KIC, Sato, and Kiewit had a joint and several obligation to defend against claims arising from Pacific Fence's acts or omissions, even where one of the indemnitees was part of the cause of the negligent act or omission. The circuit court's October 3, 2011 "Order Granting [Kiewit's] Motion for Enforcement of Order Granting [Kiewit's] Motion for Partial Summary Judgment Filed on July 1, 2011" required Pacific Fence to reimburse KIC for the pro rata share of defense fees and costs allocated to Kiewit under the May 27, 2011 order granting KIC's motion for partial summary judgment against Sato and Kiewit. In one of its May 27, 2011 orders, however, the circuit court calculated Kiewit's pro rata share of defense obligations without considering Sato's and KIC's joint and several duty to participate in the defense under the Pacific Fence Subcontract.

### [d]    Coastal's Cross-Appeal

Coastal appeals from three circuit court orders: (1) the May 22, 2007 "Order Granting Part and Denying in Part ['DHHL's Motion for Partial Summary Judgment'], Filed January 10, 2007," which concluded that no genuine issue of material fact concerning DHHL's right to a defense by KIC existed; (2) the April 27, 2007 "Order Granting in Part and Denying in Part [KIC's] Motion for Partial Summary Judgment Filed on March 5, 2001," which concluded that KIC's duty to defend DHHL passed through, jointly and severally, to Coastal and Kiewit; and

(3) the May 27, 2011 "Order Granting [KIC's] Motion for Enforcement of the Order Granting in Part and Denying in Part [KIC's] Motion for Partial Summary Judgment Filed March 25, 2007, as Against [Design Partners]."

Similar to Pacific Fence's contentions regarding pro-rata allocation of defense costs amongst Defendant Parties, Coastal contends that KIC should be required to contribute to DHHL's defense costs, "along with Coastal, Kiewit, and Pacific Fence, rather than imposing its share of those costs on Coastal and Kiewit."

Coastal contends KIC was not obliged to defend DHHL against its own negligence and could not pass that duty on to others; that their duty to defend was narrower than an insurer's duty to defend; and that apportioning defense costs amongst the Defendant Parties would implement this narrower duty.

### [i] Coastal Owed a Duty to Defend KIC and DHHL up Until the Circuit Court Granted Summary Judgment in Favor of Coastal on February 25, 2010.
Coastal contends it did not owe a duty to defend DHHL or KIC because alleged negligent acts or omissions could not have arisen from its work on the Project and, therefore, the circuit court erred by granting KIC summary judgment on Coastal's duty to defend. Coastal contends that in the First Amended Complaint, Arthur was "mistaken" and had "misidentified" Coastal as the general contractor. Coastal states that "[Arthur] had simply assumed that Coastal was the contractor responsible for grading and site improvements." Arthur's First Amended Complaint identified Coastal as "the General Contractor for this development" and did not name Kiewit as a defendant. Coastal asserts KIC and other Defendant Parties knew that it was Kiewit and not Coastal, who was responsible for the grading and site improvements that were the subject of Arthur's First Amended Complaint. Together with the narrower duty to defend that is applied in the context-of non-insurance contracts, this meant that "the allegations of the complaint did not warrant a finding by the [circuit] court that Coastal owed KIC or the DHHL any defense, let a lone [sic] a defense against all claims asserted against either of them."

The circuit court's February 25, 2010 Order Granting Coastal's Renewed Motion for Summary Judgment, as well as subsequent orders addressing Coastal's limited liability for a duty to defend, found Coastal had a duty to defend DHHL and KIC until Coastal was granted summary judgment. The circuit court also determined that Coastal's acts or omissions fell outside of the scope of claims "arising out of, resulting from or attributable to" Coastal's work under section 3.18.1 of the Coastal Contract. On May 22, 2007, the circuit court denied Coastal's first motion for summary judgment on Arthur's First Amended Complaint, finding issues of fact as to whether Coastal's scope of work might have included responsibility for the debris fence and drainage culvert. Therefore, the circuit court did not err in denying Coastal's first motion for summary judgment.

Coastal's contention that it owed no duty to defend is complicated by its agreement to settle its liability for a duty to defend KIC. On June 9, 2011, Coastal filed a "Petition for Determination of a Good Faith Settlement" under which it paid $47,500 to KIC for defense costs. The circuit court granted this petition on November 17, 2011.

The court stated it need not address Coastal's contention that it owed no duty to defend DHHL or KIC. Coastal does not (1) argue that the lack of nexus between its work on the Project and Arthur's complaint negated the basis for granting KIC's motion for summary judgment, or (2) indicate whether and how this argument was raised to the circuit court. Coastal's opening brief was required to present an "argument" that contained its contentions and citations to authorities and parts of the record relied upon, but did not do so.[455] Coastal was also required to set forth points of error in its brief that stated "where in the record the alleged error was objected to or the manner in which the alleged error was brought to the attention of the court. . . ."[456] In light of the particular circumstances under which Coastal's duty to defend was invoked in this case, Coastal's subsequent agreement to settle the issue of its liability for a duty to defend, and because Coastal failed to properly present its points of circuit court error or argument, the court disregarded this contention.[457]

**[ii]   Coastal's Obligation to Defend Extended to Claims Potentially Arising Under the Coastal Contract.**   Coastal contends that the circuit court erred by concluding that Coastal agreed to assume KIC's obligations to DHHL under the indemnity clause of the Coastal Contract, section 3.18.1, does not contain an express assumption of KIC's obligations to DHHL and was not intended to operate as a "conduit" for assuming KIC's obligations. KIC's obligations to DHHL arose under Section 17 of the KIC Contract, which provided that KIC would defend DHHL against claims related to sales, construction, or design of the Project within a year of completion; claims based on non-disclosure or inadequate disclosure of risks; and legal actions arising from KIC's development and construction work. The KIC Contract indicates, however, that KIC would not defend against DHHL's negligent acts or omissions related to the Project.

Coastal correctly asserts that KIC did not add a provision expressly stating that Coastal would assume KIC's duties to defend DHHL. Further, while broader than a duty to indemnify, the duty to defend arises "whenever any of the claims asserted may potentially come within the scope of an indemnity agreement, and the defense must continue until it is clear that the liability cannot possibly come within the scope of the indemnity."[458] Therefore, Coastal's duty to defend KIC and others extended to all of Arthur's claims that potentially arose under the Coastal Contract.[459]

---

[455] *See* HRAP Rule 28(b)(7).
[456] HRAP Rule 28(b)(4)(iii).
[457] *See* HRAP Rule 28(b).
[458] *Indemnification and Insurance*, 79 Pa. B. Ass'n Q. 156 at 178.
[459] *See Pancakes*, 85 Haw. at 293, 944 P.2d at 91.

Section 3.18.1 of the Coastal Contract required Coastal to defend KIC and DHHL against claims "arising out of, resulting from or attributable to . . . the performance of the Work and [Coastal's] duties under the Contract Documents [.]" Like Kiewit, Coastal contracted to defend KIC and DHHL for all claims "arising out of, resulting from, or attributable to . . . the performance of the Work and [Coastal's] duties under the Contract Documents, caused in whole or in part by any negligent act or omission. . . ." Coastal contends that it did not intend to assume KIC's obligations to DHHL, which is why section 3.18.1 specified it would defend only such claims.

KIC argued to the circuit court that its intent in including indemnification provisions in its contracts "was to pass the duty to indemnify and defend against any third-party claims, including those of [Arthur] and DHHL, to the persons or entities performing the actual design and construction work from which a claim might be made." Coastal contends that "the principal purpose of the [Coastal] Contract was not to provide for the defense and indemnity of KIC but instead to provide a contractor for the [Project] that would build houses for that project."

Coastal contends the Coastal Contract specified it could only be liable for claims arising from the scope of Coastal's contracted work. Coastal argues that "in construction-related litigation involving duties to defend arising between and among multiple defendants, a trial court should apportion defense costs on the basis of the claims that arise from or are attributable to the defendants' respective scope of work." Kiewit contends that Coastal's suggested rule would require "overturn[ing],"[460] insofar as the rule is applicable to "situations where the express language of the indemnity provision does not limit the defense to the indemnitor's scope of work." The court disagreed.

Pancakes held a duty to defend encompasses "claims [raised in a complaint] that fall within the coverage of the indemnity provision[.]"[461] Only those claims that could potentially be attributable to the contracted work fall under the indemnity provisions in contracts under review in the instant case. As discussed in regard to Pacific Fence's appeal, apportionment amongst indemnitor-parties as well as the indeminitee-defendant is consistent with Pancakes. A duty to defend and indemnify cannot be passed off entirely onto a subsequent contractor because that duty arises whenever a claim is made against acts or omissions attributable to the indemnitor's work. The Coastal Contract, like the Pacific Fence Subcontract, did not provide that Coastal would assume KIC's duties to defend DHHL to the exclusion of KIC's or DHHL's potential liability for its own negligence or willful acts. The Costal Contract provides:

> [Coastal] shall indemnify, defend, and hold harmless [KIC], . . . [Sato], . . . [DHHL] . . . from and against all claims, damages, losses, and expenses, including but not limited to attorney fees, arising out of, resulting

---

[460] Pancakes & First Ins. Co. of Hawaii v. State, by Minami, 66 Haw. 413, 665 P.2d 648 (1983).
[461] *Pancakes*, 85 Haw. at 292, 944 P.2d at 89.

> from or attributable to (1) the performance of the Work and [Coastal's] duties under the Contract Documents, caused in whole or in part by any negligent act or omission of [Coastal], a Subcontractor, . . . or anyone for whose acts they may be liable, regardless of whether such claim, damage, loss, or expenses is caused in part by a party indemnified hereunder[.]

Under this provision, Coastal was obligated to contribute to the defense of DHHL, shared with Sato, Kiewit, Pacific Fence, KIC, and DHHL; and the defense of KIC, shared with Kiewit, Pacific Fence, and Sato. Although Coastal is required to defend and indemnify KIC and DHHL, KIC is also obliged to provide a share of the defense of DHHL based on the independent duty created by the KIC Contract.

As Coastal properly contends, DHHL also had an independent duty to participate in its own defense under Section 17 of the KIC Contract, the last paragraph of which specified "Section 17 shall not cover the negligence or willful acts, omissions, failure to act, or misconduct of [DHHL] either related to the development of this Project or *related to the completion of [DHHL's] authorized mission.*" (Emphasis added.)

### [4]  Conclusion

The court vacated in part and affirmed in part the Circuit Court of the First Circuit's Amended Final Judgment, filed on April 2, 2013, and remanded this case for further proceedings consistent with the court's decisions on the orders, partial summary judgments, and summary judgments appealed from as specified supra.

In regard to Arthur's appeal, the circuit court's September 8, 2010 "Order Granting Defendant Kalawahine Streamside Association's Motion For Summary Judgment On Any And All Claims Asserted By Plaintiffs Due To Lack Of Causation Filed on April 8, 2010" is vacated. The May 24, 2010 "Order Granting Defendant and Third–Party Plaintiff Kamehameha Investment Corporation's Motion for Partial Summary Judgment as to Plaintiffs' Claim for Punitive Damages filed on March 2, 2010" and the August 26, 2010 "Order Denying Plaintiff Arthur's Motion For Leave To File Complaint Over and Against Third–Party Defendant Kiewit Pacific Co. Filed on March 9, 2010" are affirmed.

In regard to appeals taken by Pacific Fence and cross-appeals by Sato and Coastal, the court vacated the following circuit court orders and remanded this case for further proceedings to newly determine Defendant Parties' respective liabilities for their duties to defend under the KIC Contract, Sato Contract, Design Partners Contract, Kiewit Contract, Coastal Contract, and the Pacific Fence Subcontract:

> (1) The April 27, 2007 "Order Granting in Part and Denying in Part Defendant and Third–Party Plaintiff Kamehameha Investment Corporation's Motion for Partial Summary Judgment Filed on March 5, 2007";

(2) The May 22, 2007 "Order Granting in Part and Denying in Part 'Defendant State of Hawai'i, Department of Hawaiian Home Lands' Motion for Partial Summary Judgment' Filed January 10, 2007";

(3) The August 8, 2007 "Order Granting Third–Party Defendant and Fourth–Party Plaintiff Kiewit Pacific Co.'s Motion for Partial Summary Judgment, Filed Herein on June 8, 2007";

(4) The May 27, 2011 "Order Granting Defendant and Third–Party Plaintiff Kamehameha Investment Corporation's Motion for Partial Summary Judgment Against Fourth–Party Defendant Pacific Fence, Inc. and for Enforcement of Order Granting Motion";

(5) The May 27, 2011 "Order Granting Defendant and Third–Party Plaintiff Kamehameha Investment Corporation's Motion for Partial Summary Judgment Against Defendant Sato & Associates, Inc. and Third–Party Defendant Kiewit Pacific Co. and for Enforcement Order Granting Motion";

(6) The May 27, 2011 "Order Granting Defendant and Third–Party Plaintiff Kamehameha Investment Corporation's Motion for Enforcement of Order Granting in Part and Denying in Part Defendant and Third–Party Plaintiff Kamehameha Investment Corporation's Motion for Partial Summary Judgment Filed March 25, 2007, as Against Defendant Design Partners, Inc.";

(7) The May 27, 2011 "Order Granting Defendant and Third–Party Plaintiff Kamehameha Investment Corporation's Motion for Enforcement of Order Granting in Part and Denying in Part Defendant and Third–Party Plaintiff Kamehameha Investment Corporation's Motion for Partial Summary Judgment Filed March 25, 2007, as Against Defendant Coastal Construction Co., Inc."; and

(8) The October 3, 2011 "Order Granting Third–Party Defendant and Fourth–Party Plaintiff Kiewit Pacific Co.'s Motion for Enforcement Of Order Granting Third–Party Defendant and Fourth–Party Plaintiff Kiewit Pacific Co.'s Motion for Partial Summary Judgment Filed On July 1, 2011."

# TABLE OF CASES

*All references are to sections.*

# INDEX

*[References are to section numbers.]*

# O